A PERFORMANCE COSMOLOGY

Testimony from the Future, Evidence of the Past

A Performance Cosmology

Testimony from the Future, Evidence of the Past

Judie Christie, Richard Gough, Daniel Watt

Published for the Centre for Performance Research by

Routledge
Taylor & Francis Group

LONDON AND NEW YORK

First published 2006
by Routledge
2 Park Square, Milton Park, Abingdon, Oxon, OX14 4RN

Simultaneously published in the USA and Canada
by Routledge
270 Madison Avenue, New York, NY 10016

Routledge is an imprint of the Taylor & Francis Group an informa business

Designed by Steve Allison/The Design Stage, Cardiff Bay
Printed and bound in Wales by Harcourt Litho Limited, Fforestfach, Swansea

British Library Cataloguing in Publication Data
A catalogue record for this book is available from the British Library
Library of Congress Cataloging in Publication Data
A catalog record for this book has been applied for

ISBN 0-415-37358-5

The publisher acknowledges the financial support of the Welsh Books Council

CYNGOR LLYFRAU CYMRU
WELSH BOOKS COUNCIL

Cover: Audience Eating from The Last Supper, *Madison, Wisconsin, USA 2003*
Photo: Cody Williams

Title Page: Early CLT Streetwork in Builth Wells, Wales, UK circa 1978
Photo: unknown

To the curious
    for their openness
To all who have worked with us

Contents

3. Evidence of the Past

For the record, and with the benefit of hindsight

ACKNOWLEDGEMENTS

We should like to express our sincere gratitude to everyone who has been involved in the creation of this book. Most especially, we thank all the contributors – colleagues, scholars and practitioners who have written for Sections I and II – for their keen insight, breadth of vision and generosity. We gratefully acknowledge also all the photographers whose works illustrate and counterpoint the texts. We are particularly indebted to the many photographers across thirty years who with perspicacity and precision have captured moments and images from our own projects and productions and to the many performers who not only appeared in them but helped form the images.

As this is an anniversary book that marks thirty years' work, we take the opportunity here to gratefully acknowledge the key support of the Arts Council of Wales in the work of CLT and CPR over the years, as well as the last ten years' support from The Department of Theatre, Film and Television Studies and the University of Wales Aberystwyth. Also, we are grateful to Professor Ioan Williams and the University for the establishment of the new post of CPR Publishing Assistant, a post that has greatly enabled the preparation of this book, amongst others.

There are many people we wish to thank for their untiring personal and professional support towards the production of this book: Talia Rodgers and Minh-Ha Duong of Routledge for their continuing help and collaboration; Wayne Hill for his precise and sharp proof-reading; Steve Allison of The Design Stage in Cardiff for his ongoing sensitive creativity, collaboration and patience; and all the current members of the CPR team for their hard work and support: Electa Behrens, Jodie Bray, Helen Gethin, Joan Mills, Antony Pickthall, Cathy Piquemal and Siu-lin Rawlinson. We note here a special mention and thanks to Cathy Piquemal for her assiduous and terrier-like burrowing in the attics and to Electa Behrens for her warm, intelligent efficiency and co-ordination.

JUDIE CHRISTIE, RICHARD GOUGH, DANIEL WATT

Introduction: Plotting a Course, or Impossible Beginnings

Time present and time past
Are both perhaps present in time future,
And time future contained in time past.
If all time is eternally present
All time is unredeemable.
What might have been is an abstraction
Remaining a perpetual possibility
Only in a world of speculation.
What might have been and what has been
Point to one end, which is always present.
Footfalls echo in the memory
Down the passage which we did not take
Towards the door we never opened
Into the rose-garden. My words echo
Thus, in your mind.
But to what purpose
Disturbing the dust on a bowl of rose-leaves
I do not know.
                    Other echoes
Inhabit the garden. Shall we follow?

T. S. Eliot, 'Burnt Norton', Four Quartets

In the vast and ever-expanding cosmos of theatre and performance, there is a satellite substation, the CPR – the Centre for Performance Research (formerly Cardiff Laboratory Theatre) – which, in one form or another, has been travelling – usually expectantly, hopefully, and certainly naively – through thirty years of mutating moments of theatre, performance, and performance research. Taking the nomenclature and notion of *centre* merely to exert a certain gravitational pull – or gravitas – of its own, the CPR has been drawn on its journeys and trajectories more towards peripheries and margins, to take another look at some of the edges and boundaries as they have so far been plotted, coursed and mapped in the known performance universe. The satellite mission is sometimes flagrantly and unashamedly that of the dilettante, but to keep our iterative rose in mind, fragrantly so.

And so now, what purpose in 'disturbing the dust on a bowl of rose-leaves?' – a question that may perhaps be asked of any reflection upon the event of performance – well, there is the lingering fragrance for a start, a combination of beauty and decay evoking nostalgia and promise, but there is also the activity itself, which stands in for the past, bears witness to it and unfolds another possible version of events. Disturbing the leaves of history is about what might happen next as much as what has already passed.

We have produced this book at the moment (already an aftermath) of the thirtieth anniversary of the CPR to observe that milestone as pretext, subtext and context for consideration of a raft of interests in the cosmology of theatre, performance and performance research – a document in the present that looks back to the future and forward to the coming of the past.

The core questions explored in *A Performance Cosmology* are therefore broad, open and open-ended, and quite deliberately so. We have tried to avoid a well-trodden exercize in mapping and categorization and to offer instead a contingent content, a process – exploring possible orienteerings through sites of critical, affective and even strategic multivalency, where there may on the way, and in between, be sightings of potential and potentialities, even if they may, as we might expect, be simply footprints in the sand and snow, and remembering, of course, that in space no-one hears a scream, only its echoes.

The occasion of this book causes the CPR satellite to hover uncomfortably in *Uchronia*, over the abyss between subjectivity and objectivity as well as over the tantalizing uncertain fissures in time between *There, Here-and-Now* and onto *Where?*

Where? Well, a journey to *Ithaca* has been mooted, and a visit to the *Phoenician Markets* recommended on the way. We may – or may not, it depends – also return to one of our favourite places to visit across time, the ever-beguiling *Sea of Serendipity* whose rip tides and currents subside into gentle ripples lapping onto as yet unimagined distant shores.

Firmly rooted in Wales, and celebrating the position of Wales on the periphery of Europe, CPR seeks that which makes the marginal central and celebrates diversity and all that which exists on the periphery, on the edge, on the border between different art forms and between social and aesthetic action – that which disturbs, illuminates, challenges the norm, takes a paradoxical position, is made off-centre, off-side, on purpose.

Possible Paths through this Cosmology

We recognize that this book offers a set of curious constellations; in trying to unfold its manifold themes, through speculative essay, fiction, interview, fragmentary recollection or chronological table, it has been hard to create a necessary distance. Memory, with all her inventive tricks and turns, has still been the best vehicle for us to trace out co-ordinates, perspectives and maps that we hope might resonate and have meaning for others. In honour of our current geographical position - Aberystwyth being at the end of the railway line (or is it the beginning?) - it seems appropriate to begin a brief overview of the three sections of the book here, with the terminal co-ordinate, The End, in order to triangulate the Middle and Beginning.

The End: *Evidence of the Past*

In place of words, an image, an object or a photograph may also speak as witness and present itself alone, and also in juxtaposition, as circumstantial or contextual evidence. Despite the slipperiness of memory, the partiality and partial processes of archive and retrieval, the disappearing acts of fact, and with none of the impartiality of forensics and archaeology, in Evidence of the Past we present a bricolage of fact, fiction, image, object and interview through which CPR's stories might emerge.

It is not possible, practical or even desirable to log and retrace all the pathways and wanderings of CPR here, nor do we think a straightforward history is of much interest to you, the reader. But, for the record, and for those who like lists, we have appended some further circumstantial evidence in the form of a family album: a chronology of 'named' moments - the performances, projects and events - that have marked our journeys, as a form of evidence, a mark in the shifting sands, creating some order at last and at least. This catalogue is of course as yet incomplete. There are omissions, errors and mis-rememberings, but its construction has functioned for us partly as a navigational tool through active trajectories rather than static events, a record of encounter and discovery, and also simply and mainly as a means of remembering all those individuals and companies with whom it has been a great privilege to work.

The Middle: *The Field Stations*

You will find at the core of this book a matrix of field stations in the performance cosmology charting points of departure to the Future. Gathered from seasoned observers, at each station is a series of reflections, essays and conjectures on theatre and performance, as event and discipline, the range of which, unconstrained by topical particularity, offers a broad encounter with performance, its origins, evolution and future direction.

Entering the field station section backwards, we encounter a substation first, where two authors - both theorists and practitioners who occupy very different positions on the broad spectrum of theatre and performance - reflect on the future of the field through considering the small but elusive step of tomorrow. This substation operates like a threshold - towards tomorrow - re-presenting in textual format an 'ungrammatical text', an essay that was originally made to be spoken and also an interview that has been transcribed and edited in an attempt to retain the immediacy of conversation.

Whilst the field stations appear numerically from 1 to 9, this is just one manner of collation. Multi-directional readings can be made across the matrix and across themes and interests; there are no prescribed modes of relation. And so, whilst the cosmological framework allows a macrocosmic purchase on the material, it is also possible to consider the microcosmic, with each station as an atomic particle with further 'sub-atomic' divisions. For example, the Greek nucleoid states of being associated with each station pull back to origins but the protonic function of the other elements in each station is to continually seek valency or co-valency across stations.

The key to the field stations can be found, we feel, in their simplicity. Whilst there has, inevitably, been some editorial structuring of the essays in relation to each other, we have tried to keep this to a minimum and would prefer you to enjoy the journey where we hope you will encounter 'ports seen for the first time', enjoy 'sensual perfumes of all kinds' and ultimately, although not essentially, 'learn and learn from scholars'.

The Beginning: *Intimate Conversations*

In addition to the many ways of looking, thinking and working suggested by the field station commentators, we offer in *Intimate Conversations* a range of perspectives and commentaries on ways of working at CPR in particular. The evolution of 30 years' practical work - the collaborations, friendships and cultural and artistic encounters - is not easy to trace adequately in any text, and this is not attempted here. Instead a sample kaleidoscope of experience, viewpoint and opinion is presented, in a variety of forms - from diary fragments to memories of single events to overviews of particular areas of CPR's work - each a singular encounter with our ways of working by a colleague, associate or fellow-traveller.

On the Way

Journeys rarely end at the intended destination and even less frequently begin at their point of departure. Whilst not a simple task when the map is the same size as the terrain, we have plotted some co-ordinates and departure-points briefly here and throughout *A Performance Cosmology*. We wish you new discoveries on your journey through this cosmology - from whatever point or port you choose to enter it - and in all the spheres and cosmologies you will enter in the future.

PHOTO: RICHARD GOUGH

When you set out on your journey to Ithaca
Pray that the road is long,
full of adventure, full of knowledge.
The Lestrygonians and the Cyclops,
the angry Poseidon – do not fear them:
You will never find such as these on your path,
if your thoughts remain lofty, if a fine
emotion touches your spirit and your body.
The Lestrygonians and the Cyclops,
the fierce Poseidon you will never encounter,
if you do not carry them within your soul,
if your soul does not set them up before you.

Pray that the road is long.
That the summer mornings are many, when,
with such pleasure, with such joy
you will enter ports seen for the first time;
stop at Phoenician markets,
and purchase fine merchandise,
mother-of-pearl and coral, amber and ebony,
and sensual perfumes of all kinds,
as many sensual perfumes as you can;
visit many Egyptian cities,
to learn and learn from scholars.

Always keep Ithaca in your mind.
To arrive there is your ultimate goal.
But do not hurry the voyage at all.
It is better to let it last for many years;
and to anchor at the island when you are old,
rich with all you have gained on the way,
not expecting that Ithaca will offer you riches.

Ithaca has given you the beautiful voyage.
Without her you would have never set out on the road.
She has nothing more to give you.

And if you find her poor, Ithaca has not deceived you.
Wise as you have become, with so much experience,
you must already have understood what Ithacas mean.

Constantine P. Cavafy, Ithaca, 1911

REFERENCES

Cavafy, Constantine P. (1978) 'Ithica' in George Savidis (ed.) *C. P. Cavafy Collected Poems* transl. Edmund Keeley & Philip Sherrard, London : Chatto and Windus, p 29.
Eliot, T. S. (1944) 'Burnt Norton', *Four Quartets*, London: Faber and Faber, p. 13.

1. Intimate Conversations

Ways of working with the Centre for Performance Research

JUDIE CHRISTIE

On Ways of Working: A View from the Bridge

To see a world in a grain of sand, –
And a heaven in a wild flower,
Hold infinity in the palm of your hand, –
And eternity in an hour.
William Blake, *Auguries of Innocence* [1]

My veteran status as Chief Helmswoman on Mothership CPR affords me a particular and long view of its inside workings (as well as of its many thousands of visitors and territories visited over the years). And so, by way of introduction to this section on Ways of Working, I here offer a view from the bridge in the form of a few background notes as context to the ship's current course from *There*, to *Here-and-Now*, and onto *Where?* (But consider yourself duly warned that, having now foolishly alighted on the *Point of No Return* in the *Realm of Abject Allusion, Mixed Metaphor, Atrocious Alliteration and Irritating Italics*, I, at least, am stuck here for *multum in parvo* testing.)

Note 1 The Mission Statement

The primary mission of this ship of fools is to pan and sift through the shifting sands of theatre and performance, to dig to uncover origins and roots, to extend boundaries, perception and possibilities, seeking out the affective and the effective (the grain of sand in the oyster) of whatever complexion, shape and form and wherever it may be found. Critical to mission planning therefore (as well as writing funding applications) is an understanding of the difference between 'affect' and effect' (but we will always muddle aims and objectives as a matter of syllogistic principle).

Note 2 Destination

Well, certainly, a journey to *Ithaca* as indicated in the previous pages. And, maybe, a return to one of our favourite places to visit across time, the ever-beguiling *Sea of Serendipity* whose rip-tides and currents subside into gentle ripples lapping onto as yet unimagined distant shores. But wormhole engineering is not yet sufficiently advanced to make for an easy ride through dark matter towards the *Isles of Enchantment* and there is the increasingly present danger of the gravitational pull of *Planet Pessimism* with its *Sloughs of Doubt and Despond* and *Mires of Miserabilists*.

Note 3 The Craft

Built circa 1974, the design of the craft was quite revolutionary for its time, and now, whilst not standard, is not so unusual. Designed for reconnoitre to and between *Points* of *Not-Knowing* and *Not-knowing-Even-More* rather than as a flagship, and with carrying capacity for working passengers only, the ship is not a large model of its kind. Whilst retaining a certain metamorphic capability, it is unfortunately too large now to camouflage itself completely effectively for undercover work. Its accumulating cargoes of institutionalization also mean it cannot travel quite as lightly as it once could. The crew is small and burn-out is a constant risk (fortunately, on-board disputes are not frequent and tensions can usually be resolved into 'discourse' by a timely injection of chocolate).

Whilst having a fairly complex system of allied instruments, the ship's main engines are the twin motivators of theatre and performance; these are fuelled by curiosity and oiled by obstinacy, and for full speed both need to be firing together. They can run as single engines for a while if required, particularly for testing and maintenance reasons, but there is no back-up motor as the Drama Distributor Cable was scuttled along with the bathwater during one of the periodic *Semantic Scourges* by the *Arrogance of Youth* (under the rallying cry of 'illiterate on purpose').

The concavo-convex lens at the helm of the ship can be focused by means of a crank handle that usually takes two or more people to operate and manoeuvre, a team effort that is also required for the unwieldy steering mechanism. In fact, whilst having a certain dependence on technology – even though the projector is always breaking down and the profile lanterns have seen better days – most of the on-board systems and instruments are likewise manual and rudimentary, the preferred mode being analogue, biotic, anti-teleological and sometimes old-fashionably dialectical. This is especially true of the communications system that is in constant need of updating, with the demystifiers on permanent overdrive to unclog the build-up of too-many-words-and-not-enough-physical-practice and filter them through the *Whispering Gallery* to *Charlatans' Corner* up on the bridge.

The on-board galley and mess is unusually large and well equipped for a vessel of its kind, and is dominated by a state-of-the-art oven for baking pies in the sky. Visitors can search in vain for the sleeping quarters (which can never be found when they are needed) and are also often caught short by *The Dreaming* sign on the ship's only lavatory.

Because of the burdensome weight of its contents, for reasons of ballast *The Attic* is located deep in the hold and is kept hermetically sealed lest the thousands of stored meme-seeds – used for expeditionary barter as well as bound for the rose garden – germinate and rampage.

Casting an eye on the graphics of the ship's exterior livery – 'C.P.R.' – one might fancifully, if so taken, speculate that the curve of the 'C' is figuratively suggestive of 'continuum', 'confluence' and 'concentricity', where the rupture in circularity in the 'C' opens towards the central 'P' of 'possibility', 'potential' and 'polarity', reining in the remaining 'R' of 'return', 'remember' and 'recover'. Also barely discernable on the livery are the traces of the recently scrubbed-out numbers '30+10', which did not add up to 40, but enumerated in years the current course of CPR and its ten years at *New Base Camp* in Aberystwyth.

Note 4 The Crew

The original crew had little formal training relevant to the required tasks, drawn together more by a sense of adventure and exploratory zeal than professional calling. As the craft contained no instruction manual, muster roll or manifest of expeditions, resourcefulness, resilience and outright bravado became valued attributes.

Little formal distinction in roles and responsibilities was discernible in these early years and whilst not proclaiming or espousing a co-operative structure, a sense of ensemble emerged and 'group' decisions

PHOTO: RICHARD GOUGH

determined routes, destinations and navigational courses. And despite an ever-increasing definition of roles and distribution of responsibilities (encrusted by age and institutional maturity), to this day this ethos of working as one, mucking in (and out) and 'all hands on deck' has remained. Lacking conventional professional skills and a manual (*The Book of Manual*, as it was to become known – still under construction) necessitated extreme autodidacticism, inventiveness, acquisitiveness and a voracious appetite to learn.

Hosting another ship's crew was not only an act of generosity and companionship but more often a blatant attempt at piracy - to 'discover' how they operated and functioned, to extrapolate and 'borrow' good models of practice. Pedagogical encounters, especially those (curiously dubbed 'workshops') held in the *Public Domain*, became a way of securing 'in-house' training and an opportunity for self-development as much as an 'Educational Programme For Others'. Learning though doing, learning through trial and error, learning how to fail and how to fail better have been sustained strategies for practice-based knowledge, akin to walking the boards for the thespian, or walking the plank for the sea-farer. A suspension of disbelief for this crew was not so much a contract of imagination between spectator and event, more a *modus operandi*.

Lunging and lurking on the outer peripheries of the performance cosmology, often perplexed by and uncertain of the interdisciplinary explorations and a million miles from Broadway and the West End, the crew would occasionally lose confidence and, in a crisis of volition with a longing for a return to the familiar and an urge to give up, courage would soon be restored with the old joke *'What? And give up show business?'*

Mutinies have been seldom but are not beyond possibility. Dramas in funding, the constant need of 'Grant Maintenance and Repair' and better financial prospects elsewhere have often been the reason for departures. *Schismogenesis* – where things develop by splitting apart – as one performance cosmologist has advanced elsewhere[2], has been the mode by which fissures and differences within CPR have been resolved, giving rise to numerous other enterprises and projects.

Some crews, against all odds, retain youthful vitality, some implode, some atrophy and petrify, and some disband. Whereas the end for this crew is not yet in sight, nor envisioned, and a further thirty years' work could possibly be realized, the more likely conclusion (piracy, capture, sequestration and insolvency set aside) is *apoptosis*, where the cells of an organism mutually agree to commit suicide, down tools, scuttle the ship. But endings should not be evoked in this beginning

and *schismogenesis* is likely to continue and creatively evolve, so long as over-production and a tendency to hyperactivity does not cause burn-out.

Some time in the mid-eighties, 'less is more' was adopted as a guiding principle in reaction to a period of excessive output. For a while it functioned like a mantra, but sadly, the 'less is' section of the phrase snapped off, got lost and forgotten, leaving the crew with the single refrain 'more', as if a chorus of urchins in the musical *Oliver*!

'Less is more' has recently been rediscovered, re-constituted and revived. The crew's ambition now is to boldly go and seek those endeavours that radiate a synergistic dimension, where any one exploration fires on all cylinders, combining: cultural co-operation, collaboration and exchange; practical training, education and research; performance, production and promotion; documentation and publishing; information and resource.

Note 5 Ship's Log

Whilst empiricism has been much vaunted in remarks above, I nevertheless, in conclusion, offer the following cosmology travel tips and advice extracted from the log-book of Mothership CPR to any new theatre company thinking of touring:

... *Thereby Madness* lies in *Safe Haven*
... *Brain Storm* is not part of *The Settlement of Knowledge* but like *Llareggub* is a state of *Erehwon*
... *The Point of Paradox* may be glimpsed on a good night
... *The Limits of Patience* can be reached quite easily
... *Turning Point* is at the bottom of *The Void*
... The ascent to *Reckless Heights* is more fun than the descent
... *Cross Roads* get even crosser if you dither
... *The Indigents of Insolubilia* tell us that *The Lie of the Land* can be found but *The Sound of Silence* can't
... Bear left at *The Paths of Righteousness*
... *The Hippocampus* is more alluring than *The Campus*
... And *The Ivory Tower* is made from dead animals

NOTES

1 Blake, William (1917) "Auguries of Innocence" in (eds. D. H. S. Nicholson and A. H. E. Lee.), *The Oxford Book of English Mystical Verse*, Oxford: The Clarendon Press.
2 Schechner, Richard (1977) *Performance Theory*, New York: Routledge after Bateson, Gregory (1972) *Steps to an Ecology of Mind: Collected Essays in Anthropology, Psychiatry, Evolution, and Epistemology*, Chicago: University of Chicago Press.

CLAIRE MacDONALD

Tools for Conviviality

1

The title of this essay is taken from a book by the social critic and theologian Ivan Illich (1975). In the 1970s Illich distinguished between technologies, or tools, that allow us to live well and tools that lay waste to our future. Convivial tools favour action over consumption; they allow» us to proceed dialogically and without exploitation. Conviviality expands the possibilities of who we are; in time, non-convivial tools will kill us off. This notion has always seemed to me to apply to metaphorical as well as material tools – conversation, the exchange of skills and collaboration are all tools for conviviality, and are also tools that CPR has built into a practical discourse around performance over the past thirty years. In this sense conviviality is closely connected to the second term I want to invoke here: 'hospitality', a word whose provenance includes a place of refuge, as well as the act of hosting, giving space or providing sustenance to strangers. Conviviality and hospitality are dynamic, suggesting that practical and discursive exchange is at the centre of all social process, and that exchange is not merely optional but also a structured cultural obligation, an act, or series of acts, with consequences.

The tools for conviviality that have emerged as central to the practice of CPR after thirty years of work – creating dialogue, bringing practitioners, teachers and scholars into conversation – have thrown a rope around theory and practice, those unruly partners, and steered them into the same field. That field, or battlefield, has been the place in which the work of CPR has located itself, and the sometimes disjunctive relationship between making performance and standing back and writing and talking about it has been the tension that has driven projects.

I first saw Cardiff Lab in London in the early 1980s when they performed at the ICA. I, and the company of which I was part, Impact Theatre, got to know them after that. We regularly performed at Chapter Arts Centre in Cardiff and in some cases worked with members and ex-members of the group as it expanded to spawn other groups, or as its members moved around European festivals and centres, fostering their own dialogues and events. When I first encountered the Lab they seemed, somehow, more European than we were. They were very much a group – eccentric, extrinsic, outside the metropolitan world. They seemed almost magically exotic; they came, after all, from Wales, and were known to have travelled to Eastern Europe, to Spain, South America and Scandinavia, and to have worked with Grotowski. They evinced a kind of footlooseness, stepping around the capital, and the perhaps self-serving world of what was then called 'alternative theatre', to forge hospitable connections with companies and artists across an ever-expanding map. Their place as a company based in Wales, and not in England, gave depth to their practice. The tensions around Welshness, language and place, ensured that their practice had to address, however tangentially at times, questions of identity and language and to search for form through that tension. There was a productive disquiet in their work that disrupted easy notions of belonging, and which has continued to inform projects since. That tension has forced certain terms into play and encouraged a questioning conversation around place, memory, identity and cultural form, about what is relevant and what is not, about what kinds of tools and practices shape what kinds of work and what kinds of theory.

Like many other companies formed at the time, the Lab were not a playwrights' theatre, but a theatre in which the question of what and where the performance text was, and what constituted the theatre work itself, was open to question, as was the notion of the function and place of the artist, within both the process of making theatre and the process of shaping cultural life. Within the work of the Lab, that complex situation was never quite resolved, but instead was continuously opened up through conversations, exchanges and collaborations with others.

Laboratory. Cooperative. Their theatre was a 'lab'; ours (Impact Theatre Co-op) was a cooperative. The terms connect all of us to the development of ideas on the left – to ways of connecting art-making to political and social structures. The theoretical context for the work that connected all the companies I saw in the 1970s and early 1980s was the existence of a cultural left that took the questioning of institutions very seriously. Cardiff Lab were one of the 'laboratories' of theatre, taking nothing for granted, keeping moving, making experiments.

2

2005. I am looking at two photographs. In one, a naked woman walks across a dark stage strewn with red and pink carnations, playing an accordion. In the other, a tiny figure seems to be walking away from the viewer along a winter road lined with leafless trees and patches of snow. One is from the brochure of the recent re-showing of Pina Bausch's 1982 piece *Nelken* at Sadlers Wells, the other an image from a brochure about the Polish company Gardzienice taken by Hugo Glendinning in the winter of 1988 on a trip to the village of Gardzienice in northern Poland, as part of the CPR project to bring the company to Britain and introduce the work to UK and Irish audiences. Both images remind me of the huge changes generated in the 1980s by contact with major European work that seemed to lie outside the boundaries of either what we called 'fringe' theatre, or the kind of theatre being produced within major theatres.

The work of Bausch and Gardzienice was amongst that work. It made the boundaries between mainstream and experimental theatres, and between physical theatre and plays, more porous, encouraging the leakage between forms, and the attention to a much wider range of theatre practice, that informs the theatre culture we now see. Katie Mitchell's current 'Dream Play' at the National, the work of directors like Kathryn Hunter, Neil Bartlett and Lloyd Newson, has all been made possible by this wider, more generative conversation across borders, and Cardiff Lab and then CPR have been a crucial part of that conversation, generating their own performance work, bringing to the UK the work of artists they encountered on their own travels, and enquiring into the nature of the performance process through events and projects that have brought thinkers, writers, artists and performers together.

When Hugo Glendinning and I went to Poland in the winter of 1988 to prepare for the visit of Gardzienice to CPR's 'Points of Contact' conference the following spring, my own life had begun to shift its focus. Between the time when Impact performed in Poland in 1986, invited through the auspices of Cardiff Lab by Akademia Ruchu, a kind of cultural temperature had changed, at least in my own generation. In 1985 I was a theatre performer and maker. In 1988 I was running the Theatre Department at Dartington and writing plays and criticism. I was also involved in discussions with Richard Gough of CPR and Ric Allsopp at Dartington, about how to set up publications that would reflect the kinds of interests we had in performance and publishing. In 1993 those conversations themselves led to the founding of the journal *Performance Research*.

3

Cardiff Lab segued with customary fluidity into CPR at the end of the 1980s, as the balance between making work and making other kinds of events began to change. The centre itself had already been put in place, and in a sense it had been there since the founding of the Lab as a company, because the Lab had had a sense of the significance of the material records of theatre and performance from the start. The shift of focus seemed a natural one, and I remember thinking how timely it was, and how glad I was that someone was doing it. Now I see that in many ways it exemplified a wider cultural shift made by theatre artists in their thirties who didn't see themselves as career academics but who had an interest in ideas and criticism as well as theatre practice. It was a move from making to curating, from accepting a role on the outskirts of theatre culture, to requiring a place at the table. It was a move that re-placed discourse within a frame of reference defined by an independent performance group, and it centred its enquiry on the notion of 'research', widening the conversation about what research could look like and what its outcome might be.

The notions of place and memory and their relationship to evidence and documents have always been key to that enterprise. These have been (again) deliberately unresolved terms - terms that require a continuing process of engagement in order to keep them on the table. The kinds of events, processes, documents and exchanges that CPR has generated have always had 'form' as part of their function; that is, they have looked at how form emerges from process and practice, at how the body and the voice respond to memory and place, at how the way we write and talk evidences the ideas we talk about, and at how the places in which ideas are exchanged - a terraced house, the gateway to a grand estate, the banquet table, stage or farmyard - all frame and form discursive events.

4

Performance Research is now the third phase of my relationship with CPR. *Performance Research* is a collaborative curatorial venture embodying the notion that a publication can also 'host' a conversation, addressing the space of the page itself as a transactional space of performance.

This phase too evidences a wider cultural shift towards reflection and curation, now being made by practitioners in their forties and fifties, and it seems appropriate that it should be so. Performance is not only ephemeral, to see it as such depends on one's view of where and how performance takes place. It is also profoundly material, evidenced in records, acutely connected to the page, to the mark, to the grain of the voice, to the turn of a heel, the kiss, the sigh, the peeling off of a glove. But the status and nature of the material evidence of performance, and the archival, reading and theatre-making processes associated with it, are always in question. *Performance Research* is a response to the question of what kind of space for conversation, performance and record a page, or a book, a sequence of pages, might be, and in its almost ten-year existence it has encouraged artists and critics to use the space of the journal to curate a wide range of possible visual and written forms for the page as a space for performance.

Curation, conversation, host, hospitality, place, memory, archive, document and discourse – all of these and more have been brought into that field where theory and practice meet. CPR has been a crucial part of that meeting place and, within my own career and interests, has allowed for an ongoing engagement with experimental practice as a critic and thinker and latterly as an editor. This is what conviviality means to me. The conversation can at times be abrasive, even contradictory. It can generate disagreement, and it is certainly not leading towards a clear, preconceived outcome. What it is doing is fulfilling the reasons that I have always been involved in art – to understand better, to live well and to engage with other people through creative processes that last for the whole of our lives.

REFERENCE

Illich, Ivan (1975) *Tools for Conviviality*, London: Fontana.

The Road to Gardzienice

PHOTO: HUGO GLENDINNING

ANNA FENEMORE

Ways of Working:
Eight things I know now that I didn't know before

Sometimes we find ourselves in a space that seems familiar but violently unnerves us. That intimately engages us but that alters just at the moment we come to terms with it. The spaces of memory, of dreams, of nightmares, of fairground rides, of children's games: spaces that stop us in our tracks. We shall never collect enough of these spaces because they show us that we are real, that we are our arms and hands and fingers, eyes and tongue, imagination and memory and dreams and muscles. And so we have just discovered that we are in an unfamiliar space that seems familiar, in an explosion of our habitual manners of being. And we invent ways of dealing with these spaces that resemble the games of children – avoidance, conspiracy, confrontation, pleasure seeking, daydreaming. But the space alters, and orientations alter, and the person I am is no longer the person I was before. I began by trying to write eight things I know now that I didn't know before, eight because that is the number of years since my first contact with CPR, and ended recognizing that maybe I did know these things before, they were then not a memory, and of course the only thing absent from an experience or journey itself is the memory of it:

1 Rehearsing the distinction between comprehension and apprehension is not enough for the performance studies researcher. The distinction that matters is between conscious/visible judgment and habitual/invisible sedimentation. Knowing how to behave in a performance space is the basis of all performance knowledge and making visible the invisible (and vice versa) is the underlying theme of all the practitioners' work I have been introduced to by CPR. But this is a theme I only recognize over time and in retrospect.

2 The journey to Aberystwyth is long and seems familiar, but rarely is. The shortcut through Brithdir on the B4416 is elusive, and the T-junction at the nearby Inn is a 50/50 uncertainty.

3 In *A Thousand Plateaus*, Deleuze and Guattari cite Meinong and Russell who opposed 'distance' to 'magnitude' (1988: 483). Here a *magnitude* (the number of things I know now that I didn't know before, the map reference of Brithdir) allows itself to be measured (eight, p. 143 map ref. H1) and a *distance* (the journey between not knowing and knowing, between Aberystwyth and not Aberystwyth) can be measured only indirectly and, while not being strictly indivisible (the milometer simultaneously converts distance into numbers), 'cannot divide without changing in nature each time' (Deleuze and Guattari 1988: 483). If distance is the *difference* between knowing and not knowing, then we cannot divide that difference without it altering in nature, and we cannot measure such difference (the knowing and the not knowing have to shift as well as the difference itself). In contrast magnitudes can be easily measured (eight years, eight things I know now that I didn't know before, the shortcut through Brithdir takes off approximately 3cm/3 miles). A journey is a *difference* and so not measurable directly because it is the gap between one state (of not knowing) and another state (of knowing), and this gap cannot be divided without altering. Each workshop/symposium/performance I have attended as part of CPR has been spatial, temporal, and durational (they had a beginning and an end, each punctuated by a long drive, alone, sometimes in the dark, and once along the vertiginous coast from the south accompanied by a storm and many rainbows). When put alongside other workshops with beginnings and ends, this accumulation could never make up the journey of my knowledge acquisition, which is something quite different indeed (a familiar space made unfamiliar has no beginning, centre or end). My journey with CPR can thus be divided into different 'types' with distinguishable qualities (yodelling in Bangor, kalarippyatthu in Aberystwyth, archaeological performance in stilettos in the Preseli Mountains) but not broken down into measurable 'units' with distinguishable quantities/measurements. This journey has therefore been a 'distance' or 'difference' not a 'magnitude'. Or in fact a set of differences, as the journey doubtless continues, and on such a journey it is impossible for the space traversed to be substituted for or translated into moments. Durational learning is indivisible.

4 It is nearly impossible to walk up hills in stilettos, and absolutely impossible to do so gracefully.

5   CPR strategically queries the concept of a journey's indivisibility. By setting forward numerous ways of working, the way of working suggested by CPR attempts to break down learning into its constituent parts. Each training/performance/idea/theory facilitated by CPR attempts to physicalize the stop point (between units of knowing and between steps in the long walk up a stony hill). Each unit requires beginning and end and a pause before the next unit (a pause for a solo drive through darkness or rainbows, a pause to regain balance and to kick mud from high heels). In theory, this contradicts precisely the concept of durational activity being indivisible. Nevertheless, in practice, this contradiction or impossibility is the means by which the familiar becomes unfamiliar and knowledge is acquired. Contradictory or impossible because the journey must continue, it does not stop when each workshop, or each step of the journey up or down the hill, stops. The impulse or intensity of forward propulsion is intrinsic in every step, because the intention is to get from A to B (to cover the *distance* or the *gap between* not knowing and knowing, from top to bottom). While this intention is in place the body is constantly adapting to whatever rigid instructions it is given (whether this is Bharatanatyam, Georgian singing or hill walking). However, this is with the knowledge that the next step is about to begin and with a correspondingly altered bodily state than what might have been, had just the (hypothetical) single step been completed.

6   The concept of *jo-ha-kyu* (see Barba 1995: 33–4) establishes that the impulse (*ha*) is followed by the stop (*kyu*) and a pause or hold between the stop and the next impulse (*jo*) is already in place once the stop has been reached. For the bodies of performance this effects an altered bodily state determined by an opposition between 'holding back' and 'pushing forward' (lacking in the hypothetical single step of knowledge acquisition). In this way the body-mind continues its forward motion and adapts to the *beginning* and *ending* of a new phase of learning, by altering the *direction* of the body-mind's journey. This is an imperceptible change of direction but absolutely concrete in the processes of knowledge acquisition. All the practitioners I have worked with through CPR have made reference in one way or another to the idea of 'drawing oneself in' at the 'end' of each workshop. This process of drawing oneself in is not merely a metaphorical concept, despite the vague terminology, but rather asks that we continue the action in the opposite direction to that in which it is going. 'Pulling back' might be a more literal translation of the experience of forward propulsion littered by moments of backward directionality. Thus, the step (the single hypothetical workshop) is subordinated to the trajectory of the journey (the acquisition of knowledge) rather than the other way round.

7   I woke once in a tent at Druidstone[1] and experienced the uncanny moment of cognition; the tent was familiar but the people in it were all strangers. I instantly recognized that these were people I knew and a tent I had never before slept in.

8   CPR asks us to attempt the impossible, to take each step as it comes, to remove the single step from the realm of hypothesis. Impossible, for when I end the single workshop I must in fact place two stops in my trajectory: the stop before I 'pull back'; and the stop before I 'push forward' again. This is a *gap between* or a *distance* that is untheorizable – what happens in this gap? At each moment in the sequence of *jo-ha-kyu* there is a split again so each *jo* contains a further *jo-ha-kyu* and onwards into infinity. The impossibility or difficulty of this infinite regression in practice is apparent. What we can know as participants of CPR is that the steps we take do not simply end and then begin again immediately. Each stop within a process of acquiring knowledge alters direction, and each stop necessitated by that change of direction involves a further change of direction and so on infinitely. Thus, CPR asks of its participants the impossible twice over: the subordination of the trajectory to the point, and the ability to control and understand the infinite regression of knowledge acquisition. It is this strategic impossibility, however, that is precisely the point. The familiar made unfamiliar.

NOTES

1. Druidstone Hotel, Druidstone Haven, Pembrokeshire, Wales.

REFERENCES

Barba, Eugenio (1995) *The Paper Canoe: A Guide to Theatre Anthropology*, London: Routledge.

Deleuze, Giles and Guattari, Felix (1988) *Anti-Oedipus: A Thousand Plateaus*, London: Athlone Press.

HEIKE ROMS

Eye and Ear, Foot and Mouth: Mapping performance in three journeys and one withdrawal

Ystwyth, From Source to Sea – The River's Journey': a CPR project with Rachel Rosenthal and Simon Whitehead

First Journey: 10 –13 October 2000

On 10 October 2000, at around 10:30am, four of us stood by a waterlogged bog in the windswept uplands beyond Blaenycwm in west Wales, on the border between the two counties of Ceredigion and Powys. We had come here to search for one of the sources of Afon Ystwyth, the small river that links the outer edges of the hills of mid-Wales with the town of Aberystwyth ('The Mouth of the Ystwyth') on the Irish Sea. Among our small band of travellers were Rachel Rosenthal, performance artist from Los Angeles, and Wales-based movement artist, Simon Whitehead. The two had been brought together by the Centre for Performance Research's *Mapping Wales* project, which paired artists from within Wales with those from without for a series of performative excursions into the Welsh landscape. This was uncharted territory in many ways: Rosenthal and Whitehead had never met before, and neither knew the area they were about to map. They were accompanied by American film-maker Kate Noonan and myself as documenters of their joint journey.

Our itinerary was to trace the river from its source to the estuary in four days by walking for periods along its course. On the first day, the upland route took us from the spring, past sheep grazing on the hills to a deserted

mine near Cwmystwyth, where the river's water once fuelled the centre of the Welsh lead-mining industry. On the second day we followed the river on its highly landscaped path through the woodlands at Hafod, an eighteenth-century estate whose remarkable design was inspired by the contemporary ideals of the Picturesque movement. The lowland course on the third day ran through pastures and farmland, before on the final day we reached the estuary in Aberystwyth, where the river is now used primarily for leisure pursuits. The various uses had left their imprints on the land: We walked along ancient sheep tracks, miners' trails, romantic forest paths and disused railway lines.

Rosenthal and Whitehead collected drawings, writings, sound recordings, soil samples and organic and inorganic objects such as flowers and stones. Their assemblage

was to form an experiential 'counter-map' that was both sensual and discursive. Instead of a distant bird-eye view from above it offered a grounded perspective of close-up. Instead of permanent features it featured transient sensations. And in place of simplified abstraction it proposed detailed complexity. It sought, in the words of Jean Baudrillard, both the 'poetry of the map and the charm of the territory' (1983: 3).

What was being mapped was also the working process of two artists and their coming together. Rosenthal and Whitehead share an interest in ecology, but the manner in which their work articulates this concern is informed by their different ages, genders, artistic sensibilities, cultural backgrounds and personal histories. These differences manifested themselves in subtle ways. Rosenthal's drawings and stories were playful creations, adding captions to pictures or animating objects. Whitehead's sketches and word pieces often functioned as records, listing times and locations, impressions made, actions carried out, people met or objects gathered. And while Rosenthal focused on sketching, writing and taking photographs, Whitehead used the landscape itself as page, leaving traces through gentle interventions.

At the end of the four-day excursion, Rosenthal and Whitehead were invited by the CPR to present a performative map of the journey to an audience. A model of the Ystwyth was gradually assembled from the gathered objects, accompanied by narratives of the trip. These 'narrated adventures', as we may call them with de

Certeau (1984: 116), turned 'map' into 'tour' (119) and thereby told also of the effort of mapping itself, of the possibility or impossibility of remembering the terrain. Rather than concealing the absence of the territory in the seamlessness of representation, it revealed this absence to be the very condition of its mapping.

Second Journey: 31 October 2000

The second journey was made three weeks after the initial trip, following Rosenthal's and Noonan's return to the United States. Whitehead and I retraced our steps to take the objects that we had gathered back to their previous locations. Some of them had been transformed: the rowan berries into jam, the sloe berries into gin. Others were transposed: Spring water was poured into the sea, sea water into the spring. This time, however, access to the river was occasionally obstructed. The continuous rain during one of the wettest British autumns on record had caused the lower Ystwyth to break its banks, returning to its own remembered map of where it was before they straightened the river to make room for houses and liveable acreage.

Third Journey and Withdrawal: 25 April 2001

We returned to the river again six months later. Asked by the CPR to create a record of the journey for publication, the challenge was now to translate a three-dimensional, embodied and ephemeral performative map back into the flat, diagrammatic and a-temporal surface of the page. Barnaby Oliver, composer, designer and long-time collaborator of Whitehead's, created a simple layering of text and imagery, using the drawings and writings generated during the initial journey. These pages were to be treated as objects that could be physically shaped and altered by the river itself. The intention was to travel to the Ystwyth and douse the pages in the river, to extend the process of the journey as well as attempt to represent it. Whitehead anchored the pages in the river bed by the estuary and left them to absorb the Ystwyth water. When taken out and dried, patterns of silt and seaweed had inscribed themselves into their now undulating surfaces, creating miniature landscapes of slowly dissolving memory maps.

This process was originally to be repeated at different stretches of the river. Access to the river, however, was now completely prevented by the outbreak of the foot-and-mouth epidemic. The territory was governed by a different map – the invisible map of disease, which had drawn impassable boundaries between affected and non-affected areas and rendered all movement between them impossible.

Maps and Counter-Maps

What came into a conflict at this moment in time were two different attempts at relating to the same terrain: that of a sensitive and sensual artistic practice and that of a highly contagious disease. Both can be regarded as counter-practices to the conventional performance of cartography. Maps, states the dictionary laconically, are reduced-scale representations of territory on paper or other two-dimensional surfaces. This definition implies a seamless relation between the knowledge of a terrain and the signifying systems by which this knowledge is organized and presented. Maps thus have become synonymous with an unproblematic indexicality, with pure reference, with clean constative statements. Yet this only serves to hide maps' deeply performative nature: Denis Wood (1992), in his Barthes-inspired study of the culture of cartography entitled *The Power of Maps*, argues that maps construct, rather than reproduce, the world. Following Wood, we may say that the map is performative utterance: it constitutes a speech act of

persuasion ('this *is* here' and 'that *is not* here'), and, in soliciting a response, it both enables and constrains subsequent performances (including its everyday use, remapping, and the creation of new maps).

There are numerous examples of contemporary artworks that attempt to engage with the performative nature of the map by proposing modes of un-mapping, re-mapping and counter-cartographic practice, practices that, to borrow from Clifford Geertz (1983: 20), either redraw the cultural map or suggest an alteration of the principles of mapping. Many of them are driven by an attention to that which conventional cartography does not map, the experiential plenitude of our actual sensual and emotional encounter with a concrete environment beyond the visual, often informed by a strong ethical and ecological stance. Yet the experience of the foot-and-mouth epidemic suggested that the environment is shaped and changed by forces that may escape conventional mapmaking; but neither are they easily revealed in these artistic counter-maps.

The spread of the epidemic, and its political handling initiated a variety of spatialized practices that led to the profound reordering of the territory it affected. The governmental policy of 'isolate and destroy', for example, with its concomitant mass cull of millions of animals, many of them perfectly healthy, was based on an abstracted computer-generated 'disease map', which predicted the 'percolation' of the epidemic from one affected farm to another, yet which did not take into account how the geographical reality of the highly heterogeneous and fragmented agricultural landscape in Britain would influence the actual transmission of the virus. An initial attempt to contain the disease by halting the transportation of livestock across the country proved to be inefficient as it grossly underestimated the number of 'animal movements' generated by the complex geography of modern industrialized meat production. The choice to locate sites for mass-burials and mega-pyres in areas that appeared suitably remote and unpopulated on the Ordnance Survey map overlooked that some of these locales were deeply implicated in other, older narratives of geopolitical struggle, which now resurfaced. In Wales, for instance, the army firing range selected for the disposal of carcasses, a place in the middle of the Brecon Beacon's National Park known as the Epynt, had been a contentious site for a Welsh battle over territorial, cultural and political self-governance since the 1940s, when local villagers were moved out to make way for a British army training ground.

The epidemic thus created a new spatial relation between disparate regions, pulling some together and others apart, regardless of their specific topographies, histories, cultures or modes of social and economic organization. This too was a counter-map of sorts: unlike conventional cartography, whose function is based on the concealment of its own construction, this map was revealed in its very making, in its daily redrawing of territories, boundaries and passages and in the resistance this caused. In short, the disease exposed the otherwise hidden performances of mapping and the scientific, economic, political, personal and cultural desires that drive them.

ACKNOWLEDGEMENT S
Photo on bottom right of page 11 by Keith Morris. All other photos by Heike Roms. Maps by Barnaby Oliver.

REFERENCES
Baudrillard, Jean (1983) *Simulations*, transl. Paul Foss et.al., New York: Semiotext(e).
de Certeau, Michel (1984) *The Practice of Everyday Life*, Berkeley: University of California Press.
Geertz, Clifford (1983) *Local Knowledge: Further Essays in Interpretive Anthropology*, New York: Basic Books.
Wood, Denis with Fels, John (1992) *The Power of Maps*, New York: Guildford Press.

RIC ALLSOPP

Express Trains: Working at CPR

Digging (quite literally) through the piles of flood-damaged detritus, ephemera, un-filed old papers, photos, books, memorabilia and other dubious materials (for instance a small blue plastic elephant given to all participants in the 1991 ISTA in Brecon by Eugenio Barba) that constitute the material history of the last 30 years of my work, that seem to constitute the walls and floor of my office and that I suppose I am now meant to call my 'archive', I managed to find what I was looking for: evidence that I arrived at Cardiff Laboratory Theatre sometime in 1985 as the Assistant Editor of *Theatre Papers* in the footsteps of David Williams[1] who, before he left for Australia, had started to make an introductory listing of the Centre for Performance Research for the forthcoming (and final) 1985 series of *Theatre Papers*, edited by Peter Hulton.[2] The path from Dartington to Cardiff was by that time fairly well trodden, with connections already stretching back to the mid-1970s in the form of performers, and a more recent visit of Cardiff Lab to the Council of Europe Workshop on Theatres and Communities, which had been held at Dartington in 1982 (directed by Alan Read).[3] I remember that on my first visit Richard Gough was 'unavailable' and that the unimposing Victorian building at No. 5 Llandaff Road, where the CPR collection was housed, was as cold and un-enticing then as it probably still is today. My purpose was to complete the 'Introductory Listing', and in doing so make some sense of an eclectic collection of detritus, ephemera, un-filed old papers, photos, books, journals, memorabilia and other dubious materials.

Trying to remember particular ways of working or what were pressing motivations or interests through the veil of time and experience often seems proportional to the archival materials that remain (hence the importance of sustaining performance and theatre archives as material collections). The practices and discourses of contemporary performance have shifted radically and fundamentally over the last twenty years in all sorts of ways that I don't need to repeat here. An enthusiasm for, say, structuralist or formalist approaches, for certain training techniques, for the idea of training itself, for a particular aesthetic or conceptual perspective, are constantly off-set, impacted upon and adapted by other ways of making, of thinking, of using vocabulary, of re-considering the place of performance, its practice and its research. What better, then, than some primary textual source material in the form of the 'Preface' to the 'Introductory Listing' as a means of remembering why and how we were thinking about performance (and the Centre for Performance Research) in 1985:

> The way in which information concerning the practice of theatre & performance is categorised not only reflects what we already know about the field of theatre activity & analysis, but also enables us to define and explore its boundaries. Contemporary theatre research is concerned with areas of work which often overlap other disciplines such as social anthropology & psychology and which are sparsely documented from the point of view of theatre practice. The collection of material at the Centre for Performance Research, set up by the Cardiff Laboratory Theatre, concerns itself with the documentation and definition of these areas as well as with mainstream theatre practice. It provides an invaluable resource for both theatre performers & researchers. (Allsopp 1985: 1)

Noting that I had divided the collection into twelve categories 'for the sake of simplicity', the paper went on to list some of the more interesting parts of the collection including:

> Periodicals – Performance Magazine (Britain)/ Full set; TEATR (Russian) / Full Set. English summary;
> Audio Recordings – Old Harp Singing from Tennessee; Jerzy Grotowski / Answers Questions from the Floor; Essays – Mike Baker / On Violence and Performance. Rat Theatre (no date); and Contemporary Theatre Information – The Phantom Captain; Intimate Strangers; Triple Action; Kiss; as well as referring to 'a large collection of boxed pamphlets / leaflets / articles relating to theatre and performance worldwide by country'.

In 1984 Peter Hulton had suggested that I should think about a bibliographic system for 'the making of theatre imagery' – and, fired-up by hearing Patrice Pavis speak on the semiotic analysis of theatre at a conference at Warwick University, I set out to devise a suitable system which could form

> ... a method of classification for the resources used in the making of theatre imagery. Here, the

resources are the books, articles and periodicals that can provide access to a growing corpus of knowledge concerned - directly & indirectly - with the making of theatre. It is in a sense a secondary resource ... since theatre draws primarily on the practical and active resources of those engaged in its making. Theatre is not in the first instance a literary or theoretical art, yet books and published materials form an important means of communication between practitioners and the historical tradition of theatre making, as well as providing a vital forum for the contemporary activities of theatre ...

[A] standard classification of books used for theatre training/studies such as the sources, history, theories and craft of theatre fails to reflect, or more dynamically become a useful and integral resource for the nature of the activity of making theatre imagery. It was with this sense of the inadequacy of standard classification that I was asked to attempt a new methodology for looking at the making of theatre and find a form of bibliography that would both inform and be an integral part of that making ... I reject the notion that the individual is at the centre of theatre training. It is not centrally the individual who is being trained. Theatre occurs at the point of interaction between people and between people and the world that they dwell in. It seems to me that the individual is being trained, or trains him/herself to approach this central point of interaction and to find there the necessary imagery to make that event a piece of theatre. An undue emphasis on the individual moves away from the central fact of theatre as a 'necessary' communication through imagery.

The words that we use to describe/name this activity of a communicating imagery themselves point to a move away from the individual ... and towards a vital and interactive communication between people and their environment: 'drama' - the thing done; 'theatre' - the thing seen, the place where the unseen manifests itself; 'dance' - to draw towards one, to weave between; 'text' - that which is woven, a web, a weaving. These words imply a network, an organic system, a drawing together of people and place in an active sense, not the passive receptivity of individuals ... I have chosen to understand theatre imagery as what occurs - (that which presents itself) - at the interconnections of an organic network system, which map the dynamic field of theatre

activity. I have thus tried to formulate a model that shows an 'open systems' approach to theatre imagery. (1984: 1-3)

The 'Open Systems Model' that I went on to elaborate operated in two functional modes - active and passive - informed by three sub-systems: the textual, the contextual and the intertextual, which operated in both of the functional modes. The three sub-systems in turn operated in relation to four sub-divisions or dynamic networks: Intertextual: critical, historical, analytical, aesthetic; Contextual: psychological, ideological, behavioural, interactional; Textual: proxemic, kinesic, linguistic, scenic. The intention was to develop a model that was

more generalised and less precise [no problems there!] than some of the semiotic and structural models that have been suggested. Yet theatre imagery is never a precise art. It operates as a dynamic system and often the precise details of any part of the system are of less importance than a view of the whole - the activity of making and engaging people in theatre imagery. This model ... shows that two-thirds of the enterprise are concerned with the context and intertextuality of theatre, in other words its relationship to the world we dwell (precariously) in. It is to this sense of in-dwelling that theatre imagery must relate to enable theatre to remain vital and communicative. Perhaps a bibliography of theatre imagery is a small and insignificant move, but I would hope that ... an understanding of theatre imagery as a dynamic system will allow people to perceive how theatre can be an integral and creative means of understanding the relationships between people and our environment - a task of some urgency. A dynamic theatre is not only concerned with the recreation of its peak moments through history and their contemporary relevance, but concerned with finding the contemporary forms that will speak to and enact our present conflicts and ideals. (1984: 8)

After completing the *Introductory Listing* the following year (in 1985), it was with such idealistic and rhetorical thoughts that I wrote to Richard Gough (whom I still hadn't met) and suggested that the CPR collection might benefit from such a bibliographic categorization. Richard was enthusiastic and so, seizing the opportunity to apply the 'open systems approach to theatre imagery' that I had developed, I spent some months at Llandaff Road in 1986-87 reading and cataloguing my way through the book collection, listening to Old Harp singing and the Klezmatics (courtesy of Mike Pearson), eating fish, chips and curry sauce from Rabiotti's, breakfasting at the

Busy Bee and meeting the small but continual stream of performers, directors, academics and researchers that came up those dingy stairs at 5 Llandaff Road. I had noted in 1984 that

> [i]deally the bibliographic system should be computerised – with a facility to key-in the codeword for cross-referencing. The books/ articles would then be listed in all the appropriate categories enabling the user to search for books within specific categories ... The holding library would already have an alphabetical author index and classified index. (1984: 11)

It was of course never that straightforward, despite the initial help of an Acorn BBC B computer (with an awesome 32 Kb of ROM, a speed of 1.8Mhz, and a large pile of 5.25-inch floppy discs, which stored 360kb of data) and later an IBM PC. The collections however did gradually succumb to the onslaught of methodology, open systems and high technology, and the first cross-referencing, computer-searchable catalogue of the CPR collection was made available in 1987. The computer-searchable catalogue was programmed in BASIC, and subsequently in D-BASE II (for use with a hard-disc), by Richard Knights at Dartington.

The hard-copy *Catalogue One 1987–88* (compiled and edited by Richard Allsopp) of which only one or two copies still remain, was splendidly and extravagantly produced by a combination of dot-matrix printer and photocopier in black type on grey paper. The red and black cover showed 'a Samoyed shaman beat(ing) his drum on his journey to the underworld' and the catalogue was liberally illustrated with prints from Le Roux and Garnier's *Acrobats and Mountebanks* (London, 1890). It described the Centre for Performance Research as 'a multicultural reference library and archive that does not approach theatre from a literary perspective but emphasizes its physical, visual and interactive aspects' (1987:1) and under a heading of 'Bibliographic Design' noted that the design 'ha[d] been developed from the premise that theatre occurs at the meeting points of an interactive network of textual, contextual and intertextual factors rather than being simply the end product of a linear and historical sequence of events' (1987: 10). The *Catalogue* placed over one thousand books 'specialis[ing] in research and experimental aspects of twentieth-century Western theatre and the traditional theatre, dance and music of other cultures, particularly India, China and Japan' alongside periodicals, videos, music on cassette and disc, theatre posters and contemporary theatre information and ephemera, in a searchable matrix that attempted to wed some of the excitement of micro-computer technologies with an experimental and (for the time) radical approach to what theatre and performance research might consist of and in.

All the projects that I worked on with CPR until 1994 and the beginnings of *Performance Research* could be described, in the words of a member of the Gardzienice Theatre Association who wrote to me after the second CPR Points of Contact conference 'Performance, Nature and Culture' held at Dartington in 1988, as 'meeting like express trains stopped for a moment in one station' – people brought together in a high-energy discharge of ideas, enthusiasms, images, approaches.

Twenty years later and I am inclined to think that it is not the collection itself – which will remain held together in its material state with wood, glue, paper, metal, glass and ink, or by the always inadequate conceptual systems that give such a collection form, shape and a semblance of coherence against time and the dissipation of memory – that is of central interest, but what it has enabled people to share. This is its real cultural capital, the meetings of ordinary and remarkable people held briefly by a common enthusiasm for the possibilities of theatre and performance and the work that continues to radiate out from such meetings. The collection itself will continue to inspire as it is reworked, re-catalogued, re-archived and recorded according to the imperatives (financial, political) of the day and the enthusiasms, obsessions, and curiosities of individuals.

NOTES

1. David Williams is currently Professor of Theatre at Dartington College of Arts, Devon, UK.

2. Peter Hulton is presently Director of Arts Archives, University of Exeter. A DVD ROM of the complete Series 1-5 of *Theatre Papers* (1977-86) is available from Arts Archives.

3. Alan Read is currently Professor of Theatre at King's College, London. The twentieth anniversary revisiting of the 1982 Council of Europe Workshop on Theatres and Communities was convened in London as 'Civic Centre: reclaiming the right to performance' under the auspices of Alan Read's AHRB-funded project 'Performance Architecture Location' in April 2002 (see www.civiccentre.org).

REFERENCES

Allsopp, Ric (1984) *The Making of Theatre Imagery: a bibliography*, Dartington: Theatre Department (unpublished).

Allsopp, Ric (ed.) (1985) 'Centre for Performance Research: an introductory listing', *Theatre Papers* Series 5, No.13, Dartington: Theatre Papers.

Allsopp, Ric (ed.) (1987) *Centre for Performance Research: Catalogue One 1987-88*, Cardiff: CPR.

JOAN MILLS

A Family Affair

I am one of the people who can say that, 'the CPR changed my life', and in my case, even more than most! When Cardiff Laboratory Theatre (later to become CPR) were looking for someone to work on a project about the voice, and I met Richard Gough for an informal interview, I was unaware this would both open up a whole new way of working for me – which is still a source of study, practice and inspiration twenty-five years later – and start a working relationship between him and me that would also develop into a life partnership through marriage and parenthood. And so my involvement with CPR is a truly family affair, CPR being always the other element in our family, the third party in this marriage (to quote a certain princess), and this plainly curtails my ability to reflect on CPR ways of working in anything other than a personal or partial way. A sense of 'family' has always been one that is strong in theatre groups and networks, as well as an expanded sense of 'home' where the demands of the work, and way of life, bring together the public, the personal, the professional and the private on many levels in a complex tapestry. An interweaving and balancing act bringing great enrichment and fulfilment as well as at times frustration and exhaustion, an interweaving where intense and complicated working schedules and the needs of children and childcare have somehow to be managed and integrated (and why consequently our daughter Lilith developed from a very early age a necessary role as both discerning theatre critic and diminutive cultural ambassador and social ice-breaker).

On meeting with Richard that January in 1981, I was initially disappointed when I realized that the invitation to work with Cardiff Lab was not to perform or direct, but rather to explore and research the voice in performance, and to begin organizing a project that would bring a range of the world's vocal traditions to Cardiff. I was a theatre director and performer – with a good deal of proven administrative capability – but I certainly did not think of myself as a scholar, a theorist or a curator, nor could I then see how these could be integral to practice. But as I began to work on *Project Voice* a few days a week, over what eventually became more than a year, I began to get some clues as, from the beginning, I was offered the opportunity to develop the flexibility of both the body and the mind: I was invited to join the company's early morning training, which I would then leave at nine to begin organizational work, reading, phoning and writing,

Lilith, Richard, Joan and Kristin Linklater – Summer Retreat, Druidstone, 1996

yet with the sound of the voices, movement and breath below me in the rehearsal space and later the musical accompaniment of the group practising scales and learning a new piece. And so my thinking was always in this context of performance training, improvisation, discipline and creativity. I was also invited to join the workshops for the company led by guest teachers, where I first studied with Zygmunt Molik and Enrique Pardo and began truly to follow my voice, and where I met and began a 'singing journey' with Frankie Armstrong, a practical and intellectual dialogic exploration through the voice, which has so far lasted twenty-five years.

I soon discovered that the vision, scale and ambition of Project Voice was far beyond the financial resources of Cardiff Lab, as well as the comprehension of the Welsh Arts Council where neither 'Drama' nor 'Music' would take financial responsibility for it. We applied for the new – seemingly progressive – European funds, but applications were processed over timescales that meant a funding decision would be retrospective, and therefore useless. We did, however, receive a generous research and development grant from the Gulbenkian Foundation, which supported the research and planning phase and enabled the creation of an information resource about the voice in performance from around the world, and this was the foundation on which we have built the subsequent twenty-five years of voice activity. But an intensive three weeks of performances, workshops, lecture demonstrations and discussions about the voice had been planned, and indeed programmed: an unprecedented gathering and an amazing array of 'voices' from around the world – practitioners, vocalists in speech and song, academics, composers, voice teachers. Many had agreed to financial conditions derisory in their usual terms. But even derisory fees and expenses mount up, and when it became clear that all funding possibilities had been exhausted, we determined still to do *something*, and so invited five of the artists and a hundred people who were interested in the voice and met for a weekend. Thus *Project Voice* was born.

Over the next eight years in and around my other freelance directing and teaching work, I continued working with Cardiff Lab and later CPR, exploring my own voice-teaching and directing practices, contributing to several new performance pieces, as well as receiving extraordinary opportunities: more work with Zygmunt and Enrique; the chance to meet such influential practitioners as Jerzy Grotowski, Eugenio Barba, Roberto Bacci, Wlodzimierz Staniewski as well as to experience their work through performances and workshops; more travel and work in Europe and eastern Europe in the context of festivals where we met and collaborated with the groups producing the most exciting work of the era. Everyone we met was passionate about creating new work, developing skills, exchanging ideas and practice, and all were united in a shared dislike of various forms of 'deadly theatre'. We all felt part of a kind of 'family'. I remember Eugenio Barba once talking about why he carried on when things were disheartening or difficult, talking of the need to go on for the sake of all of us, in the past as well as now, the others who had, in their turn, also experienced struggle and troubles. It was the first time I felt that sense of connection and continuity with practitioners from the past, the future and across cultures. We were all very different individuals, groups, at odds sometimes but nevertheless a family. Very recently, I attended a talk by Eugenio on an Odin tour of British universities, and his first words were 'Who is my father?', going on to speak movingly of our ancestors, our teachers, our mentors and the deep influence they have over us, and speaking very much in terms of the family.

Through the work with CPR also came invitations: to be a representative for the UK at an International Theatre Institute meeting in Madrid and – even more significantly for me – at the Rennes Music Theatre Festival. Here I first experienced *P'ansori 'Opera'*, the extraordinary vocal form from Korea – a sung storytelling, epic folk-music

from shamanic roots – that so entranced and excited my imagination that I vowed to bring a performance to Wales, fulfilling this promise to myself eight years later for the first Giving Voice festival. And later, in 1989, participating in the extraordinary workshop with Gardzienice Theatre, staged by CPR in the perfect coastal surroundings of Druidstone Haven in Pembrokeshire, it was clear to me that access to such inspirational voice work had to be made possible on a more regular basis and to many more practitioners and scholars. And so we determined to create some kind of international voice event, even if it still could not be on the scale first envisaged in 1980. By this time, CPR had built up an expertise in creating events and gatherings that brought together practitioners and academics in dialogue through a range of activities, workshops, talks, performances, and this was clearly the way forward for the subject of the 'voice in performance'. I was determined that it should be not merely a conference where a series of academic papers are presented, nor just a performance festival, nor a few unconnected workshops. It had to encompass access to unusual and outstanding voices in performance, allow for a real meeting with the practitioners we invited and create ways for us to examine how such practices related to individuals' own work and teaching and to hear these voices in an illuminating context, juxtaposed carefully with others in a manner that stimulated discussion, interaction and understanding.

And we wanted to create an intensive experience, where a lot could be explored and shared in a short time, where the participants could receive training from world-class voice practitioners, hear presentations about a wide range of vocal techniques, see and hear unusual and outstanding examples of voice work spoken and sung, and even have a little time to talk with fellow participants. For me, as for many others, the balancing act between looking after children and working meant that opportunities for stimulus, artistic growth, and development had to be meaningful and also fast and furious: 'long' on the experiential level, but short on the temporal one.

So far Giving Voice has lasted fifteen years. The success of the first event encouraged us to continue; we developed the idea of broad contextual frames for *Giving Voice*, embarking on the first triad in the series – *A Geography, An Archaeology and A Divinity of the Voice* – moving through *A Politics and, A Philosophy and Psychology* – and leading now to the ninth session of the project, *Myths and Mythologies of the Voice*, in 2006.

Giving Voice has gathered together a wonderful array of some of the world's finest performers and voice teachers in a unique celebration of the voice. Over 1,600 performers, directors, teachers, therapists and a growing number of members of the public and non-professional voice-users have taken part in the project.

Giving Voice springs from a strong belief in the voice's ability to communicate beyond language and cultural difference and a belief that working with the voice can allow people, from wherever they come, to enjoy and value the riches of difference as well as the recognition and celebration of a common humanity.

Giving Voice is an established international event with the aim of advancing the appreciation and understanding of the voice in performance through practical research and a celebration of its many and varied manifestations throughout time and culture. It brings together those who have an interest in the voice but who will not necessarily meet in the course of their practice: academics and practitioners, performers from a variety of disciplines, teachers of spoken voice and singing teachers, those with an experimental interest and those who favour traditional methodology, those from the world of medical knowledge of the vocal mechanism and those interested in the spiritual dimensions and healing properties of voice work. This opportunity to compare, contextualize, to be able to enquire directly from another practitioner rather than speculate – this is what the CPR has given me and has allowed me to offer to others via the projects in which I have been involved.

Despite being an early graduate of the University of Hull Drama Department, I was, as a young director, very resistant to theoretical discussion and critical analysis and imagined that theorists had little or nothing to say to me. Maybe this was because I entered the profession at a time when university graduates were increasingly beating a new path 'onto the boards', but were still regarded with some suspicion by many in the profession who despised the 'intellectual' directors and actors, as their training was felt to be too much in the head and too little in the body, 'in the page' not 'on the stage'.

So it is even more strange that it was a theatre company led by a young Artistic Director – who, in order to carry on with the practice he had begun, had not taken up university places offered to him – that excited my interest in research, and in looking at the voice in a more contextual manner, to explore it through interesting juxtapositions and meetings, through a notion of 'curiosity'. Richard Gough is a genuine explorer. *He* needed to find out what it was that a project, performance, workshop, presentation or event might reveal, and it is this sense of curiosity that makes the CPR what it is. This is why so many practitioners have found themselves drawn to CPR events and equally why outstanding scholars from across the whole range of theatre and performance studies – not to mention cuisine, archaeology, anthropology, philosophy and psychology – have also responded so positively to the CPR's curiosity and way of carefully and precisely but unprescriptively balancing the mix of performance practice and theory.

Other aspects of the CPR ways of working are manifest in the day-to-day reception of visitors. Time and time again practitioners and scholars hosted at CPR have commented on how well they were looked after, how personal CPR's approach is compared to the way they have been received by other conferences or institutions. Once again I turn to the sense of family for an explanation. I think the CPR has tried to welcome each person or company as they would welcome guests to their homes. The professional and personal divide is deliberately confused. The senior staff of CPR themselves have families and appreciate all too well what it is like to be away working, missing the children or partner, staying in impersonal unwelcoming surroundings, possibly jet-lagged and maybe anxious about a presentation to be given the next day. The same imaginations that create the CPR's challenging programmes are also at work considering how guests might feel. If someone has made the gift of effort to travel, they will be received accordingly: welcomed personally given comfortable surroundings. This is not about money (nor fancy hotels, CPR's financial means being modest), but someone will have thought about the best situation for each guest, what might they need most, independence perhaps to come and go, proximity to the seaside delights of Aberystwyth, a place with room for their family, a situation where they might cook for themselves? If they hadn't taken seriously enough the warnings of how cold and wet Wales can be, someone will lend them sweaters, hot water bottles. They will be invited to our houses for supper with our families, taken to a local place of interest on a day off.

I have focused on *Giving Voice* because it is the project through which I have most contact with CPR, but in fact each project and series – whether it be *Points of Contact* or *Past Masters* or the *Summer School* or *Cross Current* events – attracts a wonderful mix of participants: scholars, performers, teachers of performance, and, increasingly, members of a wider public who enjoy this stimulating mix between practice and theory. Above all, this is what I love about CPR and its way of working. At a time when the word 'accessibility' became meaningless or, worse still, an excuse for funding something of doubtless worthiness but doubtful worth, the CPR has shown how to make practice accessible to those who might not have ventured into the studio and has certainly surprised many practitioners by the inspiration to be found in a highly-informed scholarly presentation.

My final thought on how CPR weaves a mix of practice and theory, the professional and the personal, is to give an example, recalling a conversation over lunch with Alice Lagaay, a philosopher and a guest-speaker at *GivingVoice 8, A Philosophy and Psychology of the Voice* in 2004. Alice explained that she had felt rather nervous speaking about the voice with so many voice practitioners in the audience. She was unsure that she had much to tell us, even though her own extensive research was centred on philosophies of the voice. Within five minutes we were so deep in discussion – with me sharing observations and experiences as a director and voice teacher and her commenting so pertinently and with such clarity from her research – that we hardly noticed two hours pass. Alice, heavily pregnant and needing to rest before her talk that evening, used her rest-period to re-write her presentation weaving in some of the thoughts and discoveries we had explored together that afternoon. Given this chance to meet and engage in discussion, Alice and I saw how much we had to learn from each other and how much the interaction stimulated rather than threatened our disciplines. Despite her fears, when she gave her presentation that evening her vocal delivery was so beautiful – the tone and pace, the way she communicated genuinely with her audience – that she was a paragon of the power of the voice to awaken us and to speak to both heart and mind.

CPR continues to connect me to a professional 'family' of other artists and thinkers, and its work continues to be interwoven with our own family events. The recent CPR events celebrating thirty years' work have given me a chance to reflect on my own twenty-five years' professional collaboration with the company but also on twenty-five years of family life closely woven into the rich fabric of international projects, unusual conferences, visiting performances, guests, meals, stories told, songs shared. I have, over the years, sometimes complained bitterly about this lack of division between CPR and the rest of life, between work and family, but it is a way of working and living I have also come to respect and value greatly, seeing the remarkable quality of trust, cultural exchange and artistic development in which it results.

The Meditation Room – Together Project, Copenhagen, 1983

PHOTO: JAN RUSZ

'Grandfather' at home in Gardzienice

PHOTO: HUGO GLENDINNING

PAUL ALLAIN

The Nature and Culture of Performance

My first encounter with the Gardzienice Theatre Association was at a conference organized by the Centre for Performance Research at Dartington College in 1988, entitled 'Performance, Nature, Culture'. The presence of this group sent waves of excitement through the proceedings. In a demonstration of their training, these exotic figures swirled round with their long hair flying in an exercise based on Hassidic spinning. In the evenings, beneath the apt medieval timbers of Dartington's Great Hall, they stamped heavy-booted through their sung performance *Avvakum*, based on the seventeenth-century autobiography of the eponymous Russian Orthodox priest. In 1988, both nature and culture meant something very different in Poland from what they suggested to us in the West, as these practices revealed. Gardzienice's director Wlodzimierz Staniewski has always avoided the term 'folk culture', which at that time still under Soviet domination implied state-organized presentations of mythologized Polish dances, songs and rituals. The Jewish music and Russian Orthodox hymns and Slavic laments, the 'native' songs which formed a central part of Gardzienice's canon before they went on later to explore Western European and Ancient Greek melodies, were from quite another mythology – of Poland's East and Poland's neighbours, of abandoned border villages and forgotten churches in what are for us even today culturally remote lands. Through nature especially, as well as performance of course, Gardzienice found kinship with CPR. Both were looking for new spaces and sources for theatre-making. So began also the actual realization of my own explorations into Polish theatre that until then had been at one remove: through Stanislaw Ignacy Witkiewicz's writings and paintings (he painted commissioned portraits under the influence of a cocktail of drugs) and a much thumbed copy of *Towards a Poor Theatre*.

In April 1989, CPR brought Gardzienice back to the United Kingdom for a short workshop in Druidstone Haven, Wales – a second home for many of CPR's activities. The Druidstone Hotel where we were based is perched on cliffs riddled with caves, an ideal place for focused work in the kind of 'natural environment' that Staniewski has repeatedly advocated and sought. I documented this workshop for the first-ever issue of the journal *Music Theatre Dance*, produced by Middlesex Polytechnic as it was then known (Allain 1990). In this article I describe

how we exercised on the beach and cooled our warmed up bodies in the bitterly cold sea; we sang out our names in a cave to be answered by the crashing waves; and we ran at night along the moonlit cliff-top roads. Druidstone matched perfectly the Romantic fringe spaces that had then nourished Gardzienice's work in Poland and beyond for over a decade (they were founded in 1977). As in autumn 1989 I began my doctoral research into Gardzienice's praxis at the University of London, so did the relationship between CPR and Gardzienice flourish. Jane Bell of the Druidstone Hotel was invited several times to cook celebratory dinners in Gardzienice village over a thousand miles away. And more than a decade later the relationship was cemented further when CPR presented Gardzienice's *Metamorphoses* in a Baptist chapel in Aberystwyth as part of the 1999 Performance Studies international conference.

I went to Poland and Gardzienice for the second time in early November 1989, traveling via Berlin Tegel airport and going under the Berlin wall at Friedrichstrasse to head East by train. Five weeks later I was singing in the chorus of *Avvakum* in the small Aryan chapel in Gardzienice village that was then their performance, training and workshop space, all rolled into one. Mid-way through this 45-minute performance, our chorus had to enter from outside the building (no carpeted foyers here) accompanied by icy Siberian winds of -15 degrees. Before Christmas I returned by train to Germany though this time to a united country. The Berlin Wall had fallen.

Following the dismantling of this symbolic and actual barrier, the nature of culture and performance in Poland has altered radically, changes which Gardzienice have had the fortitude to survive, though many theatre groups have not. Communism's industrial dependency had all but frozen the Eastern countryside and abandoned it to obscurity. Nature and culture in present day Poland and what is the EU now exist in much more familiar paradigms, subject to the pressures of road building, housing and light industrial developments, satellite dishes and commercialization – the steady encroachment of Capitalism that we in Britain have faced for decades. Gardzienice still sing and perform, though the songs are of a different genesis. Their metamorphosis has been extensive, and they now occupy a much larger building with small rehearsal rooms and a big performance space, as well as other houses in the village of Gardzienice.

My book on their work that evolved from my doctoral research (1997) charted just the beginning of these transformations.

As I write this, the physical sensations of that first workshop immersion still surface. CPR recognize the value of participation and practice, just as they respect the importance of reflection, as this collection of texts testifies. My research has attempted to fuse these processes in several practical accounts, to create what might be crudely termed written primary sources of experience, of practice. My work with Gardzienice took me to Toga in Japan where Tadashi Suzuki held his international festival, and then to Pontedera. In January 2005, I hosted a symposium at Kent University of the Workcenter of Jerzy Grotowski and Thomas Richards. The Workcenter, and Grotowski's emphasis on doing, hinted at also in what Staniewski has described as the 'sprawca' in Polish, all point to a certain quality of work that is not necessarily done before, with or for an audience, but is simply done. Rehearsals, training and workshops are a hidden and neglected aspect of the performance whole, our still culturally remote land. I have been drawn to this landscape not only because of the difficulty of writing clearly about it or because without it none of the performances we see might exist, but because so much of value happens there that becomes overly self-conscious or too pointed in performance. And the question of how one maintains a private, personal and focused quality of doing in public is fundamental to performing, yet little explored.

Looking back at my article for *MTD*, I read again the suspension of belief and judgment that participation necessitates and that I tried to capture in that, my first published piece. We need to be able to train with conviction and practise without inhibiting analysis, so that when we emerge the other side, when we stand back and judge, we can speak with embodied insight. Reflection can rarely be done within the flow of the work, because it is always enough just to do. We need to allow ourselves to be immersed, and yet also to know when and how to reflect. This duality is still the central challenge for those documenting performance processes. It is difficult work for which, thankfully, CPR has laid solid and significant foundations.

REFERENCES

Allain, Paul (1990) 'Gardzienice Theatre Co. - a practical account' in *MTD, a journal of the performing arts* (winter 1990), London: Middlesex Polytechnic, pp. 29-32.

Allain, Paul (1997) *Gardzienice: Polish Theatre in Transition*, Amsterdam: Harwood Academic.

Barba, Eugenio (ed.) (1968) *Towards a Poor Theatre*, Holstebro: Odin Teatrets Forlag.

Richards, Thomas (1995) *At Work with Grotowski on Physical Actions*, London: Routledge.

Staniewski, Wlodzimierz with Hodge, Alison (2004) *Hidden Territories: The Theatre of Gardzienice*, London: Routledge.

PHOTO: HUGO GLENDINNING

Gardzienice Village, Winter 1988

DANIEL WATT

Philoxenia: The Host as Parasite

And so I want to thank you for being a good host. It's not easy to host all these countries. It's particularly not easy to host, perhaps, me. (Laughter.)
George W. Bush meeting President Kirchner of Argentina, 4 November 2005
Does hospitality consist in interrogating the new arrival? Jacques Derrida *Of Hospitality*

Over thirty years the Centre for Performance Research, and its former identity as Cardiff Laboratory Theatre, have produced, invited, accommodated, introduced, facilitated and made accessible the work of countless theatre companies, scholars, theorists and practitioners from a varied range of disciplines and backgrounds, frequently from many different countries with the manifold logistic difficulties that such international collaborations entail. Many people who have encountered, and participated in, this work attest to the attentive hospitality of CPR. But the host is not always simply open to the guest, and the guest not always at home where they stay; sometimes interrogation and estrangement are responsibilities that the host must, in a sense, provide. An insight into CPR's work might, perhaps, be found in the concept of the 'host' and all of the uncanny homeliness that this role entails. This short essay inhabits (in a manner whose parasitism will, I hope, be illuminating) the writings of Jacques Derrida and J. Hillis Miller and circles around the issues of hosting, hospitality, homes, interrogation, paradox and the nature of friendship, *perhaps*.

Philoxenists *Perhaps*, or, *Yes*, Maybe

'It's particularly not easy to host, *perhaps*, me,' they said.

Words of another: of that supremely other declaring themselves as such. And, perhaps without entitlement, I have emphasized this word: *perhaps*. This word, though, shows all the concern and unease, the doubt and suspicion of the guest: that they may be a burden, an intruder, unworthy or, perhaps, deeply unexpected. This may be the duty of a guest, to acknowledge that they will be difficult and dangerous company. Danger, duty, difficulty and the unexpected - all words of a kind of future:

> The event is possible only coming from the impossible. It arises *like* the coming of the impossible, at the point where a *perhaps* deprives us of all certainty and leaves the future to the

future. This *perhaps* is necessarily allied to a yes: yes, yes to whoever or whatever comes about. (Derrida 2005: 74)

One of the ways that the Centre for Performance Research works (in the sense of to operate or to get things done) is to utilize the (im)possibility of this perhaps. It creates and offers spaces in which a fleeting community can come together. And this is frequently a 'community of those without community'.[1] The workshops, conferences, performances, special events, summer schools and other activities undertaken by what is probably thousands of participants over the years seem to have each created a community of participants who, whether the event were marginal or major, for a group of ten or for a delegation of four hundred, enjoyed or disliked, has generated memorable discussion, innovative practice, and a certain encounter that changes the status of the individual from participant to guest and frequently from guest to friend, perhaps. These terms are not used here in the sense of a frivolous camaraderie, the useless solidarity of a lazy exchange, but rather with all the potential that the friend and guest have to be critical, to provide food for thought for their host, or even their enemy. For this is also how the Centre for Performance Research allows itself not to work (in the sense of function properly): by opening the uncertainty of the future to a possible friendship.

> To think friendship with an open heart - that is, to think it as close as possible to its opposite - one must perhaps be able to think the *perhaps*, which is to say that one must be able to *say* it and to *make* of it, in saying it, an event: perhaps, *vielleicht, perhaps* - the English word refers more directly to chance (*hap, perchance*) and to the event of what *may happen*. (Derrida 1997: 30)

It's particularly not easy to host when the burden of the event depends on chance, or opens itself to the friendly gesture of letting what may happen, happen. Here there seems to be a kind of other 'duty' in terms of welcoming the friend. This would consist of allowing the guest, in the movement from guest to friend, to challenge the host, by their difference, their foreignness. To host would entail the ability to be so courteous as to allow the guest to interrogate the host, to criticize and resist the very hospitality that enables such criticism. In parentheses (itself a dutiful parasite to the text) Derrida explores the duties of hospitality:

For to be what it 'must' be, hospitality must not pay a debt or be governed by a duty: it is gracious, and 'must' not open itself to the guest [invited or visitor], either 'conforming to duty' or even, to use the Kantian distinction again, 'out of duty.' This unconditional law of hospitality, if such a thing is thinkable, would then be a law without imperative, without order and duty. A law without law, in short. For if I practice hospitality *'out of duty'* [and not only *'in conforming with duty'*], this hospitality of paying up is no longer an absolute hospitality, it is no longer graciously offered beyond debt and economy, offered to the other, a hospitality invented for the singularity of the new arrival, of the unexpected visitor. (Derrida, in Derrida and Dufourmantelle 2000: 83)

It is not easy to escape the cycle of economy that seems to follow the duties of hospitality. It is always, of course, generous to return favours, but it must never be expected. Looking back on all the many guests that CPR has hosted, I wonder if finally they have all been 'unexpected' because their engagement with the organization was never rigorously prescribed, and in this manner the ground between host and guest, friend and enemy, interrogator and new arrival slips and changes, is rewritten and offered as another encounter with culture and singularity, with identity and power. This event of hospitality is not without its own reaffirmation of territory and borders though, or indeed without suspicion of the visitor: what stakes itself on a chance encounter is that the visitor may reveal themselves to be in search of a new home; one that the host has *perhaps* already gambled in the grace of the game. It is in that sense of chance that the pathology of the host emerges: is the host a philoxenist (one who loves strangers - or loves hospitality and hosting) or perhaps a secret xenophobe (one who fears strangers) who conquers such fear through xenodochy (receiving strangers)? In that tension between the love and reception of strangers, which begs further questions concerning obligation and obsession, there will always be the issue of the home. But aren't all homes more like the xenodochium (a house of reception for strangers and pilgrims; a hostel, guest-house, esp. in a monastery): a chance refuge, a place for passing through?

Home from Home

CPR is based in Wales, previously in Cardiff and now in Aberystwyth. Wales has been their home, and yet in a sense they do not dwell there comfortably. Their outlook has been precisely that: out. Continued conferences and artistic collaborations have attested to the fluidity of borders, the ephemeral nature of maps, the illusion of belonging. By embedding themselves deeper into the heart of Wales by the move to Aberystwyth - frequently referred to in the Centre's literature as both the *end* and the *beginning* of the line - the Centre challenges the status of home and makes it in a sense negotiable. So CPR has succeeded in making their home a place in which they are themselves guests. J. Hillis Miller in his essay 'The Critic as Host' follows the implications of the reversibility of the host and the guest: 'A Host in the sense of a guest, moreover, is both a friendly visitor in the house and at the same time an alien presence who turns the home into a hotel, a neutral territory' (Miller 1979: 221). As we have ample evidence of a neutral territory is frequently a site of contestation. At the heart of many territorial disputes is the question of language, and home is intimately determined by the language that is used there, be it foul, foreign or familiar.

I do not have the record of how many of CPR's staff have been Welsh-speakers. It is, *perhaps*, not many. And of the present company none would list Welsh as their 'mother tongue', and none, I suspect, would consider themselves fluent in the language. Language renders an irreconcilable problem in the heart of the home:

What in fact does language name, the so-called mother tongue, the language you carry with you, the one that also carries us from birth to death? Doesn't it figure the home that never leaves us? The proper or property, at least the *fantasy* of property that, as close as could be to our bodies, and we always come back there, would give place to the most inalienable place, to a sort of mobile habitat, a garment or a tent? Wouldn't this mother tongue be a sort of second skin you wear on yourself, a mobile home? But also an immobile home since it moves about with us? (Derrida, in Derrida and Dufourmantelle 2000: 89)

So it might be better to consider all the 'mother tongues' that CPR staff, and interns, have brought - as 'second skin' - to their Welsh home from home: Dutch, French, Finnish, German, Italian, Mandarin, Polish, Portuguese, Spanish, Swedish. And alongside this all the languages that have required translation through CPR events and through the journal Performance Research, far too many to list here. The language that they have been translated into is English, the language of another country from the one that CPR calls home. Yet English is not simply the 'other' language in Wales, it is an equal language. Wales is truly bi-lingual in that respect.[2] English is not simply a language that is *accepted* in Wales - as a guest - as the parasite upon a natural Welsh medium. The relationship between English and Welsh is so closely bound in Wales that it illustrates the complex interdependence of the host and the parasite: indiscernible double identities whose edges are difficult to discern. Again here it will be useful to unfold a little more of Miller's exploration of this curious relationship.

Miller's etymological journey carries him through the 'para' of parasite, from *parasitos*, beside the grain, with an originally positive sense of sharing. This later underwent transformation into a professional dinner guest, one who is able to elicit invitations without returning the favour. Later still this transformed into the modern social and biological meanings. He interestingly follows through the implications of the co-habitation of the parasite with its host, again through the etymology of the Eucharistic host as sacrifice or victim. This itself undergoes the complex paradoxical inversion of the host becoming a stranger, even an enemy (Miller 1979: 218 –21).

The host and the parasite are bound together then:

> Each word in itself becomes divided by the strange logic of the 'para,' membrane which divides inside from outside and yet joins them in a hymenal bond, or which allows an osmotic mixing, making the stranger friend, the distant near, the Unheimlich Heimlich, the homely homey, without, for all its closeness and similarity, ceasing to be strange, distant and dissimilar (Ibid.: 221)

The home that CPR creates, for itself and its guests, is therefore one that carries all the uncanny unease that should mark the reciprocity of the host and their guest. For without the challenge to the guest - physically manifested in the difficulty of travelling to Aberystwyth - that retains the right to criticize, and reciprocally to be challenged, to uncover new modes of disseminating knowledge (that specifically target the entrenched emphasis on the written), there will be no research, and especially none that *performs*. The Centre is not a *centre*, it gathers to disperse. When CPR *hosts* it does not cease to interrogate. What is particularly not easy to discern is where the CPR is most at home: as the outside turns inside, it seems that CPR must also be *welcomed* by those who visit it; incurably alien (like the circus of its early performance *Moths in Amber*), a para-site.

CPR is itself a guest of the University of Wales, Aberystwyth, who in hosting them welcome into academia, into the institution, a foreign body[3] that is both critical of institutions and any easy formulae for dissemination of the strange discipline of Performance. This is itself to be welcomed, like the unexpected dinner guest, and seems more at home with that earlier definition of the parasite who shares the meal beside their host. If such proximity, and equity, of these table fellows can be maintained it will obviously profit both, for they will find much to discuss and in the 'open heart' of friendship much may be generated through estrangement and foreignness. At this fragile border it may be necessary to interrogate all new arrivals, who, feeling strangely at ease, will perhaps find in the Centre for Performance Research an uncanny home - a xenodochium - where theory and practice eat side by side.

NOTES

1. It is not possible here to trace through all the legacies of thought concerning the community, friendship, the host and parasite. The words are Bataille's taken up by Blanchot and Nancy, Derrida and Lingis, grounded in work on the friend (and enemy) from Aristotle to Nietzsche. A *critical* genealogy of the community would, perhaps, be impossible. But considering this impossibility (at the very foundation of community) it would be interesting to trace - and in some part this book, perhaps, does that - the communities made possible by Cardiff Laboratory Theatre and the Centre for Performance Research.
2. Thanks to Richard Gough for his comments and discussion of the nature of English-speaking in Wales.
3. The foreign body is explored thoroughly, in the context of criticism and the institution, in chapter 7 of Nicholas Royle's *After Derrida* (1995).

REFERENCES

Miller, J. Hillis (1979) 'The Critic as Host' in *Deconstruction and Criticism*, Harold Bloom et al. eds., New York: Continuum, pp. 217-53.

Derrida, Jacques (1997) *Politics of Friendship*, trans. George Collins, London: Verso.

Derrida, Jacques and Dufourmantelle, Anne (2000) *Of Hospitality*, trans. Rachel Bowlby, Stanford: Stanford University Press.

Derrida, Jacques (2005) *Paper Machine*, trans. Rachel Bowlby, Stanford: Stanford University Press.

Royle, Nicholas (1995) *After Derrida*, Manchester: Manchester University Press.

HELEN IBALL

A Little Big Boots: On participating in Summer Shift 2004

Pre-(r)amble

The 2004 Summer Shift was my first *actual* experience of CPR. The very fact that this surprises me, and that I have to double-check with myself, says much about the significant role of the Centre in performance praxis nationally and internationally. I feel like I grew-up with CPR. In fact, I've had irregular contact by telephone with the archive and the bookshop and contributed on a couple of occasions to *Performance Research*. I've chatted to Richard at the odd symposium. A precious handful of my days working as a design tutor in Theatr Y Castell, Aberystwyth were occupied with an Italian company[1] brought over by CPR, who took up temporary residence with us, and joyfully disrupted University of Wales health and safety regulations with indoor fires and dodgy means of perambulating themselves around the lighting rig. The year I left the Department and moved away was the year that CPR arrived in Aberystwyth.

What they *aren't* is at least as important as what they are: they aren't a training or degree course, they aren't a receiving house, they aren't just a library or museum, they aren't based in a capital city or any kind of city. They know all about being a Centre without striving to be in the centre. Their conferences: until attending 'Towards Tomorrow' this year, I've missed all of these. On each occasion I planned to go, but personal and professional commitments always conspired against me. It wasn't until July 2004 that my life found such a place as to enable me to consummate its relationship with CPR. Mike Pearson's performative expedition, 'If you go down to the woods today', was the first event in which I participated during that first experience, so that is my focus here. This testimony looks back at moving forward, and so it felt apt that two sections be ordered as a reversal of the title – first 'Big Boots' and then 'A Little' – in order to begin at the end and make the end continue.

1 Big Boots

I begin with an A. A. Milne analogy in tribute to *Performance Research*, who published my first writing to appear in print; an article whose opening gambit was 'Winnie-the-Pooh is a stop and think kind of bear' (Iball 1999: 70). In the chapter 'In Which Christopher Robin leads an expotition [sic] to the North Pole', Winnie-the-Pooh recognizes that when Christopher Robin pulls on his big boots an adventure is going to happen (Milne 1986 [1928]: 104). That sense of focused anticipation is part of the atmosphere amongst the cluster of participants gathered at the designated meeting place on the steps of Theatr Y Castell, Aberystwyth. From here we are divided into teams and given the maps and tasks that will take us on our journey, stopping at three sites before arriving at the Penquoit Centre in Pembrokeshire by nightfall.

The Summer Shift is a change of gear, where gear refers both to the style of outfitting and to altering the speed or direction of transmitted motion. I wear walking boots and waterproof trousers. The vista shifts from the seminar rooms and workshop spaces and offices I inhabit day-in-day-out on the day-job. Mike Pearson is taking us on an expedition. Mike is Christopher Robin and Baden-Powell and then some. He is Brith Gof and *Theatre/Archaeology* (2001) made flesh. He asks us to think on a different scale, contemplating performance in the middle distance, zooming-out from habitual (theatrical) foreshortening. Or getting right-up close. He refers with reverence to Tim Ingold's notion of 'taskscape' in *The Perceptions of the Environment* (2000). It is by what we *do* that landscape makes itself apparent. And the landscape that appears natural may be artificial; as at Hafod, the first site we visit.

Artifice is not a replacement for something real. That common misconception is what connects artifice to accusations of theatricality, and the theatre to accusations of artifice. Rather, artifice is something made by us. It is by what we *did* that performance made itself apparent in that Welsh landscape: and by what we didn't do but plotted and imagined into hypothetical futures from this generative retreat.

2 A Little

The intention of this testimony is to contribute a little (my 'two-penneth') to making apparent the landscape of CPR. CPR is landscaped thinking: bringing together international experiences to collaborate in a manner of immense benefit to the individual practitioner. We were shift workers taking our part in that ongoing endeavour. Mike's workshop was the penultimate event of the 2004 programme. People worked double and multiple shifts. Many of the other participants had attended some or all of the earlier events in various combinations. I went on to Richard Gough's finale, 'Full Board' (22–25 July 2004), which some of the group did not. A chatted mythology was developed: tasters of other workshops, and other participants I had never met, materialized in my peripheral vision. Shifts began to morph into overlap. Here and now, I get a little dizzy with the fear of misrepresenting the experience. My take is partial for sure.

An expedition is, for the inhabitants of Hundred Acre Wood, 'a long line of everybody' (Milne 1986 [1928]: 108). Rabbit's friends and relations tagged onto the end of the line. The line persists in emails and phone calls, in thoughts and intentions, in visits to shows, in reunions at workshops and conferences. And the Chinese whispers of our anecdotes: the idiosyncratic spin-offs of collective memories. The line is fractured and incomplete, but full of a persistent sense of possibility, of re-acquaintance and future collaboration. At times it is dotted and there are branch lines; peopled by some I know very little and yet somehow very well indeed through our engagement with the set tasks:

Thinking in maps and storyboards,
Capturing atmospheres in Polaroid,
Writing postcards in our heads in steamed-up cars.
Planning to take people who aren't here on guided tours of places they can't visit.
Making archives in our minds of performances we know will never be made.

And being taken to a place where a 'known' performance has been made. Mike revisited Esgair Fraith with us, as interventionalist guests at the site-specific theatre work *Tri Bywyd* (October 1995). How did that work make itself apparent? In Mike's anecdotes and in the slab that marked where they had buried a dead sheep and in the memories I had of the performance as documented by Clifford McLucas (2000: 125-37) and of the descriptions of the piece by Mike in *Theatre/Archeology* (Pearson and Shanks 2001: 154-62). I was imagining live performance through written description whilst standing in the place where it was made and hearing someone who had made it re-invoke it when I'd first read of it whilst sitting on a sofa in Hull.

We worked in teams to create the proposal for a piece of theatre that took an audience through this landscape. My group looked to the horizon and envisioned a long line of everybody being drawn down the track towards the ruin, snaking from distance into close up.

Back at Penquoit, we shifted it all again, envisioning the essences and narratives of Esgair Fraith transported to a boat journey past warehouses lining the side of a canal somewhere on the outskirts of Birmingham. One of the group lived on a narrow boat and her coffee-break tales had captured our imaginations. Thus we practised what Mike had preached: conceiving site specificity and performance that is 'not of necessity congruent with its site' and where 'interpenetrating narratives jostle to create meanings' (Pearson in Pearson and Shanks 2001: 23).

Nevertheless, even in the very first hours of the first day, we had some difficulties in moving through these landscapes at a consistently creative pitch.

As in our efforts to a settle upon a performance concept at a Neolithic burial mound, Pentre Ifan, as rain that can only be described as horizontal drenched us – and the standing stones took on far too great an attraction as a shelter. Whilst we were receiving expert guidance in reclaiming 'eventness' (Pearson and Shanks 2001: xiv), at times it seemed we were being hotly pursued in that activity by the eventful; most memorably the interns' flukey car crash in Tesco's car park in Haverfordwest.

We were, however, most often frustrated and wryly amused by the physical limitations of ourselves:

Trying to keep scribing for the group in the back of the car on twisting lanes
and feeling car sick
and being defeated by nausea
and relying on recalling it all later
and almost managing it

and floating when we fell in the river (a metaphor for risk, failure, a wet personality) because it took us by surprise, as we had been expecting to tumble out of a tree.

Or, as Roo exclaimed once rescued from drowning, without realizing he had been: 'did you see me swimming? ... That's called swimming what I was doing' (Milne 1986 [1928]: 122).

And so you see, in the writing of it, my testimony has become occupied with the qualities of the experiences, rather than any narrative wholeness to be claimed by anecdotes. Such is the Summer Shift that the most telling place to recap is not the story but its generative source.

Which means I am not going to divulge the syncronicity with which the Milne analogy extends (on expotition [sic] to the North Pole it is only a matter of time before one of the adventurers is in the river).

So here I am, reaching for the moments that grow stories. That is the heart of it: telling of the generative energy arising from the Summer Shift as an opportunity to conceptualize, to be inspired by guidance and through collaboration. The brevity of such an experience is very precious when a little goes such a long way.

For the record, one more little thing: the river was shallow. The rest of the group didn't have to find the North Pole to fish me out.

NOTES

1. Compagnia Laboratorio di Pontedera in Fratelli Dei Cani (The Brothers of Dogs) and Il Cielo Per Terra (The Sky Underground) at St Donat' Arts Centre, St Donat's Castle, Llantwit Major, Vale of Glamorgan, Theatr Y Castell, St Michael's Place, Aberystwyth and John Phillips Hall, College Road, Bangor on 2 - 5, 8 - 9 and 11 - 12 February 1994

REFERENCES

Iball, Helen (1999) 'Melting Moments: Bodies Upstaged by the Foodie Gaze', *Performance Research* 4.1: 70–81.

Ingold, Tim (2000) *The Perceptions of the Environment: Essays in Livelihood, Dwelling and Skill*, London: Routledge.

McLucas, Clifford (2000) 'Ten Feet and Three Quarters of an Inch of Theatre', in Nick Kaye (ed.) *Site-Specific Art*, London: Routledge, pp. 125-137.

Milne, A. A. (1986 [1928]) 'Winnie-the-Pooh', in *The Complete Winnie-the-Pooh*, London: Chancellor Press.

Pearson, Mike and Shanks, Michael (2001) *Theatre/Archaeology*, London: Routledge.

PHOTO: KEITH MORRIS

Expedition across the Preseli Mountains

SIBYLLE PETERS

Performances of Truth

What I shall have to say here is neither difficult nor contentious, the only merit I should like to claim for it is that of being true, at least in parts. The phenomenon to be discussed is very widespread and obvious, and it cannot fail to have been already noticed, at least here and there, by others. Yet I have not found attention paid to it specifically.

It was for too long the assumption, that the business of a 'statement' can only be to 'describe' some state of affairs, or to 'state some fact', which it must do either truly or falsely ... But now in recent years ... it has come to be commonly held that many utterances which look like statements are either not intended at all, or only intended in part, to record or impart straightforward information about facts ... The utterances we are to consider here do not 'describe' or 'report' or constate anything at all, are not 'true or false'; and the uttering of the sentence is, or is a part of, the doing of an action, which again would not normally be described as, or as 'just', saying something ... What are we to call a sentence or an utterance of this type?

John L. Austin

In spring 2004 CPR invited me to Aberystwyth to work on a research project that dealt with the academic lecture as performance. The first weeks were wonderfully calm and peaceful shifting between library, beach and the friendly countryside house of Lucy and Ric's. I prepared a lecture that began with a long quotation from John L. Austin's lecture series 'How to do things with Words'. I decided not to mark the quotation as such but simply to begin by delivering Austin's lecture instead of my own – thereby *performing a lecture* instead of *fulfilling the performance of academic lecturing*. That gave me the opportunity to reflect upon this strange difference and its historical background.

The lecture was to be presented, amongst other venues, at the SCUDD (Standing Conference of University Drama Departments) conference 04 that took place in Aberystwyth under the title of 'Articulating Practice', just a few days before the start of the CPR's *Giving Voice Festival 04* ('Philosophy of the Voice'), and I took the chance to take part in a four-day workshop in experimental voice-and-body work by Enrique Pardo. Absorbed by my research I didn't manage to take a closer look into the programme of the workshop until the night before it started. Then I discovered that participants were requested to bring along a text learned by heart. My despair – would I have to stay awake all night to learn an appropriate text? – soon turned into relief: I already knew some words by heart: the beginning of 'How to do things with Words'! Thus I became the only participant working not with dramatic or narrative material but with an academic text. This turned out to be a challenging experience and a kind of shortcut into the problem dealt with by my own lecture. In short: academic lectures usually tell something about something – a relation that is called 'knowledge', but sometimes this relation is crossed by a different level of attention focused on the correspondences between the referential claims and the way the lecture is conducted, or performed. I was especially interested in the way evidence is configured in this kind of crossing.

The lectures presented in the evening sessions of the Giving -Voice Festival were well suited to build a bridge in this respect. There I heard the sentence (I think it was Ralf Peters who uttered it): 'Whenever I tell something about the voice, all of a sudden the voice tells something about me'. Wasn't that exactly what I wanted to show? – that this principle, usually denied by academic discourse, still takes part in the production of knowledge via the neglected performance of the lecture. Ralf Peters was followed by Alice Lagaay, who argued that the performative use of language turns the relation between voice and language inside-out. Whereas in the constative use of language the voice can be seen as the medium of language, the performative use makes the language the medium of the voice.

This happened to be exactly what Enrique Pardo's workshop was about. We learned to go against the dominance of textual reference and use the text as a medium for our voices – their sounds, colours, atmospheres, movements. But strangely enough this 'turning around' in a way still matched with the content of Austin's famous text that, for the first time, stated: whereas the constative use of language is ruled by the formal difference of true and false, there is another use of language that ca•'t be judged in such referential terms. So, paradoxically, just because of this correspondence I couldn't deny that in the end there was a complex dimension of truth in our voice-experiments.

Thus the voice work made me think about Austin's argument the other way round. When Austin says that philosophers for too long assumed that 'the business of a "statement" can only be to "describe" some state of affairs, or to "state some fact", which it must do either truly or falsely', this seems to imply that they did so because this is true of the way academic discourse itself uses language. Consequently a wrong opinion about the use of language was caused by a philosophical discourse that generalized its own use of language. This implication highlights the need to deal with the performative use of language in philosophical terms. But still it tends to exclude the performative dimension from the academic discourse itself. And indeed the question – whether Austin's lecture series is or is not reflecting its own performative use of language – still provokes debate today. So finally I came to pose my question like this: can we, in paying respect to Austin as the first ever lecturer on performativity, accept his distinction between a truth-bound use of language and a performative dimension that is actually defined by not dealing with truth? And if not, what kind of truth is dealt with in performance? Or even more important for my topic: what are performances of truth?

During the following days I took part in the Giving Voice workshop and the SCUDD conference more or less at the same time, constantly changing between the rehearsal stage (where the workshop participants more and more turned into a crawling, howling, haunting, crying, laughing crowd) and the academic lecture theatre (where everything seemed to be under control, but sometimes was all the more bewildering) – well, you know what academic conferences can be like! Two worlds, which by appearances could not be more distinct, were still deeply connected for me in those days: a connection that was not easy to stand or to follow, but still a connection, which for me is nothing else but 'the way of working'.

Epilogue: 'Performances of Truth'

At this point things took a surprising turn. Enrique Pardo at that time was almost obsessed by the ancient medium the Sibyl of Cumae and planned a project about the voice in the context of truth telling. Therefore, I became aware of the connection between my first name and this special kind of 'performing truth'. An accidental hint in regard to the questions raised?

As tends to happen when issues of work are associated with personal history, my brain was slowly scattered by complexities. The last day of my visit came (dolphins were spotted in the bay that morning) and culminated in one of the famous CPR performance dinners, really a last supper for me. In this enchanted setting, both worlds – conference and festival crowds – collided, until around midnight representatives of both sides performed a phantasmatic tango on the dinner table. In a dreamlike state I gave my edition of *How to do things with Words* to a beautiful member of the Pantheatre and caught the first bus to London.

PHOTO: ALINE VASQUEZ KELLER

Eating Words, Aberystwyth, 2004

Frankie Armstrong and Joan Mills – Lost Voices, 1986

Singing Praise

The phone rings. It could be of no consequence, a delightful chance to chat with a friend or one of those phone calls that may have a major affect on your life. Such was the call from Ceri Llewellyn, Administrator of Cardiff Lab around 1983.

I'd been singing professionally since 1964, mostly in the Folk Revival and the anti-war and women's movements. During the sixties I'd been involved for seven years with Ewan McColl and Peggy Seeger, mounting a range of theatrical, recording and radio productions featuring both traditional songs and those written by Ewan and Peggy. Ewan remained very influenced by Stanislavski, and hence we explored a range of Stanislavskian approaches to both songs and theatrical productions. I left Ewan's group in 1970 and concentrated on singing as well as having my day jobs in social and youth work and as a trainer.

I started pioneering (a grand word for learning on the job!) my voice workshops based on ethnic styles of singing in 1975. To my amazement, something I started as a one evening experiment turned into a major part of my working life. Amongst the groups who invited me to run workshops for them was the occasional theatre company, but largely I worked with community groups, in mental health, with teenage girls, women's groups and in the folk scene.

And then came the phone call from Cardiff. I was invited to run a weekend for the members of the Lab. I liked the sound of the organization, especially when Ceri said that the admin and secretarial staff were to join in too. I can recall arriving on Cardiff Station to be met by the secretary who confessed to being petrified, saying that she'd never done anything like a voice workshop before. In the event, she turned out to have a great natural voice and initially found the workshop easier than some of the formally trained singers. That first weekend seemed to go with great energy and enthusiasm. All of the participants loved the Eastern European part-songs. They got very excited listening to the variety of song and vocal styles on tape, including some of Shamanic chanting and Tuvan overtone and split-voice singing.

It was clear that I had met with kindred spirits, and I started a friendship and collaboration with Joan Mills that lasts to this day. The exact sequence of my continuing contact with the CPR now eludes me, and I'm also not sure when Joan and I realized that whenever we sang together, something very extraordinary happened.

It may even have been at that first workshop. To this day when I listen to some of our recordings, I often can't tell which voice is which. The strange thing is that when we sing individually there is no difficulty at all telling who is who, but some strange metamorphosis happens when our overtones meet and mingle.

In 1985, Joan had written to ask me if I would co-create a vocal theatre piece with her for a Cardiff Lab festival of new work the following year. I was thrilled and delighted at the prospect. I had found myself involved in theatre again a few years earlier with Graeae Theatre making a show that the cast devised with the fine director Nigel Jamieson. We toured the piece in India, and it had been an extraordinary time. I had loved the experience but wondered if I'd get another chance outside the sphere of theatre for the disabled. And here it was. For over a month I lived with Joan and Richard, being treated to their wonderful hospitality and cooking. The food and the conversation at meal times were gifts for stomach, heart and head.

Chapter must still resound with the myriad of sounds and songs we experimented with over those weeks. In the evenings, Joan read to me from a wide range of historical sources on the silencing of women down the centuries, which was the subject of our piece Lost Voices. Their library overflowed into corridors and hallways. When time allowed, Richard directed us (I think this was when he was creating and directing Table Manners, too). I felt to be in the heart of the Lab's process – never enough time, ideas flying in and out like moths at twilight, last-minute decisions and panics, and then, miraculously, it all comes together at the final hour.

The connection between us was truly cemented, and I recall saying – prophetically – during that stay in 1986 'I like Cardiff, I think I could even live here'. After this, I periodically went to Cardiff to run day or weekend workshops, and Joan and I increased our repertoire, finding a few occasions to sing publicly.

I was on one of my many trips to Australia when the first of the Giving Voice events happened. It had sounded wonderful from the reports I got from colleagues who had attended. By the second festival, I had moved to Cardiff (it was a sad day for me personally when the CPR was lured to Aberystwyth a few years later – as the crow flies it is not a great distance from Cardiff, but as public transport goes it can take longer than flying to Africa) and was able to offer hospitality to a number of friends including Vivien Ellis and the late, much missed, Venice Manley. A birch tree and a honeysuckle vine that we all planted at that time are still thriving in my garden. And, as well as a tree to commemorate my first *Giving Voice*, there were all the workshops I participated in – what a feast of stimulating talks and discussions, presentations and concerts.

Since then I have made sure that I've been back in the UK for each and every *Giving Voice*, teaching, presenting and participating. The extraordinary teachers and performers I have met through *Giving Voice* over the years are too numerous to mention. Suffice it to say that they have played a central role in the development of my work and reflections on voice. To mention but a few of my absolute high points, unforgettable concerts include those by A Filetta from Corsica, Mtiebe from Georgia, the Bistritsa Grannies from Bulgaria, the extraordinary Trang Quang Hai and his wife – Hai doing astonishing overtone singing as well as playing twelve instruments and the spoons like you have never heard. Then there was the magic of Bernice Johnson-Reagon's contextual talk and participatory concert of spirituals and gospel singing, and most recently, spell-binding concerts by Marianna Sadowska from the Ukraine, Stepanida from Siberia and Jonathan Hart from New York. And these are just a few of the concerts, out of a whole range of events, talks, and workshops! It has been an honour and a gift to participate in these events.

My informal relationship with CPR has continued through my work with Joan, teaching weekend courses together as well as recording: with other Cardiff-based singers and musicians we put together *The Fair Moon Rejoices* CD, and later Joan also joined me with John Kirkpatrick and Leon Rosselson on *The Garden of Love* CD.

The National Voice Practitioners Network [NVPN][1], which I helped establish, has had a rich symbiotic relationship with CPR's *Giving Voice* over the years and we have a strong Welsh contingent, in part due to the input of CPR's *Local Voices, World of Song* projects, and I trust that this rich interplay between myself, CPR and *Giving Voice* will continue to bear fruit.

NOTES

1. The Network began as a reunion of voice teachers who had trained with me. A group of us formulated a statement of our ethos, principles and practice, which I still find to be a moving and powerful statement (see www.naturalvoice.net). We opened out the Network to others who agreed with and practised this approach. Four years ago we formalized ourselves into a constituted organization, providing information, support, networking and training for those running voice/singing groups or community choirs.

Joan Mills and Frankie Armstrong – The Wild Girl, 1987

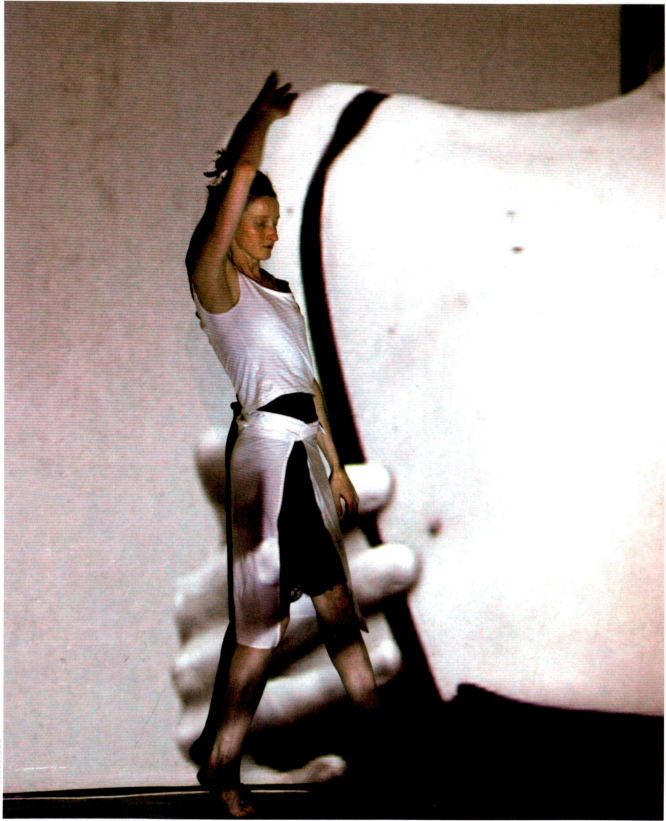

PHOTO: FUTOSHI SAKAUCHI

Ailsa Richardson in re-member(3)

AILSA RICHARDSON

Pro-found and Impossible

Could I be so bold as to create my own mini field station as a response to this invitation: using an existing structure (found) to hang my reflections on and around; observing from a different perspective; following a lead; taking an idea and running with it; starting small; reflecting; mirroring; simultaneously obeying and disobeying, following and resisting.

> My imagined field station is:
> *Profundia, impossibilia*
> *Collecting (gathering)*
> *Base/Basis/Site, Support, Melt, Mould, Fuse/ Fusion, Failure*

Starting point: December party

I attend the CPR 30th birthday party. I think of my own 30th birthday party. My invitation to people was to dress either from a past life or a future reincarnation. At 30 the party seems, by nature, to be poised between past and future, in a place where a balance is struck between the two.

The two things that stick in my mind from that weekend are a meeting with Melanie Thompson and a discussion around failure i.e. the nature and necessity of failure. This piece follows on directly from my notes on these occurrences, and I knew that these would be

Melanie Thompson

the impetus for this writing and that my engagement with that event would begin a reflection upon my own experiences of CPR.

I didn't contribute much or anything to public discussions that weekend. I kept very quiet – holding the birthday cake, contributing music and ideas to the planning of the event, washing up (I'm proud that my first performance at Chapter took place behind the scenes between the kitchen sink and the dishwasher). I witnessed and waited to see what would come to the fore (in terms of significance and profundity) – what would stand in relief against the background of other people's celebration and reminiscences.

Where I found myself

(apart from at Chapter's kitchen sink)

1. wanting only to reflect on past and future in a way that can actively shift and change in the present.
> *History is always written from the perspective*
> *of the present: history fulfils a need of the present*
> *(Lechte 111)*
(in the of case of the CPR party history fulfilled the needs of the event and now in the event of this writing it must fulfil my task of recollection and reflection).

2. in conversation with Melanie – finding she is connected to two of the key artistic collaborators in my life and is now researching her Ph.D. at the University of the West of England where I began my formal training as an artist. We discussed artistic interests and through conversation found similarities in our present concerns and the connection of these to our history and potential future as artists. This became more profoundly apparent when Melanie handed me a card and the image on it had a marked similarity to some from my most recent performance *re-member me.*
> We can only operate in the present, which holds
> the past and the future at the heart of a network
> of connections. (Tolle 48)

3. at an event acting as a site of potential connections cutting across times and processes: a site of arrival and departure. A base.

Pro-found
found
a foundry: melts, moulds, fuses
founded, established, coming of age (30)
foundling: rescued from obscurity, from
potential neglect

I think about how these may relate to CPR's activities.

For some reason (beyond reason) I look for 'foundry' in an encyclopaedia. Of course, I don't find foundry, but in the place where foundry should have been there is Foucault. I have neglected Foucault in favour of other things in life. I love philosophy, but I am not well read. I like to happen upon philosophers and philosophical thought in the course of other actions and lines of enquiry (the thrill of happening upon something relevant rather than seeking it out intentionally). I read about Foucault, genealogy, epistemology and Nietzsche's 'effective history'.

Foucault recognizes that if history is always genealogy and an intervention, frameworks of knowledge and modes of understanding are themselves always changing. Epistemology studies these changes as the grammar of knowledge-production and is revealed by the practices of science, philosophy, art and literature. Epistemology is also a way of connecting material events to thought or ideas. That a particular practice embodies an idea is not self-evident: the connection has to be made evident within the practice of epistemology itself (Lechte 112).

Where I find myself

At this juncture, I find myself working for CPR temporarily. I am placed within the organization and although this is a step towards the inside of the organization it also enables a step back and an opportunity to overview its operations. The aim of CPR (as quoted in the invitation for this piece) is to 'attempt an open and rigorous examination of physical expression (in the context of performance)'.

From here, CPR appears (remaining true to its beginnings as a theatre company) to operate as an artist does. I have taken a step into the mind/body of this artist as it collects, assembles, recollects, re-assembles; as it creates pieces of work that manifest as events and publications which act as sites of connection (of artists, scholars and their ideas) enabling people to come together to train, present and exchange ideas and perhaps more pertinently enabling research in various forms - as training, lecture, performance, writing, image-making etc.

Alongside these affective operations exist other elements - chaos, creative ideas/imagination unbounded, open-endedness and the impossibility of closing the gap between vision and material manifestation (Duchamp's 'art coefficient'). The trick is to exist in the gap - with the pain, the hard work, the necessity of failure.

Susan Melrose, as part of her essay 'the curiosity of writing (or, who cares about performance mastery?)' examines the issue of epistemic practices in the context of practice-driven research. She recognizes the fact that the inventiveness of professional arts-creative practitioners means they are inevitably involved in epistemic practices but asks the question: can they be shown to 'operate to the power of speculation and interrogative auto-reflection' - not necessarily as writing but as a 'logics of production' and 'practice mastered through practice'.

I FIND MYSELF observing CPR engaged in the task of attempting to be as responsive as this *as an organization* (in its artistic and epistemic practice). It faces the same challenges as the arts-creative practitioner engaged in practice-driven research within the academy. Speculation and reflection on CPR will find it to some extent resisting definition and also working towards a clear 'logics of production'. The operation of CPR as arts-creative practitioner simultaneously embraces functionality and dysfunctionality, as, to an extent, it resists definition by the institution it is part of but not completely owned by. As the academy (as part of the knowledge economy) is always attempting an explanation, an analysis, a justification of its operations in relation to research, so CPR maintains the inventiveness and mutability of the artist. As a site *at the heart of a network of connections*, perhaps CPR's most valuable asset is as an artist who enables research. It is perhaps this enabling process, i.e. the enabling ability of the arts-creative practitioner (*where foundling processes and ideas become rescued from obscurity*), that is the most valuable thing a creative artist can offer, and thus it must become a fundamental aspect of practice at every level of operations.

REFERENCES
Lechte, John (1994) *Fifty Key Contemporary Thinkers: From Structuralism to Postmodernity*, London: Routledge.
Tolle, Eckhart (2004) *The Power of Now: A Guide to Spiritual Enlightenment*, USA: New World Library.
Melrose, Susan "the curiosity of writing (or, who cares about performance mastery?)", paper given at PARIP 2003, National Conference, University of Bristol.

JILL GREENHALGH

And before I know it

Mad in pursuit, and in possession so
A bliss in proof, and proved, [sometimes] a very
woe;
Before, a joy proposed; behind, a dream.

Circa 1981

It is past midnight, I am utterly exhausted, spent, a rag. I, we, have been rushing from meetings with locals, dignitaries and actors, to rehearsals, to shopping for stuff, to building the spaces, to more meetings, for weeks. (I think we forgot to eat today.) Anyway I am, as they say, at the end of my tether. I have borrowed the van (midnight being the only time it was free) and I am sitting among bracken in a pine forest, three miles out of town, holding a pair of secateurs and it's pouring with rain (and I forgot my coat). I am collecting a vanload of bracken and soil to cover the floor of a cave, in an underground slate mine, in Blaenau Ffestiniog, Snowdonia, North Wales. The performance of 'The Widow's Dream' opens tomorrow and I still haven't a clue what I am doing in 'my' bit.

This, I decide, is the worst moment in all my time with this company; the reigning chaos is unbearable, again, I will protest, again, I will leave, again. Enough. I am suddenly feeling very, very sorry for myself and start to cry, the big kind of cry that doesn't happen so often. *WHAT THE **** AM I DOING HERE?*, I scream to the owls.

Clearly no one is listening to me (except those owls), so I stop crying, carry a dozen armfuls of bracken to the van, go back to the little cottage I am staying in with Julia and Phillip, and go to bed.

Next morning we finish making the performance. Was it three or four days we had to make the whole thing? Some of the Odin actors had joined us - they are not used to making performances in three days - it's a joy to witness their panic.

That evening we perform. It is the strongest and most beautiful piece we have ever made.

The spectator takes a journey underground through a once very productive slate mine - now a tourist attraction.

The Widow's Dream, *Llechwedd Slate Caverns, Blaenau Ffestiniog, 1981*

PHOTO: PAUL ROYLANCE

The spectators pass through a labyrinth of caves and passageways led by a sound and light sequence. We have timed and choreographed the whole performance to the light changes and turned off the sound. My cave image lasts just two minutes and is the evocation of the graveside vigil of a miner's wife. The spectators pass many different scenes and images. At the end the performance the tour opens up into a spectacular underground lake on which we launch a boat set on fire - a floating funeral pyre, a ritual, for the death of all miners. Did someone sing? I can't remember, perhaps John played his trumpet. Our audience, some of whom had lost family members in disasters in this very mine, are tearful and thankful.

I worked with Cardiff Laboratory Theatre for seven years (1979–86). I was always busy. We sped from one project to the next - one country to the next - it was exciting, exhilarating. Richard Gough is able to envisage strong and resonant images, he has the capacity to persuade you to do anything, he is a seducer, always. He has ideas, big ones, always, exciting ones, impossible ones... we throw in our bits, we spew ideas - caught in the excitement of anything is possible. And we never learn - we each find ourselves fighting our corner for the stupidest, craziest notions and before we know it we are responsible for actually constructing the image, scene, action, performance for tomorrow lunchtime.

We had a device we called the 'fish tank' (cannot recall why it was so-called). Basically on *'GO!'* everyone would shout everything they could think of that they might do in [for example] a toilet. And before I know it, I am driving a 1940s Norton motorbike, with side car, in a wedding dress, through the streets of Leicester, after a mock wedding to Handel's Water Music in the two halves of the newly furbished public toilets. And before I know it, I am singing temperance songs in a pub in the centre of Loughborough, or Stand by Your Man in a working man's club in the Rhondda (that one was a bit close to the wind), or playing the dragon keeper on stilts leading a twenty-foot dragon through Llandysul, or performing in boats on Lake Bracciano near Rome (no one can see what we are doing - we are too far away), or re-staging Faust, or playing Captain von Trapp in the Sound of Musak, our Christmas panto in Chapter Arts Centre (and fulfilling a life-long ambition to sing Edelweiss), or playing clarinet on allotments in Denmark, or driving the massive Lethal Red Truck (that we bought from the People Show) around Europe, or restaging the Jarrow March, or hosting a series of community barters throughout rural Wales, or preparing a feast for three hundred people. Or ... or ... or ... and ... and ... and ... each event more tiring than the last ... each event always worth it - almost always.

I have a fondest memory of a summer in Italy, playing

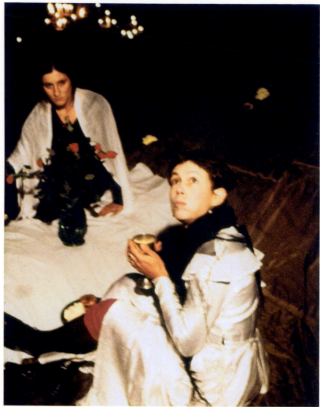

The Widow's Dream, *Llechwedd Slate Caverns, Blaenau Ffestiniog, 1981*

in Volterra, meeting and working with Akademia Ruchu and Roberto Bacci's group in Pontedera: in our billet, a building that was once a (so-named) lunatic asylum, it's evening, and we are all in our pyjamas, sitting in a kitchen, drinking wine and eating pasta, a long, laughing evening and I most clearly remember the feeling of having stopped, not working (for once). And another (weirdly fond) memory of the time when I drove Lethal Red Truck to Madrid and arrived just in time to perform *The Orchestra* in some suburb square. The rest of the group had eaten a dodgy seafood paella the evening before. We start the performance and suddenly the sax player rises and shuffles off stage. We carry on, and then the cello player leaves, the French horn too... we are three instruments down... the conductor looks at us, and mournfully mouths 'sorry' and leaves as well. Needless to say the whole thing fell apart as our poisoned colleagues threw up behind us.

Twenty-five years on, this process of reflecting on ways of working dredges only a series of nostalgic rememberings on my part, forgiven, from the far away that is right now. I still cannot stand the madness of organizational chaos, and the legacy that I carry with me from those halcyon days with Cardiff Lab is that anything is possible but even more so if you see it coming.

FRANC CHAMBERLAIN

Ways of Working: Ten Fragments from Sixteen Years of Interaction [1]

Prologue

In the ten fragments that follow, I draw on my memories and my journals to pick out moments of involvement or ways of working with CPR since 1988. Rather than attempt to gather the pieces into a coherent narrative, I wanted to catch something of the differences of approach of the work, as well as a sense of a personal encounter, which speaks in different voices. I don't attempt to evaluate the work of CPR in a general sense or to offer a typology of ways of working. Nor do I trace in any detailed or systematic way the impact of these encounters on my own ways as a practitioner, teacher, writer, editor and human being. Perhaps though, I should offer a generalization: CPR has made a greater contribution to the development of research into performance practice in the United Kingdom than any other single organization in the past thirty years. I don't think that this research contribution is always recognized or acknowledged and I'm not even sure that a volume such as this, welcome though it is, can do that contribution justice.

These fragments are not intended to be paradigms of either my own experience at an event or of the event itself. They are not holographic fragments from which a whole can be generated. Occasionally the texts I quote from my journals are unrecognizable to me; they bring no memory of the experience they refer to, only links to other texts and concepts. At other times I find myself engaged in a reverie where I'm immersed in a sensory experience that I hesitate to call a 're-experiencing' because I have a sense that the once-living is being re-worked as in a dream. I have refused the temptation to re-work the words of the past in the language of the present, although they are, of course, re-contextualized.

Each fragment seems to me to be a momentary crystallization of a trajectory that is a mixture of both singular and ordinary. The notes from the past indicate what appeared significant then, implying an attractor that drew each articulation. Sometimes it takes time for us to be able to tell the difference between what's important and what's unimportant, and frequently it requires the engagement of others to point out the obvious or draw out the obscured.

I offer these pieces in the hope that they will stimulate others' recollections, offer something of a flavour of events to those who weren't there, provide small moments of connection with other texts in the volume, point towards different ways of working, and, perhaps, open out onto areas that have yet to be discussed.

One

Points of Contact 1: Theatre, Anthropology and Theatre Anthropology,
held at Leicester Polytechnic's School of Performing Arts,
from 30 September to 2 October 1988.

Eugenio Barba, Franco Ruffini, Ferdinando Taviani, and Nicola Savarese presented the results of the research that they had been conducting at ISTA [International School of Theatre Anthropology] since 1979 for the first time in the UK. Mette Bovin, an anthropologist closely associated with Barba at the time discussed her practice of provocation anthropology and showed her ethnographic film *Dances in the Sand*. Roberta Carreri, collaborator with both Barba and Bovin, performed *Judith* as well as giving a demonstration of her training process. This line-up on its own would have been outstanding, but Richard Schechner and John Blacking were also speaking and offering different perspectives on the relationship between anthropology and theatre.

This was my first encounter with the work of CPR and the richness of this symposium fed into my explorations of the points of contact between theatre and anthropology and into classes and courses in the field that I've taught ever since.

Two

Points of Contact 2: Performance-Nature-Culture,
held at Dartington College of Arts, April 1989.

We're told to wrap up warm and go for a walk led by Richard and Judie … We reach the grass rectangle with terraces of grass. A clear sky, half moon, and sharp stars. We stand, talk, and look … Three Poles amidst us, whispering … Then, opposite the moon, which is silver in the branches of a cedar, along the path, two torches appear between the trees, accompanied by the sound of bells, or finger cymbals. The red-orange flame of the torches contrasts with the moon as the newcomers move along one side of the rectangle and then descend the steps in the middle of the second … The sound of their boots on the steps is a good percussive accompaniment to their arrival. We move to mark a vague semi-circle to accommodate them … They sing, bodies expressive, contorting but not with excess tension, making shapes with body and sound … they sing in a group, a moving sculpture of bodies. They have blankets wrapped around them, one or two carry censers; the smell is of Frankincense/Myrrh … the feeling for me is like Christmas or bonfire night; a special, communal, festive occasion.

Staniewski steps forward, wearing a greatcoat, and speaks through an interpreter. He wants a 'meeting' before the performance. We are a small group (about seventy) and he wants us to look at each other, at the sky…to 'look at the heavens with new eyes' and to keep looking. 'He who seeks will surely find' becomes changed into: 'He who walks will not be lost' and we retrace the route of the performers' entrance with them amongst us and we are led into the Great Hall and they show us where to sit.

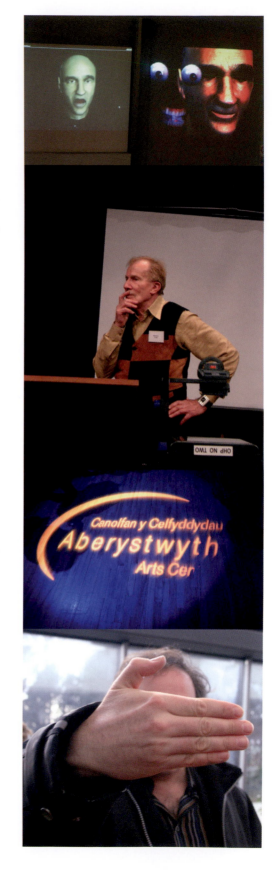

Three

Gardzienice Workshop, Druidstone Haven, Wales,
from Wednesday to Sunday, 19–23 April 1989.

After watching CPR's company perform at Chapter in Cardiff we were driven two-and-a-half hours West, arriving at Druidstone at 1a.m.

A beautiful place. We were met by the company and told that we had three minutes to get ready for a night run.

Running: gentle joy finding sound rhythms, changing the body movements but always loose and staying with each other in the same rhythm. Members of the company would link arms with one of us and emphasize the rhythm. Moments where we stop and hang loose. We ran for about thirty minutes ending with a hanging loose and then went in to eat.

It took me a while to get my rhythms together, but I enjoyed the run. We were told to stay aware of our surroundings.

After food Dom, Steve and I went down to the beach; tide out, full moon, beautiful and refreshing. We met Judie on the way down; hair loose and salt-watered.

Slept in a double bed with Paul. Bed at 0230, up at 0745. At 0815 we jog to a square piece of grass overlooking the sea where we performed a series of warm-up exercises. Mariusz leads: 'Too much talking in the morning is annoying.'

After the warm up Wlodek gave a little talk. Sometimes, he said, it is not necessary to talk but for us English it is. So we do. We need to tune our inner music to the outer music.

«»

Note for me: All singing/actions are gifts to others. I was getting into movements that were for myself.

«»

The idea of the Greek chorus is important for the whole work. Individuals make propositions, come out of the chorus, 'shine brightly like a star' and then, 'extinguishing' return to the chorus.

«»

As I look at these notes from 1989 in November 2004, I notice how my memory tells different stories. It tells me of running at night and a white horse appearing in the moonlight, of being told to notice the horse. But I also remember a resistance, a sense of being patronized. I wasn't a city person and felt that the instruction to 'notice' created an unwelcome dissonance in my environmental tuning; I was already noticing. My memory tells a story of being impressed by the training processes of the company but feeling uncomfortable with the politics of experience.

Four

Points Of Contact 3: Performance, Politics and Ideology, held at the University of Lancaster, Thursday to Sunday, 5–7 April 1990.

One of the intentions of this conference was that is would be 'organised to enable all participants, as far as possible, to play a significant part in the formation of its findings'. One of my memories is of a session where people were making complaints about the organisation of the event, missing the point that they weren't taking responsibility for making the event be more what they wanted.

Utpal Dutt, defended Marxism as Eastern European regimes fell arguing that it was 'utterly stupid' for the East Germans to destroy their social system because they wanted a better car than the Trabant. Peter Oslzly, on the other hand, spoke of the theatre's role in the liberation of Czechoslovakia in the velvet revolution.

During the course of this symposium there were practical workshops with Hugo Medina (Chile) and Augusto Boal (Brazil), but the most interesting moment for me took place in a group exploring gender politics. I volunteered to participate in a role-play in the middle of the group; a conflict between a man and a woman. I'll sometimes shout when I'm in a conflict and don't mind other people shouting at me. However, in the process of the role-play, I noticed that the woman I was working with had raised her volume and, in role, I shouted: 'Don't you shout at me!' I can no longer remember what the imagined conflict was about but I was struck by the feedback from those watching that my partner had raised her voice to match mine, whereas my perception was that she'd raised it above mine. A little reminder of how, occasionally, a role-play can enable us to see something in ourselves that is usually hidden.

Boal said later that any person can go into themselves to find the self they need; if they are timid, for example, they can get in touch with a courageous person. In the role-play, however, I wasn't looking for anything new. I was playing an oppressive man, easy enough to find and easy enough to distance myself from. My characteristic response would have been very different from the oppressive man's, but my perception was the same and the perception was, in fact, a misperception.

Five

Working on Performance East and West, Brecon and Cardiff, from Saturday to Sunday, 4–11 April 1992.

This was the seventh session of ISTA and the first to be held in the UK. It was unsatisfactory in some ways because there were no workshops to participate in, and there was also less debate than is customary at a CPR symposium. My notes have much more argument in them than normal, perhaps because there was so little space to debate.

My last notes:
The 'mannerisms' of the Odin actors may be defences to change, but they are neither 'conventional' in the sense of handed-down, nor 'natural' in the sense of everyday. They are therefore, certainly extra-daily gestures, but is this enough? The gestures are repeated by the actors throughout several performances, and they become fixed signs without referents. This frees them for montage but removes a sense of a physical language or, rather, of an affective language. The burning up of the body in Grotowski's texts is turned into a reification of the body; the body becomes an object to be cut up like a piece of celluloid. A grammar of empty signs means that the combination is based on the aesthetics of the director. Any underscore has to be created by the actor to generate an internal coherence (Why? Why not be fragmented? Schizo?)

There is no communication from actor to audience. The audience fill the signs (or create referents with their own imagination). The emperor's new clothes ...

Six

*Points of Contact 4: Performance Ritual and Shamanism, Cardiff (?),
from Friday to Sunday, 8–10 January 1993.*

Nicolás Núñez has us jogging and then freezing in a squat with our thumbs against our foreheads. We're looking for an animal ally to emerge. When it does, we develop a dance from the qualities we associate with it. For the time being mine fits perfectly.

I ask Nicolás about the possibility of publishing his book in Harwood's Contemporary Theatre Studies: it appears in 1996.

Núñez's work led me back to the experiences I'd had with Rena Mirecka in 1984 in a way that Staniewski's hadn't. Within a few weeks of the conference I received a letter from Mirecka, the first contact for nine years, inviting me to attend an event in Sardinia that September. I went.

Seven

*Process and Documentation, Brecon, from Thursday to Sunday,
26–29 August 1993.*

Anna O, Hijinx, Forced Entertainment, Black Mime, Roland Miller, Scala Review Fantasia. Opportunities for participants to investigate working practices of at least three companies. I chose to be with Scala Review, Hijinx and Anna O. I remember only fragments. From Scala Review, the idea of incorporating disagreement and conflict, avoiding the dangers of a flattening consensus in devised work. Working with Hijinx, I stuff my mouth with a stone wrapped round and round with duct tape, wedge myself high in a corner on the outside of the building to descend and leap towards a paper effigy of myself with a dangling, bleeding heart.

Susan Melrose is ill. Cathy Naden and Claire Marshall perform her paper. All I can remember is something about sheep. At the end, David Hughes asks: 'What do you call your Art?'. Hearing 'arse' rather than 'art', I replied:

'I call my arse "my arse", what do you call yours?' At some point, I remember (imagine?) Roland Miller entering through a window.

I only attended a day of the second session on process and documentation at the University of Lancaster but the explorations into the documentation at both of these sessions fed directly into the courses in documentation we teach at UCN.

I haven't attended a *Points of Contact* event since 1993.

Eight

Past Masters 5: Michael Chekhov, The University of Birmingham, from Friday to Sunday, 5–7 November 1999.

My first CPR event for six years. It is the only one of the *Past Masters* series that I've attended although I wish I'd been able to get to more. I gave a paper at this one and got interrupted by the videographer asking me to stop moving about so much. When I'm giving lectures I place ideas/images in the space and map a journey between them using the width of the audience as a limit.

Nine

The Summer Shift, Aberystwyth, July 2002.

There were some difficulties in the workshop with New World Performance Laboratory. One participant commented on a particular difficulty: 'There was something in the dynamic of the whole course that was about male power. Jim gave a song to a female singer, but at every other point he'd started the songs. In the moment the female singer couldn't take it, a male singer picked it up, and Jim closed the whole sequence down. He said later to justify it that it never worked when started by a male ...'.

Ten

Eating Words, A Performative Banquet by Richard Gough, Aberystwyth, Saturday, 3 April 2004.

A fragment from my writing on *Eating Words* published in NTQ, November 2004:

> This will stay in my memory as a wonderful performance event. I don't know what will happen to it though. Will it become more elaborate and detailed? Will I suddenly remember the food and the colours, the name of the woman next to me, the music? Will my imagination continue to work on these things and produce versions that I can't distinguish from the reality? In my mind's eye there is a woman in an ice-blue silk ballgown, turning. Was she there? I really don't know.

All photographs taken by Franc Chamberlain during 'Towards Tomorrow', April 2005, Aberystwyth, Wales

Chris Rowbury – From Honey and Ashes, *1991*

The Courage to Create:
Food, Alchemy, Objects and Performance[1]

MT: How or when did you first start getting interested in food in performance and food as performance? Do you remember what sparked your interest in it?

RG: I've been citing the major conference gathering/ festival we organized in January 1994 in Cardiff as one of the Points of Contact conferences as a significant departure (this was a series that we'd launched several years before, which was simply to bring theatre and performance into contact with other disciplines). The title was 'Points of Contact: Performance, Food, and Cookery'. We'd started the series with one on theatre and anthropology. We did one on nature and culture, on politics and ideology and one on shamanism and ritual. But sometime in 1992 or 1993, I began to think of organizing a major gathering to bring scholars, food historians, restaurateurs, performance artists, theatre-makers and food artists together in a festival. It was bigger than a conference because it was a whole programme of performance works, very much inspired by some of the discussions I'd had with Barbara Kirschenblatt-Gimblett on my trips to New York. And it was an extraordinary

gathering, truly, in terms of the range of presentations we garnered. We had papers, such as one on Napoleon's banquets, we had a lecture on the archaeology of the trifle. Some major food historians gave some very serious, detailed, academic presentations on food preparation and culinary history. But we also had food demonstrations, demonstrations of gadgets, Barbara Kirschenblatt-Gimblett curated a whole programme of short films, and we had a whole evening of screenings of some of the best moments from all the great foodie films. We had presentations from people like Bobby Baker. Richard Schechner was there with *Faust Gastronome*. Günter Berghaus did a whole project on Futurist performances with food. It was a very full programme, and we had special commissions. For example, we brought Alicía Rios across for the first time from Madrid to curate *A Temperate Garden*. We brought two extraordinary teachers, Edisher Garakanidze and Josef Jordania, from Tblisi to work with us to form a Georgian choir and then staged a full Georgian banquet with fifteen different courses and fifteen toasts each with a song, extraordinary, ancient polyphony in between each course.

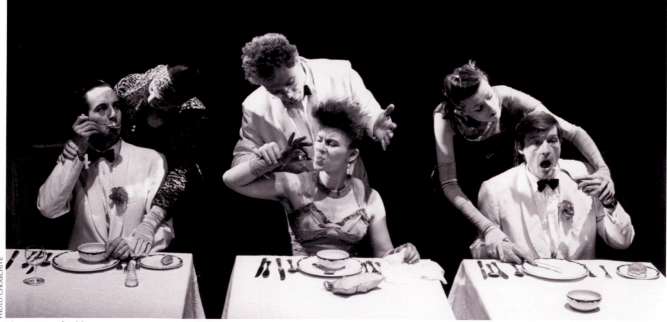

PHOTO: CPR ARCHIVE

The Origin of Table Manners (*First Version*), 1985

The First Performance Banquet – Mold Event, Mold, 1979

Whilst that was a catalyst, and a whole number of issues have emerged for me since that event, my interest precedes that considerably. Mike Pearson reminded me that, actually, one of the very first projects I did back in 1976, was a sort of banquet or certainly a performance that involved the serving of food to the audience. And then he reminded me that during our residency in Mold in North Wales, in 1979, we staged a banquet, a performance banquet. And I remember being very inspired by Japanese food, not that I had ever been to Japan or even a Japanese restaurant. But I just looked at all these extraordinary photographs of Japanese food and the simple, colourful presentation on the plate. This was just at the time when, of course, nouvelle cuisine was just beginning to emerge, partly through the influence of Japanese cuisine. And at this banquet I remember the audience was sat in two halves, transverse. Mike and I were performing in the middle, and yet they were also eating. And we worked with a cook who made these extraordinarily delicate, fragile pieces of food that were served to them as they ate. So, somewhere right at the beginning for me, there was a fascination in the participatory aspect of theatre, food, and eating.

When we were preparing the conference 'Performance, Food and Cookery', one our great hopes was to get Margaret Visser, the Canadian cultural critic who's written *Much Depends on Dinner*[2] and several books about the sociology of eating. And through reading her material, it explains a lot to me about my early interest in the occasion of eating. I stress that, because I'm not a chef. I'm not a cook. I'm interested in the processes of cooking, but the foodstuff, the actual material that we've often served in these events has not been particularly special. I say this to create a distinction between someone like Peter De Bie, for example, the Belgian-based chef, performance artist and theatre maker, who is a remarkable cook. What is absolutely remarkable about that work and that tradition of work - there's several other chefs/artists working this way - is that as well as the theatre, the food is extraordinary. I think in my work, the food is sometimes quite basic and rudimentary. It's not that I'm trying to make a case for the food element being that spectacular or extraordinary. In that sense, I'm more interested in the event around the food.

MT: So is this, then, where food and performance intersect for you? Because initially, you think about food and performance, or food in performance, and on one hand it seems unusual, and you think, "Where do they connect?" and on the other hand it seems, "Where *don't* they connect?" So where are those intersections for you between food and performance?

The White Dinner, *DasArts, Amsterdam, 1999*

RG: I think it is interesting – it's one of the things I began to notice in putting together 'Performance Food, and Cookery' – how many theatre-makers, theatre directors are often very keen about food and also use food as an analogy for their work and the process of creating. And I think on one level, there's something about the very process of transformation that connects the two. I think so much of what we do in theatre and performance is about transformation of one material into another material. One might hope that there's some form of transmutation or even transubstantiation, the turning of base metal into gold, a sort of alchemical approach there. Certainly when you witness the work of a master chef, you see how he or she, through knife or flame or a combination of both, transforms that raw material into something extraordinary: the ordinary into the extra-ordinary. Although perhaps glib and rather literal, I think the analogy there between what goes on in terms of making theatre, making performance, is very close, so if we are dealing with ordinary energy, ordinary presence, ordinary fragments of work and trying to transform them, transmute them into something extraordinary through our skills as performers – whether that's as a dance, with our voices, with our bodies, in terms of how we construct the gesture, in terms of how we point out the image, deliver the text, sing the song or whatever – that we are dealing with raw material in the same way

and transforming it. And so there's a strong process of alchemical transformation there that for me connects between the process of cooking and the processes of theatre making.

Then on another level, there is the whole aspect of how a restaurant functions and how a theatre functions in the sense of preparation of something, whether it's a show or whether it's a dinner, for an audience to watch or eat. Now obviously, in the theatre, often the audience is passive, sitting in a seat, mainly listening and watching. In the restaurant, and what I really love about the work of the restaurant, is that it's multi-sensory. All that is customary in theatre, plus taste and smell and touch. So in a way, what I'm suggesting here is that – and I know this is a generalization – in the main theatre and performance are often restricted to two senses. In food work, you have the possibility to engage all five senses. What I want to emphasize here is that in addition to the process of transformation and process, there's also the participatory aspect of the audience or the diner. People are going to the restaurant to experience something, and in the restaurant it's much more tactile, immediate; they consume. In the theatre, they receive. They receive those images, the sounds, that information, those texts. But both are operating on that level of a group of people making something for other people to consume. So there's that connection, too.

I think it's interesting to note how a whole new range of restaurants are becoming much more theatrical in their approach to the 'staging' of food and food preparation. But traditionally, restaurants obviously focus more on taste and smell. Then gradually in some ways certain cuisines have also paid attention to the look of the food on the plate. But it's that multi-sensory experience that food and performance begin to offer. So one of the things I've become interested in is how we raise the performative aspect of the food event, in terms of how the event is staged; the choices of how people sit, how they approach the food, how they're served the food, it all offers great potential for the performer, for the scenographer, for the theatre-maker. The ideal combination would be that one was working with a brilliant chef who's working on the taste of the food and the look of the food and the quality of the drinks and the wine, etc. That doesn't often happen, so I've accepted that a lot of the work that I've been able to do has not been able to work with high quality food preparation. It's been perfectly adequate; it's been perfectly edible, but it isn't on the level of some of the other food artists whose work I know.

I think of that whole aspect of transformation, of the process, and also – as we've ended up talking about the skill of the chef – the connection between training and theatre. In some ways the skills required to know how to transform that raw material through the processes of cutting or cooking are similes to the performance art of creative transformation. Those skills – that virtuosity, that knack, know-how, knowledge – are very similar to the skills and attitude, physically and mentally, required of the performer.

MT: When we talk about performance, particularly any kind of experimental performance, the idea of risk and danger comes up, and not entirely in a metaphorical way because there is a very particular element of risk in what you ask of your audience, let alone what you ask of your performers. But it does stop at a certain point, whereas with food it doesn't necessarily stop. So in a way, combining performance with food seems to then make that element of risk really immediate and visceral.

RG: It does always surprise me how willing people are to try, how 'game' they are. There are always a couple of people who, even though they know they're coming to a performance banquet or edible food installation, won't touch a thing. That's interesting as well in itself – really, why come? But the other thing that's also interesting is people who will just eat anything that's put down in front of them without pausing to think, 'Hold on, where is this coming from? Or where is it being prepared?' But that, for me, points to a much more basic ritual of what we're tapping into through this work, the joy, the pleasure of communally sharing the food together, whether it's simply a loaf of bread broken into bits and put onto the table or whether it's something more complex.

However, as I've kept saying, sometimes for me the work has not even been about the food. I should perhaps mention another piece, a very ambitious project leading to a production called *The Origin of Table Manners*, which I was doing in the mid-1980s and the late 1980s. We did two completely different versions of it with different casts, and it toured quite extensively. We had tremendous fun in the making of it. It was a piece that paralleled or came

Dinner Talk, DasArts, Amsterdam, 1999

out of the process of *The Heart of the Mirror* and then *The Burning of the Dancers*, which were two much darker, disturbing, and rather more difficult pieces to make. But two other pieces – *The Wedding* and *The Origin of Table Manners* – were two shows that were lighter, happier, more creative productions. And in the process of making *The Origin of Table Manners* we had some wonderful meals and events and performances, many of which didn't involve much food. It was always focusing on the rituals of eating, the customs, the etiquette, and I think that again has been quite a major fascination for me and was certainly the main subject of that show. The question we were asking ourselves in that piece is, 'What happens to manners in a moment of crisis? What happens to your etiquette at a moment when your life is in danger? How do you continue to behave in front of others?' And also how are manners and the customs surrounding eating – this is specifically and peculiarly from a British perspective, a Western European perspective, I should say – how are they inculcated? How are they formed? How are you trained in your manners in the first place? So a whole show emerged that was looking at table manners but was nothing to do with food. We only ever used bits of stale bread throughout the whole of the show. It was a show that was made for a black box studio where the audience, in a conventional theatre sense, sat and watched it. It was a piece that we toured extensively throughout Europe, and we took it to South America, had a huge success with it in many different cultures and cultural contexts. As I said, it never dealt with food; it dealt with issues of manners and etiquette connected with eating food.

MT: Food, and then food and performance, obviously carries lots of social, cultural and political baggage along with it. Is this one of the things that interests you the most? What are the meanings that you find most compelling?

RG: Very much so, as raw material, it fascinates me because it's so charged. As Barbara Kirschenblatt-Gimblett has said, 'Food is substance with strong presence.' It is both actual and metaphorical. As soon as you begin to work with food, you move into an area of some controversy. You're accused of playing with your food, and you act and think again as a little kid at table – the whole notion of playing with food is forbidden territory. It's the fact that using it as raw material also seems to be wasteful. It raises issues. It is immediately problematic. I remember one of the things we did at DasArts [was] create a whole screen of rice falling from the ceiling.[3] It lasted about five minutes, and it lasted long enough for a whole sequence of projected images to be played against this screen of raining rice. And the images that the artist chose to project were to do with starvation and famine, and yet of course, the very fact of using rice in a way that was causing it to be unusable – because it was being used several times; we did recycle it, but it was always picking up dust and dirt – was in itself wasteful. And yet this was the very thing that he, a Romanian artist, Iulian Baltatescu, who was working on that, was trying to point out. It interests me how some people become very uneasy in using food as raw material, even though the cost of ten sacks of potatoes, which would be enough raw material for a whole workshop to work on, is probably less than two tubes of oil paint.

PHOTO: CPR ARCHIVE

The Origin of Table Manners (*Second Version*), 1989

Again, at DasArts, we had some visitors once from the Rijks Academy who were very outraged in a rather earnest and self-righteous way about the wasteful aspect of using food, and yet when we pointed out that actually, the money that had been spent was probably one-tenth of what they would spend on clay or oil paint - somehow that didn't connect for them. The fact is that you don't make the economic equation. What we see is material of substance and material of sustenance, of substance and sustenance, being used in a wasteful way. But I find that is what is very special about working with food and staple produce, the fact that it is charged, the fact that it is 'substance with strong presence' because it is both sustenance - it is edible and sustains life - and yet is being used in a way that seems to be wasteful that makes it highly charged and political from the outset, even before whatever you do with it. That is the nature of the material, the dangerous nature of the material that you're actually using. It not only represents sustenance, it is sustenance. It actually is what it is a symbol of.

MT: It actually *is* its function. It is its own sign.

RG: It is its own sign, yes. Food is immediately charged. It's a big issue, though, and one that we should pursue more because I think sometimes I'm not necessarily as politically charged or sharp as I should be on those issues. And I'm well aware now, for example, when we are seeing the misery in Darfur in Sudan, that one must think, 'Well, yes, how can we make food performance? Should we 'play' with food?' But the point of it is that we have to go much deeper than that rather superficial criticism, because we really do have to look at the whole way that industries and nations use their own power and riches and differences in distribution. And I was horrified recently to learn that many of the big supermarket chains deliberately destroy their food at the end of the day or the end of the week, rather than give it to homeless charities, hostels or homes, because they don't wish to interfere with the process of supply and demand or to in any way alter the market economy.

MT: You started to talk about DasArts and the work some of your students did with staple foods there. Maybe we should shift gears. You've done a series of projects based on the ideas of last suppers - partly Christ's last supper, not only Christ's last supper, the idea of last meals in general, one's last supper. And there have been four so far: one in Wales, one in the Netherlands, one in Italy, and one in the United States in Wisconsin. I was wondering if you could talk about this idea in general - what interests you about a last supper?

Cookery Demonstration, DasArts, Amsterdam, 1999

PHOTO: RICHARD GOUGH

RG: Well, it started at DasArts. That was version one, DasArts in autumn '99. The second one was here in Aberystwyth in October 2000 as part of the Restless Gravity Festival. Then the third one was in Florence at the Fabrica Europa Festival in May 2002, and the fourth one, but not the last, was in Madison in November of 2003. So yes, it did start at Amsterdam and start within the context of the DasArts block entitled 'What's Cooking?' However, having said that, I think the very simple tableau of the *Last Supper* had featured in my work earlier. I mentioned to you about *The Origin of Table Manners*. Although we were only six performers in that, with a seventh mysterious presence of the ship's captain at the table, there was a contemplative scene sustained for the last twenty minutes of the whole show. It came out of a whole project based on an interpretation of Leonardo da Vinci's 'Last Supper' image. As you're probably getting a sense of, there are ideas and images that trundle on and reappear and disappear and then emerge about ten years later on, so it isn't as if at DasArts I suddenly came up with the idea. I'd wanted to do a project loosely based on the idea of last supper, but as you say, more on the notion

The White Dinner, *DasArts, Amsterdam, 1999*

PHOTO: REYN VAN KOOLWIJK

of an individual's last supper? Whose last supper? Is it your last supper? The reason why I got invited in the first place to DasArts to do this entire block is I had done a project there with Judie [Christie] two years earlier when I had done a black dinner.[4]

MT: Please explain what a 'black dinner' is.

RG: There's an extraordinary text, Huysmans' *Against Nature*, written in the nineteenth century.[5] It was a text that Oscar Wilde was very influenced by. It's a description of bohemian decadence, and there's a section in this extraordinary novel where he describes a fabulous dinner that the anti-hero prepares because he is a sort of aesthete, a decadent, extraordinary dandy. And he constructs this most extraordinary, exotic black dinner where all the food and all the wine and how it's served is black. And it was my proposal to Ritsaert ten Cate to actually prepare a black dinner for part of an opening of an earlier block at DasArts. The interesting thing about DasArts at that point is that it was based in an old gasworks in the west of Amsterdam, an old, disused factory that subsequently turned out to be polluted and is now going through the whole process of being cleansed. But they had several different out-buildings on this site, including this massive gas holder that I eventually did a piece in 1999. But what was very clear from the early visit to DasArts was that we were to make a peripatetic dinner, which would be a journey, that you would create different courses in different rooms. And this was a very practical solution because in a way we only had two days to make this event. Judie and I were there over the weekend to purchase and to plan, and we then met the students on a Monday morning, and I think the dinner was on the Tuesday evening, so it was a two- or three-day turnaround. And we got the students to work in small groups of twos or threes, and they were first of all assigned a different room, a different building, a different moment in the evening, a different course, whether that was to be the aperitifs or the appetizers or the first soup course or the fish course or the main meal. They got different stations within the structure, and they worked on different projects, separate but interdependent components. Ritsaert ten Cate was to going to give a 'black speech' at the end of the meal. I think there were about eleven different stations in the journey.

I enjoyed the structure of a meal happening in different locations and the students having the opportunity to work in very particular environments, in very particular locations. These were very unusual buildings. Sadly, I think most of it's been knocked down now, but the architecture was very peculiar. They were clearly bits of industrial archaeology, so they were very much late-nineteenth-century. It had this sense of decay – the pungent smell, big huge pipes appearing outside and inside certain buildings. It was the sense that something industrial had gone on in these spaces. So that gave the idea for a structure for *The Last Supper*. [It] would be a journey, that the audience would literally go on a journey and that through the journey, as in any good journey, things would be revealed. So first of all, you made the decision to go on the journey and then, through the journeying, hopefully have these moments of epiphany, of revelation. And I like that very much as a structure, and I've used that several times now, and I definitely wanted to develop and explore that strategy given the opportunities that DasArts presented.

The theme was very simply about last suppers. And as it turned out, in a way, the project at DasArts had the most strongly Christian connotations, and that was just by a peculiar set of circumstances, through some of the lectures that we received about Christian art and about the interest in iconography of the Last Supper, and that influenced students together with some of the things that we had seen, like the ritual slaughter of lambs. That profoundly affected them, disturbed some and inspired others.

Now, another thing about why that happened, which was a profound experience for all of us ... because when

I mentioned to people I did an entire fourteen weeks on performance, food, and cookery, I think people get the image that we just ate a lot, which wasn't the case at all because, for example, for at least four days we went to a monastery on the border between Belgium and Germany. We followed the process of fasting. Some of the men were allowed to live in the monastery in the guest rooms with the monks. Some of us, and for sure all the women, lived in a hotel close by, but during the day we went up and spent the day with the monks, following the routine and system of prayer. It's funny, I say four or five days; it might have been a bit shorter. It felt like a long time, and we followed the system of fasting, and finally the fast was broken. But that had a very big impression on a number of us for all sorts of peculiar reasons. And again, it's about this aspect of detail I was going to mention, because I do remember one thing that we were all struck by was the slurping, the noise, the torrent, the unleashed passion of the slurping of the soup.

MT: Moving on from *The Last Supper*, there's a significant body of scholarship, obviously, on the politics of food but also specifically on food and performance. You've mentioned before the work of Barbara Kirschenblatt-Gimblett and the journal *Gastronomica*.[6] I was wondering if you find that your practical work with food and performance is influenced by this scholarship? Would

The Origin of Table Manners (*First Version*), 1985

PHOTO: REYN VAN KOOLWIJK

Richard Gough in The Last Supper, *DasArts, Amsterdam, 1999*

you say that your work with food and performance combines theory and practice? This is one of our constant questions in academia - is it possible to combine theory and practice? So with this very specific body of theory out there, does it find its way into the work that you do?

RG: Yes, yes, and yes to those questions. Yes, whether it's in relation to food or not, I find reading, encountering performance theory and theories of practice very invigorating in a practical sense, so that relationship is one of imbrication, as when tiles are laid on roofs and there's that continuous overlap between the two. But in relation to food, particularly, my partner, Joan Mills, has always been amazed at how many cookery books I have. How could one man need that many cookery books? Why do I need that many cook books? Have I ever cooked from half of them? No, I haven't. I haven't ever followed the recipe, but I can actually enjoy reading a cookery book at night, and not because I was thinking about the food, but I actually enjoy reading the recipes. I actually enjoy imagining the product, and following the process, if it's good. However there are some awful ways of writing about recipes and food preparation.

There is, of course, an art of reading play scripts so that when you've read a lot of plays, and this must be the case for musicians in looking at a composition, there is a mental facility to imagine, to almost realize in your

mind, the physical reality of that play. So it's no longer just a text; it's no longer just a script. You can, though the reading of it, imagine the staging. But I don't just mean the staging. I mean the physical reality of it. In a way, I think chefs must feel that in reading recipes. And I love to read about food history and food culture, and you mentioned *Gastronomica*, which is a wonderful journal and addition to the whole notion of the study of gastronomy and the place of gastronomy within culture. And I think over the next few years we're going to see more and more institutions include the study of culture and gastronomy within their curricula. It's always been, I suppose, an object of study within cultural studies, but to value it as study of gastronomy, art, and culture is fascinating, I think, and exciting.

So that's yes to that bit. And yes to the writings and the reflections on food and performance. Yes, it literally invigorates my work, as I'm sure it does many others. Although sadly there isn't a great deal of literature out there. Yes, there are certain key scholars like Barbara Kirschenblatt-Gimblett and Darra Goldstein and others who have written and certain scholars who have written on practitioners like Bobby Baker and Alicía Rios, but there still isn't a great deal of description or analysis of work, and I think there needs to be. There could be a lot more written about the subject and about the history and the historical precedents of this work. I think it's often the case that people think they're being innovative and experimental and they're creating something new, but then you see just how much the Futurists were exploring in relation to performance, food and cookery back in the 1920s and early '30s. And I would love to be more informed by some of that scholarship, some of those historical descriptions and analysis of earlier work and invention.

MT: There are also the series of performance banquets that you've done, like the SCUDD [Standing Conference of University Drama Departments] banquet. Is there anything you'd like to add about them?

RG: They emerged, really, as a way of concluding in a celebratory way the Summer Schools and the Summer Retreats. They marked out certain occasions, moments to celebrate, to mark an achievement. We would have a 'singing supper', which came out of the occasions that we had around some of the Giving Voice festivals, with some extraordinary singers around a table at a conference banquet or meal. But on a simple level, just the eating of food, and for me the occasion of just being together and having a meal is enough.

There's always a conference meal. It's usually in the university or the hotel in the town, so I thought, 'Well, let's make something of the occasion. Let's let it function as the conference banquet, but let's make it a performance as well.' At the root of that is simply the strategy of saying, 'Let's make the familiar unfamiliar. Let's just change the rituals, the habits, the etiquette that usually functions at these occasions.' What if the first thing that happens is that you all stand on the table that you're going to eventually eat off? What if your aperitif drink or your cocktail is served on a high bar that is actually structured into the very table that you're going to eat off? And you just begin to play with the format a little.

What's often the case in those structures, which again I like almost as much as the cyclical and the journey-type projects, is that they begin to break down, that the evening might begin in quite a tightly structured way and that you clearly are cast in a role and you're going to witness certain events. Maybe you're going to see certain events or be taken on a journey through an installation, but then it seems to slide, and I like the sense of it being a rather slippery slope, too, that sometimes it might get a little bit out of control. But most of all it begins to blur. The edges begin to break away. Then it slips into being a meal, and yet there are still some performance elements. And then the performers are still present, but they're no longer being that much of a performer. They could just be ordinary members of the banquet. And then the guests,

the diners, seem to be more the centre of focus. This happened very much in the SCUDD banquet, in that we managed to structure it in such a way that the banqueters, the delegates actually, became the main dancers at the end of the event. It was they who were dancing on the table. The performers were sitting watching. I like that sort of slippery slope of these structures. One of the Obscure pieces of music that I liked very much was a piece called 'Decay Music', by Michael Nyman, and it was simply a series of sounds that gradually decayed into silence. And that notion of a structure that at first is very precise and formatted and gradually decays, that its structure decays, that the very fabric of the scenario, of the performance format, is built to decay and then is allowed seemingly to fall apart. It goes against everything that we might demand, as theatre-makers, you'd think we'd want a certain structure to it so there would be a beginning, middle, and end. But I've become more interested in structures that have a beginning, a sort of shifting, restless middle, and then go wrong.

Hospital Ward – The Last Supper, Madison, Wisconsin, 2003

PHOTO: JILL CASID

MT: And then who knows what's going to happen?

RG: And then it begins to fall apart, and yes, who knows what's going to happen? And then it blurs also those divisions between, when you sort of know it's a performance, and it is a performance, but then it isn't any longer. It's an event. It's a social event that is beginning to perform itself and that those divisions between art and everyday life have really become confused in a creative and provocative way.

DW: What aspects of food and its sociality remain a concern for you? And how does the medium of performance enable their exploration more thoroughly than, for example, a written examination of the sociology, history or philosophical structures of eating and socializing?

RG: The G8 summit is meeting in Gleneagles in a few days. What will they eat at Gleneagles and who is arranging how they are to sit around their banquet table, their positions in relation to each other? And what will they eat at such a forum, or discussion, that is hopefully to discuss poverty in Africa? Does it concern us what they eat and how lavish the food will be and how the arrangements will be at the table? I think that is quite an interesting starting point. What fascinates me is how food is prepared and how the occasion of eating food is presented and how much of society, its power structures and symbolism, is expressed through, confirmed and galvanized by that.

In earlier times royal banquets, even in the UK, used to be public occasions. You could go along and watch your royal family eat. So many of these state occasions were much more public and I think it's a shame in a way that we're not getting an insight into the Gleneagles banquet. So I start from that point because it does seem to me that whether it's state occasion, G8 summit, or family dinner, or two lovers going out for a meal together that so much is attached to that occasion. I remember Sunday lunch becoming this terribly tense occasion because it was the only time we ate together as a family. It became an occasion around which all sorts of tensions attached themselves in terms of preparation of, and for, the Sunday lunch. Nothing violent happened, no plates were smashed, but it was a crucible around which all sorts of issues were played out.

As material food has immense presence: put a plate of potatoes or rice on this table and it has huge significance.

Judgement of the chefs – The Last Supper, *Madison, Wisconsin, 2003*

PHOTO: CODY WILLIAMS

In theatre work as soon as you begin to play with your food, it has all sorts of significance. Even in a workshop context when we destroy six lettuces, there is the sense that despite how little they cost the fact that we were playing with food has a real, strong, substantial, political dimension. The point is that food, as substance, has 'strong presence'. That connects with all those issues of sustenance and poverty. As material to work with, it's really powerful and strong.

So there are two aspects to begin with: the substance, the food itself, the material presence of the food itself. Then there's the social significance that attaches to the social occasion of eating and dining. It's interesting that so many of the important events, if you think in terms of your life, are marked by meals. How going out for a meal with your lover is either the start of a relationship or the end. Why is there a need to do that publicly? That's where I think restaurants are also very fascinating as subcategories of theatre and performance. Wonderful domestic dramas are being played out in restaurants. What's also interesting in restaurants recently is how the kitchen – the activity and business of cooking – has come forward into the public gaze.

The third aspect that's of interest from a performance point of view is that raw material is transformed, not always through heat or flame because in Japanese cuisine it's as much in the cut as the cooking. So it's not always about cooking the material but it is a process of transformation that takes place by a chef, or someone who's technically expert, at transforming that. But equally, even in the domestic kitchen, there's an act of alchemy that takes place in small domestic moments. That lamb chop and the two veg are transformed into an occasion for family celebration.

DW: Hopefully we can pick up on ideas of transformation and politics when we start talking about objects. In the two talks you have given at 30+10 events, in Cardiff and Aberystwyth, *Thirty-one Objects*[7] and *Perfect Time, Imperfect Tense*[8], you revisit a fascination you have held over these thirty years with objects. Your summer workshop this year and a July event – *A Hundred Years in Boxes*[9] – also focus on the status of objects, in the tradition of Duchamp and the Surrealists and the work of Joseph Cornell. This work prefigured your work with food. Can you explain this return to the object in terms of a collector consolidating and reflecting on their collection - retrieving the action and status of each piece and, as you said in your talk, 'liberating them from their moribund existence' – or has there been a particular turn in your conceptual and artistic thought that has led to this return of the object? And is it a political object?

The Last Supper, *Aberystwyth, 2000*

PHOTO: KEITH MORRIS

RG: Depending on their use, all objects are political. I see the approach to food and the material of food in much the same way as I used to work with objects so in that sense it's not so much of a shift. The work on objects - at the very beginning, as an eighteen-, nineteen-, twenty-year old - was very much inspired by Duchamp and Magritte. As I mention in the talk you're referring to, at that point I was working with Mike Pearson, and it was a very steep learning curve for me. To learn about Grotowski, Peter Brook and Eugenio Barba and the training techniques of those practitioners, and then also the Open Theatre, the Living Theatre. We were working in a studio with those very physical techniques. I was struggling, because I was one of those kids in school who was always the last to be chosen at sports so I never thought of myself as particularly athletic. So in the early days of working with Mike, who was very athletic and had been working with R[itual] A[nd] T[ribal] theatre, with these techniques, that central European tradition of physical training, there was an aesthetic and a rigour of creating physical training and physical imagery without objects. I became interested in the objects not because I had any training in that area at all.

There was an interview between David Sylvester and Francis Bacon. It might seem odd to mention Bacon, because his paintings don't contain many objects but there are a few significant ones. The way that Sylvester talked to him about his studio and how Francis Bacon arranged his studio was very interesting to me, and at the same time I was encountering the work of Magritte. I should say that there's a whole aspect of Surrealism and Surrealist work that has never touched me, moved me or fascinated me. The work of Salvador Dali, for example, I have never felt drawn towards. But the composition in Magritte's work and the way that certain very specific

Andrzej Borkowski – The Origin of Table Manners, *1985*

objects - the umbrella, the bowler hat, or the fish, or the roller skate, or the bird cage. There's one particular image where there's a man sitting on an armchair with a birdcage in front of him and a cloak around him. That made a huge impact on me. Then I went back and read Andre Breton's texts. Because often when we're talking about Surrealism we forget about the political dimension of Surrealism and the roots of Surrealism in the way that Breton and the whole early Surrealist group were animated and excited. That took me back then to reading Lautremont and the texts that the Surrealists referred to. 'The chance encounter of a sewing machine and an umbrella in an operating theatre' - that was in Lautremont's text that inspired Breton and indicated a direction for Surrealism, this chance encounter between two very diverse objects. Last night I finally saw the Guinness advert of the fish riding the bicycle, and you think, 'This is how far we've come after eighty years of Surrealism.' It's finally contained and commodified by the industry of commerce - advertising. Going back to the root, it is that collision and juxtaposition that became very fascinating for me.

I began just to seek out certain objects, some of which were in my family's attic or in the garden shed, but then I began to seek things out from around Cowbridge Road in Canton, Cardiff. In the late 70s and early 80s there were several antique shops and junk shops. Again we have to remember that there's a realpolitik happening here. Our colleagues, Odin Teatret, could buy masks from Bali or get these wonderful silks. They seemed to have the funds to do that. We had £10 as a production budget. So to go along to the junkshop on Cowbridge road was really the only possibility we had. But it was a good possibility, because within that junkshop there were these extraordinary discarded objects that someone had decided they no longer wanted so they didn't have a function. I often didn't know what the function was. Some objects you just simply no longer know what their purpose was. So the possibility is to invent a purpose for them, on one hand. The other possibility is to subvert the purpose that they had.

This is where the Surrealist project comes in: to release them from their moribund existence. I do like that idea: that there is a second order, a second life. So long as one worked *with* them. I saw many companies that would take an object and the exercise seemed to be one of dominance. It seemed to suggest that the individual, the performer could make a hundred and one things with that object. So for example a chair becomes a canoe. Well, I was more interested in the canoe: the actual canoe, or the actual chair. I never saw the point of the performer's ability to achieve dominance over an object. What seemed a greater possibility was to accept its existence as a chair, or as a birdcage and then say 'what happens between what I do and what it is?' In that sense it taps into the found object, of that sense of finding an object and through your action creating a dialogue with that object. I became interested in that creative dialogue that still allowed the object its dimension and place in the world, but that through a behaviour something else was released. I do think that in the essence there's a Surrealist project there, in the political sense of the Surrealist object: to discover the fabulous. It was years later that I was to come across Brecht writing on making the familiar unfamiliar. That is another aspect of what I'm talking about here. The familiar use of that roller skate, or umbrella, could be used in a way that made it unfamiliar, that didn't undermine its use as an umbrella but that brought about another possibility for its use.

DW: In trying to raise the status of the object to the same level as the performer, were you trying to exceed the performer? This is what Kantor did with the 'machine of annihilation'[10], which totally crushed the performers offstage.

RG: There was a certain phase where I certainly felt the objects were far superior to the performer. They were consistent. As I joked in the talk, they were always ready to work. They weren't going to complain. They were there at 9 o'clock in the morning. They were ready to go and they were keen to perform their *objectness* on stage! That sounds like a joke comment, but in a funny sort of way I believe that. If theatre performance is about constructing ways of seeing and really working with the imagination of the spectator, then in a way the potential of 'the object' is very great and [is] functioning in our everyday lives continuously in any case. I think if one really develops a way of looking, it's very exciting in terms of how you see the moribund and mundane existence of an object in a different way.

I actually enjoyed that work with objects. I did leave it in one sense. There was a feeling that came as a second phase in the work that this was all getting a bit 'prop'-oriented. I always had problems with this word 'prop', this notion of a 'requisite'. I never saw them as props. I find [the double-meaning] an interesting notion in any case: that these objects were there to 'prop' up what one did. I didn't see them like that. But there was a sense in which we getting a bit cluttered by this stuff. The interesting thing in relation to your question - and maybe this is very sad - is that I haven't thrown them away. I can actually locate objects that I used thirty years ago, and bring one out that I've managed to keep in this immense collection. So there is a collection, there is also this collector within me. There is also another tradition that we should mention, that Mike and I talked a lot about in the late 70s, that is the *bricoleur*. The French concept of the *bricoleur* is someone who uses what's available. So the maker says, 'Well, I need to make this, so I purchase this wheel and those bolts and wire and I construct that object'. The *bricoleur* says, 'Well, what have I got?' and 'what can I make- do with?' and 'how can I use this thing, as it is, and perhaps adapt it or change it, to allow me to do what I need to?' I think the French notion of the *bricoleur* connected to the British notion of the eccentric and that Surrealist strand running through does create something quite distinctive.

I wasn't to see Kantor's work until about two or three years in, which is still comparatively early. Thankfully then, Geoffrey Axworthy, the director of the Sherman Theatre, brought Kantor's *Dead Class* to Cardiff in 1976, which was a major coup for Cardiff and [proved] to be a huge influence on me. To see Kantor's work at that time was significant and subversive, because remember that the work then was driven by a very austere non-object based work - Grotowski, Barba, Brook, then to suddenly see Tadeusz Kantor's work and see the way in which objects were being used - some of which were adapted and montaged objects, but some really were

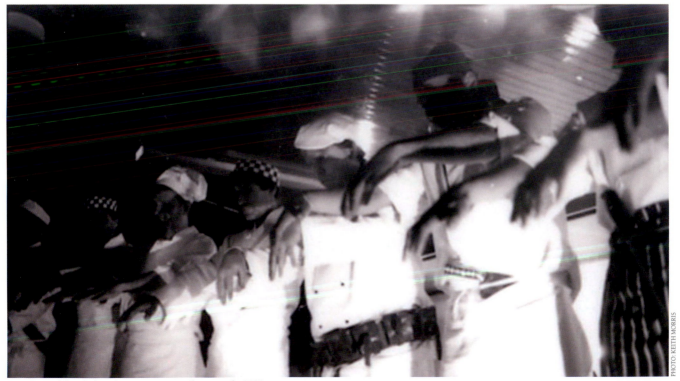

Inspection of the Chefs - The Last Supper, Aberystwyth, 2000

PHOTO: KEITH MORRIS

Sad Happy Party – The Last Supper, Madison, Wisconsin, 2003

just the school desk or the blackboard. This was a real revelation to me, because it was what I had hoped for or dreamed of from the reading of Magritte and Duchamp. Suddenly to see it in performance and then, years later, to read about Tadeusz Kantor and learn about Tadeusz Kantor's trajectory and his relationships with objects: how he moved through a fine art tradition, as a maker, scholar and a scenographer into engaging with objects in that way.

DW: There's something in the title of the workshop 'Still Life' and all the meanings that plays with. Is it the sense that the object is *still*, after all, life, that you're trying to retrieve a possible life from it that it never probably had, that it has an alternative life? And doesn't that always play back into the death of the human? It's also a kind of death of the narrative of the collector of objects. For example, in the talk on Thirty-one Objects there's a certain nostalgia to do with the narrative that's being created: is that being questioned alongside the identity of the object that's being presented?

RG: Of course in the French it's [not 'still life' but] 'dead nature', which I've always found quite alarming. The original definition of nostalgia is the pain to return, and I think in relation to these objects, yes, for me there really is a pain to return. As you picked up, in the talk I gave in December 2004 it was very emotionally charged. Whilst

I had entitled it 'Thirty-one Objects to Aid a Forgetting', it really was more a process of *remembering*, because as soon as I began to invoke the history of these objects, the reality of when I worked with Sian Thomas or Mike Pearson was very present. So those objects have a very powerful presence. I think that some of those objects that have remained in a collection really do have strong presence with the power to provoke that pain of return. What I'm trying to cancel out is that sense within nostalgia of a rather sweet and sickly notion. I don't think it's about that. I think in some ways it's a very harsh pain.

In terms of the collector and a collection, I think there's something very fascinating in the notion of a collection as an attempt to avoid death. There is a sense of resilience and defiance in maintaining that collection. Recently there has been a programme on British television where two people come into the house and tell you how you should declutter and throw away all this stuff, and they go through every person's belongings. I find this process absolutely horrific. It didn't take into account what symbolic significance those things might have. That's what we're also talking about, a kind of symbolism that's embedded in some of these objects. In this programme of so called cleansing and decluttering, they have this big machine that they chucked all these objects in and they were destroyed, lost forever. Not only do I not *want* to do that, I think it would be *wrong* to do that. I felt there was something so puritan and earnest in this process. What if the clutter goes some way to defining who you are? However, Michael Landy did this wonderful project where he destroyed all his possessions.[11] That is when it is transformed into something that is both political and poetic.

DW: As a member of Cardiff Laboratory Theatre, a performer, director and producer, over many years you have witnessed many changes in Performance as a discipline. Have the necessities to develop disciplinary theoretical codes overwritten the potential of practical performance or have they enhanced its reception?

RG: I think Performance as a discipline has a problem now – and I want to make a very clear distinction between Performance *Studies* as an approach to understanding the world, using performance as an optic, and Performance *Practice* as an aesthetic practice. I think the blurring of the two can be both dangerous and fecund. Your question begins 'As a member of Cardiff Laboratory Theatre...' and we were that: a laboratory theatre. I still like the fact that more recently CPR has reasserted that it *is*, primarily, a theatre organization – to the point where I would begin to question whether we do Performance Studies. Richard Schechner, along with a number of colleagues, primarily Barbara Kirshenblatt-Gimblett and also many others who were involved in the New York project developed the notion of Performance Studies, using performance as a way of looking at the world. So one began to look at other aspects in cultural life, as performance, whether that's (going back to the earlier question) restaurants as performance, social etiquette as performance, a riot as performance, G8 summit as performance. To the point at which one begins to say, 'Well, if everything's performance then what's left?' If the optic becomes wholly encompassing then where is *theatre* and the *practice* of performance within that.

But Schechner is always very clear at what point he is talking about Performance *Studies* and at what point he is talking about Performance *Practice* and aesthetic practice. He always makes a separation in terms of his own work. On the one hand he makes theatre, whether it's with Performance Garage or with East Coast Artists; on the other hand he is Professor at New York University in Performance Studies. He makes a very clear distinction between those two. When we move closer to home, with what we're doing here, and partly what we're doing at University of Wales Aberystwyth, I think sometimes we're mixing Performance Studies, as an approach and way of understanding, with practice: as aesthetic practice. I think what we're very strong at here, in terms of what

I do, what Mike Pearson does, what Jill Greenhalgh does, is actually great work in terms of aesthetic practice as performance and the developing of the aesthetics of performance and the strategies and tactics that can be used to create performance. I think there are a few colleagues coming in who are much more in tune to a Performance Studies approach, to conceptual practice, as a way of looking.

Where I think within the discipline things have become a little skewed is that the adaptation of performance as a way of looking at the world has actually left a vacuum, and we haven't developed critical faculties within the domain of performance, so that theatre as a practice, and certainly music and fine art practice are far more developed critically, in terms of having a language and a way of apprehending and engaging with practice to be able to analyse it. So for example in performance work what worries me now, and I think it needs to become a project pursued urgently, is to really develop the theoretical and analytical skills to apply to performance practice. Not so much to apply the model of performance to understanding the world or using performance as an optic but much more within the practice of performance to gain greater rigour in terms of how to analyse performance. There's a lack of definition in analytic terms

The Last Supper, *DasArts, Amsterdam, 1999*

PHOTO: REYN VAN KOOLWIJK

to apply to performance. I think that's the next phase of performance as a discipline: to strengthen, galvanize, and maybe it needs to borrow from fine art, particularly from theatre, certain technical and analytical tools to be able to expand and make more vital and rigorous its critical capacity.

What I'm missing is that when we talk about scenography or choreography, what is the 'ography' of performance, what might it be? There was an attempt in France, from Jean-Marie Pradier to create ethnoscenology, which was study of the *skene*, but that hasn't quite embraced what I'm saying is missing, what would really embrace scenography and choreography, but what would also speak from the aspect of theatricality, from performance. I think Performance Studies is developing well and that what we are identifying here needs to be addressed by those of us coming more from Performance Practice. From this perspective within the discipline, we need to bring more technical knowledge and practitioner 'know how' into the academy. When I think of the discipline of fine art, or the language that musicians or composers utilize I feel envious. I wish we had that sort of precision in our critical dialogue with the work.

DW: So what is it about theatre or performance that's so valuable to you? What is the particular quality of theatre that makes it different from other ways of changing perception?

RG: I have to answer that on a couple of levels actually. One is about a process of making – which we've not covered in our interviews – it's funny that not many people talk about it either: the process of creation, and the courage to create. I was trying to think recently: why do I do workshops? Why have we spent so much time in the last thirty years organizing workshops? Why have we tried to give a lot of emphasis to process? I think it is the value of the collective process of making theatre. I'm not dismissing the individual, the dramatist, the writer or the scenographer. I'm talking about the difficult processes of collectively creating. I suppose that's why I've spent my life working on devised theatre. A group of people come together and struggle to work together, through dips and troughs and peaks and find the 'courage to create'. That phrase is quite important to me. That is a political act too, sometimes against the spirit of the times, or at odds with professional demands. Spaces can be created where a group of individuals can come together to make something and to discover something. Within that, for me, there are so many positive lessons. If only some of those skills and processes could be transferred to other aspects of life and professionalism, then there could be a lot of hope in the world.

One of the things we used to do frequently in the early years was special events. We used to take over the use of something. For example the London to Nottingham Express train or the Crosville bus company in Mold.

PHOTO: REYN VAN KOOLWIJK

Kneading Bread – The Last Supper, DasArts, Amsterdam, 1999

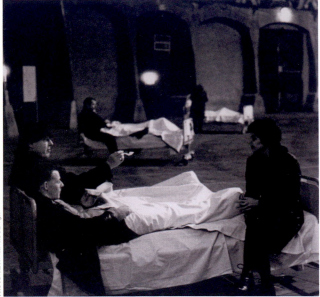

PHOTO: REYN VAN KOOLWIJK

The White Dinner, *DasArts, Amsterdam, 1999*

We would ask the managers if we could use their bus or train. Initially the response would always be no. The second phase was always to go through a series of negotiations and get permissions, do it, and then see how their perspective had been changed. I've always found great satisfaction in that: the creation of theatre and performance as another form of transformation. Transformation in terms of small communities, and how and where it takes place, and how it affects beyond the confines of an enclosed studio into work outside in the real world and affects the perceptions of others. That aspect of the economies of production and how those ripples of production, which spread out from a black box studio, can affect others, is important. Then you get to the audiences, the viewers, the spectators, seeing the work. For me theatre still has the power to change people, their lives and imagination. That's still why I still do it. That's not to say that all other arts don't do it; they do. The area that I'm particularly interested in is work that is fragile and that disappears. For me there's something very special about that disappearance and that ephemerality.

In a way the witnessing of the theatre event is just one aspect, a really important aspect of course. But having said that, all else that goes on - if that's a permanent ensemble or a group that works together for [only] five days - that sense of creating despite all the odds a little community that generates, for this brief moment, a safe world where you can really explore your own creativity is really important. I firmly believe that if you can find that courage, you can transfer that into other aspects of life and make changes.

NOTES

1. This is a selection of material from interviews Richard Gough gave with Melissa Thompson on 25 August 2004 and with Daniel Watt on 30 June 2005.
2. Visser, Margaret (1988) *Much Depends on Dinner: The Extraordinary History and Mythology, Allure and Obsessions, Perils and Taboos, of an Ordinary Meal*, New York: Grove Press.
3. The DasArts Foundation - 'De Amsterdamse School/Advanced Research in Theatre and dance Studies' - is an international advanced study for theatremakers. DasArts was founded under the aegis of the Dutch Ministry of Education, Culture and Science and is affiliated with the Amsterdam School of the Arts. The DasArts study programme concentrates on all disciplines in the performing arts. DasArts has no fixed curriculum. Twice each year a guest curator/mentor designs a new programme based upon a theme to be explored in depth by a maximum of fourteen participants. The mentor, a prominent artist or group of artists, works with DasArts for a period of three months and chooses the theme and guest lecturers in consultation with the artistic staff of DasArts. DasArts, Amsterdam, Block 11, *What's Cooking? Still Life, Turbulent Recipes*, 20 September - 26 November 1999, Tutors: Rob Berends and Richard Gough.
4. 22 September - 28 November 1997, *A Hunger Artist*, DasArts, Amsterdam.
5. Huysmans, Karl-Joris (2003) *Against Nature*, trans. Robert Baldick, London: Penguin.
6. *Gastronomica, The Journal of Food and Culture*, Berkeley: University of California Press.
7. *Fifth Column, Forth Wall, Third Theatre (or Thirty-one Objects to Aid a Forgetting): Cardiff Lab and CPR 1974-2004* at 'C/O The Gym' 4-5 December 2004, Chapter Studio, Cardiff.
8. *Perfect Time: Imperfect Tense: An Object Exercise in Conditional Remembrance*, at 'Towards Tomorrow?', 6-10 April 2005, University of Wales, Aberystwyth.
9. The Summer Shift 2005, 27 June-1 July, 'Still Life - Inside and Outside the Box'
10. A structure of folding chairs, used in the Cricot 2 1963 production of Witkiewicz's *The Madman and the Nun*, would expand, forcing the actors from the limited performance space.
11. Michael Landy, *Break Down*, 9-23 February 2001, Artangel (former C&A shop), Oxford Street, London.
12. Pradier, Jean-Marie (2001) 'Ethnoscenology: The Flesh is Spirit', in Günter Berghaus (ed.) *New Approaches to Theatre Studies and Performance Analysis*, Bristol: The Colston Symposium and Tübingen: Max Niemeyer Verlag, pp. 61-81.

2. Testimony from the Future

Field Station dispatches and soundings Towards Tomorrow

The Field Stations: Ways of Reading

Many attempts have been made to introduce, or highlight, the performative aspect of reading. Most frequently these experiments have utilized the increasing flexibility of typography to create a different path of reading across the page. We have decided to leave such decisions to the authors of each text and concentrated on developing an overall conceptual schema that would enable a diversity of reading methods. The reading strategies for the field stations are myriad, and we would encourage readers to approach them as creatively as possible.

Two influences are worth noting, the first being the Luò Shu square, and the second the Sator magic square. Whilst these do not themselves describe either a numerological or anagrammatic programme through which we envisaged the stations being read, they do demonstrate some of the fluidity of reading 'directions' that we hoped might be employed.

The Luò Shu square is obviously the most apparent, as its map of numbers remains in the grid of stations.

The sum of the numbers in each row, whether diagonal, vertical or horizontal, totals 15. Each reading is therefore, conceptually, afforded the same value. However we hope that each different ordering will demonstrate its own series of connections and contestations through and between the essays.

The architectural, cosmological and lunar aspects of significance in the Luò Shu square have been replaced by dual words that indicate an overarching opposition or tension, e.g. utopia/hysteria, and these are further elaborated by three keywords, e.g. politics, ethics, ideology, that describe areas of research interest or obsession that indicate the pertinence of the essays within that station.

For readers of a more anagrammatic and occult persuasion, we also site the potential of the Sator square, which is a Latin palindrome:

It is possible to produce a number of anagrams from the letters, but the most conclusive is a double Paternoster Greek cross, with Alpha and Omega at the start and end of the vertical and horizontal. Reading itself is already active in this arche-teleology and asserts itself as finitude.

Talking of time, that is another burden that the field stations attempt to relieve: the linear evolution of an editorial model.

So, because time is pressing, immerse yourselves in the field stations wherever you feel compelled and read across, up, down, diagonally and between, tracing lines we could not see.

ACKNOWLEDGEMENT

We would like to take this opportunity to thank Jo Riley, author of *Chinese Theatre and the actor in performance* (1997, Cambridge: Cambridge University Press) for introducing us to Luò Shū square.

The Nine Field Stations

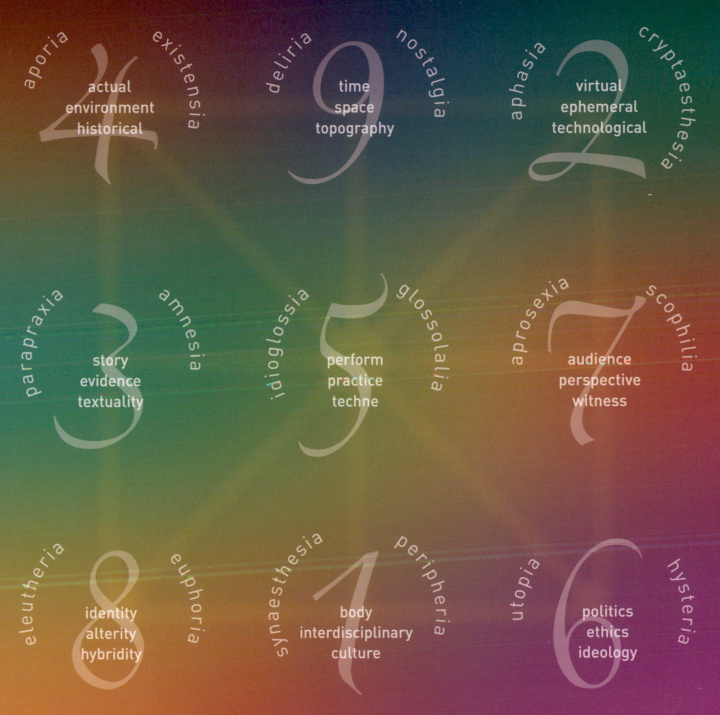

4
aporia
existensia
actual
environment
historical

9
deliria
nostalgia
time
space
topography

2
aphasia
cryptaesthesia
virtual
ephemeral
technological

3
parapraxia
amnesia
story
evidence
textuality

5
idioglossia
glossolalia
perform
practice
techne

7
aprosexia
scophilia
audience
perspective
witness

8
eleutheria
euphoria
identity
alterity
hybridity

1
synaesthesia
peripheria
body
interdisciplinary
culture

6
utopia
hysteria
politics
ethics
ideology

A River of Senses and a Touch of Otherness

(Keywords: periphery, synaesthesia, body, inter-disciplinarity, culture, becoming)

在 四 官 者 不 欲 利 於 生 者 則 為 …
耳目鼻口不得擅行必有所制

If the four officials are not desirous of what advantages life, they must so become ... The ears, eyes, nose and mouth must not stir unauthorized; something must be in place regulating them. Lüshi Chunqiu 2/2.1

A river chart and the place of the lowliest

Luò Shū (洛 書) means 'River Document', and the number one slot at its bottom cartographically indicates the 'water phase' in the cycles of the 'five phases'[1] (洛 書, 'wǔxìng'), which is how classical Chinese thinkers vied to concretize, and thus to manage, an analogous intuition to Heraclitus' in Greece: that existence is but becoming, flux and flow. The water phase characterizes that moment in becoming when animated things acquire a propensity to go down and spurn no place, however lowly or uninviting. It is associated with reaching death, danger and abstruse things. It is visualized as scurrying into a lair, or entering a chasm or pit. It is sensed as becoming cold, fearful, silent, dark, musty, bland and still. It portrays the watery function of the kidneys lodged in their rear bodily pit, as well as the ears and the feet, because both are shaped like kidneys, the feet situated lowest in the body and the ears furthest back in the head, and both sound and feet, like urine, are things that move and flow. It marks the abode of sorcerers, diviners and magicians; healers, alchemists and mediums; thieves, murderers and executioners; swindlers, strategists and conspirators. It is the burrow of the 'Rat' (鼠, 'shǔ'), the lowliest ranked sign in the Chinese zodiac, a being of the winter solstice, dens and midnight. And it is the aquatic lodging of 'Zi', the lowest rank granted to heads of subject states in early Zhou dynasty times. As a 'barbarian' chieftain, Fan Li, is said to have remarked to an emissary pleading clemency on behalf of the central state of Wu just defeated by his armies:

> Long ago ... our rulers would not even get the Zi rank from the Zhou; hence they dwelt with turtles, alligators, fish and tortoises, spent the time with frogs and amphibians. Thus, to my shame although I have a human face, I am still

a bird and a beast; how can I understand your refined words? (Guoyu, 21.7, in Pines 2005)

The Luò Shū also documents a legendary domesticating process accomplished by the great legendary rulers of pre-dynastic China, culminating with Yu the Great (大禹, pinyin 'Dà Yǔ), direct ancestor of the first documented Chinese dynasty: the Xia (twenty-first to sixteenth centuries BC). By 'going with' instead of against the propensity of water – which is 'to go down' (*Mengzi* 1960: 42) – Yu the Great succeeded in domesticating the waters of the Yellow River.

> The inundating waters seemed to assail the heavens, and in their vast extent embraced the hills and overtopped the great mounds, so that the people were bewildered and overwhelmed. I opened passages for the streams and conducted them to the four seas. (*Shujing* IV: 1)

The colour of the central square in the 'River Document' is yellow. It represents both the Yellow River basin as well as China: 中國 ('zhǒng guó'), the 'middle kingdom' or 'central land'. The number five at its centre is a rotating axle that cranks an intricate machinery of pentagonic correlations that endlessly rotates, in a pulsating flux, around its periphery: the 'five cardinal duties', the 'five jade symbols of rank', the 'five ceremonies', the 'five forbidden inflictions', the 'five orders of relationship', the 'five punishments', the 'five seasons', the 'five courses of honourable conduct', the 'five colours', the 'five musical notes', the 'five land tenures', the 'five presidents', and so on (*Shujing* II - IV). Each instance within all those sets of fives is disseminated from the grid's central square to its octagonal periphery, according to a correlative logic which, at least it its original ordaining formulation, is strongly synaesthetic. As the *Shujing* makes abundantly clear, the purpose was proper governance: to tidy up and bolster the Middle Kingdom's eight outlying provinces against savagery and misrule. The Luò Shū is but a mechanism that extends Yu's mythical 'going along with the propensity of things' logic, so successfully applied to taming the mighty river's waters, to the domestication of everything 'under heaven' (天下, 'tiānxià'). *Everything*, from the cadences of insect metamorphosis, which were so crucial to a culture whose principal route to other civilizations is still known as the 'silk-route', to the no less important, yet so unruly, throbs of the senses.

Taming nature by nature's ways

物 動 則 萌 萌而
衰 乃 殺 殺乃藏
生生而長長而大大而成成乃衰

Things first stir, and then they sprout. Sprouting, they are born. Being born, they grow. Growing, they expand. Expanding, they reach their hale. In their hale, they must wane. Waning, they are slaughtered. Once slaughtered, they are put away. *Lüshi Chunqiu* 3/5.2

Read peripherally in a clockwise direction (assuming an observer situated in the northern hemisphere), the Luò Shū correlates human activity, natural processes and the eight compass points (with south above and north below). Through a great arc starting at the number eight slot on the northeastern side and ending at the number six slot on the northwest, it traces the daily path of the sun. Depending on the season, sunrises happen at numbers eight, three or four and sunsets at numbers six, seven or two; only water at number one, in the northern direction, remains untouched by the sun. By including the number one slot, so that the arc becomes a full circle, the diagram also registers the monthly cycles of the moon (new moon is at number one, waxing at three, full at nine and waning at seven); the yearly cycles of the seasons (winter at one, spring at three, summer at nine and autumn at seven) and the twelve-year cycles of the planet Jupiter (with the meridian, or zero degrees ecliptic longitude, intersecting number one). It also directionally correlates key biotic paths (circulatory, excretive, nourishing, etc.), agriculturally important cycles (like precipitation patterns and plant growth and decay) and the anatomical distribution of the bodily organs.

All these ordered arrays of circular correlations enact what is called the 'nurturing cycle of the five phases' (or 'five moments of becoming'). When things are going through a 'wood phase' (three and four, due east), they tend to nurture other things that are undergoing moments of becoming that make them act like fire (nine, due south); the latter nurture things whose moment of becoming make them act like soil (two, at southwest), which in their turn nurture things that are undergoing a 'metal phase' (seven and six, due west); and the latter nurture things whose moments of becoming make them act like water (one, due north). There, at times like midwinter, the nurturing cycle stops, and waits – as in nature. The stopping principle is enforced by things that, partaking not in phases, have a mountain-like stability. So, eight at northeast is the place of *Gen*, the 'mountain' or 'obstacle' in the *Zhōuyì*[2]. It only permits the renewal of the cycle at times like the onset of spring, by allowing things that are going through phases of acting 'like water (one), not from rain, but from

a [mountain] source' (*Mengzi*), to nurture things that are in phases of acting like wood (three and four).

If we read the Luò Shū numbers in arithmetical sequence rather than peripherally, other, more intricate, correlative cycles are conjured into sight. A pattern resembling a butterfly (see diagram) can be traced, which evokes the daoist Chuangzi's famous 'butterfly' dream, and the moth of the silkworm (*Bombyx mori*) – whose nymph weaves its cocoon in double loops resembling number eights, which are also the patterns drawn by silk harvesters' hands when unravelling the cocoon and the patterns traced by the warp yarn as it criss-crosses the weft yarn when weaving silk. The figure also mimics the analemma (the reclining double loop traced by the sun on the sky throughout the seasons) swaying across the Milky Way – as the latter can be spied at nightfall between the winter and summer solstices[3]. And it also apes the looping patterns traced on the firmament by the forward and retrograde motions of the planets, patterns that ancient Chinese astrology correlated with the abstruse loops of fate.

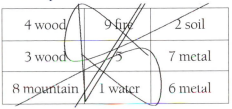

4 wood	9 fire	2 soil
3 wood	5	7 metal
8 mountain	1 water	6 metal

In ancient China all such patterns expressed an erotic dance that wove together the circular ways of heaven and the square ways of earth (*Lüshi Chunqiu* 3/5). Its mythical protagonists were the stars Vega (in Lyra), called by them the 'seamstress', and Altair (in Aquila), her 'cowherd' lover, who are separated by the 'Heavenly River' (天河, 'tiānhé') but once a year surreptitiously consort. This amorous dance inserts the warp of what is traditionally called the 'regulating cycle of the five phases', on the weft of earth: actions like those of fire (nine) are regulated by actions like those of water (one), which are themselves regulated by actions like those of soil (2) which are, in their turn, regulated by those like wood's (three and four), which are themselves regulated (skipping five, which is neutral at the centre) by actions like those of metal (six and seven), and so on.

How are such correlations important in harnessing nature? If you kick a natural but inanimate thing, like a stone lying on your path (this is a simile from Gregory Bateson), the laws of mechanical causation can predict the effects of your kick. But if you chance to try to kick an animated natural thing, say a dog, out of your way, such laws no longer apply. The creature's reaction will be dictated by its own dynamism, or propensities, and by its own patterns of relationship (Bateson 1980). A dog is a peculiarly animated, changing and interrelated thing, whose actions are dictated less by causes than by reasons, as Wittgenstein might have said. (In classical Chinese investigations of nature, reasons rather than causes were the privileged term.) Since it would require omniscience to know the moment in its dynamism that every dog is going through, as well as its current pattern of relationships, and also since a dog cannot declare its reasons (at least not in a language intelligible to us), the best manner of steering action in such cases is by correlating dogs with other things. In ancient Chinese correlative cosmology, the 'Dog' (狗, 'gǒu' – eleventh sign in their zodiac) is assigned to the northwest direction and the 'metal phase' in the Luò Shū[4]. So its 'natural' dynamism and manner of interrelating are like those of metal: its reasons and its motives move between pliable docility, reliability and a lethal cutting edge. It follows that a dog sitting in one's way is a thing better left unkicked, as doing so is either superfluous or perilous.

The Chinese tradition, after Mencius, has a clever name for volitional interventions that do not heed the peculiar phases of becoming that animated things are going through and motivate them. They call them 'pulling sprouts', after a famous parable of a farmer who, upset that his sprouts would not grow, 'helped' them to do so by pulling them upwards - with the result that they all withered and died. The Luò Shū endeavours to help avoid 'pulling sprouts' by correlating the diverse propensities, motives and patterns of interrelation of animated things, including, crucially, our animated senses. This is done in a manner not unlike what Lévi-Strauss calls the 'classificatory science of the concrete' but in a version with two twists. It does not stay trapped in binary oppositions and, albeit decidedly orientated towards sense perception, it also and no less emphatically strives to re-orient sense perception itself.

Synaesthesia and the cosmological domestication of the senses

子曰無為 而 治 者其舜也與夫何為
哉 恭己 正 南 面 而 已 矣

The Master said: 'One who governed without acting was Shun. Why act, now! He just reverently aligned himself facing south, and that's all!' Confucius, *Analects* XV,4

故曰丹之所藏者赤烏之所藏者黑

Therefore it is said: 'Whoever stores cinnabar, reddens; whoever stores ravens, blackens.' Liú Xiàng, *Garden of Tales* 17

In China, south is the direction of sunlight and warmth.

Accordingly it signifies for them the direction of summer and of splendour, recognition and success. These are no mere metaphors but tactile synaesthesias that many inhabitants of the northern hemisphere will readily endorse, together no doubt with the contrasting ones that perceptually associate north with winter and hence with feelings of descent, termination, gloom and cold[5]. Insofar as splendour and success, on the one hand, and termination and oblivion, on the other, are not just abstractions but physically perceivable events, the former can be sensed in others as a glow, and in ourselves as warmth. And the latter can be sensed as others' gloom and our own cold. These two sets of sensations can actually be perceived as physically emanating from the south and north directions respectively. Therefore, since high antiquity sovereigns in China faced south to govern, so that their 'illuminated governments could become as splendid as summer and fire' (*Wuxing Dayi*). And, as the ruler sat on the throne facing south, 'spring enacted life on his left (east), autumn death on his right (west), summer growth before him, and winter burying to his rear' (*Guanzi* I: 138).

If on a sunny winter day we sit, as a Chinese monarch would have done, facing our midday sun (south if we are in the northern hemisphere and north otherwise), it should not be so difficult perceptually to apprehend subtle correspondences between the sunny dazzle on our chest and the smouldering within it brought about by plenitude and success; neither should it be so taxing palpably to feel similar correspondences between the coldness on our backs and the icy grip of fear upon the spine.

We could find it slightly harder, but by no means impossible, to go on from there to apprehend sensations akin to spring emanating to us from the east direction, i.e. surging feelings of vitality bursting ebulliently out, as shoots from the soil. Even more, at the specific day and time of the spring equinox it should even be possible for us - by reverently aligning ourselves with east, as Confucius might have said - to feel spontaneously grasped by a universal balance then prevailing on earth, and encounter a precious if fleeting sense of perfect poise and equanimity. Allowing such sensations to complement the other ones of surging life, we should then be able to feel invaded by: 仁 ('rén'): benevolence, humaneness. 'Rén' is Confucianism's most important virtue; it comes from the east and is described as being naturally born in us in spring. Even if our senses are not so keen, we can still avail ourselves of the vitality mixed with harmony prevailing in the world at springtime, naturally to cultivate our benevolence, and calibrate our measuring and levelling tools:

In this month, protect sprouting shoots, nurture the delicate young, and preserve all orphaned things ... dispense with shackles and manacles, allow no executions or floggings and put an end to litigation ... When day and night are equal in length, standardize weights and measures, calibrate the balances and weights, adjust the measures for the peck and bushel and rectify the steelyard and the levelling instrument (*Lüshi Chunqiu* 77–8).

Conversely, the west direction is associated with the autumn equinox and the equinoctial sunset, events that correlate with the impartiality of justice in an evenly balanced world. It is thus the time and direction of 義 ('yì'): justice, righteousness – Confucianism's second capital virtue, complementary of 'rén'. 'Yì' comes from the west. It can be felt (so long as our senses are well trained) naturally to manifest in us during autumn.

[During the first month of autumn] the Son of Heaven orders to punish the oppressive and insolent, to revise the laws and ordinances, to put the prisons in good repair, to provide handcuffs and fetters, to repress and stop villainy, to maintain a watch against crime and wickedness. (*Yueling, Monthly Ordinances*, revised by me)

The above are not mere legislative admonitions. In the original texts they come propped up by elaborate ritual ordinances, 禮 ('lǐ'), which had the burden of fleshing up, through enactment, what was in origin a very skeletal synaesthesia. The classical Chinese verb 為 ('wéi') in my initial epigraph means 'to become', 'to enact', 'to act', 'to appear to', 'to serve' and to 'act for the sake of.' Ancient China's classificatory science was predicated on ritual performative enactment, because the senses, which are its guides, themselves necessitated regulation and control. Such enactment's task was to put synaesthesia 'into the whole body' of China, as Grotowski might have said.

The first month of spring's creatures are the scaly. Its musical note is Kio. Its taste is sour; its smell is rank. Its sacrifice is that at the 'door'[6], and the spleen has the foremost place[7]. The Son of Heaven [the Emperor] rides in the carriage drawn by the green-dragon horses, and carrying the green flag; wears the green robes and the green jade. He eats wheat and mutton. The dynamism of the season is fully seen in wood. On the day, the Son of Heaven leads his ministers and officers to meet the spring in the eastern suburb ...

The first month of autumn's creatures are the hairy. Its musical note is Shang. Its taste is bitter. Its smell is putrid. Its sacrifice is that at the 'gate'[8], and the liver has the foremost place[9]. The Son of Heaven rides in the war chariot, drawn by the white horses with black manes, and bearing the white flag. He is clothed in the white robes, and wears the white jade. He eats hemp-seeds and dog's flesh[10]. In this month there takes place the inauguration of autumn. The character of the season is fully seen in metal. On the day, he leads in person his ministers to meet the autumn in the western suburb. (*Yueling*)

That the correlations with sense perception in these ancient alignment – directional - rituals were meant not as abstractions but as actual concrete training sessions for the senses, is attested by the attention paid in them to the lush deployment of actual sensuousness. Here is an example from a trance possession dance in honour of the supreme deity of the east, taken from the *Chuci*, (*Songs of the South*) (*Chuci* 102):

We grasp the long sword's haft of jade,
And our girdle pendants clash and chime.
From the God's jewelled mat with treasures laden
Take up the fragrant flower-offerings,
The meats cooked in melilotus, served on orchid mats,
And libations of cinnamon wine and pepper sauces!
Flourish the drumsticks, beat the drums!

The fifth sense and the touch of otherness

墨子曰鬼神之明智於聖人猶
聰耳明目之與 聾 瞽 也

Mozi said: the wisdom of ghosts and spirits is to that of the sages as the sharp of hearing and keen of sight are to the deaf and blind. (Mozi, XI, 46/3-4)

In dancing ... I come to participate in the being of others, the *other* dances in me. Bakhtin, *Art and Answerability* 131

Intriguingly, touch is excluded from the senses in the fragment from the *Lüshi Chunqiu* quoted in my first epigraph, as well as from the correlations with the compass points ritually enacted in the *Yueling*. Indeed, we may ask, why do so many Chinese classics, despite the pentagonic cosmology that so comprehensively informs them, when it comes to the senses, speak not of five, but of (literally) 'four officials'? The reason is, I think, that sight, hearing, smell and taste, as residents of the River Document's periphery, are conceived as subservient to touch – that fifth sense – which 'ministers' to them from the centre, and which is assigned to the 'soil phase'. That is why the synaesthesias invoked earlier as issuing from the four directions - such as warmth, cold and vitality – are tactile, self-perceptive and kinaesthetic in kind. The other four senses are, I think, in the service of allowing the sensorium synaesthetically *to be touched*, by success, by glory, by humaneness, by righteousness and so on.

But there is a risk involved. The Luò Shū ultimately expresses sets of unstable and precarious, because ever flowing, equilibriums. From their peripheral assignments, the other senses may also render the receptive centre vulnerable to the touch of *otherness*. That touch may be erotic, and resolve in unmanageable carnal passion, as in the illicit unions across the heavenly river of the weaver and the cowherd. It may be ecological, resolving in a blurring of distinctions between humanity and beasts, as in Fan Li's remonstration to the Zhou envoy. It may be cultural, and resolve in dangerous pressures from strange ways of life marauding in the Middle Kingdom's peripheries[11]. Or it may be kinaesthetic and supernatural, resolving in a frenzied dancing abdicating governance altogether to some awesome power, as in the possession songs like the one quoted above. In the latter (as well as in the later commentaries on them) a cliff-hanging standoff between rulership and disorder is all too evidently played out - with a gestus that exudes sensuousness, yet is uneasily *touched* by strangeness.

In all such cases, the risk of the synaesthesias affecting touch is that of its leaking down from the Luò Shū's central square to its lowliest one, the place of water and the Rat, and a concurrent *de-yellowing* of the mighty river - blackened and overrun by night.

NOTES

1. In line with their pentagonic cosmology, ancient China from the times of the Warring States to those of the Han Dynasty observed five seasons, with a late summer intercalated between summer and autumn.

2. Zhōuyì: The *Zhou Dynasty Changes*, also known as Yìjīng or *Classic of Changes*.

3. For striking images of the analemma, visit: http://solar-center.stanford.edu/art/analemma.html

4. As the palace guard is pictured facing south, the dog stands guard to his right-hand side and slightly behind, i.e. to his northwest.

5. C.f. Shakespeare: 'Now is the winter of our discontent Made glorious summer by this son of York; And all the clouds that lowered upon our house In the deep bosom of the ocean buried.' (*King Richard the Third* I, 1, 1-4).

6. 'Door': the direction of sunrise at this time of year, east by southeast in the northern hemisphere.

7. When facing south our spleen, which is located on the left of the body, is towards east.

8. 'Gate': the direction of sunset at this time of year, west by northwest in the northern hemisphere.

9. When facing south our liver, being on the right side of the body, is located toward west.

10. The 'dog', you will remember, pertains to the westerly directions.

11. The historicity of this ethnic anxiety is well attested by classics such as *Tianwen, Shanhaijing* and *Huainanzi*. In the latter it is actually correlated with strange - real or imaginary - peoples inhabiting the lands beyond the eight outlying provinces of Han Dynasty China (Huainanzi V).

REFERENCES

Allan, Sarah 1997: *The Way of Water and the Sprouts of Virtue*, New York: State University of New York.

Bakhtin, Mikhail 1990: *Art and Answerability. Early philosophical essays*, Austin: University of Texas Press

Bateson, Gregory 2000: *Steps to an Ecology of Mind: Collected Essays in Anthropology, Psychiatry, Evolution and Epistemology*, Chicago: University of Chicago Press.

Birrell, Ann 1999: *The Classic of Mountains and Seas*, Harmondsworth, Middlesex: Penguin.

Chen Qiyou, ed. 1984: *Lüshi chunqiu jiaoshi*, Shanghai: Xuelin Chubanshe.

Cheng Shude, ed. 1990: *Lunyu jishi*, Beijing: Zhonghua Shuju.

Ebrey, Patricia 1993: *Chinese Civilization: A Sourcebook*, New York: Free Press.

Field, Stephen, trans. 1984: *Tian Wen. A Chinese book of origins*, New York: New Directions.

Hawkes, David, trans. 1985: *The Songs of the South. An ancient Chinese anthology of poems by Qu Yuan and other poets*, Harmondsworth, Middlesex: Penguin Books.

Kalinowski Marc trans. 1991: *Cosmologie et divination dans la Chine ancienne: Le compendium des cinq agents, Wuxing dayi, VIe siècle, Xiao Ji*, Paris: École française d'Extrême-Orient.

Knoblock, John & Riegel, Jeffrey 2000: *The Annals of Lü Buwei. A Complete translation and study*, Stanford, California: Stanford University Press.

Legge, James, trans. 1960: *Shujing*, Hong Kong: Hong Kong University Press.

Legge, James, trans. 2004: *The Li Ki*, Whitefish, Montana: Kessinger Publishing

Lévi-Strauss, Claude 1972: *The Savage Mind*, Chicago: University of Chicago Press.

Major, John 1993: *Heaven and Earth in Early Han Thought: Chapters Three, Four and Five of the Huainanzi*, New York: State University of New York Press.

Naijing Yuan, Haitao Tang & James Geiss 2004: *Classical Chinese: a basic reader*, New Jersey: Princeton University Press.

Pines, Yuri 2005: 'Beasts or Humans: pre-imperial origins of the "Sino-barbarian" dichotomy', in Amitai, Reuven & Biran, Michael, *Mongols, Turks and Others. Eurasian nomads and the sedentary world*, Leiden and Boston: Brill.

Rickett, W. Allyn, trans. 1998: *Guanzi: Political, Economic, and Philosophical Essays from Early China*, New Jersey: Princeton University Press.

Sun Yirang, ed. no date: *Mozi jiangu*, Taibei: Helu Tushu Chubanshe.

Wittgenstein, Ludwig 1968: *Philosophical Investigations*, Oxford: Blackwell.

Yang Boyun, ed. 1960: *Mengzi yizhu*, Beijing: Zhonghua Shuju.

GUILLERMO GÓMEZ-PEÑA

FIELD STATION 1

Declaration of Poetic Disobedience

Guillermo Gómez-Peña XTavera

As a 'Post-Mexican' performance artist operating out of the U.S. for over twenty years, one of my conceptual obsessions has been to constantly reposition myself within the hegemonic maps. Whether this map is the Americas, the larger cartography of art or my personal biography, one of my jobs has been to move around, cross dangerous borders, disappear and reappear somewhere else and in the process create 'imaginary cartographies' capable of containing the complexities of my multiple and ever-changing identities, voices, communities and performative bodies.

This 'cartographic project' came to an impasse on 9/11, when suddenly all our geo-political-cultural certainties went berserk. Overnight, theological cowboy emperor Jorge W. Bush imposed a new simplistic and binary map dividing the world into 'us' and 'them': 'us' meaning strictly those who agreed unconditionally with his imperial policies, and 'them', meaning all savages determined to destroy "democracy" and 'western civilization'. Bush's 'America' became a euphemism for a place inhabited by warmongers and savage capitalists disguised as freedom-loving patriots and innocent victims of evil. And those invested in destroying Bush's "America" were not only all terrorist-sympathizers – even indirect sponsors – but eventually everyone who

criticized his fascist policies, including 'us', the critical intellectuals and artists from throughout the world. 'We' no longer had a place in Bush's cartography. 'We' were not to question his worldview.

In November of 2003 I began to write this text. It was my clumsy attempt at finding a post-9/11 voice and place in another map – an imaginary one drafted by me. As I drafted this poetic cartography my goal was to rescue the pronoun 'we' (our multiple communities) and in the process establish symbolic connections between my psyche, body, language, dreams and aspirations, and those of my contemporaries. My new map began to expand to include migrants, bohemians, activists and critical intellectuals from this and other countries. I was fully aware that it was an exercise in radical imagination that could only become a temporary reality in performance mode. At the end of my four-month literary adventure, I titled the piece 'A Declaration of Poetic Disobedience from the New Border'.

Part chant poetry and part political exorcism, this 'declaration' could be described as both performance and performative literature. It was meant to be declared publicly and ritually, to be activated and performed within a civic dimension. It required multiple surgical interventions into the human/political body.

I performed this piece in many contexts throughout 2004: town meetings, street demonstrations, art museums, theatre festivals and conferences. Sometimes I performed it as a solo chant, other times as a call and response community ritual. I asked my audiences: 'As I perform it, if you feel that the text addresses your anger and concerns, please stand up'. Once I even asked the audience to come on stage and join me when they felt their personal 'concerns were implicated in the text'. On special occasions I performed the piece in dialogue with *Mapa/Corpo*, a ritual performance piece I developed with my colleague, Japanese-American performance artist Emiko R. Lewis, 'the apocalyptic geisha'.

Mapa/Corpo has been referred to as 'an interactive ritual' that explores neo-colonization/de-colonization through acupuncture and the symbolic representation of the post-9/11 *body politic*. As the audience enters the space (a gallery or black box theatre without seats) they come across a troubling, yet familiar image: a human body (Lewis) lies on a surgical table covered by the U.S.

flag. Standing over her, an acupuncturist dressed in a lab coat intently prepares for 'surgery' by laying out forty needles. On closer observation it becomes apparent that a small flag is attached to the tip of each needle, each flag representing one of the nations belonging to the alleged 'coalition forces'.

In my techno-shaman-in-drag persona, I walk around the tableau, and throughout the space, erasing the boundaries between audience and performers.

At one point I begin to slowly reveal Emiko's body, working from the feet up, section by section, until her body is exposed, but her eyes are still blindfolded by the U.S. flag. The acupuncturist methodically follows my path, inserting the forty needles/flags one by one into her exposed body, leaving the audience with the after-image of a 'colonized' female body/world to ponder.

I then step behind a lectern and deliver my 'Declaration of Poetic Disobedience'. At the end of the declaration, I invite audience members to 'de-colonize Emiko's body' by carefully removing the flags with the assistance of the acupuncturist. One by one each flag is lifted, displaying the power that each individual has to make a change. *What follows is the complete text of Declaration, which was originally published in my book* Ethno-techno *(Routledge 2005).*

A declaration of poetic disobedience from the New Border

This "Declaration of Poetic Disobedience from the New Border" is part chant poetry and part political exorcism. I wrote it as a homage to some of my spiritual ancestors, Martin Luther King, Jose Marti and the Beat Poets.

(GP facing the ceiling of the gallery, theatre or auditorium while chanting in tongues)

1. – To the Masterminds of Paranoid Nationalism
I say, we say:
'We', the Other people
We, the migrants, exiles, nomads & wetbacks
in permanent process of voluntary deportation
We, the transient orphans of dying nation-states
la otra America; l'autre Europe y anexas
We, the citizens of the outer limits and crevasses
of 'Western civilization'
We, who have no government;
no flag or national anthem
We, fingerprinted, imprisoned, under surveillance
We, evicted from your gardens & beaches
We, interracial lovers,

children of interracial lovers, ad infinitum
We, who defy your fraudulent polls & statistics
We, in constant flux,
from Patagonia to Alaska,
from Juarez to Ramalla,
We millions abound,
We continue to talk back...continue, continue (in loupe)
(Shamanic tongues)

2. – To those up there who make dangerous decisions for mankind
I say, we say:
We, the unemployed, who work so pinche hard
so you don't have to work that much
We, whose taxes send your CEOs & armies
on vacation to the South
We, the homeless, faceless vatos aquellos
in the great American metropolis
little Mexico, little Cambodia, little purgatory
We, the West Bank & Gaza strip of Gringolandia
We, within your system, without your mercy
We, without health or car insurance,
without bank accounts & credit cards,
We, scared shitless at ground level,
but only at ground level
We will outlive your project X, Y, Z, culeros
(Shamanic tongues)

3. – To the Lords of Censorship & Intolerance
I say, we say:
We, mud people, snake people, tar people
We, Living Museum of Modern Oddities & Sacred Monsters
We, vatos cromados y chucas neo-barrocas
We, the permanently unsatisfied subcultural typos
We, the immoral majority sieging your dreams
of purity & order

We, against the corruption of formalized religion & art
We, bohemians walking on millennial thin ice
Our bodies pierced, tattooed, martyred, scarred
Our skin covered with hieroglyphs & flaming
questions
We, indomitable drag queens, transcendental putas
waiting for love and better conditions in the shade
We, 'subject matter' of fringe documentaries
We, the Hollywood refusniks,
los greaser bandits & holy outlaws
of advanced Capitalism
We, without guns, without Bibles
We, who never pray to the police or to the army
We, who barter and exchange favors & talismans
We, who still believe in community, another
community,
a much stranger and wider community
We, community of illness, madness & dissent
We, scared and defiant
We shape your desire while you contract our services
to postpone the real discussion
(Shamanic tongues)

**4. – To those who have conveniently
ignored our voice:**
I say, we say:
We, who talk back in rarefied symbols & metaphors
We, the artists & intellectuals who still don't wish to
comply
We, bastard children of two humongous nouns:
'heterodoxia' e 'iconoclastia'
We, radical theorists in the academic trenches
We, the urban monks who pray in tongues & rap in
Esperanto
We, who put on masks, penachos & wigs to shout
We, standing still in our underwear
right in the center of the stage
with the words carved on our chests:
'Performance artist: will bleed for food'
We, critical brain mass
We, fuga inminente de cerebros y hormonas
We, spoken word profética, sintética
(Shamanic tongues)

I take off headdress and put on ski mask

**5. – To those who are as afraid of us
as we are of them**
I say, we say:
We, generic brown & black males who fit all
taxonomic descriptions

We, who have no name whatsoever in the news
We, edited out, pixilated, censored, postponed
We, beyond the video frame, behind the caution tape
We, tabloid subject matter par excellence
We, involuntary actors of 'The Best of Cops'
We, eternally stalking mythical blonds in the parking
lot,
We, mistaken identities in your computer memory
We, black & brown nude bodies in the morgue
We, embalmed bodies in the Museum of Mankind
We, one strike & we're out; two strikes and you're in
We, prisoners of war in times of peace;
prisoners of consciousness without a trial
We, prime targets of ethnic profiling (your favorite
sport)
We, of the turban, burka, sombrero, bandana, leather
pants
We surround your neon architecture
While you call the FBI, and the Homeland Security
Office
(pause)
Yes, we are equally scared of one another ... Your
move ... (Howling)

6. – To the share-holders of mono-culture
I say, we say:
We, bilingual, polylingual, cunnilingual,
Nosotros, los otros del mas allá
del otro lado de la línea y el puente
We, rapeando border mistery; a broader history
We, mistranslated señorrita,
eternally mispronounced
We, lost and found in the translation
lost & found between the layers of this text
We speak therefore you cease to be
even if only for a moment
I am, US, you sir, no ser
Nosotros seremos

Nosotros, we stand not united
We, matriots not patriots
We, Americans with foreign accents
We, Americans in the largest sense of the term
(from the many other Americas)
We, in cahoots with the original Americans
who speak hundreds of beautiful languages
incomprehensible to you
in cahoots with dozens of millions of displaced
Latinos, Arabs, blacks & Asians
who live so pinche far away from their land
& their language
(Shamanic tongues)
We feel utter contempt for your myopia
& when we talk back, you loose your grounds
(Shamanic tongues)
I speak, therefore we continue to be...on the same page
on the same strange planet

7. – To the masters and apologists of war & their pitiful 'Coalition of the Willing'
I say, we say:
We, caught in the crossfire,
between Christian fear & Muslim rage,
We, rebels, not mercenaries
We, labeled 'extremists' for merely disagreeing with you
We, thinking majority against unilateral stupidity
We, against preemptive strikes & premature ejaculation
We reject your arms sales & oil deals
We, distrust your orange alert & your white privilege
We, oppose the Patriot Act patrioticamente
the largest surveillance system ever,
the biggest prison complex to date
We, oppose your 'full spectrum dominance'
We, who are never polled by Fox News
We, who never get to debate Chris Matthews
We, whose opinions are never on the front page
of your morning paper
We did not vote for you, Magister Dixit
do not support your wars, Master Cannibal
do not believe in your Infinite Justice
We demand your total TOTAL withdrawal
from our minds and bodies ipso-facto
We demand the total restructuring
of the world economic system
in the name of democracy & freedom, las nuestras
(pause)
And you, Mad Cowboy, are you taking note?
or are you already on your way to Mars?
(Shamanic tongues much longer & wild)
I speak in tongues therefore you evaporate, evaporate,
adios

I take off ski mask & gather myself

8. – Finale:
(Finally facing the audience)
We, baaaad poetry,
We, poliglotas en la oscuridad
We, (Tongues)
We, (Tongues)
We, (Tongues)
We, the shamans exorcising Enron
the brujos against Microsoft
We, dervishes under the arch of McDonalds
We, the ghosts of the past
in cahoots with the future warriors
in cahoots with all innocent civilians killed
on both sides of the useless War on Terror
We, literally dying for new ideas
performing against all odds
(pause)
We dedicate these burning words
to our homeboys and homegirls;
the rejects of all dysfunctional communities
embarking on a great political campaign
against the enemies of difference
(Shamanic tongues)
I speak, we speak, therefore we continue to be ...
together
even if only in the realm of the poetic
even if only for the duration of this most unusual mass

AMELIA JONES   **FIELD STATION 1**

Rupture

rupture

> – n. 1. the act of breaking or bursting ... 2. the state of being broken or burst ... 3. a breach of harmonious, friendly, or peaceful relations ... 4. *Pathol.* Hernia, esp. abdominal hernia. – v.t. 5. to break or burst ... 6. to cause a breach of ... 7. *Pathol.*, to affect with hernia. – v.i. 8. to suffer a break or rupture.
> – **Syn.** 2. fracture, break, split, burst. 5. fracture, split, disrupt. – **Ant.** 2. seam, union. 5. unite.
> *Random House Dictionary of the English Language*, 2nd edn, unabridged, p. 1684.

Two stories open this essay about fracturing, splitting, mutilated and bursting flesh:

1) Ovid's 2000-year-old rendering of the myth of Marsyas, where the unfortunate satyr by this name is stripped of his skin by Apollo as a punishment for his arrogance in challenging the god to a music-playing contest. 2) Franz Kafka's 1914 'In the Penal Colony', where a man who has supposedly broken the law is inscribed with gothic letters spelling out the code he has transgressed.

We are dealing with bodies that burst, bodies whose contours have been removed or punctured, bodies that have lost the clear differentiation between inside and out. The flesh of the convict in Kafka's story (guilty only of falling asleep while on duty) loses its capacity to differentiate inside and outside of the body; the internal flesh literally seeps out through the innumerable incisions and abrasions in his skin. In contrast, Marsyas loses his skin altogether.

The machine of retribution is described in horrific detail in Kafka's story: the 'harrow' part, which consists of a plane of needles embedded in glass (so that the torture can be rendered visible to spectators), inscribes the condemned man's disobeyed commandment into his flesh in stages of increasing depth over a twelve-hour period. The man is never sentenced and never has a chance to defend himself, nor is he apprised of what is going on. ('There would be no point in telling him', says the machine's master; 'He'll learn it on his body' [Kafka 1961 (1914): 197].) The ultimate point seems to be to 'teach' the offender his putative offense by literally writing it into his flesh. However, given that he inevitably dies of the pain and bloodletting (the carving, by writing, of his flesh), such instruction seems pointless in a truly Kafka-esque way.

Ovid's tale is, of course, equally gruesome though in a mythical rather than cynical way. The crucial moment occurs when Marsyas clamors (to Apollo), 'Help! Why are you stripping me from myself?' Ovid continues:

> But in spite of his cries the skin was torn off the whole surface of his body: it was all one raw wound. Blood flowed everywhere, his nerves were exposed, unprotected, his veins pulsed with no skin to cover them. It was possible to count his throbbing organs, and the chambers of the lungs, clearly visible within his breast. (Ovid 1955 [c. AD 8]: 145)

Crucially, the peeling away of skin is the peeling away of the very self. Flesh = Self. Without the flesh, the self presumably disappears.

The brutal realism, minute detail and horrific goriness of these gripping stories of bodily destruction bring corporeal pain into a metaphoric dimension. As theorist of bodily pain, Elaine Scarry, notes, such metaphorization is crucial to the identification of pain *as* pain – that is, as something that comes to have personal but also, via communication, social meaning: 'If the felt-attributes of pain are... lifted into the visible world, *and if the referent for these now objectified attributes is understood to be the human body*, then the sentient fact of the person's suffering will become knowable to a second person' (1985: 13, 16).

Most important for my purposes, the Marsyas and Penal Colony stories mark the shocking ambiguity of bodily rupture in relation to the real. Both are metaphorical tales about the rending of the skin that nonetheless rely on the visceral narration of brute material damage to convey their symbolic messages. [1] The stories thus open up a series of issues key to this essay: the impossibility of separating the metaphorical from the material/physical dimensions of bodily rupture; the crucial role of symbolic action and narration in conveying stories about human psychic pain (which is also, at the same time, physical pain); and, most crucially, the continuum of the not-real and the not-fake in acts involving corporeal splitting.

I could have used the terms 'real' and 'fake' rather than their negations; however, I prefer to invoke the increased ambiguity of the boundaries between what we imagine to be real and what we experience as fake that the negative forms provide. In this essay, then, I explore this continuum of the not-real and the not-fake through an impassioned and at some points intentionally dream-like narrative about body works that explore the limits of human presence and absence (and, in an abyssal telescoping of impossibilities, the inextricability of the two – and of life and death). I deploy a feverish language that moves back and forth between moments of 'rational' (scholarly) discussion and passages of obvious irrationality. This writing exposes itself as embarrassingly not-fake and not-real at the same time, uttering from my body yet conveying itself as abstract black marks on a computer screen (and ultimately on paper, for you to read).

As Kafka's story suggests, bodily enunciation is itself a kind of wounding. As Viennese performance artist and theorist Michaela Poeschl has written, 'my mouth [is] a gash, every sentence an open wound [and the] wound is the switch point or crash point between inside or outside' (1997: 2, 14)[2]. In this sense writing ruptures (breaks, bursts, fractures) the clean surface of the paper (the skin of inscription) by puncturing its surface, intentionally making holes where rationality can seep away – like Marsyas's or the convict's blood and tissue. Blood is both the sign of life and (in excess, flowing out) the harbinger of gruesome death. Rivers of life-blood, hot and red, carving the page. Black marks turned red with effort and corporeal/mental pain.

The Not-Fake

There is no such thing as 'the real.' By not-fake, then, I do not mean to suggest a definitively determinable category of body art practice. Rather, I want to point to a kind of body art gesture that pushes in the direction of what may seem to be not-fake (by posing itself as 'authentic') while sustaining the possibility of the not-real.

Trying to 'prove' she is alive, the body artist slices and dices the skin. Trying to externalize internal pain (of the physical/psychic variety), the artist slashes, punctures or otherwise ravages the exterior of the body. He makes psychic pain into a visible sign of/on the body. He marks physical pain (writing it, as if with Kafka's inscription machine) as a readable text. The artist (through the invocation or negotiation of pain) enacts the inextricability of emotions, thoughts, and embodiment.

Gina Pane: in *L'Escalade* (1971) she climbed a ladder the rungs of which had been adorned with razor blades; in *Sentimental Action* (1974) she traced rosettes of blood onto her arms with razors. 'The red rose', she wrote, 'transformed into a vagina by a reconstitution in its most present state, the painful one' (quoted in Vergine 2000:

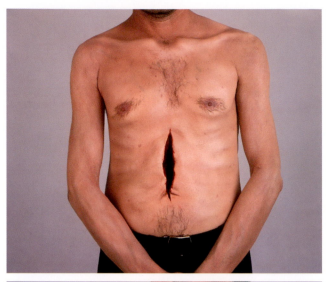

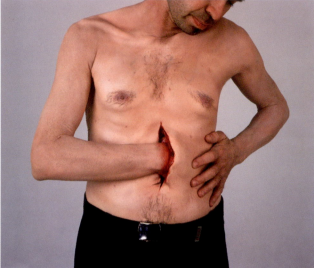

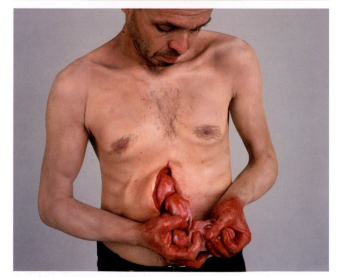

Daniel Joseph Martinez : Self Portrait #9a, #9b and #9c

80

197). In *Le Lait Chaud* (Warm Milk) (1972), she first cut her back (the blood rosettes spreading into rivulets only partly absorbed by her white shirt) and then her face, then showed the audience members a videotape of their reactions to her acts of self-mutilation.

Through her use of video and other representational devices, Pane narrates bodily rupture – so insistently marked as not-fake by the resulting eruption of bodily fluids (here, blood) – as incurring representational effects (effects of the not-real). Pane's bleeding body creates a body of illustration: the shirt, marked (inscribed) with blood; photographs of her acts-in-process; videotapes of audience reactions. The latter strategy, in fact, serves to point to the unreality of all levels of the putative real – to the fact that Pane's brute embodiment (her 'existence', there, at that time, as a corporeal subject with pulsating organs and flesh) manifested itself in and through others (shown on the videotape reacting to her).

Even in the most not-fake of body art events, the body is experienced as an effect of representation, an effect of the perceptions of others (as these bounce back to the exhibitionist and become part of her self-perception). (Of course, theorists such as Christian Metz (1985) have noted that the photographic or filmic representation is itself a *cut inside the real*, and thus a violent castration or severing; the photograph itself, then, perpetrates a kind of wounding.)[3]

And yet ...

Pane's pain (homonyms that do not seem coincidental) would have been immediate and viscerally experienced by 'herself' but not by her audience, who would only see her body *over there*, bleeding and rent; identification with perceived pain, after all, is not the same thing as bleeding oneself. Except for the fact that, as Scarry points out, pain is always already narrated through bodily transformations that express it symbolically for the other. If nothing else, masochistic body art makes this explicitly clear.

As Kurt Krens has noted, 'No wound ever speaks for itself' (quoted in Poeschl 1997: 25). It *means* only in relation to those who 'read' it as a bodily sign (the body is read/red with blood). Including the person whose body it ruptures? No, there's a distinction here (I'm waffling, I know): the person whose body is ruptured by the wound experiences rapidly firing synaptic messages that make her extremely uncomfortable and, unless she is a masochist (thereby experiencing a kind of orgasmic bliss), unhappy. The synaptic firings are a kind of analogue pulsation, conveying bodily signification through a different means than in the exchange of meaning from subject to subject (an exchange that can, after all, occur through seeing or hearing the pained body 'live') or through any of these three modes of perception

in relation to representations. Pane's audience imagines and, through identification, perhaps even (symbolically, but not synaptically) *feels* such discomfort. A distinction, but not a clear one (again: the continuum of experience is marked by practices of not-fake bodily rupture).

Male body artists are known for more explicit and far more dramatic (histrionic) bodily mutilations than female ones (Pane and Marina Abramović, with her equally menacing stagings of potential bodily rupture, such her similar deployment of knife-edged stairs in her recent New York performance, *The House with the Ocean View* (see McEvilley 2003), being striking exceptions). I have written at length elsewhere (see 1994) about the potential effects and meanings of masochistic male body art. Suffice it to say here, men have told the story of an especially violent relationship to their own flesh in their body art works.

It's as if male artists violate their bodies in order to prove they are, impossibly and paradoxically, both *alive* and *transcendent* – they both 'are' embodied and 'are not' immanent. (As Simone de Beauvoir famously pointed out in *The Second Sex*, it is precisely this equivocation – this capacity to deny immanence in the face of its effects – that points to the privilege of being a masculine subject in Western patriarchy.) Thus: externalizing the internally felt pain of living with cystic fibrosis, in a decade-long series of public performances Bob Flanagan (with the help of dominatrix Sheree Rose) punctured his penis, had himself burnt, tied up, whipped, and hung upside down until his head turned an alarming shade of red (a sack of blood ready to burst); theatricalizing the psychic pain of his socially-marked *différence*, and his stigmatized and vulnerable status as an HIV-positive subject, Ron Athey stages elaborate ritual performances involving the wounding of his body by himself and others (by long needles threaded through his skin and other violent events) choreographed into what he calls pageants of 'erotic torture and penance' (in Goldberg 1998: 119); in a paean both to suicide and to fashion shows (a paean that enacts the fashion show as deadly), Franko B., in his 'I miss you' performances, paints his body a ghastly white and has a doctor put shunts to let blood flow from his wrists, allowing drops and streams of red to drip along a catwalk as he promenades ritualistically back and forth; dramatizing the painful recognition of the bodily contour as permeable and mortal rather than as a firm boundary ensuring bodily coherence, German artist Micha Brendel, in a 1989 performance, carved, sliced, and cut his flesh with knives, allowing blood to run through the cracks made in the 'crust of egg and asphalt' covering his body and in the mask that covered his face.[4]

Ouch.

Ironically, male body artists seem especially to relish the appearance of *blood*, as if it confirmed their masculinity, their prowess, their live-ness (while also – as our two opening stories make exquisitely clear – projecting the opposite, their immanence as enfleshed beings and thus beings destined to die). This is an ironic gesture not the least in that it produces the male body as a kind of menstruating (permeable), ruptured sack. Paul McCarthy's blatantly not-real ritualistic rupturings of his bodily coherence, and his smearing of ketchup in place of 'real' blood around his crotch like menstrual blood (about which more below), seem to comment wryly on this masculine fixation, as well as to point to the limits of men's attempts to eschew their immanence (his acts point to the contradiction between blood-letting and claims of transcendence).

But sometimes body acts are both deeply violent and non-bloody. Perhaps the ultimate in body violation are acts perpetrated in the name of western medicine and the law (Kafka certainly plays on the latter). Slovenian artist Ive Tabar explored the violating dimension of western medicine in his 1990s performance in which he enlisted a seven-member medical team to anaesthetize him – turning him into a brute object to be manipulated or even potentially put to death.[5]

Ripped, severed, smashed, dismembered, ravaged, torn, split, burst, flayed, devoured, carved, sliced, cut, hacked, slivered, popped, incised, stabbed, torn. Pain rendered visible. The body a vessel of communication. Per Paul McCarthy: 'the sack is cut open – the human sack is cut open – the body sack or the animal sack, the sack meaning the skin. We search for what can't be gotten at in the interior of the body, cutting open the body to peer inside' (quoted in Stiles 1985: 36; 1996: 14). What will we find there? Surely brute material (billions of cells bound into flesh and blood and bone) rather than some ethereal matter confirming our transcendence of the flesh.

Halfway between the Not-Fake and the Not-Real

Many artists have flirted with the indeterminacy of the distinction between the not-fake and the not-real. Cathy Opie, in her self portraits from the 1990s, depicted her own body carved with wounds suggestive of those inflicted by a society suspicious of or hostile to queer subjects. Yet she conveyed her bleeding flesh entirely through color photographs (the public staging that was so crucial to the complex effects of Pane's works is left out of the picture, as it were). The not-fake of the bodily inscription is rendered through the not-real of the photograph (which is paradoxically in its indexicality the least not-real – the most 'real' – of all modes of representation).

Opie's oozing flesh, marked in one case with a cutting image of a house with two stick-figure women out in front holding hands, is known to us 'only' as a picture (and, especially in the age of the digital photograph, how easily this could have been faked!). As in Kafka's story and the 1998 movie *The Pillow Book* (directed by Peter Greenaway), bodily inscription becomes a means of proving the sensual live-ness of the body while paradoxically turning it into an abstract site of writing (it becomes, as it were, a piece of paper, the elusive intangibility of which is indicated by Ferdinand de Saussure's concept of the signifier and the signified functioning like two sides of the same piece of paper). The female protagonist of *The Pillow Book* desperately writes the bodies of her male lovers as if, through this act of willful penetration, she is claiming them for her own. Yet, as the movie narrates it, she is forced to recognize the impossibility of 'having' the other in this way, through the penetratory act of 'taking' his body.[6]

Other halfway works, which insist on the not-fake status of the wounded body while also depending on the not-real capacity of visual and/or textual representation to substantiate these wounds, include:

1) Yoko Ono's *Cut Piece*, performed both in New York and in Tokyo in the 1960s and recently restaged in Paris, in which she has audience members come on stage and, slice by slice, cut away her clothing to reveal her naked body. The cutting never reaches her actual flesh, but metaphorically the violence of cutting mimics the violence of the gaze as it shriekingly violates the female body, at least as feminist theories of representation from the 1970s would have it.

2) Chris Burden's self-wounding performances from the early 1970s, in which he placed himself in the path of danger, having himself hurt or almost hurt. In these works, such as the infamous 1971 *Shoot*, in which he orders a friend to shoot him in the arm, Burden scrupulously orchestrated the wounding/potential wounding and its documentation. The wounding is apparently not-fake (as attested, in *Shoot*, by a rivulet of blood visible in the black and white photograph documenting the piece). Yet because it began and ended as an act choreographed to function *as art* (and so *as representation*), resulting in a marketable photograph captioned with deadpan descriptive text, it is difficult, if not impossible, for it to claim status as fully not-fake.

3) In Hannah Wilke's mid 1970s *S.O.S.* performances she offered audience members gum, stripped off her clothes, then took the chewed gum from the audience and formed the wads into 'cunts' which she pasted all over her naked flesh. She documented the resulting image of (not-real) self-wounding in photographs (see my 1998:

182-3). Here, the not-real dimension is literally marked through the representational status of the 'wounds' and then, in a doubling structure, through the status of photographic representation. (At the same time, at the original performances the not-fake would have emerged in the mingling of saliva and flesh – the emanation of a smell of bodies interweaving in a public space.)

4) Wilke's 1990s *Intra-Venus* series of performative self-portrait photographs documenting her body's reaction to the devastating effects of cancer and chemotherapy; again, the not-real yet also not-fake status of the photograph as index marks the image of her illness in its full ambiguity, an effect she played up by performing herself in playful ways, contradicting the horror of the illness and the devastating effects of chemotherapy making their deadly marks on her flesh. Her actual death from cancer shortly thereafter, in 1993, testifies to the ultimate impossibility of the not-real to sustain the flesh forever (yet, the pictures remain in their immortality ...).

4) Nao Bustamante's twist on Pane's and Abramović's cutting ladders in her circa 2000 performance piece *America the Beautiful*, in which she tightly binds her voluptuous naked flesh and, 'severely handicapped by her requirements of feminine guile and beauty pageant pretensions', climbs the 'ladder of success in high heels' (Topiary c. 2000). Ranting and raving, she tosses her trussed body around on the ladder, threatening to do herself terrible bodily harm but never actually breaking her bones or flesh.

5) Most ambiguously, Orlan's 1990s series of cosmetic surgery performances, gathered together under the conceptual title *The Reincarnation of Saint Orlan*, involve plastic-surgery events in which her body is sliced, diced and rearranged in a horrifyingly not-fake way. Yet, once again the not-fakeness of the project is usefully compromised by her dependence on modes of representation to convey the resulting imagery and 'relics' (satellite video imagery, faxes, photographs etc.). And the effect of these surgical interventions is disturbingly reliant on the not-real – the whole point of plastic surgery being the reconfiguration of the given body in an attempt to match a pre-given (if also internalized) bodily ideal: the making of the body and/or face into a superficial picture of 'beauty'. Since any bodily ideal is, by definition, not-real (i.e. born and bred in fantasy), we might argue that Orlan's project brilliantly navigates the inseparability of the not-real and the not-fake. Having a surgeon enter into her flesh, scraping, cutting, reshaping it and turning it inside out, as it were, she also tantalizingly takes the ultimate risk (like Tabar) of the demise of the body. She performs a yearning toward the ideal (the ultimate form of which is immortality) while tempting death.

Perhaps death *is* the ideal? Or the only place the ideal resides is in death?

More than anything, the works that play in the gray area between the not-fake and the not-real thus confuse the very differences between presence and absence, life and death, that we want to assume exist. It is the belief in (and insistence on) these distinctions that allows us to pretend, from lived moment to lived moment, that we are immortal. Without these distinctions – and this is why these works (especially Orlan's) are so disturbing – we would have to admit to the tenuousness not only of our status as living but of our very sense of who we are (our sense of being bounded and, so, coherent subjects in the world).

Such acts of ambiguity thus create or express another kind of pain: the pain of acknowledging that we are, as Western philosophy would have it, flesh of the world, inextricably intertwined with it, and yet mortal.[7] We will thus eventually merge (again) with the earth.

Alternatively, Eastern philosophy offers a less frightening way of thinking this through. In yogic philosophy, the notion of 'removing your face' (so apt when addressing the case of Orlan!) has to do with severing one's superficial self from one's 'true' self (a concept that does not sustain the implications of transcendence that define it in western ideology).[8] In yogic philosophy the true self can never be reached without at the same time giving it up (relinquishing consciousness and intelligence and mind, one reaches a state of *nirbijah samadhi* [Iyengar 1996: 97]). Removing one's face is about dissolving the masks through which the subject performs her social identities, allowing for – even embracing – the lack (i.e. the non-coherence of the self) that joins her to the flesh of the world.[9]

This gesture of removing the face in yogic terms is about accepting mortality and our fundamental incoherence as subjects; it is about embracing the indistinguishability of the not-fake and the not-real. In some sense, for me, the not-fake/not-real projects described here navigate the same terrain.

The Not-Real

Life vs. death and presence vs. absence are, in projects that insistently expose the not-real, presented as false oppositions, inspiring the ontological questioning of being (and of the price of existence). The emphasis here is on ritual, the staging on and through bodily signs whose status as representational signs is emphasized through the blatant use of mediating representational devices.

Explored and played out: the status of the body as surface, as representation. Picture/skin continuum.

Around 1970 Judy Chicago produced a number of works expressing through various representational devices (text, photography, drawing) her emotional (defined as bodily) pain as a woman living in Western patriarchy and in particular as one attempting to make her way in the white male-dominated U.S. artworld. One way to look at these (for example: a lithograph showing a woman's naked ass being assaulted by a gun held by a presumably male hand) is to understand them as responding to the idea of violence as representational, as inexorably leading to real acts (per Catherine Makinnon's and Andrea Dworkin's anti-pornography arguments in North America). In the color lithograph *Peeling Back* (1974), part of the 'Rejection Quintet', Chicago uses a less literal strategy. Here, a gorgeous, flower-like array of peeling layers of color reveal a central core; a handwritten text below describes a woman's (presumably Chicago's) experience of being mistreated (violated) by the male-dominated art world.

These are representations that imply bodily harm without explicitly depicting or enacting it. Chicago's concern with the signifying effects of indexical or abstracted imagery encourages the inclusion of explicit texts describing what the images are intended to reveal. The continuum of verbal (representational) rape with actual (embodied) rape.

The problem with such a conflation? Many feminists have countered MacKinnon's and Dworkin's arguments by pointing out that it does not serve feminism to assume that representation equals the real (see Adams and Cousins 1996). [10] To conflate them is to deny the possibility of countering (intervening in, critiquing, shifting the meanings and values of) representations. They are inextricably linked on the one hand (as the above section pointed out) and yet not the same: they are ontologically and semiotically distinct. So much Cindy Sherman's seemingly endless streams of self-imaging, in which her body is staged and reiterated as a picture, makes clear. [11] The not-real dimension of the picture (which parallels the not-real aspect of the feminine masquerade) simply points to the inexorable human desire to *know* the person who occupies the focal point of our gaze.

Fake wounds engage this conundrum at the level of embodiment. There are fake wounds that mark the body *as image*, affirming its status as a picture for the other: George Maciunas's stick-on scars from the late 1960s; [12] Viennese Actionist artist Rudolf Schwarzkogler's infamous faked castration event in 1965-6 (itself exemplifying the general Actionist tendency towards staging non-real violence, veiled in Catholic overtones, in public); [13] Vito Acconci's *Trademarks*, a performance work in which he clamped his teeth down into his skin making bite marks in his arms (the signs of wounds, but left incipient with no blood drawn); and, as described above, Hannah Wilke's explicitly symbolic 'wounds' – the bubble-gum cunts she stuck to her skin in her 'S.O.S.' performances in the mid-1970s. More recently, the not-real is viscerally evoked in Osline's bizarre 'Deeper Skin' series (c. 2000), polaroids depicting variously mutated bodies, seemingly sliced or pierced from within by fleshy knobs, spikes or cancerous lesions (2001). Joanna Roche has sparred with Osline's work elegantly in a poem, aptly describing her images: 'Surrealism, drunk on Francis Bacon, / meets the Human Genome Project.'

There are two projects of the not-real that I want to focus on because they exemplify the most powerful effects of eschewing the promise of presence and authenticity seemingly secured by the not-fake. Paul McCarthy's histrionic stagings of male violation – such as the videotape *Rocky* (1976), in which he unhinges the simulated heroism of the popular movie by the same name by smearing his genitals and ass with menstrual-blood-like ketchup – insist on the simulacral nature of masculinity (its status as a 'feminine' masquerade of phallic plenitude which continually fails). Ketchup is confused with blood, just as other stinky food products can be confused in productive ways, producing unreal expectations. (McCarthy notes wryly: 'The bottle of mayonnaise within the action is no longer a bottle of mayonnaise; it is now a woman's genitals. Or it is now a phallus' [quoted in Stiles 1996: 14].) Insisting on the fakeness even of 'concrete performance[s]' of the masculine body, McCarthy exposes the masquerade as the self-performance of not-real attributes which are then taken as guarantors of the not-fake. [14] The whining, ruptured, bloody body in McCarthy's performances – as not-real as fake can be – is (like Marsyas, like the convict in Kafka's story) ultimately masculine.

McCarthy's work reminds us that it is, after all, threats to the *male* body (not the female) that motivate patriarchy to shore up the boundaries of masculine subjectivity in a seemingly endless operation of reconstructive phallocentrism. McCarthy, precisely through the insistently not-real dimension of his enactment of the wounded male subject, exposes this operation for what it is.

In a similar fashion, Danny Martinez's fantastic self-portrait triptych of photographs (subtitled *Fifth Attempt to Clone Mental Disorder, or How One Philosophizes with a Hammer / After Moreau and Cronenberg*, 2000) depicts him ripping a hole in his stomach and pulling out his guts. [15] He literally *cores* himself, and then exposes his viscera to public view.

Or does he? Of course not. [16]

Ovid's and Kafka's explicitly not-real body acts are not pictures (or video images) that seek to convince us that the body is 'really' wounded. Rather, they insistently expose the simulacral (representational) dimension of all bodily wounding.

This is not to say that people don't suffer in 'real life' or that no wounds 'really' rupture the body's surface. (The works of Franko B. and Gina Pane, not to mention the horrifically ruptured bodies we are never allowed to see from the US 'defense' of Iraq, and so on, tell us otherwise.) Rather, as Scarry suggested, it is to point out that the level on which pain can be transmitted to others is representational. Even our own experience of pain is sifted through the representational field (our neurons fire, yet our understanding of these impulses is filtered through our culturally determined notions about pain and bodily coherence). Not to mention the level on which our *memory* of pain takes place.

For example. I've given birth to two babies. One with an epidural and one without any drugs whatsoever. In the former case, I watched my body as if it belonged to someone else – I could not *feel* the very efforts my own muscles were exerting in order to expel this horrifically large foreign object from my body's interior. In the second case, I *lived* my pain in the deepest way. And yet, in trying to access that experience, I can only do so through the sieve of representation. It exists in my mind in the form of a movie of someone else (but viewed from the strangest perspective of the actual sufferer – like the subjective point of view deployed in a Joan Semmel painting). So I see my body as if from my own perspective, and yet the *feeling* of the pain as my limbs were being (or felt like they were being) ripped asunder has escaped me. I know rationally that it hurt – a lot – but except through my own representations I have no access to that experience (if I did, I would be, by definition, experiencing it again). So which pain was more 'real' (or, in the terms of this essay, less not-fake) – that masked by drugs or that experienced 'directly'?

Puncturing the Page

Coagulated, diced, dismembered, sutured, fissured, scraped, perforated. I'm a bit dried out by these ruminations about rupture – everything has leaked away. Whether in drips (Franko B.), in torrents (Marsyas) or in sugary red globs (McCarthy), the bloody river has run dry.

Clive Barker has written, '[e]very body is a book of blood; wherever we're opened we are red' (Poeschl 1997: 14, n58).

I feel as I felt when I had just given birth the second time (as I remember the feeling through words and images, which are like pictures made by my own eyes). Bone tired, white through loss of blood (my own or hers? Who's to say?... she wanted her warm dark home back, was the feeling).

I've been re[a]d out.

I 'know' (insofar as one can grasp anything other than as second- or third-hand rendering) only that the not-real and the not-fake cannot be differentiated. That the body is and isn't 'transcended' through performances of extreme masculinity and/or that it is and isn't inexorably immanent in reiterative representations of women's bodies and wounds. Holes are never wholes, and yet maybe the hole is as close as we can get to proving to ourselves the possibility of wholeness (McCarthy again: 'I've made this hole metaphor as a metaphor of cultural control, what you can see and what you can't see' [quoted in Stiles 1996: 16–17]). Not an insignificant lesson from a bunch of ruptured bodies.

NOTES

1. In these stories, this narration takes place in words. Elsewhere, as in Titian's *Flaying of Marsyas* (1575-76), pictures attempt to narrate such messages.

2. I am indebted to Poeschl for sharing this text with me; in its frenzy and fearlessness it has been an inspiration for this essay.

3. Metz argues: 'an instantaneous abduction of the object out of the world into another world, into another kind of time ... [the photographic take] is immediate and definitive, like death and like the constitution of the fetish in the unconscious, fixed by a glance in childhood, unchanged and always active later. *Photography is a cut inside the referent*, it cuts off a piece of it, a fragment, a part object, for a long immobile travel of no return' (1985: 84, emphasis added).

4. Brendel describes the piece entitled *Der Mutterseelenalleinering*, performed at the Galerie Elefant, Berlin, in *Body and the East* (1998: 120).

5. See Jurij Krpan, 'Stressing the Extent of the Body as the Answer to the Terrible Fall into the Culture' (1998: 120). Bob Flanagan planned to have his partner Sheree Rose insert a video camera into his coffin after his death (he was very ill all his life with cystic fibrosis), which could be activated by an external viewer so that images of Flanagan's decaying body could be viewed on a monitor. Sadly, he died before he could work out the logistics for this horrifying but fascinating piece, which also explores non-bloody bodily violation – but in this case by representational technologies themselves. I discuss this piece in my book *Body Art / Performing the Subject* (1998: 237).

6. In fact, the man she truly loves dies from the internal wounding caused by a drug overdose, not by the wounding of the flesh the film seems to point towards.

7. It is Merleau-Ponty who extensively theorized our being as flesh in

the world. See especially *Visible and the Invisible* (1968 [1964]).

8. On removing one's face, I am indebted to the wisdom of yoga teacher and philosopher Paul Cabanis.

9. In facial surgery the face is removed only to be refigured into a rictus and reapplied to the meat of the body. Motivated by the desire to attain a kind of selfhood that is predicated entirely on the shape and appearance of the external image of the body, this process is blatantly opposed in its materialism to the dematerialized facelessness yogic philosophy encourages as a goal.

10.

11. I have written extensively about Sherman's photographs, most recently in 'The "Eternal Return": Self-Portrait Photography as a Technology of Embodiment' (2002).

12. I learned of these 1967 proto-types, which may have been actualized in 1969, from Fluxus expert Dore Bowen, whose work on the movement brilliantly restages it in relation to theories of mass reproduction. They are noted under the Maciunas entry in the *Fluxus Codex*.

13. In his important book *The Skin Ego*, Anzieu gravely discusses this as a 'real' event and interprets the 'victim' as Schwarzkogler himself, when it was actually another man, Heinz Cibulka, and the castration was faked. Anzieu extrapolates by arguing that Schwarzkogler 'perceived his own body as the object of his art, amputated his own skin, inch by inch, until finally he killed himself. He was photographed throughout the process ...' (1989: 20). See Kristine Stiles's exposure of this myth in 'Performance and Its Objects' (1990: 35-47).

14. See McCarthy on 'concrete performance' in Stiles 1996.

15. These images were not manipulated after they were taken. Martinez used body make-up to stage his ritual hara-kiri (its unreality is exposed by the flat look of unconcern on his face as he seemingly views his own viscera).

16. But I am reminded of the time after I had just met Bob Flanagan and he invited me to his studio to view tapes of some of his performances. Showing me a clip of a music video he performed for the rock group 'Nine Inch Nails', he had no idea that I thought for a moment that the evisceration of his abdomen shown on the tape was not-fake. I am not sure why my disbelief was suspended so thoroughly for those moments, but, once he started to laugh and joke about the images, I snapped out of it quickly.

REFERENCES

Adams, Parveen and Cousins, Mark (1996) 'The Truth on Assault', in Parveen Adams (ed.) *The Emptiness of the Inmage: Psychoanalysis and Sexual Differences*, London: Routledge, pp. 57-69.

Anzieu, Didier (1989) *The Skin Ego*, (trans. Chris Turner), New Haven and London: Yale University Press.

Beauvoir, Simone de (1953 [1949]) *The Second Sex*, (ed. and trans. H. M. Parshley), New York: Alfred A. Knopf.

Brendel, Micha (1998) *Body and the East*, Ljubljana, Slovenia: Museum of Modern Art and London and Cambridge, Massachusetts: MIT Press.

Goldberg, Roselee (1998) *Performance: Live Art Since 1960*, New York: Harry N. Abrams.

Hendricks, Jon, Ed. (1988) *Fluxus Codex*, Detroit: Gilbert and Lila Silverman Collection and New York: Harry N. Abrams.

Iyengar, B. K. S. (1996) *Light on the Yoga Sutras of Patañjali*, London and San Francisco: Thorsons.

Jones, Amelia (1994) 'Dis/Playing the Phallus: Male Artists Perform their Masculinities', *Art History* 17.4 (December).

Jones, Amelia (1998) *Body Art / Performing the Subject*, Minneapolis: University of Minnesota.

Jones, Amelia (2002) 'The "Eternal Return": Self-Portrait Photography as a Technology of Embodiment', *Signs: Journal of Women in Culture and Society* 27.4 (Summer).

Kafka, Franz (1961 [1914]) 'In the Penal Colony', in *The Penal Colony: Stories and Short Pieces*, (trans. Willa and Edwin Muir), New York: Schocken Books, pp. 191-227.

Krpan, Jurij 'Stressing the Extent of the Body as an Answer to the Terrible Fall into the Culture', in *Body and the East*, ed. Zdenka Badovinac, Ljubljana, Slovenia: Museum of Modern Art and London and Cambridge, Massachusetts: MIT Press p. 170.

McEvilley, Thomas (2003) 'Performing the Present Tense', *Art in America* 91.4 (April), pp. 114-117, 153.

Merleau-Ponty, Maurice (1968 [1964]) *Visible and the Invisible*, ed. Claude Lefort, (trans. Alphonso Lingis), Evanston: Northwestern University Press.

Metz, Christian (1985) 'Photography and Fetish', October 34 (Fall), pp. 81-90.

Osline, Naida (2001) *Deeper Skin: Photographs*, Santa Ana, California: Grand Central Art Center, California State University, Fullerton.

Ovid [Ovidius Naso] (1955 [c. AD 8]) The Flaying of Marsyus, in *Metamorphoses*, trans. Mary M. Innes, Harmondsworth, Middlesex: Penguin Books, p. 145.

Poeschl, Michaela (1997) 'Let's Make it Halloween. Get Out Your Knife, Carve me Like a Pumpkin, and Then Let's Fuck', unpublished paper, pp. 2, 14.

Roche, Joanna (2001) 'Death in an Era of Decapitation (or, the perfection of painting)', unpublished poem (September).

Scarry, Elaine (1985) *The Body in Pain: The Making and Umaking of the World*, Oxford: Oxford University Press.

Stiles, Kristine in conversation with Paul McCarthy, 'Interview', in *Paul McCarthy*, London: Phaidon.

Stiles, Kristine (1985) 'Imploring Silence,' *High Performance* 8, 29.1, p. 36.

Stiles, Kristine (1990) 'Performance and Its Objects', *Arts Magazine* 65 (November), pp. 35-47.

Topiary, Samuael (c. 2000) 'Wobbling in High Places' *San Francisco Bay Times*, quoted on Nao Bustamante's web page <http://www.sfgate.com/offbeat/naobeauty.html>.

Vergine, Lea (2000) *Body Art and Performance: The Body as Language*, Milan: Skira.

JOHANNES BIRRINGER   FIELD STATION 2

Interactive Environments and Digital Perception

At the turn of the twenty-first century, digital tools have become an almost unavoidable presence in the creation, recording and dissemination of performance. Digital processes involved in performance, such as interactive programming and physical computing, sampling and real-time processing, sensory feedback, animation, data streaming and distributed networks (telepresence) produce new physical experiences and perceptions, which are the result of the hybridization of virtual and real spaces. Introducing this 'Field Station' and its inquiries into the virtual, the ephemeral and the technological, I look at changing contexts of performance by treating performance as environment and as system. I refer to contemporary performance and dance that use digital processes and are affected, in particular, by the transformations of audio-visual space and bodily perceptions within interactive and streaming media environments. Dance, more comprehensively than theatre and live art, has played a pioneering role in adapting digital tools and exploring new synergies with electronic music, sound art, media and installation art, which in turn means that dancers have also collaborated more effectively with adjacent practices in computer engineering, visual technology and the sciences. Thus, contemporary choreography and explicitly computer-driven performance reflect new conceptual models of hybrid mediatization, positioning the experience of dance less in relation to its traditional kinesphere than to an expanded notion of information/data space and an evolving digital phenomenology.

Rather than introducing a wider context of interactive art and various forms of interactive design, I proceed from a few concrete examples.[1] My emphasis will be on the ways in which digital environments affect our senses and on how performance can be understood as transmedial, implying cognitive and affective notions of perception beyond the representational apparatus of theatre or cinema (perspectival vision) and thus beyond the 'image' or visuality of movement. The future of performance not only promises new models of transcultural collaboration and exchange, it also implies more complex distributed systems of sentience, communication and interaction.[2]

1 Transmediality

The notion of 'interactivity' – connecting bodies to digital interfaces – gains its meaning if we read it in the context of design processes that build an extended, trans-individual nervous system, which is intrinsically changeable and malleable. One could also call it a condition or state, and as such it harbors certain dynamic behaviours. Practitioners in interactive art, dance and music have referred to their networked and computer-rigged laboratories as 'intelligent stages', but I consider the theatrical metaphor misleading. Responsive and interactive environments can be created in many diverse configurations, bounded (installations, site-specific work, theatre stages) and unbounded (urban space, networked space). What concerns us here is the perceptional process within such 'systems'.

The discourse on the body in live art, dance and representational theatre relied on notions of subjectivity, identity, reference, physicality, nature, technical artifice, etc., which had to be refocused in recent performance and media theory, especially in regard to the properties of digital media and pervasive computing that no longer maintain materially mimetic qualities (still prevailing in analog film and photography). Information theory, concerned with abstract, disembodied and decontextualized transmissions and simulations, construes a post-human cybernetic world (see Hayles 1999 and Whitelaw 2004), whereas digital performance recovers embodiment and agency in the particular physical, affective, proprioceptive and tactile dimensions of experience, with which interaction constitutes its space through computer processing and internal bodily processing. Transmediality, at the same time, points away from the anthropocentric view of the performer–body in real space to the interspatiality of virtual environments and complex human–machine communications that involve programming and various media applications. The technical simulation of vision and other sensory perceptions in turn affects our knowledge and experience of human perception.

As a mode of technical mediation within such an infrastructure, interactivity points to a new under-

PHOTO: LISA RASTL

Willi Dorner Company, 'back to return', Nottingham 2004.

standing of environments of relations, a relational aesthetic based on physical interaction as well as a new technological kinesthetic. Designing digital interfaces in dance means organizing a sensory and intelligent space for communicative acts that are inherently dynamic and unpredictable. The space is not 'set' for a fixed choreography, but programmed for potential interactions and movements in which partners behave within a network of relays and responses, and in which technologies and media generate perceivable realities. Interaction thus involves the whole environment, and it maps its 'world' through the continuous biofeedback it receives via direct sensory stimuli that are also technically mediated (sound, image projection, tactile sensors, wearable computing built into textiles, etc).

Ephemerality is no longer a concern. Digital objects can be collected and stored in databases, and perform-ance thrives on re-organizing, using, interfering with the information space, adapting to it in ever-open, improvisational ways. In terms of composition, interactive dance is processual, and as a transmedia form it can be embodied in different ways and shapes. But as an aesthetic event it implies a sensory and sense-

making body-brain activity. Interactive movement and play involve behaviors that I describe in human and social terms rather than machinic and functional ones, even though the programming of an environment implies assigning functions and values of recording/recorded data, as the software uses the input from the tools of connection and manipulates, mixes and remixes the input, which in the case of dance includes bodily movements, gestures, sensations. We use a mixed language if we speak of 'sampling sensations' or 'framing affects', and the sensorial and technical levels of interactivity often get confused. But it is apparent that aesthetic emphasis has shifted from the object of representation (choreography) to the emergent situation itself, the performative interplay, the materialization of technology. We see dance and 'digital objects' in the environment (projections, 3D virtual worlds, artifacts that serve as interface, etc), but real time computing in interactive installations generally shifts the 'process' to the physical involvement of the user and thus alters conventional distinctions between 'artwork' and 'observer'. This is not the case in interactive performances staged for a spectating audience. Interactivity, in general, offers and assigns roles to the users when interacting becomes an essential component in the condition of the situation, its actualization and reception.

2 back to return

Willi Dorner Company's 'back to return', a continuous three-hour exhibition of dance, film and sound installations, was performed in and around the entire Lakeside Arts Center during the recent 2004 NOTT Dance festival (Nottingham). The audience was handed a schedule and location plan and was invited to roam freely and explore the various aspects of the installation, which comprised nine solos, a duo, a trio, as well as a number of audio and video pieces, which, in some cases, functioned like a solo (in one a voice spoke a monologue in three different tempi, in another the recorded footsteps of a dance were audible). Although this environmental installation did not use any direct real-time interactive processing, the conceptual treatment of the 'dance material' (both live and recorded) as database or as samples indicated a digital approach to a locational and temporal structuring and dispersion of information, which required each visitor to form her own synaesthetic picture of the whole.

The relationship between micro-elements and macrostructure is transmedial, and since individual components of the installation are performed repeatedly, and thus can be viewed more than once, from different angles and in an accumulative manner, the process of reception is both nonlinear and gradual, without a center of gravity and perspective. The perspective distortion of the multi-layered (frame)work is deliberate.

Solo 3 was performed in the Green Room for one visitor at a time. I had to sign up and wait my turn, and was then asked to close my eyes upon entering the room where the dancer was waiting for me. I was led to a chair and told to keep my eyes closed. As the dance unfolded, I found myself in the challenging situation of having to accept this sense deprivation (without the conventional visual perception of movement) and rely on my other senses and my imagination. It was an extraordinary experience, however simple the parameter for this interaction, but I remember this solo as the most interactive piece of the entire installation. I heard the dancer move, in close proximity, sometimes further away, I followed her breath and energy expenditure, I sensed movement and began to form 'mental pictures' of what this movement might be like based on my calculation of its speed, energy, strength and subtlety. My sense apparatus began to perform complex operations, activating my body while my fantasy

drifted into other areas of association and interpretation. I could not see this dance but I heard soft and hard motion, my temptation to look decreased as I imagined myself in a darkroom, necessary to develop film. In this case I developed a space in which my attention shifted to breath and circumference. I sensed movement all around me, and I became enveloped. The intimacy was exhilarating and erotic; instead of clear pictures I formed a tactile apprehension of the world of felt movement in which I was submerged. Such an interactive performance animates the audience to reciprocate with a kind of 'movement processing': it is not a virtual dance, but the visitor's bodily perception is itself virtualized.

3 World Modeling

I emphasize the phenomenological weight of this sensory processing to distinguish it from fashionable but misleading notions that digital performance today is overwhelmingly predicated on 'virtuality' and on the 'body' being digitized, its movements and enunciations captured and coded for algorithmic processing (Carver and Beardon 2004: 167-71). In my example, there is a shared real-time environment in which 'images' (perceptions) are extravisual, generative, synaesthetic – contingent on sensori-motoric, haptic and auditory apprehensions. Dorner's playing with the 'blind' viewer only underlines that in most cases of contemporary digital dance the interactive relationship involves the dancer's or participant's intervention into the world of projected media (video, 3D virtual reality, animation) which is apprehended through the whole body. If 'back to return' is a model of immersive performance, it indicates how dance can activate bodily modalities apart from

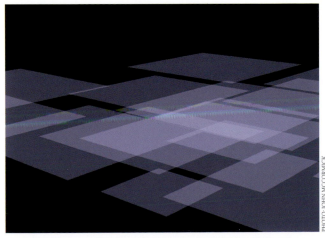

Company in Space (Hellen Sky, John McCormick) with Igloo (Ruth Gibson, Bruno Martelli), 'Sentient Space', 3DVR World, Essexdance 2004.

PHOTO: JOHN MCCORMICK

ADaPT, 'Self-Talking', multi-site telepresence performance, 22 January 2005

sight.[3] The process (proprioception, tactility, affectivity) through which human perception constructs images does not depend on the visual mode. My other examples of interactive dance point to a similar expansion of the visual image and our optical experience. Dancing with virtual worlds opens up a perspectival flexibility that transforms the photographic and cinematic projection of the real. It challenges choreographers to think of the relations between dance and projected image in different ways, especially regarding the familiar and redundant back-projections of video on stage. Some choreographers (including Pablo Ventura, Klaus Obermaier, Vim Vandekeybus and Frédéric Flamand.) have experimented with projections directly onto the bodies of the dancers or used video as a lighting source. At the 2004 Monaco Dance Forum, the Multimedia Workshops and TechLab ('Extending Perception') were specifically dedicated to the haptic effects of video-sound projection and to motion-sensing technologies and their kinesthetic impact.

The processing speed of digital technologies has reached a point at which motion sensing systems can now transform data in real time. Programmers and digital architects working with dancers have started to use 'movement information' for the construction of synthetic image worlds and modelization that enable the dancer to act upon a 'living' data environment that is as fluidly evolving, elastic and changing as physical movement, but in which the projected images are no longer representational. The virtual world, which Hellen Sky and John McCormick (Company in Space) in their recent collaboration with Ruth Gibson and Bruno Martelli (Igloo) called 'Sentient Space', affords a different mental experience of the image–space.[4] Their experiments with telepresence and motion-capture took a complex conceptual turn towards real-time dynamic systems in which the image–environment is generated by the crossing of several networked morphogenetic processes. Sky and McCormick explored telematic performance based on the idea of visual world-modeling. Movement data, captured in real time from Sky and Gibson (in exoskeletal motion sensing suits), were transmitted and processed to create 'soft bodies', i.e. the data were not mapped onto animated figures but stretched, folded and manipulated to create topological models – images that act like the congealment of the space in-between the two dancers performing in remote locations.

McCormick thinks of the composite mass of the dancers as shared volume – and this visual mass is made out of the connection between the dancers' motions (e.g. the motions of hands, pelvis or upper body). As I watch the projected environment of warped space, I am perplexed by this dance, which has been utterly transformed into a kind of biomorphic architecture. The changing shapes of volume are a direct expression of the movement–distance between the dancers who are generating the motion data, but 'bodies' here become spatialized energy, floating topologies in torsion. My own perception is alienated to a certain extent, as I cannot rationally grasp it but need to let myself float with the anamorphic qualities of these motions.

Dancing in responsive environments that use telepresence and 3D VR interactivity means participating in virtual or distributed space: to enter into image–space and kinesthetically experience the body somewhere else (and as something else) requires different kinds of intuition. The term 'sensing' gains a dimension beyond the habitual physical and organic understanding of bodily anatomy, musculature, cellular consciousness and proprioceptive spatial awareness of moving-within-the-kinesphere. The convergence of interface design and movement perception here extends (Laban-derived) structural explorations of the body's kinespheric repertoire for movement with regard to space, shape, effort, dynamics, rhythm, and expressive qualities. In the digital laboratory these qualities are intuited in or between data–space, projected space (video/animation) or other virtual topologies (VR, nongeometric virtual space). The performer learns to 'see' with the whole body, projecting herself into the entire space that surrounds her.

4 Dancing across Spaces: Telepresence

Finally, the transformation of site into multi-sitedness in streaming media performance can be illuminated through the phenomenal experience of synaesthetic perception. 'Dancing across' here means that digital technologies can connect and fuse different spheres of activity, but delays and interferences in Internet transmission also play tricks on our perception. This encourages us to play with synchronicity and recursion, and to invent dramaturgies that use lags, loops, discrepancies and peripheral perceptions aesthetically. At the first interactive laboratory in the former coal mine Göttelborn (2003), I created a six-minute film of a solo by Koala Yip on the roof of the immense sinking pond rotunda. Entitled 'Oracle', the edited film was not shown at the concluding exhibition. Rather, I asked Koala to question the 'oracle' again in her native language. Her voice (via wireless microphone) then animated sections of the film in real time, processed in a Max/Msp software patch created by Marlon Barrios Solano. The algorithmic process translates Koala's voice into new shapes of light – distorted, pulsating, curved, exploding and shrinking picture-animations that bear little relation to the original dancefilm, even though we still recognize Koala's movement and her mirror reflection in the watery vortex of the sinking pond. The film became a virtual environment that lit the imaginary world, echoes of Koala's vocal intonations pulling, stretching and scratching the digital emulsion of the filmstrip (http://interaktionslabor.de).

In the telematic dancework 'Self Talking' (2005), collaboratively created with Kelly Gottesman and his team, the live stream connects his movement (in Detroit) with my voice and sound (generated in Nottingham) across the distance. I am the voice in his head which he hears as he dances, a voice remembering and anticipating the movements I feel as I receive them in my incoming stream. Telepresence creates an interactive environment allowing the real-time synthesis of various media acting upon each other in a shared virtual reality (the Internet) which needs to be spatialized through projection. I see a projected dance, I move with it, and there are other systems of reference in play: memory, physical consciousness and orientation, sensing of color, light, shapes and sound, one sense modulating another as I speak through the movement of Kelly's body and begin to play the piano keyboard on my end. In our studios the emphasis is on the dancer's actions, how he or she incorporates the projected light and sound of the stream into an extended sense of the world, an extended body.

One aesthetic challenge in telepresence is the conscious

Koala Yip, 'Oracle', Interaktionslabor Göttelborn 2003

VIDEOSTILL J. BIRRINGER

VIDEOSTILL: J. BIRRINGER

ADaPT rehearsal of 'Saira Virous' (Nottingham)

incorporation of the camera interface into the performance, with dancer and cameraperson working very closely together in a restricted area under subtly diffused light. The choreographic relationship to the streaming environment, and to the frame compositions of the virtual images created by the cameras, suggests that the dancer insert herself into a moving architecture and move 'through' the filmspaces.[5] It is perhaps also appropriate to say that she 'frames' herself. The other challenge is to orient in a media-rich space by focusing on the expressive quality of the proprioceptive system, on the potential variations and associations the dancer makes with sounds, shapes, and rhythms, on implicit form which cannot really be measured and quantified by computers and tracking devices. Space fills with voices and resonances, performance emotions, changing and transforming from one medium to an other, spilling fantasies.

As an emergent system, the telepresence event cannot be controlled. It is an 'adaptive system': we re-adapt existing media and bodily techniques to the new interface, playing with the real-time synthesis of various media forms in an evolving space of emotions in which we perceive our own vitality. We are separate but appear together in a shared world where we need to intuit the other presences. The emphasis is on our actions, not on avatars who journey in pure data environments like the synthetic worlds of games. Digital perception however implies that the dancer inserts herself into the moving architecture. I would venture to suggest that the dancer in this case has to 'wear' the digital environment, the image environment, the sensual presences she feels. Thus the perceptional experience is closer to the kind of sensation we have when we wear certain clothes that heighten our awareness of our surroundings, the effect we have on our surroundings or the eyes we feel on our own

bodies. Digital environments, in this way, can be worn or experienced as a second skin. For the dancer herself this means that she develops a (virtual) proprioceptive and tactile vision that goes beyond vision, since she may not recognize herself in the stream nor all the sonic and visual information that continuously flows through it. To a large extent, this dance is an imaginary activity, a fantasy of self and other, a perceptional 'modeling' in the way in which wear ourselves for the environment which clothes or undresses us.

In the future, we may develop new digital 'scripts,' devise interplay methods to incorporate audiences as active participants who want to join the interface, enter the story. I imagine that such performance-scripts involve interactive storytelling, distributed narratives and game-like structures for the audience's direct collaboration in the fiction or in spatialized play.[6] In a recent online performance with partners in Detroit and Tempe, we tested such a 'game engine.' 'Saira Virous' explores a collaborative process involving both programming (Max/Msp and Isadora patches creating a game-landscape with different levels for movements and behaviours in a surreal game) and open participatory performance by multiple players. Players enter unprepared into a game–scenario in which the networked environment acts as a fantasy space (any other social space of interaction could also serve as a model). Strange tasks are engaged in by the players who interact with each other and the streams that are filtered through the patches. While my earlier work with the ADaPT collective, similar to that with Company in Space and other telematic choreographers (like Lisa Naugle, Sita Popat, Laura Knott, Wayne McGregor, Paul Sermon and Susan Kozel), was focused on camera-generated telepresence, I now prefer a more sensuous engagement with the digital plasticity and modular interactional possibilities of the medium itself, treating tactile and spatial movement through the images in the manner in which textile and fashion designers work with transformable fabrics on the body.[7] I envision the live web-streams to be playful, erotic and fantastical digital processes we sense on the skin and through the pores. In such dancing we absorb the digital environment: the virtual and the fantastic are not strange to us when we incorporate them as physical sensations. Movement-images, even when they are abstracted and filtered through visual and sonic processing, continuously merge with our consciousness. They affect us to create a reaction, and even if the complexity and density of the continual flow overwhelms us, blinds us, we also discover through such interactive art how our neurobiological bodies adapt to information-rich environments and organize their creativity beyond our perceptual habits.

NOTES

1. For an extended discussion, see 'Dance and Interactivity' (Birringer 2004a) and 'Dancing with Technologies' and 'Impossible Anatomies' (Birringer 1998: 27-144). For a laboratory report on the workshop on interactive tools and systems, see http://www.dance.osu.edu/~jbirringer/Dance_and_Technology/ttreport.html. A bibliography on interactive dance is at: http://www.notam02.no/icma/interactivesystems/dance.html

2. My reflections on a new digital phenomenology are inspired by Mark B.N. Hansen's theorization of the 'digital image' (extending Henri Bergson's theory of perception) and his approach to interactive information environments that become a bodily process of filtering and composing images (Hansen 2004: 93-124). For an examination of transcultural media performance, see Birringer 2004b.

3. Cf. Grau 2003: 343-4. For important insights into affective perception, see Massumi 2002; for the cybernetic aspects of interactive art, see Ascott 2003. A pragmatic study of rehearsal methods for digital dance is available in Dinkla and Leeker 2003, and for the history and theory of interactive art see Dinkla 1997, Hünnekens 1997 and Manovich 2001.

4. 'Sentient Space' was created as an experiment at the Digilounge Workshop in Chelmsford (UK) in February 2004. The workshop was convened by Scott deLahunta and produced by Essexdance and the British Arts Council. I am grateful to deLahunta for inviting me to the workshop, and to the artists for sharing their findings. Another experiment at the workshop was conducted by Carol Brown and her dancers. In their collaboration, Brown and digital architect Mette Ramsgard Thomsen devised an interactive environment (SPAWN) to explore how kinetic information informs the behavior of virtual architectures. The dancers created duets or trios with the projected light of the architectures computed by the software Thomsen had written. Their bodily contours were tracked by the camera and processed by the computer program, and they affected the morphological shapes of the image-light and image-color as their movement dynamics became embodied architecture. They literally enacted the virtualization of/in their bodies.

5. The telematic performances described here are produced by the Association of Dance and Performance Telematics (ADaPT). Partner sites since 2001 include Columbus (Ohio), Tempe (Arizona), Salt Lake City (Utah), Madison (Wisconsin), Detroit (Michigan), Irvine (California), Brasilia and São Paulo (Brazil), Nottingham (UK) and Tokyo (Japan). The ADaPT online performances are documented and archived at: http://www.dance.ohio-state.edu/dance_and_technology/ips3.html, : http://dance.asu.edu/adapt/ and http://www.dance.osu.edu/~jbirringer/Dance_and_Technology/workshops/ips3.html.

6. New theories on gaming and interaction design (Copier and Raessens 2003; Newman 2004) address the overlap between media, as do festivals on computer games such as 'Screenplay', held every February at Nottingham's Broadway Cinema. Apart from its various games contests and exhibitions, the festival features seminars, webcasts and performances exploring interactive digital technology and its impact on culture today. See http://www.broadway.org.uk.

7. For example, Alexander McQueen, Hussein Chalayan, Lucy Orta or Vexed Generation (Quinn 2002: 117-39). In this context, it is also interesting to look at the work of textile/performance artist Regina Frank who has explored the intersections between textile/text, fabric and Internet communications in her durational exhibitions, in which she stitches email messages or text files into the garments she wears. See www.regina-frank.de/. The relationship between costume design and wearable computing is also explored in the choreography of Yacov Sharir and other practitioners in the dance and technology field and by design artists such as Jane Harris.

REFERENCES

Ascott, R. (2003) *Telematic Embrace: Visionary Theories of Art, Technology and Consciousness,* (ed. E. A. Shanken),. Berkeley: University of California Press.

Birringer, J. (1998) *Media and Performance: along the border*, Baltimore: Johns Hopkins University Press.

Birringer, J. (2004a) 'Dance and Interactivity', *Dance Research Journal 35(2)/36(1)*: 88-111.

Birringer, J. (2004b) 'Der transmediale Tanz', in Krassimira Kruschkova, Nele Lipp (eds.) *Tanz Anders Wo: Tanz intra- und interkulturell. Jahrbuch der Gesellschaft für Tanzforschung*, Hamburg: LIT Verlag, pp. 23-56.

Brouwer, J., Mulder, A., Charlton, S., eds. (2003) *Information is Alive: Art and Theory on Archiving and Retrieving Data,* Rotterdam: V2_Publishing/NAI Publishers.

Brouwer, J., Mulder, A., Charlton, S., eds. (2003) *Making Art of Databases*, Rotterdam: V2_ Publishing/NAI Publishers.

Carver, G. and Beardon, C., (eds. (2004) *New Visions in Performance: The Impact of Digital Technologies*, Lisse: Svets & Zeitlinger.

Copier, M., Raessens, J., eds. (2003) *Level Up: Digital Games Research Conference*, Utrecht: Diagra/University of Utrecht.

Dinkla D., Leeker, M., eds. (2003) *Dance and Technology/Tanz und Technologie: Moving towards Media Productions/Auf dem Weg zu medialen Inszenierungen*, Berlin: Alexander Verlag.

Dinkla, S. (1997) *Pioniere interaktiver Kunst*, Ostfildern: Cantz Verlag.

Grau, O. (2003) *Virtual Art: From Illusion to Immersion*, Cambridge (Massachusetts): MIT Press.

Hayles, K. N. (1999) *How We Became Posthuman: Virtual Bodies in Cybernetics, Literature and Informatics*, Chicago: University of Chicago Press.

Manovich, L. (2001) *The Language of New Media*, Cambridge (Massachusetts): MIT Press.

Massumi, B. (2002) *Parables for the Virtual: Movement, Affect, Sensation*, Durham: Duke University Press.

Newman, J. (2004) *Videogames*, London: Routledge.

Quinn, B. (2002) *Techno Fashion*, Oxford: Berg.

Whitelaw, M. (2004) *Metacreation: Art and Artificial Life*, Cambridge (Massachusetts): MIT Press.

PHILIP AUSLANDER   FIELD STATION 2

AnimalCam: Ocularcentrism and Non-Human Performance

The arts section of the New York Times for 30 November 2004 serendipitously juxtaposed two articles. The first concerned GuitarBot, a self-playing digital musical instrument that has performed both with human accompanists and in solo recitals. One of the latter, at the Juilliard School in New York City, was billed as a 'Robo Recital: No Human Performers' (Beckerman 2004). The second article was about *Cavalia: A Magical Encounter Between Man and Horse*, an extravaganza produced by one of the founders of Cirque du Soleil, intended to show 'the horse unfettered' (Sharkey 2004). Together, these two articles suggested the two sides of posthuman performance: the technological (performance by machines) and the zoological (performance by animals other than human beings).

Neither phenomenon is new, of course. Animals have been pressed into service as performers, often in blood sports, for millennia, and the dream, if not the reality, of machine performers has been around for centuries. But the idea of non-human performers has acquired fresh currency in the age of digital technology. Now that we may converse with chat bots, employ avatars to act in our behalf, and watch films in which human performers share screen time with CGI figures, the need to theorize the non-human in performance feels more urgent. To date, much of the work in performance studies to take up these questions has revolved around technology and the concept of the cyborg. More recently, animal performers have come into focus: *Performance Research* devoted an issue to the theme and most major academic conferences in theatre or performance studies now feature at least one 'animal panel' on their programs.

Looking back from the future, I believe we will see that machine and animal performance are overlapping areas of inquiry, in part because the animal is always technologically mediated in performance, if only through such technologies as bits and bridles. More crucially, performing animals and machines, while different in obvious and important ways, raise similar theoretical and critical issues. For me, these issues revolve around questions of agency, autonomy and subjectivity in performance, questions that pertain equally to human performers. I therefore prefer the term 'non-human' to the term 'posthuman' and am more interested in the shared

characteristics of human and non-human performance than in cyborgian hybridization. Most of the work I have done in this area has been on the technological side of the equation (see Auslander 2001, 2002a, 2002b, and forthcoming) but I have had occasion recently to give some thought to the zoological side as well.[1]

Here, I will discuss two human-enabled performances by animals, both achieved through technological mediation. The first is the identity performed by Koko, the famous 'talking' gorilla, on 'her' website (www.koko.org). I will argue that the website emphasizes the importance of vision to Koko, a priority she shares with humans, thus downplaying her status as an animal in favor of presenting her as (almost) human. By contrast, Stanley the dog, the main character of Jana Sterbak's video installation *From Here to There* (2003), enjoys greater control over the technology that frames his performance and is thus able to perform a more specifically animal sensorium and identity, albeit for an exclusively human audience.

The role that Koko is made to perform on the website is that of 'ambassador for her critically endangered species'. Like any good ambassador, Koko is able to communicate with her hosts: the first text on the homepage of the website describes her as 'a 33-year-old lowland gorilla who learned to speak American Sign Language' (ASL); another page identifies her main diplomatic qualification by saying, 'she can speak to us humans in our own language'. Koko's ability to acquire human language is emphasized continuously and the message is clear: we humans can no longer use our capacity for language as a way of distinguishing ourselves from other animals. But the idea that language is a defining human trait remains in force nevertheless: the presentation strongly suggests that Koko's linguistic ability makes her more like us, not us more like her. She had to acquire human language to effect inter-species communication – the researchers who work with Koko communicate with her by using a combination of ASL and spoken English and express no interest in learning to speak gorilla, whatever that might mean. We're much happier to acknowledge Koko's putative humanity than our own animality.

While treating Koko as an honorary human may cause us to be more respectful of animals (or at least the higher primates) and treat them as beings possessing subjectivity, if not subjecthood, we continue to define subjectivity, like language, in human terms. On the website, Koko is shown interacting primarily with human beings, including such celebrities as Mr. Rogers, the late host of a children's television program popular in the US, and Robin Williams, the actor and comedian. Her interactions with other animals are framed as human relationships: Michael, another gorilla (now deceased), was her 'best friend' and she selected 'potential mate' Ndume by means of video dating (the implication of a monogamous relationship belies male gorillas' normal polygamy). She is also shown with a cat identified as her pet. One of Koko's hobbies is painting pictures that are described in terms of familiar stylistic categories: according to the website, gorillas can produce images that are both 'representational (based on what they see) and impressionistic (based on what they feel)'.

Gorillas' sensorium is very similar to that of human beings: they see and hear well and are not as dependent on the sense of smell as some other animals. The importance of sight to the gorilla is subtly emphasized on Koko's website as a means of making her seem human. She produces visual art, looks at videos of potential mates and gazes fondly at the kitten she holds in her arms. Koko looks at the same kinds of things, and for the same reasons, as we do, and we look at Koko looking. We permit ourselves to believe that she is (nearly) one of us in large part because she apparently places the same premium on the sense of sight as we do. Ocularcentrism is thus bound up with anthropomorphism, even with respect to Koko's linguistic achievement, since Koko's acquisition of language is confirmed visually. Although we human beings cannot hear Koko communicate, we can see that she is linguistically competent because she is trained in ASL, a visual form of verbal language.

Our ocular relationship to Koko is different, however, from the ocular relationship between human beings and animals described by John Berger in 'Looking at Animals'. Berger identifies a modern, technologized human gaze that objectifies animals: 'animals are always the observed. The fact that they can observe us has lost all significance' (1980: 14). Berger contrasts this condition with an earlier one characterized by 'that look between animal and man, which may have played a crucial role in the development of human society, and which, in any case, all men had always lived with' (1980: 26). The case of Koko challenges Berger's account of this transition somewhat. As the various interactions with human beings on Koko's website show, she is not simply the observed. Her ability to observe us actually is important to us, and the fact that we are interested in exchanging gazes with her is an index to a new way of thinking about (at least some)

animals. But Koko's ability to observe us is important to us primarily because we want to believe that she is one of us. Cary Wolfe suggests, 'the figure of vision is . . . ineluctably tied to the specifically human' (2003: 3). The emphasis on vision in the way Koko is presented allows us to regard her as (almost) human; when she looks at us, we implicitly believe that we are exchanging the same kind of gaze – a human gaze. We do not feel ourselves to be the object of an Other's gaze, an animal's gaze, which is what Berger is talking about. While granted a degree of subjecthood, Koko is not permitted to perform a distinctly animal subjectivity, only a quasi-human one. [2]

Given the classic status of Berger's writing on this subject, dare I say that while I find his account of the progressive physical and cultural marginalization of animals useful and convincing, I also find his account of ocularity in human/animal relationships to be surprisingly anthropocentric? In his descriptions, the exchange of gazes between 'man' and animal always works to humanity's advantage without providing any clear benefit for the animal. In arguing that the 'look between animal and man' may have contributed to the development of human society, Berger distinguishes the human response to the animal's gaze from that of other animals by saying, 'man becomes aware of himself returning the look' (1980: 3). So, man gains self-consciousness from this exchange, but what does the animal get? The framing of Koko's performance as a gorilla ambassador to humanity sidesteps this issue: since Koko's animality is suppressed in this performance, her audience need not be troubled by the question of parity in ocular transactions between humans and animals.

The close association of the visual with the human raises difficult questions for artistic practices, including performance, seeking a critical stance with respect to anthropocentrism and speciesism. Since performances produced by humans inevitably reflect the priority of vision in the human sensorium, 'it is ... tempting', as Wolfe notes, 'to abandon the figure of vision altogether' (2003: 3) and insist that only performances that engage other senses can be considered truly posthumanist in outlook. But Wolfe is not quite ready for such a radical rejection of ocularity, and neither am I. He proposes instead that 'one way to recast the figure of vision (and therefore the figure of the human with which it is ineluctably associated) is to resituate it as only one sense among many in a more general – and not necessarily human – bodily sensorium' (2003: 3). In conclusion, I shall discuss a video installation I saw at the Venice Biennale in 2003 that constitutes a step in the direction Wolfe indicates.

The installation, entitled *From Here to There*, was by Jana Sterbak, the Canadian representative to that

Biennale. I will simply quote the description from the press release: 'made up of a series of short segments, the work chronicles the adventures of Stanley the dog in the City of the Doges, as well as on the banks of the St. Lawrence River. Without conventional plot development or predictable aesthetic choices, spectators will observe life as it appears from a height of 35 cm above the ground'. Sterbak made her video using a puppy-cam attached to the adventurous Stanley, a young Jack Russell terrier. The resulting images are slurred and oddly cropped; the frame bounces and vibrates according to the rhythms of the dog's movements.

John W. Locke, in a catalog essay for the exhibition, argues that we should not see the images in this video as subjective camera shots from the dog's point of view. (In fact, he argues against the whole concept of the subjective camera on the grounds that the camera's version of vision is true neither to human nor canine perception and subjectivity.) To call the puppy-cam a subjective camera would be to imply that we understand and can recognize canine subjectivity. The video camera replicates neither a dog's subjectivity nor the way a dog sees, of course, and its emphasis on sight belies the dog's perceptual world (although sound plays a large part in this piece as well). Nevertheless, the video serves, in Locke's words, as 'a record of Stanley's visual attention. The image precisely follows every movement of the dog's head. We don't know what he is thinking, or even if thinking is the right concept, but we are seeing where he is looking and the speed of his shifts of attention' (2003: 10). Whereas Koko is always shown directing her attention to things that would also attract a human being's interest, Sterbak's puppy-cam allows us to see what a dog chooses to look at when left to his own devices.

In a different essay in the same catalog, Gilles Godmer claims provocatively that Stanley's attention is not visual in nature at all. 'Through Stanley', writes Godmer, 'the image subjects us to the animal nature of smell' (2003: 88). The camera's position (35 cm above the ground) is that of a non-human being for whom olfaction is the primary sense. In *From Here to There*, 'the camera serves interests that rely to a great extent on the olfactory and that are foreign to us' (2003: 88). For Godmer, then, the video is a visual record of Stanley's olfactory attention. There is, of course, no way of enabling Stanley's human artistic collaborator and audience to share in or understand his sensorium. Arguably, by presenting images of the things to which a creature driven more by smell than by sight chooses to give his attention in a way that traces the trajectory of his shifting interests, the installation at least allows us humans to experience what vision looks like when it is subordinated to another sense.

Oh, and it may interest Berger to learn that Stanley exhibits no inclination whatsoever to observe the people around him, who appear only as vague, momentary presences. As opposed to Koko, who is always represented as interacting with human beings, Stanley displays no desire to exchange meaningful looks with man – his own interests direct his attention elsewhere.

NOTES

1. This essay is based on the response I presented as part of a panel on non-human performance at the 2003 meeting of the Association for Theatre in Higher Education. Although I do not refer directly to the papers presented on that occasion by panelists Una Chaudhuri, Jennifer Parker-Starbuck and Erika Rundle, I thank them all for their inspiring work without which I would never have engaged with these ideas.

2. I wish to emphasize that my critique of how Koko is represented is not intended as a critique either of the scientific research of which she is a subject or the efforts to protect endangered gorillas undertaken in her name.

REFERENCES

Auslander, Philip (2001) 'Cyberspace as a Performance Art Venue', *Performance Research* 38: 123-6.

Auslander, Philip (2002a) 'Live from Cyberspace, or I was sitting at my computer this guy appeared he thought I was a bot', *Performing Arts Journal* 24: 16-21.

Auslander, Philip (2002b) 'Live from Cyberspace: Performance on the Internet', in Jutta Eming, Annette Jael Lehmann and Irmgard Maassen (eds.) *Mediale Performanzen: Historische Konzepte und Perspektiven*, Freiburg: Rombach Verlag, pp. 321-35.

Auslander, Philip (Forthcoming) 'Humanoid Boogie: Reflections on Robotic Performance', in David Krasner and David Saltz (eds.) *Staging Philosophy: New Approaches to Theater and Performance*, Ann Arbor: University of Michigan Press.

Beckerman, M. (2004) 'The Guitarist is Metal. No, Not Heavy Metal', New York Times, 30 November.

Berger, John (1980) *About Looking*, New York: Pantheon.

Godmer, Gilles (2003) 'Roving Photographer', in *Jana Sterbak: From Here to There*, Montréal: Musée d'Art Contemporain de Montréal, pp. 77-91.

Locke, John W. (2003) 'Experiments in Camera Movement: Venice 1896 to Venice 2003/Lumière to Sterbak', in *Jana Sterbak: From Here to There*, Montréal: Musée d'Art Contemporain de Montréal, pp. 99-109.

Sharkey, J. (2004) 'The Stage Is Set: Enter Horses at Full Gallop', New York Times, 30 November.

Wolfe, Cary (2003) *Animal Rites: American Culture, the Discourse of Species, and Posthumanist Theory*, Chicago: University of Chicago Press.

Global Feeling: (Almost) All You Need Is Love

On 25 June 1967, the Beatles performed a new song, 'All You Need is Love', before an intimate yet immense audience, one numbering approximately 350 million people – an audience composed of dozens of invited celebrities and guests sitting around the band in a London BBC studio and the millions upon millions of TV viewers watching from sites around the world. The performance was part of the BBC show *Our World*, considered by some to have been the first global television program.

One might approach the performance of 'All You Need is Love' using Philip Auslander's concept of 'liveness' (1999), for John Lennon sang the song live while listening to taped tracks the band had recorded days earlier at Abbey Road Studios, tapes also listened to through headphones by Paul, George and Ringo, as well as the half-dozen classical musicians also sitting-in that day. One might also approach the performance through at least four paradigms of performance research: the cultural performance of rock music, the technological performance of satellite television, the organizational performance of the British Broadcasting Corporation and Capitol Records, and, lastly, the financial performance of these two entities, as well as that of the Fab Four themselves (McKenzie 2001, 2004). (Significantly, when 'All You Need You is Love' was released shortly afterwards as a 45 single in more than a dozen countries, the B-side selection was the song 'Baby, You're A Rich Man'.

I will consider 'All You Need is Love' from another angle, however, that of *global feeling* and a certain futural perfumance.

Though there's been much discussion about the political, economic, and cultural dimensions of globalization over the past decade, less attention has been given to the dimension of feeling. A few scholars have addressed it: anthropologist Arjun Appadurai has analyzed the complex 'structures of feeling' that globalization entails (1996), while literary scholar Bruce Robbins has begun theorizing a hypothetical, posthumanist way of 'feeling global' (1999). I wish to approach this affective dimension in terms of performance, in order to begin thinking about 'global feeling'.

By 'global feeling', I mean at least two things. First: the possibility that feelings can be transmitted globally in unprecedented ways. Much of this possibility has to do with profound changes in migration, tourism, transportation, international trade and communication technologies. Even if not felt by everyone on the planet, emotions and affects can be communicated and shared around the world in ways that were never before possible, at least not with such immediacy and intensity. I am not arguing that everyone feels the same thing or that they interpret shared feelings in the same way. This first sense of the term 'global feeling' simply refers to the possibility of affects and emotions being transmitted around the world.

Second, by 'global feeling', I also mean the sense of 'feeling global', feeling a/part of and from global events, both local and distant. By 'global feeling' I do not mean 'we are the world', much less 'I am the world'. Rather, I want to stress this pun 'a/part': global feeling means both feeling a part of the world and feeling apart from it at the same time. 'Feeling global' is feeling a/part: it's feeling both localized and globalized, situated and detached, a sort of passion or pathos at a distance: *telepathos*. It is not necessarily feeling the same 'thing', but it is feeling connected – and thus also disconnected. In some ways, this second sense of global feeling entails an awareness of the first sense; it's a feeling that one is feeling something with others around the world. The 1967 performance of 'All You Need is Love', I want to suggest, can be approached as an instance of global feeling.

But let me offer a more recent and very different performance of global feeling, one whose repercussions are still with us today, though we may feel them in different ways. The terrorist attacks of September 11 have been analyzed and discussed from many perspectives. In terms of global feeling, the crash of four airliners into the World Trade Center, the Pentagon and a field in Pennsylvania sent out a wave of shock around the world, a shock transmitted by television, radio and internet, as well as word of mouth and frantic telephone calls. Though I was in Manhattan when the planes struck the towers, I first heard about it from my mother, who telephoned me from Florida.

Now this global wave of shock was itself complex, and it produced a wide variety of feelings in a very short period of time. Many people in the US felt intense fear and confusion, others revulsion, sadness, anger – or some mix of these emotions. Such feelings were felt around the world, as the United States received many messages of sympathy from abroad. However, for some people, the initial wave of shock produced very different feelings: feelings of joy and amazement, of triumph and satisfaction. The attacks were obviously carefully planned and executed in order to produce widespread impact.

If we can think of September 11 in terms of global feeling, can we also think of it in terms of performance?

Here let me draw upon the work of sociologist Mark Jurgensmeyer, author of the book *Terror in the Mind of God: The Global Rise of Religious Violence*. Jurgensmeyer analyzes an extensive set of case studies, including terrorist acts by Christian, Zionist, Islamic, Hindu, and Buddhist groups. Significantly, he uses performance as an analytical lens to identify patterns of religious violence. In a chapter titled 'Theater of Terror', he stresses that such violence strives to be spectacular. He writes:

> At centre stage are the acts of violence themselves – stunning, abnormal, and outrageous murders carried out in a way that graphically displays the awful power of violence – set within grand scenarios of conflict and proclamation [...] By their demonstrative nature, they elicit feelings of revulsion and anger in those who witness them. (2000: 122)

Significantly, Jurgensmeyer calls such theatrical forms of terrorism 'performance violence'. Terrorist acts, he argues, function as both performance events and performative speech acts. Performance violence makes dramatic, symbolic statements and also attempts to change things.

The setting and timing of performance violence may themselves be symbolic. The Pentagon and World Trade Center, for instance, were potent symbols of the US military and international trade and finance. In terms of timing, the writer Christopher Hitchens suggested in *The Guardian* a few days after the attack that September 11 marks a significant date in European and Islamic history: 'It was on September 11, 1683 that the conquering armies of Islam were met, held, and thrown back at the gates of Vienna' (2001). This military reversal, by the way, was soon followed by what, until recently, has been called the last Christian crusade against Islam.

Jurgensmeyer also argues that performance violence usually has multiple audiences and that its perpetrators are often very media savvy. Using television and other media, they may seek to strike terror into a general public, while at the same signaling strength and determination to a narrower audience. Following Jurgensmeyer's line of inquiry, the attacks of September 11 can be understood as a performance designed to produce a specific set of global feelings: feelings of terror and revulsion for a wide, general audience, and feelings of triumph and determination for another audience whose size would surprise most Americans. One of most striking things about the attacks on the World Trade Center was that they were recorded by helicopters taking images of the city for broadcast on the morning news shows. These cameras produced broadcast quality images of the attacks that were quickly transmitted around the world. It was largely through such images that the world felt the shock and awe of September 11.

I use this term 'shock and awe' here because it takes me to another, closely related example of global feeling: the US 'shock and awe' bombing of Baghdad. I am not equating the September 11 attacks and the 21 March bombing of the Iraqi capital. But I do think that these coordinated, even choreographed, missile strikes can be understood as a direct response to the spectacle of the World Trade Center attacks. The US military campaign produced carefully-targeted, large-scale explosions in a major metropolitan area, explosions captured and transmitted by broadcast quality media to a worldwide audience. As the name indicates, this campaign was explicitly designed to create a specific set of feelings: shock and awe.

Many, if not most, Americans would not like to think of the shock and awe campaign in terms of terrorism; it was, after all, portrayed at the time by the US media as a turning point in America's triumph over the Iraqi army and Saddam Hussein's government. But though its stated goal was to shock, awe and confuse the Iraqi leadership, there is little doubt that the campaign also produced terror on the population. One might also consider both the effects and affects it produced elsewhere: in other Mideast countries, in Asia, Africa, Europe and also in the Western hemisphere. One thing is evident today: the war against Iraq has cost the US government and the American people the global feelings of sympathy and support that were expressed immediately after September 11, and in the wake of torture scandal at Abu Ghraib prison, the assault on Fallujah, and the continued violence elsewhere in Iraq, one wonders when, if ever, such feelings will return to displace the anger and suspicions now felt around the world towards the United States.

Though I have been discussing the global feelings associated with terror and war, I want to return to the Beatles' performance of 'All You Need is Love'. Today, almost forty years later, the televized performance and the song's sentiment may seem naïve, fanciful, even quaint and old-fashioned. Confronted with the complexities of contemporary globalization, American imperialism and the two-headed monster of terrorism and the 'global war on terror', surely something more is needed than love.

There's nothing you can do that can't be done.
Nothing you can sing that can't be sung.

Nothing you can say but you can learn how to play the game.
It's easy.

Nothing you can make that can't be made.
No one you can save that can't be saved.
Nothing you can do but you can learn how to be you in time.
It's easy.

All you need is love.
All you need is love.
All you need is love, love.
Love is all you need. (1967)

Almost. One also needs to consider *what sort of love* is needed. Lennon's notion of love was not restricted to commonplace understandings of this emotion. The song was written especially for the broadcast of *Our World*, with its intimate and immense audience. While we can and should critique the commercialism associated with the Beatles – and rock music generally – we should recognize that the band not only used musical instruments and magnetic tape as creative media, they also used Capitol Records and the BBC in a similar manner – and not only as creative media but also as *political* media. For 'All You Need is Love' was a political anthem, a song sung worldwide during that summer of 1967, a season actively promoted as the 'Summer of Love' from hippie-central San Francisco. Lennon's love was precisely a political love.

I am not waxing nostalgic here. Rather, I want to suggest that a resistant performativity – a perfumance of the present, yet attuned to the future – cannot do without a global feeling of political love. In their latest book, *Multitude*, Hardt and Negri write:

> People today seem unable to understand love as a political concept, but a concept of love is just what we need to grasp the constituent power of the multitude. The modern concept of love is almost exclusively limited to the bourgeois couple and the claustrophobic confines of the nuclear family. Love has become a strictly private affair. We need a more generous and more unrestrained conception of love. We need to recuperate the public and political conception of love common to premodern traditions. (2004: 351)

Because they argue that the multitude consists of singular desires, singular bodies, singular situations and struggles, Hardt and Negri contend that what is needed is a *common language of singularities*. The global feeling of love or, more accurately, multiple global feelings of love constitute an affective medium for creating such a language.

What other sort of performances might be relevant to creating these global feelings of political love? Though Hardt and Negri suggest that the political concept of love is difficult for many people to understand, the twentieth century contained several well-known embodiments of such love. They can be found in the legacy of modern civil disobedience practised in countries around the world. Though there are a wide range of emotions associated with the practice of civil disobedience articulated by Thoreau and developed by Gandhi, King and so many others, perhaps no emotion is more important than love.

Love was crucial for Gandhi, whose term for nonviolence was *ahimsa*, which he defined in both negative and positive terms. Negatively, it means not injuring any living being; positively, it means 'the largest love, the greatest charity', even towards one's opponents (1993: 95-6). Thus for Gandhi, nonviolence, *ahimsa*, was closely related to love. Martin Luther King likewise stressed the overriding value of love, and he drew upon the Greeks to define it. King stressed not *eros* or sensual love, nor *philia*, the reciprocal love between friends. Instead, King valorized *agape*, which he defined as 'understanding, creative, redemptive good will for all men [...] It is the type of love that stands at the centre of the movement we are trying to carry on in the Southland' (1992: 22-3). Of course, for Gandhi and King, these practices of love resonated with their respective Hindu and Christian beliefs, and though they both preached love, it was a confrontational love that they taught and practiced.

A more secular version of such confrontational love can be found in the political protests of ACT-UP. Before his death in 1993, AIDS activist Jon Greenberg wrote that, although ACT-UP is united in anger, its protests function as primal scream therapy, getting the anger out so as to 'open up to love, knowledge and power' (1992). And it is striking in this context that the 1997 collection of essays devoted to ACT-UP founder Larry Kramer, often seen as the angriest of AIDS activists, is titled *We Must Love One Another or Die*.

If love has been a crucial emotion for traditional forms of civil disobedience, what role might it have for more contemporary, global forms?

I have been teaching courses on civil disobedience for several years, focusing especially on the emergence of electronic civil obedience and 'hacktivism'. In contrast to more traditional forms of activism, electronic civil disobedience is not limited to local actions undertaken by long-standing communities. Its campaigns often work through global networks, bringing together short-term coalitions from around the world for direct actions against the web sites of multinational corporations and transnational entities such as the International Monetary Fund and the World Trade Organization. Such protests, however, are usually coordinated with actions on the ground, in the streets, and, in the case of the 2003 protests against the WTO, on the shores of Cancun, Mexico, where nude protestors used their bodies to write 'NO WTO' on the white sandy beach.

The possibility of creating performances that elicit global feelings of political love faces many challenges in getting beyond private, familial, and bourgeois notions of love. What is a love that is both intimate and immense, both personal and public, both proximate and distant? Such a love, while drawing on premodern traditions (Hardt and Negri cite Christian and Jewish love – oddly leaving out Islam – but, again, there are obviously many, many other forms of love), involves creating truly postmodern structures of feeling, and here I do not limit the postmodern to aesthetics but include the very problematic economic and technological dimensions of postmodernity.

Here I come to another type of performance that may help us think – indeed feel – this global feeling. Counter-intuitively, I refer here to organizational performance, the performance of workers, managers and entire organizations. In *Perform or Else*, I argue that this performance paradigm is highly normative, both formally and politically, yet that it also contains mutant and potentially transgressive forces as well.

In *Multitude*, Hardt and Negri explicitly connect up with this mutant dimension of organizational performance, affirming its creative and productive potential. Indeed, such performance is for them crucial for the creation of the common, the medium that connects the multitude's singularities of difference without universalizing or transcending them. In contrast to habit, which Hardt and Negri argue is the common produced alongside the material labor of industrial, Fordist economies, performance is the common produced by immaterial labor, which characterizes today's service and information economies. They write that:

> post-Fordism and the immaterial paradigm adopt performativity, communication, and collaboration as central characteristics. Performance has been put to work. Every form of labor that produces an immaterial good, such as a relationship or an affect, solving problems or providing information, from sales work to financial services, is fundamentally a performance: the product is the act itself. The economic context makes clear that all of these discussions of habit and performance have to be given the sense of doing or making, linking them to the creative capacity of the laboring subject. (200–201)

I must stress here that the material labor found in mines and factories, the labor theorized by Marx and Engels, still obviously exists, especially in sites in Asia and Latin America. Yet such labor – and the hard wares or commodities it produces – is now wrapped in 'soft wares', in flows of information and finance, in the flexible accumulation of capital described by David Harvey (*The Condition of Postmodernity* 1989). Indeed, the manufacturing of 'hard wares' presupposes the 'soft wares' of contemporary communication, finance and management. But, again, my main point here is that Hardt and Negri emphasize not the normative dimension of organizational performance but its accompanying creative and transformational dimension.

Now the cultural performances that performance scholars know and love are not as distant from these organizational performances as we may like to think. One place they mix and intermingle is in 'experience design', the crafting and eliciting of affective and social experiences in such spaces as museums and retail stores, private homes and public spaces, video games and websites. Indeed, 'experience design' may be a key form of immaterial labor. Brenda Laurel helped articulate the practice of experience design in her book *Computers as Theater* (1993), using Aristotle's *Poetics* to write her own poetics of human-computer interaction. I have long argued that contemporary forms of theatre and cultural performance might offer more appropriate models for experience design, something my new media students have experimented with.

Others, too, have explored alternative forms of performance, while at the same time moving from the intimacies of 'experience design' to the larger structural complexities of the 'experience economy'. Joseph Pine and James Gilmore are authors of a book published by the Harvard Business School called *The Experience Economy* (1999). Its subtitle: *Work Is Theater & Every Business a Stage*. If Laurel theorizes human-computer interactions as theatre, Pine and Gilmore theorize *all* economic activity in terms of theatre and, like Laurel, they focus on designing experiences. Though they concentrate on the experience of consumers, such as those drinking coffee in Starbucks or vacationing at Disney World, they also discuss designing the experiences of workers, managers and top executives.

Significantly, to explain how 'work is theater and every business a stage', Pine and Gilmore turn to Schechner's theory of 'enactments'. Schechner proposes a nested structure: at the core is *drama* or the underlying scenario; surrounding this is the *script*, the basic code of events that interprets the drama; surrounding both drama and script is *theatre*, the actual enactment of the script by the actors; finally, surrounding them all is *performance*, which for Schechner includes the whole constellation of events that pass between actors and audience. In Pine and Gilmore's theory of experience economy, the central drama becomes the core business strategy; the script becomes the production process; the theatre becomes the work that carries out these process; and, finally, the surrounding performance becomes what Pine and Gilmore call 'the offering', that is, 'the economic values [that] businesses create for customers' (109). Thus, in *The Experience Economy*, business performance is equated with theatrical performance, and customers with participatory audiences.

While one can critique business' appropriation of theatre and cultural performance through experience design, one can also 'design back', ex-appropriating or refunctioning corporate experience design in order to produce different effects. Let me give you an example.

One of the most famous TV ads ever sought to evoke a global feeling: I refer to a 1971 Coca-Cola ad, often referred to as 'I'd Like to Teach the World to Sing'. Produced by the advertising firm McCann-Erickson, it featured several hundred young people on a sunny Italian hilltop singing a jingle that ended: 'Coca-Cola – It's the real thing'. The song was a worldwide hit – minus the Coke reference – for a band called The New Seekers, and it reached #7 on the US charts and #1 in the UK.

Thirty-two years later, on a London hillside, I saw not the real thing, but a really surreal thing: a giant can of Mecca-Cola. In many ways, this can brings together a number of elements: experience design, performance, political philosophy and global feeling. The day I saw the big Mecca Cola was 15 February 2003, and I was surrounded not by hundreds of people, but by hundreds of thousands, indeed, over 1.7 million people, all of them protesting the impending war on Iraq. The protest event had numerous sponsors and planners, and its overall experience design was emergent, distributed and immanent to the event itself. Nonetheless, using Schechner's notion of enactments, we can read the experience design thus: at the core was the unfolding drama of the war protest, surrounded by the scripts or plans for the protest event; this script was embodied in the theatre of everyday life by the protestors themselves, while the performance passes not only from the stage to the audience, but from one site to many others.

For though it was located in Hyde Park, the protest was a networked, global event: not only did it concern an international crisis, not only were there speakers from different nations and cultures, but also we were connected via satellite television to millions upon millions of others at protests around the world, in Australia, Germany, Italy, South Korea, Spain, Turkey and the United States. As a number of these protests began appearing on the large projection screens in Hyde Park, there was a palpable feeling that a wave of sentiment was circling the globe and that we were experiencing it live, in mediation. The complex of feelings differed in different places: festive and laid-back in London, tense and violent in New York.

A truly global feeling would entail a post-human love, a sentiment of care and affection that is not restricted to family and friends, or to communities and nations, or even to the human species. I have in mind an ecology of love, one that extends to animals and plant-life, to flocks and herds and forests and plains. A love that even includes the inorganic, an amorous feeling that swells up to the height of mountains, that follows the bends of a river, that's carried on and on by an ocean breeze or the sound of falling rain. Perhaps such a sense beckons even from the stars, the black holes, the deep void of the cosmos. Thus beyond global feeling: a schizo, cosmocraving.

And yet, remaining earthly, perhaps the most challenging aspect of a global feeling of political love is, finally, initially, all too human. For Gandhi's *ahimsa* entailed a love for the British colonial officials he so opposed, while King's *agape* involved loving the Southern sheriffs who beat and arrested him and his fellow civil rights activists. Who, today, can imagine taking such feelings global – and thus learning to love Shell Oil or IMF officials, George W. Bush and Osama bin Laden? These are things perhaps even Lennon would have a hard time imagining – or perhaps not.

In the spirit of three dreamers – Lennon, Ghandi and King – who in a sense both died for their dreams and live on in ours, I will finish sketching a performative poetics of global feeling. As I suggest elsewhere, resistant performativity – which I sometimes call perfumance – involves 'scaling up' Butler's strategy of resignifying or queering normative discourses and practices. How does one queer a war machine, a terror network, a fascist regime?

Butler herself provides a clue, for she connects resignification to Brecht's tactic of refunctioning (*Bodies that Matter* 1993). But while Butler's resignification targets discrete words and gestures, Brecht's refunctioning targets social and technical apparatuses. Moreover, refunctioning works at a different level than signification or semantics, for it involves pragmatic transformation of concrete structures *and* processes, and here we are considering structures and processes of feeling. And yet while Brecht sought to refunction the apparatus of German theatre, the perfumance I have in mind must not limit itself to cultural institutions but instead seek to displace a much wider range of performance systems: corporate, technological, financial, educational, medical, governmental – indeed any sociotechnical system dominated by performance measures and incentives, by normative demands to perform – or else.

In a broader sense, I refer here to what Marcuse called the 'performance principle'. In 1973, almost twenty years after he first introduced this concept, Marcuse wrote:

> According to this principle, everyone has to earn his living in alienating but socially necessary performances, and one's reward, one's status in society will be determined by this performance (the work-income relation). The rejection of the Performance Principle also rejects the notion of progress which has up to now characterized the development of Western civilization, namely, progress as increasingly productive exploitation and mastery of nature, external and human, a progress which has turned out to be self-propelling destruction and domination (2001: 197).

I am the first to admit that the feelings such performance systems usually evoke in me are not love and affection; quite the opposite: they are the feelings of alienation and disaffection which Marcuse associates with the performance principle. And yet, such performance systems are nonetheless lined with desires, passions, and, yes, even love at times. Anyone who has worked in them – and that would certainly include students and professors, artists and curators, activists and advocates – has very likely felt such love from time to time, even if she or he has trouble articulating or even admitting it. I have also seen – and felt – it among workers on the assembly line and in the small retail store, as well as the large accounting and new media firms where I have worked during my life.

The challenge, then, is not only to elicit such emotions but also to sustain and interconnect them, and not only with those found in other institutions, but also in other, far-distant places, and not only in the margins of societies and cultures, but also in the more centralized nodes of high performance sociotechnical systems. Since love has traditionally been conceived in terms of immediacy, proximity and presence, one must imagine a global feeling of political love that is also mediated, distant and marked by absence. Referring back again to Auslander's notion of 'liveness', perhaps we need to give some thought to 'loveness'. But I will let Marcuse have the last word, for where did he locate the most promising resistance to the performance principle, that reality principle of postindustrial societies? Here, there, in *Eros*. All you need is Eros. Almost.

REFERENCES

Appadurai, Arjun (1996) *Modernity at Large: Cultural Dimensions of Globalization*, Minneapolis: University of Minnesota Press.

Auslander, Philip (1999) *Liveness: Performance in a Mediatized Culture*, London: Routledge.

The Beatles (1967) 'All You Need is Love / Baby You're a Rich Man', Parlophone.

Butler, Judith (1993) Bodies that Matter: On the Discursive Limits of "Sex." New York: Routledge.

Gandhi, M. K. (1993) 'On Ahimsa', in Rudrangshu Mukherjee (ed.) *The Penguin Gandhi Reader*, New York: Penguin Books, pp. 95-6.

Greenberg, Jon (1992) 'ACT-UP Explained', <http://www.actupny.org/documents/greenbergAU.html>

Hardt, Michael and Negri, Antonio (2004) *Multitude: War and Democracy in the Age of Empire*, New York: The Penguin Press.

Harvey, David (1989) *The Condition of Postmodernity: An Enquiry into the Origins of Cultural Change*. Oxford: Blackwell.

Hitchens, Christopher (2001) 'Why the suicide killers chose September 11', *The Guardian*, 3 October.

Jurgensmeyer, Mark (2000) *Terror in the Mind of God: The Global Rise of Religious Violence*, Berkeley: University of California Press.

King, Martin Luther (1992) 'Facing the Challenge of a New Age', in *I Have a Dream: Writings and Speeches that Changed the World*, San Francisco: HarperCollins, pp. 22-3.

Kramer, Larry (1997) *We Must Love One Another or Die: The Life and Legacies of Larry Kramer.* (ed. Lawrence D. Mass), New York: St. Martin's Press.

Laurel, Brenda (1993) *Computers as Theater.* Reading, MA: Addison-Wesley.

Marcuse, Herbert (2001) 'A Revolution in Values', in *Towards a Critical Theory of Society*, London: Routledge, p. 197.

McKenzie, Jon (2001) *Performance or Else*, London: Routledge.

McKenzie, Jon (2004) 'High Performance Schooling', *Parallax 31* (April-June): 50-62.

Pine, Joseph and Gilmore, James (1999) *The Experience Economy: Work is Theater & Every Business a Stage.* Cambridge, MA: Harvard Business School.

Robbins, Bruce (1999) *Feeling Global: Internationalism in Distress*, New York: New York University Press.

DAVID WILLIAMS   **FIELD STATION 3**

Writing (After) the Event:
Notes on Appearance, Passage and Hope

This week marks the twentieth anniversary of the horrors of the Union Carbide chemical disaster in Bhopal, the world's worst recorded industrial accident, in which an explosive release of toxic gases killed thousands of people. To date, no one has accepted responsibility for cleaning up the poisons (including mercury, lead and a wide range of carcinogens) that still leak from the abandoned site into the surrounding air and the groundwater, and people are still suffering and dying. Meanwhile countless other dangerous emissions are dispersed into land, sea and sky on a daily basis, the world heats up, and the misery plains of the world's refugee camps proliferate ... In a cultural context characterized in part by diminishing memory and institutionalized histories of oversight and forgetting, such infernos generate questions in me as to the functions, possibilities and limits of our privileged lives and work as performance-makers, writers, teachers. Although I conceive of each of these as practices of (modest) hope – with attendant responsibilities - misgivings and questions multiply and provoke turbulences and flows. Questions about how to negotiate the delicate struggle to 'work out some livable unison between panic and grace' (Blau 1982: 84). Questions about history and historiography, about memory, ethics, connectivity, responsibility and, perhaps above all, hope.

In a particular philosophical tradition, hope has been conceived as a negative condition, implying a negation or deferral of life. For Spinoza or Nietzsche, for example, hope suggested an absence of the pursuit of joy, an ethic of surrender to the logic of deferral in which pleasure and gratification are postponed: an acceptance of suffering now in the hope of enjoyment later, as in religious hope. For Nietzsche, such *ressentiment* – a reduction of joy to a practice of hope – was against life itself. So how might one think hope differently? 'In impossible times when one does not know how old one is or how young one is yet to be', as Nietzsche wrote in *Will to Power*, what would be a practice of hope on the side of life?

'Spaces of appearance'

One of the primary impulses in Western philosophy has been to look for a reality that is not subject to turbulences

and flows. In the face of the impermanence and flux of the phenomenal world of 'appearances' as perceived pejoratively, i.e. as illusory surface, many thinkers have pursued an essential(ist) 'Being' that transcends the instabilities and mortalities of cultural forms and mores, opinions, sensory impressions, subjective ideals. Amongst others, the Stoics, Plato, Descartes and logical positivists have conceived of 'appearance' and 'reality' as hierarchical opposites that draw their meaning from each other. For such philosophical dispositions, 'true Being' is the lack of (illusory) appearance.

Hannah Arendt was one of a number of twentieth-century philosophers who conceived of the diversity and confusion of appearances as primary reality, our common world, rather than as fugitive illusions. For her, such idealist cleftings were instances of 'frozen thought which thinking must unfreeze' (Arendt 1971: 431). She located meanings not as fixed concepts, but moving measures inviting active negotiation. If truth is not a pre-existent, primal ready-made, but a function of multiple perspectives on the reality of appearances, Arendt suggested, all truths invite critical examination and responses that allow for revision. Appearances appear to someone, they are relational. Their shifts and changes are responses directed to others, performative displays in turn inviting diverse responses: affirmation, say, or contestation, the will for things to be different. Each appearance thus contains the potentiality for beginning something new, for remaking relations and selves. In this way, Arendt located appearances as positive dialogic events in the unfolding of civic life rather than as failed reflections of some transcendent 'Being'. Although Arendt, like Brecht, recognized that the instruments and ideological structures of perception would change the appearance of what is seen to appear, here social existence is conceived as plural, inter-subjective and contextual. Its objects of 'inter-est' are constituted by relationships, by passages *between* (Arendt 1958: 182–3); and the play of appearance in this in-between affords the possibility of communicative and interrogative exchange, connection *and* distinction.

For Arendt, endeavouring in the wake of Nazism to articulate the conditions of a participatory politics within which commonality is dependent upon diversity, one of the primary conditions was the existence of spaces of free speech and interaction, 'spaces of appearance'. Such spaces, which Arendt extrapolated from her reflections on the Greek *polis*, are founded on an ideal of civic encounter, responsibility, ethical engagement and self-revelation with and in particular contexts:

> The space of appearance [is] the space where I appear to others as others appear to me, where men [sic] exist not merely like other living or inanimate things but make their appearance explicitly.
>
> (Arendt 1958: 198–9)

Can theatre still be one such 'space of appearance'? The director of the Paris-based Théâtre du Soleil, Ariane Mnouckine, has sometimes used this same phrase – *espace d'apparition* [1] – to describe her own ideal of a dynamically interactive socio-political agora for embodying and exploring thought-in-action. Yet, as Herbert Blau and Peggy Phelan *inter alia* have reiterated in their subtle articulations of the double-binds of representation, the play of appearances in performance (and of recursive reappearances and disappearances) is complex indeed. As a performance-maker and teacher, I have been haunted by Blau's question: how to effect 'the liberation of the performer as an *actor* who, laminated with appearance, struggles to *appear*' (Blau 1990: 257; emphasis in original)? The struggle is all,

> at the dubious end of ideology, at the possible end of history, when our lives are still dominated (incredibly) by the prospect of an actual disappearance. All theatre comes against the inevitability of disappearance from the struggle to appear. The only theatre worth seeing – that can be seen rather than stared through – is that which struggles to appear. The rest is all bad makeup. (Blau 1982: 298; emphasis in original)

What is the nature of the event – what happens – at those moments of a flaring into visibility *through* appearance, of an ephemeral visitation in the active vanishing of performance, like that of a ghost (*apparition*) erupting through the walls of appearance to take (its) place? At the intersection of visible appearance and invisible happening, dream and event, the 'doing' and the 'thing done' (Diamond 1996: 1), what then appears and to whom?

One of my primary interests as performance-maker and writer emerges from an interrogative pragmatism focused on the *happening in appearance*, above all in terms of what Blau has described as 'the fugitive relationship between the premonitory act and the actualization, the incipience and the immanence' (Blau 1990: 264). So, for example, one's experience of watching performers at

work in this in-between is never uniform in terms of its *density*. What then are the conditions within which the qualitative particularities or peculiarities of a performer – their micro-rhythms, dynamics, energies, desires, needs, not-knowings, modes of embodiment and so on – seem to be aligned, refracted or 'thickly' layered in such a way that that person, as multiplicity and singularity, *seems* to come into focus, i.e. they *appear to appear*? What are the conditions within which they seem to be uncovered, to (come to) matter, and to be enabled to take (a) place here now? How might one make space for something akin to Lyotard's theatre of energetics, in which what appears is 'the highest intensity ... of what there is' (Lyotard 1997: 288), as well as for the energetic perception of its volatility, its 'heat'? Similar questions about apparent eruptive emergence could be formulated and asked of an image, an object, a site, a memory, an instance of composition, a process of devising, an act of writing, as well as of (say) the education of a student, the training of a sports team or of a horse, the design of a garden, the unfolding of a relationship – all of them at least potentially 'spaces of appearance' for the becomings of identities in process. In each of these contexts, one's responsibility is to try to invent the conditions of invention, to navigate and discriminate according to what one might call a situational or localized ethics, or an 'eco-logic' (Guattari 1989: 136), [2] and to make (a) space that is generative, encouraging and hope-ful in the face of unpredictability:

> There are two ways to escape [the inferno]. The first is easy for many: accept the inferno and become such a part of it that you can no longer see it. The second is risky and demands constant vigilance and apprehension: seek and learn to recognise who and what, in the midst of the inferno, are not inferno, then make them endure, give them space.
>
> (Calvino 1972: 165)

Writing (after) the event

In this discourse of appearance and its flarings in performance, it is important to clarify that I am not proposing a return to a metaphysics of 'presence'. The *seeming* in *appearing to appear* is crucial if one is to avoid privileging any singular, original 'authenticity' here. I write in the shadow of the recurrent post-structuralist discourse of disappearance as foundational event in the ontology of performance, with which I am broadly sympathetic, for it can act as an enabling strategic proposition in articulating what remains in the wake of performance. Such critical dispositions deconstruct the hegemony of the ocularcentric in cultural histories, for example, or 'celebrate disappearance as a powerful source of compositional and hermeneutical information' (Gilpin 1996: 106). Furthermore, they can problematize persistent traditions of non-reflexive description as solipsistic representation of representation, and thereby find ways to write out (of) this conceptual cul-de-sac.

'We can never know what took place', suggests Heidi Gilpin, William Forsythe's former dramaturg, 'because the image etched in memory is transformed the moment we attempt to reexamine it' (106). Yes, agreed, at an absolutist level: but does that mean one cannot endeavour to account for what appeared or might (have) appear(ed), aware of its very appearing as effect or product of a way of seeing and knowing, and of the incremental fictionality generated in the remembering? It rather depends on how one conceives of what such writing *does*, and whether appearance's disappearance is failure of permanence, or active if ephemeral emergence. In writing (after) the event, memory *troubles* the past in the way that colour is 'troubled light' (Berger and Christie 1999: n.p.), a spectral refraction that allows partial and differential tonalities to appear. Transformation only constitutes loss, rather than, say, productive *poiesis* or *kinesis*, if one's project is recuperative, reproductive, restorative – i.e. the conservative *mimesis* of a historiography in thrall to Realism's truth claims - and 'why is it better to *last* than to *burn*?' (Barthes 1990: 23; emphasis in original). If the practice of memory is conceived as an 'art', as Michel de Certeau suggests (1988: 86–9), a *poiesis* defined by the active play of alteration (which only ceases when memory is in decay), a 'confusing and guileful mobility' (memory 'moves things about' [87]), and a metonymic singularity of details in relation to an absent 'whole', then:

> Far from being the reliquary or trash can of the past, [memory] sustains itself by believing in the existence of possibilities and by vigilantly awaiting them, constantly on the watch for their appearance (87).

According to Peggy Phelan, performance 'becomes itself through disappearance' (Phelan 1993: 146); and for Herbert Blau, 'in theatre, as in love, the subject is disappearance' (Blau 1982: 94). However disappearance is the function of appearance, it subtends appearance in the way that forgetting creates the ground for remembering's possibility: an imbricated loop of concentration and evaporation, emergence and dissolution, form and *informe*. Appearances, like love, can be transformative becomings. Although perhaps their burning may not last, they leave traces in their 'wake' (a-wakening, passage and mourning) in our memories, desires, bodies, imaginations.[3] These traces

will never be registered empirically, empiricism being the resilient, revenant myth of a liberal humanist desire for unmediated originary 'truth', a quantity surveying approach to reality that denies the disturbance effected by observance, and the contingent assumptions and partialities of modes of seeing and their blind spots. Instead they will be new texts, translations, partial re-enactments and re-fashionings, at best the fictional, dynamic products of memories, desires, bodies, imaginings having taken place or to come: what the poet Paul Celan referred to as 'Singbarer Rest' (Celan 1995: 100), the 'singable remains'. The return to the event in representation cannot effect recovery of what is lost, but it is in this very irrecuperability that there lies the possibility of an ongoing, unfinishable historiographic project, an enabling 'decomposition' (Wood 2000: 202),[4] a critically reflexive thinking and working through of memory and history, embodiment and inscription, as process:

> If historicism narrates the continuity of the winners, secured in a homogeneous understanding of time and knowledge, a *critical, open and vulnerable history* might, on the contrary, be conceived as a narration, an account, suspended between inclusion and exclusion, between representation and repression, *in which the final word never arrives*. (Chambers 2001: 11; emphasis added).

In order to give a future to the virtual space of the future (*l'avenir*), we need a philosophy and practice of inter-located *passage* rather than of fixed ground or territory, in the present unfolding of a democracy that is, as Jacques Derrida, Chantal Mouffe and others have suggested, always provisional, insufficient, in process, always 'to come' (*l'à-venir*). It is apparent that location and identity, for example, are produced as much through narration as through what already exists: they are more to do with doing than knowing. A(n un)certain kind of critical writing provides opportunities to rehearse and play-fully refashion those heterogeneous personal mappings that we are continuously making up and over, and out of which we constitute our-'selves': a kind of fluid performative 'auto-topography' that creates senses of self and of space and place, rather than the 'self' or the 'world' occurring preformed, as if they were pre-existent entities rubbing up against each other. If space, time, self are conceived as 'a multiple foldable diversity' (Serres and Latour 1995: 59), a field of flows and intensities – *spacing, timing, selfing* – then perhaps a dynamically spatialized (and fictionalized) self-in-process and in-relation can fray just a little the dualist territorial imaginaries of inside and outside, of self-identity in opposition to radical alterity. If the continuity of identity is secured through movement and the capacity to change rather than the ability to cling to what is already established, as Zygmunt Bauman suggests (1999: xiv), then one's responsibility is to abandon the logics of mastery and let untimely elements of outside in-here. Here identity becomes 'a point of departure for a voyage without guarantees, and not a port of arrival' (Chambers 2001: 25); and one is invited to consider 'home' no longer as a 'fixed structure', but as 'a contingent passage, a way that literally carries [one] elsewhere' (26).

For my own part, in recent years I have drawn on elements of contemporary philosophy and cultural theory in an attempt to explore the mutable parameters of identity, location and performance. This writing has proposed tentative mappings of certain unpredictable, energetic events 'in proximity of performance', to borrow Matthew Goulish's phrase: the shifting point of contact in contact improvisation, and the activated ethics of a relational axis in-between; fire energetics and their implications for writing about the active vanishings of performance; place as contested and heterotopic, and the possibilities of an aberrant 'animal geography'; 'skywritings', a proliferative critical historiography of ways in which skies have been conceived, contested, and practised in contemporary art and socio-politics, and their implications for a performance epistemology; and, in particular, alterity as productive event in human/animal interactions, affording an enquiry into the constitutive horizons of the 'human' in terms of its animal others. In these texts, I have endeavoured to explore more performative modes of writing critical histories, particularly in relation to what resists historiographic inscription – the qualitative, the fugitive, the unpredictable, the overlooked – and in this way minimally 'to redirect the geometry of attention', to borrow a phrase from Joan Retallack.[5] Such redirection goes hand in hand with a conviction that one can never recuperate a disappeared world, one can simply try to write (into) a new one, and try to find resonant forms for the singable remains. The act of writing therefore seeks to 'do' or perform something of the moment(um) or affect of movement in absent bodies, or at least to rehearse aspects of the ambiguities, pluralities, displacements and ephemeralities of live performance through the conjunction of diverse modes of writing and voices.[6] I conceive of such writing as a material discursive practice, in which the page is a public space for enactments or instantiations of critical performance, rather than a matter of formal or modish 'style', or writing to be consigned to the 'merely' creative: to quote Retallack once again, 'a space to be playful in a purposeful way'.

As a tentative articulation of malleable relationships in process and of a topology of passages of connectivity, such writing might be read as the preparation of conditions for critically resistant thought and of 'a place to welcome ... the face of the absent' (Berger 2001: 32): a space of appearance characterized by an uncertain but resilient hope.

The evolving trajectory of this work reflects a gradual displacement from the relatively 'solid ground' of theatre studies and theatre history towards more fluid and tentative articulations of the shifting 'lie of the land' in an expanded field of contemporary performance and its intersections with philosophy, politics and historiography. This trajectory marks an unravelling of conviction as to theatre as the singular site of concern, and at the same time a growing fascination with present process, conditions, practices, perceptions 'in the middle', and ways of thinking through performance as inter-subjective and ephemeral event. Perhaps these materials also suggest a certain scepticism about particular claims to knowledge and its 'finishability', and, to borrow Jean-François Lyotard's terms, a desire to become a 'philosopher' rather than an 'expert' (Lyotard 1984: xxv): to know how not to know with interrogative momentum, to travel critically between different modalities of knowing and not-knowing in a relational field, a place of unstable ground, a landscape of the passage:

> Ordinary human beings do not like mystery since you cannot put a bridle on it, and therefore, in general they exclude it, they repress it, they eliminate it – and it's *settled*. But if on the contrary one remains open and susceptible to all the phenomena of overflowing, beginning with natural phenomena, one discovers the immense landscape of the *trans-*, of the passage. Which does not mean that everything will be adrift, our thinking, our choices, etc. But it means that the factor of instability, the factor of uncertainty, or what Derrida calls the *undecidable*, is indissociable from human life. This ought to oblige us to have an attitude that is at once rigorous and tolerant and doubly so on each side: all the more rigorous than open, all the more demanding since it must lead to openness, leave passage: all the more mobile and rapid as the ground will always give way, always. A thought which leads to what is the element of writing: the necessity of only being the citizen of an extremely inappropriable unmasterable country or ground (Hélène Cixous in Cixous and Calle-Gruber 1997: 51-2; emphasis in original).

NOTES

1 *Apparition*: appearance of a person; manifestation of a sign; outbreak of a symptom; also vision, apparition, spectre. (From *Collins Robert French-English Dictionary*, New York: HarperCollins, 1998). In Patrice Pavis's *Dictionary of the Theatre*, the entry for 'APPARITION' reads: 'Fr.: *apparition*; Ger.: *Erscheinung*; Sp.: *aparición*. See GHOST' (Pavis 1998: 28). Mysteriously, and fittingly, there is no entry for GHOST; it has disappeared.

2 'The logic of intensities – or eco-logic – concerns itself solely with the movement and intensity of evolutive processes ... Praxic openness constitutes the essence of the art of the "eco"' (Guattari 1989: 136, 140).

3 See Schneider (2001) for a remarkable discussion of performance as interrogation of archival thinking, in which performance is figured as both 'the act of remaining and a means of appearance' (103).

4 '[A]n act of decomposition: one that breaks up or disintegrates things already composite – things that have adhered or become coherent.... Decomposition can thereby effect and perform further acts and ceremonies of composition and allow other possibilities or expansions of understanding and reciprocation to take place' (Wood 2000: 202).

5 Retallack used this phrase during an inter-disciplinary writing round-table, 'Partly Writing', at Dartington College of Arts (19-20 January 2002), in the context of a discussion of D.W. Winnicott's notion of 'in-between' spaces as spaces of cultural intervention.

6 For a productive account of performative writing, see Pollock 1998. Pollock proposes six porous frames for 'performing writing': it is 'evocative', 'metonymic', 'subjective', 'nervous', 'citational' and 'consequential'. 'Performative writing ... is for relatives, not identities; it is for space and time; it is for a truly good laugh, for the boundary, banal pleasures that twine bodies in action; it is for writing, for writing ourselves out of our-selves, for writing our-selves into what (never) was and may (never) be. It is/is it for love?' (98).

REFERENCES

Arendt, Hannah (1958) *The Human Condition*, Chicago: University of Chicago Press.

Arendt, Hannah (1971) 'Thinking and moral considerations', *Social Research*, 38.3, Autumn, 417-46.

Barthes, Roland (1990) *A Lover's Discourse: Fragments*, trans. Richard Howard, London: Penguin.

Bauman, Zygmunt (1999) *Culture as Praxis*, London: Sage.

Berger, John (2001) *The Shape of a Pocket*, London: Bloomsbury.

Berger, John and Christie, John (1999) *I Send You This Cadmium Red*, Barcelona: ACTAR.

Blau, Herbert (1982) *Take up the Bodies: Theatre at the Vanishing Point*, Urbana,Illinois: University of Illinois Press.

Blau, Herbert (1990) 'Universals of performance: or amortising play', in Richard Schechner and Willa Appel (eds.) *By Means of Performance: Intercultural Studies of Theatre and Ritual*, Cambridge: Cambridge University Press, pp. 250-72.

Calvino, Italo (1972) *Invisible Cities*, trans. Warren Weaver, New York: HarcourtBrace Jovanovich.

Celan, Paul (1995) *Breathturn*, trans. Pierre Joris, Los Angeles: Sun and Moon Press.

Certeau, Michel de (1988) *The Practice of Everyday Life*, trans. Steven Rendall, Berkeley: University of California Press.

Chambers, Iain (2001) 'A Question of History', in *Culture after Humanism: History, Culture, Subjectivity*, London and New York: Routledge, pp. 7-46.

Cixous, Hélène with Calle-Gruber, Mireille (1997) *Rootprints: Memory and Life Writing*, trans. Eric Prenowitz, London: Routledge.

Diamond, Elin (1996) 'Introduction', in Elin Diamond (ed.) *Performance and Cultural Politics*, London: Routledge, pp. 1-12.

Gilpin, Heidi (1996) 'Lifelessness in movement, or how do the dead move? Tracing displacement and disappearance for movement performance', in Susan Leigh Foster (ed.) *Corporealities: Dancing Knowledge, Culture and Power*, London: Routledge, pp. 106-28.

Guattari, Félix (1989) 'The three ecologies', trans. Chris Turner, *New Formations* 8, Summer, 131-47.

Lyotard, Jean-François (1997) 'The Tooth, The Palm', trans. Anne Knab and Michel Benamou, in Timothy Murray (ed.) *Mimesis, Masochism and Mime: ThePolitics of Theatricality in Contemporary French Thought*, Ann Arbor: University of Michigan Press, pp. 282-8.

Lyotard, Jean-François (1984) *The Postmodern Condition: A Report on Knowledge*, trans. Geoffrey Bennington and Brian Massumi, Manchester: Manchester University Press.

Pavis, Patrice (1998) *Dictionary of the Theatre: Terms, Concepts, and Analysis* trans. Christine Schantz, Toronto: University of Toronto Press.

Phelan, Peggy (1993) *Unmarked: The Politics of Performance*, London and New York: Routledge.

Pollock, Della (1998) 'Performing writing', in Peggy Phelan and Jill Lane (eds.) *The Ends of Performance*, New York: New York University Press, pp. 73-103.

Schneider, Rebecca (2001) 'Performance remains', *Performance Research* ('On Maps and Mapping') 6.2, Summer, 100-108.

Serres, Michel and Latour, Bruno (1995) *Conversations on Science, Culture and Time*, trans. Roxanne Lapidus, Ann Arbor: University of Michigan Press.

Wood, Elizabeth (2000) 'Decomposition', in Sue-Ellen Case, Philip Brett and Susan Leigh-Foster (eds.) *Decomposition: Post-Disciplinary Performance*, Bloomington: Indiana University Press, pp. 200-13.

The Scribes of Merlin (An obscure lecture)

1. fire
2. breaking the glass part one: LS 2
3. the doubting baron's threefold death
4. Secret Archive
5.1 swing away part one
X. Bonus track: *Signs* (remix)
5.2 swing away part two
6. parapraxia
7. twenty-three
    [Amnesia digression]
8. breaking the glass part two: demons
9. faith

1

In *The Great Fire of London*, Jacques Roubaud asks a question.

Merlin predicts the future 'in obscure words' whose meaning is only understood once the events they've announced have 'come about.'

Roubaud wonders why Merlin 'surrenders to speech' that only the future can apprehend at a moment when, once the prediction has been fulfilled, it no longer holds the slightest importance.

He proposes a moral answer: Merlin's knowledge of the future can remain innocent only if he doesn't play with it in order to act upon the world.

If his future actions are inconsistent with how he saw he was supposed to act, he will lose both honor, and, far worse, certainty.

I accept the question (Why speak in obscure words?), but have other answers.

Merlin's 'power to know the future' was a secondary gift, bestowed by God in response to his primary gift – 'to know all things said and done in the past' – which Merlin received from his father, a demon.

Jacques Roubaud wrote *The Great Fire of London* to mourn his wife's death: 'I've devoted myself to the enterprise of destroying my memory ... I set fire to it, and with its debris I charcoal-scrawl the paper.'

Merlin, I believe, spoke obscurely for two reasons: 1) as in the case of his creation of King Arthur, 'to act upon the world'; 2) as in the case of his prediction of the doubting baron's threefold death, to procure the faith of the witness.

2

Douglas wrote me in an email dated 9/30/04: *I want to give you a copy of LJS senior thesis show from college, I think you would recognize the early stages of certain themes you are mining.*

The next time I saw him, he held a red plastic binder containing his working script from Lawrence's 1983 Antioch College production *The Mimi Gabor Variety Show*, in which Douglas acted.

He flipped to the last page of the last scene, and read aloud.

Larry: 'Look, metaphor is where it's at, isn't it?'
(Smashes wine glass with hammer).

'It's just like the wine glass in the last scene of *The Swans*,' said Douglas, insisting that two performances, with fifteen years intervening, ended with the same glass.

'One more thing,' said Douglas, handing me the red binder like evidence, 'Larry's first lover died of a brain tumor - Larry wrote *The Mimi Gabor Show* to mourn his death.'

A baron insisted that 'all of (Merlin's) knowledge comes from the Devil,' so King Pendragon granted him leave to test Merlin's powers - story number one.

The baron asked Merlin to tell him how he would die, and with the King's permission, Merlin replied, 'Know then, sir, that you'll die by falling from your horse and breaking your neck - that's how you'll leave this world.'

3

The King brought Merlin to the chamber of an invalid (the disguised baron) who struggled to speak, '... sir, how shall I die?' and Merlin replied, 'The day you die, you'll be found hanging.'

When they visited an ailing monk in an abbey, Merlin took the King aside: 'Do you think I don't know how this fool who's testing me is going to die?

If he doesn't die so, don't believe anything else I say.'

He said to King Pendragon in the monk's presence, 'He will die in the two ways I've already described, but now I'll tell him the third, more surprising than either; for know this: on the day he dies, he'll break his neck, and hang, and drown - and those who live will see him die this threefold death.'

The baron believed this impossible prediction proved Merlin a fraud, but soon, riding with a company of men, he came to a wooden bridge spanning a river - suddenly his palfrey stumbled; thrown forward, he fell on his neck; his body tumbled, his gown snagged on a jagged bridge support, and legs in the air and head in the river, he died: hanged, drowned and neck broken.

Then Merlin came to King Pendragon and told him very openly that he loved him dearly and was eager to see him thrive.

The King, amazed to hear Merlin speak so humbly, asked him to keep nothing secret that concerned him.

'I will tell you nothing that I should not,' said Merlin, and the King said, 'I am at your command.'

At the end of *The Swans*, Lawrence holds the glass while wearing the coat of King Ludwig II of Bavaria.

4

King Ludwig's Secret Diary, discovered posthumously, was stored in a Secret Archive until its destruction - only passages quoted in a 1955 biography survive.

Historians note the 'mental deterioration' and 'acute sense of carnal guilt' with which the diary links unexplained sexual episodes, referred to as 'falls', to numerological calendar calculations.

'Soon I will be a spirit; heavenly airs are around me ... I repeat it, and as truly as I am the King, I will keep it, not again until the 21st of September.

Remember the 9th of May 3 times 3! - Feb. - April - June - Septemb. Fragrance of the lilies! The King's delight ... This oath has its binding power, as well as its potency by

De Par le Roy

LR

DP LR

Before number XII of the year of my reign was completed, and therefore the miserable fatal number 13 was still in the ascendant, the "last" fall occurred! - Shortly before I became 33 years of age.'

33's digits, multiplied, give 9, 'the number of steps of the *throne* power of self-command achieved when I have reached this number...'

The other performers exit, Lawrence, glass in hand, watches the backdrop screen, where on video the performers walk the hall to the dressing room, joined by Lawrence.

Lawrence, on stage, seeing an image of himself leave the stage, says: *That's me.*

Graham Hess (Mel Gibson), a former priest, has suffered a crisis of faith - story number two.

5.1

Worldwide agriglyphs guide hostile aliens whose wrists emit poison gas; however, abruptly after invading, they inexplicably depart.

One alien, earlier wounded by Graham, remains, invading Graham's home.

Graham and family display 'tics,' behavioral weaknesses: daughter Bo leaves glasses of water everywhere; son Morgan suffers overstimulation asthma attacks; brother Merrill, failed baseball star, keeps his bat mounted on the wall; Graham considers his wife's vaguely intelligible dying words proof of God's callousness.

With Alien clutching Morgan, and the family paralyzed in its orbit, Graham sees Merrill near his trophy bat, perceives the living room as a trap awaiting a trigger, and intones Colleen's last words, baseball lingo for *hit as good as a miss*.

bonus track

Monster in my room - can I have a glass of water? Water by your bed. Dust. Hair. Contaminated. Five minor league home run records. Strike-out record. Lumberjack chopping down a tree. It felt wrong not to. Bo has this thing about drinking water. Her whole life. A tic people have, except it's not a tic. 'See,' her eyes glazed, 'Swing away.' Nerve endings her brain firing as she died, and some random memory of your baseball. There is no one watching out for us, Merrill. We are all on our own. Ray fell asleep. She's not in an ambulance, father. Swerved off the road, and hit Collen, and then a tree. The truck has severed most of her lower half. She won't be saved. Her body is pinned in such a way that it's alive when it shouldn't be alive, and the truck is holding her together. Talking almost like normal. We wanted you to come down here as long as she's awake.

Does it hurt?

I don't feel much.

Good.

Tell Morgan to play games. It's ok to be silly.

I will.

Tell Bo to listen to her brother who'll always take care of her.

I will.

And tell Graham -

I'm here.

Tell him to see.

...

And tell Merrill to swing away.

Are you the kind that sees signs? Or do you believe that people just get lucky? Is it possible there are no coincidences? Swing away, Merrill. Merrill, swing away.

5.2

Merrill takes down his bat; Alien, perceiving hostility, gasses Morgan; Merrill swings, hits Alien who drops Morgan; Alien falls, toppling a glass, the water of which burns him.

Graham and Bo see her proliferation of glasses, and realize water induced the aliens' retreat.

Graham carries Morgan outside, Bo following, as Merrill hits Alien into a glass, or misses Alien and smashes a glass spraying water, until, drenched, Alien dies; Graham injects Morgan's medicine, understanding that his asthma-constricted lungs prevented inhalation of Alien's gas.

Morgan revives, Merrill joins, and Graham experiences catastrophic revelations: Colleen's death started a Morgan-saving clock ticking, the confluence of bat + water + asthma; the astrolabe of faith decoded Colleen's last words, obscure speech, revealed as retroactively prophetic, predicting the four weaknesses as rehearsals, transformed into strengths by this reversal apotheosis.

Graham's faith returns.

6

Parapraxia: the faulty performance of an intended act; in psychoanalysis, a minor error revealing a subconscious motive – practice beside practice.

Paranoia: the belief that parapraxia enfolds past and future – knowledge beside knowledge, Merlin's gifts.

The decentered subject's role (to see) resorbs into a universal mechanism: Graham's faith returns him to his family as one of the *Elucidarium's* four elements: earth (Merrill), air (Morgan), water (Bo), fire (Graham).

Yet the re-centered subject's ability, to read the world's hidden pattern, fuels the mechanism – the powerless/ omnipotent subject becomes a figure the great significance of which nobody understands.

Creativity, mathematics, religion, or delirium reconciles the paradox – story number three.

He considered his twenty lost years schizophrenia only retroactively: at the onset he did not descend into disease; he ascended into enlightenment.

Before announcing his solution (erroneous) to Riemann's Hypothesis for the pattern of prime number occurrence – a number-theory problem the intractability of which, some believe, contributed to his breakdown – he told a friend that, as validation of his proof, Life Magazine featured him on the cover; when the friend said that's Pope John XXIII, he replied it was himself in disguise, since his name was John, and twenty-three his favorite prime number.

Analogy, signifying deep identity, animates meta-morphosis: thinking becomes hallucinated, reflects upon its hallucinations, and frees itself to 'fall' again, like King Ludwig, into a delirium that extends to its reflection: immortality at the price of identity.

The dream contains the waking.

7

'Anxious,' he asked his former French professor for Jean Cocteau's address, and was 'very disappointed' to learn Cocteau had died.

Uncovering Cocteau's secret identity (twenty-third Grand Master of the Priory of Sion), he may have believed (John (Jean) twenty-three...) that Cocteau, like the Pope, was himself disguised.

Cocteau's art encrypted Priory beliefs, employing the structural Fibonacci series, the birth of number theory, evoked by Leonardo da Vinci, 9th Grand Master.

Secrets included *twin Christ* – a crucified double allowed Jesus to escape and start a family with Mary Magdelene in southern France, from whom the order of the Priory descend, worshipping Christ, and Mary, disguised in the image of the Grail, equally.

He called himself as 'the left foot of God on earth.'

On his way to the Nobel ceremony, after recovering and receiving the prize for his economic theory of competitive game equilibrium, he indicated to friends a Stockholm bank to which he had once wired money to defend against alien invasion.

Gödel proposed that points inside a multi-dimensional set compactify in relation to an excluded point, i.e. an outside; similarly, Alien coheres Graham's family and belief system – only by Alien's exclusion can Graham's closed set exist, and it consolidates through a mathematical/ritualistic mechanism for Alien's destruction, its endpoint signaled by a breaking glass.

In a well-known Jewish wedding tradition, the groom breaks a glass at the ceremony's conclusion; modern explanations include relationship fragility, ushering celebration, or recalling the temple's destruction.

Archaic beliefs hold that breaking a glass frightens demons.

Amnesia digression

In 1690 philosopher John Locke proposed the following. A child grows and becomes a lieutenant. The lieutenant remembers when he was a child. The lieutenant becomes a general. The general remembers when he was a lieutenant, but not when he was a child. Personhood requires continuity of memory; therefore – as A remembers B, and B remembers C, but A has forgotten C – the general and lieutenant are the same person, and the lieutenant and child are the same person, but the general and child are different people. One person over the course of a life is therefore both one and two. Edward Stillingfleet, Bishop of Worcester, found Locke's position unacceptable, attacking it as 'inconsistent with the resurrection of the body and hence with the Christian faith.'

8

Merlin's words reach us via dictation to handpicked scribes, starting with Northumberland monastic Blaise.

The thirteenth-century Viennese *Prophecies of Merlin* records plans for a house in the Caledonian forest to observe the heavens, plans in which Merlin conceives the number of scribes according to the same logic as doors and windows.

> You will offer six hundred sacrifices and as many windows to the one whom I may see through those windows – fire-spitting Phoebus Apollo with Venus, And I may examine the constellations sliding through the sky by night, Which will teach me about the people of the kingdom in times to come, And let as many esteemed men, having been taught to

Lawrence Steger backstage at the Museum of Contemporary Art, Chicago, 'The Swans'

write down those things I may say, Be present, and let them learn how to entrust a poem to writing tablets.However, scholar Lucy Allen Paton's 1926 commentary concludes: The mechanism examined in this chapter belongs to a consistent whole, so united in its parts that it is manifestly the work of one hand; therefore, the scribes are fictitious authorities for whom we have no prototypes, standing in for imaginary descendents of Maistre Blaise.

'Everything that's happened – and is still to happen – has significance,' said Merlin.

He calculated meaning in the frequency of dogs and red-necktied men passing; imagined himself a go board with corners at Los Angeles, Boston, Seattle, and Bluefield, West Virginia.

God wrote the book of Creation to reveal his existence: beings along the pilgrimage road of the world are signs, at first puzzling, but if examined carefully, faith, with the aid of reason, deciphers, under differing characters, a single word.

Hydrophobe Alien or demon burned by holy water; Merlin's demon gift to see the past or John Nash's space alien messages in algebra?

He travels great distances with no loss of energy; produces art without intention.

9

Obscure speech is a tool in the pedagogy of faith.

As the expression of perfect form, a medieval edifice surrounds it, manifesting a universal mechanism, collapsing time, supplanting 'world' and 'nature' with 'book.'

My life closed, I proclaim: this was beauty, that was fear, these the gestures of which I made myself; from outside, I see the pattern of my journeys, inscribed as a sign on the earth's surface, recording and guiding my peregrination; the tics and loops that suffused my work like the sourceless light of dreams, concealed Merlin's prophecy; I: their scribe.

Lawrence Steger did not see Mel Gibson mourn his wife in *Signs*, nor America mourn other deaths with statements like: the New Jersey commuter's chronic tardiness saved his life that Tuesday morning.

Had he lived long enough, Lawrence might have pinpointed the haunting feeling that Merlin's threefold prediction caused the doubting baron's threefold death – one death to repay each test – and trapped us in a reversal: proof a product of the imagination; reason a circle-shaped prison.

The end of *The Swans* – Lawrence, glass, King Ludwig's coat, demons departing - he watches himself leave, and he says: *That's me.*

But it's not me.

His body is pinned in such a way that it's alive when it shouldn't be alive, and the performance is holding him together.

Live-Lawrence exits, video-Lawrence waves the camera away and smiles, the camera switches off, and the monitor glitches and goes to black.

ACKNOWLEDGEMENTS

Thanks to Douglas Grew; Bryan Wildenthal Memorial Library, Sul Ross State University, Alpine, Texas; The School of the Art Institute of Chicago; The Lannan Foundation.
Photo: Lawrence Steger backstage at the Museum of Contemporary Art, Chicago, *The Swans*. Latin translation by Matthew Hunter Griffin. Photo: unknown.

SOURCE NOTES

This essay grew out of a larger writing project: a response to the work of theatre/performance artist Lawrence Steger (1961–1999). Texts, images and ideas derive from the two specific performances noted below, while themes present in his body of work, overlaid with the grid of Field Station 3, inspired the essay's concept and shape.

Arimethea, Merlin, Perceval', in *Arthurian Studies* XLVIII, trans. Nigel Bryant, D. S. Brewer, Cambridge: Cambridge University Press.

Genet, Jean (1963) *Our Lady of the Flowers*, introduction by Jean-Paul Sartre, trans. Bernard Frechtman, New York: Grove Press.

McIntosh, Christopher (2003) *The Swan King: Ludwig II of Bavaria*, London: Tauris Parke.

Nasar, Sylvia (1998) *A Beautiful Mind*, New York: Simon & Schuster.

Paton, Lucy Allen, ed. (1926) Les Prophecies de Merlin, from ms. 593, Bibliothèque Municipale de Rennes, in *Modern Language Association of America Studies in Content, Part Two*, New York: D. C. Heath and Company; Oxford: Oxford University Press.

Pesic, Peter (2002) *Seeing Double*, Cambridge (Massachusetts) and London: MIT Press.

Roubaud, Jacques (1992) *The Great Fire of London*, trans. Dominic Di Bernardi, Chicago: Dalkey Archive Press.

Shyamalan, M. Night (2002) *Signs*.

Steger, Lawrence (1983) 'The Mimi Gabor Variety Show', unpublished manuscript in possession of the author.

Steger, Lawrence (1998) 'The Swans (remix)', unpublished manuscript in possession of the author.

Twyman, Tracy (2002) 'Jean Cocteau: Man of the Century and 23rd Grand Master of the Priory of Sion', in *Dagobert's Revenge* 4:2.

de Boron, Robert, attrib. (2001) 'Merlin and the Grail: Joseph of

REBECCA SCHNEIDER   FIELD STATION 3

What I Can't Recall

Ihr naht euch wieder, schwankende Gestalten,
Die früh sich einst dem trüben Blick gezeigt.
Versuch ich wohl, euch diesmal feszuhalten?[1]

I had decided to write about a performance that I could not recall. And I decided that any performance would do. Not being able to recall the performance, however, I had no performance in mind. So I sat down and said: Show yourself! I did! I sat right here in my study, in my robe, by my fire,[2] and I said: Be Revealed! I should not have been surprised when the first performance to come to mind as forgotten was *Faust*. Now – which *Faust*, you ask? Ahh. That took a moment to reappear.

Strasse. Faust. Margarete vorubergehend[3]

I had only to recall Margaret – which was relatively easy to do. If the seamstress had been there, then I knew it was Goethe's *Faust*, or an Auteur's version of Goethe's version of Marlowe's version of the chapbook on the well-known tale of the Late Medieval Student and Professor of Magic himself. How powerful I felt. Indeed, I had apprehended Performance in my Study!

Mephistopheles: So seh ich wahrlich ein Theater.
Was gibt's denn da?[4]

Now, truth be told, when this particular performance showed up at my hearth, I was not pleased. It had taken place long ago, but it seemed too easy. I knew the Director and so with a simple phone call or email or a search in the archive I could have retrieved information to spark my memory and buoy my flailing recall back to solid surface. But I was interested in the *wavering* of the forms, their aspect of 'almost gone but not quite' (I can't be completely sure, for example, that it was Margaret in my memory – but it surely wasn't Helen of Troy). I was interested in the completely chalky, overwritten aspect of slate so often used that it can no longer be erased, but neither can it comfortably record – like some sticky Mystic Writing Pad left out too long in the hot Amnesia of the Modern Day sun. I was, that is, interested in my own powers (or lack thereof) of conjure.

Nevertheless, the moment *Faust* showed up, I wanted to leave this particular performance and chose another. To be sure, there are many more performances I remember even less well! The moment – *the very second* – that this production appeared to memory as a name – *Faust* – so did events of an entire day and, swirling round that, the eventuality of an entire *time*. And fast as cold air to

warm lung, details of my own life crowded in sharply and clearly, in direct proportion to the dim and wavering specifics of the production itself.

Mit segenduftenden Schwingen
Vom Himmel durch die Erde dringen
Harmonisch all das all durchklingen[5]

I tried to ignore the flap flapping of personal narrative, the scrappy tunes of this and that, of here and there, and trained my thoughts on the performance – but I could recall very little beyond a memory of Margaret, the theatre space itself, a long pine table in the playing area, one other vaguely raucous scene (lots of bodies running and shouting and hurling food) and – that is all. Nothing more. Not a very helpful scrapbook in the least.

I did, however, remember my own body in the seat. Quite exactly. And I recalled quite clearly my 'point of view' and even the walls of the theatre space (a large rectangular room), the lights up in the house and the din of the audience before the show. The force and clarity of this aspect struck me as odd. So I tried another magic trick: a quick tour through as many performances as I could revisit, at the speed of light, around the world. Many marvels were revealed to me, and in almost all of them I remember most clearly the same things: my body in the seat, *where* I was sitting, the theatre around me, my point of view and the hum of the audience (or the lack of hum if sparsely attended) just before the show. Is this peculiar to me?

My question became: What does it mean to recall the periphery? How is the edge of the Magic Gulf of any interest without the scene on stage? What does it do to remember the rim? If I recall to the side, am I forgetting? *Was gibt's denn da?*

Let me return to *Faust* and do my best. The performance I was trying to recall seemed umbilically linked to, or was somehow swaddled in, the 'eventness' of the entire day on which it took place. Then again, one day would hardly contain it. The *tale*, which the performance we were headed to see on that day would reenact, was old (as these things are measured). Marlowe rendered it just shy of a cycle play, a hair from morality – a play that would catch us wavering somewhere between *Everyman* and 'the play's the thing' – turning – just over the limen of Middle Age into rampant youth (as these things are measured). And Goethe's *Faust* seems to gesture from deeper within the flames of youth, as if grasping Magic and Myth and Morality from afar. For Goethe the Subject is equipped with Guilt, the Devil no match for Romantic Love, the Passion Played interior. Just as the Choir of Spirits recommends: It's 'built again within' (1620). My point is that the play we would see *later* on the day I am about to describe had come quite *early*, and taken many travels outside and in, while the paltry details I will gather here seem certainly to lag behind, 'post-', one could say if one had faith in a prefix, or *dust*, scampering across this hearth, distracting me from the ash and embers and flame.

> *Forgetting forward and behind, the Angel is turning*
> *to the side.*

The performance I speak of, which I do not recall, took place at least ten years ago. It was, in fact, twelve or thirteen years from this writing. It is hard to say how long it will have been from your reading – though I suspect, it will still have been somewhere between twelve and thirteen – a very dangerous time. In America (and that is where we were at the time), clocks never make it through that passage. Neither do most timepieces in Germany (where we may have begun), though the people continue to speak of it: somewhere between 12 and 13. But we did not speak of it then. One tends to remark a passage only after or before, forward or behind, once across the many thresholds of its passing.

> *Amnesia is a house with many mansions, with niches*
> *for all sorts of tableaux of winking stone in partial*
> *light. Amnesia only returns when you remember it.*

The day before, I had traveled to the city where this performance was to take place. Or, I had traveled to this city where the performance was to take place the day after. I recall that I was with someone – not you – but someone whom, like the performance, I have also almost forgotten. I recall that we awoke in the apartment of my ex-husband

> (so you see where all of this is going, or has gone,
> the tumble and detritus caught up in the event,
> the clutter and toss of life's drips and bits, the
> 'oceanic rumble'[6] now like static on your pristine
> screen)

in the apartment of my ex-husband, we awoke. For some reason I remember the clutter of that tiny place far better than the faces of the actors we were to encounter twelve or thirteen hours later in the theatre. Was that because I had lived for years with that flat's affects – that gnarled afghan, that soddy towel, that piqued pot, that particular odor – and here they all were again, on a slightly different set, across town, playing out a similar script in which the only thing missing was...

Beside the point. Now the difficulty is remembering the order of things.

I do recall that: We went out for the day, Walking in the City.

I had only one task, to go to the library at some point in the afternoon. In the evening we would go to the theatre. So we walked to the East, and as we walked the Numbers began to reemerge. Somewhere between Second and Third we stopped for lunch, marching through the noisy underbrush of a café's main room to look for a Back Garden. We wanted to sit outside. It was somewhere early in April, April 3rd? Perhaps. Maybe somewhere between the 8th and the 9th, or the 9th and the 10th. As before, it was one of the first fully warm days of that year.

Dear Reader: The events that I am about to have narrated are true, and happened exactly as recorded here.

We found the Garden.

The Garden was filled with long pine tables. We then found a spot on one of the tables at the back by the fence, under a tree. We shared the table with a woman and a young boy who were already there when we arrived.

Now here's a surprise, just at this moment in writing, I have recalled that my cousin Barry was with us. Hello Barry! He must have joined us somewhere in the morning. My cousin was interested in magic, and so the conversation began to turn to the side, and fix us in its sights.

> *It seems possible that we were dead and didn't know*
> *it. But then, what difference would that have made?*
> *Death, it seems, is the issue of least import, so full of*
> *returns as to make it completely beside the point.*

I do not recall when it was that the Boy turned to us and said to me – pointedly to me: I will give you one wish.

He put on the table before me three or four small plastic Native talismans and one dream catcher. His mother was smiling awkwardly, but she was beginning to seem very, very far away. Something in the Boy's eyes made a funnel out of time and to look into it was to see such a dizzying array of possibility, both before and behind, that one's bearings are immediately tossed and only the effort to swallow and frown simultaneously could begin to bring one back to the present.

> *Faust: Du kannst mich, O kleiner Engel, wieder*
> *Gleich als ich in den Garten kam?*
> *Margarete: Saht Ihr es nicht? Ich schlug die Augen*
> *nieder.*[7]

Something in the Boy's gaze pulled me in. He told me to pick a 'shield' and make a wish. It would come true, he said. Indeed he did. He said, 'It will come true.'

Time now made itself into an April toad and hopped away, taking the sense of 'this is here' and 'this is now' with it, back to some hole in the fence. She sat there blinking at me, thriving in Empire's amphybiries.[8]

I mistakenly thought: I've already wished my Wish to myself – again and again and again and again – so what can it matter to make a bargain like this, a pact, that '*it will come true*'?

> *Mephistopheles: So hab ich dich schon unbedingt.*
> *[...]*
> *Durch flache Unbedeutenheit,*
> *Er soll mir zappeln, starren, kleben,*
> *Und seiner Unersättlichkeit*
> *Soll Speis und Trank vor gier'gen Lippen schweben* [9]

As we were about to leave, me with my talisman, the child with my wish (though I never spoke it aloud), he said: There will be a price.

Now, this boy was somewhere between eight and nine, or seven and eight. Perhaps he was six. He was impossibly young for the words that came out of his mouth. And though we laughed as we left – my cousin, my lover, and myself – we talked about it quietly outside. Perhaps I should not have wished, I asked? Perhaps not, my companions said. I kept the token in my pocket. We walked West.

The library faces a park and from the fourth or fifth floor, in a comfortable chair, one can look out just atop the trees toward the Triumphal Arch. From years of living in that library, I'd found a secret solace in glancing up occasionally from this book or that book to take in the trees. But my reading was choppy that day. And I do not recall the text. *This is the only place at which I doubt my memory.* In it, I am following Susan Buck-Morss through Walter Benjamin through Baudelaire. Between the fourth and fifth floor, I was riveted to a page, contemplating the image of the Frontispiece of Baudelaire's Les Epaves (Buck-Morss 1989: 200).

Looking up, I thought:

> Why had I not wished for world peace? Why not wished for prosperity for all? I had wished only to see you again. I had only wished to see you one more time.

I consoled myself to think that the Wish and the Boy were absurd on the one hand and childish on the other. I thought: A product of the Enlightenment, like myself, does not invest in the crippled mode 'belief' without qualification – and certainly not belief in magic. Nor, to add to that, I added, should one believe precocious but possibly very disturbed six-year-old boys with overly silent mothers in backyard Gardens over hummus and olives on April afternoons in the churning bowels of very big cities.

It was then, looking out the window, that I heard the screams. People in the park were running and shouting. A car was hurtling onto the green, East to West, at top speed, careening out of control before slamming to a stop. An accident. Someone was hit.

I was out of my chair, as was everyone on the fourth or fifth floor. We were all pressed against the glass looking down. The sirens, now – their reenactment of wolf howl – getting closer.

I don't recall if I met up with my lover again that afternoon – probably so, but it hardly matters. I don't recall, that is, what happened between the library and the theatre. Then again, what happens between libraries and theatres is often given up for gone. In any case, it was time to go to the performance. Hours had passed since the accident, and the sun had set. I remember approaching the theatre building, though I can't recall the precise locale (it was not a major venue). It was East of the Park. So, again we walked East.

In my next memory I am seated, several rows back. The theatre is a large room with white walls, and there are rows of seats against the long side of the rectangle. Entering the theatre, one had to cross the playing space to take a seat, so we must have crossed that space, as I am now, in my mind, looking out from the third row back, slightly left of centre.

The house is filling up.

Thinking about the audience, I actually recall coats – it was early in April after all. The memory of the coats brings back the chill in the evening – yes, there it is! The director is marching about. He is coming toward me. He asks me – Is that seat taken beside you? It is not. Then he asks: Will you save it for someone named –

He says your name.

Did you see this coming, O Erzengel? Did you catch this careening, this out of control precision – this shadow of agency passed by, bypassed, this fall, not taken, left forgotten on the rim?

'It will come true.' 'There will be a price.'

> So, here it is. As I wait in my seat before the stage I know it will take place. Even if you don't come, you will have come, and so it will have been as if you had been here in your absence. You can not not have come, as you'd already arrived early. I begin to hope for this – to lust for the opening, the first words, intake of breath that will bring the play to the Greedy Lip to float in the space before. It remains for you to come or not to come and both will have been the same. It is already past the time of commencement. The rim has been reached and more. The Director can no longer hold the House. The lights are dimming, and I am thinking – yes – we will have come to –

Just after the last minute, somewhere between fade and out, you enter the theatre. I see you. I watch you see that you have to cross the stage, that you have no choice. As you cross the stage, I see you see that there is only one seat left.

As I have said: In the theatre, there was a long table. There were actors and they fulfilled their roles. There were and there are rows and rows and rows of seats where we – now you and I – take part as well. I remember watching in extreme detail - my body beside your body incidentally, accidentally, incrementally – each minute passed eyes front but side by side. It is the watching I remember – *I do not remember what I watched.* Did Faust destroy Gretchen? Was Gretchen destroyed? Who can say?

I do remember one more odd bit of that night's flotsam: I stood to leave as people clapped. I left the theatre silently and alone. I recall, then, quite distinctly: The kiss of cool against my neck in the night air. The deadly scent of winter still on the prowl. Walking North.

> *Shau alle Wirkenskraft und Samen*
> *Und tu nicht mehr in Worten kramen.* [10]

NOTES

1 'Again you show yourselves, you wavering Forms, / Revealed, as you once were, to clouded vision. / Shall I attempt to hold you fast once more?' (1–3). I will cite repeatedly from Goethe's *Faust* (1961). The line number from the German text appears beside the English translation. Except where indicated, the translations are Walter Kaufmann's.

2 Echo: Descartes (1992: 89).

3 'Street. Faust. Margaret passing by.' (2605)

4 'There is a theatre I see. / What will it be?' (4213)

5 'Bliss-scented, they are winging / Through sky and earth - their singing / Is ringing through the world.' (450)

6 Echo: Certeau (1984: 5).

7 'Faust: Did you know me again, little Angel, as soon as I entered the garden? Margaret: Didn't you notice? I cast down my eyes.' (3165) My translation.

8 Echo: Wilbur (1950).

9 'And, pact or no, I hold you tight.' (1855). My own translation would read: 'You are already mine without condition. / [He who has a spirit such as yours –] / I'll drag him kicking and staring and sticking through flat triviality / as in his insatiable desire food and drink float just beyond his greedy lips.'

10 'Envisage the creative blazes / Instead of rummaging in phrases.' (385)

REFERENCES

Buck-Morss, Susan (1989) *The Dialectics of Seeing*, Cambridge, Massachusetts: MIT Press.

Certeau, Michel de (1984) *The Practice of Everyday Life*, (trans. Steven F. Rendall), Berkeley: University of California Press.

Descartes, Renée (1992) *Meditations on First Philosophy*, (trans. George Heffernan), South Bend, Indiana: University of Notre Dame Press.

Goethe, Johann Wolfgang von (1961) *Faust*, (trans. Walter Kaufmann), New York: Doubleday.

Wilbur, Richard (1950) 'The Death of a Toad', in *Ceremony, and Other Poems*, New York: Harcourt, Brace.

Stones in the Mind

Aporia/Existentia

The Greek word ἀπορία means impassable and applies literally to a terrain that offers no way through; figuratively it connotes states of dilemma or perplexity. As a metaphor, then, it invites comparison between states of the mind and states of the land. On this theme, there is a story about the Zen master Hogen interrupting some young monks who are arguing about mind and matter. Hogen points to a round stone on the ground, about the size of a human skull, and says: 'That is a big stone. Is it inside or outside your mind?' There is earnest consideration all round, before one of the monks attempts a reply. To a Buddhist, he reasons, everything is mind. 'So I would say that the stone is inside my mind.' Hogen looks at him pityingly. 'Your head must feel very heavy, when you are walking around with that stone in it.'[1] Zen storytelling specializes in dilemma and irresolvable paradox. Aporia. The Zen koan, a riddling story or question, can sit in the mind like a heavy stone (or a tickling feather), sabotaging thought processes. This particular story about Hogen encapsulates the aporia of trying to work out the relationship between the ground on which we walk and the mind in which we think.

There is a surprising reversibility, it suggests, in any cause and effect account that we might compose for ourselves. As Australian Zen teacher Susan Murphy says, 'I love the way that places become places by drawing us into their stories. This requires a particular honed receptiveness in us, an opening' (Murphy 2003). We can tell stories about places, but sometimes it may be that they are producing stories we are drawn into as tellers. That is, if we meet the requirement of 'a particular honed receptiveness.' Zen practice might assist in this, but so might certain kinds of performance practice. I'm interested in how some performers are contributing to a turn in public consciousness of the mind/land relationship in Australia, a turn that is as much atavistic as futuristic, and is the subject of a range of recent books and essay collections (including Cameron 2003, Read 2003, Gibson 2002).

Dwelling

Non-indigenous Australians face the existential dilemma of being dwellers in a terrain that will remain in important respects impenetrable to them, because the land itself requires the kind of ancestral connection described by the Aboriginal painter Ivan Namirrkki:

> This place, the creek and the water, we love this country, we Aboriginal people. We love it. The old people were the same, attached to the land. The people, our grandfathers and grandmothers, great grandparents, our ancestors, they lived here in this place, put here for them. That's how we talk about our land. Our spirits lie in the water... We didn't create this culture recently. It lies in the ground. It lies in the earth, but we are bringing it out. We bring it out and paint it on bark, where we can see it. (2004: 112-13)

Namirrkki is from Arnhem Land, a spectacular expanse of terrain in what is known as the 'Top End' of Australia - the extreme north of the Northern Territory - where for centuries the gigantic sandstone and granite formations have been the surfaces on which indigenous painters brought out the secret images harboured in the land. Namirrkki's statements are from an interview given for a recent major exhibition of Arnhem Land painting at the Art Gallery of New South Wales. The exhibition, titled *Crossing Country: The Alchemy of West Arnhem Land Art*, draws together the works of dozens of artists who share this atavistic belonging.

Walking around *Crossing Country* is an overwhelming experience. First because of the number, scale and complexity of the works included. Second, because of their subject matter, which immediately presents the term *matter* as something to be reckoned with. Here are paintings of moons and waterholes, mammalian intestines, stick insects and birds of paradise, of serpents actual and mythical, meat dead and alive, of wind and its movements. The pervasive subjects are spirit beings, and they come in myriad forms. Some have the white faces and hollow eyes reminiscent to the western eye of gothic spectres, but others have an exaggerated anatomical presence. They are skeletons who carry their flesh and blood about with them in bulbous appendages; or fecund, tentacled beings whose swollen sex organs reach down towards the earth. They tell of places where the boundaries between the living and the dead are uncertain, but where the boundaries between cultural traditions - between those who belong and those who do not - seem absolute. And that is the third overwhelming aspect of this display: the city dwellers who are wandering round the gallery are presented with testaments of a belonging from which we are radically excluded.

Performing aporia

This haunted sense of exclusion may be experienced as an aporia, but aporia does not have to be an experience of deprivation. Doubt, dilemma and impasse can serve to strip away some of the narrowing influences on human consciousness and so enlarge the dimensions of experience. In the performing arts, the aporia of living as adopted beings in a land so fiercely expressive of its genetic authority can provoke some of the most exhilarating forms of experiment, cultivating that 'honed receptiveness' Susan Murphy identifies as a precondition for two-way dialogue with places. It is a convention in Australia to speak of relationship to the land as a matter of 'spirituality', but there is more to be learned by focusing on physicality - or even physiology - as the dimension of being that implicates us in the land and the landscapes we inhabit. It is a matter of matter. In his monologue performance *Shadows* (2002), William Yang talks about how many Australian city-dwellers tell themselves they have had a 'spiritual' experience in the bush, but really, the bush itself is the experience. You just happen to be the one standing in it.

In a series of performances narrating the history of his Chinese Australian family across the continents of Australia, Asia and America, Yang - a fine photographer - uses images to record his travels through the Australian landscape as if this were some missing other relation: always present, occasionally intrusive, and sometimes steering his course with a compelling power that he acknowledges with a characteristic lightness of touch. Shadows tells the story of an Aboriginal boy who has been adopted into the family of Sydney artist George Gittoes, and at the heart of the narrative is a visit Yang pays to the remote town of Engonnia in north-western New South Wales, the home of the boy's Aboriginal family.

One of the older women in the family tells Yang about a local massacre site, on the land of a farmer named Bob. He asks to be taken there but the response is puzzling. No-one wants to call Bob. They keep making excuses. Eventually, Yang manages to confirm an arrangement for the next day. But the next day it is cloudy and on cloudy days, the family tells him, the spirits follow you home. So no one is willing to go with him and he sets off on his own. He fails to find the site and returns frustrated, then sets off again the next day, when he manages to meet up with Bob the farmer. Bob, however is 'very angry' that Yang has come unaccompanied.

Subtly, cumulatively, a drama is built up around this quest. Yang doesn't ask himself why he is compelled to keep going in search of the site; his aboriginal friends avoid acknowledging their fears about it; and finally, Bob delivers a throwaway statement that is also loaded. The site, he says, is 'a big nothing. A Joke.' The episode culminates with Yang finding and photographing the location.

In the performance, he recounts this experience as a shadowy figure in front of two panoramic slides, showing what at first glance might indeed look like a big nothing - a patch of raised stony ground surrounded by barbed wire - but as he talks, he points to small white shapes at the lower edge of the slides. Bones, amongst them the clearly identifiable bones of a child's hand.

The story works on the audience at many levels but it is, amongst other things, a story of being unable to find the way to the heart of a mystery, and of encountering strange blockages and divergences in the human agents who might be able to provide guidance towards it. Yet Yang, the migrant Australian in the story, is the one under strange orders to find his way through. Where do these orders come from? The stones in the mind, or the mind in the stones? The land itself? Is the fact that he has no native connection to it the reason he is its chosen witness?

In *Shadows*, the process of live story telling traces a path that enables psychical engagement to occur in a meandering pattern, holding to the peripheries of a core experience that can't be approached directly. It is the art of tracing and holding this pattern that is Yang's genius. At the end of an earlier work, *Blood Links* (1999), which follows the lines of diaspora in his family, he reveals that he is a Taoist. This gives a certain detachment to his view of the directions lives may take. Perhaps it also underlies the wry sense of permeability that he manages to convey about his own role in the various journeys of Shadows. He is a curiously transparent presence on the stage, with the persona of a slightly fey uncle who turns up to do the inevitable family slide show and introduces, perhaps quite unintentionally, a whole new take on inevitability.

The physiological dimensions of our relationship to the land may be those that most persistently elude our awareness. If this is an inevitable but unintentional theme in *Shadows*, it is a conscious focus of Tess de Quincey's Body Weather practice. De Quincey trained in Japan with Min Tanaka in the mid-1980s before starting to create performances in Australia. 'Looking back to 1988 when my individual practice started to emerge,' she says, 'I now realize that I have been gradually weaving a field of research which pendulates between the city and the desert' (2002).

In 1996, I was involved in the documentation for the city-based project, *Compresssion 100*, co-devised by de Quincey and Stuart Lynch. The original goal was to create a hundred site-specific performances (in the event there were over 160) throughout the Sydney metropolitan area during the thirty-one days of May, in collaboration with a range of local artists. 'Can the city's geist and consciousness be tapped?' was the question driving the experiment. The performers sought to be porous to the diverse energies of the locations and their inhabitants, past and present. There were events on Bondi Beach, at a soup kitchen by Central Station, in a tunnel under the footings of the Harbour Bridge, on Observatory Hill overlooking the harbour, at the zoo and the animal shelter, in a kindergarten and a jail, on a ferry, in a bathing shed and along the Parramatta Road. The Parramatta Road became a framing symbol for the overall project. Always known as Sydney's worst road, it is also the earliest city-to-city travelling route since colonization and it points due west, towards the other Australia, the remote deserts and bushlands of the centre, where de Quincey located her next major project, *Triple Alice*. Working in central Australia was, she says, 'the inevitable consequence of being in this country.' There was 'an inevitable drawing towards the centre, the burning point.'[2]

The Company organized three extended periods of residence at Hamilton Downs, about sixty kilometres from Alice Springs. The site itself is a set of wooden buildings constructed by early settlers, and is surrounded by a creek bed. Most of the time this is dry, but when there are prolonged rains, the bed becomes a running river. 'Energy comes up from the earth', someone told me as I was preparing to go there. 'You can feel it.'

What is under the earth are silica crystals, a vast bed of them, so perhaps there is something literally true about this. I arrived with a friend from Sydney about half way through the residency. We were there as writers, with only a week to spare from our academic jobs, in contrast to the performers who had committed to six weeks or more of work in the location.

Every morning began with an hour of 'MB' - muscle and bone work - a set of routines performed outdoors on a raked area of flat ground. These strengthen, ground and energize the body and, as I discovered even through my rather incompetent attempts to participate in the back row, have the side effect of sensitizing you to the lights, airs, movements and sounds around you. The work of sensitization continued through the day, with 'Manipulations' - exercises done in pairs to re-examine the weight, breath and alignment of the body - followed by improvisations to sharpen the connection with particular areas of the land around the camp site. Simple as it may sound, it is work that calls for the strongest levels of courage and discipline because, as de Quincey puts it, 'meeting this place is so huge. It ain't no pussy. It's a tiger.'[3]

Meteorologists talk about weather systems - systems plural, she emphasizes - multiple and overlapping. The Triple Alice residencies fostered awareness of the overlapping climatologies of the body with its immediate environment, bringing in visiting speakers with special knowledge of the physical and cultural properties of the area. The group began to work on a 'Dictionary of Atmospheres', which would include a section called 'The Silica Tales'.

The disciplinary formations of Yang's Taoism and de Quincey's Body Weather, with its parallels and echoes of the butoh tradition, draw on different cultural heritages, but in the Australian context they exhibit some convergences, especially through their cultivation of receptiveness: the body and the mind, almost indistinguishable from each other, tuning in to the cross currents of the wider environment. De Quincey calls this 'inhabitation', and in explaining the word, she like Susan Murphy reverses the conventional terms of relationship between persons and places. 'Places enter and inhabit people and determine their language and being.' This is the kind of perception Yang communicates in his challenge to notions of 'having a spiritual experience' in the bush. De Quincey speaks of 'physical and conceptual impermeation'. Existence is also *existentia*, the act of being - distinguished in philosophy from the more passive *esse*, to be. In Latin, the verb *existere* also has connotations of emergence, becoming visible or manifest, a process that is both active and passive. It may involve arduous work in order only to reach a point of resignation, the finely honed receptiveness of aporia.

NOTES

1 A succinct version of this story is told in Marc de Smedt, The Wisdom of Zen (New York: Abeville press, 1996), unpaginated.
2 Tess de Quincey, in conversation with Jane Goodall, Sydney, 29 December, 2004.
3 ibid.

REFERENCES

Ross Gibson, Seven Versions of an Australian Badland (St.Lucia: University of Queensland Press, 2002).
Susan Murphy, 'The Practice of Stories and Places' in John Cameron, ed., Changing Places: Re-imagining Australia (Sydney: Longueville Books, 2003).
Ivan Namirrkki, 'Our Spirits Lie in the Water,' in Crossing Country: the Alchemy of West Arnhem Land Art (Sydney: Art Gallery of New South Wales, 2004), 112-13.
Marc de Smedt, The Wisdom of Zen (New York: Abeville press, 1996)
Tess de Quincey, 'Sites of Multiplicity and Permeation,' notes for the Place and Performance Research Seminar, Sydney University, December 2002.
Peter Read, Haunted Earth (Sydney: University of New South Wales Press, 2003)

MIKE PEARSON   FIELD STATION 4

Marking Time

Trace and aura. The trace is appearance of a nearness, however far removed the thing that left it behind may be. The aura is appearance of a distance, however close the thing that calls it forth. In the trace, we gain possession of the thing; in the aura, it takes possession of us. Walter Benjamin (1999: 447)

In *Theatre/Archaeology* (2001) Michael Shanks and I outline a series of possible convergencies between the two disciplines, examining variously the documentation of devised performance, the employment of theatre in heritage contexts and the discernment of performative practices in prehistory. The work commences with a borrowing and appropriation of notions and procedures to help expand and illuminate extant disciplinary perceptions and stances and culminates in the elaboration - after Clifford Geertz (2000: 19-35) - of a *blurred genre*, a mixture of performative and scientific practices in an integrated approach to recording, writing and illustrating the past. We express a desire to create live expositions in which archaeology and performance are jointly active in mobilizing the past, in making creative use of its various fragments and in developing cultural ecologies out of varied interests and remains, relating different fields of social and personal experience in the context of diverse and contradictory interests. This, we suggest, necessitates a broader definition of possible objects of retrieval, new approaches to the characterization of behaviour and action, different ways of telling and different types of recording and inscription that can incorporate different orders of narrative: documents, ruins and traces are reconstituted as elements of real-time events. In forms of hybrid presentation - in a combined address to particular sites and themes involving personal narrative, polemic provocation and critical reflection, and in an *interpenetration* of scientific and performative - we have presented conference papers together, devised formal, mediated performances at significant places and organized guided tours of ephemeral locations. But our closest collaboration may yet result from a shared interest in the apparently oxymoronic notion of 'archaeologies of the contemporary past' and their exposition.

At the most intimate of scales we inscribe the urban fabric with varying degrees of permanence. The physical surroundings of both private and public domain are marked by our presence ... and by our passing. From 'Kilroy was here' to modern graffiti, we deliberately 'tag' the environment: proclaiming identities and affiliations, demarcating territory. But inadvertently, quietly, continuously - in the touch of flesh on metal and stone - we also leave signature *traces*: the prints of our bodies. In certain places, our marks accumulate - the signs of our regular and habitual contact: grubby handprints around door-handles, greasy smears on the street outside the fish-and-chip shop. In others, our bodies abrade and erode. We wear things out with our hands, our feet, our backs, our bottoms, our lips: the step is worn shallow, the handrail rubbed naked of paint; the wall is scored by generations of resting bicycle handlebars. In the very passage of pedestrians, in places of multitudinous swarming, the pavement is ground down. Elsewhere, there are the marks of singular actions - scuffs, scratches, cuts, stains; of traumatic events - accidents of fire and explosion, incidents of anarchy and unrest; of transitory occurrences - dropped groceries, vomited kebab. Sometimes they are no more than the faintest swish and sometimes, awful to behold, scenes of crime - 'arcs of blood, quantities of semen'. And on the street corner, dogs sniffed urgently, cocked their legs, left a jumble of spoor in the wet concrete. The unintentional, the random, the intimate unplanned touch of history's passing ...

These are the authentic traces of the performance of everyday life: the result of routine, tradition, habit, accident, event, ritual; of long-term evolution and unconnected short-term ruptures and singularities; of nearness; of dwelling. And they are ineffably archaeological, constituents of what has been termed an 'archaeology of us' (Buchli and Lucas 2001: 8-9). French archaeologist Laurent Olivier first coined the term 'archaeology of the contemporary past' - of the recent, of the short-term - to describe a 'relationship of proximity maintained regarding places, objects, ways of life or practices that are still ours and still nourish our collective identity' (Olivier 2001: 175). As a field of enquiry, it involves a renewed sensitivity to the fabric of the present and attention to those details - distinct and differentiated - that signal our presence but which we consciously disattend or casually ignore or commit to collective amnesia.

There is an implicit re-politicization here of a discipline that had its nascence in foundational processes of nation-state building as a form of active apprehension, a particular sensibility to traces. As it poses the question 'Who made these marks?' it addresses social and ethical issues, engaging with questions of identity, community, class and gender. In an examination of the relationship between material culture and human behaviour, it inevitably concerns aspects of activity and experience that are non-discursive, resulting from practices of labour, trade and social life. It might reveal inarticulate, unregarded or disregarded practices – anonymous, silent, silenced, suppressed, forgotten, ignored – such as patterns of social smoking or profligate street urination or covert sexual activity. It might challenge familiar categorizations – such as assigned usage and the spatially constructed order – through the identification of delinquent events and practices – shortcuts, transgressions and acts of trespass that privilege the route over the inventory: the lateral skids of skate-boarders, places where the bye-laws of the city are clearly broken by chewing-gum chewers and public drinkers and drug users. It might presence absence, indicating the traces of those departed or who live a life of a different timetable, such as night workers and club-goers. It might indicate small acts of vernacular defiance in the personalization of domicile and business. It might demonstrate the partiality of our understanding of the occupancy of the city, revealing that which escapes usual discourses of urban apprehension and planning. It might be redemptive and therapeutic, but equally troubling and disruptive. With the accent on detail – on that which we barely notice – the archaeologist might enquire of inhabitants and workers about the marks their activities and occupations produce and about how such traces reveal difference and distinctiveness; about the genesis and history of existing marks within the locale and how they serve as a mnemonic for the events that caused them, leading to a fuller appreciation – through the stories and experiences of others – of the micro-chronologies and polyphonic geographies that make up the urban present, to the city as a temporal as well as a spatial phenomenon.

In these traces, can we discern the movements, moments and encounters involved in their making: 'maps of practices and behaviours'? If our very walking is archaeological, then these are surely the true spoor of archetypal figures of the modern city: Benjamin's *flaneur* (1999: 416-55); Certeau's *walker* (1998: 91-114); Deleuze and Guattari's *nomad* shifting across the smooth space of the urban desert (1998: 380-7); Jane Rendell's *rambler* with his swaggering masculine gait (1998: 108-22); Debord's *dérivists* cut loose (1996: 22-32); Canetti's surging crowd (1973: 15-105). And all somehow enmeshed in Marc Augé's paths, crossroads and centres (1995: 56-8). But to track them we may need a taxonomy, a field guide of marks ordered and identified according to type, location, density and time-scale.

In the city, public and private come apart. 'Doors stop and separate ... On one side, me and my place, the private, the domestic ... on the other side, other people, the world, the public, politics' (Perec 1997: 37). But the marking does not stop indoors. As I look up from writing, I am aware of blocked fire-places and doors, added alcoves – stratifications of the past, operating on various time-scales of preservation and decay: layers of decoration and structural alterations, complex sequences revealed in the domestic and the ordinary. The house was built in 1905, one of a multitude of terraces built as part of the expansion to accommodate the workers of the burgeoning city of Cardiff, Wales: in the false-roof you can see the jerry-building, bricks roughly stacked on bricks. Throughout are the heterogeneous traces – the patinas

of occupancy – of the many who have lived here and their decisive actions: to knock down walls, to lay new floors. With each new layer of wallpaper, each new lick of paint, each new change of surface, colour, texture, a palimpsest is created. Each repair or decoration records a crucial moment of discussion, argument and communal action. Even the most mundane set of circumstances has a particular kind of depth or density: the character of the place. But recognizing this depends upon looking at them in unfamiliar ways. For what is banal at one scale of viewing may be minutely patterned and textured in close-up, '[m]emories not programmatically preserved but elusive and densely overlaid, of many lives which surface momentarily in old paint, obsolete wiring, and forgotten cupboards ...' (Harbison: 1997: 190).

I know that others have lived and died here before me; I see their ghostly handiwork and it is uncanny, unsettling (see Giard 1998: 133–43) This 'living with history' might cause us to ask with Benjamin, 'What lives and loves, dramas and deaths, have been enacted here, in this room?' 'There used to be no house, hardly a room in which someone had not once died.' 'Today people live in rooms that have never been touched by death, dry dwellers of eternity, and when their end approaches they are stored away in sanitaria or hospitals by their heirs' (Benjamin 1992: 93). It is these very heirs who are in thrall to the current spate of television 'makeover' programmes, busily engaged in do-it-yourself activities, in constant exorcism, in a stripping away that threatens the small-scale, though tangible, domestic heritage: its aura.

If the unturned calendars in the sandwich bar were anything to go by, 44 and 46 James Street, Cardiff were abandoned, boarded up – and protected from vandals – in August 1989. After breaking in, we found traces of those who lived and worked there. Wear patterns around

doorways and stains on skirting boards attested to their presence, and also to their absence. They indicated how the habitual actions and chance moments have shaped the place. But we should beware. The life-story of these shops did not cease simply because they were removed from the histories of the people who once worked there. They began to decompose, to fall apart – significantly and confusingly for us – of their own volition, visibly changing as we visited them, drawing our attention to the way that nothing in the material world is ever fixed, always tending towards entropy: slates became dislodged, paint peeled, a veneer of dust settled, pigeon droppings accumulated. Michael Shanks has called this – in that we do not perceive it – the secret life of things. Places and objects are constantly in motion, changing in ways that condition how we observe and make use of them.

In the attic a man's suit quietly rotted beside three Coca-Cola cans and a tray of cutlery spilled across the floor in an unwitnessed moment. But can we ever be sure that human agency was involved in what appears now as an event? Were the chair knocked over and the cutlery scattered in an emotional outburst, or as an accident during evacuation, or later as the result of perching birds? Accidental arrangements of objects – particularly when framed in the viewfinder of the camera – suggested narratives for an eye adjusted by the forensic 'turn': pen, four cups, knife; shoe, bird's nest, wooden cash till, betting slips, jacket; single knife; single toothbrush. Tools and utensils bore chips and abrasions that attest to their usage, to events they had witnessed, things that had happened to them, signs of ageing, time and use – the carving knife ground thin on the doorstep, a favourite mug cracked and handleless ... We removed them, intending to integrate them into performances elsewhere.

But out of context they became so much detritus, already left as surplus to requirements by their former owners; we threw them away. Artist Emma Lawton intended to hack into the shops – to cut, hammer, slice their fabric – and then order and reorder the fragments of brick and mortar by size and colour elsewhere. But they were demolished quickly, without our knowing, to make way for a car park for the Cardiff Bay Development Agency. But I can still stand on the street and tell the story of our forced entry and the story too of Lynette White who was murdered in 5 James Street opposite: an evocation of aura through the performative.

And now as I look up from writing, I see the carton of milk I bought this morning, week-old flowers, last month's *The Wire* magazine, a photograph taken ten years ago, a two-hundred-year-old family heirloom. Few of us live – choose to live – in a space of minimalist rectitude. Most of us engage in small, daily acts of curation. Whatever our economic status, I contend, we value things. Our present is multi-temporal.

In (site) works of performance that evince the transitory and the mundane, we might demonstrate for the popular imagination how we ourselves and our immediate environment are part of historical process, how constituents of material culture exist within overlapping frames and trajectories of time, drawing attention to how we are continuously generating the archaeological record. Whilst little is at risk here, everything of value – communality, generational communication, sense of place – might be at stake. As modes of cultural production, archaeology and performance might take up the fragments of the past and make something out of them in the present, in an attitude critical and suspicious of orthodoxy, of any final accounts of things.

Why? Such works might resemble small acts of resistance to the excesses of mediated, global culture, drawing attention to the local and particular, identifying and energizing regionalized identities, without monopolizing interpretation. In a renewed sensitivity to ephemerality, to an everyday rendered unfamiliar, an enacted archaeology might provide insights into the personal and the emotive, at scales that as yet escape the scrutiny of CCTV surveillance: 'to address tensions, contradictions, exclusions, pains' (Buchli and Lucas 2001: 14). It might celebrate the fact that we do and can still mark – insubordinate to the imperatives of public cleansing, architectural sanitization, social decorum – in acts that are colloquial, vernacular, detailed, social and that, in this, we are not alone. And perhaps this concern with the dirty and the discarded is a symptom of late modernism, a nostalgia for a public domain in dynamic dialogue with its inhabitants, counter to the current genrefication and gentrification of the urban landscape, the deterritorialization of social life and retreat into the unmarked domain of cyberspace. A restoration of the absent present ...

REFERENCES

Augé, Marc (1995) *Non-Places: Introduction to an Anthropology of Supermodernity*, London: Verso.

Benjamin, Walter (1992) 'The Storyteller', in *Illuminations*, London: Fontana Press.

Benjamin, Walter (1999) *The Arcades Project,* Cambridge, MA: Harvard Belknap.

Buchli, Victor and Lucas, Gavin (eds.) (2001) *Archaeologies of the Contemporary Past*, London: Routledge.

Canetti, Elias (1973) *Crowds and Power,* London: Penguin.

Certeau, Michel de. (1988) *The Practice of Everyday Life*, Berkeley and Los Angeles: University of California Press.

Debord, Guy (1996) 'Theory of the Dérive' and 'Two Accounts of the Dérive', in Libero Andreotti and Xavier Costa (eds.) *Theory of the Dérive and Other Situationist Writings on the City*, Barcelona: Museu d'Art Contemporani de Barcelona/ACTAR.

Deleuze, Gilles and Guattari, Felix (1988) *A Thousand Plateaux*, trans. B. Massumi, London: Athlone Press.

Geertz, Clifford (1983) *Local Knowledge: Further Essays in Interpretive Anthropology*, New York: Basic Books.

Giard, Luce (1998) 'Ghosts in the city', in Michel de Certeau, Luce Giard and Pierre Mayol (eds.) *The Practice of Everyday Life, Volume 2: Living and Cooking*, Minneapolis: University of Minnesota Press.

Harbison, Robert (1997) *Thirteen Ways: Theoretical Investigations in Architecture*, Chicago: Graham foundation/MIT Press.

Hernandez, Anthony (1995) *Landscapes for the Homeless*, Hannover, Germany: Sprengel Museum.

Olivier, Laurent (2001) 'The Archaeology of the Contemporary Past', in Victor Buchli and Gavin Lucas (eds.) *Archaeologies of the Contemporary Past*, London: Routledge.

Pearson, Mike and Shanks, Michael (2001) *Theatre/Archaeology*, London: Routledge.

Perec, Georges (1997) *Species of Spaces and other Pieces*, trans. J. Sturrock, London: Penguin.

Rendell, Jane (1998) 'West End Rambling: Gender and Architectural Space in London 1880–1830', *Leisure Studies* Vol. 17, No. 2.

All photographs taken by Mike Pearson

CHRISTOPHER BALME   FIELD STATION 4

Aporias of Ekphrasis: The Performance Archive – Archiving the Performance

Among the many functions and goals of the Centre for Performance Research, its desire to archive the ephemeral and transitory art of performance is one of its most valuable but aporetic tasks. To define Field Station 4 between the actual and the historical and aporia and existensia is to set out some of the central and productive tensions in the field of performance studies. If we define aporia - following *Webster's Dictionary* - as an insoluble because contradictory but therefore productive philosophical puzzle, then we are also describing some of the intractable problems facing performance studies in general.

In the following remarks I want to discuss the apparent aporias of archiving performance from historical and contemporary perspectives. I wish to demonstrate that these problems, although apparently intractable, are by no means novel but have a history reaching back to antiquity. As the title of my essay indicates, I want to add a further Greek word to the plethora already suggested. This term, *ekphrasis*, refers to the old question of how to render in words visual images - the art of describing pictures. Although ekphrasis with its emphasis on the visual by no means exhausts the manifold signs and energies emanating from performance, it does grapple with one very central question as performance usually makes a substantial appeal to the visual senses of the spectator. As we shall see, the function of archiving the performance through words and visual images can result in artistic products in their own right.

Before the advent of moving image media there were three ways of preserving the experience of performance: describing the event in words, rendering it in a visual image, or passing on the information verbally and physically by direct demonstration, usually in a master-pupil situation. If the latter is a pedagogical project, the former are situated on the cusp of art and scholarship. It is on the latter I wish to concentrate because it relates most directly to CPR's project of archiving performance traditions. The following remarks are associative ruminations on the apparent aporias of archiving performance.

Ekphrasis

In his famous essay on aesthetics, the *Laokoon* (1766), the German dramatist and theatre theorist Gotthold Lessing established an influential dichotomy between temporal and spatial arts, i.e. between poetry and painting or sculpture. It is among other things a treatise on the aesthetic rules or limits governing the representation of the human body in different artistic media in Greek culture, with very clear normative rules legislating how the body *ought* to be represented by modern artists. Although this theory's application to the theatre is tantalizingly hinted at but never theoretically elaborated in the *Laokoon*, Lessing returns to the problem a few years later in his writing for and about the new Hamburg National theatre. In the fifth chapter of the *Hamburg Dramaturgy*, he speaks famously of acting as 'transitory painting', 'suspended between the visual arts and poetry' (Lessing 1966: 36). This is an indirect reference to the *Laokoon*. If Lessing's essay in aesthetics elaborates an influential doctrine of media specificity, requiring that verbal and visual arts perform separate tasks suited to their capabilities, then this poses problems for any attempt to render in words adequately responses to visual artworks. The ancient Greek concept of ekphrasis provides one remedy to this dilemma, as Murray Krieger suggests in his study *Ekphrasis: The Illusion of the Natural Sign* (1992). Originally the genre of ekphrasis, or more generally the ekphrastic principle, referred in its simplest form to the epigrams added to early Greek statues. Krieger presents the possibility of a simultaneous perception of motion and stasis by critiquing the Lessing tradition with its neat separateness of the mutually delimiting arts. Krieger sees in the plasticity of the language of poetry a means of overcoming Lessing's dichotomy. This language tries to become an object with as much substance as the medium of the plastic arts, the words thus establishing a plastic aesthetic for themselves.

The plasticity of words to describe bodies in motion, speech in full flow, is an extension of the ekphrastic principle considered neither by the Greeks nor by literary scholars such as Krieger. Yet, as any critic of performance knows, this is a basic requirement of the job. And ever since the eighteenth century, when theatre criticism began to emerge, writers have been painting word pictures of performances that today provide an invaluable archive for scholars. This applies equally to vocal performances where critics have striven to capture the sensuality of singers 'giving voice', particularly in operatic performance. Whether we look at Lessing's own attempts to describe actors and acting in the *Hamburg Dramaturgy*, or think of Aaron Hill's early eighteenth-century journal *The Promptor* (Appleton and Burnim 1966) and its many successors, the ekphrastic principle abounds in their descriptions of bodies in performance. For many actors and actresses we have only this evidence, and we construct our historiographical narratives around this archive. Finally, I would like to argue that every performance scholar engaged in describing and analyzing performance is by definition performing ekphrasis: trying to render the fleeting images of bodies and spatial arrangements in a sculptural language that probably by definition moves towards metaphor.

Ocular proof: The Iconography of Performance

Judging by cave paintings discovered in Australia, North Africa and Southern Europe, the representation of the performing body in visual images appears to be an anthropological norm. Whatever 'function' these images may have performed for the originators (and must we always think in terms of 'functions' for artwork outside our narrow Kantian perimeters?), they are part of an archive of performance iconography. The field of theatre iconography (Balme et al. 2002) devotes itself to collecting and analyzing the many categories of images resulting from theatrical performances, but it is especially interested in those that are produced post factum, as records of the event. With its overt Eurocentric focus theatre iconography's own canon begins with the famous Southern Italian vases depicting dancing maenads, actors in masks and costumes, and satyr plays. These images provide perhaps the earliest substantial and purely visual record of performance culture in the western tradition. But visual images are notoriously unreliable from the historian's point of view. As Ernst Gombrich famously put it, images make for unreliable evidence because, unlike language, they lack the ability to make propositions: 'It is in the nature of things that images need much more of a context to be unambiguous than do statements. Language can form propositions, pictures cannot ... Art can present and juxtapose images, ... but it cannot specify their relationship.' (1969: 97). This may be true from the perspective of linguistic philosophy, and when the two media are strictly separated. Performance

however integrates rather than separates media, and therefore images do not necessarily always have to 'speak for themselves' in splendid isolation. They are frequently supported by language, even if it is only a title, but often it is much more. In one of CPR's most widely read publications, Eugenio Barba's *A Dictionary of Theatre Anthropology: The Secret Art of the Performer* (1991), Barba and other contributors make extensive use of the visual archive to demonstrate the rich history of performance traditions from a transcultural perspective. These images range from the famous Receuil Fossard of early Commedia dell'arte imagery to photographs taken by ISTA of their own workshops. Particularly striking in the publication are the many serial images that attempt to document the process of performance in its temporal flow.

Moving Media

The third and most effective means of archiving performance is the moving image. This only became possible with the invention of the cinema in the 1890s. It is perhaps not surprising that some of the earliest film documents to have survived are of dance. Both Lumière and Edison made films of dances by epigones of Loïe Fuller in 1895 (Balme 1992). Although comparatively few film documents of early theatre performances have survived, a large body of material depicting 'primitive dance' was collected by anthropologists. The film camera had hardly been invented before anthropologists were taking these initially cumbersome devices with them into the field. Again, favoured objects were dances and ceremonies. Visual anthropology archives contain a considerable amount of performance-related film material dating from the early twentieth century. Yet here, too, we are confronted with another interesting aporia. The National Film and Sound Archive in Canberra contains, for example, footage of rituals performed by Aboriginal men and women which are so sacred that it is not actually allowed to be viewed by anyone.[1] While the footage exists on the archive catalogue, it is, phenomenologically speaking, non-existent because beyond actual apprehension by anyone (including the curators). While this prohibition certainly reflects a major achievement in terms of recognizing indigenous rights and respecting religious customs, it poses an interesting conundrum for archivists. What is the good of an archive that cannot be consulted? The logical step to destroy the *tapu* material (to use a Polynesian term) is not possible either. Archivalists by nature do not destroy archives, nor indeed does the step seem to be necessary as the existence of the film footage is not per se offensive or illegal, only its apprehension.

Students of performance are often confronted by similar if not quite so extreme problems. Researchers seeking to view in-house video material of performance are frequently faced with a similar paradox. The material exists but may not be accessible for copyright problems.[2] In the age of cheap videotaping procedures most theatres and performing artists record their work on videotape. In fact, performing artists are becoming masters of their own audiovisual archiving - producing video promotions and demo tapes without which participation at festivals is scarcely possible. This is particularly the case of groups working at the interstices of commercial and subsidized theatre. Nowadays, the functions of promotion and archiving seem to be more closely allied than ever before. Of course most smaller theatre and performance groups do not have the resources to maintain properly organized archives.

At this point, CPR's audiovisual archive becomes such an important resource for scholars. In many ways it resolves or at least defuses some of the aporias discussed above. It combines the purely iconographic with the media archives and in fact makes productive use of both as its valuable publications demonstrate. It alleviates the need to rely entirely on the ekphrastic principle of describing pictures. Although, as most scholars of performance would acknowledge, a little bit of ekphrasis is essential for writing about performance. The ephemerality of performance must be counter-acted by the plasticity of language.

NOTES

1. This refers to the Baldwin Spencer expeditions conducted in the first decade of the twentieth century. In 2005 a selection of scenes was made available to researchers.
2. The copyright question pertaining to audiovisual material is complicated and certainly not yet subject to international norms. A widely advocated position is, however, that in order to view a tape of a performance, all the performing artists involved have to give written permission. This is not necessary for so-called in-house which are produced to facilitate rehearsals and are by definition not for public consumption.

REFERENCES

Appleton, William and Kalman A. Burnim (eds.) (1966) *The Prompter: A Theatrical Paper* (1734-36), New York: B. Blom.

Balme, Christopher, Robert Erenstein and Cesare Molinari (eds.) (2002) *European Theatre Iconography*, Rome: Bulzoni.

Balme, Christopher (2002) 'Moving Media: Theatre Iconography and its Limits', in Christopher Balme, Robert Erenstein and Cesare Molinari (eds.) *European Theatre Iconography*, Rome: Bulzoni, pp. 351-60.

Gombrich, Ernst (1969) 'The Evidence of Images', in Charles S. Singleton (ed.) *Interpretation: Theory and Practice*, Baltimore: Johns Hopkins.

Krieger, Murray (1992) *Ekphrasis: The Illusion of the Natural Sign*, Baltimore: Johns Hopkins.

Lessing, G.E. (1962) *Hamburg Dramaturgy*, intro. Victor Lange, trans. Helen Zimmern, New York: Dover Publications.

JOE KELLEHER   FIELD STATION 5

Legwork – Thinking Showing Doing

Kinkaleri, from 'West' (video project 2002-2006)

The room is pitch black. When I enter I have to walk like a zombie, a sort of conscious zombie, arms out in front and shuffling along so as not to bump into other people who are probably here as well, even if I can't see them yet. The only illumination is from a large screen on the far wall where still images are being projected. Each image appears on the screen for about a minute before fading into the next one. The colours are washed out or saturated in ways that seem old-fashioned-familiar, the modern taking on already a patina of antiquity, which goes along with the unconvincingly 'up to date' aspirations of the images themselves. I presume I've come in towards the end of the hundred-minute sequence. The topic at the moment appears to be transport. A silver-coloured train has been photographed from overhead. White arrows pasted onto the image mark out the length of one of the carriages in units of 'm'. Metres probably. This is followed by an image of a passenger airplane on the ground. And then another airplane – the same or similar – suspended among clouds and blue sky. That's fantastic. The airliner is followed by a picture of people on bicycles – on solid ground again – but again going somewhere: cheerfully cycling past a clutch of enormous satellite receiver dishes. A polar expedition negotiates a crevasse. A book is open at a page with a diagram of our solar system. I assume it's our solar system. An astronaut, at the end of a curling umbilicus, floats in deep space. A space rocket is blasting off. Wild geese are in flight over a darkening landscape. A string quartet is captured scraping and plucking silently. A violin is pictured next to a page of sheet music. And then a black circle appears upon a white background, which is when I imagine that we are either at the end of the world or back at the start of the image sequence.

This is also where the voices begin, piped into the same dark room. Given the context we might take the voices as a commentary on the images. A sort of performance-studies discourse, if you will, 'explaining "showing doing"' (Schechner 2002: 22). [1] There are several voices, but only one speaks at a time. They sound as if they are saying something, sound at least as if they are speaking human languages, even if none of them is a language known to me. As it happens, though, the voices are not saying anything, not even using languages. This is not Babel but sheer babble. These are glossolalic voices,

recordings of 'speaking in tongues'. What they are doing is talking nonsense, so that – even if I don't at first hear it as such – the panorama of human knowledge that passes on the screen, all of that evidence of making and doing, all of that work that has got us (some of us at least) from there to here, from the primal division of light and dark to Thanksgiving and space exploration and string quartets, is little by little deviously inflected. At least it is for me, the spectator, who remains here a while, in the dark looking and listening, trying to think about all this.

The work I've been describing is *Once Upon a Time* by British artist Steve McQueen, exhibited at the South London Gallery in Peckham during autumn 2004. The voices are from an archive of glossolalic speech collected by linguist William Samarin, and the images are a selection of data inscribed on a gold-plated analogue disc that was attached to the Voyager space probes and blasted into space in 1977 (around the same time, give or take half a decade, that the performance studies discipline took off in the USA [2]). Both probes are still speeding into the far distance – the furthest man-made objects from earth, as the NASA website likes to remark. [3] The hundred or so images on the Voyager disc are parts of a message intended for space travellers from other worlds than this one and destined for a playback in the far distant future. Between them they tell a story of humanity. More precisely, they depict the earth as a stage upon which the human story is very much the headline feature, slanted it has to be said (given that the messengers are NASA and their associates) towards a western telling of that tale, which is to say a story of progress and enlightenment.

On the one hand this is a cultural and technological 'progress' at the level of the images themselves – so that for example totems of white, western civilization occupy a certain place at the climax of the sequence, juxtaposed with 'traditional' Asian dancers and African carvers of wooden elephants. To this extent the story is partial, and it should be added that the interstellar spectator – once they have worked out how to play the disc and how to understand what it has to show – will learn little from these images about the other sides of technology's cutting edge, not least the military-political agendas that sustain the NASA programme, nor the figures of death, pestilence, starvation and war that, in another telling, might have a more prominent part in this drama. Which brings us onto the other hand, the way in which the image sequence constructs a pedagogic progress by which a stranger, a foreigner, an alien might learn how to look, learn how to read, instructing the viewer how, for instance, to understand juxtapositions of scale, or how to experience a two-dimensional image as a three-dimensional scene, or how to compute multiplicity and comprehend sequentiality as such. And, as I watch and am instructed in how to read my own species-history, I find it hard to keep my distance. The effect is of being called towards a determinedly realist fiction where the more or less adequate match of image and world won't quite allow me to disbelieve it completely; but where, if I were to speak, if I were to attempt to join in and play my part, it would have to be in one of those glossolalic voices that only *sounds* like language, that only *seems* to touch, in its indivisible murmur, upon an exact and manifold sense of things, and where the speaker appears and disappears like an ache, like a mouthful of air, at once here and nowhere, unable to do anything but sustain this performance, for fear of disappearing completely, for good as it were.

In an interview that appears in the book accompanying the exhibition, McQueen speaks of his interest in an art that touches 'what is happening in your head', that articulates a present tense of experience, a suspension between past and future that might be compared with the everyday experience of reading a book:

> you only understand the book as far as the last words you've read. Each time you turn the page, you're somewhere else. It's a journey.... So when interesting things happen, it's immediate, and is just there; and it reinforces your presence. There is a relationship with the image. (McQueen 2003: 24–7)

I imagine this suspension as a mode of transit, a way of passing amongst images, as if one were sitting on a train or a plane or a bicycle, or maybe even floating in space attached to a craft that is in orbit around the moon: going places without ostensibly doing anything oneself. As if that illusion were sustainable, if only for the duration of a 'train of thought'.

Kinkaleri, from 'West' (video project 2002-2006)

McQueen's evocation of what he calls a 'limbo' of thinking between past and future experience recalls Hannah Arendt's pages (published a few years prior to the Voyager expeditions) at the close of the first volume of her last work *The Life of the Mind*, pages that seek to address the question 'Where are we when we think?' Here Arendt summarizes her view of thinking as an activity that 'is its own end' and for which there is no better metaphor than the everyday 'sensation of being alive'. That does not mean, though, that thinking is anything less than extraordinary. Indeed it is most likely 'always out of order' as far as the world goes, tending to interrupt ordinary activities of production and consumption and be interrupted by them (Arendt 1978: 197). Rather than a more intimate engagement with reality, thinking might be understood as a mode of 'de-sensing' so as to gather up the 'essences' of things as concepts, a sort of withdrawal from actual 'doing' similar to the withdrawal of a theatrical spectator from the world of speech and appearances so as to better reflect upon these things as they are rendered as images (92).

Arendt proposes that the thinker's tendency to deal in generalized essences leads them to privilege what is 'applicable anywhere', which is to say, 'spatially speaking a "nowhere"', so that the 'thinking ego', all things considered, 'is, strictly speaking, nowhere; it is homeless in an emphatic sense' (199). The emphasis, though, will be not so much on a where as a when. Arendt turns upon her own formulations and suggests that to ask after the 'where' of thinking is perhaps the wrong question, overdetermined as it is by a prejudice towards spatially-oriented thought. She recalls Kant's position according to which the 'intuition of ourselves and of our inner state' is strictly temporal, time having, as Arendt explains, 'nothing to do with appearances as such ... but only with appearances as affecting our "inner state", in which time determines "the relation of representation"' (Arendt 1978: 201; Kant 1986: 49). We arrive then at an insight similar to McQueen's, for whom the 'relationship with the image' has to do with an experience of what Arendt refers to now as 'the gap between past and future' or the *nunc stans*, the 'standing now' of medieval philosophy. And, like McQueen with his figure of the relaxed reader, Arendt attempts to image this gap – which is only conceivable to the extent that someone is there, experiencing it, in the gap so to speak – with a series of scenic metaphors including a line graph in which a 'thought-train' cuts a diagonal between the axes of 'past' and 'future', all three lines appearing to head off into the 'infinite' like the tracks of space probes anticipating their final rest in a silence akin to that 'immobile quiet in which the mind is active without doing anything'. For the thinker, who follows the middle track in the diagram, this would be what Kant calls a 'land of pure intellect' sustaining itself according to Arendt as 'an enduring presence in the midst of the world's ever-changing transitoriness' (Arendt 1978: 206, 211). Until, that is, the surrounding world intervenes, as it will; until perhaps even the silence of deep space is interrupted by the interstellar DJ, who will put the needle on the record and start the whole babble and spectacle of messages and appearances going again.

In the gallery, though, rather than a 'line of thought' created out of 'a *succession* of soundless words – the only medium in which we can think' (Arendt 1978: 202), we have an apparently thoughtless stream of wordless sounds in concert with an ambered frieze of happy island earth and its leaf-gathering, elephant-carving, bicycle-riding citizens. If thinking undoes appearance, glossolalia goes one further, appearing to undo the very substance of thought. Not that the glossolalic voices themselves are not doing anything. Indeed they are doing expression, doing passion, doing communication even, and doing them as if they have never been done before. As if a world depends upon it. But doing these things a world away from where they might happen for anyone else, except as a sort of overwhelming impressiveness or (depending on one's taste and patience) numbing superfluity. Or so we might say, if we accept Michel de Certeau's suggestion that what is isolated and authorized in glossolalia, and thereby set apart from the social, is the 'opera' of everything that is prolix, uncontrolled, and fragile in human dialogue, which is to say the essence of the dialogic utterance as such, but removed from actual dialogue and performed upon 'the stage of verbal exchange' where the 'abjection of meaning' is 'prerequisite to this *vocal utopia* of speaking' (de Certeau 1996: 30).

Kinkaleri, from 'West' (video project 2002-2006)

Notwithstanding the abjection of meaning the performative capacities of glossolalia are legion, not the least significant of which would be its capacity to articulate a generally resistant performative, that of 'a non-linguistic ego, which... cannot pass from one individual to another. It is outside the social system, and belongs to the speaker, who takes possession of language by this means' (Yaguello 1991: 96. Cited in Shamdasani 1994: 39). Even such recalcitrance, though, is caught after all in the net of interpretation (written interpretation usually), which aims to credit (or expose) the *work* that is supposed to go into the glossolalic performance and the worker who is supposed to have performed it: a performance that catches us out – as we in turn perform the values of the interpretation system, 'some *meaning*, a *real*, the *work*' (de Certeau 1996: 36) – by exposing us as theatre-workers too; and the glossolalic 'vocal utopia' as the projection of an altogether realist theatre at that. Only thinking perhaps, if we knew how to do that, would be capable of resisting the temptation to rush onto that stage right now and talk itself silly. Thinking, and – in the midst of all – a certain sort of legwork.

Legwork is an ordinary term for the most prosaic labour, an altogether forward-looking way of getting the job done that involves slogging around from place to place, checking facts, comparing appearances, getting involved, making sense of things, and expending time and energy as one does so. It is the sort of work that is supposed to come before thinking, to support it and then make itself scarce – the sort of everyday doing upon which thinking depends but from which it is supposed nevertheless to remove itself – arcane labour, necessary labour, the work let's say of ploughing, going to the end of the field at the right time of the year and then turning around to do it again.

The old word for that turn into the furrow is *versus*, which generates the no less venerable term 'verse', a term that still circulates here and there to refer to a particular (written) mode of the sort of work that, as it happens, sets itself against the prosaic: the ambiguous work of poetic making. At a technical level, the suspension between the prosaic and the poetic is effected by that straddling of the end of the verse line known as *enjambment*, which, in the momentary disconnection it effects - in Giorgio Agamben's account - 'between the metrical and syntactic elements, between sounding rhythm and meaning', turns in two directions at once, forwards and backwards, catching the reader in an intimate suspension between past and future. For Agamben '[t]his hanging-back, this sublime hesitation between meaning and sound is the poetic inheritance with which thought must come to terms'(Agamben 1995: 39-41).

Jacques Rancière takes up this inheritance in his brief history of utopian political endeavour *Short Voyages to the Land of the People*. More exactly, he writes of endeavours where an actual setting out, on foot for the most part and therefore 'not so much to far-off isles or exotic vistas as to those much closer lands that offer the visitor the image of another world', shades into a way of imagining, a way of seeing and saying and a way of believing in what is seen and said that remains as it were in transit: specifically the way of a 'foreigner' who persists in undoing 'the certainties of place, and thereby reawakens the power present in each of us to become a foreigner on the map of places and paths generally known as reality' (Rancière 2003: 1, 3). Indeed rather than utopian we might do better to shuffle that word again and say something like transutopian endeavour, since for Rancière the 'truly utopian point: the wordless evidence of the thing given in itself, the exact coincidence of word and thing' is not an issue of the labours of poets and political visionaries but of a prose 'realism'. 'For the modern utopia, in its very principle, is not the happy islands but the production of a *place* where separation is erased, where the order of discourse exactly and naturally corresponds to the order of things and their properties.' Only the poem, with its foreign accent, its stop and start, its divisions and deviations, its reflections and lettings-go, its momentary suspensions of the representational economy, threatening 'to tip over into nothingness at the end of each line and after the last verse ... is what best denounces the modern utopia', even if the prose of the world in the next moment 'enjambs the line, chases away blankness, makes us forget the myth by making it real' (98-9).

At the end of his book Rancière imagines a walk. He writes of 'an interminable walk in the course of which the subject exceeds everything that it intelligibly could

Kinkaleri, from 'West' (video project 2002-2006)

PHOTO: KINKALERI

be said to be at one with.' He describes the wanderings of the 'foreign' woman played by the actress Ingrid Bergman in Rossellini's film *Europe 51* who, in an attempt to get to know the people, goes astray in an unfamiliar European city and, as she does so, undoes the capacity of the realist film to speak with any assurance (scientifically, politically) on behalf of the things and people that it represents. Hers is a stepping out of the frame, an undoing of knowledge, not unlike the extravagant progress, Rancière suggests, of the thinker Socrates in his 'own' city, stopping at certain moments only to 'restart forward - questioning and defying - under the sign of this interruption.' For Rancière the motto of such reflective labour resides in the advice that Rossellini's heroine gives to a young tearaway: '*think* about what you are doing!' (Rancière 2003: 118).

Now, when I imagine a performance - a 'showing doing' - that might suture action and reflection according to such a command, it is not a walk and a commentary that comes to mind but a sort of interruptive standing-still, against an occasional buzz of background noise. A sort of *nunc stans* after all, which stands up for about fifteen or twenty seconds and then collapses. That is, rather than a stepping forth there is a buckling of the legs, a body - occasionally two bodies - falling onto the pavement and lying down where they fall, for all the world as if dead. And all of it for the sake of another who watches, records and says nothing: the gaze of an immobile camera that captures whatever happens to appear of what we do, while the life of the city carries on doing what it does, going about its business, passing in and out of view.

Italian performance group Kinkaleri's ongoing video project *West* (like McQueen's *Once Upon a Time*, a work that addresses the times according to the conventions of an archive or atlas of sequenced images) is produced as a series of episodes made on the streets of particular western European cities: so far, Paris, Rome, Amsterdam, Vienna, Athens. Capital cities. Visitor towns. Places where everybody's everyday impinges, in countless unforeseen ways, upon somebody else's. Places where it is possible to ignore that fact. Famous, familiar places that could just as well be anywhere, but which happen - in these particular moments - to be right here. Each episode of *West* consists of a string of relatively simple shots that follow an identical format. In every shot the metropolis is rendered as a 'living' picture postcard, the frame filled either with the banality of the monumental (the Parthenon, the base of the Eiffel Tower, a corner of the Olympic stadium) or else the monumentality of the ordinary (the frontage of a fast food shop, a playground, a suburban train platform), at the centre of which a video camera records a person - or maybe two people together, anyway different people in every shot - standing on the spot, about twenty yards away, staring back into the lens.

These are people who have interrupted their journey, their itinerary, their work to do this. They have removed themselves from the busy world of appearance and doing that they occupied before - and which everyone around them occupies still - so as to give themselves up, for however short a time, to *this* appearing, here in front of a recording eye that puts them in the centre of things (or at least the centre of the shot) and waits upon their performance. The performances are unimprovable. After a period of gazing back at the camera the subject 'dies'. That is they fall over, with no particular behaviour (although no two people crumple the same way), simply doing that as best they can, showing themselves doing that. The camera does not follow their fall. It continues to look in the direction it was looking, allowing whatever time it takes for a scurrying or dawdling pedestrian to pass out of the frame, or else a van or a moped or a train or a massive articulated barge, these movements constituting a sort of environmental choreography that seems to compose itself briefly around the minimum event. The moment is, though, brief. The body is on the ground now, somewhere at the bottom of the frame, a minor inflection upon a scene that - already - carries on regardless. I wonder what is going through the mind of that person, in that moment, lying by the road. Did I do that right? Have they stopped filming yet? Is it time to stand up yet? Is anybody looking at me? I imagine thinking being done, a voice in the head, the merest thinking, the merest showing, the merest doing, alone and right in the very midst of things. I imagine the one who is playing dead alive to every moment, a world away from how they might imagine themselves to appear right now, setting out on 'the path paved by thinking, the small

Kinkaleri, from 'West' (video project 2002-2006)

inconspicuous track of non-time beaten by the activity of thought within the time-space given to natal and mortal' humanity (Arendt 1978: 210). I imagine something going on.

NOTES

1 '"Being" is existence itself. "Doing" is the activity of all that exists, from quarks to sentient beings to super galactic strings. "Showing doing" is performing: pointing to, underlining, and displaying doing. "Explaining 'showing doing'" is the work of performance studies.'
2 The first edition of Schechner's *Performance Theory* appeared in 1977.
3 See NASA's Voyager website.<http://voyager.jpl.nasa.gov>

REFERENCES

Agamben, Giorgio (1995) *Idea of Prose*, (trans. M. Sullivan and S. Whitsitt), New York: State University of New York Press.
Arendt, Hannah (1978) *The Life of the Mind*, San Diego: Harcourt.
de Certeau, Michel (1996) 'Vocal Utopias: Glossolalias', *Representations 56*: 29-47.
Kant, Immanuel (1986) *Critique of Pure Reason*, (trans. J. M. D. Meiklejohn), London: Dent.
McQueen, Steve (2003) *Speaking in Tongues*, Paris: Éditions des musées de la Ville de Paris.
Rancière, Jacques (2003) *Short Voyages to the Land of the People*, (trans. J. B. Swenson), Stanford: Stanford University Press.
Schechner, Richard (2002) *Performance Studies. An Introduction*, London: Routledge.
Shamdasani, Sonu (1994) 'Encountering Hélène: Théodore Flournoy and the Genesis of Subliminal Psychology', in Théodore Flournoy, *From India to the Planet Mars: A Case of Multiple Personality with Imaginary Languages*, (ed. Sonu Shamdasani), Princeton: Princeton University Press, pp. xi-li.
Yaguello, Marina (1991) *Lunatic Lovers of Language: Imaginary Languages and their Inventors*, (trans. C. Slater), London: Athlone.

SUSAN MELROSE   FIELD STATION 5

Who Knows – *and who cares* – about performance mastery (?) [1]

First, there is the question of value invested in the canons of twentieth-century art. This value is not set: there is always formal invention to be redeployed ... [and] cultural capital to be reinvested. Simply to surrender this value is a great mistake, aesthetically and strategically. Second, there is the question of expertise ... Hal Foster (1996: xii)

Introduction

My title here alludes to *attitude* ('who cares ...?'), as well as to *knowledge-in* and of, and *knowledge-about*. Attitude is extremely difficult to calculate, impossible to grasp *as such*, since all we can see are actions - discursive or other - practices, of one kind or another, from which attitude (or posture, or inclination) is, rightly or wrongly, deduced from a position of external observation. Yet attitude, which some might argue to be totally lacking in objectivity, which is experienced as subjective, might well also constitute a 'durably installed' [2] *dis*-position - a 'state of mind' [3] liable to predetermine what sorts of options seem to be available, what sorts of actions might be taken, and from what sorts of positions. A mechanism, then, involving position, inflection, posture and inclination; constructed from the apparently intangible but liable to determine certain sorts of orientations, certain sorts of observations, the sense that certain sorts of options are available, reasonable and appropriate, and others not. If we are concerned with *who knows*, and *who cares* (about performance mastery) in relation to certain sorts of inclinations, actions and interpretations, then we are dealing not simply with episteme, but with technê, which in Aristotelian philosophy, according to Richard Parry, 'is itself also *epistêmê* or knowledge because it is a practice grounded in an "account" - something involving theoretical understanding' (Parry 2003).

When some of us look back from a future time at some of the curiosities of the second half of the twentieth century - as did Hal Foster, with the tools he had available, from its final decade - we might note not simply the historically-specific emergence and widespread expansion of a 'textual *turn*', said to have 'refashioned much art and criticism on the model of the text' (with

certain ongoing implications [4]), but, progressively, an 'interdisciplinary *turn*' [5], an 'ethnographic *turn*' [6], a 'visual turn' [7], and, more recently, a 'practice *turn*'. (Schatzki, Knorr Cetina and Savigny 2001). Turn - and turn again: turns might be said to articulate dispositions and to include inclinations as well as orientations; turns might well be attitudinally marked, as much as some would argue that they are ideologically in-formed, productive and reproductive. In Hal Foster's account, the 'textual turn', applied in the specific context of contemporary (visual) art practices, was viewed, from the final decade of the twentieth century, both as symptom of an ongoing trouble, and as one for which the writer himself could propose no cure. Some of us, in other words, *suffer the turns* within which we are caught up.

Knowledge (of turns), from this perspective, does not necessarily heal ancient attitude in present-day writers. In this paper I qualify successive *turns*, produced by expert-writers and educators within the university, as constitutively ambiguous: while each has seemed, momentarily, to provide a coping mechanism for and to illuminate some aspect of the 'knowledge-political problematic' posed, for the university, by writing's other, each has nonetheless failed expert practitioners, to the extent that each turn, '*in turn*', has been unable to reach those parts of academic writers where ancient inclinations, dispositions, postures, prejudices and ways of seeing are lodged. Academic writers are themselves masters of certain sorts of practice modes, after all, and they bring writing's technê - its inclinations and its virtues together with its mechanisms - as well as its epistêmê, to their task.

From the point of view of the history of academic (*writerly* and *pedagogic*) turns, then, I am proposing that we consider (the knowledge-problematic posed by) virtuosity and performance mastery in the university, not simply as a matter of a disciplinary expertise whose name has largely been erased from the discourses (and aspirations) of Performance Studies [8] (while remaining central to ongoing and widely-celebrated activity in performance-making), but as (academic) writing's *trouble* in the later twentieth century [9]. That trouble is best represented, here, by widespread uses in performance writing of the casually abusive, generalizing, deprofessionalizing and anonymizing term 'the body'. Uses of the term 'the body' are contagious, as we have seen in the emergence of Dance Studies over recent decades, where they infect expert dancers-become academic researchers, as well as expert dance-critical writers. More importantly, in the present situation, is the fact that widely-proliferating uses of the term 'the body' betray a posture, an inclination, a positioning, an attitude and a thematization, which are not those of 'the practitioner' *at work*, but specific, rather, to the (expert and objectifying) spectator-contemplator, to spectator theories of knowledge, to shifting (if not fickle) spectator attitude and to her modes of (discursive) productivity.

1 I am not 'Darcey Bussell' (or, 'the *turn* of "the body"')

The 'knowledge-political problematic' to which Foster and I differently refer, above, is properly ancient; it was durably installed, in, through and for writing, from that moment when technê and epistêmê were formally named and separated, in ancient Greek wordage, such that the one was taken to stand for 'craft or art', and the other for 'knowledge'. In his six-part account of the fortunes of epistêmê and technê in the Ancient Greek - it ranges chronologically from the writing of Xenophon, via Plato, Aristotle and the Stoics, through to Alexander of Aphrodisias and Plotinus - Richard Parry indicates an ongoing contestation concerning the 'knowledge status' of technê:

> It is in Aristotle that we find the basis for something like the modern opposition between *epistêmê* as pure theory and *technê* as practice. Yet even Aristotle refers to *technê* or craft as itself also *epistêmê* or knowledge because it is a practice grounded in an 'account' - something involving theoretical understanding.

In my argument, which takes up the changing definition of 'theory' (as an account of / accounting for) appearing in Theodore Schatzki's 'millennial' *Practice Turn* ... (Schatzki, Knorr Cetina and Savigny 2001), technê might well be viewed as an *accounting for* expert practices, where that 'accounting for', will tend in the first instance to be other than discursive - although it may well include the verbal elements of orality - prior to discourse, except in those instances where what is at stake is the expert or disciplinary practice of writing itself. Rather than discursively accounted-for, the expert accounting (or 'theoretical practice') of technê is articulated, and elaborated, by the expert practitioner's *undertaking them* (*appropriately*). Disciplinary appropriateness is part of

techne and involves a range of material mechanisms and productive and evaluative apparatuses - not least those through which spectators identify and adjudge production values, the qualities particular to the event, 'professionalism', radical performance-making, liminality and/or 'cultural performance' (McKenzie 2001), and 'good (or 'bad') acting'. Appropriateness can be as readily identified in the master craftswork of Mnouchkine's *1789*, in The Wooster Group's *To You, The Birdie*, as it can in Wheeldon's *Tryst*, danced by Jonathon Cope and Darcey Bussell for the Royal Ballet. Darcey Bussell's artistry and signature practice, by the way, not least in Wheeldon's choreographic im-press for *Tryst* (1990) is doubly ill-served by dance writing, once when it is excluded by Dance Studies because of the institutional set-up that enables its invention, and a second time when that signature practice in its complexity is identified in terms of 'the body', "the [knowing or articulate] body', the 'body-knowing' or 'body memory' - through which sorts of verbal tactics some dance writers have tried (foolishly, to my eye) to identify dance mastery in terms of body (rather than brain). I have observed elsewhere that to the extent that Darcey Bussell and I are both professionals, and that we both 'have bodies', and practise our expertise in public, the term 'the body' should be applied as readily to my performances as to hers ... I come back to this issue of the specificity of disciplinary mastery in section 3, below, in order to suggest that our different ('embodied') expert performances activate quite different parts of our brains.

For the moment, I want to argue that disciplinary mastery and expert practice, *always* informed and conditioned by judgement, and often affectively-invested, accounts for, by enacting and by elaborating (and reaffirming) them, its own knowledges. Even Plato, Parry argues, 'whose theory of forms seems an arch example of pure theoretical knowledge - nevertheless is fascinated by the idea of a kind of *technê* that is informed by knowledge of forms' (Parry 2003). In the Stoics (who judged themselves to be 'proficients', and for whom the four virtues of insight, bravery, self-control and justice are founded upon reason, and so upon knowledge) we find the idea 'that virtue is a kind of *technê* or craft of life, one that is based on an understanding of the universe'. There is, then, 'an intimate positive relationship between *epistêmê* and *technê*, in these ancients, 'as well as a fundamental contrast'. It is in Alexander, whose writings are thought to have emerged in the period 198–209 AD, that a change begins to be marked: 'wisdom is knowledge without practical utility, an end in itself' (except of course in the late-twentieth-century university, where research audit means that the concrete performances of knowledge are quantified, qualified and rewarded). In his commentary on the Aristotelian tradition, Parry notes that 'Alexander interprets ... arguments [on the knowledge-status of *technê*] as showing that pure knowledge is superior to action'. 'But there is a difference', Parry adds, 'between the claim that there is a kind of knowledge which is an end in itself and the claim that pure knowledge is superior to action':

> The latter idea is a distinct development in thinking about the relation between knowledge and craft. This development rests on the notion that action implies need and it is better to be without need. So knowledge that fills no need is superior to action, which fills some need or other. We see this idea at work in the auxiliary arguments which Alexander offers to back up or explicate claims made in Aristotle's text. For instance, when Alexander first claims that Aristotle means to show that knowledge is more honorable than action, he says that action aims at some end other than itself.

Action might be honourable or virtuous, to the extent that it 'has no end outside itself', yet for Alexander, Parry notes, 'even virtuous actions have reference to the passions':

> Divine beings, who are without passions, have no need of virtue. Those who have passions need the virtues in order to control the passions (*In Metaph*. 2, 1-10). Obviously, to have passions is to be in need.

Arts-disciplinary performance mastery is teleo-affective [10], in the sense that it is driven in part, and in the event, by the aspiration to shared affective experience, one aspect of which, for the expert performer herself, is qualitative transformation – which performers may well allude to in commonsensical terms such as 'stretching myself', 'risk-taking', 'getting something [unexpected] out of me'. Affect (and the teleo-affective) is bound up in the Old French *parformer* or 'accomplish', to the extent that the latter is striven after, and only ever achieved in part, in momentary instantiations, unlike the aspiration to qualitative transformations that drives them (Knorr Cetina 2001). On the other hand when, in passing, Parry notes, 'Aristotle says that one might justifiably think that wisdom is beyond human ability because in many ways human nature is in slavery', it is Alexander who qualifies 'slavery' by saying that humans are slaves in that they 'need such things as health and prosperity. But [that] what is divine is free of all need (*In Metaph*. 17, 15-20)'. From this perspective, virtuosity in its fragility and its aspiration exceeds performance mastery, yet it is 'in' performance mastery to the extent that the expert practitioner chases angels, to the extent that the expert practitioner seeks that degree of qualitative transformation that enables her to continue to work, and to work in speculative rather than merely elaborative mode. The divine, in our late-pragmatic age, lies in striving for the performance exemplary, the exceptional, the singular experience shared in the public event (Massumi 2002).

2 Becoming Liz LeCompte (or, 'the emergent turn')

Will registering for advanced Performance Studies enable me to *become Liz LeCompte*? Performance singularity, expert mastery and the performance divine (or chasing angels [11]) are both incommensurable with certain dominant discourses and preferred practices of a Performance Studies that struggled to emerge in the university in the later decades of the twentieth century, and they lurk within these, where they are widely misrecognized (closet virtuosity) as such. I have qualified this observation with 'certain', because the sum of Performance Studies is internally differentiated rather than uniform.

Not simply 'internally differentiated': Performance Studies includes practices and attitudes still informed and/or coloured by 'the collapse of the distinction ... between critical-theoretical reflection and creative practice', celebrated by Gregory Ulmer (1985) in the mid-1980s, alongside both the (democratically-inflected) *pedestrian turn* – the pedestrian arts [12] of performance in everyday life – and the performance expertise of the expert, signature practitioner whose work educators attempt to display to and critique as though on behalf of our students. My observation is that these dominant discourses and practices of Performance Studies are actually constitutively ambiguous to the extent that they are informed by the Beuysian 'everyone an artist!', by an ongoing and unresolved anti-institutionality and by the celebration of the singularity of the proper-named, hence marketable, signature practitioner.

Constitutive ambiguity is not simply the mark of a broad church. Rather, the assemblage of apparatuses and mechanisms that produce performance studies writing (its *technê*) includes exclusivist positioning, inclination, dispositifs (or set-ups), attitude and triumphalist posturing, to such an extent that the study of performance (as distinct from Performance Studies) is split apart and fails to communicate internally.

When Ulmer writes with such ease, then, in his timely *Internet and Invention: From Literacy to Electracy*, that 'Joseph Beuys demonstrated how to **do theory** as sculpture, or rather, **as craft**, working with felt and fat,

researching their reality or "Gestalt'" (my emphases), in order to examine 'such materials as figures or relays for a theory of social organization ("social sculpture" [Ulmer 2003: 35])". I find it even more difficult to move on in my reading than I did when Foster, above, worded a ready distinction between a set of practices nominalized (hence ontologized) in terms of 'art', and another set identified as 'criticism', in order to proceed then to declare that in that particular framework, 'theoretical production became as important as artistic production' (Foster 1999: xiv). Writing becomes opaque for me, at these sorts of *turns*, rather more than it serves to illuminate for me one or another aspect of the expert or disciplinary or professional performance mastery about which I remain inexhaustibly curious.

In Ulmer's writing particular words, and the combinatory sets in which they appear, are rendered opaque to me: '*doing* theory' – hence practising 'it' (whatever that 'it' might refer to) – starts well; 'theory *as craft*' is crafty in its own way; but his 'materials as figures or relays *for a theory of*', not only renominalizes 'theory', but locates it in a particular, hierarchical relation to what is given as its object ('social organization'). There are effects and causes aplenty here, and I find it hard not to conclude that in Ulmer *the writer* the nominalized and hypostasized 'theory' is given as independent (and arguably transcendent) of the material practices given as the means to its effect. '[A] theory of social organization' is provided here *by a writer* (positioned, inclined and predisposed, as professional writers tend to be, to belief in the orders of writing), as the objective of the consummately expert, singular, signature-art practitioner's material engagement.

I wonder if there might not be a lesson here that I might

learn *to the end of my becoming Liz LeCompte, expert arts practitioner?* Or is it actually the case that, *educator-writer that I am*, and regardless of the happy notion of emergence, my technê means that I will continue to 'experience [performance expert] entities as independent of [my] instrumental coping practices'? Writers concerned with the 'practice turn' have noted that this happens in cases of 'equipmental breakdown', where the understanding of equipment as 'available' is replaced by an understanding of equipment in terms of 'occurrentness'. 'Occurrent beings', Dreyfus notes, are revealed in their apparently independent 'resistant materiality', whenever a blockage to constructive process or breakdown occurs. At such a moment, we suddenly experience these occurrent entities as substances with properties, independent of our own being, attitude, inclination and doing, and as a consequence a *wholly constitutive and professional anxiety comes into the practice framework* – whether 'we' are expert writers '*about performance*' or expert arts practitioners.

The emergent anxiety, constitutive of certain stages then in certain sorts of multi-participant creative practices as well as of expert writing '*about*' its other, tends to 'disclose ... beings in their full but heretofore concealed strangeness as what is radically other' (Heidegger 1977:105, cited by Dreyfus 2001). That anxiety, and what results from it, is included in a Heideggerian account (technê) of ordered 'coping strategies', which range from an initial 'absorbed coping' to 'envisaging'; from envisaging to 'deliberate coping' (Knorr Cetina 2001). A 'concerned coping' will precede the emergence of a 'detached attitude' in the practitioner, which is identified in Heideggerian terms as 'deworlding'. It is 'deworlding' and its detachments – the shift into an objectifying position from within complex creative processes themselves – that will allow us to seem to cope by introducing a process of thematization which Knorr Cetina describes as 'itself a form of [expert] practice'. Yet 'thematization', for all that it is a form of practice, and regardless of the fact that it is in thematization that expert practitioners meet across disciplines, and communicate, is not prioritized in those sorts of expert practice that professionally employ not just the currently fashionable 'embodiment', but a professional multi-dimensional (and often multi-participant, parallactic) schematics that provides a range of micro- as well as macro-*measures*. It is through the ceaseless operation of these measures (brought by the disciplinary set-up, rather more than by the urge to overtake it) that actional choices are grasped, made, tested and modulated in the processes leading up to performance events. But I want to come briefly back to choice-making in expert practice in my conclusion.

3 The Limits of (expert) Writing (or, in/adequate descriptions of equipmental operations)

I can't dance, don't ask me. –
Jerome Kern

To make new work, one should 'personalize ... a composed singularity of vital movements in [such] a way that it could collectively spread.
Brian Massumi (in Melrose 2003)

Certain of us 'deworld' more readily than others, not least when there are political issues at stake (such as argument for the 'knowledge status' of expert performance practice and mastery in the university). If my argument that anciently-inflected *attitude* to performance mastery continues to resonate through the ways in which some of us, with the very best of intentions, approach expert disciplinary practices, then we are caught up in something finer and more insidious than knowledge-political argument can overcome. It is on this sort of basis that I have intuited the need to exit from some of the available cultural studies discourses, within which, on the strength of emerging *turns*, I might otherwise seem to be dancing on the spot. Intuition is no stranger to certain processes in academic writing, even if it remains the case that it has been largely overlooked as a vital *professional* tool specific to the techne of practitioner expertise. I often enough experience the shiver of insight, when 'the materials of a disciplinary problem are brought into sudden unexpected relationship' (Ulmer 1994) with other process elements at work, to want to keep on working. My point of departure, here, is the banal (but politically delicate) conviction that expert practitioners, working to professional criteria, are differently 'wired' [13] from those lacking that expertise, coupled with the *sense* that I need different means, from those available via one or another cultural-studies trope, to make that case effectively.

When Ulmer wrote in the early 1990s that memory stores information (and, I am assuming, the knowledges specific to professional expertise) in 'emotional sets', on the basis of 'common feelings ... based in eccentric, subjective, idiosyncratic physiognomic perceptions' (Ulmer 1994: 142–3), he had not had the 'benefit' of reading the findings published in 2004 and relating to fMRI scanning and data analysis. The observations coming from cognitive neuroscience when it interfaces with professional dance practices are appropriately tentative: 'When we watch someone performing an action, our brains may simulate performance of the action we observe', and '[t]his simulation process could underpin' – 'underpin' marks the difficulties of writing – 'sophisticated mental functions ...'. Now, for myself, I'd prefer not to have introduced the qualifier 'mental', since I have no idea whatsoever what these cognitive neuroscientists mean by the term. Nonetheless, I persist:

> The network underlying [sic] human action observation seen in functional magnetic resonance imaging (fMRI) includes premotor cortex, parietal areas and the superior temporal sulcus ... The supplementary motor area and motor cortex are typically not activated, unless an element of movement preparation is also involved. (Calvo-Merino, et al. 2005: 1)

'This might suggest', note the writers, 'that action observation' (such as occurs when a professional choreographer works with trained dancers) 'activates only high-level [sic] motor representations, at one remove from actual motor commands'.

> However, transcranial magenetic stimulation (TMS) studies suggest that action observation *can* directly influence the final cortical stage of action control in the motor cortex ... [The results obtained] suggest a brain process of motor simulation based on direct correspondance between the neural codes for action observation [in the expert practitioner] and for execution.

Aha! As Ulmer notes, if 'an emotional set occurs' – in, for example, practitioner experience in devising – 'which is similar to the original "problem" emotional set, ... then a new link is made. [A] pathway is opened up and the present "solution" emotional set is combined with the "problem" emotional set (Bastick 1982). What the new combining of emotional sets effects is, in the best of cases, a 'recentring insight, characterized by recognition of the possible solution'.

A 'sudden recognition' of this sort, Ulmer goes on, ' ... produces a strong feeling of certainty, of being "right", a feeling of knowing' and an operation of judgement vital to the production of performance work. Together these operations themselves produce different and tentative action options, and will lead to choices made which, where they are retained, are likely to be experienced by all participants as different degrees of release in the tension and anxiety to which Dreyfus and other practise-turn writers have drawn attention. Nonetheless, Ulmer's account, like those emerging later from writers of the 'practice turn', might seem to lack a vital factor that might take their insights beyond the speculative, linked to human activity in general, into the order of the *speculative-singular and exemplary*, linked to expert or disciplinary arts-making practices. From this perspective, then, the writers observe – in terms that are carefully limited – that '[a] particular action may figure in the motor repertoire of a trained expert but not in the motor repertoire of someone [such as an expert spectator] who has not been so trained':

> We tested this hypothesis using a factorial fMRI design in which expert ballet and capoeira dancers watched videos of ballet and capoeira movements. In this way, both groups of expert subjects saw identical action stimuli, but only had motor experience of the actions of their own dance style.

The 'motor repertoire' seems to me to be limiting, inasmuch as the researchers' concern is with expert and inexpert observations of expert action and not with what might emerge from expert observation coupled with the production of new work, and/or with writing 'about'. Nor can it help us with an account of the ways in which expert observation links through to invention – in the signature practices of a choreographer like Wheeldon, or Butcher, or Brandstrup. Nonetheless, I persist: in the course of this carefully controlled experiment [14], then, 'any differences [observed] between groups of [trained] dancers must reflect effects of expertise on action observation, and not on the representation of the object or location to which the action is directed'. A third control group was also tested, in order to determine whether or not 'non-expert control subjects [might] show similar [brain] activity when watching either style of dance'. The results of a series of carefully controlled experiments suggested that the brain's mirror system is sensitive to 'much more abstract levels of action observation, such as those that differentiate dance styles' executed by experts, than had previously been thought by cognitive neuroscientists. Not only 'much more abstract levels', however: '[O]ur results show that the [brain's] mirror system is concerned with observing skilled movements, not muscles' as such, and 'are linked to [those] *learned* motor skills' which figure so strongly in the expert practitioner's knowledge system. If past research in the same field had suggested 'that premotor cortex may encode detailed action plans for complex movement ...', the writers add, '[o]ur results suggest *such action plans may also be activated by action observation*' (my emphasis). Finally, then,

> we identified a second set of areas influenced by expertise ... consistent with other findings relating these areas to emotional experience ... [T]his area is routinely activated in emotion processing ... In particular, it shows strong responses to pleasurable and rewarding stimuli ... Second [it has been suggested] that this area contributes to social judgement and the regulation of social

behaviour ... [Third, the] influence of expertise on cingulate, retrosplenial and parahippocampal activation is also consistent with these areas' role in episodic memory ... The greater familiarity of experts with their own movement style may lead to stronger activation of brain mechanisms of episodic memory, even when watching another [expert at work].

The influence of expertise, they conclude, 'suggests that, taken together as a network, activation of...midline areas reflects a combination of episodic memory processes and the *degree of engagement* between the viewer and the stimuli during action observation' (my emphasis). It follows that:

> the parietal and premotor cortex system does not respond simply to visual kinematics of body movement, but transforms visual inputs into the specific motor capabilities of the observer. While all the subjects in our study saw the same actions, the mirror areas of their brains responded quite differently [and were illuminated or not] according to whether they could do the actions ...

Not just doing, then, but *doing in expert (and potentially singular) manner*, in the cases that interest me. That is, in ways which engage a number of areas of brain activity in the expert practitioner-observer and which work the interface, calling upon the intuitive processing as well as the established repertoire and the logics of performance production, specific to arts-disciplinary expertise. When, therefore, the choreographer Kim Brandstrup writes, first, about dance-making processes, that 'a dancer's specialized sense of the duration of motion and sound in space and time is an analytic competence, in the way that a sense of pitch is to a musician', and, second, that '[i]n my perception of each passing moment [in choreographic activity] I feel there is a fleeting sensorial echo prompting my anticipation of what will follow' [15], he is writing on the basis of twenty to thirty years of expert, professional activity. On this basis, although we sit together to watch a rehearsal, and watch with a similar intensity of attention to detail, I am pleased to be able to conclude that 'watching dancers at work' reaches parts of his expert-practitioner's brain – where practical expertise, the repertoire of already-existing dance options, the aspiration to qualitative transformation, affective investment and judgement intertwine – that in my own *were never developed*. [16] On the other hand, when in 'Objectual Practice' (2001:187) Knorr Cetina approaches creative and constructive 'epistemic practices' in terms of a relational idiom linked to the researcher's own position within an 'interlocking structure or chain of wantings'

and when she writes, then, about the researcher's own technê, I am equally happy to conclude that it is in the experience of this interlocking chain of wantings, which 'entails the possibility of a deep emotional investment in [research] objects', that the brain activities of the expert choreographer as researcher and mine meet. This is a meagre beginning, but it's a beginning, for all that. Attitudinal change will tend to follow, slowly, as we acquire the means to step outside of the various turns and tropes of twentieth century critical and cultural theoretical writing.

NOTES

1. The simplest answer to my opening question is The Centre for Performance Research, whose mixed-mode public enquiries into performance mastery are internationally renowned. The first essay taking this title was presented at a symposium held at Middlesex University in 2003, and can be found at <http://www.mdx.ac.uk/www/epai/>

2 Bourdieu defines habitus, which contributes to attitude and actional potential, as 'durably installed'; see, for example, Pierre Bourdieu, *Outline of a Theory of Practice* (1977).

3. I use the term 'mind' here with misgiving, since I remain unconvinced by the various attempts at definition. Nonetheless, the 'durably installed' must be installed in a 'somewhere' of the human brain. See Joseph Dumit 2004 for a critical enquiry into some of the terms of this debate.

4. Notions such as the '*text* of the stage', the '*discourse* of the mise en scene', and '*reading* theatre', are actually afterimages of the *textual* turn applied to theatre and performance.

5. Peter Osborne (see 2000) has written about some of the excesses of the interdisciplinary turn and its reduction of heterogeneous practices to a single, 'post-Saussurean' model.

6. Texts representing the ethnographic turn emerged after James Clifford's mid-1980s critical enquiry into writing in anthropology and ethnography. See, for example, Alex Coles 2000.

7. Few writers engage critically, from within Performance Studies, with the 'visual turn', even if it is the case that performances are only a matter of visual culture to those who spectate upon them (as distinct from performing within them). Recent indicative texts include Barbara Stafford 1999 and Gary Shapiro 2003.

8. There are notable exceptions here, in the work of Phillip Zarrilli (see for example 2000a, 2000b, 1995), Eugenio Barba and the various activities, publications and events of CPR itself.

9. The later twentieth century was still characterized both by the hermeneutics of suspicion and by certain expectations with regard to the ways in which the ideological function of certain modes of arts-expert practice might be identified in and by writing.

10. I owe the term to Theodore Schatzki (2001), who fails however to develop it in that volume.

11. <http://www.sfmelrose.u-net.com/chasingangels/> (2003)

12. A number of academic writers in recent years, myself included, have taken up the complex tropes (and the political implications) of de Certeau's writing: see especially Alan Read 1992 and Nick Kaye 2000.

13. I acknowledge that the trope in turn conceals a knowledge-gap, as did 'cognitive mapping', in its day – in Frederic Jameson's writing the cognitive map is 'that mental map of the social and global totality we all carry around in our heads in variously garbled forms'.

14. The writers point out that the research activity, which focused on nineteen professional dancers and ten non-expert control subjects, was carried out according to the protocol approved by the Ethics Committee of the Institute of Neurology, London.

15. K. Brandstrup and N. Pollard, unpublished, 2005.

16. I would argue that they never could have been developed in terms of the criteria applied to the assessment of professional expertise in the arts-disciplinary fields.

REFERENCES

Bastick, Tony (1982) *Intuition: How We Think and Act,* New York: John Wiley.

Bourdieu, Pierre (1977) *Outline of a Theory of Practice,* (trans. R. Nice), Cambridge: Cambridge University Press.

Calvo-Merino, B., Glaser, D. E., Grezes, J., Passingham, R. E. and Haggard, P. (2005) 'Action Observation and Acquired Motor Skills: An fMRI Study with Expert Dancers', *Cerebral Cortex,* Oxford: Oxford University Press.

Coles, Alex (ed.) (2000) *Site-Specificity: The Ethnographic Turn,* de-,dis-,ex-, Vol.4, London: Black Dog Publishing Ltd.

Dreyfus, Hubert (2001) 'How Heidegger defends the possibility of a correspondence theory of truth with respect to the entities of natural science', in Schatzki, Knorr Cetina and Savigny (eds.) (2001) *The Practice Turn in Contemporary Theory,* London and New York: Routledge.

Dumit, Joseph. (2004) *Picturing Personhood: Brain Scans and Biomedical Identity,* Princeton and Oxford: Princeton University Press.

Foster, Hal (1996) *The Return of the Real: The Avant-Garde at the End of the Century,* Cambridge and London: MIT Press.

Heidegger, Martin (1977) *The Question Concerning Technology and Other Essays,* trans. W. Lovitt, New York: Harper Torchbooks.

Kaye, Nick (2000) *Site-specific Art,* London and New York: Routledge.

Knorr Cetina, Karin (2001) 'Objectual Practice', in T. Schatzki, K. Knorr Cetina and E. von Savigny (eds.), *The Practice Turn in Contemporary Theory,* London and New York: Routledge.

Massumi, Brian. (2002) *Parables for the Virtual: Movement, Affect, Sensation,* Durham and London: Duke University Press.

McKenzie, Jon. (2001) *Perform ... or Else: From Discipline to Performance,* London and New York: Routledge.

Melrose, Susan (2003)<http://www.sfmelrose.u-net.com/chasingangels/>

Osborne, Peter (2000) *Philosophy in Cultural Theory,* London and New York: Routledge.

Parry, Richard. (Summer 2003) '*Episteme* and *Techne*' in Edward N. Zalta (ed.) *The Stanford Encyclopedia of Philosophy,* http://plato.stanford.edu/archives/sum2003/entries/episteme-techne/

Read, Alan (1992) *Theatre and Everyday Life,* London and New York: Routledge.

Schatzki, Theodore, Knorr Cetina, Karin. and von Savigny, Eike. von (eds.) (2001) *The Practice Turn in Contemporary Theory,* London and New York: Routledge.

Schatzki, Theodore (2001) 'Practice Mind-ed Orders', in T. Schatzki, K. Knorr Cetina and E. von Savigny (eds.), *The Practice Turn in Contemporary Theory,* London and New York: Routledge,

Shapiro, Gary (2003) *Archaeologies of Vision: Foucault and Nietzsche on Seeing and Saying,* Chicago and London: University of Chicago Press.

Stafford, Barbara M. (1999) *Visual Analogy: Consciousness as the Art of Connecting,* Cambridge and London: MIT Press.

Ulmer, Gregory (1985) *Applied Grammatology: Post(e)-Pedagogy from Jacques Derrida to Joseph Beuys,* Baltimore and London: Johns Hopkins University Press.

Ulmer, Gregory (1994) *Heuretics: The Logic of Invention,* Baltimore and London: Johns Hopkins University.

Ulmer, Gregory (2003) *Internet and Invention: From Literacy to Electracy,* New York: Longman.

Wheeldon, Charles. (1990) *Tryst,* Dancers: Darcy Bussell and Jonathan Cope, London: Royal Opera House; Music © 1990 James Macmillan, performed by the Scottish Chamber Orchestra.

Zarrilli, Phillip (ed.) (1995) *Acting (Re)Considered: Theories and Practices,* London and New York: Routledge.

Zarrilli, Phillip (2000) *When the Body Becomes All Eyes: Paradigms, Practices and Discourses of Power in Kalarippayattu, A South Indian Martial Art,* Oxford: Oxford University Press.

Zarrilli, Phillip (2000) *Kathakali Dance-Drama: Where Gods and Demons Come to Play,* London and NY: Routledge.

VIDEO IMAGES (page 133) Photos © Rosemary Butcher
Eun Hi Kim, performing in Rosemary Butchers 'The Return' (2004/5: unpublished). Eun Hi is dance-trained, to professional standard, even though the work produced might well not be identified by the spectator, as 'dance', as such.

According to Butcher, that dance-training, and the performer's (professional) singularity, are vital to her own ongoing enquiry into the means to transfer dance-disciplinary specificity to the screen. Equally vital is Butcher's recourse to the post-production work of the independent film-maker, Martin Otter. Butcher works here between different instances of disciplinary mastery, and the production values that apply in each instance. She takes these as given. In performative terms, she seeks to draw the spectator's attention to (and thereby to constitute) the sight of 'someone experiencing something, over time'. On just what that 'something' might be, the artist remains wholly reticent.

Incomplete Alphabet Some notes after twenty years of Forced Entertainment

Introduction

In what follows the words that start with A come first, those that start with B come second, etc., but within the category of any particular letter, the sequence is not strictly alphabetical. Like I need the structure of the lexicon, but I'm not fully prepared to live with its tyranny.

Audience

In the first five years we could not deal with the audience directly, more or less pretending, in the construction of the work, that they were not there. These early shows – with heavy cinematic soundtracks and room-like stage constructions creating a sense of fictional 'elsewhere' – almost had the fourth wall in place. Dynamics were across the stage – play structures, game or ritual structures, which meant that the performance personas could be caught up in their own logic, their own reasons for doing things above and beyond the presence of the audience. 'Private reasons' as we used to say, half joking to explain the events, 'private reasons'. The audience was simply a witness to a set of compulsions, actions or whims and their consequences played out between the performers.

In the later work, though, (from say *Speak Bitterness* in 1995 through *First Night* in 2001 and even *Bloody Mess* in 2004) the audience has often come at the very top of our agenda. Indeed, perhaps the format of the chorus-like line-up – all performers at the front of the stage and addressing the public directly in turns – has been the most common recurring structure, appearing in project after project, especially as a way to begin. Here at the top of the show, the line-up is an act of mutual revelation and confirmation for both performers and audience – we are all here, all in place, all present and correct. The performers are stood before you in a line at the edge of the stage. You, at the same time are all there in the auditorium, sat in your rows and facing us. A blank face-off. The moment at the start of the football match where the two teams stand for the national anthems, gazing at the crowd. The zero of theatre. Us facing them. Them facing us. Watching. Waiting, ready. A space of expectation.

It is 24 April 2004 at 15:39 p.m. I face the computer screen that, by the time you read this, will have become a page. You face the page. We watch each other for a moment. Imagining. And then it begins.

From time to time as this essay unfolds we will return to this face-off. The zero of our situation. My speaking, writing. Your reading me, witnessing. And between us a space that shifts and undulates, sometimes appearing as a vast unbridgeable distance, sometimes as an almost traversable microscopic fraction.

This, my love, my enemy, my friend, my stranger, is performance.

Absence

Inside the theatre there are only the performers and the audience. Onstage the performers have some material items – flimsy or not-so-flimsy scenery, various props and costume stuff. The audience, for their part, have their coats and their handbags and the contents of their pockets. But that's all. *The whole of the rest of the world* – its physical locations and landscapes, its entire population, its complete set of objects and its unfolding events – is invariably outside, *emphatically absent.*

Theatre then must always (?) be: the summoning of presence in the context of absence. A bringing in of the world.

Blankness

I am watching her sleep, in Brussels, in the hotel, her face toward the pillow and shrouded in her hair. Unable to 'read' this blankness, this lack of information, *I imagine her.*

In many ways we saw theatre increasingly as a space for projection, a projection occasioned always by blankness, by lack of information, by repetition, by silence. Constructed through the manipulation and coding of these deliberate emptinesses, the stage is a screen – the viewer both projectionist and audience. The other, before you, can never be known. Only guessed at. Mistaken. Projected upon.

I think of the unreadable faces of Jerome Bel's dancers as they look towards the audience in *the show must go on* ... I think of the extraordinary stillness and blankness of Raimund Hoghe's masterpiece *Meinwarts*. I think of the darkness and the deserted stage that one faces from time to time in Elevator Repair Service's *Room Tone*, and of the timed silence in our own work *Bloody Mess*. As if theatre in the end were only a set of emptinesses, left there to be filled by the viewer.

What did Peter Handke say in *The Story of the Pencil*?

'The best thing, storyteller: get others, gently, to tell stories. Make this your goal. And do it in a way that, afterwards, they feel that they had a story told to them, a wonderful one.'

Editing

In the end perhaps we had only two tools, two modes - the elemental now-ness of improvising and its more considered afterwards of editing.

For us improvising was always an unbroken timeline, a block of pure contingency, pure causality. The clock ticks as performers hoist themselves by their own bootstraps, surfing the silence with a stuttering ebb and flow of actions and texts, finding something, anything, to do. Building from impulses and lucky chances to consolidation and achievement, this architecture of improvisation passes temporary blocks, boredoms and periods of slender progress before these, too, give way to new discoveries or extraordinary moments. In its pure form - in the rehearsal room, or in the improvised durational works like *Quizoola!* and And on the *Thousandth Night* ... - there is a tentativeness to this process, an organic rhythm of failure, discovery, consolidation and eventual collapse that a spectator feels (knows, intuits) is real. Things, as I'll no doubt say later when it comes to 'T', take their own time.

In creating the theatre work, our task shifts eventually from improvising to editing. In this later phase we cut, shift and change material that has been generated in real-time improvisation into a new place in a controlled repeatable structure. In this transformation, the material - forged in a particular moment - is taken from its context and its true place in time, in order to be defined, altered and replayed at the service of a larger dramaturgy.

The trick of this, the true craft of it, at least as we have pursued it over twenty years, has been to treat the raw material with considerable respect. Not just to cherry-pick the 'best bits' from improv, but to look as well to the context - at the dynamics of the emerging conversation between performers, or the sequence of unfolding events and associations that might have led

to or framed something beautiful, strange or hilarious. Collaging material from different sources and from the diverse sensibilities and intentionalities of many performers, we did not want an arbitrary or meaningless collection of fragments. We did not seek a world set loose from all logic. Instead, there, in the heart of what often looked chaotic, playful, preposterous, there was an extraordinary and scrupulous paying heed to context, reasons and interconnections.

Hours and hours and hours of scrutiny of the video tapes. Hours and hours of discussion about what went where and who went when and why.

Energy

It wasn't all intellect. In fact, at times theatre for us was hardly intellect at all. More often it was the wound, the cry, the thrash, the crash and burn or simply the complex layering of too much to look at too fast, too much at the same time, too many levels, layers, collisions of materials, discourses, sense. Go straight for the pit of the stomach, the heart, the balls. The raw post-apocalypse of Impact Theatre and Russel Hoban's *The Carrier Frequency*, the precise delirium of the Wooster Group's *L.S.D. Just the High Points*, the mood-swings of Anne Theresa De Keersmaker's *Stella*, the unflinching nightmare of Pina Bausch's *On Listening to a Recording of Bluebeard's Castle*. Each of these was a turning point for us, a pushing to or encounter with an edge.

As if the point you're looking for, the point the work must to get to, the point you are seeking in the theatre is the edge of discourse itself, something raw, direct and pure. Now, we would say, *now, now*, that's the point where it all starts to bite. Or no, we would say, of things we did not like, no, 'it never really bites'. There was Brecht in what we did and what we loved. But there was Artaud in there, too.

Forgetting

In *First Night* (2001) Terry stands firm in her high heels, sequined dress and rigor-mortis smile, imploring the audience not to think about the world outside the theatre, to try to forget all of the many worries, troubles, banalities and cares that might distract them from the disastrous vaudeville of the show as it stumbles and crashes on the stage before them. Her text, in the end, like so many other texts in our work, becomes a long list of things, in this case a catalogue of things that must not be thought about.

Forget about the wind rushing through trees and fire engines rushing to an accident. Try to forget about rivers flooding and cars – cars on a motorway piling into one another. Try to forget about footsteps walking on pavements and broken heels. And poison and rusty knives. And guns. Try not to think about guns. And daggers and letter bombs. And nail bombs. And chemical warfare. Try not to think about chemical warfare. And chemotherapy. And the common cold. Try not to think about the common cold. And hospitals. And nurses. And surgeons and rubber gloves and trolleys and serums and cupboards. And expensive drugs that whole countries can't afford ...

The list continues some twelve to fifteen minutes, and as Terry speaks the public have no choice but to see, and to think of, the absent things that she mentions. Bringing in the world.

Names

The core group: Robin Arthur, Richard Lowdon, Claire Marshall, Cathy Naden, Terry O'Connor, and the person writing these words: Tim Etchells. Significant others: Huw Chadbourn, Deborah Chadbourn, Susie Williams, Tim Hall, Sue Marshall, John Rowley, Jerry Killick, Hugo Glendinning, John Avery, Nigel Edwards. And others of course. And then the rest of the world.

The obscene, the unspeakable

Sometime in 1997 I downloaded a list from the Internet: a catalogue of some 2,433 obscene words – slang and euphemisms for body parts, bodily fluids and sex acts.

Blow Job
Butt Fuck
Get Your Manhole Inspected
Gonads
Fist Your Monster

Like many obscene or unspeakable objects, the list combines the effect of both repulsion and attraction – an object that *must not be* and yet *cannot not be* seen. As the text printed for rehearsals of our project *Pleasure*, performers, technicians and the office team alike all gathered at the printer reading from the sheets of paper, reading out the most disgusting terms they could find, performing their amusement and repulsion, reading, reacting and shaking their heads to turn away and yet eagerly demanding each new sheet as it fell to the floor.

The obscene, the unspeakable – the thing that cannot but must be seen, the thing that cannot but must be said – these were driving forces in many of the shows. There were the excessive and grisly hysterias in *Hidden J* (1994) and *Bloody Mess* (2004) The predictions of death and personal disaster for the audience in *First Night* (2001), The blood-and-gore splattered bodies and faces in *Showtime* (1996), *Some Confusions ...* (1989) and *Let the Water ...* (1986). The methodical descriptions of accident, suicide and autopsy in *Dirty Work* (1998). The horrible violence and danger of *Club of No Regrets* (1993). Time and time again, we played our way to that edge of theatre that would have you turn your head away.

Even addressing the subject and situation of theatre itself, like moths drawn to a flame, we often tended to what we called the illegal: that which could not or should not be done in public, that which could not or should not be said. There were the playful extremities of abuse heaped on the audience in *First Night* and in *Showtime*. The near-chaos of collage-based pieces like *Marina & Lee* (1991) or *Bloody Mess*. The lack of immediately recognizable theatricality in documentary works like *Instructions for Forgetting* (2001) and *The Travels* (2002). The unexpected drunken privacy of the performers in *Disco Relax* (1999) and *Pleasure* – their faces turned down and away from those watching.

I remember the first days of *Pleasure* rehearsals where this drunken, slow-motion energy set in. As Terry and Cathy were dancing without apparent care to the sloweddown music from the record player at 16 rpm, Richard was making an indifferent introduction, eyes down and away from me saying 'Whatever, whatever, whatever, whatever ...' I simply could not believe that they were behaving like that in front of me. And I loved it.

Logic

And together we loved the consequent, too – the following of an idea or a structure through to its inevitable end. We loved the always particular and idiosyncratic logics that belonged to particular artists, works or fictional worlds. We loved works that avoided the arbitrary and, instead, had the courage of their convictions. The way that each good work (performance, book, film, whatever) constructs and at the same time speaks through its own logic, its own grammar. The work is the forging of a language, and a statement in it. And at the same time, perhaps most important, most political, of all, it is a question about language, meaning, culture, the social and how they operate.

Pause

We face each other again, you and I. The one of us reading, the other writing. It's late night for me now. Tired. In a different city than the one in which I began. I search for you. I search. I search for you, and these words like eyes flicker as they try to find and get the measure of your face. With one word or phrase, or another perhaps, maybe this one, we make eye contact. There is something that might be called 'electric' – a glimpse, a connection, a charge that passes between us. Then it's gone.

Performers/Process

Think about it this way. With each new project you are not creating a character, more creating a new version of yourself. As if the you of daily life has a series of ghosts, partial surrogates, doubles, echoes, remixes, even opposites that can exist, perhaps only in the unusual climates, landscapes, worlds of performance. You, stood naked in front of a curtain. You, 'drunk' and talking nonsense language. You, answering impossible questions. You, wearing a series of animal costumes. You, reading a text you have not seen before into a microphone while other people do unexpected things all around you. You don't create a fiction perhaps but rather, for each new project, articulate a version of yourself that can exist in that particular world, under that particular constraint, under that particular duress, a version of yourself that can exist in that particular unstable, strange, and semi-fictitious place of the stage.

You don't make someone else. You make *you*, if different, if exaggerated, if distorted, if shrunk, if restricted. But you, nonetheless. It is you that you make, it must be you that you make, because, when all is said and done, it's you that has to be to seen, shown, encountered, revealed.

Starting from 'nothing' in the rehearsal space on day one, there is nothing to guide the work except desire. The group as a collection of people, who agree to drift openly towards topics, images, themes, actions, texts. A falling in love. The pursuit of a certain openness.

You make you, and because of this your instincts are vital, your interests, your passions, your phobias. Not because you'll want to forget, hide or get over these facts of yourself in pursuit of the other, the fiction, the 'character' as perhaps they might have taught in other kinds of acting, but because, for the most part and with exceptions from time to time, your interests, passions, phobias and instincts alone can guide you. They'll be the basis of what you do, from show to show, from moment to moment.

A least favourite question from working with students: 'What do you want?' And a favourite answer: 'What have you got?'

Time

It takes us many years to realize that time, more than anything else, is what we are dealing with. The unfolding of actions over duration, the economy of events in the frame of hours, minutes, seconds and split-seconds. Our work, our trade, our business, like that of drug dealers, certain doctors and psychiatrists perhaps, musicians, filmmakers and choreographers is the slowing of time, the shattering of it, the stretching and the speeding of it. The forgetting of time, the strange yet necessary job of making time drip, pulse, echo, loop, freeze, shimmer, explode.

And if we were, as a strategy and as a manifesto commitment, offhand about the other materials in and with which we worked (crudely-hewn fragments of text, second-hand costumes, homemade props, a halogen lamp for lighting, a bunch of cardboard boxes stacked to make a wall), we learned that time at least could not be cheated or faked, that the good things (good shows, good actions, good gags, good moments, good lives, meaningful encounters) take their own time, the time they need.

Trash

A favourite dream was that all the material used in a particular project could be 'weightless', trash, nonsense or throw-away, but that somehow the arrangement of these pieces would make them sing. The dream was that somehow the fact of a work's arrangement alone could make it a hundred or a thousand times more articulate than any of its raw materials.

Thinking this way, performance for us was always closer to certain schools of painting or musical composition than it might be to drama. Less a case of narrative structure than an art form based on the dynamic deployment of pictorial and non-pictorial elements across the surface of a stage, building layers, contrasts, echoes, repetitions or the structured unfolding of text and image over time.

This fantasy show constructed from trash would resist scrutiny, so that any part of it, if pulled from the 'mess', would seem unsubstantial, weak, disposable, even absurd, but once placed back in the whole would continue to play its part in the confoundingly articulate structure. In some ways perhaps, each show we have ever made has been an attempt to realize this fantasy; some more overtly so than others.

Years

We are sat in someone's front room in Sheffield, watching a pornography of night-vision fragments punctuated with tracer fire (1991). We are watching back the video tape of a *Hidden J* rehearsal (1994), watching back the tape we shot in some terrible hotel corridor (1986), watching back the video tape of a *Club of No Regrets* rehearsal (1998), arguing about the rhythm of a section in *Nighthawks* (1985), playing fast-forward a tape of Richard and Claire pretending to fuck in the shower (1999). We are searching through a box for the tape of us walking through a small section of *First Night* on the stage in Rotterdamse Schouwburg (2001), watching back the tape of the first performance of *Who Can Sing a Song to Unfrighten Me?*, laughing so much at the antics on the stage in the recording that our motive in watching the thing is pretty well forgotten (1999). We are in a transit van (soundtrack quite possibly Tom Waits) (1984), we are in a theatre (2000), in a dressing room (1991), in bar late at night (1988), in a taxi to an airport (1989). We are walking in a strange city looking for a place where we can eat (2002), we are repeatedly drawing diagrams of the structure of a show on paper napkins (or on beer mats or in a notebook) in the corner of a small bar, with furrowed brows and shaking heads (soundtrack quite possibly The Fall) (1987). Or else we are in a restaurant, mentally rearranging scenes, sections and other elements of some performance or another, passing paper down the table to get a comment or a raised eyebrow from someone else (1990), we are drinking in the last Godforsaken bar left open in some town, wherever we are, whatever show we have just done (1998). We are covered in tomato ketchup (1986), tins of spaghetti (1996) and talcum powder (1989 and 1993), subjected to dousings in cold water (1993, 2004). We are blasted in fake blood (1986, 1989, 1993), subjected to showers of leaves (1993), or soap flakes (1988), or lager (1988, 1997, 1999) or half-chewed peanuts (1999). We are wearing ill-fitting second-hand clothes as costumes (1992), or we are dressed not even as humans but as animals (1997, 1999), or dressed not even as animals but as trees in brown painted cardboard cylinders (1996). We are bedecked in joke-shop plastic masks (1999), in pathetic party hats (1994). We are stripped naked and not looking great on it (1994). We are making reluctant confessions (1995), answering impossible questions (1996), telling improbable stories

(2000). We are looking foolish (1991), we are looking awkward (1999), we are looking weak (2000), we are looking nervous (1985), we are looking half drunk (2004), we are looking silly (1994), we are looking pretty stupid (2001). We are in a dressing room, playing cards or reading, talking about yet another pointless, twisted and incompetent war (1990). We are talking about some movie (1987) or about Bhopal (1984) or about some totally crap performance we saw, or about Columbine (1999). We are reading aloud from the newspaper one deception and one lie at a time, one outrageous description of atrocity after another, shaking our heads, making tasteless jokes (1995). We are hoping without hope. We are passing the bottle, yelling despondent abuse at the slew of idiot TV anchormen, pundits and commentators (1987, 1992, 1995, 2001, 2002, 2003, 2004).

Zero

The zero of theatre. The line-up at the front of the stage, this time at the end of the performance. Actors facing audience. Audience facing actors. Watching. Waiting. Thinking back on what has happened.

It is 2 Jan 2005 at 11:43 a.m., and I face the computer screen, which, by the time you read this, will have become a page. You face the page. We watch each other for a moment, as we have done from time to time in this encounter. Imagining. Thinking now about what has passed between us.

And then, with the last clicks and clatters of my fingers on the keyboard, the scanning movement of your eyes across the page and the unconscious movements of your lips as they shape these last unspoken words, it ends.

ACKNOWLEDGEMENT

An earlier version of this text, on video, formed my contribution to the LIFT enquiry in April 2004. A subsequent version was published in German in Theatre Heute later the same year.

Hounded Buildings:
Site, performance and traumatic memory

Performance sites are fragile spaces, prone to be affected by fire and urban development, shifts of the local economy, altered demography and occasionally by major upheavals and catastrophes. Traumatic memories assert themselves in and around those spaces, reshape them and modify their function. I am focusing here on two related, paradoxical cases, one from my post-Yugoslav exile in Amsterdam, another from my own remote ex-Yugoslav past.

1

Hollandse Schouwburg was erected in 1892 in the Plantage Middenlaan, the main street of a predominantly Jewish area of Amsterdam, housing some smaller entertainment venues. Exploited commercially, it offered a varied repertory of comedies, melodramas, revues and an occasional tragedy or drama. In 1940, after the Nazi occupation of the Netherlands, it became the only functioning theatre, accessible to Jews, both as performers and as spectators, in the newly established ghetto, an urban area sealed away with barbed wire and sentries from the rest of the city. In 1942, after most Amsterdam Jews were relocated in the ghetto, performances were discontinued and the venue became a deportation point. Deportations took place weekly, according to the lists made by the Jewish Council, a body whose function was stretched between self-governance and collaboration, for it sought to appease the Nazi authorities and tame their haste to make the Netherlands *Judenrein*. Entire families had to report in the theatre in the morning, carrying only minimal luggage, and were then taken by streetcars to the Muiderpoort station at the periphery of the city, from where a train took them to the Westerbork concentration camp in the north-east of the country, the last stop before Auschwitz. In this manner, 110,000 people were systematically deported in 1942–43, and only 6,000 came back.

Even after the deportations had started, a secret performance was taking place outside the playhouse, probably at dusk. I replay it in my imagination whenever I come to the site. I stand in front of the building where the Nazi guard stood. The streetcar comes from the left and stops at the street corner, blocking my view of the building across the street. It used to be a Jewish orphanage and it is still a daycare centre. During the occupation, the streetcar would cover the view of the Wehrmacht or SS soldier standing in front of the theatre, where I now stand. In that precious moment the students from the Walter Süskind underground network, hiding behind the corner, would dash to the door, grab a baby from the orphanage, offered by the staff in a precisely-timed operation, and disappear behind the corner into hiding before the streetcar started moving again. Many children were saved in that way, others disappeared via back alleys and courtyards. Today, passersby, hurrying to the nearby zoo, even the visitors of the monument are oblivious to this bizarre story, the replacement of some melodramatic scene unraveling on the stage (think of Sheridan's *Pizzaro*, for instance) by a condensed, rushed, real life, secret performance of far-reaching consequences, repeated daily with the passing of the streetcars. Until the orphanage was closed, its staff and orphans also deported in 1943.

After the liberation, the theatre was hastily destroyed, except its street façade and the entrance lobby, as if physical traces of the collecting point were unbearable to the survivors and yet impossible to erase completely. Or perhaps because the reminder of the original theatre function devalued the piety that was to be assigned to the place for its role in the holocaust. Perhaps the back of the building was destroyed because evidently it could never be used again as a performance site, its role in the deportation process pre-empting the restitution of the original theatre function. Marked by a crime of huge proportions, the building presumably could not serve as a playhouse again, it could never fill with laughter of a comedy nor serve to stage anyone's private sorrow. But it was equally unconceivable to build an apartment house or an office building on the same spot.

The site remained an enclosed, haunted courtyard, then a monument with an eternal flame was erected in 1962, so at least there was a place to lay flowers. In the remaining lobby a wall with the names of all the deportees was built. The memory function that the place acquired was expanded with the opening of an educational exhibit in the 1993, about persecution, hiding and deportation of Jews in the Netherlands during the Nazi occupation. Only on the staircase leading to the exhibit room, some posters, programs, props and costumes from the museum collection of Theater Instituut Nederland remind of the former theatre usage of this building. Theatre is historically relegated to a prologue to the real-life mass humiliation, pain and suffering that the exhibit invokes and documents.

The enmeshment of a theatre and holocaust logistic is striking. There are in Europe several theatre buildings that were the sites of riots, revolutions and wars, places of assassinations and proclamations and of other important political events, but this conjunction of entertainment and mass deportation is unique. To most visitors today, the site is just another holocaust memorial. Only to the theatre history buffs it is also a memorial to a theatre made impossible by racial persecution, performances discontinued by mass deportation of both performers and the spectators, stage acts displaced forcefully to the Westerbork camp – where singers, musicians and actors among the inmates staged revue performances on the eve of the weekly departure of another transport to Auschwitz. Were it left as a theatre building in 1945, albeit devastated and empty, Hollandse Schouwburg would today display its functional disjunction in an astonishing manner, convey its extinguished theatricality and its holocaust drama more eloquently than the wall with names and the educational exhibit, that, anyhow, could have stood as well in some other spot.

2

In 1902 architects Marcel Komor and Dezsö Jakab built the magnificent synagogue in Subotica/Szabadka (former Yugoslavia, now Serbia), remarkable for its floral ornaments and vivid colors of a Panonian Secession style that marks several other synagogues they constructed at the turn of the century in what was then the southern part of the Austro-Hungarian Empire. The long decline of the city, still ongoing, started in 1918, when a new state of Serbs, Croats and Slovenes was established and its border with Hungary drawn a bit north of the city's periphery. The city's Jewish community of several thousand people sought to adjust to the new political circumstances, felt the consequences of the economic crisis of the 1930's, saw the first anti-Semitic laws imposed by the Yugoslav government in 1940 and lived through the brisk Nazi occupation in 1941 and the ensuing Hungarian annexation. In March 1944, with the Arrow Cross, the Hungarian fascists, in power, mass deportations of Jews started all over Hungary and were meticulously carried out in Subotica as everywhere else. By October, when Tito's partisan army and the Soviet troops entered Subotica, its Jewish community was practically eliminated, and very few of its members returned later from the concentration camps and hiding.

During Tito's Yugoslavia, only a few dozen Jewish families lived in the town, most of them non-religious. The synagogue remained closed as a tacit memento of a disappeared community. S.L. claims however that as a little girl in the 1950s she was brought occasionally by her grandmother to the synagogue for some high holiday service held there (probably in the summer because the heating system was broken) and remembers hiding in the abandoned upper gallery. J.B. remembers entering the building secretly as a small girl, sometimes in the late 1950s, through a broken window, and getting very scared, for she had trouble climbing out.

In 1985, Ljubiša Ristić, a maverick theatre director, took over the ailing National Theater in Subotica, merged its separate Hungarian and Serbo-Croat language ensembles and proclaimed a new era of intercultural theatre, multilingual performances, staged on various local sites and frequent guest productions and tours. As his opening production he decide to stage Imre Madách's *A Tragedy of Man* (Az ember tragédiája 1861), a late romantic epic drama about Adam and Eve's march through time in the pursuit of hope, from the Eden exile to some collectivist colony in the remote future. This cult play of the Hungarian stage, written as an echo of Goethe's *Faust*, resonates a positive philosophy of history though its para-human protagonists, caught in the bet of Lucifer and God, facing challenges of various epochs and yet replenishing their supply of hope and persistence with each tragic twist and historic defeat.

Our production – time to admit here that I served as its dramaturg, together with László Végel – sought to recycle some basic situations and main dramatic lines but also to extend the record by filling in additional episodes of the last 120 years, derived from world and local history, to update the practice of revolution since the clash of Robespierre and Danton, described by Madách, and offer new emblematic situations of betrayal, perfidy and baseness against which to test Adam and Eve's unwavering hope. The performance started in the courtyard of the crumbling theatre building, moved to the main square where the kidnapping of Aldo Moro was restaged with the use of several cars and much shooting, and turned into a processional play along the corridors and courtyards of the magnificent town hall, another Komor and Jakab masterpiece, with installations and short, repeated scenes. Finally, close to midnight, the old synagogue was for the first time in decades lit, unlocked and filled with people, and there the last dinner of European revolutionaries was staged, as an alternative Passover. Bakunin, Marx, Hugo and Garibaldi, poets Vörosmarty and Petöfi, and Lajos Kossuth and his defeated Hungarian revolutionaries of 1848 were seated at the table as apostles of freedom, approached by two children, Anne Frank and Daniel Cohn Bendit, who posed the question on the special character of this night to connect the past and the future and redeem the project hope from the exhausted eschatology of Adam and Eve. The multilingual production ended with the chorus of Subotica pensioners singing from the gallery Verdi's 'Va pensiero' from *Nabucco*. In 1988 this production was remade into 'Berlin Subversion' and staged in Wilmerdorf town hall, a former Goering's Ministry of Luftwaffe in Berlin.

In the ensuing few seasons, the synagogue in Subotica was used as a chief theatre venue by Ristić and his cohorts, while the plans were developed to adapt the old inadequate theatre building on the main city square. Some local Jews felt offended by its use, claiming that the performances violated the spiritual character of the synagogue. Others argued that the space had been de-consecrated ever since the holocaust and that its current artistic use revalorized the splendid architecture of this long-neglected building and pleaded for its thorough renovation. Indeed, excellent acoustics and the old glory of elegant arches and floral ornaments, recognizable in traces on the ceiling, endowed the venue with special magic – despite improvized heating, not very comfortable seats and the absence of rudimentary backstage comfort for the performers. Anyhow, stating rightly that any use of the building violates all norms of occupational and public safety, the city authorities stopped further performances in the late 1980s, promising conservation, if not full restoration or adaptation into a concert hall or theatre venue.

No plans were ever developed, no conservation work was ever carried out, the synagogue has remained ever since closed, abandoned and exposed to further decay. With the disintegration of the former Yugoslavia, Ristić's intercultural artistic project lost its grounding, while military operations nearby, Milošević's regime and the UN sanctions brought isolation and misery to the entire region, and in 1994 Ristić left Subotica to embark on political instead of theatre adventures, becoming the president of JUL, the party of Mrs. Milošević. In the ensuing chaos, crisis and overall pauperization, most inhabitants of Subotica had to write off any hopeful promises of Cohn Bendit and Anne Frank. Other local sites used by Ristić shared the destiny of the synagogue. The old theatre building remains closed as dangerous for public use, various locations around the nearby Palić lake succumbed to wilderness or were possessed by commercial interests. With the worsening of inter-ethnic relations in the city and the Serbian, Croat and Hungarian nationalisms caught in a pattern of mutual escalation, the Hungarian and Serbo-Croat ensembles were re-established as separate entities, the National Theater slid back into its provincial insignificance and started playing boulevard plays in a former movie house, adapted cheaply in an appropriate kitschy style.

3

Both the Hollandse Schouwburg and the Subotica synagogue hide the ghosts of their respective theatrical past, their original functions made impossible by the holocaust. The remains of a former playhouse in Amsterdam live through its substitute function of an educational exhibit space and a memorial. The cupolas of the Subotica synagogue still can impress an accidental visitor, but the inner space remains inaccessible and the decay continues. Soon, with most of the remaining Jews gone from the town, there will be no voice to add a narrative to the venue and the short-lasting and failed effort to re-instate the public function of the building through performance, to revive it as a playhouse, will be forgotten as well. In both sites, performance has become an impossibility: in Amsterdam by the prevalence of attentive memory, in Subotica by indifference ushering oblivion. What remains defined and unambiguous is the empty space caused by the holocaust, the thoroughness of its eliminatory drive, which both buildings keep witnessing, each in its own way.

ADRIAN KEAR   **FIELD STATION 6**

The Memory of Promise:
Theatre and the Ethic of the Future

The other is the future. The very relationship with the other is the relationship with the future. (Levinas 1987: 77)

We are appealing to this entirely other in the memory of a promise or the promise of a memory. That's the truth of what we have always said, heard, tried to make heard ... through flame or ash, but as entirely other, inevitably. (Derrida 1989: 113)

The embers of this image are still smouldering; dampened by time, but not extinguished entirely. It comes at the end of the final episode in the marathon theatre series by Societas Rafaello Sanzio (SRS), *Tragedia Endogonigia* (C#11, 'Cesena', December 2004). Maybe it's not a conclusion, but a beginning – or, rather, a restaging of the necessary confusion and interrelation of the two. Although the environment in which it takes place is cold and wet, the image itself is nonetheless striking, and illuminating. The scene is a wood, a dense congregation of trees, leaves, mud, briar and bracken brought from outside the theatre to transform the space within. Its realism is utterly convincing, with the dark of the night penetrating its depth-perspective unmistakably. The temperature inside the building has been dropped several degrees to just above freezing, confirming somatically the folding of the outside in. Rain – or, at least, water made to fall 'atmospherically' – descends onto the stage with an unremitting rhythm. The noise it makes is braided, augmented even, by the sound of cars passing along a road adjacent to the wood, their headlights throwing chiaroscuros over the scene through the filter of the cross of beams. This is therefore not an isolated forest but a border area existing somewhere on the edge of a town, village or other form of community settlement. It is populated, so to speak, by more than just bark and twigs. The static naturalism of the stage environment is disturbed, in fact, by a faint but audible sobbing emanating from downstage left. It is a child's presence – heard but not seen – that interrupts the image of the landscape and introduces narrative into it as well: 'Alone, lost in the woods ...'. In the distance, a group of men can be heard calling, shouting. They enter at the back of the

stage with high-powered torches, looking, searching, for something or *someone*. But the child remains silent, hidden. The auditory and visual impact of the rain is amplified as it falls against the men's waterproof capes, splattering off their artificial skins and dancing in the light before them. The men move closer to the audience – and the child – pointing their lights into the recesses of the undergrowth and canopy. As they get nearer to where the child is secreted, it becomes clear that this is not a rescue but a hunt. The child is either being forcibly restrained or simply does not want to be found. The search team, distracted by an off-stage 'discovery', turn their backs and move purposefully towards the exit. Once they have gone the stage returns to its 'natural' state, an environment in which time remains in suspension. The child crawls out from his hiding place and occupies the space singularly: a small boy in white pyjamas, alone and drenched to the skin. As he lies there, crying, one of the men comes back in. The boy scuttles towards his sanctuary, but he has now been sighted. The man holds out his open hand to him, seemingly encouraging him to return home, to rejoin the community. But it is not taken. Instead the man grabs him, holds him down and with dull, deadly sweeps of his arm stabs the boy in the neck repeatedly.

This Abrahamic gesture – no less disturbing for its familiarity – acts as a reminder of the sacrificial violence underpinning the foundations of this *future* society. It therefore looks back at the audience at the same time as the audience looks ahead to it, codifying theatrically the exchange of meanings and temporalities. The actor on-stage appears to sever the boy's head, but the one he holds up to confront the audience with belongs instead to his cat. The point is made nonetheless: what we are witnessing is a repetition of the sacrifice of otherness.[1] In this respect the child and the animal are interchangeable – at least metonymically – in the anthropomorphic machinery that both inaugurates and suspends 'the human' as the subject of theatrical representation (Agamben 2004: 92). The moment itself seems to invoke the a priori nature of image's point of reference, its conjuring of the ur-past into the present tense of performance. It therefore exists within two temporalities simultaneously: both a reconfigured sense of history and an anticipated promise of futurity. Likewise, it operates across the boundaries of what might be called, following the schematization offered by the philosopher Jacques Rancière, otherwise historically incompatible 'regimes of identification' (2004: 20). The image, as *image*, might be read first and foremost tendentiously; that is, in terms of its purpose, direction, and the organization of the domain of its effects. Or, at least, in terms of the tendentiousness that the image itself represents: the ways in which images affect the construction of the community's ethical mode of being as such. The foundational significance of what Rancière calls 'the ethical regime of images' is therefore made present once again through the operation of *mimesis*, the institutionalization in artistic practice of a certain 'regime of visibility' (2004: 22). But at the same time the intentionality of the image-making process, its orchestration within the theatrical *mise-en-scène*, is characteristic of an 'aesthetic regime' which moves outside the limits of the mimetic to purposefully reconfigure the 'distribution of the sensible'. Rancière describes this manoeuvre as typically avant-garde, contrasting 'two regimes of historicity' in imaging a future that 'incessantly restages the past' (2004: 24). The gesture here would seem to be consistent with this approach – not so much inaugurating 'the new' and differentiating it from 'the now', as finding a form in which to represent its historical rupturing contemporaneously.

Societas Rafaello Sanzio's *Tragedia* project is to this extent an elaboration of the fundamental social significance of tragedy as the pre-eminent form of cultural representation. In this episode, and with this image in particular, the company appear to have taken up Walter Benjamin's claim that tragic performance is 'based on the idea of sacrifice' – a sacrifice whose split temporality renders it both 'first' and 'final'. According to Benjamin, it is 'final' to the extent that it atones for some historical error, but also 'first' in inaugurating a new dispensation formative of future community relations. The sacrifice that tragedy represents is in this regard 'representative', and tragedy itself is endowed with the task of making 'new aspects of the life of the nation become manifest' (1985: 106–8). Already, then, the ethical potentiality of the image is stabilized theatrically, turned from memory into ideology through being given narrative consistency. Importantly, though, the tragic hero's sacrifice is made silently; and silence, says Benjamin, maintains a corresponding possibility of resistance. In producing an affective contrast between 'image and speech', tragedy creates a political distance between the situation it represents and the discourse it uses to describe it – a distance re-inscribed by its claim to historiography. Benjamin suggests that the tragic hero's silence not only encodes 'the unarticulated necessity

of defiance', but enfolds an 'unknown' word within its secret vocabulary. Sacrifice, it would seem, addresses itself to a future society capable of understanding its gesture appropriately; the audience of the tragic drama might well come to see itself as just such a constituency. Tragic form translates such immanence into materiality, and through it 'the community learns reverence and gratitude for the word' which the tragic hero's death has 'endowed' it (Benjamin 1985: 109). Its temporality is therefore irremediably split: directed towards a future which it appears to anticipate, the sacrificial gesture testifies against the atavistic violence that seems to bring it about; at the same time, its representation in the theatre figures it historically as well, a still image of an excluded foundation whose remembrance in the present operates with the force of an interruption.

Benjamin's analysis is therefore conducted with an understanding of time hinged upon the theatrical ethic of the present being constructed in relation to the future – a future which discloses the forgotten memory of repressed history as 'protest' against the current *ideological* configuration. Although the economy of representation, within which the theatre operates, consigns *mimesis* to the re-presentation of past events, it also reanimates their latent potentiality as missed opportunities to construct an alternative vision of future possibility. So in the theatre, the effect of representation is to disrupt the present moment by creating the memory of promise within it: memory, because what is to come is something past, forgotten; promise, because what is past is to be rescued, recovered, made present once again through the movement of 'redemption'. From this perspective, the past continues to preserve an element of its significance as a 'seizing in the instant' of the future's performativity – maintaining 'a trace of the latter's power' as it returns to disrupt the present (Düttmann 2002: 22–3). Because the past has been a future, to some extent, it is the future itself that is disclosed in the representation of past events. Not the future as actuality, but the future as potentiality: the promise of what has been returning as what is to come. In this respect, Benjamin's approach to tragedy is consistent with his broader cultural materialism, which seeks in its objects 'a consciousness of the present which explodes the continuum of history' (1982: 227). The key to this is his identification of the 'dialectical image' as that which flashes into flame in the 'now' of recognition. This moment brings with it the prospect of a political actualization that might turn the memory of promise into the grounds of new settlement, an *ethical* re-foundation. Thus, for Benjamin, 'the utopian images that accompany the emergence of the new always concurrently reach back to the ur-past. In the dream in which every epoch sees in images before its eyes the one that follows it, the images appear wedded to ur-history' (cited in Buck-Morss 1989: 116). The reappearance of the past in the form of theatrical memory harbours also the promise of a political awakening; its fire erupts as the dream of futurity breaks through the prism of historicity.

The function of avant-garde performance in drawing attention, once again, to the utopian dimension of image-making practices, is, it would seem, to refract into artistic form the material 'redistribution of the sensible' that accompanies them. Rancière is unequivocal about this, arguing that 'aesthetic anticipation of the future' is orientated less towards 'artistic innovation' than the 'invention of sensible forms and material structures' required by the 'community to come' (2004: 30). The avant-garde mobilizes the experimentation inherent in the 'aesthetic regime' and orients it towards the construction of a *political* subjectivity – subjectivity brought about through fidelity to a constitutive event and on-going adherence to its transformative possibilities. This aligns its practices with what Alain Badiou terms the 'ethic of truths': a process of subjectivation in which the subject is 'induced' as an effect of their commitment to thinking through the implications of the interruptive emergence of the radically new. Artistic invention is, according to Badiou, one of four generic procedures capable of producing critical cognizance of the truths immanent within an historical situation – their ideological organization – and converting this into a commitment to creating 'a new way of being and acting' reflective of its materially engendered reconfiguration (2001: 39–44). Badiou calls this active, anticipatory, *thinking* an activity of speculative 'forcing'. He invokes the term to illustrate the hypothetical nature of a truth procedure in constructing 'the powerful fiction' of its completion axiomatically in order to augment its 'potency' in forcing – or performatively producing – new knowledge of the situation (2003: 62–5). Its operation might therefore be characterized theatrically as the imaginary representation of alterity, of changed social relations and disrupted ideology. To this extent, 'the ethic of truths' might be said to function through anticipation of a moment to come as much as through sustaining the logic of an event that has happened already [2]. Its utopian vision is as such simultaneously backward- and forward-looking, highlighting the fact that ethos is never simply a shared space of being or dwelling but the strategic occupation of conflicting territories and the necessary composition of alternate possibilities. Rancière clarifies this by demonstrating that its construction is always more or less motivated, 'polemical' – which is to say, in a certain contradictory way, *utopian*. For utopia is the space of a dynamic ambiguity: the relationship between the world

as it is and as it 'ought' to be in the interests of common humanity. It is, on the one hand, as non-place, inexistent, 'the extreme point of a polemical reconfiguration of the sensible', radical, category-breaking; on the other, it is also 'a proper place, a non-polemical distribution of the sensible universe where what one sees, what one says, and what one does are rigorously adapted to one another' or played out tactically (Rancière 2004: 40–2). The dream of avant-garde performance-making is, perhaps, to navigate in-between these positions, disrupting and disturbing 'the relationship between the visible, the sayable, and the thinkable without having to use the terms of a message as a vehicle' (Rancière 2004: 63). The rupturing, or interruption, of the current ideological distribution might therefore take the form of an eruption of the image from the future, from ur-history, which punctures a hole in the situation's temporal logic of meaningful sense-making.

Just such an image – or, rather, the image of just such a possibility – occurs repeatedly in the *Tragedia Endogonigia* series [3]. In episode #9, 'London' (May 2004), an instance of it is given material form, shape and body. A woman dressed in an opalescent period gown stands with her back turned to the audience, waiting. She's been here before, right at the beginning, her nape draped in cascades of strawberry-blonde hair as she hangs with hands tied to a golden thread of rope in front of a decoratively flocked curtain. But this time she is free from such constraint, unencumbered by 'historical' ties and blinds, released for a journey into the future. With a sudden, muscular snap of her neck she looks back at the audience, confronting us with something like the fact of otherness – or the fact of its representation historically. Her face is blacked-up, shockingly: set deep within the frame of the dress and wig, focussing the audience's gaze on the startlingly large pair of eyes staring back at us, unwaveringly. They appear to return our look and yet at the same time look straight through us, fixed on the horizon beyond or the void of an encroaching abyss. There is something uncanny about their animalistic quality – they appear veiled by the film that can sometimes be seen behind the eyes of a horse or pig – hinting at a potentiality dulled by domesticity and the memory of a long-remembered promise. Their stare is accusatory, hurt: a reflection of both the realization of oppression and its reduplication in hysteria as the failed attempt to look good in the eyes of the other. And yet it is addressed externally nonetheless, directed out to an audience whose presence there acts as a reminder of the materiality of history – the material history of subjectivity embodied in the face. This confrontation of stage and audience, representation and affect, appears to facilitate something like an encounter with the *fact* of history, with history as the fact of otherness. Or rather, once again, an encounter with the fact of otherness as subject to representation. For it is clear that the woman in this scene is not presented 'phantasmagorically' as a shard or fragment left-over from history, or even 'realistically' as a character or representative figure: her black-face functions theatrically as a *sign* of otherness within this specular economy and, moreover, as an mark of the theatre's implication in the historical *problematic* of racial representation. But, somewhat paradoxically, at the same time as it explicates this rather dodgy cultural politics, the scene itself seems to represent a call for the renewal of the necessary injunction to futurity which Levinas claims accompanies the ethical 'face-to-face': a relationship to the future grounded in the material relation to the other in their materiality (1987: 77). The function of this image, then, as it ghosts the theatrical space, is to act as a reminder of the basic ethic of performance: to temporalize the present.

In this respect, the work of SRS seems to proceed meta-theatrically. The shows they make and bring forward to be seen adopt a logic of performance clearly avant-garde in orientation. This is not to say that their theatre is particularly innovative, but rather that it seeks to archive the 'ethic of images' underpinning the 'aesthetic regime'. *Their Tragedia Endogonigia* looks back to the theatre's primary form, ancient tragedy, in order to resuscitate some of its archaic potentiality in re-imagining performance's *future* direction and capability. This appears to hinge on a double-movement in which the ur-theatricality of tragic image is reanimated to disrupt the self-understanding of Enlightened modernity and its ideological 'distribution of the sensible', whilst at the same time representing the return of the promise of alternative possibilities. That the hysterical figure of the other is at the forefront of this, is itself indicative that the tragedy of the future is not the ceaseless narrative of a permanent catastrophe but rather the prospect of the situation being destabilized and transformed by the utopian redemption of missed opportunities. The company's commitment to maintaining fidelity to this as the theatre's fundamental purpose and ethic is salutary and clear: to temporalize the present by invoking the past as future possibility, staging thereby the memory of a promise and promise of a memory. Through flame or ash, its potentiality remains inextinguishable.

ACKNOWLEDGEMENTS

The author gratefully acknowledges the support of the Arts and Humanities Research Board. Thanks are due also to Joe Kelleher, Nick Ridout and Alan Read for their collegial support of my engagement with the work of SRS.

NOTES

1. This has already been presaged earlier in the performance, in two other images that appear to make a similar statement. Both are set in an interior environment, seen before the 'interval' during which the audience were ushered into the space described above. It is a wood-panelled room, furnished with an armchair, side-table, and bed-a child's bed, in which the boy who appears in the second half had earlier been put to sleep, with his cat. It is empty when a black chambermaid enters in the morning, to do the hoovering. Afterwards she rests awhile in the armchair, massaging her feet. Time elapses; her neck wrenches back suddenly, and her eyes and mouth gape as she sits there, lynched. Later the point is reinforced once again when, partially seen behind a screen, the child's mother is restrained by two or three men, has her underwear removed and is stood in front of us as the bloody evidence of rape trickles down her leg. Here again it is clear that what is being constituted in these sacrifices is the community of *men*.

2. For a more detailed discussion of temporality in Badiou's philosophy, and its relationship to the theatre, see Kear (2004).

3. For an overview of this work see Joe Kelleher's and Nick Ridout's on-going writing for the journal which accompanies the company's productions, *Idioma Clima Crono* (2002–).

REFERENCES

Agamben, Giorgio (2004) *The Open*, (trans. K. Attell), Stanford: Stanford University Press.

Badiou, Alain (2001) *Ethics: An Essay on the Understanding of Evil*, (trans. Peter Hallward), London: Verso.

Badiou, Alain (2003) *Infinite Thought: Truth and the Return of Philosophy*, (ed. and trans. Oliver Feltham and Justin Clemens), London and New York: Continuum.

Benjamin, Walter (1982) 'Eduard Fuchs: Collector and Historian' in Andrew Arato and Eike Gebhardt (eds.) *The Essential Fankfurt School Reader*, New York: Continuum.

Benjamin, Walter (1985) *The Origin of the German Tragic Drama*, (trans. J. Osborne), London: Verso.

Buck-Morss, Susan (1989) *The Dialectics of Seeing: Walter Benjamin and the Arcades Project*, Cambridge (Massachusetts): MIT Press.

Derrida, Jacques (1989) *Of Spirit: Heidegger and the Question*, (trans. G. Bennington and R. Bowlby), Chicago: Chicago University Press.

Düttmann, Alexander Garcia (2002) *The Memory of Thought: An essay on Heidegger and Adorno*, (trans. N. Walker), London and New York: Continuum.

Kear, Adrian (2004) 'Thinking out of Time: Theatre and the ethic of interruption' in *Performance Research*, Vol. 9 No. 4, 'On Civility', London: Routledge.

Levinas, Emmanuel (1987) *Time and the Other*, (trans. R.A. Cohen), Pittsburgh: Duquesne University Press.

Rancière, Jacques (2004) *The Politics of Aesthetics*, (trans. G. Rockhill), New York and London: Continuum.

ALPHONSO LINGIS   FIELD STATION 6

Open Wounds

From as far back as we can peer into our history, cultural performances – rituals, initiations, ceremonies, parades, dances – were performed 'to promote and increase fertility of men, crops and animals, domestic and wild; to cure illness; to avert plague; to obtain success in raiding; to turn boys into men and girls into women; to make chiefs out of commoners; to transform ordinary people into shamans and shamanins; to 'cool' those 'hot' from the warpath, to ensure the proper succession of seasons and the hunting and agricultural responses of human beings to them' (Turner 1982: 32). These performances were animal and cosmic epiphanies, awesome and terrifying revelations of dark compulsions and cruelties that are unleashed in tabooed places and sacred times. Anthropologists have emphasized that they were also entertainments; people laugh freely at the grotesqueries and parodies that reverse the social and sacred hierarchies in Balinese temple ceremonies, in African rituals, in Papuan initiation ceremonies so lavish in cruelties to the initiates; they laughingly recognize village louts arrayed in fancy costume and spouting pompous declamations, they gossip and indulge in lavish meals.

But what were the effects of these performances? Scientific anthropologists have dismissed their efficacy to increase fertility of men, crops and animals, or to ensure the proper succession of seasons. Claude Lévi-Strauss declared that there is nothing to be learned about nature from the study of myths. Since the Romantics, anthropologists have especially focused on the function of myths and rituals to consolidate a community and its hierarchies. But the myths and rituals engender heretics, break-off sects, eccentrics, scoffers, charlatans and profiteers. Anthropologists have little studied the ways individuals resist, neutralize, and protect themselves from the visions and forces of collective cultural performances.

In modern societies, industrialization, urbanization, literacy, labor migration, specialization, professionalization, bureaucracy and the demarcation of the work sphere by the firm's clock have constituted a leisure time devoted to entertainment. In the great bulk of performances developed for leisure time – theatre, ballet, opera, film, the novel, printed poetry, the art exhibition, classical music, rock music, carnivals, processions, folk drama and major sports events – entertainment has become the dominant concern. But entertainment is a vague word that covers a multitude of effects and responses to these performances.

That small trend that has come to be called performance art repudiates entertainment to pursue instead exploration by and of the performer, exploration of what can be revealed in the human psyche and body split-open and exhibited. From the beginning they featured the grotesque and disgusting – Paul McCarthy stuffing raw hamburger and mayonnaise into his mouth; Artur Barrio leaving bundles of blood, fingernails, hair, spit, urine, shit, bones, toilet paper on city streets; Vito Acconci masturbating for days under the floor of an art gallery; Chris Burden having himself shot, electrocuted, impaled, cut, drowned, incarcerated and sequestered. These performances are known by those who follow the art avant-garde, though they typically repudiate the institutions of high art and are performed in public places – shopping malls, factories and public streets. But these 'artists' also used the media to impose their performances on the public. They understood that the electronic media – all images, all simulacra according to Baudrillard – also imposes raw physical contact with a body that words, painting and even theatre does not.

Reports of these performances in the media entertain the public. But attention to the responses they provoke can also reveal how we receive or protect ourselves from these explorations and discoveries. Are not the effects of contemporary performances as multiple as those of the ancient collective performances?

Sonia is a 35-year-old black woman from the Dominican Republic whom I met one evening at a gathering of graduate students in Chicago. Beautiful, with a soft feminine voice, she has a full, mature woman's body, though she had shaved her head. She made art objects and was auditing some philosophy classes. Her artwork was boxes, small theatres, in which she exhibited small found objects. She survived on welfare. We exchanged addresses and exchanged letters occasionally. Two years later I learned from a third party that she was diagnosed with breast cancer and was terrified at the possibility of dying. Later I learned that she moved back to her mother's in Florida. I saw her again two years ago, at a meeting on Culture Studies in Sydney, Australia. She told me she had received funding to come. The first day of the meeting, at midday, she did a performance. In the downstairs entrance hall of the building, in the centre of a circle of academics with Ph.D. degrees and secure jobs, she appeared, naked save for a skullcap of white feathers. To a short piece of Latin music, she danced. It was a shock to see her naked: her left breast was a mound of discoloured flesh with no nipple, a thick crooked scar extended across her lower abdomen. It was from her lower abdomen, she told me later, that they had extracted the substance to reconstruct her breast. We saw the botched work done on a welfare patient who could not pay for a competent surgeon. She exhibited completely her mutilated body and its ineffaceable scars, the issue of so many months of visceral anxiety over her cancerous and mortal body, and the pain, after surgery and the healing, of seeing her disfigured body. But today she danced. This body could dance, and in the dance it was transfigured. This woman danced at a distance from where we stood, but across that distance her nakedness made contact with our bodies. Her fear for mortal flesh infected us; we felt a visceral sense of the vulnerability of our bodies sheathed with clothing renewed each day. The shadow of death closed in upon us. At the same time, her nakedness revealed her courage and her determination.

Now that the healing and scarring of her body were over, she was not turned to the future and the array of things open to her, she was not turned to the intellectual fascination with philosophy and to the making of art objects, as though she had never contracted the cancer. In the present she was in the past, reduced just to her body, the body denuded for breast oblation and then for reconstructive surgery. Out of the initial shock upon seeing her mutilated body the rhythms and melodies of the dancing body held us. Dance: it's movement that is not going anywhere. This absolute movement, wholly in the present, transfigured her body; in all her nakedness she was wholly beautiful. A beauty that enthralled us and as we glanced at one another, somehow the beauty of our bodies, young and old, thick or thin, slender or sagging, glowed.

Actions that explore the human psyche and body split open and exhibited are also communications. Expressions - verbal, conceptual expressions, but also the smiles, grimaces, quizzical and skeptical looks, shrugs, scowls, thrusts which show how the conceptual expressions are to be taken and which often substitute for them - expressions fascinate us and arouse the investigations of physiology, psychology and the philosophy of mind - because, for our natural and cultural sciences, there is something exasperatingly enigmatic in the emergence of expressions in the nervous circuitry and musculature of our physical bodies.

But performances not only exhibit the emergence of meaning out of physical movements and vocalizations; they exhibit the frailty of expression, its engulfment in unmappable spasms and in the meltdown of pleasure and the opacity of pain. They release irrational and infantile compulsions where expressions are submerged in blind forces. They exhibit the intolerable and fateful menace of sickness, madness and death. Culture has trained us to execute socially-acceptable positions, postures and movements: how few these are! A performance in which a living body exhibits itself naked, cleaves itself open, and reveals uncultured, artless and impulsive possibilities that are latent in our bodies, does not only induce in us the delight of discovery. It also induces anxiety and provokes us to turn away in fear and revulsion, provokes us to neutralize the impact of the performance on us.

I had gone one evening to see an exhibition of photographs taken by a student in the fine arts department. But passing, with others, to a room behind the photograph exhibit, I saw a man, very muscular and virile, naked, who was suspended upside down on a rope hung from the ceiling. Around the small room there were two stands containing an assortment of knives - butcher knives, serrated knives, hunting knives - and two stands containing guns with boxes of bullets next to them, and over them maps of the country with the numbers of people shot to death in each of the states. For an hour and a half we stood around, looking at the man hung from the ceiling and viewing the stands in a kind of brutalized silence. The muscular young man naked and hung upside down exhibited human life at its strongest, now in a position of extreme vulnerability. The provocation, the temptation, to cruelty surged in us, as we looked at the arrayed knives and guns and the maps of the people killed with such weapons everywhere in the country. We trembled before the abyss that gaped open before us. Finally one of us grabbed a knife and cut the rope; the man fell to the floor. A student I knew, Andy, who was standing next to me, muttered 'the show is not over like that', and sprung forward, grabbed a knife and brought it down with full force into the floor, grazing the arm of the fallen man. But he had thrust so violently that, without realizing it or feeling it, his hand had slipped off the handle and down the blade, which cut deeply into the palm of his own hand and fingers. Seeing the blood flowing from his hand, he had the theatrical presence of mind to shake his hand over the fallen man, splattering him everywhere with his blood.

Then he slipped off to go to the emergency room of the hospital. He is a musician, and, several surgeries later the doctors had not been able to restore the tendons of his fingers enough for him ever to play again. He had a gathering of friends before the first surgery; he was if anything more energized and ebullient than before.

Georges Bataille explained that in sacrifice, there is a fundamental identification of the priest and the people, in whose stead he acts, with the victim. This is most visible in Aztec sacrifice, where the victim is arrayed and feted as a prince for a year before he is killed on the high altar of the sun pyramid. We in the room felt this identification with the man suspended and then fallen before us; his nakedness made us feel the nakedness of our bodies under our clothing, which protects them only from looks, and we felt his vulnerability with and in our flesh. The anxiety that infected us could be broken only by violence, and finally one of us seized a knife to cut the rope and lower the man. But Andy felt most the intensity of violence that was not so easily spent, and seized a knife to cut the arm of the man at our feet. When his knife slashed his own hand, it realized the identification with the man he struck; then he anointed the body of the fallen man with his blood.

Andy's act was an identification with the performance, extending it. And it was a more complete exploration and release of his body and its compulsions than the explorations of Vito Acconci in the seventies, who bit hard on his body everywhere, leaving bruised teeth marks on his body – but alone, without witnesses – then smearing printer's ink on the teeth marks and making imprints of them, which, afterwards, he showed to the public. We felt shock but also exhilaration at Andy's act; he acted in our stead, both realizing the temptation to cruelty upon the fallen man we felt and enacting our impulse to release the tension with a cruel release of the blood from our bodies.

In Rio de Janeiro Avenida Atlântica extends along Copacabana beach, with a broad walkway on one side where restaurants and cafés extend their tables and tourists gather, facing the beach and the sunny ocean beyond. Around the tables, about which people are dining, local people circulate selling paper cones of peanuts, small sausages, candies, cigarettes and tourist souvenirs – straw hats, t-shirts, postcards. One day as I was seated there, I saw a man approaching and saw he had both hands amputated, the one at the wrist, the other above the elbow; he was going from table to table badgering the people at their dinners.

As he approached, my eyes were drawn to him, as we always are before people with amputated limbs or crippled bodies; the sight of them arouses in us a wonder how they cope, especially if they do not look feeble and despondent but, instead, energetic and enterprising. There is something deeper: it is not in the nature of our bodies to tend always to a state of equilibrium like inert things; the excess energies our bodies generate prepare them for hard tasks and for dangers. But they also launch our bodies gratuitously into obstructed ways and on perilous paths. They drove our ancestors to cross the glaciers from Asia to North America during the last Ice Age; they drive our contemporaries to descend to the ocean abysses and rocket into outer space. Subliminally our bodies see in amputees a premonition of wounds and mutilations and eventually incapacitation that lurks as a possibility in our most energetic drives.

When the man got closer, I saw that what he was selling, thrusting the stumps of his arms before the diners, were – knives. His performance was in the public space, but his audience had not expected or agreed to watch this demanding and grotesque act. The diners at the tables were first repelled by another peddler offering them tourist souvenirs, then revolted by the sight of the stumps the man thrust under their eyes. Their horror was blocked by surges of sympathy for not just another impoverished local but a mutilated human being. But then their horror and revulsion before the sight of his handless and fingerless stumps returned before the sight of the knives he was offering them. Offering them, superficially, for sale, but also as a tourist souvenir of the knives that had cut off his hands, and an invitation to use them not simply to cut bread but to cut their flesh.

There are wounds cut open that do not heal. I have not been able to forget this man, his stumps, and his knives; each time I recall him I see him as vividly as the first time and the violent emotions his performance aroused surge up again. No doubt some of those vacationers in Copacabana have been able to wipe out the sight of him from their memories. They would have had to stifle the passions, of empathy, of morbid fascination, of cruelty to him and to themselves that he had awakened in them. What can drive out an impassioned state is only another passion. When he moved on, they would look at him from a distance, and remind themselves that they indeed had sympathy for any unfortunate human being. They would recall the times, back home, in their gated communities, when they gave to charities, indeed, volunteered on Saturdays at the information desk of the hospital. They reassured themselves of the kindness of their hearts.

Francisco de Goya's set of eighty etchings, *The Disasters of War*, finished in 1808 but not published until 1863, depict the invasion of the Napoleonic armies into Spain. They depict close-up men cornered and disarmed and then castrated and dismembered, the butchering of the infirm and aged unable to fight or flee, the mutilation and slaughter of children. The great causes of the war – the Napoleonic armies heralding the Enlightenment advancing into the darkness and superstition of rural Spain, the resistance of the indigenous people and their loyalties, traditions, and values – are invisible; soldiers, peasants, women and children tear at one another like so many rabid dogs. Goya depicts mutilated corpses covered with flies and picked at by vultures under dark skies, where there is no god above to witness, pity and redeem so much agony, so many deaths.

The classical art of wars and battlefields depicted, in and through the spectacle of mass slaughter, a transcendent sphere of the good – they invoked the victorious Alexander, Charlemagne or Joan of Arc absorbing the agony and death of the brave and redeeming them with his or her glory, or else invoked a transcendent God pitying and honouring and redeeming those fallen in battle. With Goya both the glorious Napoleon and the glorious King of Spain have disappeared; God has disappeared. Their place is taken by the viewer, who, in his horror and disgust, feels rising from his depths his core moral instincts, an immanent sphere of the good. Thus, after having been first suppressed until thirty-five years after his death, Goya's *The Disasters of War*, depicting nothing but mutilation and pointless slaughter, now rose to displace classical art and to be proclaimed the great and essential humanist art of our time.

Although Goya's pictures of war have been recognized as truthful to the point that they have virtually put an end to the classical art that glorified and redeemed agony and death in war, they had no effect on the forces that drive Europeans to war. Europe was soon to launch itself into war again, and twice most of the world with it. Does this make us think that humanist art has no power to effect the course of human conduct – or does it rather make us think that the humanist sentiment it provokes –the conviction of an instinctual moral decency in us – actually functions to serve the war industry in our times, by convincing us that military operations launched in our name are driven by the core moral instincts such art makes us feel in ourselves?

A student, Daniel, alerted me to an evening offered by the Department of Performance Studies at the university. Having misunderstood the time, I arrived an hour early. It was All Soul's Day on the Catholic calendar, and the space – a very long corridor connecting two buildings - had been furnished to evoke the Mexican Day of the Dead. There were altars decorated with folk-art saints, and even trays offering cookies in the shape of skulls, as one would see in Mexico. People gathered, and the performances began. On the far end there was a pile of white sand – which, in fact, I had almost stepped on earlier. The space was darkened, and an assistant began dropping drops of water into a glass dish of water; the sounds of the drops of water were amplified. From below the ripples were lit and then projected upon the far wall, where they spread in luminous circles. This went on for a very long time, monotonous, and we were absorbed with the sense of time itself, endless time, the time of death. Then we saw a movement in the pile of white sand, and slowly a man

rose; I recognized Daniel. He was very slender, naked, and his body sparkled with particles of sand stuck to his body hair. His head was wrapped like the head of a mummy. He slowly rose to full height, and then moved around the sand pile in widening circles until he disappeared behind a screen. He was a dead man, and what we had experienced, not in horror but in awe, an impersonal and strangely blissful awe, was the time of dying.

Each of us does something with our life – does something for himself or herself, does something for and to and against others. Each of us also has this to do: to die. Unless our life is cut short abruptly by some chance blow of force – automobile accident or heart attack – we have to conduct our own dying, by ourselves, alone. Dying takes time, we find ourselves suspended in time, waiting for death to come, as it will. All the skills and experiences we have had have become inoperative, the past and all we have learned and become skilled at fall away. There is no future, nothing to foresee, no possibilities to seize hold of, there is nothing to hope for or prepare for, for what is coming is – nothing, nothingness. We find ourselves suspended in a now that is going nowhere, but goes on, until death, of itself, comes.

But in the way we die, lucidly, bravely, with acceptance, or fearfully, cowardly, cringing, clinging, we do something for others, to others, sometimes against those who still live. We can even give them an experience of beauty.

Before he committed *seppuku*, Yukio Mishima made a film, titled in English *Rites of Love and Death*, in which he played the role of a samurai who, in an irresolvable conflict of loyalty, commits *seppuku* with his wife. The film shows the action set in a Noh stage. But after the two actors have wielded their swords on themselves and fallen, the camera rises over their bodies, and we see them now lying in the concentric waves of a Japanese sand garden, such as the one at the Rionji temple in Kyoto. When I first saw the film, afterwards, I asked a Japanese man in the audience what meaning he gave to this shift of the setting. He answered that in Japan the notion of beauty is so intimately bound to the notion of simplicity that it is almost inevitable that a Japanese person would see death as beautiful.

There are those who can do little, or nothing, by living, but who can do much by dying.

Military historians have shown that every advance in weapons technology provokes the production of a weapon to defend against it or destroy it, and in less time than it took to devise that new weapon: horses and then crossbows, tanks and then mortars, aircraft to drop bombs and then anti-aircraft guns, the ever-more destructive thermonuclear bombs and ever-more accurate antimissile missiles. But there is another dialectic in contemporary technological history, which is the more striking in that it defies our paradigms of understanding: the bigger the productive enterprises of today, works of vast teams of highly-educated inventors, engineers, electrical technicians, protected by ingenious systems of electronic surveillance, the more vulnerable they have turned out to be to ever smaller numbers of low-tech saboteurs, even to single individuals. In the sixties giant jetliners were seized by skyjackers. Then giant pharmaceutical companies were destroyed by single individuals injecting rat poison in a few bottles on the shelves of a supermarket in some provincial town. The Internet was first set up in the Pentagon to coordinate military information, and then vastly expanded for commercial use. Then youthful hackers found the most secured systems vulnerable to viruses. Two high-school dropouts in Karachi shut down the supercomputers of the Pentagon.

The hacker finds his individual mind is superior to that of the experts in whole industries. The skyjacker or industrial saboteur realizes exceptional resolve, patience and boldness. The realization of possessing not only exceptional power but also exceptional intelligence and exceptional character traits, this realization of intense individual identity, has always been the inner reward of military and industrial spies.

Everything depended on something ineffable and utterly individual: their will. They lived in the country for a year, spoke English well. They socialized with other student pilots and with their neighbours in the suburbs, shopped in the supermarkets, socialized in local bars, relaxed at home with videos of Hollywood movies.

Their weapons were their bodies - they had had martial arts training - and their will. On the planes just three of them - on one plane two of them - were in charge of subduing the flight attendants and passengers with small box cutters. Two of them overpowered the pilots as soon as the giant jetliners had reached maximum altitude and speed, and took over the controls. The one plane they directed to the command centre of the greatest war machine the planet has ever seen. As the minutes passed the capital and then the target came into view, and the men at the controls of the plane knew they would succeed. Two of the other planes were turned toward Manhattan, which the new pilots had not seen before from this airspace. The life in the man now piloting the jetliner, his will driven by all his surging emotions was on the brink of annihilation, yet he was able to command his attention and his newly-learned skills flawlessly. As the World Trade Center tower zooms into the centre of his vision, his heart blazes a moment before the impact, his exultation screams in the roar of the plane he directs. At the moment of impact and exploding fuel he is still

able to turn the jetliner so that its wings sever girders in the tower. The individual and his will are annihilated in the exploding jet fuel; then the upper floors falling into the flames turns the entire tower itself into a colossal self-destroying automatism.

The second plane had been timed to hit the second tower some minutes later so that video cameras would record it. For the rest of the day the world media showed over and over again the strike and the collapse of the towers. The destruction of a wing of the Pentagon and of both World Trade Center towers by this small commando of individuals is to all prior acts of infiltration and sabotage what the atomic bomb detonated on Hiroshima was to all prior bombings. It was an act on a world scale, being an attack on the command centres of the world's only superpower - a feat, Jake and Dinos Chapman said, of global performance art. The greatest fortresses of technologically-equipped collectives proved vulnerable to individuals using the most low-tech means and the most primitive of weapons, their bodies driven by their individual wills, which are determined to sacrifice themselves.

Within a week a New York Times reporter discovered that young Muslim men in Saudi Arabia, Egypt and Germany were wearing digital watches on whose faces there were pictures of the towers of the World Trade Center collapsing, again and again and again. The commando of 9/11 revealed an exultant and terrifying power in human bodies, a power they possess in being able to die.

The first riposte of the global superpower was to deny this human power; the military budget was increased to $500 billion, equal to that of all the other countries of the world combined, a dominance unprecedented in human history. It set out to demonstrate at once that it is capable of reducing Afghanistan to rubble, by high-altitude bombers taking off from remote locations launching smart bombs, a war of machines without the loss of a single American soldier. Then came the Shock and Awe assault on Iraq.

The public had long been informed of a succession of conflicts for which the European nations had formed alliances that led to the outbreak of the First World War; the public was well informed of the economic crisis and the rearmament of Germany that issued in the Second World War. But with the end of the Cold War, all the news media cut back most of their foreign correspondents; the public was quite uninformed about deep conflicts arising from the global struggle for markets and energy sources. The attack of 9/11 was thus sudden and unexpected; the media showed it as a multitude of deaths of ordinary Americans who simply wanted to live and make a living and had no idea they were participants in any kind of struggle. The intense visceral feelings of horror and fear for life aroused, periodically intensified by repeated Red Alerts, functioned as evidence in individuals across the land of their will to live, which appeared sacred to them, an innate core goodness – such that the force that struck such horror and fear in them could only be evil, be Evil itself. The question as to whether this sacred will to live could be a cause worth dying for did not arise: the high-tech arsenal the superpower already had and quickly increased would shock, awe and exterminate populations in Afghanistan, in Iraq, Iran and North Korea. Indeed this war would require not even economic sacrifice: while the military budget soared, taxes were cut across the board.

The man or woman on a suicide mission judges that he or she can do little or nothing for his or her own life or for his or her people by living, but can do something for them by dying, if only to counter in them the shame of their impotent existence. With what could one threaten the sacrificial individual? One cannot terrorize a commando that is determined to die. What one set out to do is hunt them down and exterminate them before they can die in their own way, with their own act. One sets out to demonstrate that they do nothing even if they succeed in their suicide mission. One does so by demonstrating that their existence, and the shame of the impotent and abject existence of their people, is and shall be worthless. One sets out to demonstrate that their deaths as their lives are worthless.

In the assault on Afghanistan and then on Iraq, the public watched the high-tech military juggernaut where soldiers did not risk their lives; six months later there appeared on television screens over the world the performances of soldiers – in the prisons of Iraq and Afghanistan. But a fraction of the photographs were shown, the US Senate which viewed 1800 photographs from Abu Ghraib suppressed public access to them, and the army immediately banned the use of digital cameras by soldiers, and no doubt many soldiers destroyed their films.

Ethics, from Aristotle to Heidegger, had made courage, the steadfastness in the face of death, the first virtue and the condition for the possibility of all the other virtues. Those who flee from battle, from seeking to kill others at the risk of their own lives, are cowards. Cowardice far from the battlefield is pure and abject when an armed man or woman lashes out upon one unarmed and defeated, forcing him to perform acts utterly degrading in his own eyes and take from him what he thought was his courage, even the courage to die, because he will not be allowed to die. The picture of the Iraq war is a picture of this extreme cowardice: the torture of unarmed and captive people, a young woman dragging a naked captive on the floor by a leash around his neck, young men stripping naked an old woman and sodomizing her with a stick. Cowardice doubling over itself in derisive laughter, cowardice doubling over upon itself, photographing itself, contemplating itself.

In the United States former high military and intelligence officials did explain that the long history of torture in military and civil conflicts has established that torture is not a reliable method of extracting information from captives. In captives who are committed and strong, torture arouses hatred and contempt of the torturers and hardens resolve. Those whom torture can break down physically and psychologically will admit to anything and invent whatever information is demanded in order to obtain a stop to the torture. It is clear that the torture practised in Abu Ghraib, where up to ninety percent of the captives knew nothing, was not practised because of the yield in information, and the commander of the intelligence agents there has now reported that little of interest was ever obtained. Although officially the hundreds of prisoners in Guantánamo are not yet charged because they are still being interrogated, it is clear that now three years later they have nothing useful to tell about the locations and operations of al-Qaeda. They will not be released because what their long incarceration and torture has produced is hatred and a hardened resolve that they would spread wherever they are released. The State Department is now searching for foreign countries that will accept them and can be reliably committed to keep them incarcerated without charge or trial for the rest of their lives.

In fact torture is inflicted in order to force the captive to confess that whatever he has to say is worthless. To force him to confess that his analysis of the socio-economic and political situation and the beliefs of his comrades are lies and delusions. The captive is kept in locations deprived of any contact with the outside and told he will never again see his comrades or his homeland or the outside world again. The torture works to break down his mind with sleep deprivation and blaring junk music such that the captive finds he can no longer think or remember. Beatings, electrical shocks, deprivation of pain killers and of food and water make him realize he can no longer maintain lucid consciousness, his very sense organs are shown to be untrustworthy. He is being forced to confess that he is incapable of truth. Stripping him naked, chaining him to lie in his own urine and shit force him to see that he is a body, useless, refuse in the way of others and of himself, excrement. The photographs taken by British soldiers in Basra show their captives naked entangled in nets, being beaten, lying in their own blood and urine and shit – for having stolen bread from the compound.

What dominates in the photographs taken at Abu Ghraib and the recent FBI report of practices at Guantánamo is the bizarre sexual degradation of the captives. This was aimed at what is taken to be the ideological framework of their minds and conduct: their Islamic faith. Female interrogators dressed in thongs and halters that rub their genitals and then rub menstrual blood onto the faces of the captives are very knowingly intended to make the Muslim captive polluted and thus unable to pray and invoke his God. The photographs feature men forced into homosexual acts and piled up naked penis upon buttocks in a grotesque forced homosexual orgy before the gleeful smirks of young American women. These are not the kind of cruelties sadistic individuals think up; you and I know that the macho bullies in high school locker rooms who humiliate the weak by calling them queer do not find young women to watch forced homosexual acts. These were scenarios of degradation enjoined by military intelligence officials who had read anthropological accounts of Islamic culture and mores; they were staged as specifically Muslim degradations. Their source-book was soon identified by anthropologists, a book entitled *The Arab Mind*, published by Zionist anthropologist Raphael Patai in 1973, much studied in the Pentagon.

Wherever torture is a state practice, from time to time a member of the insurgency is shown to the press and the cameras confessing that all he had believed in is lies and delusion. From time to time a captive is released to show his comrades his subhuman condition. The captives in Abu Ghraib were told that the photographs of their sexual degradation would be shown in their Muslim home communities, such that they would henceforth be pariahs and could survive only as stooles of their captors.

Totalitarian states, which include as part of their subjugation of their citizens the suppression of information, suppress knowledge of the state practice of torture. When, after the defeat, the German public learned of the existence of the Nazi death camps, the new German government institutionalized scrupulous respect for human rights. But what was the effect of the photographs of torture on the American public?

Artists Jake and Dinos Chapman spoke insightfully about the secret pleasure of Goya barely concealed in his set of etchings of the horrors of war drawn with such artistic perfection. They exhibited their set of Goya's etchings on which they had painted grinning clown and puppy-dog faces over the faces Goya had depicted stricken with heart-wrenching pathos. Barely concealed too is the excitement and triumph of the war reporters and news anchorman over some particularly wantonly vicious image of a war.

The media had suppressed the Abu Ghraib torture photographs for two weeks after they received them; now every news hour projected them again and again; the media and the public could not have enough of them. There was certainly an unavowed pleasure of several kinds in the media, in the public, with them.

The insistent projection of the photographs to the American public was contrived to provoke intense feelings of disgust and repugnance. President Bush gave the watchword: Americans view these images with disgust and repugnance. The intensity of disgust and repugnance across the land functioned as evidence, in each viewer, of his or her own core decency, his or her instinctual moral integrity. Americans looked about themselves, and could not imagine anybody they knew, any of the young men and women in the streets and in the mall, indulging in such depraved and disgusting acts. The aroused feeling of their own core moral integrity convinced them that, apart from these few perverts, the 150,000 National Guardsmen and enlisted servicemen and women there are brave, generous, idealistic liberators – Senator Lieberman even insisted: 'kind'. In his first public statement after the release of the photographs, Secretary of State Colin Powell declared: Now the world will see American Justice. The army itself was charged with the investigation and with punishing these few of its troops, for violation of its own code of conduct. The public was reassured of the irreproachable integrity of the army, whose procedures would be now installed in the interim Iraqi government, for the public trial of Saddam Hussein, immediately arraigned. The photographs had functioned to convince the American public of their intrinsic righteousness and the intrinsic righteousness of a collective action taken in their name by citizens like themselves.

Immediately after the attack of 9/11 on the control centres of American military and economic power, the American war president had identified the attackers as evil, irrationally motivated by pure evil, and, by contrast, the American population as good. But launching, from Florida, long-range high-altitude bombers to reduce Afghanistan to rubble was too obviously a massive outburst of revenge to convince the Americans of their intrinsic goodness. It was the photographs, the disgust and revulsion they aroused, that made their intrinsic goodness evident to them. They returned President Bush to office by a majority, seeing in him one like themselves.

REFERENCE

Turner, Victor (1982) *From Ritual to Theatre: The Human Seriousness of Play*, New York: PAJ.

Ramblers Associations
Witness / scopophilia / aprosexia / sight

But what might aesthetic performance bear witness to? Class, experience, godhead, secular power, History, complexity, process, suffering, injustice, coincidence, human vitality, intellect, Truth, racism, the concealment of Truth, community, the communitas of the performance event, a life, the kinaesthetic, form, liminality, the primary processes of human figuring, the presence of the King, the problem with presence, embarrassment, wit, historical materialism, a structure of feeling, the Party, Sensibility, a sense of fun, tradition, an invented tradition, synaesthesia, the slipperiness of signification, the redundancy of Theatre, the feminist struggle, virtuosity, martyrdom, the everyday, the struggle between stage and auditorium, alienation, this or that ideology, difference, the gut, the phenomenological, the stage's capacity to stage the phenomenological, the abject, paying attention …

The basic aesthetic of the US TV drama series *CSI Miami* (dir. Dick Wolf, CBS, 2002) was situated somewhere between documentary and commercial. It constructed a commodified present. Whenever the forensic investigator heroes thought they could bear witness to the actual events of the murder, the forward narrative of investigation would break for a flashback to the turn of events as presently hypothesized. The retrospective glimpse-episode was visually and aurally grainy, blurred, crowded and fast – a mediation, perhaps, between dream and documentary. As the series developed, the style of flashback changed. As the camera, we and the detectives gazed on the scene of evidence in the televised here-and-now, ghostly figures flowed through it, enacting in their possible present the reconstructed events.

The UK detective drama series *Miss Marple* (dir. John Strickland et al., LWT, 2004) bears witness to the modernity of the 1930s – superficiality, lesbianism, cars; fresh sound and much light – in its mediation of Agatha Christie's fiction. It simultaneously deploys the techniques of costume drama to produce Christie and her fiction as heritage, a commodified past. Here, in the evidential flashback to, say, a dinner-dance, the bodies are so much more immediate than in the glossy heritage-present, the 'past' so much more lived than the 'present' – to bear witness, perhaps, that the forensic imagination wants to recapture a source it can never access in its own moment.

I think first of feet. Until his feet got very bad, my friend Lewis did most of his seeing with his feet and intellect. With little sensory capacity in his eyes and ears, his feet would guide him through domestic, work and dance performance space, and his intellect through the ontological and social, from family to philosophy. He had and he has a prehensile intellect. And the whole of him bore insistent witness to the facts, both that perspective was not dependent on sight; and that the haptic (be it of sight, touch or smell) was as pertinent to living as was the perspectival. And that meant that time had to be taken. Not taken up; but taken at its proper pace so as to bear witness not only to the nuances of life, but also to the blindingly obvious … if only we take the time. But let's not be romantic: Lewis is very much a subject in a world of objects, a body informed by the Western art – or maybe trap – of perspective.

(Also, he would, sitting – projecting the real and into the real – stamp-gallop his enthusiasms-in-repose. Conjure the picture and re-embody the moment.)

So Lewis's feet, in my experience of him, were instruments both of the haptic and of the perspectival. It's surely also so for the rambler; or maybe here most aptly (getting a perspective on things, matching self to self) the Rambler of the 1930s. Bearing witness to public right (or ancient way; or rambling between the two?), the Rambler's feet (is this a movie now, a costume drama?) refind and redefine the immemorial route, the right of way – generated and sustained equally by infinitesimal negotiation of pitch or quality of land and some end in sight – as instances of field, pasture, woodland (when was it Nature?) become reterritorialized as path.

Samuel Johnson *Rambled* from 1750 to 1752 (reflecting in Number 89 on 22 January 1751, how, 'when a man shuts himself up in his closet, and bends his thoughts to the discussion of any abstruse question, he will find his faculties constantly stealing away' so that 'attention' is lost), *Adventured* from 1742 to 1754 and *Idled* from 1758 to 1760. And, on the way, in 1755, he published the first standard English dictionary. Its successor, the *Oxford English Dictionary* – in its *Shorter* form – gives us a perspective on 'pica', thus: '2. *Typogr.* A size of type, next below English … '; but then gives up on the projections of language to bear witness to the real thing:

In the innovative Jacobean masque, King James

This is Pica type.
This is small Pica type.

appears both as witness and to be witnessed. Placed

A digression: I've rambled across Google and even

at the point of perspective, he sees exactly what is to

some academic search engines, but I can't find the

be seen. And so placed, he is seen as full Presence.

work that will satisfy my fetish about fetish. My own

And as the masque turns to communal dancing, the

fetish is a bit smellier than feet (even Lewis's), though

courtly feet prance out the rhythms of peasant dances,

penis / baby / *foot* seems to me quite a nice Freudian

projected into the more genteel register of courtly style.

series. (A footing, perhaps? What are those rubber

Invigorated by the borrowed energy of honest labour,

socks *for*?) It's just that when Freud says that the

the aristos stamp on those from whom they steal. The

fetishist mistakes the part for the whole, the whole he

Brechtian performer appears as witness to a critical

has in mind is the human individual whole, corpus

attitude that sees beyond the obvious; bears witness to

and subject. Which of course makes Freud a fetishist.

the real divisions in the audience; bears witness to the

At the end of Volume VI (1761), the narrator of

need for communal action that recognizes the present

Tristram Shandy looks back on the shapes of his

as an historical moment. The Brechtian perfomer

narrative projections, 'the lines I moved in through

invokes the theological authority of the Party and of

my first, second, third, and fourth volumes'. He

Marxism as master text. Or, The Brechtian performer

bears witness to the partiality and constructedness of

does it by drawing squiggly lines on the page. He

what appears on the Brechtian stage.

makes no comment – they are supposed speak for

Montagu Slater first wrote a documentary account,

themselves. But looking back on Volume V (also 1761),

and then a play, *Stay Down Miner* (1937), to bear

he distinguishes between different orders of his own

digression from the intended story:

While A, a trip to Navarre, was an admitted distraction

witness to the recent stay-down strikes in South

from his purpose, B was an 'intended curve' to relate

Wales, where miners occupied their pits. The play

an interesting episode, and D was an interruption to

includes a verse passage that fashions a metaphor as

his purposed line, caused by agents within the narrative. And 'as for c c c c c they are nothing but parentheses, and the common *ins* and *outs* incident to the lives of the greatest ministers of state; and when compared with what men have done, – or with my own transgressions at the letters A B D – they vanish into nothing.' Finally, he looks forward to writing the ultimately straight line of narrative, and presents such a line there on the page, 'as straight a line as I could draw it, by a writing-master's ruler (borrowed for that purpose), turning neither to the right hand or to the left' (Sterne 1967: 454).

Sterne plays with the pretended presence of the narrator, his own real presence as writer and the limits of the novelistic form – even as it is being fairly-newly fashioned. He bears witness to the materiality of the book; to a drive to bear accurate witness, to pay proper attention; and to the overload that such a drive implies. And he bears witness to rambling, to the creative necessity of not paying attention.

At the start of Volume VII (1765), the narrator of *Tristram Shandy* sets out on a trip to France. He stays overnight at Calais, arriving and leaving in the dark. But he wagers with the reader that, on the basis of what his barber has told him, he could make as good an account of Calais as any travel writer ever did, who 'wrote and galloped ... galloped and wrote, ... wrote-galloping'. And such a chapter follows. Coming, in his account, to the Square, he comments, 'could there have been a fountain in all Calais, which it seems there cannot, as such an object would have been a great ornament, it is not to be doubted, but that the inhabitants would have had it in the very centre of this square' – which actually is 40 feet longer in one direction than the other, so not actually square, and therefore very aptly called *place* in French rather than *square* (Sterne 1967: 462-4).

In 1907, Freud wrote a letter to his family from his hotel room on the Piazza Colonna in Rome. He described his own experience and that of the crowd of the Piazza and its many calls on his attention, including advertisements and entertainments. But in his absorbed recollection of the evening, he could not remember whether or not there was a fountain there. Jonathan Crary makes an account of the letter and of Freud at the end of his *Suspensions of Perception* (1999).

Pay attention. That's what Crary says Western subjects have been increasingly refashioned to do, since the late nineteenth century. If Benjamin's

powerful, to my mind, as Benjamin's Angel of History. Slater figures History as 'Time, in the shape of a mine'. He contrasts the 'lighted roads of the past' with the 'blank wall of the future' and with the present, 'where workings narrow'. (Slater 1936: 251-3) The perspectively-focused present offers itself up only to haptic grapple, the negotiation of local affordances. And, from this perspective at least, there's a rhetorical uncertainty about those 'lighted roads'. Do they figure a history that gives up its linear clarity to retrospective view? Or the narrow vision of searchlights?

Writing on architecture, Puglisi (1999: 30-41) considers 'projection' as a shared term. For architects it means the geometrical translations of plans; for philosophers reflection on reality and for scientists its replication in models; for Freudians it means *empathy*; and for artists some form or another of *mimesis*. As a meta-term, projection is that which is necessary for the passage from 'one medium of representation to another'. And so both art and (mediatized) reality are 'based on a series of projective relations, each of which permits the representation of the object, but alone can never succeed in exhausting its content'. Reality for us now is 'articulated and structured in a metaphoric continuum'. The local *coup* in Puglisi's architectural argument comes with his citation of Borges and Cesares's fable of the architect Verdussen, who, recognizing that architecture, as a non-figurative art, 'cannot escape the confines of art by presenting the real object', projects and builds a structure of 'walls, windows, door and roof' that resists human habitation. Puglisi here strategically forgets what else architects properly project into their work, so as to identify such a building that happened for real.

J. J. Engel's prescription for gesture on the Neoclassical stage in the 1780s was that it should be true both to Nature and to Art. For example, the posture for Terror bore witness to the need to keep the object of terror in sight and at bay – and to the need to take extra breath. But it also bore witness – in the skewed symmetry, easeful grace and general tidiness of the body – to Art, on the model of classical statuary.

Letter VIII of Henry Siddons' adaptation of Engel's treatise ends with advice to the actor making a 'Passage from Repose to Attention': 'The attitude most expressive of nonchalance ... is when the body is seated at its ease, and leaning against any supporting object, the arms folded, and the legs crossed. Thus, the last moment of the tranquil attitude, I mean that approaching the nearest to coming activity, is the reraising the body directed towards the object that excites our interest, placing the hands equally separated upon the knees ...; and by these methods disposing the whole frame to exert itself and enter into immediate action' (Siddons 1822 [1807]: 49-54).

In 1981, in the opening chapter of *The Political Unconscious*, Frederic Jameson addresses the problem of historical interpretation. In particular, he asks questions about the historiographic drive to make narratives of the past, and generation experienced modernity in terms of fragmentation and dispersal, ours needs to recognize that, in fact, 'distraction can only be understood through its reciprocal relation to the rise of attentive norms and practices'. The disciplinary organization of labour, what Althusser called Ideological State Apparatuses, and the culture of spectacle require that we concentrate our attention, focus on a reduced number of stimuli at a time. But he goes on to say that if sustained attentiveness is a form of subjection, it is also a tool for resistant praxis, the enactment of a 'creative and free subjectivity' (Crary 1999: 2-3).

From this perspective, Freud's analytical technique of 'evenly suspended attention' is for Crary 'one of the most formidable techniques of attention to emerge in the twentieth century'. The analyst focuses on nothing in particular, in order to maintain a degree of attention to everything and anything. They bear witness to the analysand's own witness, while not going mad through deliberate attention. Freud's modernity 'is that he proposes a technique for dealing with a stream of information that has no evident structure or coherence' in 'a full reversal of the "searchlight" hypothesis of attention, which risks only finding out that which one already knows'. The aim is to find 'a way of decoding the historical genesis of an indecipherable present, in terms of an individual human subject' (Crary 1999: 367-8).

Lewis Jones, Salamanda Tandem Bodycam Project (1996)

argues that novelistic narratives have value as partial textualizations of past social realities that resist recovery in their totality, a totality that anyhow would be unfigurable. This, then, might for us be a flashback from a time where Foucault's champions make sharp distinctions between Althusser and him, to one where Jameson, at the hazy edge of his writing (a framing footnote), identifies Althusser, Foucault, Deleuze and Guattari, Kristeva and Derrida as part of a quasi-coherent 'anti-interpretative' assemblage, which despite itself deals precisely in hermeneutics (Jameson 1981: 23 n7).

In passing, let's note that Jameson regards those basic units of narrative he calls 'ideologemes' as 'free-floating', in the sense that they are never actually present in any novel. Though they might, he suggests, be found in minor literary forms. As interpretation plays its game of monument and ornament, major form and minor, figured history and so resistance again takes the shape of the dominant.

Crary follows both the hermeneutically-inclined Jameson and the hermeneutically-disinclined Deleuze and Guattari - and many others - to suggest that 'visuality' is itself a product of 'forces of specialisation and separation'. Life, and our experience of it, is composed of 'irreducibly *mixed* modalities', gathered up in our historical embodiments. For him, modern critical theory was 'derived from a now pointless critique of presence' and has been blind to the fact that 'whether or not one has direct perceptual access to self-presence is intrinsically irrelevant within modern disciplinary and spectacular culture'. Attention had already become the compensation for 'the *historical* obliteration of the possibility of thinking the idea of presence in perception' (Crary 1999: 2-4).

In '1981: A skewed symmetry', part of *A Thousand Plateaus*, Deleuze and Guattari bear witness to the moment when the front paw of the beast becomes

Lewis Jones, Salamanda Tandem Bodycam Project (1996)

There's another significant datum that Crary wants us to pay attention to: that attention is not encompassed by the realm of the visual. 'Spectacular culture is not founded on the necessity of making a subject see, but rather on strategies in which individuals are isolated, separated and *inhabit time* as disempowered'. It's a matter of disciplined embodiment. So the feet that dance to trance can be engines of resistance. (Consider the composed body as a synchronic narrativization of prior experience, a particular gathering up of the distributed archive of Foucauldian infrastructures). And 'Attention Deficit Syndrome' - indeed, the whole gamut of 'aprosexia' and its counterpart obsessive attention - is part and parcel of the medicalization of non-normative embodiments in the modern West - to which fact autistic subject Wendy Lawson (2001) will readily bear witness.

prehensile and grasps the branch of the tree as an implement. In their schema, there is here a process of mutual deterritorialization and reterritorialization. The assemblage that has been paw dissolves and flows into the assemblage that has been branch, which dissolves and flows in the complementary or coincidental direction, at its own particular pace. There is a mutual reterritorialization, as hand and implement. What de/reterritorializations might we imagine or engineer between our assemblages of performance - at the levels of being-on stage; witnessing; forgetting; dissolving; convening; acting on the Real; writing histories ... What machines can we access, or might access us, to engender such drifts, gallops, dissolutions, focusings?

If we're in the business here of taking performance as a perspective and getting a perspective on - and projection for - performance, then Lewis for me figures as much as monument as he might as ornament.

REFERENCES

Crary, Jonathan (1999) *Suspensions of Perception*, London: MIT Press.

Jameson, Frederic (1981) *The Political Unconscious: Narrative as a Socially Symbolic Act*, London: Methuen.

Lawson, Wendy (2001) *Understanding and Working With the Spectrum of Autism: An Insider's View*, London and Philadelphia: Jessica Kingsley.

Puglisi, Luigi Prestinenza (1999) *Hyper Architecture: Spaces in the Electronic Age*, trans. Lucinda Byatt. Basel, Boston and Berlin: Birkhäuser.

Siddons, Henry (1822 [1807]) *Practical Illustrations of Rhetorical Gesture and Action, adapted to the English drama. From a work on the same subject by M. Engel*, London: Richard Phillips.

Slater, Montagu (1978 [1936]) 'Stay Down Miner' in John Lucas (ed.) *The 1930s: A Challenge to Orthodoxy*, Brighton: Harvester Press.

Sterne, Laurence (1967) *The Life and Opinions of Tristram Shandy*, Harmondsworth: Penguin.

LAURIE BETH CLARK **FIELD STATION 7**

Dear Friends and Family

Dear Friends and Family:

I am writing to you from field station number seven, the field station of Seeing, where I have been stationed for the last thirty years, if one can date one's postings from the time we leave home and choose a professional alignment. The landscape is the rolling hills and grassy plains of Visual Arts and, more recently, Visual Culture. Within my domain are the unincorporated districts of Audience, Perspective and Witnessing. I've visited many of the other stations at one point or another, partly because the station itself is characterized by restlessness, but Visuality is what I come home to.

The field station resembles a fire tower, a single large room on stilts, the highest point in this vicinity, with windows on all sides, outfitted for single occupancy. It's key that the station is meant only for one occupant, as that is the conceit necessary for the proper functioning of perspectival vision in its dominant human and mechanized incarnations. But this isolated contemplation of the landscape, while in a great North American tradition of Thoreau and Abbey, has been an impediment to producing my report. I've more often traveled to gatherings of other 'rangers' and in the past been more motivated to discourse by sociality.

From here, I can just barely see another tower in each direction, as the stations are positioned in such a way as to allow us to relay signals from one to another and thus pass messages over a long distance. Some months ago, such a signal did arrive asking me to write a descriptive and predictive report of the view from my station taking into account both Scopophilia (love of looking) and Aprosexia (inability to concentrate).

Both terms have some elements of deviance: the former is aligned with 'unusual' sexual practices, the latter with an 'abnormal' lack of attentiveness. Neither scopophilia nor aprosexia have been burning questions for performance theory or practice to date. Scopophilia was a *cause célèbre* for media studies and aprosexia has been a primary concern of child psychology. Both, interestingly, are gendered maladies. Voyeurism is most often prosecuted in adult men, attention deficit disorder most frequently diagnosed in boy children. Through my field glasses, I can spot the grown man who cannot stop looking, walking hand in hand with the boy child who cannot pay attention.

It's surprising that performance has not paid more attention to visuality, given that it found something of an institutional home in Art Schools and University Art Departments, at least where it is taught. Performance *theory* pedagogy (a.k.a. Performance Studies) emerged and has been more situated in a relationship with theatre studies. Performance is *practised* and *produced* in a wider range of contexts than it is taught. Dancers, poets, musicians and actors are as likely as visual artists to find something useful in the hybrid practices of live art, and the venues for dissemination are as likely to be theatres as galleries. But it is rare (in the US anyway) to find a course, let alone

Dear Kind Stranger:

In the time since I began writing this report, the landscape as I imagine it has changed substantially. What I had visualized as savanna is now alluvial. It's like the flood plain of the South American pantanal, traversed by truck in one season and by boat in another. I always knew that the request for the report was relayed here from overseas and that some of the others who would produce reports were across other oceans, though from this landlocked US state it was hard to keep in mind. Even from the island of Manhattan, which gives the frame of reference to much of this report, the water was hard to see from the street-level performance spaces. But the power of water was brought into our domestic spaces most intensely this year first by the Indian Ocean tsunami and then by Hurricane Katrina, making our safe and dry stations seem not so much like rooms on stilts as arks on high ground. The shift, however, is not caused merely by external communications; it's a place I've written myself towards, the need for a different metaphor. The communication I want to make has less in common with a signal to a station I can locate on the horizon, with whose operator I have communicated frequently in the past, than with a message placed in a bottle in hopes of eliciting a response from a stranger.

If you find this message, would you consider writing an ethnographic study of performance art spectators? I want someone to study our demographic, both statistically and anecdotally. Beyond friends and family, practitioners and critics, who are the strangers filling our seats (or standing or wherever we've positioned them)? Who responds to ads in the paper or to the posters we design? Who regularly turns to the performance art listings in *Time Out* and goes to see unfamiliar work? And what does this group of interested strangers like about the genre? Is performance consumption constituted like music? Do audience members follow particular artists? How do scopophilia and aprosexia line up with loyalty and promiscuity?

In the phrase 'we go to see performance' – who are 'we'? Do we know the first thing about audiences for live art? I recently had dinner with a friend and her partner, whom I was meeting for the first time. When asked where they had met, they said they first noticed one another as regular audience members at the same performance art events. Now my friend is a performance artist and producer, so I was not the least surprised to learn that she regularly attends live art events. But her friend was not, and I realized in this moment that I had never imagined people who are not practitioners but who regularly go to live art events.

Is there a *general* public for performance art? Prior to this small epiphany, whom did I imagine I was making my work for? I certainly always assumed there were practitioners in the audience. I go to see as much performance as I can and expect that other performance-makers do the same. I know that family and friends are there and always hope there are critics and curators. I think I did imagine spectators who were drawn in by an investment in the content or attracted by compelling graphics to single events. I also had a clear picture in my mind of identity-based spectatorship, like the regular audience members at WOW café. What I had failed to imagine was

a comprehensive curriculum, in performance anywhere but in an art school. Why should this be the case? Arguably the skill set for making performance has no more in common with painting and printmaking than it does with voice and scenography.

The institutionalization of performance *practice* pedagogy in a *visual* milieu suggests that we might have explored a unique set of relationships. Forty years of institutional cohabitation – North American genealogies of performance tend to start with 1960s happenings while giving lip service to Renaissance and futurist antecedents – ought to be enough for us to see some mutual concerns. But influence seems to have gone largely one way; that is, installational strategies have thoroughly permeated visual arts practice, but questions of visuality have remained marginal to performance practice.

Live art has been rather aprosexic with regard to vision; it has not consistently paid attention. Performances exploring the privilege of spectatorship have been sporadic at best, driven by individual artist's interests and concentrated in feminist performances, when the film studies theorization of the gaze was given its due. What performance has more wholeheartedly embraced than 'seeing' is 'being seen' (and heard). This may be said of the predominance of solo self-referential performance, but that will have to be addressed from other field stations. What falls in my purview is live art's incestuous relationship with the camera, as demonstrated by the ubiquity of televisions on stage, especially with live feed video. Conveniently, the syndrome of scopophilia includes not only the erotics of seeing but the erotics of being seen as well.

Neither a critique of the dominance of the gaze nor a reflexive study of it, performance has nevertheless explored its relationship to vision extensively (if unsystematically) through documentation. Some argue that it is the simultaneous emergence of these media that so intimately coupled performance with video. The earliest portable consumer video recorders became available for artistic experimentation around the same time as performance appeared, and so it seemed 'natural' to investigate these emerging, experimental, time-based media together. Others fault visual arts for fetishizing permanence by trying to make a stable object of something as transient as the gaze. Regardless of cause, this heightened awareness of being seen, along with the high value placed on task-based rather than dramatic structures, may be live art's most perspicuous contribution to mass culture. Reality television as the apotheosis of performance art?

The naming of the practice as performance is arguably due to its visual arts (and poetry) circumstances, since liveness hardly distinguishes performance from theatre, music or dance. You'd have to use modifiers like 'experimental' or 'non-dramatic' to modify the term to differentiate it from other performing arts. It's interesting to note that the relationship between performance and seeing (or for that matter between theatre and seeing, or even, illogically, between music and seeing) is established linguistically in other ways as well. For example, we go to 'see' performance. Even if that is not what we do there, it's how we discuss the total experience, which may be in fact dominated by hearing texts and/or sounds (and include other sensory elements as well).

a 'subscriber public', people with a loyalty to the genre, or the discipline of live art.

My question here is not about who forms the base for the Brooklyn Academy of Music's Next Wave series or the Lincoln Center Festival. These crowds seem to be the same cultured, liberal-bourgeoisie audiences that support Broadway and take season tickets for the Opera. What I'm curious about is who is in the audience at those small and persistent-against-all-odds alternative spaces like Franklin Furnace or PS 122 or Dixon Place. Could we devise the term 'genral' public for a public that invests in and cultivates a genre? Is there a 'genral' public for performance art rather than a general public? Who deliberately reads the listings in the *Village Voice*, the *Reader* or *Time Out* looking for performance as the category of work s/he would like to 'see'?

I want to know who is watching, who is looking, who is paying attention, who is witnessing, and from what perspective. How does our public structure participation? Is the manner of spectatorship as hybrid as the terms of production? Several colleagues in the past (notably Suzanne Lacy and Rob Witting) have encouraged me to think about at least five modes of spectatorship (1-performer, 2-witness, 3-direct spectator, 4-indirect recipient and 5-viewer of documentation), though new technologies are troubling these distinctions. Does this hypothesis correspond to actual audience accounts experience?

I had been thinking that, to stimulate your imagination, I would send you a Viewmaster or educational filmstrip of thirty commemorative 'stills' from performances, most ones I have never seen, yet I carry in my imagination as though I had been there – performances for which I am a category 4 spectator. These would be paradigmatic moments in (mostly) U.S. performance art history, the performances that comprise the idiosyncratic histories we teach when we initiate students into the genre. Mine includes: John Cage's silent composition, Yves Klein's leap, an Allan Kaprow happening, Gilbert and George's living sculptures, Charlotte Moorman playing a Nam June Paik cello, William Wegman's dogs, Geoffrey Hendricks's and Bici Forbes's 'Flux Divorce', Vito Acconci masturbating, Christo and Jeanne Claude's 'Running Fence', Joseph Beuys speaking to the hare, Hermann Nitsch's castration, Chris Burden's crucifixion, Carolee Schneeman's interior scroll, Philip Glass's and Robert Wilson's project 'Einstein on the Beach', Marina Abamović and Ulay naked in a doorway, Laurie Anderson playing the violin, Stelarc's suspensions, Anna Mendieta's silhouette, Mierle Laderman Ukeles shaking the hands of sanitation workers, the Guerrilla Girls's masked lectures, members of Sankai Juku hanging upside down, Karen Finley covered in chocolate, Teching Hsieh roped to Linda Montano, Suzanne Lacy's women on the beach, looking at Annie Sprinkle's cervix, Guillermo Gómez-Peña and Coco Fusco in a cage, Cindy Sherman's disguises, Spaulding Gray seated at a table, Tim Miller in the lap of an audience member, William Pope.L crawling up Broadway. And yours?

Witnessing the Witness

Oh woe is me
T'have seen what I have seen, see what I see.
Ophelia, in Hamlet

But my dear Sir, my dear Sir, look – at the world
– and look – at my TROUSERS!
Nagg, in Endgame

I want to argue for an ethical position in the labour we do as spectators and researchers of theatre and performance, as well as in our capacities as artists in these fields. My aim is to propose a (very) preliminary framework for examining our positions as witnesses, not merely as onlookers and observers but as active and engaged witnesses. I want to argue that by consciously taking on a witnessing position when doing or watching performances as well as when participating in or watching the world in which we live, we can at least begin to establish such a moral stance. Performances as well as other artistic expressions, and today also the electronic media in conjunction with other social and cultural institutions, show and teach us what it means to become a witness. And by witnessing the witnesses we learn how to become witnesses ourselves. Drawing attention to our own role as witnesses within the larger field, where much of the knowledge we have about the world is mediated by other witnesses, is a form of empowerment with evident ethical consequences.

The route I want to take, and obviously only a very rough map can be presented here, will take me from Nietzsche's challenging speculations on the origins of tragedy through the narrow needle's eye of the Freudian primal scene. From there I will move on to Brecht's first insights into how a primary epic theatre can be modeled. My aim is to demarcate the significance of the witness within the cultural and critical discourses we pursue and attempt to sketch briefly how the protocols of witnessing are constituted and how they have been transformed, in particular in relation to theatre and performance. Regardless of whether the witness is finally supporting or subverting the officially accepted narratives in our societies (and as I will indicate later there are still deep-seated religious undercurrents in the term 'witnessing'), the position of the witness is of crucial importance for the cultural negotiations that are triggered by performances.[1]

Witnessing is based on a dialectic between the private and the public spheres, fluctuating between the intimate forms of witnessing outlined by Freud and the formation of the libido as well as individual trauma on the basis of the primal scene, on the one hand, and the Brechtian forms of testimony or official reports about a public event, a street accident, which is retold by a story-teller, regulating public opinion as well as ideological positions, on the other. Even if the mutual relevance of these two intellectual endeavors is perhaps not immediately apparent, it is my contention that examining them in tandem is productive for the development of such an ethical approach to theatre and performance.

Peggy Phelan has also implicitly pointed at such a dialectic between the private and the public, arguing that even if 'theatre has borrowed the understanding of witnessing from psychoanalysis and political ethics, it seems to me that theatre has been somewhat shy in pursuing what it can add to the force of witnessing itself' (1999: 13). Witnessing, she claims is so rich with nuances, that 'to solicit an ethical witness in a theatre event requires one to trust that the border of performance exceeds its spatial and temporal boundaries' (13). Following this important insight, I am interested in the protocols that transform us into conscious witnesses exactly at that liminal borderline where we are simultaneously watching both the performance and the world.

Performances invite us to 'look at the world' but also at the trousers, as the tailor in the joke told by Nagg, Hamm's father in Beckett's *Endgame*, commands his frustrated customer to do. When the tailor after several weeks of hard work has not yet finished the trousers the customer who has ordered them finally complains that God made the world in six days and 'you are not bloody well capable of making me a pair of trousers in three months'. To this the tailor makes his cynical remark: 'But my dear Sir, my dear Sir, look – at the world – and look – at my TROUSERS!' (1990:103). Look we apparently must in order to present a testimony about this world. And we are always asked to compare the world with the trousers – the work of art.

The annals of the theatre and the performing arts contain the histories of how spectator-witnesses have been positioned vis-à-vis something we/they are watching and are invited or even required to respond to or react to. The witnesses presented on the stage are witnessed by spectators, who, just like the performers, are also witnessing the events in the world around us. In *The Birth of Tragedy* Nietzsche developed this triangular relationship on the basis of Schlegel's notion that the chorus in Greek tragedy - a kind of collective witness - is an 'ideal spectator'. Nietzsche proposed a multi-focal vision where the spectator, at least on an ideal level, is at the same time viewing the performance both from inside and outside the fictional world, both as a member of the chorus and as an external spectator.

The Dionysian condition, 'with its annihilation of the ordinary bounds and limits of existence' (Nietzsche 1967: 59), as well as the magical power of art itself are Nietzsche's guarantees that the spectator will neither be completely separated from nor totally absorbed by the world of illusion, but will be able to develop a viewpoint that examines both the performance and the world from such a witnessing position. Nietzsche concludes his argument by saying that

> the chorus is the 'ideal spectator' insofar as it is the only beholder, the beholder of the visionary world of the scene. A public of spectators as we know it was unknown to the Greeks: in their theatres the terraced structure of concentric arcs made it possible for everybody to actually *overlook* the whole world of culture around him and to imagine in absorbed contemplation, that he himself is a chorist. In the light of this insight we may call the chorus in its primitive form, in proto-tragedy, the mirror image in which the Dionysian man contemplates himself. (1967: 62-3)

Nietzsche's bifocal theatrical vision, looking at the performance and the world simultaneously, creating an almost narcissistic self-awareness for and of the spectator, also contains a word-play on the double sense of 'overlook' in English as well as in the German original - *übersehen* - meaning both to survey and to ignore. This double sense can also facilitate the establishment of an ethical position. Our viewing hovers between an investigative surveying position of heightened attention of what we are actually seeing, but at the same time it also includes something that we have become used to overlooking in the sense of ignoring. The function of the witness in performance is to undo this ignorance through the investigative protocols of witnessing.

«»

In his essay 'The Street Scene' Bertolt Brecht drafted a model for a '"natural" epic theatre' where the witness of a traffic accident, an event that is only a metaphor for those failures of the past we have been taught to call history, transforms herself into a performer. This epic performance is based on

an incident such as can be seen at any street corner: an eyewitness demonstrating to a collection of people how a traffic accident took place. The bystanders may not have observed what happened, or they may simply not agree with him, may 'see things a different way'; the point is that the demonstrator acts the behaviour of driver or victim or both in such a way that the bystanders are able to form an opinion about the accident. (Brecht 1982: 121)

The bystander-spectators who have not seen the accident itself thus become secondary witnesses to this event, watching and listening to the eyewitness. One of the crucial points in this context is that through this procedure performances will enable the spectators to participate in an ethical discourse, making it possible for them 'to form an opinion' about events where questions of right or wrong, justice and injustice are contested. Or as Tim Etchells has argued,

> to witness an event is to present it in some fundamentally ethical way, to feel the weight of things and one's own place in them, even if that place is simply, for the moment, as an onlooker ... The art-work that turns us into witnesses leaves us, above all, unable to stop thinking, talking and reporting what we've seen. (1999: 17-18)

Brecht's model, when transferred from the street-corner of the outside world to the theatre stage, clearly challenges the position expressed by Paul Celan in his poem 'Aschenglorie' about the possibility of bearing witness about the Shoah, after the survivors have become old and died:

> *Niemand*
> *zeugt für den*
> *Zeugen*

Nobody can bear witness for the witnesses, says Celan. In performances, however, it is imperative to do so, because this is the way in which the actor will in some sense take on the responsibility of a witness in order to report about the failures of the past.

For Celan, the consequences of a personal trauma, having witnessed something that cannot be communicated by others, is transformed into a moral position where the survivor becomes a witness. For Primo Levi, however, even

> we the survivors, are not the true witnesses ...
> We survivors are not only an exiguous but also anomalous minority: we are those who by their prevarications or good luck did not touch the bottom. Those who did so, those who saw the Gorgon, have not returned to tell about it or have returned mute, but they are the 'Muselmans',

the submerged, the complete witnesses, the ones whose depositions would have a general significance. (1989: 63-4)

For Levi only the victim whose imminent/immanent death makes him or her completely mute can become a witness.

Something of this traumatic muteness, but on a very different scale, is also generated by the Freudian primal scene, a paradigm for witnessing that emphasizes its private, most intimate dimensions. Freud's principal objective was to point at the deep-going consequences of this 'scene', a kind of proto-theatrical scene, for the moral-psychological formation of the individual. The repressed aggressions initiated by such a real or even imagined primal scene, as Freud himself even claimed, can lead to an outburst of violence and illicit sexual relations. Whereas Brecht located the origins of the Epic theatre with a actor-demonstrator who from having witnessed a public catastrophe gradually becomes a scientist (like e.g. Galileo), for Freud the witness is a (male) child triggered by the scientific curiosity about his own source of origin, who seeks out the intimate relations between his parents as the answer to this curiosity. However, this child-witness/scientist is gradually transformed into a potential murderer of his own father and a *tyrannus*.

The dialectics between the Freudian and Brechtian points of departure for the notion of witnessing show how broad its range and its shifts of meaning are. Also, when examining the etymology of the notion of the witness from a broader historical perspective, the fact that in the Greek of the New Testament the word *martus/marturion* actually means both 'witness' and 'martyr' is very significant. From a religious-theological perspective a witness is someone who was ready to become a martyr, proving the strength of his faith in Christ by submitting himself or herself to a violent death. A martyr bears witness to his or her beliefs and willingly becomes a victim because of this faith; it is someone who by his or her death bears witness to the truth of a holy writ, someone who is put to death for his or her religion, or sacrifices his or her life for the sake of a principle, or to sustain a certain cause. As the monotheistic religions gradually consolidated their belief systems, the martyr/witness became someone who wanted to expose his or her inner subjective self to the world as a believer and was willing to pay with his or her own life by bearing testimony and witnessing to that inner truth.

At some point, and here we need the historians for the exact details, through the processes of secularization as well as other developments, this kind of witness gradually shifted to become someone who had seen the suffering or the death of another person, a messenger of someone else's affliction, rather than the victim himself or herself,

strengthening the legal implications of this notion. This also made it possible for the witness to become a moral agent who is acting from an ethical position based on universal human values rather than figuring as a religious martyr attempting to demonstrate the superiority of his or her own faith by supernatural powers.

But the proximity of the witness to the victim remained. True, the theatre developed strategies through which this theological Gordian knot of the martyr and the witness were questioned and criticized. It is possible to discern a gradual separation of the witness from the victim on the stages, but they remained closely connected on the narrative level, even while their respective roles gradually shifted. In such performative contexts, the witness frequently becomes victimized but not to prove the existence of any supernatural power. Rather, the act of witnessing, or eavesdropping, as it is called in the theatre, was seen as a form of transgression, no doubt closely related to the widespread ambivalence towards the theatre as an institution where all the spectators are actually eavesdropping in one way or another, for which the eavesdropper was punished.

The interactions between the audience-spectator and the on-stage witness establish meta-theatrical performance features that in different ways simultaneously disclose and evoke the workings of a specific performance as well as the ways in which the theatrical machineries of this performance are constructed. These interactions, I claim, are an integral aspect of the theatrical communication of a specific performance. The fact that some of the fictional characters are watching or witnessing what the other characters on the stage are saying and doing while the spectators in the auditorium are also watching the performance (including of course the performances of these witnesses), establishes the hermeneutic perspective from which a performance implicitly 'invites' its spectators to watch and interpret this performance. This invitation, or sometimes even seduction, subliminally induces the spectators to reflect or to react to their own experience as spectators, hopefully transforming the passive theatregoers into active spectator-witnesses with a clear ethical agenda.

There are at least three forms through which a character on the stage becomes such a viewer or witness. The most obvious one is by presenting a play or a performance-within-the performance like *The Mousetrap* in the third act of *Hamlet* or Kostia's play in the first act of *The Seagull*. The second is a witness who is an eavesdropper like Polonius in many of the scenes of Hamlet, e.g., in the closet scene where Hamlet kills him while he is hiding behind the arras spying on Hamlet's and Gertrude's conversation, or like Orgon hiding under the table in *Tartuffe*. When

Polonius spies on Hamlet in Gertrude's closet after a long and intricate series of scenes where he and others have been spying, he is victimized, and it is important to add that he becomes a victim who is ridiculed rather than becoming a martyr. Also Ophelia undergoes a process of victimization. After she has witnessed Hamlet's 'madness' in the 'Nunnery' scene, she soliloquizes 'Oh woe is me / T'have seen what I have seen'. The anguish of having seen what she has seen is no doubt one of the reasons for her madness and suicide.

Eavesdropping appears both in tragedies and comedies, and it is clearly a transgressive activity. In tragedy the eavesdropper is usually punished; in comedy the eavesdropper does not always understand the full implications of what he or she learns by this transgression.

The third manner in which a viewer or witness can be introduced is through the appearance of a supernatural character, like for example the ghost in *Hamlet*, who we somehow must assume witnesses the events of the whole play from the very beginning. The invisible presence of the ghost triggers the action of the play, but as a creature from a supernatural world, he is not able fully to control the development of the events. Sometimes, however, such an otherworldly creature, who is also a witness, appears at the very end of a play to set things right again, as a *Deus ex Machina*.

The first form of viewing on the stage, the performance-within-the-performance, emphasizes the aesthetic dimension of witnessing; the second, exemplified by the eavesdropper, draws attention to its psychological aspects; and the third, introducing the more or less omniscient, supernatural witness, emphasizes the metaphysical aspects of viewing. In practice they are however not always clearly separated but interact in different ways. Shakespeare's *Hamlet* abounds in all the three forms of witnessing and eavesdropping on the stage, all of which in different ways draw our attention to a certain aspect of the medium of the theater, its inherent dependence on watching. Thus, at the same time as these forms of witnessing expose the theatricality of a performance, they also assist us in establishing the specific hermeneutic perspectives from which it can be watched, thus empowering the spectator to become an active witness.

«»

Before concluding this short presentation of the witness in and of performance, it is necessary to say something about myself as an Israeli. I live in a country that has suppressed more than three million Palestinians for almost four decades now, and is still occupying that part of the land which the majority from both peoples have agreed will eventually become the independent state of Palestine. Regardless of what the future holds, the years of occupation will no doubt remain a very difficult-to-heal wound for many generations. So far, both peoples are living in a situation of vicious circles where any kind of progress towards a peaceful solution – like negotiations, reaching agreements, coordinating Israeli withdrawals, establishing institutions that will become the infrastructure for a future Palestinian state – are constantly disrupted by the mutual drive for retaliation and sacrifice. Looking at myself within this conflict, I also realize that it is impossible for me to be fully objective, because the notion of witnessing is so closely connected to the narratives of suffering, sacrifice, victimization and retaliation that have been feeding the conflict. This is one of the reasons why we so frequently use the word 'tragic' when we are talking about the Israeli-Palestinian conflict. It implies a sacrificial pattern where human lives are at risk.

Trying to understand the implications of this conflict and the actions and discourses it generates in relation to the notion of the witnessing, it is possible to draw the following very tentative conclusions:

1. The religious and the ideological forces at work within this conflict as well as in the region at large, and perhaps in the whole world, are gradually bringing us back to the earliest forms of the witness-martyr, undoing the critical distance between the witness and the victim initiated by the processes of secularization and theatrical performativity.

- On the Israeli side the Shoah in a way 'transformed' all Jews into victims/martyrs/witnesses. As a state, Israel has become a 'survivor-witness', frequently only expressing itself through military force so that the Jews will supposedly never become victimized again. The universal understanding we must draw from the Shoah has not been emphasized clearly enough.

- On the Palestinian side Islamic fundamentalism has reformulated the 'shahid' as the true martyr committing suicide for his or her faith, in order to kill others, blindly.

2. At the same time documentaries, photographs, human rights organizations on both sides, fact-finding missions, demonstrations, films, theatre performances, dance, the visual arts – in short all the media, journalistic and aesthetic, as well as the critical discourses accompanying and commenting on them, informing us about the atrocities committed by the Israeli army, the

settlers and the different security organizations – serve as our witnesses. And recently, a gradually growing number of very impressive documentary films and exhibitions has appeared, showing us the ugliest aspects of the occupation.

3. The religious and the nationalistic discourses are manipulated in such a way that it is very difficult to distinguish between them and the supposedly more objective media discourses. The Brechtian street-corner witness, who was supposed to give such an objective report so that we could form our own opinion about what he or she has seen, frequently becomes a preacher, while the media relate to what they are reporting as if they have witnessed a mythical primal scene.

«»

The difficulties raised by the fact that today we are witnessing wars and famines as well as festive occasions through images broadcast to us on television or still photographs have not yet been fully accounted for. There are some recent attempts to do this, like Susan Sontag's reflections on the complexities of witnessing in the modern global media world in her book *Regarding the Pain of Others*. According to Sontag, 'in a system based on the maximal reproduction and diffusion of images, witnessing requires the creation of star witnesses, renowned for their bravery and zeal in procuring important, disturbing photographs' (2004: 33; see also Boltansky 1999). This form of witnessing has 'regarded', i.e., witnessed the suffering of others and is now bringing it to the attention of the public. What the consequences of this will be for the future of performance and witnessing is impossible to say.

However, in order to reconstitute and to revive the moral force of the witness, a combination of two rhetorical positions must be reclaimed and re-developed. First, the legal status of the witness as someone who is supposedly giving testimony in a court of justice has to be more clearly distinguished in the performance contexts. And second, it is important to regard the witness in a trans-historical, even metaphysically determined context, as proposed by Walter Benjamin in his famous meditation on the Paul Klee painting 'Angelus Novus'. This painting, Benjamin says,

shows an angel looking as though he is about to move away from something he is fixedly contemplating. His eyes are staring, his mouth is open, his wings are spread. This is how one pictures the angel of history. His face is turned towards the past. Where we perceive a chain of

events, he sees one single catastrophe which keeps piling wreckage upon wreckage and hurls it in front of his feet. The angel would like to stay, awaken the dead, and make whole what has been smashed. (1969: 257)

This angel is also a witness, looking back at us, who are situated in the past. A storm blowing from Paradise, where history began, has got caught in his wings and it 'irresistibly propels him into the future to which his back is turned' (258). This means that we are looking into the future behind the back of this angel-witness. What we will see there is up to the next generation of theatre- and performance-artists to show.

NOTES

1. In terms of the Field Stations, this positions my contribution in the lower right hand corner of the map, connecting between #6 and #7: exploring the visualities of performance as a key to moral issues.

REFERENCES

Beckett, Samuel (1990) *Endgame* in *The Complete Dramatic Works*, London: Faber and Faber.

Benjamin, Walter (1969) 'Theses on the Philosophy of History' in *Illuminations*, New York: Schocken Books.

Boltansky, Luc (1999) *Distant Suffering: Morality, Media and Politics*, Cambridge: Cambridge University Press.

Brecht, Bertolt (1982) 'The Street Scene: A Basic Model for an Epic Theatre', in John Willet (ed. and trans.) *Brecht on Theatre*, London: Methuen, London.

Etchells, Tim (1999) *Certain Fragments: Contemporary Performance and Forced Entertainment*, London and New York: Routledge.

Levi, Primo (1989) *The Drowned and the Saved*, London: Abacus.

Nietzsche, Friedrich (1967) *The Birth of Tragedy*, (trans. Walter Kaufmann), New York: Vintage Books.

Phelan, Peggy (1999) 'Performing Questions, Producing Witnesses', Foreword to Tim Etchells, *Certain Fragments: Contemporary Performance and Forced Entertainment*, London and New York: Routledge.

Sontag, Susan (2004) *Regarding the Pain of Others*, New York: Picador.

The Effect Produced

I would like to thank Paul Allain for his help with my own translation of this article. Thanks also to Jean-Marie Avril and Cathy Piquemal who have also worked on translating 'The Effect Produced'.

The notion of the produced effect (in German: *Wirkung*) has been little used by theories on theatre and yet it is very useful in examining how theatre acts on society, on the audience or on the individual spectator. Normally associated with it, in opposition, is the notion of reception, namely the manner in which society, audience or spectator responds to the dramatic text or the performance. These two notions of produced effect and reception, which in ordinary use aren't always distinguished from one another, make us grasp how theatre influences us and how we influence it.

In the sixties and seventies of the last century, German aesthetic theory was opposing a *Wirkungsästhetik* (an aesthetic of the produced effect) to a *Rezeptionästhetik* (an aesthetic of reception) and the question was to know whether we had to – for an analysis of the text – take into account the production's mechanisms or rather deal with the act of reading and reception. The aesthetic of reception (Jauss 1977, Warning 1975, Grimm 1977) came to fill in a gap that the study of authors and their writing techniques had often concealed: a lack of knowledge of the audience and their horizon of expectation. Nowadays we recognize that one must approach the production and the reception of the work, literary or theatrical, together and that one shouldn't separate the production of the effects from the manner in which they are received by the reader or the spectator.

The notion of effect has a long classical tradition behind it. The produced effect can be easily observed on the spectator (rather than on the reader), and it is in this field that classical theatre engages with this notion (as though to confirm theatre's efficacy). For instance, Molière advises: 'let us only consider, in a comedy, the effect it has on us' (*La Critique de l'École des Femmes*, scene 6). And Racine, for his part, stresses that the effect of his theatre is universal and lasting: 'I have recognized with pleasure, in the effect produced on your theatre by everything of Homer and Euripides that I have imitated, that common sense and reason were the same in every century' (Preface of *Iphigénie*).

Whether it concerns comedy or tragedy of the French or the Greek, of the seventeenth-century audience or that of the twenty-first century, theatre produces an effect on the audience distinct from the other arts. The performance is necessarily 'live'. It makes the whole of the scene (actor, spoken text, 'stage effects') and the spectator coincide, if only for a brief moment, in a unique and non-repeatable event. During this event, there is even a communication and a movement back and forth between stage and auditorium, and the produced effect is perceptible from the feedback on the actors' performance.

The 'good' or the 'bad' reception-reaction rebounds onto the performance, either facilitating it or slowing it down. A history of audiences and societies and their influence on dramatic texts, performances or productions remains to be written. And what is the *mise-en-scène* if not a mechanism, become indispensable by the end of the nineteenth century, to adapt the performance to the specific intended audience, and thus a taking into account of the receiver for the creation of the stage performance?

In order to imagine this history of the produced effects (of the theatre on the audience as well as of the audience on the theatre), one should start to specify what exactly generates this effect on the spectator: theatre in general? Reading the play? The performance? The style of the *mise-en-scène*? One should distinguish the effect produced according to the type of receiver as well as the mode of reception and in particular its duration.

1) *From the individual points of view of the spectators*, who are moved by the story most of the time, identifying themselves with a character or a conflict. We know that – since Aristotle – the pleasure of the spectator of tragedy is linked with a feeling of pity and terror: pity and compassion *vis-à-vis* the unfortunate hero, terror and masochism toward oneself. This mixed feeling gives rise to a catharsis, or 'purification of the passions'. But this cathartic effect can only be produced if the spectator knows that the theatrical action is not real, which produces in them a denial: 'It is necessary that it is not true, that we know it is not true, so that the images of the unconscious may be truly free' (Mannoni 1969). It is therefore very difficult to evaluate the impact of the performance on the spectator: it is more or less direct, immediate, invisible or deferred.

2) *From the collective point of view of the audience*, the produced effect is equally difficult to grasp, for theatre

is 'a rooted art, the most committed of all the arts in the living web of the collective experience' (Duvignaud 1965: 11). The audience's reactions differ from the totality of individual responses, for if 'the theatre performance is organized so as to have an effect in the moment' (15), the audience is often undecided or even divided. How far can we push the audience? Everything has been tried to shock them, to get the audience out of their torpor by all kinds of performances. Nowadays, in certain limit experiences, one simulates the violence perpetrated against the actors in order to disturb the audience, to almost force them to intervene in a physical fashion (Fura dels Baus). And, if theatre audiences have historically been relatively homogeneous, for the last twenty years audiences have been extremely varied, by genres, and its consequent reception will be equally heterogeneous: so what exactly has the theatre had an impact on? A community of theatre lovers? An audience made up of regular customers? Isolated individuals? Tourists?

3) *From the point of view of society as a whole*, the effect of a play or a performance will be equally powerful and significant, whether the impact is immediate and visible or postponed and hidden. It remains for historians to tell us how great plays or unforgettable stage events have influenced the course of history (as with the Greek tragedies or romantic theatre in Poland). As to the success of the plays, depending on historical circumstance, they are sometimes immediate (Racine, Rostand), at other times deferred and unimaginable (Kleist, Büchner, Musset).

Factors and Markers of the Produced Effect

The produced effects are as countless as they are unpredictable. At best, we can predict at which levels they are identifiable. By distinguishing the different levels of the text during the reader-spectator 'textual co-operation' (Pavis 2002), the following components and factors of the produced effect become apparent:

- *The place of enunciation*. The space of the event determines the overall impression: is it an Italianate theatre or a 'site-specific performance', a found place that determines the *mise-en-scène*?

- *The plot*. Is what we are being told credible enough to make the reader/spectator uneasy or must we 'invent our own story'?

- *The dramaturgy*. Does the creation of an action by characters result in a fable that will be understood by all (once and for all) or, on the contrary, that will be extremely changeable? Each new reading or production constitutes what was in the past called a 'concretization'.

It is a useful notion if it suggests that every reading is necessarily new, evolves in the course of time and only concretizes in history, that is to say, if it suggests that every reading specifies and constructs what before was only general and abstract and had not been made concrete by a situation of relative and new reading. A problematic notion indeed, if the concretization suggests that the work is unique, stable, essential, but that it is manifested in different times according to various modalities. Indeed, the different realizations are not variants of a same work, but original productions each time, derived from a work, due to the changes of context and of our modes of reading, and of the construction-deconstruction that we make of it.

- *The level of the unconscious and ideology*. The effect of the same play or performance will be different according to each receiver, for the effect depends as much on their unconscious as their relation to ideology. Which finds expression, for instance, in:

a) *An identification* with the character, to the triggering of a fantasy or of daydreaming.

b) *An interpellation*, in the meaning of Althusser (1965), is a manner of forcing the spectator to 'respond' to the portrait that is made of them and of their situation through the characters.

c) *A legitimation*, which is the stage following the 'interpellation', when the involved subject confirms and legitimates the order given by fiction depending on their own situation.

d) *A disorientation of the spectator* is always possible, frequently as the first reaction; when prolonged, it prevents recognition or identification of a known situation. This is especially possible with shows from cultures that are foreign to us.

At whatever level we approach text or performance, we can see that the effect they have on the reader or the spectator depends as much on the object itself (its configuration) as on the receiver (their identity). The notion of produced effect functions as a mediation between production and reception. To determine the effect produced by a performance, we must establish the manner in which it has been produced whilst imagining the expectations with which it was received and understood. Taking only one example, the *mise-en-scène*, there are two ways to approach it: through describing the tasks and the working process of the director, or through reconstructing the role of the spectator according to their expectations and their real situation. Production and reception are intimately linked and interdependent. Production anticipates its effects on the spectator and imagines what the spectator is going to understand of the received object; it reconstructs the project or even the intentions of the *mise-en-scène*. Thus, shaping a production is as much about fashioning a subject matter and its elaboration by actors and all the other artists as it is taking into account the changing viewpoint of the spectator according to their habits, their expectations, their new situation. Thus giving attention to the produced effect keeps us from privileging only one of the two sides of the theatrical event – production or reception – by reintroducing a dual model in applying the model of communication (sender/receiver) onto the theatre work.

Therefore we can clearly see that directing fosters and maintains the spectator's interest, bringing about in them the desire to see and understand, without ever being able to achieve this. There is however no universal theory of the effects or failsafe method to touch the spectator (Pavis 2000). For what is important is not the intrinsic value of the signs and effects of each 'scenographic language' (music, space, aesthetic, language etc.) but the combination of all materials proper to each staging (and even to each 'scene' of the show). Only a 'militant' and political aesthetics, such as that of Brecht, will attempt to quantify the respective effects of each language. Thus Brecht recommends that the worker assigned to set-building draw up a 'table of the possible effects', and he suggests the worker indicate for each scene of each play the quanta of effects (*Wirkungsquanten*), for example: 'the social marks, the historical marks, the alienation effects, the aesthetic effects, the poetic effects, the technical innovations, the effects of tradition, the destruction of illusion, the values of exposition' (1967: vol. 16: 467). This set-builder's checklist seems somewhat mechanical and hard to corroborate, but it has the merit of quantifying the force of the effects and making tangible their variety.

Theatre effects are thus innumerable. But measuring the effects produced on the spectator is not obvious, for there is no clear, final typology of effects. It would be better – albeit metaphorically – to imagine what 'inner *mise-en-scène*' the spectator performs as soon as they are affected by the *mise-en-scène*: how does the *mise-en-scène* embed itself, carve itself, sculpt itself, in them. Cognitive psychology might help us to see how the stage configuration stamps itself in the imagination and the body of the spectator, as a 'negative' of the perceived or hallucinated figure coming from the stage. The spectator perceives and experiences it as a re-play, as an inner mime, especially through the actors' moves on the stage. The spectator possesses the faculty to comprehend an imaginary network that the *mise-en-scène* endeavoured to establish. The spectator has the awareness, an embodied awareness, that the performance in the process of the *mise-en-scène*, always leaves traces in them, be it a sensation,

an aesthetic pleasure, a figure, or an overall score. This effect produced on the spectator gives them the certainty that everything has been organized around them, but without being totally explainable or communicable.

The director always asks herself or himself: what should I do so that something emerges for them, the spectator, '*mon semblable, mon frère* [my fellow-creature, my brother]' (Baudelaire), so that my art has an effect on them.

REFERENCES

Althusser, Louis (1965) *Pour Marx*, Maspero.

Brecht, Bertolt (1967) *Gesammelte Werke*, Suhkamp.

Duvignaud, Jean (1965) *Sociologie du Theatre*, P.U.F.

Grimm, Gunter (1977) *Rezeptiongeschichte*, Fink.

Jauss, Hans Robert (1977) *Asthetische Erfarung und Literarische Hermeneutik*, Fink.

Mannoni, Octave (1969) *Clefs pour l'Imaginaire*, Le Seuil.

Pavis, Patrice (2000) *Vers une Theorie de la Pratique Theatrale*, P.U., Lille.

Pavis, Patrice (2002) *Le théâtre contemporain*, Nathan, Paris.

Warning, Rainer (1975) *Rezeptionsasthetik*, Fink.

Woyzeck effet produit

The pleasure of looking freely is one of the greatest pleasures imaginable. It blossoms most fully in the theatre. The spectator looks at what he wants without guilt, without any obligation to have results or to buy anything. He is protected by a contract. However his taboos, his habits, his unspoken laws restrict this complete freedom, for can one look into somebody's soul for a long time? And look into that which does not concern us? It certainly takes some strength, some courage too.

In those performances that I do not understand or that bore me stiff because I do not see what they are getting at, I can at least look in my own way, against the tide, far away from any semiological tyranny and mapped-out meaning. I love looking at women speaking a foreign language or with a look that is foreign to me. The same thing happens with foreign performances. One can look at the stage as a field of experimentation in looking. Let's not deprive ourselves of this!

Often, stagings of the last thirty years, stagings of avant-(re)garde, are so arranged that the spectator's gaze can wander back and forth, from surface to depth, from moment to moment.

Can one, should one, theorize this wandering of the gaze? No doubt psychologists would do so successfully. But theatre exists precisely *not* to reduce everything to a theory, i.e., etymologically to a contemplation, a consideration and ultimately an abstract speculation. Theatre, the *teatron* of Greek tradition, is the place from which one watches a show. As important as the object being looked at is the place from which and the attitude with which one looks at it.

In July 2004 in Mainz, directing Büchner's *Woyzeck*, I decided directly to use the dirty and various locations put at my disposal: a class-room, a cellar, an interior space, a garden where I could accommodate about thirty people, who were ready to follow the character moving around. I chose not to change anything in these 'found places' and to take into account the symbolic location we were in: the university photo lab, in which, because of the digital simplifications, there is nothing left to develop. I tried to put myself in the spectators' place, that is to see things from their perspective, to imagine what they would see from the interaction between these dirty walls and the story about the soldier Woyzeck. So I went back and forth between these different ways in which everyone looked at each other. Every spectator was encouraged to take pictures during the performance, to contribute to the symbolic murder of the killing gaze, Woyzeck's gaze on Marie, through the camera rather than the usual knife, the remnants of a primeval technology and scene.

Pursued by everyone with these surveillance and registration machines, Woyzeck himself becomes the camera that kills. He takes his revenge on the world which observed him and which has given him proof of Marie's unfaithfulness.

We are all Woyzecks: spectators ready to kill, to look and to see and get proof of the other's guilt.

But how to avoid the gaze as a revolver, a knife or a camera, to let our gaze be cast gently over the body of the performance? *Mise-en-scène*, this pitting against each other all the elements of the performance in relation to the spectator, has accustomed us to follow the spatio-temporal unfolding of the performance. But it sometimes happens that it frees our gaze and that we get lost in the image without being able to leave it. *Mise-en-scène* then has nothing left of a privileged vector; we are thus encouraged to reconstruct ourselves and to refind ourselves again through it.

I wrote a foreword to the play: Woyzeck and Marie welcomed every spectator of the opposite sex into a sinister cellar in front of an old fashioned camera masking as a Polaroid. He or she started the monologue with 'tell me that you love me!' The future spectator, and current victim, did not know where to put themselves, were made to feel very uncomfortable, he or she was seized upon as a desiring subject and rejected as a spectator equipped with heavy semiotic know-how. What Marie or Woyzeck said to each other is what the actor always says to his or her mute and unfeeling spectator: 'Tell me that you love me!' Which is also what everybody says to everybody else.

So this is what I understood of the scopophilia and aprosexia of Field Station 7. Not to mention aporia, existensia, amnesia, parapraxia, aphasia, cryptaesthesia, idioglosia euphoria, eleuctheria, peripheria, synesthesia, utopia and, of course, hysteria.

I ask you all to witness the fact that I respected the terms of our contract, that I have been a good voyeur, keen to look like a reliable witness, regardless of the cost, thereby testing the ways of dispersing my attention, and yours.

The ACTOR playing Woyzeck, to a female spectator on her own.
Tell me you love me.
wait, not straightaway.
let me first make the camera ready
to record your voice
to draw your outline
to freeze forever the features of your face
here in the darkness of the cellar.
Let me tell you
why I want to take your portrait
before it is too late.

Tell me you love me:
Marie, she never told me
that she loved me.
Had she told me,
it might have calmed me down
calmed me forever.
Because deep down
Deep down in the cellar
I, Woyzeck, born with photography
Pursued by the photographs
Tormented by the photocrats,
I am not a bad guy.
It's just that they never tell me anything
they never tell me they love me
I never told it either
not to Marie, not to you, not to anybody.
And yet it was so simple:
'Marie, I love you' or 'Hello, Madam, I love you'
Yes, I know, it seems simple, but it is comical.
Never ever did I speak that fateful phrase: 'I love you'.
Never did I have the time to think about
what would give her great pleasure
or what would do her good
too observed, too pressed, too oppressed
never a kind word
neither for her nor for me.
Had she stopped at least for a while
stopped running after her image
chased by those blokes with their dirty and hairy hands,
by this trendy photocrat
half drum half major
half photo half labo
half photomate half photopimp

Maybe I would not have bought my camera
if only I had told her 'I love you'
like I am telling you right now
and if she had told me as you do right now: 'I love you'
we would have avoided a lot of trouble.

So here we are face to face, silent
You are saying nothing to me because I am saying nothing to you
I am saying nothing to you because you are saying nothing to me
Subject? Object?
The camera is loaded
The words too are loaded
Loaded with meaning.
Careful that everything does not blow up
'Tell me you love me'

The FEMALE SPECTATOR, understanding that in order to be admitted she has to say 'I love you!'
Here is your ID picture.
Stick it into your passport.
You will need it when entering and leaving the photo lab.
That's all. Thank you. Farewell.

ACTRESS, playing Marie to a male spectator on his own.
Tell me you love me
I know: one does not say those things
That's not a thing you can ask the other
Certainly not to a man like you
Who looks so well-bred.
This should come from you.
But wait, don't be so hasty.
Anyway nothing is ready
I must set up the camera
To freeze your face forever
and your surprise, and your fear, and your desire.

You can still go home
You run the risk of having your photo taken
Like that, by anybody
Your image will take a blow
A blow beneath the belt
A blow you might never recover from
Because the gaze of the objective is without mercy
Just as the gaze has no mercy
That men cast on me
No mercy and no love.

The photocrats devour me with their eyes
It seems I am photogenic
But they don't say a word
Or only empty words, obscenely empty
Therefore please: tell me you love me
Woyzeck, he never said it to me
But he always rushes in

And me, too, I never said it to Woyzeck
that I love him:
hey, you, Woyzeck, I see you and I am telling you:
I love you.
But I never could tell him anything
Too late
You can still get out of it
By closing your eyes
By leaving the place
On tiptoes
Not seen not caught
'I could not find the right building'
A developer revealing the world's bruises
You, you may leave when you want
I have to stay and be finished on the spot
Because I am the Woyzeck of the Woyzeck
The photocrat's gaze pins me down
Pierces me
In spite of my seven buckskins
'Bin ich ein Mensch'
I would not go that far

I never dared to tell you
Something really simple
I love you, you, Woyzeck
Because you only wanted to see me
Because you talked to me in your delirium

But if you had only told me
You Marie, I love you,
You and your body on edge
I love you
With your eyes, with your hands, with your words
If you had told me that
Things would have come to pass
You and me

But never mind
Since everything goes to hell, man and woman
Well, well, it's ready
Come on: tell me that you love me

The MALE SPECTATOR, understanding that in order to be admitted he has to say 'I love you'.
Here is your ID picture
Stick it into your passport
You will need it when entering and leaving the photo lab.
That's all. Thank you. Farewell.

Woyzeck cast: Jana Chiellino, Johanna Gerhards, Jens P. Gust, Doris Mucha, Christiane Kirchner, Hoger Tapp, Robert Teufel, Simone Horn.

ADRIAN HEATHFIELD   FIELD STATION 8

Writing of the Event

These fragments are assembled from writings that took place over a number of years. In most instances they were not included within the writing projects, but occurred beside them, as reflections on the practice of writing itself. So, an essay composed of process reflections, marginal notes and out-takes. The practice that these writings discuss, is diversely referred to as performative writing, event-text, event-writing and impossible writing. I have not attempted to erase this incoherence in categorization and nomination here, since formal insecurity and ontological instability are important dynamics of the writing practice I wish to invoke.

«»

How *outside* the writer's language is in relation to the event; how lacking in that which would turn inside, make the thing flow and burn, touch and weigh again. How utterly significant, unique and unforgettable is the event. How lost it is now. All that one can do is proceed inside this tear; vibrate at the borders of memory. The writer casts word-nets towards the event-residues of memory; ghost images lodged in the frayed screens of the mind's eye; sense traces harboured in the recesses of flesh. To write the event conscious of writing's internal failure, its mnemonic and ontological insecurity, but nonetheless invested in its impossible object. It is the annulment of the life of the event by time, and the belatedness of language itself, that makes the event's recall in writing necessary, vibrant and continuously possible.

«»

Perhaps the relation between writing and the event of performance is something like the relation that Maurice Blanchot finds between writing and disaster in his exquisite work, *The Writing of the Disaster* (1995). The phrase evokes the tensions of force, agency and direction, the pull of paradox, located in all such scriptural acts. The writing of the disaster – the writing of the event. This writing is not simply upon a subject or about it but, rather, is 'of' it in the sense that it issues from it, is subject to its force and conditions. The writing of the event emerges, then, from an imperative in the event and is subject, like Blanchot's writing, to the relentless negative force of its radically elusive origin.

«»

Event-writing is interested in a set of binary relations at play in the encounter with the artwork: the relation of the self to the work, the relation of the self to the artist who made the work, and the relation of the self to the other person who also encounters or speaks of the work. How each of these selves encounters otherness in each instance of relation becomes my main concern. And within this writing, through the interplay of these relations, the extent to which this author can stage a limit experience of 'his own', pressing his thought towards that which it does not yet know.

Writing otherwise than he writes, he writes in such a way that the other might come to words, as approach and response.

«»

This turning, this inclination of thought and writing towards that which it excludes, requires not just a self-referential gesture, the writing's announcement of itself as writing, but a thorough deconstitution and erasure of itself as writing, in form and content. Listen, for instance, to the laceration and negation of writing that Edmond Jabès finds necessary and so writes, in his turning toward the outsides of the book:

- a book – he said – that I'll never write because nobody can, it being a book:
- against the book.
- against thought.
- against truth and against the word.
- a book, then, that crumbles even while it forms.
- against the book because the book has no content but itself, and it is nothing.
- against thought because it is incapable of thinking its totality, let alone nothing.
- against truth because truth is god, and god escapes thought; against truth, then, which for us remains legendary, an unknown quantity.
- against the word, finally, because the word says only what little it can, and this little is nothing and only nothing could express it (2000: 99).

Can you feel the precise cut of these negations? The plurality of meaning that arises here? With sublime eloquence Jabès says a great deal about language and its referential powers: he says it says very little in relation to its object. Is his 'finally' merely the marking of the last phrase in a list, indicating the word as the ultimate unit of language to have its power negated? Or is it that we should be against the word 'finally' itself? This sense slips over the commas of Jabès's already broken incantatory style. Whatever, it seems that it is the closure of and around infinity that is the source of the word's poverty.

Whether it is the word that is set against itself, or against its own finality, this word is in any case, according to Jabès, saying 'only what little it can'. He pities the poor word, and then goes on to degrade it further by saying that even this little is nothing. And here I am sure you identify with the word, and recognize the feeling of sad insufficiency; you once gave something, what little you could, but that little amounted to nothing. And finally, it seems that all of this cancellation is itself cancelled by an unspeakable foundational absence that no word can ever approximate.

The kind of writing Jabès is trying to write of and with is, like performative writing, a negative affirmation; it is forever promissory, it asserts as it cancels itself. It is not even clear to whom this little masochistic cycle belongs, to Jabès or to his book? '- a book - he said - that I'll never write because nobody can, it being a book: / - against the book.'

«»

A recurrent trope of the event-text will be the interleaving of autobiographical writing with critical discourse. This gesture is not simply the insertion of excluded or subordinate terms within the purified space of the language of critique: the subjective within the objective, the specific and the situated within the general and the abstract, the emotional and the sensual within the rational and the perceptual. Though it may be each or all of these things. It is a gesture that calls into question the cultural place and social function of writing itself. It perturbs the relations of distinction and action that found writing, the operation of the writer upon and through writing, the operation of writing upon its object. Of what does the text speak when its writing subject is spoken rather than the text speaking of its object? It speaks the dissolution of the place of its author in the event of writing towards an object. Writing becomes a multi-dimensional space of agency and reflection in this disturbance of the proprieties of relation between author, writing and object. A vehicle that implicates its reader, and its author, the writing and its object, in a fluid exchange where the position of each in relation to each other is destabilized. Should we call this writing 'autobiographical', even if we understand autobiography as fiction? Perhaps only if we understand the fiction of autobiography as a critical site of limit testing in which the feelings, memories, experiences, and thoughts of the writing subject are brought to their outsides.

This writing should not be misunderstood by its author (quite likely) or its reader (more likely) as the occasion for anecdote, or the bolstering of the stories the self tells itself about itself: the reification of the author's values. Its only validity rests in its failure to deliver the self through writing, in what it speaks at the edges of its own articulacy. It is not employed in the service of the author's powers, but in a counter-mythology, by which the author may dissolve in the face of relation: relation to the other of the self, found in the contemplation of the other in art. Of this necessary self-negation Blanchot writes,

A writer in spite of himself: it is not a matter of writing despite or against oneself in a relation of contradiction - indeed, of incompatibility - with oneself, or with life, or with writing (that is all merely the biography of the writer, and he has only anecdotal significance). Rather, it is a matter of writing *in another relation*, from which the other dismisses himself and has always dismissed us, even in the movement of attraction. (1995, my italics)

How to write in another relation? What is at stake in event-writing then, is an attitude, an inclination; a being beside oneself, a turning towards the imminent, a waiting with vigilance, a patience, a taste for becoming.

«»

This writing is like an act of friendship: it can only half-know the other, but proceeds all the same, in the suspension of trust and distrust, founded in the indeterminacy of the word.

«»

Performative writing does not see cultural events or artworks as objects, but rather as situations, manifestations, articulations of ideas. As such they are rarely static and final, but highly dynamic and provisional. They are seen not just as representations but also as sayings. What they say is said in relation to, and partly determined by, their context: historical and present, material and spatial (in terms of the institutions or social settings in which they are presented), and embodied (in terms of the physical and sensual relation between the spectator and the object, and the spectator and its other recipients). To address such sayings in writing is to say back, to respond, to engage in a process relation that is corporeal, animate and transformative. In other words it is to stage a crossing: a dialogue. Dialogue manifests a form of discourse that is within and partly about the present context of encounter; an intensely social and provisional affair that is not subject to closure. Here language is gripped by differentiation: as Blanchot says,

To converse is to turn language away from itself, maintaining it outside of all unity, outside even the unity of that which is. To converse is to divert language from itself by letting it differ and defer, answering with an always already to a never yet. (1995: 4)

In performative writing this dialogue may simply be between an author and a work, or it may be the product of an author imagining and scripting distinct voices in relation to a work, or it may indeed be a dialogue between authors, which takes the work as its intermediary subject. Each form has its own problematics of relation and encounter.

The intangible gift that is given in this exchange evades name and number, it is not a quantifiable phenomena, nor is it an object of knowledge. It cannot be assured. It is the gift of time spent entwined with the ideas of others, heart in hand, ear in mouth, eyes at the horizons of thought, words slipping over lips and dissolving into air. The 'imaginative communion': the art of dialogue / the dialogue of art. Given time the gift returns.

In this last context particularly – a dialogue between authors – obstacles, blockage and disagreement are generative sources in a creative process. The limit relation is not an endless and effortless flow of inspirational enlightenment. It is, after all, a zone of difficulty and risk, a tiresome and messy business. Dialogue is a space in which one often encounters the ice hard facts of personal, philosophical, ideological, somatic and cultural difference. The encounter with misunderstanding, the acknowledgement of disagreement is significant here because it becomes a moment in which one can register and test difference, articulate the mutability of what seems fixed, re-articulate relation. Dialogue proceeds in the miss as much as the hit, in the passing over and the turning away, in refusal and sometimes most testily in silence, which is not to be mistaken for non-communication. Dialogue in the face of the work, in the face of the other who also encounters the work, is that *vital failure* that one must perform again, in order to make the failure of the work meaningful. Dialogue is a convention of failures – author, work, interlocutor, reader – a meeting of the undone, a beautiful catastrophe of misunderstanding.

«»

dear you
unlettered
who will have been not this
and so
who will have been misspelled and re-worded

dear you

with whom I am always beginning
always to say
to say

words will undo us and bind us tame
with notions
that barely touch the skin between us

you are elements of light, unseen
you haunt waking moments and whisper me to sleep
you rest beside me in the deep night of dreams

words lap and fall at us
dumb-fuck things

am I nothing
to you
but this letter?

«»

Were a didactic note on the methodology of this impossible writing possible, it might go like this:

Do not develop a set of conceptual frameworks or questions and then look for interesting works to illustrate, exemplify or even contest them.

Do not approach cultural artefacts or performances that manifest specific ideas in order to elaborate their meanings and consequences.

Discourse and object: neither should be subservient to the other, each has a life of its own. Each life should find itself in your writing in a relation of mutual vibration.

Do not choose objects of study at all. Allow them to choose you, and allow them to write themselves. This is the written equivalent of the found object: its occurrence in the work is not the product of an intentional consciousness, it enters the work by chance, it surprises its author, and its movement into the work is one of displacement. It comes to speak both in and of itself, and otherwise, by dint of its relocation, its extraction from its natural context of meaning, its habitual discourse-world. It is the subject of a thorough disarticulation.

Better still be seduced by an object, write because it is impossible to avoid its vortex of meaning. Be taken by the unnameable thing you sense inside of you because of it. Write this thing attentive to the way it recesses as you write.

Do not do this writing yourself; allow the force of the object its consequence in you, the unthought thought to write itself.

These processes can only be secured by the most acutely vigilant passivity.

«»

The text that is oriented towards the other reconfigures the relation between writing and speaking, asserting writing as speech. This is not in order to reinstitute speech as a direct conduit to being, distinct from or before writing. But is, rather, in order to recognize saying as a means through which writing can enter evident conditions of productive instability. 1. I write to say. 2. I write as I would say. In each instance this is a text in which there is an emphasis upon the saying rather than the said, a recurrence of the voice. Roland Barthes named this practice 'writing aloud': an act that is intimately concerned with the erotics of language (1980). This voicing is a perturbation, a manifestation of repressed phenomenological content within a textual economy. In the context of a live reading of the author's text the saying produces a surplus that the text cannot contain. This excess is encountered by its auditors, including its author, who hears his voice dissolving into the ears of others, his text deconstituted in the face of their imagined and real words. The writer instantly resents the prematurity and impatience of his written thoughts. The field of senses and emotions agitates against the holding force of words. The relation, as now, is dilatory, terrifying, exciting. In the context of silent reading this recurrence of voice is subject to the imaginative projection of the reader, who hears this voice, through the filtration of their own voice slipping through their mind's mouth. The relation is a textual consummation: tongue over tongue, words trickling into dissolution in the sensate, meaning atomized.

«»

The event-text is a text in which the temporality of language is called into question. Derridean deconstruction has asserted the notion that speech is itself always already written (Derrida 1978). The many linguistic and aesthetic tactics of experimental theatre writing have affirmed this notion by announcing the predetermination by writing of their spontaneities. Both of these critical and aesthetic moves are designed to undermine the notion of the present, by inserting within it a before. The event-text is not content however simply to affirm this division of the present. It brings writing into proximity with the now, offering up and playing with the possibility of escape from the imprisonment of the 'forever before' of linguistic structures.

How would language become now? (*Here the author speaks for an indeterminate period of time, trying to attune himself to, and immediately articulate, the moment in the presence of others: broken observations emerge, from sounds, looks and perceptions. There is a great deal of silence.*)

More or less in proximity to now? But somehow always anticipating something else, always also belated.

«»

I find something shattering: a cultural scene, a work of art, an instance of articulation. I am compelled to relay the force of this deconstitution, which vaporizes form, rips open discourse, draws me out and in. Event-writing in this context is both an answer to and a perpetuation of the force of this shattering. It aims to honour the call inherent in the instance of the breach, not by subjecting it to discourse, but by re-iterating, the only way it knows how, in different terms, the force of thought's disintegration. This can be seen as similar to the act of testimony, an opening to the forgotten within, and as commemoration, where the bearing witness re-iterates that the experience of the event is constituted by the dissolution of language itself.

«»

Last night I came upon an event that made me feel the most present, the most connected, the most alive that I have ever felt. I want to tell you the life of this event, but I cannot. Because the I that speaks, that would tell you, was not there. Was not there but witnessed something nonetheless, felt something nonetheless, that is still with me now, past but full of potential, unforgettable yet unrecallable, resident in me, but untouched by the lulling assurance of words. Were I ever to speak it, I would shatter and dissolve before you, become like the thing itself, which has no itself. And yet the words keep coming, keep coming to approximate that life lived, unseen, felt in the crevices of thought, felt between desire and its realization, between loss and hope, between you and I. An impossible thing at once singular and multiple. There and not there. Forever now and never again. It continues without continuity. I want to say what this life is, I want to spell it out like others try to, to re-present it. But all I can do is cast words in thin air.

«»

REFERENCES

Barthes, Roland (1980) *The Pleasure of the Text*, (trans. Richard Miller), New York: Hill and Wang.

Blanchot, Maurice (1995) *The Writing of the Disaster*, (trans. Ann Smock), New Bison Book Edition, Lincoln: University of Nebraska Press.

Derrida, Jacques (1978) *Writing and Difference*, (trans. Alan Bass), London: Routledge.

Jabès, Edmond (2000) 'Desire for a Beginning, Dread of One Single End', in Jerome Rothenberg and Steven Clay (eds.) *A Book of the Book*, trans. Rosemarie Waldrop, New York: Granary Books.

MICHAEL PETERSON   **FIELD STATION 8**

an untenable identity formation:
Eleutheria in eight parts

1 Admission to Eleutheria

A vacation on the site of being – what 'american' could resist? Once there, to inquire after identity, alterity, hybridity. How different these terms sound now than fifteen years ago – not to mention thirty. When the Centre for Performance Research began I was ten years old and identity to me was literally a black and white issue, as I struggled without success to make sense of the *de facto* segregation of my southern US town. Twenty years later I was trying to critique 'identity privilege' and performance.

Thirty years on, it seems like privilege isn't the half of it. For example, Americans have two ways of understanding the relation of identity and martyrdom. On the one hand, we rehearse daily the paranoid fantasies of death through someone else's misguided martyrdom; fear is the staple of our political season, and it's a bumper crop. On the other hand, privilege in US society can increasingly be measured by how one experiences the demand to establish identity. For the under-documented, it can be a threat to life and livelihood. For the over-documented, an annoyance whose futility establishes just how important we are. As a child, in my family, a 'martyr' was one who ostentatiously performed an unpleasant chore – the dishwashing martyr, etc. In today's security queue, the over-documented produce their own identification with a sigh, identity martyrs in the cause of keeping everyone sorted out.

'Authenticity' as a matter of identity politics has been on the wane, they tell us, for some time. In its less essentialist modes, authenticity contributed to critical epistemologies, but today authenticity seems on the verge of eclipse by verifiability. The new ontology of identity is guaranteed by the validation of the state. In this bleak outlook, the context of performance seems to be the (forcibly) united states of *being*.

And the euphoria on offer? For the over-documented, at least, it is a euphoria of escape *into*, not from, identity. The relief of being airborne, or inside the conference room or on vacation – identity confirmed, we receive admission to what Marc Auge has with some justification called 'non-places'.

The violence of this production of identity is increasingly explained away with the curious all-purpose slogan of new-style US adventurism. 'Freedom isn't Free' is a rhetoric that invokes sacrifice but in fact expresses *expenditure*. As in the spending of the expendable, whether that means abridging the petty civil liberties of the frequent-flying classes or the literal shackling of those 'positively identified.'

2 Wilde Identity: Freedom-Loving Like a Formalist

The first section of Oscar Wilde's first collection of poems is headed 'Eleutheria,' after the Greek personification of liberty. 'Sonnet to Liberty' explains the relationship between identity ('my passion') and liberty (eleutheria):

> NOT that I love thy children, whose dull eyes
> See nothing save their own unlovely woe,
> Whose minds know nothing, nothing care to know, –
> But that the roar of thy Democracies,
> Thy reigns of Terror, thy great Anarchies,
> Mirror my wildest passions like the sea, –
> And give my rage a brother – ! Liberty!

The wild manifestations of liberty *mirror* the wild(e) passions of the speaker; this twinning, the brother to his rage, is the only reason given why the speaker cares for liberty at all. If the figure of Eleutheria began as a personification of liberty – a notionally present reminder of it – then the Greek figure is also the mascot of a history of *aestheticizing* freedom.

This sort of romantic fascination (even as ironized by Wilde) with which the elite regard those struggling for freedom seems harder to come by, these days. Along with our beautiful but so often melancholy copies of *Performance Research,* we import from the UK outraging evidence of our own misdeeds, like the documentary play *Guantanamo: Honor Bound to Defend Freedom*, which while moving, seemed to provoke in my fellow spectators sighs of futile embarrassment. Or *We Will Rock You*, the enjoyable West End musical fantasy pastiched from the music of Queen and now in an indefinite run at the 'Paris, Las Vegas' casino. Just as in so many Hollywood sci-fi films, there the oppressive state is a kitsch joke, to be overcome simply by fulfilling the mythology of freedom so celebrated in Rock and Roll. Culturally we celebrate liberators, libertarians and even libertines, but so central is 'liberation' to both our dramaturgy and our national mythology that seemingly every narrative ends up being one of self-congratulatory freedom.

3 Eleutheria: Offshore from America

Eleutheria was the original name of the narrow strip of island in the Bahamas, now spelled Eleuthera. It was settled in 1647 by a luckless colony of 'Independent' congregationalists fleeing religious conformity in Bermuda. What began as the pursuit of freedom of religion soon factionalized; the colonists lost all their supplies and were saved only by shipments of food from New England. A literally untenable geological *and* social formation.

Eleuthera is now a tourist colony, one of the quiet 'out islands' of the Bahamas, no longer as popular with the very rich as it once was but still sustained by imports from the colder mainland. Rather than a 'freedom of', its visitors now seek a freedom from, an outsourcing of libertine experience built on the vestiges of slavery and colonial expansion.

4 Freedom: Where the Marginal Action Is

Like Eleuthera, Eleutheria is much longer than it is wide. As used in English, the term amounts to an obfuscation of liberty, a way of not saying it. Greekness states one's high-mindedness but not much else. Freedom: 'it's Greek to me'. The long history of a shallow concept.

Eleuthéria is the title of 'Samuel Beckett's first play', unproduced, and only just barely published in 1995. This is an unwieldy three-act satire of bourgeois Paris. Of particular interest is the concern the adult characters express for the idle Victor Krap (perhaps an ancestor of a later Beckett character, the old archivist of Krapp's *Last Tape*). Victor lives idly in 'a hole' in an alley, emerging only to scavenge food from waste bins. Much of the action of the play consists of others' attempts to clarify his character, but Victor remains, in a way, stubbornly unclear, free from identity. Victor, and this play as a whole, with its monologues about 'the problem of existence', comes down, with Wilde, on the side of an anti-social experience of freedom.

Eleuthéria is also of interest for its evidence of the playwright searching for a dramatic freedom in the construction of his work. In addition to metatheatrical touches that include a spectator climbing on to the stage in the final scene, the text displays a recognizably Beckettian interest in quotidian behavior. While the first act is almost a drawing-room comedy, centered on the Krap family's discussion of the absent Victor, Beckett also specifies extensive 'marginal action' that occurs on the other side of the stage. In Act 1 Victor is visible moving about his dingy room; in Act 2 the main action is at Victor's place, but the servant Jacques and later Victor move through the family's room. The playwright further dictates that 'in each act, Victor's room is presented from another angle... [T]his also explains why there is no marginal action in the third act, the Krap side having fallen into the pit' (4). While Victor's withdrawal from the world typifies the bourgeois existentialist, the play also graphically demonstrates its disdain for society, as the bourgeois scene literally drops off of the stage. As the play ends, Victor 'looks perseveringly at the audience... Then he gets into bed, his scrawny back turned on mankind' (191).

5 Hybridity and Banality

Much later, the musician Lenny Kravitz was inspired to write a lackluster song named after the resort island of Eleuthera, where he has a home. 'Eleutheria' is strikingly unconvincing reggae: note on his successful 1993 rock album *'Are You Gonna Go My Way'*. It is notable for its insipid lyrics and a rhyme scheme fulfilled even less imaginatively than Wilde's: 'Eleutheria, the fire is burning / Eleutheria, the tables are turning.'

Kravitz was already famous when he wrote this, and well-known as a hyphenated American and musical hybrid. (He is the son of a Russian Jewish television producer and the Bahamian-American actress Roxie Roker, an Obie Award winner best known for her role as Helen, one half of the ground-breaking interracial couple on the American TV sitcom *The Jeffersons*.) Why should an engagement with his 'roots' produce such disappointment from one of the US's most celebrated artists of hybridity? The problem on this album isn't one of identity or authenticity but of politics. Lacking the energy and even the political engagement of some of his songs, 'Eleutheria' celebrates the freedom that comes with acceptance. 'My life is perfect, because I accept it as it is,' Kravitz sings. Functionally, it's a happy update of Billy Joel's annoying 1989 hand-washing hit, 'We Didn't Start the Fire,' which juxtaposed a list of historical names and events (Brando and the H-Bomb, Hemingway and the Bay of Pigs) with a chorus that fuses rock 'n roll freedom with Joel's own brand of patriotic self-justification:

We didn't start the fire

It was always burning since the world's been
turning
We didn't start the fire
No, we didn't light it
But we tried to fight it

6 Euphoric Loss

In contrast, the US division of this field station has
certainly seen plenty of performance that constructs the
possibilities of identity freedom as something other than
historical innocence or commodity fetish. For example,
the engagement of Guillermo Gómez-Peña and others
with disruptive potential of border culture has been
justly celebrated. But US culture feels more and more a
stranger to the world of performance research, to world
performance; more and more awash in an ideology of
'American exceptionalism' and martyr complex.

Even our 'alternative' establishment indulges. *Lost
Objects*, an oratorio at BAM's 'Bang on a Can' festival in
the autumn of 2004 (music by Michael Gordon, David
Lang and Julia Wolfe; libretto by Deborah Artman) is
symptomatic. The tone is elegiac, mournful; the visual
style indebted to the cinematic semi-surrealism of Théâtre
de Complicité. The difficulty is that while the piece (like
much of the country) is still trading on a national sense of
injury lingering since 11 September 2001, it has nothing
explicit to say about that or any other sense of loss. The
chorus gravely intones a litany of loss at the beginning:
'I lost my hat ... I lost my keys ... I lost my mind'. Later
passages lament lost languages, lost technologies
(mostly disused rather than lost to knowledge) and so
on. The size of the cast and orchestra, the multi-layered
scaffolding filling the enormous proscenium, and the
incongruous DJ Spooky, elevating from the fog-filled pit
between movements to offer brief remixes – all suggest
that something important has happened, but the work
has nothing to say about it. Attuned to the mood of their
cultured, liberal audience, the creators celebrate loss,
creating a convenient loss without objects and seemingly
without subjects or contexts. We are invited to sit in the
dark and enjoy feeling sorry for ourselves.

7 'Freedom is on the March'

So threatens our president. Part of the difficulty of
understanding what he means by this in a global
context is that the notion of freedom within the US
is so thoroughly bound up with plain, old-fashioned
nationalism rejuvenated by the exploitation of communal

loss rendered as abstraction. While researching a project
on Las Vegas culture, I attended numerous performances
in casino showrooms after both the US invasion of
Afghanistan (October 2001) and the second invasion of
Iraq (March 2003). Like the attack on the World Trade
Center, these events occasioned curtain speeches, tribute
messages on casino marquees and other gestures, but
some performances went further, incorporating as a
tribute to US troops a durable hit song by country music
star and former Vegas blackjack dealer Lee Greenwood,
'God Bless the USA'. The verses of this song invoke
patriotism primarily through a listing of US place names,
but its chorus highlights the vagueness of its principles:
'I'm proud to be an American, where at least I know I'm
free ...'

If Greenwood's lyric has little to say about the meaning
of freedom, another recent appearance on the Las Vegas
scene thematizes liberty explicitly, if complexly. The
magicians Penn and Teller, whose shtick is based on
revealing the workings of classic magic tricks, have
recently included a bit in their Vegas show in which they
appear to set fire to a US flag wrapped in a large copy of
the Bill of Rights. In typical fashion, the bombastic Penn
then restages the trick, illustrating on the always silent
Teller how the feat is accomplished.

Penn and Teller (especially the bombastic Penn, 'the
one who talks') embody the rock and roll libertarianism
that might be said to be the official mainstream ideology
of Las Vegas culture. Just as their use of firearms in
other tricks is wrapped in discourse about the second
amendment to the US constitution (read by some as
guaranteeing unrestricted gun ownership), this trick
is explicitly about the first amendment and appears
to assert that without actions such as flag-burning the
freedoms of the Bill of Rights are at risk. As Penn says,
'even though the flag is gone, the Bill of Rights remains'.
Still, the final twist in the act is that the disappeared flag
is transported in an instant across the stage and seen
waving on a flagpole, completing the libertarian pose of
wrapping one's critique in the nationalism which seems
to make it possible. This ideological sleight of hand lets
Penn and Teller have it both ways; they celebrate their
freedom and daring and at the same time make available
to nationalistic viewers their reverence for an abstraction
of freedom. I find in this piece a political as well as
theatrical demystification, but it is certainly vulnerable
to the charge of pandering, like the variety acts singing
Greenwood's song, to freedom as an abstraction rather
than a practice.

8 'Stress and Duress' and Empathy as a last resort

A broader understanding of what this march of freedom means might be glimpsed by pairing the 'failure' of *Eleuthéria* with the very concentrated success of a late Beckett text, 'Catastrophe'. If in his first play the choice seemed to be between ludicrous society and a misanthropic turning of one's back to the world, in 'Catastrophe' (1982, published 1984) Beckett perhaps foresees the material consequences of either form of disengagement. In this brief work, an authoritarian director (D) instructs an assistant (A) in how to pose the Protagonist, who stands center stage on a platform, dressed in black, face downturned. It is clear that a work of theatre is being staged, as when the director instructs the assistant that the protagonist's cranium 'needs whitening'. At the same time, 'P' is clearly not protected by an effective performer's union: 'He's shivering', notes the assistant; 'Bless his heart', says the director, with apparent sarcasm. The assistant then suggests 'a little gag', which the director angrily rejects: 'this craze for explication!' 'Sure he won't utter?' worries the assistant; 'not a squeak', D replies (299). 'Catastrophe' reverses one of the metatheatrical devices of *Eleuthéria*, with the director going out into the audience space to evaluate the tableau. 'There's our catastrophe' he approves, 'in the bag' (300).

Viewed today, 'Catastrophe' now theatricalizes the kind of performative abuses that the US disavows (in claiming that reports of prisoner abuse are exceptions to military discipline), exports (in defending the practice of 'stress and duress' techniques) and outsources (in the use of 'extraordinary rendition' to deliver captives to the security forces of nations known to use even more extreme methods). Beckett calls attention to the theatricality of torture without abandoning the philosophical austerity of his *oeuvre*. Indeed, as with Pozzo's abuse of Lucky in *Waiting for Godot*, Beckett could be said to imply that atrocity is in part a response to the implacability of time. The plays themselves may withhold explicit judgment of these acts, but in a play dedicated to Vaclav Havel, as 'Catastrophe' was, the resemblance of state power to 'the problem of existence' hardly means the work is without moral stance. In my reading, the play both allows for empathy with the object of theatricalization and also observes the cruelty inherent in that production of empathy.

But if there is always the risk that theatrical empathy will amount to participation in a commodity culture of alterity, as in Kravitz's flight to an abstraction of freedom as a 'last resort,' this cannot mean that empathy is bankrupt as a strategy. Preceding *Guantanamo: Honor*

Bound on the stage at the same stage of The Culture Project's 45 Bleecker Theater was Sarah Jones's solo performance, *Bridge and Tunnel*. Jones's work imagines a slam poetry event featuring a global assortment of immigrant amateur writers, all performed on her own body. In the varied tradition of solo work about the multiplicity of identity (which includes Anna Deveare Smith and Danny Hoch, among others), work like *Bridge and Tunnel* can seem to market 'diversity,' often to a largely identity-privileged audience. This is especially true in Jones's use of the humour of cultural difference. But at their most successful, performances like these at least *model* empathy on the body of the performer and suggest that at a minimum (as a last resort) loving the other need not be limited to consumption of difference.

Between the production of highly commercial demystification produced by Penn and Teller and the model of a critical embrace of difference to be glimpsed in Jones, performance might help keep open the increasingly claustrophobic discourse on 'american' identity and freedom. If US military performance in the globalized 'battlespace' continues unchecked, it may be that pleasurable demystification or the evocation of empathy will always seem insufficient. But it also means that performance that solidifies identity privilege, confuses nationalism with liberty or consoles the boredom of conquest with the memory of a wound – such performance sets an untenable stage.

REFERENCES

Auge, Marc (1995) *Non-Places: Introduction to an Anthropology of Supermodernity*, (trans. John Howe), New York: Verso.

Beckett, Samuel (1995) *Eleuthéria*, (trans. Michael Brodsky), New York: Foxrock.

Beckett, Samuel (1984) 'Catastrophe,' in *The Collected Shorter Plays of Samuel Beckett*, New York: Grove: 295-301.

Wilde, Oscar (2000) 'Sonnet to Liberty,' in *The Complete Works of Oscar Wilde*, Vol. 1, (ed. Bobby Fong and Karl Beckson), Oxford: Oxford University Press: 149.

EDWARD SCHEER   **FIELD STATION 8**

Eleutheromania: Performance Art and the War on Terror

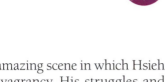

Eleutheromania: mad zeal for freedom. Eleutheromaniac: one possessed by a mad zeal for freedom. <http://dictionary.oed.com/>

I will not yield; I will not rest; I will not relent in waging this struggle for freedom ... (Applause.)
G. W. Bush, 2001

I escaped Afghanistan in 1999 because I was afraid for my life. I spent ten days in the ocean in a small boat with forty strangers. After three days, we lost our way because of the storm. For six days and six nights it was dark, we could not see the sky. On day ten, we ran out of oil and food, the boat broke down, but the sun came out and so did the Australian police. I still have trouble sleeping when I think of the journey.... I spent seven months in Woomera Detention Centre with no communication to the outside world. We just waited and waited and no one would answer our questions. I now have many health problems because of my time spent there. I was eventually granted a Temporary Protection Visa and sent to Melbourne.
Mohammed Arif

Carceral Performance I, Tehching Hsieh

In 1974 Tehching or Sam Hsieh was working on an oil tanker as a business administrator when he jumped ship in Philadelphia to enter the USA illegally. Later he arrived in New York and lived there without an ID card as an illegal immigrant until the amnesty in 1988. As if to enhance the effect of this dubious liberty during those years, he produced a number of year-long durational performances that severely restricted his freedom of movement. Between September 1978 and July 1986, he performed five of these, five years spent in a state of voluntary confinement. In the first of these Hsieh lived in a cage in a studio at 111 Hudson Street deprived of conversation, reading material, TV or radio and even writing instruments. In a subsequent piece he punched a time clock on the wall of his studio every hour of every day for one year. In the third of these, in 1981–82, Hsieh remained outside and never willingly went inside a building. The video documentation

of these events records an amazing scene in which Hsieh is arrested seemingly for vagrancy. His struggles and screams as he is dragged away by the police are decidedly non-theatrical. He knows he will be incarcerated and his project will be compromised. But this scene dramatizes something that only performance art can make visible in the age of compassion fatigue.

The irony of these events anticipates an experience that has become emblematic of the new millennium, not only in the experience of illegal immigrants but in what that experience signifies to these immigrants, by no means possible to summarize, and to the Western democracies who so graciously receive them. Hsieh's performance art suggests that it is something to do with an experience of freedom: glimpsed but thwarted, freedom asserted by negation, freedom abreacted: acted out in order to negate its effects, to depotentiate it, domesticate it, neuroticize it. Freedom so desperately desired one would live the compromised liberty of the illegal immigrant to experience it and then, in living this, to assert one's own power to further deny it for oneself in performance art. This is surely the essence of Hsieh's work, that he gets to choose what to do with his freedom. The corollary to this is that the violent imposition of freedom on other people is a meaningless gesture in terms of freedom (but not in terms of violence). Hsieh could certainly deal with arrest and incarceration; after all he had considerable experience of it, but only as a function of his own will.

Artists such as Hsieh remind us of what is at stake in this term. I suspect that people who take their freedom for granted can never fully understand the dialectic he sets up in his work to do with liberty and incarceration. The OED doesn't list *eleutheria*, the Greek word for freedom, but it lists 'eleutheromania'. It's as if we Anglo-Saxons only ever get this concept *in extremis*, in its sudden withdrawal (incarceration) or in its most extravagant productions: performance art. It only becomes visible when it is abreacted: violently negated or shoved down someone else's throat. Performance art is perhaps the most useful cultural form we can rely on to remind us of the meaning of freedom in a historical context in which the political leaders of the West suck all the meaning out of the term on a daily basis.

Close the Concentration Camps

On Saturday 15 June 2002 at the Monash University Museum of Art in Melbourne, Australia, Mike Parr's face was sewn up with stitches through the lips, ears and eyebrows. Parr also had the word 'Alien' branded into his right thigh. For five hours, from 1–6 p.m., he sat with his right trouser leg ripped open to reveal the fresh mark on his leg. He was positioned in the gallery space beneath enormous black lettering which read, 'CLOSE THE CONCENTRATION CAMPS.' This image was webcast for the entire five-hour duration of the event.

In another gallery, extracts of text chosen by Parr from the Immigration Detention Centre Inspection Report of 2000, bizarrely titled 'Not the Hilton', were projected onto the walls. These observations and recommendations made by the Joint Standing Committee on Migration for the Parliament of the Commonwealth of Australia noted details such as the fact that the managers of the facilities, ACM (Australian Correctional Management), used six-week contracts for staff to 'ensure that they take an essential break from the stress of the job and the climate' and 'to prevent staff from identifying closely with the detainees' position.'

The Museum's publicity for the event focused on the political issues that informed it and included Parr's brief explanation of his action: 'Like many Australians I feel outrage at the way we are treating asylum seekers, and I think their treatment in so-called 'detention centres' requires that we do something. I want to use the language of my 'body art' to make the strongest possible statement in support of the detainees'. The Museum's publicity also made an attempt to describe the experience of the visitors to the gallery, 'witnessing Parr's performance will encourage reflection on the realities of detention, in contrast to the mediated and sanitized representation of asylum seekers by politicians and the media.'

Life Crisis Ritual

Artists such as Parr and Hsieh are driven to imagine and perform rituals which can transcribe the crisis of the time, embody it and make it livable, both for the artist and for others who choose to let this work speak to them and for them. This is the specific potency of performance art, that it develops what Victor Turner calls 'life crisis rituals' (Turner 1986: 101, Scheer 2001) in response to drastically changing social and personal conditions. The rituals of these two artists are separated by two decades, but both speak to the same experience of the singular

alienation of the illegal immigrant and their thwarted liberty. Both facilitate the perception of the precisely regulated suffering of the Other in our midst. For Parr, the crisis he is acting out involves nothing less than the symbolic representation of national identity in Australia in the new millennium.

Australia 2000–2005

The euphoric nationalism of the Sydney Olympics in 2000 has disappeared in favour of a kind of neo-Orwellian ambience marked by terror and the repercussions of the war against it. The neo-Conservative government of John Howard, in power since 1996, has maintained its domestic popularity by manipulating a discourse of subtle racism. This discourse developed gradually over the early Howard years, reaching maturity in the Liberal party's campaign slogan for the 2001 election: 'We decide who comes to this country and the circumstances in which they come.'[1]

This statement has been matched by an immigration policy that is perhaps best described by one of the government's own members as 'an immigration policy that fails the fundamental test of upholding human dignity. It causes trauma in people fleeing regimes that in some cases we've sent troops in to resolve.'[2] The policy referred to is the mandatory detention of asylum seekers in concentration camps or 'detention centres'. These are often located in barren and isolated areas far from large conurbations in places like Woomera in South Australia and Port Hedland in the far northwest, though there is one small centre at Villawood in Sydney's western suburbs. They are all places where those asylum seekers who manage to survive the journey from Afghanistan or Iraq are held behind razor wire until they either go mad and are hospitalized or are deported or in some rare cases freed on temporary protection visas.

This issue has been the most visible aspect of Australian public life in the years up to 2005. No Australian artist could avoid it, but few have taken as direct an approach as Mike Parr who has tackled it head-on in his performance art after 2000. Parr has a 35-year career as an iconic image-maker in Australian and international art circles. His performances of the 1970s, often violent, mono-structural solo events, were followed by more poetic, surreal performances through the 1990s featuring the artist as a bride figure. In the most recent phase of performance, Parr has shifted towards a forceful and violent engagement with the issue of asylum seekers as an emblematic case for the issue of Australian national identity.

Water from the Mouth – Carceral Performance II

The first of these works was a ten-day performance entitled *Water from the Mouth*, which took place at Artspace in Sydney (26 April - 5 May 2001). This piece establishes the language of the new durational works in its use of new media and its political themes. A large wood and cardboard structure contained the body of Parr who did not eat for the ten days of the piece. Visitors to the gallery could not see him directly. There was only one hole in the wall that contained a video camera recording Parr's movements. The continuous realtime video image of Parr was projected onto a wall of the gallery and streamed onto the Internet. There was no interaction with visitors and no activity for the artist other than occupying the space for the set time.

One visitor on the ninth day described seeing Parr's 'sickly shuffle, his pale, clammy skin' and felt he looked 'vegetative, and flicked his right arm to his cheek and lip corners in a compulsive repetition.' Another said he appeared 'sad, but peaceful like a hospital patient who's going to die soon.'[3] Parr himself described the experience of the gradual loss of language, the descent into 'that whirlpool of dissociation that must be the most disorientating aspect of solitary confinement. The fact that the lights never went out added enormously to the stress' (Parr 2004).

Ten metal buckets were arranged just inside the doors of Artspace. These were progressively filled with urine during the progress of the performance, a counterpoint to the depthless, odourless screen image. A visitor to the gallery could hear Parr shuffling around through the thin walls of the box. As the days went by and Parr lost his control over language, he could be heard involuntarily muttering through the speakers around the space. Visitors could also smell the urine but could only see the image of Parr as a mediated representation. Walking around the gallery reinforced a kind of synaesthetic experience of the work, in that the senses were given too many stimuli and tended to overlap onto each other, so an image came with a smell and a sound.

The structure of *Water from the Mouth* lends itself to a reading in terms of the Lacanian structure of the psyche: the symbolic, which is the domain of the signifier, the social order, the law etc; the imaginary, the realm of illusion, where the images, phantasies and dreams, which are the stuff of everyday life are taken as facts; and the real, which is unavailable for symbolization. These various orders: the real is that which is hidden behind the wall of the symbolic, Parr's body and its intimate interior experiences. In entering the symbolic space (the institution of the gallery), we forfeit a relation to the real.

What takes its place are signs, images projected into a wall or a screen. The image this generates, 'peaceful like a hospital patient who's going to die soon' is an imaginary, that is, illusory but necessary, product of the entire system.

Making visible, even palpable, the essential experience that psychoanalysis describes, in which a subject becomes aware of the existence of 'the other economy', that one is divided into two, simultaneously self and other, is an ever-present theme for Parr, in evidence from the very first works. But Parr is also taking a position on the recent resurgence of racist language in Australian politics and elsewhere. This language constructs a mythic collective identity based on a series of exclusions. Refugees and asylum seekers were the focus of this tactic in 2001 and were characterized as the 'other' by this discourse, that is, as a group of outsiders whose values (evident in behaviours such as throwing children overboard, or not joining the queue) were constructed as 'un-Australian'. The conditions for empathy with these people and their plight were actively negated by the Government, for instance in imposing media bans on the publishing of close-up photographs of the asylum seekers. In the process the national self was represented as an undivided homogeneous entity confronted with a disturbingly amorphous non-self (terrorism, refugees, illegal aliens etc) that must be kept at bay. In this context the performative representation of the divided self, which is everywhere in evidence in the forms of Parr's recent work, and in which self and other are part of the same entity, can be read as a form of dissent.

Water from the Mouth did not make explicit references to the issue of the policy of mandatory detention of asylum seekers, as the later works would do. Yet its themes of incarceration, the careful management of the manner in which the inmate was perceived, the experience of a long duration for the performer as well as the visitor, mark it as the first of Parr's new phase of political works, in which Parr's body became the field for the metonymic set of displacements. His stillness and awkward silence (despite the microphone in the room) evoke, at the same time, the confused spectator watching as the 'crisis' is endlessly redefined and administered and the asylum seeker in the detention centre locked up for long and indeterminate periods with no access to the media to make their case public, or with lips sewn together in mute protest.

Discourse of the Body

Why would an artist such as Parr embark on such an uncompromisingly critical and physically demanding performance practice late in his career? The physical and mental demands of the recent performances have been immense. They have all entailed a personal ordeal for the artist: the ten-day hunger strike of *Water from the Mouth*; the nailing of Parr's right arm into the gallery wall in *Malevich (A Political Arm) Performance For As Long As Possible*; the sewing of Parr's face with stiches through the skin and lips in *Aussie Aussie Aussie Oi Oi Oi (Democratic Torture)* and *Close the Concentration Camps*, the use of electric shock on the artist's body in both *Aussie Aussie Aussie Oi Oi Oi (Democratic Torture)* and *Kingdom Come, Or Punch Holes in the Body Politic*. After this latter performance Parr described the debilitating effects of the work, which involved 'sleep deprivation (i was without sleep for more than forty hours), nothing but liquids for four days and more than thirty hours of continual shocks' and which towards the end of the piece produced 'extreme paranoia ... i had begun to hate the audience and could barely contain myself' (Parr 12 April 2005). His partner Felizitas worries about what his body can withstand as he ages, and Parr himself was concerned enough about the extended use of electric shock in his most recent work to update his will just prior to undertaking the performance. So why do it?

As a performance artist Parr has always understood that the body is a key site anchoring the chain of associations that underwrites the social contract between subjectivity and power and that the most direct route to a creative violation of that contract is to create a disturbance in the flesh. Parr's own experience of physical disturbance, suffered at birth with the mangling of his left arm, makes him peculiarly sensitive to the fact remarked upon by structuralists that the body is discursively inscribed by power, written on and coded by social forces and institutions. The family, the law, the compulsory performances of consumerism and gender identity all shape the body in different ways. All have, at one time or another, become the focus of critique in Parr's performances. His renewed attack on his body in the recent work reasserts an attempt to negate the determining influences of those institutions at a time in history when they are becoming increasingly conservative and brutalizing.

Parr's recent performances remind us of the significance of performance art in its capacity to generate difference by working the seam of language and the body. The relentless flattening of language in the war on terror is perhaps the most insidious of the raft of renewed socio-cultural processes that manufacture normativity and docility. The Australian context reveals how people can be led to negotiate away their own freedoms and diminish their own institutions and how easily everyday anxieties can be placed at the disposal of the politics of division. In this environment Mike Parr's renewed ordeals are an affirmation of liberty, his own and others.

NOTES

1. While there were other slogans in use, this was, as Ross Gittins (2003) argues, 'the centrepiece of his last election campaign triumph'.
2. Judy Moylan (2005) is the Liberal member for Pearce in Western Australia.
3. Briony Trezise (4 May 2001) 'Review of Mike Parr's *Water from the Mouth*', unpublished.

REFERENCES

Arif, Mohammed <http://www.fitzroylearningnetwork.org.au/story1.html>

Bush, G.W. (September 2001) Address to a Joint Session of Congress and the American People, United States Capitol Washington, DC. <http://www.whitehouse.gov/news/releases/2001/09/20010920-8.html>

Gittins, Ross (2003) 'Honest John's Migrant Twostep' *The Age*, 20 August <http://www.theage.com.au/articles/2003/08/19/1061261148920.html>

Hsieh, Tehching, One Year Performance Art Documents 1978-99 <http://www.one-year-performance.com/>

Moylan, Judy (2005) quoted in 'This week' *New Matilda*: 39. Wednesday 25 May <http://www.newmatilda.com/home/>

The Oxford English Dictionary online <http://dictionary.oed.com/>

Parr, Mike (2004) Interview with Edward Scheer, 21 April, unpublished.

Scheer, Edward (2001) 'The Veil of the Liminal: Mike Parr's Brides', *Parkett* 62 (September) 157-66.

Turner, Victor. (1986) *The Anthropology of Performance*, New York: PAJ Publications.

Deleria/Nostalgia; Time, Space, Topography

Time. Space. Topography. These three words epitomize the immanence of the field of performance. More than that, topography, which includes every movement of bodies as well as every arrangement of places or sites of performance, is always accompanied by a certain experience of time and space, which is implicit in it and, maybe more important, conditions it. This is why, as I wish to contend, at least in terms of a theoretical discussion, no new topography of performance is possible without taking into consideration how time and space are experienced mentally and physically under specific and specifiable historical (that is, political, social and ideological) circumstances.

If such a proposition is tenable, any new topography of performance will be linked to the whole spectrum of emotions from delirium to nostalgia, which, unless perturbed by the most self-reflexive and self-critical forms of criticism within the space of discourse, will domesticate any artistic expression, halt a movement of thought, or freeze a gesture of thinking. This space of discourse is not a passive receptacle, but, as postmodern theory put forth, an open field of specifiable relationships (Foucault), a dynamic and open space of potentialities (Bourdieu), a space of close-range vision (Deleuze), a territory in which objects can be situated but never classified (de Certeau), a space where words, concepts and objects need to be wrestled from their 'proper' meaning and place (Spivak), a space of enunciative possibilities (Bhabha), a configuration that escapes the confines of the vulgar representation of time (Agamben) – thus, a dynamic space of thought and practice wherein any formulation, or any movement of bodies, is realigned with other elements positioned within it.

Time. Space. Topography. The fundamental concepts of classical physics – time and space, which used to be thought of as empty and absolute since Newton's *Principia* (1687) – were questioned toward the end of the nineteenth and the beginning of the twentieth century with the introduction of Maxwell's field theory, Mach's idea of relative spaces, Lorentz's experiments with objects moving through a motionless ether, Riemann's notion of an n-dimensional geometry, Minkowski's space-time manifold, Einstein's theory of relativity, and quantum mechanics (Kobialka 1991). Absolute space was deemed to be an illusion, though a powerful one, indeed so powerful and 'so fruitful that the concepts

of absolute space absolute and time will ever remain in the background of our daily experience' (Jammer 1969: 173). Classical perceptions of space clashed with the concept of quantum space. Einstein's famous dictum – 'time and space are modes of thinking and not the conditions by which to live' (quoted in Forsee 1963: 81) – not only challenged the existing scientific model but also freed many thinkers from the constraints of Newton's Principia that had been a controlling force in the fields of epistemology and ontology as well as perception and representation of objects.

These developments in science (specifically mathematics and physics) not only organized a scientific sense of perception, but also Western art and philosophy. The Fauvism of Matisse, the Cubism of Braque and Picasso, the abstract art of Kandinsky, Malevich and Mondrian, the Futurism of Balla, Boccioni, Russolo and Severini, and the expressionist art of Kokoschka exemplify the changes that took place in the pictorial avant-garde as well as in performance art associated with these movements and which centered on the dismantling the surface of a picture and an object that up till that time functioned within the domain of Euclidean time and space.

This revolutionary concept of time and space held the promise of exposing the fissures in the bourgeois order of things by challenging and replacing the existing and often-antiquated political forces. Constructivism, the political theatre of Piscator and Brecht, and German Expressionist art/theatre offered new representational topography that resonated with new concepts of time and space, new post-1917 ideology and new post-World War I historical conditions. This new representational topography was defended by Walter Benjamin in the name of collective, open, experimental, technically-innovative political art forms such as Brecht's dramatic laboratory, which uses all of its sophistication to make the self-education of audiences possible. As he noted in his example about Dadaism: the revolutionary strength of Dadaism consisted in testing art for its authenticity. However, if the work of the art is to be wrenched from commerce, it needs to be given a revolutionary use-value. Thus, technical progress should be the foundation of political progress. In other words, 'only by transcending the specialization in the process of production, which in the bourgeois view constitutes its order, is this production made politically valuable' (Benjamin 1937, 1978: 263). Brecht's Epic Theatre fostered the necessary two dialogues: between the producers of the play and the advanced technical means of communication; and between the actor, author, technical personnel and the 'reduced men of today.'

Time. Space. Topography. The events of World War II in general and the nightmare of concentration camps in particular necessitated a different, but equally profound, reconceptualization of space and spatial practices in Europe. How was it possible to create art after Auschwitz so that the process of creation did not participate in perpetuating that civilization (and its artistic conventions) that had led to the war? This question has received a careful treatment in Theodor Adorno's 'Commitment', Gilles Deleuze's 'Discussions or Phrasing "after Auschwitz"' and Giorgio Agamben's *Remnants of Auschwitz*. If there is no return from the camps, what are the consequences of this no-return? Tadeusz Kantor, a Polish theatre director and visual artist, writes:

> 1944. KRAKÓW. CLANDESTINE THEATRE.
> THE RETURN OF ODYSSEUS FROM THE
> SIEGE OF STALINGRAD.
> Abstraction, which existed in Poland until the outbreak of World War II, disappeared in the period of mass genocide. This is a common phenomenon. Bestiality, brought to the fore by this war, was too alien to this pure idea ...
> Realness was stronger.
> Also, any attempt to go beyond it came to naught.
> The work of art lost its power.
> Aesthetic re-production lost its power.
> The anger of a human being trapped by other human beasts cursed A R T. We had only the strength to grab the nearest thing,
> THE REAL OBJECT
> and to call it a work of art!
> Yet,
> it was a P O O R object, unable to perform any functions in life, an object about to be discarded.
> An object which was bereft of a life function that would save it.
> An object which was stripped, functionless, a r t i s t i c !
> (Kantor 1993: 211)

It was not only the object that can no longer be appropriated. Also, and maybe more important, space and reality, which in Kantor's vocabulary are places of the lowest rank, can no longer be appropriated by

the dominant conventions. In this space, existing outside the normative categories of law, urban design, and history, the object ceased to be represented by the subject – that is to say, the objects and people were freed from the bondage of history and utility, dissociated from the assumed or imposed functions and entered into a network of possible relationships with other objects/people in the space that had been destroyed by war.

The generation of Sartre, Camus, Arendt, Beckett and Kantor needed to create a space (literally and metaphorically) in which all categories and concepts were wrestled from the pre-assigned use-value so that they could enter into the closest possible relationships with other categories and objects in order to reinvent and rearticulate themselves. In this sense, Adorno's definition of autonomous art expresses a mode of thinking and doing things that rejects the culture industry and its fetishized art, which protects society from social revolution and transformation: 'the principle that governs autonomous works of art is not the totality of their effects but their own inherent structure. They are knowledge as nonconceptual objects. This is the source of their greatness. It is not something of which they have to persuade men, because it should be given to them' (Adorno 1962, 1978: 317).

They abandoned visual sovereignty of the eye, which had produced the representational image in a classical, three-dimensional, pictorial space. Instead, they adopted the non-representative, non-figurative and non-illustrative process, in which the eye did not perform a visual/ordering function: rather, it followed the contours of that which organized its field of perception to invoke what Jean-François Lyotard calls 'the unrepresentable in presentation itself, that which refuses the consolation of correct forms, refuses the consensus of taste permitting a common experience of nostalgia for the impossible, and inquires into new presentations – not to take pleasure in them, but to better produce the feeling that there is something unpresentable' (Lyotard 1992: 15). This feeling that there is something unpresentable is invariably accompanied by an enunciation of becoming, rather than being, an enunciation that perturbs the order of things. The very existence of that something that is becoming or taking its course – as Beckett would have it – is not a progressive movement on a historical trajectory. Rather, it is a procedure 'establishing a conception of the present as the "time of the now"' (Benjamin 1969: 263).

Time. Space. Topography. In one of his recent essays, Fredric Jameson offers a critique of the current artistic conditions by noting that

the very sphere of culture itself has expanded,

becoming coterminous with market society in such a way that the cultural is no longer limited to its earlier, traditional or experimental forms, but is consumed throughout daily life itself, in shopping, in professional activities, in the various often televisual forms of leisure, in production for the market and in the consumption of those market products, indeed in the most secret folds and corners of the quotidian. (Jameson 1998: 111)

If Jameson is right about the stage of postmodern sensation and about social space, which is now completely penetrated, colonized, and saturated with the culture of the image, how are we to think about these artists who have decided not to follow art that essentially finds itself complicit with a globalization of the image in the service of capitalism? Capitalism, as Lyotard observes, "in itself has such a capacity to derealize familiar objects, social roles and institutions that so-called realist representations can no longer evoke reality except through nostalgia or derision' (Lyotard 1993: 5). The implications are clearly marked in the ever-present aesthetic of the sublime, which 'allows the unpresentable to be invoked only as absent content, while form, thanks to its recognizable consistency, continues to offer the reader or the spectator material for consolation and pleasure' (Lyotard 1993: 15). This aesthetic of the sublime, according to Lyotard, can be challenged if a work of art is seen as a gesture of space-time-matter – the exchange between art and place in which its 'presence' is defined in the encounter. If a work of art is a gesture, this gesture should not be confused with a process of representing an object or with a means of addressing a goal or a purpose of an action; neither should it be viewed in terms of aesthetics. 'The gesture,' as Agamben notes, 'is the exhibition of mediality: it is a process of making a means visible as such' – a thought that Adorno put forth in another context and under different geo-historical conditions (Agamben 2000: 57). Consider such diverse works as, for example, the Happening which, at least in Europe, was a consequence of a rebellion against the consumer society and/or figurative representation of reality, both of which shaped the new urban culture and cityscape [thus, New Realism found and processed fragments of reality and materials not commonly associated with high art (Pierre Restany, Yves Klein, Mimo Rotella, Raymond Hains, Arman, Niki de Saint-Phalle, Christo); Informel Paintings abandoned representation to the delirium and the jubilation of materials (Michel Tapié, Piero Manzoni); The Zero Group in Düsseldorf (1957; Otto Piene, Heinz Mack, Günter Vecker) explored

the words indicating a zone of silence and of pure possibilities in 'Zero Happenings'; Wolf Vostell's décollage (1964–66) and open-air Happenings ('No-nine dé-coll/age', 9/14/1963, for example) became the events of change or decomposition of the life principles that surround us; Joseph Beuys's FLUXUS experiments; Bazon Brock's Railway Poems and Agit-Pop (1959–62) were fragments of everyday reality that were framed or slightly altered or collaged to create an alienating effect to confront the problem of the evolving mass consumer society; Jean-Jacques Lebel's 'Festivals of Free Expression' challenged the existing standards and modes of operation] – or the site-specific art of Richard Serra, Michael Asher, Daniel Buren, Hans Haacke and Renée Green; or Body Art of Chris Burden, Vito Acconci, Gina Pane, Marina Abramović, and Ron Athey; or urban projections of Krzysztof Wodiczko in order to recognize the tension between the inherent structure of a work of art and a social striation; between the unpresentable and the need for correct forms; between a site within a network of sites and its belonging to greater economic and political structures; and, finally, between that which cannot be grasped, because in the most concrete form it shows nothing, and the process of turning these works into cultural products that are positioned within the observable phenomena of historical reality, social mutations, economic changes and academic disputes over race, gender, ethnicity or sexuality.

Time. Space. Topography. If indeed, as some critics claim and political events seem to suggest, it is true that the twentieth century taught us that radical projects to accomplish social goals in the service of grand visions are no longer possible in the age of technocapitalism and proliferation of new political subjectivities, these past experiments with time, space and topography in the field of performance are a possible radical alternative holding the place open for new performance practices to materialize in it.

Time, space, topography – as modes of thinking, rather than conditions of living – turn a performance into an immense site wherein many poetics proliferate, coalesce and diverge. This site does not function as an organizing force within a particular system of cultural consumption but draws attention to a process of making the means visible; to a system of the formation and transformation of objects and thoughts articulating an experience of actualness or aporia that challenges the increasingly mediated surface image of global capitalism; to the field of performance reclaiming its right to be a trial arena for alternatives. Time, space, topography (space/place) cannot return to their classical forms and definitions. Rather, the modalities of being, seeing and movement proliferate in the unregulated, dynamic (mental and physical) space that offers an escape from the landscape of postmodern sensation as defined by Jameson and its clichés of difference, hybridity, pluralism, relativism, and the multitude.

REFERENCES

Adorno, Theodor (1962, 1978) 'Commitment', in Andrew Arato and Eike Gebhardt (eds.) *The Essential Frankfurt School Reader*, Oxford: Basil Blackwell, pp. 300-18.

Agamben, Giorgio (1999) *Remnants of Auschwitz: The Witness and the Archive*, (trans. Daniel Heller-Roazen), New York: Zone.

Agamben, Giorgio (2000) *Means Without End: Notes on Politics*, (trans. Vicenzo Binetti and Cesare Casarino), Minneapolis: University of Minnesota Press.

Benjamin, Walter (1969) 'Thesis on the Philosophy of History', in *Illuminations*, (trans. Harry Zohn), New York: Schocken.

Benjamin, Walter (1937, 1978) 'The Author as Producer', in Andrew Arato and Eike Gebhardt (eds.) *The Essential Frankfurt School Reader*, Oxford: Basil Blackwell, pp. 254-69.

Forsee, A. (1963) *Albert Einstein: Theoretical Physicist*, New York: Macmillan.

Jammer, Max (1969) *Concepts of Space*, Cambridge, MA: Harvard University Press.

Jameson, Fredric (1998) *The Cultural Turn*, London: Verso.

Kantor, Tadeusz (1993) 'The Milano Lessons: Lesson 1', in Michal Kobialka (ed. and trans.) *A Journey Through Other Spaces: Essays and Manifestos, 1944-1990*, Berkeley: University of California Press, pp. 208-12.

Kantor, Tadeusz (1993) 'The Milano Lessons: Lesson 3', in Michal Kobialka (ed. and trans.) *A Journey Through Other Spaces: Essays and Manifestos, 1944-1990*, Berkeley: University of California Press, pp. 216-19.

Kobialka, Michal (Spring 1991) 'Inbetweenness': Spatial Folds in Theatre Historiography', *Journal of Dramatic Theory and Criticism* 5.2: 85-100.

Lefebvre, Henri (1991) *The Production of Space*, (trans. Donald Nicholson-Smith), Oxford: Basil Blackwell.

Lyotard, Jean-François (1993) *The Postmodern Explained*, (eds. Julian Pefanis and Morgan Thomas), Minneapolis: University of Minnesota Press.

Arrested Life: A Sadness Without an Object

> *Nostalgia is the repetition that mourns the inauthenticity of all repetition and denies the repetition's capacity to form identity.*
> Susan Stewart (1993: 23)

This interest began early. I was seven years old and my mother happened to be my teacher at the local school. I had written my news in a microscopic script, a feat of craft and discipline that only I could read. My mother had written on my exercise book in red ink: *See Me*, which was a beguiling imperative given that, as her child, I lived with her. I presented myself at her desk in the front of the class. I could see her but could she *see me*? I was retreating from view, and this was one of the first measures of departure. I was already aware of what the maestro of the miniature, Susan Stewart, meant when she says: 'Such experiments with the scale of writing as we find in micrographia ... exaggerate the divergent relation between the abstract and the material nature of the sign. A reduction in dimensions does not reproduce a corresponding reduction in significance' (1993: 43)'. Indeed, I would propose here according to this vector of meaning the closer to the invisible the *more* the signification.

I begin with anecdote if only to reinforce the essential 'narrative' impulse of nostalgic reconstruction. Through this process Susan Stewart suggests 'the present is denied and the past takes on an authenticity of being', an authenticity that is only available to it as narrative. '

> Nostalgia is a sadness without an object, a sadness which creates a longing that of necessity is inauthentic because it does not take part in lived experience. Rather, it remains behind and before that experience. Nostalgia, like any form of narrative, is always ideological: the past it seeks has never existed except as a narrative, and hence, always absent, that past continually threatens to reproduce itself as a felt lack.
> (Stewart 1993: 23)

Thus, inhabiting terrain adjacent to Rene Girard's mimetic compulsion, nostalgia is the desire for desire. In this reading, Stewart suggests nostalgia's primary motif is the erasure of the gap between nature and culture: 'and hence a return to the utopia of biology and symbol united within the walled city of the maternal'.

This small essay evolves from this scriptural encounter in that city-state and continues my current interest in that which *resists* representation: things that don't need representing, that cannot be represented, that are between and beyond representations, things that are too near too far too quick or too slow for representation, and perhaps most significantly things that have deliberately been kept *from* representation. This impulse has been drawing me for a short time to infants and other animals who remind us that human adult animals occupy an often predictable and less than dynamic range of scales that limits much thinking about performance to a predictable and less than dynamic range of scales.

Theatre in the expanded field of performance might consider this amplification to include the possible registers of the infinitesimal at both its limits, of gigantism and miniature. This is naturally an anti-Aristotelian enterprise – Aristotle making clear in *The Poetics* what the appropriate size of an artwork is, neither too minute nor too immense. The scale being intimated in Aristotle is of course the scale of the first-person, able-bodied Athenian human-subject. But here I want to dwell on one example of many 'barely there' art manifestations in order to approach the disappearance of performance from view, if not from thought. I hope this materialist analysis might skirt and cross Peggy Phelan's writing on the ontology of performance in fruitful ways. If, as Phelan says in *Unmarked*, 'performance is the art form which most fully understands the generative possibilities of disappearance', what if this is a double disappearance, a mimesis of an original 'barely there' state, what if presence and resistance to re-production were ghosted by the inherent insubstantiability of an object beyond scrutiny? As Susan Stewart says, 'Ontology is not the point here so much as the necessity of exploring these relations either through the fantastic or the real' (110). I would simply add, why not both? The 'natural fantastic' perhaps.

Thinking big, or small, does not in itself guarantee any special status to the enterprise: it simply reminds us of the ubiquity of middle-sized, averaged-out, human-centred performance discussion. The kind of discussion that has allowed some of us to get away with that banal, idealised and utterly unimaginable term 'the body' for far too long. Whose body are we talking about? I hope for your sake it is not mine. No, Susan Stewart has already warned us against 'the poverty of any naïve materialism confusing physical scale with subjective or social importance'. But, that reservation understood, we might still acknowledge those who have recovered multifarious bodies for consideration against the size-blind grain. From Robert Hooke in 1665, whose first use of the microscope exposed the dialectic that 'a flea, a mite and a gnat' could be compared to such 'greater and more beautiful works of nature' as 'a Horse, an Elephant or a Lyon', to Martin Heidegger in his 1930s lecture series in which he assiduously avoided the larger, advanced and 'intelligent' species for 'the poor of world', the rock-bound lizard and crab and their respective senses of world-less-ness, a philosophy of scale has always been embedded in constructions of knowledge, epistemologies and their relations to species.

It would be curious if there were not now a special regard for the micro-organic. Indeed technology and its miniaturisation are one of the defining novelties of modernity. In a corollary to this minimalist movement, the art critic Ralph Rugoff describes the twentieth century as an age when 'expressive power in art was correlated with impressive size' (1997: 11). As Joe Kelleher pointed out in response to some images being shown to us by Jennifer Parker-Starbuck: *impressive* is a word to be further fathomed in performance. From the Mexican Muralists to Abstract Expressionists and Earth Art, these visual art scales have been replicated by the gigantism of theatre and its spectacular imperative. Every generalization has its contradictions and none more so than this one. For instance, there is the counter tradition of artists such as Marcel Duchamp whose concept of the 'infra-thin' – a term used to denote the almost immeasurable variation between two nearly identical things or experiences, the weighing of a shirt, for instance, before and after its day's wearing – might be a place to begin a small history of modest modernity. From this promisingly tenuous opener, Duchamp once proposed a transformer that would recycle inconsequential expenditures of energy such as a giggle. But caution again, as Bachelard warned us, for fear of deceiving ourselves that: 'The cleverer I am at miniaturising the world, the better I possess it' (1968: 165).

Small, blood-sucking organisms play a significant part in these control mechanisms that fear reprisal from unwitting subjects. They would appear to disturb Gaston Bachelard's contention that thinking scale operates in a single direction: 'Our animalized oneirism, which is so powerful as regards large animals, has not recorded the doings and gestures of tiny animals' (164).

The history of marking the previously hidden is galvanized by the Dutch scientist van Leuwenhoek who pioneered the development of the microscope in the seventeenth century. For my purposes here, it is significant that he chose to study fleas, and the

microscope was, in all its earliest manifestations, known as the 'flea-glass'. By the turn of the nineteenth century, rooms for viewing the previously unimaginable on film were being called 'flea pits'. More recently the zoologist-baron Jacob von Uexkull conducted what he called 'excursions into unknowable worlds' by recounting the environment of *Ixodes ricinus*, commonly called the tick, a description that Giorgio Agamben describes as 'a high point of modern antihumanism':

> This eyeless animal finds the way to her watchpost with the help of only her skin's general sensitivity to light. The approach of her prey becomes apparent to this blind and deaf bandit only through her sense of smell. The odour of butyric acid, which emanates from the sebaceous follicles of all mammals, works on the tick that causes her to abandon her post and fall blindly downward toward her prey. Uexkull, quoted in Agamben 2004: 46)

The tick is a blood-sucker but not a blood-lover; blood simply fulfils the exact liquid temperature required by the tick to suck, at which point she deposits her eggs and dies. Agamben summarizes these conditions of life: odour, temperature and skin type are the three precise conditions to which the tick unites in what Agamben describes as 'an intense and passionate relationship'

The Ghost of the Flea: William Blake

unknown to man. And even when imprisoned from this relationship on a scientist's desk, in a box for eighteen years, it waits for it. An arrested life, without an apparent subject, Uexkull says, for this tick time cannot exist. What is it waiting for, without time or world Agamben wonders? It is surely waiting to 'come on'.

If, as Bachelard said, 'grandeur progresses in the world in proportion to the deepening of intimacy', there is surely no more evocative image than William Blake's early-nineteenth-century portrait of *The Ghost of the Flea*. This image bears out the Bachelardian tension of scales and plays nostalgia off against deleria: 'Whereas the miniature represents closure, interiority, the domestic and the overly cultural, the gigantic represents infinity, exteriority, the public and overly natural' (Stewart 1993: 70). Just returned from the grandest of grand tours, where it has been showing as part of the Blake retrospective in New York and elsewhere, this tiny, 20 cm x 16 cm image has for years drawn thousands across the Tate Gallery floor to peer into its lustrous depths. But in the eighty books of Blake scholarship that discuss this image, only one acknowledges its *staged* setting. [1] If Susan Stewart is right that 'the miniature becomes a stage on which we project, by means of association or intertextuality, a deliberately framed series of actions' I too, like Derrida, am interested in 'a ghost that is the phantom of no flesh' (Derrida 1983, quoted in Phelan 1993: 13). Here of course there is the added pleasure of a double loss, as the tick that finally gets its break cannot exist except in the story that survives it.

This image was for Blake part of a series of drawings entitled *Visionary Heads*, portrayals of the heads of figures, the supposed manifestations of historical persons seen during séances at the London home of his friend John Varley in the years 1819 and 1820. 'The tempera painting of The Ghost of the Flea presumably originated from one of these seances but could have been done at a later date' (Butlin 1969: 20). The inscription on the back of the painting reads: 'The Vision of the spirit which inhabits the body of a Flea and which appeared to the Lte Mr Blake ... The Vision first appeared to him in my presence and afterwards till he had finished this picture. A flea he said drew blood on this ...' and the rest is illegible. In his *A Treatise on Zodiacal Physiognomy* of 1828, John Varley wrote:

> on hearing of this spritual apparition of a Flea, I asked him (Blake) if he could draw for me the resemblance of what he saw: he instantly said 'I see him now before me.' I therefore gave him paper and pencil, with which he drew the portrait, of which a fac-simile is given in this number. I felt convinced by the mode of proceeding that he had a real image before him, for he left off and began on another part of the paper, to make a separate drawing of the mouth of the flea, which the spirit having opened, he was prevented from proceeding with the first sketch, till he had closed it. During the time occupied in completing the drawing, the flea told him that all fleas were inhabited by the souls of such men, as were by nature blood thirsty to excess, and were therefore providentially confined to the size and form of insects; otherwise were he himself for instance, the size of a horse, he would depopulate a great portion of the country. He added that if in attempting to leap from one island to another, he should fall into the sea, he could swim and should not be lost. This spirit afterward appeared to Blake, and afforded him a view of his whole figure; an engraving of which I shall give in this work. (1828: xi)

While Blake would appear to be humouring Varley's credulous belief in the material presence of such visions, Joseph Burke, another contemporary present, has suggested the possibility that they may have been 'genuine eidetic images of physiological origin' (12). But in pursuit of this material mental debate, what is Blake seeing before him? He would appear to be seeing the ghost of a flea, who is the ghosting of the rhetorical, melodramatic stage actor of the period, adjusting the scale of their work to the new demands of cavernous, immense theatrical space.

The Drury Lane Theatre, for instance, reopened in 1812 after fire, had been developed by its architect Henry Holland into a vast stage and auditorium seating 3,611 that disconcerted players and playgoers alike. Stage practice here grew to meet the demands of what one contemporary wit called 'those covered Salisbury Plains'. On seeing Edmund Kean at Covent Garden in his first Shylock of 1814, Coleridge said it was like reading Shakespeare by flashes of lightning. In 1819, just prior to Blake's séance at Varley's house, Robert William Elliston had taken over the Drury Lane Theatre, a great actor of heroic comedy, his first hit being the melodrama *The Cataract of the Ganges* where the 'real' waterfall drew more money than the assembled talent of his illustrious company, which included Kean, Pope and Holland. Simultaneously at Covent Garden, William Charles Macready made his stage debut as Orestes. Less pursued by a mystical meteor, as suggested by art critics, and more arrested by sun-bright flashes of limelight in which his immense frame is further enlarged, here is illuminated the gorged predecessor of Artaud's wildest imaginings of the plague, inviting us to consider a true 'theatre of cruelty', the real promise masked by contagion. 'At this point' as Artaud says in 'Theatre and the Plague': 'theatre establishes itself. Theatre, that is to say that momentary pointlessness that drives men to useless acts without immediate profit' (see Artaud 1968). Despite the ratcheting up of the performances that took place in them and the prices to witness them, none of these massive theatres broke even.

The flea here might be standing in for an immense viral apparition carrying plague across the boards of history, the great exterminator of the years 542, 1346-1665 and 1880-1903. But we know, or at least those of us who have children and dogs with hair know, that beyond Blake's anthropomorphic, dramatic vision, the flea is a small, laterally compressed *holometabolous* insect. It is apterous. In other words it has a complete metamorphosis and is flightless. Despite what we see here, it has no eyes. And in keeping with what we see here, it is a blood-sucking ecto-parasite. But before you feel sorry for it, a flea can pull 160,000 times its own weight, can jump 150 times its own size, and can hop 30,000 times without stopping. Flea copulation lasts about three hours.

It is in this Blakean 'tableau' that we become aware of the essential theatricality of all miniatures, borne out by the nativity crib and the dolls house. Susan Stewart, like a new-dance theorist of the 1970s recognizes the potential for movement in this apparent stillness: 'the state of the arrested life that we see in the tableau and in the fixity and exteriority of writing and print always bears the hesitation of a beginning, a hesitation that speaks the movement which is its contrary' (Stewart 1993: 54 and Fulkerson 1976). If the miniature is a 'world of arrested time': 'The miniature, linked to nostalgic versions of childhood and history, presents a diminutive, and thereby manipulable, version of experience, a version which is domesticated and protected from contamination' (Stewart 1993: 61). This manipulation is no more evident than in the staging of the flea circus: 'a seemingly pure animation, a life-from-death in which the apparatuses of the circus appear to move of their own accord.' But is this so much a 'life from death' as 'a life' itself, an immanent life of performance.

Here, lives too small for representation except by acts of proxy: the Cardosa Flea Circus founded by Maria Fernanda Cardosa from Bogota. I was aware that they had been touring in Sydney, Paris and New York and were due in London, but they never arrived. This does not for a moment mean that I should not write about them any more than the version of *The Cherry Orchard* you thought was there was never there. Of course it never came, something else did. I was at a party one Saturday, a curious English riverside tradition where one very old University races another in a long slender boat, a massive torque-machine steered by a miniature cox in a cap too small, and I was introduced to Vanessa Redgrave, who had recently been 'starring' as Madame Ranevskaia in *The Cherry Orchard* at the National Theatre in London. But she all too rarely in reality was, she was often indisposed, in the curious parlance of theatre managements facing a potentially hostile crowd, and I found myself inverting a popular theatre greeting: 'I thought your *Cherry Orchard* was wonderful, without you.' And led by her mischievous eyes, we set off on a spirited riff on the nature of infirmity, disappearance and the immortality of the understudy. No absence more forcefully invites us to speak about the nature of performance than the disappointingly literal presence of any actor could engender.

The classic flea circus trope of the fleas escaping their masters and running rampant in the audience was being evoked on a global scale with the venue in London, just along the river from where I had met Vanessa Redgrave, claiming that the troupe had disappeared without trace. Lack now loaded onto loss, for I knew from others who had found this fragile ensemble that the opening runs: 'Today is a very sad day for the Cardosa Flea Circus. Fearless Alfredo dove to his death. It is a great loss for the circus'. Loss too for the microscopic Mr and Mrs Magu who hold a marital cotton-ball lifting competition, Tini and Tiny walking the high wire with balancing poles, Harry Fleadini the escapologist, and Brutus 'the strongest flea on earth'.

Naming here bears out the anthropocentric universe the miniature assumes. Here the nature/culture elision described earlier is further complicated by a Moebian-like braiding of human and inhuman, in which the microscopic vision of the world confirms the daydream of microcosmic life. As Gaston Bachelard said of this history: 'the first microscopic observations were legends about small objects, and when the objects were endowed with life, legends of life. Indeed one observer, still in the domain of naïveté saw human forms in 'spermatazoic animals!' (1968: 156). And further inversions abound as, Susan Stewart points out, the evasion of blood-spilling by the lion tamer in the circus is inverted to become the *blood-giving* of the trainer in the flea circus. The infinity of the miniscule is here as threatening as the depths of the big cat's jaws.

The flea circuses I have seen are ones that I have heard, for they uniformly fill the absence of size with a surfeit of speech. Here the narratives of nostalgia in the miniature begin to multiply detail in a vertiginous verbality. The flea circus begins to take on the character that Michel Foucault identified in the strange death of Victorian sex enveloped in proliferating discourses. This would seem to bear out Susan Stewart's persuasive link between the titillation of the micrographic and the titillation of the pornographic. Here visual and tactile experiences are sundered; both are 'compensatory to reality' and both exaggerate 'non-reciprocity and mastery'. This may account for the distinct unease one feels as a father taking children to these events. These discourses of replacement and compensation for what is lost to sight are often further complicated by the faux 'exotic' origin. Languages of Latin America, Eastern Europe or Asia are the common parlance of the flea circus, and each unleashes a torrent of post-colonial signifiers as the human enterprise of mastering the invisible and the 'impossibly small' fails and fails again to bring order under the regime of the eye. There is more than a trace of Homi Bhabha's 'sly civility' at work in the etiquette and abandonment of the flea-ring.

Susan Stewart says 'the miniature always tends towards tableau rather than toward narrative, toward silence and spatial boundaries rather than toward expository closure' (1993: xviii). But as the peripatetic shadow of the stable doll's house, the itinerant flea circus came into being with the advent and advance of the railway and in turn its miniaturisation in the 'oo/ho' scale model ubiquitous to the nineteenth century nursery. Between the 1830s circus of the celebrated flea master Signo Bertolotto, who toured Europe, and the American Magazine's 1920s pursuit of the travelling Professor Hechler's Trained Fleas, the flea circus simultaneously traversed the taming of wilderness and nature.

Here the inanimate and the animate remind us of the toy and its unnervingly related verb: 'to toy' with something or someone. The diminution of scale inherent here endorses a nostalgic reverie of childhood where experience could once be manipulated without fear of contamination. As the architectural theorist Anthony Vidler says, 'nostalgia for a fixed abode inevitably falls into the paradox of all nostalgia, that consciousness that, despite a yearning for concrete place and time, the object of desire is neither here nor there, present or absent, now or then ... it is ... caught in the irreversibility of time, and thus is fundamentally unsettled' (1996: 63).

A natural history of performance comes to the flea circus warily. The miniature is of course always a cultural product; it cannot by definition be of nature but rather is the engagement of a human eye working upon the physical world in a particular way. But this humanist limit should not consign the project to the margins. There is an inevitable scaling up and down of all performance, as witnessed from the distance that Walter Benjamin spoke of as the pre-requisite for criticism to occur. The rock gigs of yesteryear, the Rolling Stones at Earls Court or Madison Square Garden, the Beatles at Shea Stadium,

Bob Dylan at the Isle of White are the most forceful reminder of this vector of distancing effects, which brings with it more or less alienation. As Jonathan Swift said in the words of Gulliver: 'Nature hath adapted the eyes of the Lilliputians to all Objects proper for their view: they see with great exactness, but at no great distance' (quoted in Stewart 1993: 45). But of course this distancing also allowed us to participate in the arena of our denim gods, and few of these events were witnessed without copious doses of pharmaceutical powder that did a grave disservice to the cause of proper proportion. Thus, in effect, all performance is miniaturized in degree, and thereby the transcendences offered by it occur, following Stewart, because of an distortion not a recognition of time. Performance is inherently nostalgic, its miniature aspect erasing not only labour but 'causality and effect'. The raised seating of the audience to the performer below defines the present lived reality from which the object is always to be nostalgically distanced. And despite arguments of presence, on the contrary the giant stage-side screen, characterized by Philip Auslander in his book *Liveness*, where mediatized communion is at play, mirrors the screening magnitude of the looking glass in another age. Bachelard might have been describing an edenic Woodstock when he wrote: 'The botanist's magnifying glass is youth recaptured. It gives him back the enlarging gaze of the child. With this glass in hand, he returns to the garden 'where children see enlarged" (1968: 10).

All theatre is smaller than it was first envisaged to be, and the presence of opera glasses in some older auditoria is a reminder to re-establish the proximity and scale that one loses through the economy of far-away cheaper seating. This economic/phenomenological history of the visual frame may yet be conducive to scholarship beyond such works as Stephen Orgel's Renaissance studies of spectacle and politics and Herbert Blau's philosophical reflections on the audience. This phenomenology of perception is rarely encountered, there often being a presumption that what we have seen is somehow restored to its original scale by theorization. This is borne out most markedly by a rash of theorising of theatre as a 'face to face' encounter. While this work often draws ethical implications from Emmanuel Levinas' work in *Totality and Infinity*, it can do little to convince us that theatre *really* operates through this dimension. It is a certain clichéd presumption of humanness that foregrounds the face, when theatre itself, from distance, appears much more markedly as a play of surfaces in which ear, nose and eye give way to throat, limbs and torso before moving out towards 'dispersed bodies' and their relationship to 'distributed things'. Georges Bataille wrote about this curiosity some years ago when, commenting on the peculiar forwardness of the mouth of the animal, what he referred to as the 'prow of animals', he said 'man does not have a simple architecture like beasts, and it is not even possible to say where he begins. He possibly starts at the top of the skull, but the top of the skull is an insignificant part, incapable of catching one's attention' (1985: 59). If we were able to think performance with a sense of this contingency, to rethink the apparent relevance of features, a stronger sense of our complicating animality and in-humaness might pervade an otherwise continuing preference for the panoptical first-person unified subject. The miniature dislocates us from our normal field of reference and jeopardises our delusional status as the centred spectator of the Copernican space.

Microminiature art takes everything I have said so far and hurls it into another more concentrated, sculptural dimension. The fashioning of slivers of human hair or baroque structures mounted on a grain of rice by Hagop Sandaldjian (1931-1990), like the flea circus but apparently more material, raises questions as to whether the work exists in anything but a mental landscape. Reality here begins to embrace an endless succession of orders of magnitude that lie beyond the individual viewpoint. Work of this kind invites us to consider the precariousness of being, our sense of dependency and in turn performance's radically disabled qualities. Performance is always performance by proxy; there is always someone speaking for performance, in the name of performance. But what happens when one begins to speak for something that may not be there? In this category I have considered fleas, but also ghosts, deep-sea cephalopods that have never been witnessed alive in their infathomable habitat, the performative disappearance of J. D. Salinger and, in another register, the disappeared of the military junta of Pinochet's Chile. Beyond the collective these beings are marked out and then left unmarked for different reasons that the term 'Unmarked' only partly explains. They singly and collectively remind us of those to whom performance has not quite come, yet.

If the first natural historian, Pliny, was confused when he wrote: 'fleas arise from the action of sunlight on filth', I suggest we might conclude by looking again, not at the detritus below but the sun above, if only to blink through and think through the shadows it casts. As Artaud says: 'In theatre, as in the plague, there is a kind of strange sun, an unusually bright light by which the difficult, even the impossible suddenly appears to be our natural medium' (1968: 21). It would be through this antithesis of the miniature, the most 'elevated conception', as Georges Bataille described the sun, the most abstract of objects, that we might grasp the significance of scale in

the two performances evoked above, from the miniature evasiveness of the flea circus to the massive void of Drury Lane. The 'horror emanating from a brilliant arc lamp', the ghost that Blake painted, a form of contemporary painting that Bataille described as: 'the search for that which most ruptures the highest elevation, and for a blinding brilliance, has a share in the elaboration or decomposition of forms' (1985: 58). Between elaboration and decomposition, a high-noon tall tale. Midday, moment of the shortest shadow, for Nietzsche 'end of the longest error, zenith of mankind', where nostalgia meets deliria perhaps, a condition of arrested life.

ACKNOWLEDGEMENT

Thanks to Sally Banes and Michael Peterson who joined me on the scales of theatre panel at Performance Studies international Mainz where this writing first arose, and to Wayne Hill for his assiduous copy editing.

NOTE

1. The sketches for the tempera exist in the Blake-Varley Sketchbook of 1819. There Martin Butlin, the Blake authority, says, 'The tempera is … much more dramatic than the drawing showing the flea striding across what looks like a stage with a night sky illuminated by stars and a falling meteor behind.' (1969: 15).

REFERENCES

Agamben, Giorgio (2004) *The Open: Man and Animal*, (trans. Kevin Attell), Stanford: Stanford University Press.

Artaud, Antonin (1968) *The Theatre and Its Double*, London: Calder.

Bachelard, Gaston (1968) *The Poetics of Space*, Boston: Beacon Press.

Bataille Georges (1985) 'The Rotten Sun', in *Visions of Excess*, Minneapolis, University of Minnesota Press, p. 58.

Bataille, Georges (1985) 'The Mouth', in *Visions of Excess*, Minneapolis, University of Minnesota Press, p. 59.

Butlin, Martin (1969) *The Blake-Varley Sketchbook* of 1819, London: Heinemann.

Derrida, Jacques (1983) 'The Double Session', in *Dissemination*, (trans. Barbara Johnson), Chicago: Chicago University Press, p. 206.

Fulkerson, Mary (1976) 'In the Midst of Standing Still', in *Theatre Papers*, Dartington: Dartington College of Arts.

Phelan, Peggy (1993) *Unmarked*, London: Routledge.

Rugoff, Ralph (1997) "Homeopathic Strategies", in *At The Threshold of the Visible: Miniscule and Small Scale Art 1964-1996*, with Susan Stewart, New York: Independent Curators Inc, p. 11.

Stewart, Susan (1993) *On Longing*, Durham and London: Duke University Press.

Varley John (1828) *A Treatise on Zodiacal Physiognomy*, London: Longman and Co.

Vidler, Anthony (1996) *The Architectural Uncanny*, Cambridge, Massachusetts: MIT Press.

PAUL CARTER   **FIELD STATION 9**

Delirium: Nostalgia, Theatre and Public Space

Figure 1 : Delirium

Non si puo ipotecare il futuro
Arthur Schnitzler (1977: 114)

To plunge *in media res*: 'The poet can with impunity leap across bounds' - remarks like these pepper the Master's speech. The theatre, he says, should be a murmur, a gust of memory petalled with syllables overheard Chez Crucifix - 'The Towers are the streets ... the Wells are the streets.'[1] This is how the 'conscience of his country' (as one journalist put it) lives in retirement - off the stage, as on it, a seasoned impersonator: I say to him, 'In your production, *Delirium*, why did you introduce the character 'Descartes'? He answers me: 'The key to philosophy is performance' (Honegger 2001: 186). I explain again that his retirement has left a gap in discussions about the future of theatre. People are curious about his views.

While it is true that the publication of an interview with him will bring me some small financial reward, this is not my motive in seeking him out. I want to know, I say, in a poor attempt at humour, why he no longer finds diversion *either in walking or in society*.[2] In response, he draws my attention to the book on the table. I open it and read.

> '*DESCARTES (His imagination feels itself struck by the representation of some ghosts who present themselves to him and who so frighten him that, thinking he is walking down a street, he has to lean to his left side in order to be able to reach the place where he wants to go, because he feels a great weakness on his right side, so that he cannot hold himself upright. Because he is ashamed to walk in this way, he tries to straighten up, but he is buffeted*

by gusts that carry him off in a sort of whirlwind that spins him around three or four times on his left foot. Even this is not what alarms him. His difficulty in dragging himself along means that he thinks he will fall at each step until, noticing a school open along his way ...)'

It amuses him, the Master says, that none of his critics recognized the source of *Delirium*'s opening scene. If the people ought to obey reason, they should at least know where it comes from.[3] His audiences, he says, gesturing to the sea, receive his plays as melons from a foreign land. I notice below us in the direction of the church a group of figures. Although perched precariously close to the cliff's edge, they are upright and steady on their feet. One detaches himself from the group and climbs towards us. In reply to the Master's question, Mr N (that is his name) says: 'The wind has abated.' The Master appears relieved, and I understand that, already, before our interview has begun, it has been terminated, and that Mr N's weather-report is a cue for me to leave.

I retrace my steps down the steep road that leads from his tower down to the village. The author of *Agoraphobia*, I reflect, would have no difficulty in explaining Descartes' distress. Stumbling towards his revelation of a new world, the young man was assailed by space fear. Sufferers from

Figure 2 : Nostalgia

this condition feel tolerably well in a room but are gripped by dizziness as soon as they reach a wide street or open space. They are either frightened of falling or filled with such anxiety that they do not dare to traverse the space at all. Standing at the threshold of his new, geometrically-rationalized world, Descartes was like a man entering a city in which all the signs have been removed. There was nothing to steer by. Abysses opened up on every side. His plodding step-by-step reason was a massive act of the will designed to overcome his sensation of being rooted to the spot.

If I were writing a play about Descartes, I would begin here. Descartes said that the discovery of his Method was preceded by three dreams – the first of them inspiring the opening pantomime of *Delirium*. Everyone finds Descartes' derivation of his Method from the unreason of his dreams paradoxical. But, in eliminating the usual props of tradition, common usage and received opinion, Descartes was like a performer who insists on acting without script, stage or audience. There is nothing odd about this condition: each one of us experiences it everyday in the theatre of public space. Descartes' novelty was to render the phrase *theatrum mundi* a tautology. This was why he experienced stage fright: he inaugurated a performance without a script, a society of *actators*. The plot of daily life was suddenly riddled with missed opportunities. Every possible meeting was balanced by the chance of being lost. No wonder the new public space that his Method produced made him feel giddy.

This is what I would have said, and it indicates that I am not a novice in this area. If the Master would hear me out, he would discover this. His tradition of theatre has passed its use-by date. The future of theatre lies in the street. Perhaps the last three centuries of classical theatre have been a holding operation against this obvious fact. In comparison with the true theatre of everyday life, the theatre is a netherworld. It can only be a form of ancestor worship that draws audiences to it.[4] If I am in the audience, I look at the audience: the antics on the stage belong to another world.

The second day dawns overcast. Drops of rain seed the dust on the side of the road, and when I reach the crest of the hill, I observe beyond Cape Palinurus curtains of rain. Today I plan a different tack. I want to show the Master that I am not a complete fool.

'The place where I am staying rejoices in the curious name, Pensione Tages. With time on my hands yesterday, I looked into its origin. The story goes that a certain peasant was ploughing the land hereabouts when he chanced to make a furrow deeper than usual, whereupon there sprang up from it a wondrous being, 'a boy in appearance, but a patriarch in wisdom – Tages by name' (Dennis 1907: 418).[5] Tages was remarkable both for his performance *and* what he performed. Singing, dancing and inditing, he gave the Etruscans their civil and religious code, showing them the spot where they should build their city. Isn't it remarkable, I say to the Master, that, according to this myth, the origins of theatrical representation and public space are one: the histrioi were legislators, the clowns architects, and saltimbanques ran the courts?'

'Last night,' the Master replies, 'I dreamt I was awoken by thunder. When I opened my eyes in the dark, I noticed many sparks of fire scattered around the room. What is the meaning of this, do you think?'[6]

I ignore his infernal rudeness and blunder on with my argument. A divine representation so frightening a man that he cannot plough a straight furrow; it is essentially the opening scene of *Delirium*. In deciding to spend his last years in this part of Italy, was the Master indulging his nostalgia? Was he – a man notorious for mythologising his origins – returning to his 'native land', the home of Western theatre. The title of his selected drama, *Histrionics*, entitles us to think as much. *Histrio*, or actor, is not the only Etruscan word that might have influenced him: *mundus* (our 'world') is said to come from an Etruscan word *muth* or *mund*, meaning 'a trench for offerings, near an Etruscan temple'. It signified 'the entrance to the underworld.'[7] Having openly announced that his final project would be the staging of his own death, these infernal connotations of *theatrum mundi* cannot have been lost on the Master ...

With thunder and lightning, the rain sweeps in off the sea; and I notice that, despite the sudden, loud noise, the Master has fallen asleep. Mr N discreetly ushers me out and, as if to compensate me for my trouble, gives me a book.

In a kind of delirium of humiliation, frustration and anger, I retrace my steps to the village. Alone with my thoughts, in the tomb of my head (that fine and private place, etc.), I work out a theatre of my own. If there is any point in making a side trip to interview the Master, it is to fund research for a production I shall call – why not? – *Public Space*. It is an evocation of the global city populated by *histrioi* – 'tight-rope walkers (funambuli), bareback riders (desultores), tumblers, jugglers and possibly contortionists' together with those who have 'mastered the fixed and flying trapeze.'[8] Their gyrations, their wobbling perambulations, their human towers and plunges into bucket-sized wells are said to be less realistic than the gestures prescribed in the Master's stage works. But this is an error. The impression they give of running in pre-ordained grooves represents the anxiety of millennial life. 'The true way goes over a rope which is stretched not at any great height but just above the ground. It seems more designed to make people stumble than to be walked upon' (Goodman 1947: 9). Yes, only now the rope is laid over the ground, and you cannot tell the difference.

When I reach the pensione, I am struck by the unreality of it all. If this journey has any purpose, if it's anything other than an excuse for not writing *Public Space*, it must be about making the mental room where something can happen, getting in the groove, whatever that may be, of the writing that is not about the world but of it. I am used to this sense of longing. I don't think it can be assuaged. Meaning, if there is any, 'continuously appears and continuously fades'. It's like perceiving the city as a stage-set, the buildings the 'empty husks' of a repressed pathology of everyday life (Carter 2002: 180).[9] In another period the weakness it produces would have made it a medical condition, like nostalgia or delirium. Its symptoms are: a sequence of dreams for once memorable; something in the street that you cannot explain *and cannot forget*; a 'site' as architects call it, with something that draws you to linger; and a lightning bolt (a news item) that breaks in from outside severing and fusing these elements, producing an ungovernable agitation that only traveling without a plan can tranquilize.

Here there should be a scene break, a telephone call. But nothing happens. In the café, over a bottle of wine, I open the book. It is a new translation of the Master's novel *Nostalgia*. I scan the first page, my eye quickly jumping from line to line: 'In the year 17–, while I lay in barracks at T-- in the north of England, a recruit who had lately joined the regiment was returned in sick list ... He had only been a few months a soldier; was young, handsome and well-made for the service; but a melancholy hung over his countenance, and wanness preyed on his cheeks. He complained of a universal weakness, but no fixed pain; a noise in his ears and giddiness of his head ... in the hospital three months ... quite emaciated, like one in the last stage of consumption ... One morning the nurse mentioned the strong notions he had got in his head of home ... He was able to speak constantly on this topic. He revived at the very thought of it ...'[10]

Nostalgia is an afternoon illness, a longing for the youth of the day. Crossing over the border of noon, one enters the underworld of recollection, the realm of lost hopes. The way there is not untenanted. Sleeping off the wine, it seems to me that Tages stands at my side, takes my hand, and, gently helping me up from my couch, beckons me to follow him. I have the strongest impression he is taking me home. I remember a woodcutter's path, then a clearing. Finally, we come out into a public square

PHOTO: PAUL AND ED CARTER

Figure 3 : Theatre

that bears an uncanny resemblance to a stage set. A man walks across from the other side. There is nothing memorable about his appearance. When he reaches me he says, 'The border cuts through the forest, through the brook, through a kitchen' (Specht 1994: 45). And I suddenly notice a furrow unzipping behind him, and out of it a wall, like a row of wheat, and I realize that everywhere he walks a wall springs up behind him.

At some point a border was instituted between the audience and actor. There was cut in the forest of bodies, the proscenium arch and its border guard of footlights, spots and defensive curtains. Why we think our view of the stage takes place through a removed wall, I cannot imagine. We have ignored the division in our lives that this prescribed domain represents. We, the imagined outsiders without scripts, applaud (or not) on cue; we, pushed back into a kind of oral longing (silenced, speechless, but succoured by the sound and fury), look into death's gaping mouth, the Luna Park of our illusions.

'For a stationary piece of street theatre ... a plain wall immediately behind is extremely important ... The more neutral the back wall the better; it is difficult to transform the space if the show is dominated by a huge advertisement' (Mason 1992: 89). For thirty years, in the name of theatrical emancipation, we have been putting up walls. In thirty years of producing a theatre of public space, we have not liberated ourselves from a nostalgia for the backdrop. Cartesians to the end, we have behaved outside the theatre as we behaved inside, erasing the advertisements of everyday life in order to draw the well-ordered towns and squares of our productions 'on a vacant plan according to [our] free imaginings.'

When, much later on my return to Vienna, I related this dream to a friend, she said, 'The interpretation is clear. You were suffering from delirium. It is the work of the dream to turn words into actions. Delirium, from a Latin phrase 'out of the furrow', means wander off the straight and narrow. It is the experience of being trackless, disoriented, dizzy. But you should not be dismayed. The presence of Tages, the genius of the furrow, in your dream is significant. Leading you out into the agora of modern life, he shows you the unreason of reason, of a life from which memory has been banished. The delirium of modern life is to stay in the groove, to submit oneself to the pathology of the path.

'When the Doctors first became aware that the actors in the new spaces of public life were frightened of falling or filled with such anxiety that they did not dare to inhabit them, they were confident of finding a cure. The new citizen, they said, had to learn to imagine a furrow, to draw a straight line where there was none. A good exercise was to fix their attention on railings, or a wall, going in their direction. At all costs they should shut out of consciousness the chaos of events impinging on their peripheral vision. And the good Doctors invented a device that public space sufferers could wear: a pair of spectacles to whose sides were attached vertical plates of very dark glass.[11] Inside this tunnel vision, the sufferer could advance undistracted by his surroundings. You see,' she concluded, 'when he directed all his attention on what lay in the luminous square of space ahead of him, he had the impression he was safely secured inside a darkened theatre.'

'Over the thirty years since its first production, the influence of *Delirium* on performance practice has been considerable. The opening scene of Stanya Kahn's *Delirium*, in which she staggers out onto the stage, spike-heel shoes round her ankles and a pillowcase over her head, clearly recalls the gust-buffeted Descartes of *your Delirium*. Antero Alli's vision of 'Angels descending and ascending, angels rising and falling all around us, all the time, melting into the ground', in *Orphans of Delirium* is another interpretation of your Cartesian somnambule.[12]

Works like these represent an attempt to recall theatre to its roots ...'

This is the speech I plan to deliver on the third day. The vanity of the Master is legendary. I feel these evidences of his continuing influence will break down his reserve. But my attempt to stage-manage our final meeting fails when Mr N explains that the Master is not well enough to answer my questions. He has, however, suggested that he, Mr N, may answer my questions on his behalf. I am suddenly reminded of the Doctor's remark in *Nostalgia*: to speak of oneself is to speak posthumously. 'Then,' I say, 'can we go back to where I first came in? What does the Master mean when he says, 'The poet can with impunity leap across bounds'?

'His theatre,' says Mr N, 'is the theatre of other voices. His is the discourse of other speech, the language of allegory. "If you have one, two, three or four voices ringing in your ears," the Master used to say, quoting an observation of Elias Canetti, "the interplay among them produces the most surprising effects ..."'

Figure 4 : Public Space

'O, we believe this as well,' I say, 'to us all sounds are voices, the universe is full of words: railways, birds and aeroplanes – they all speak. The script of the street is written for all with ears to hear' (paraphrasing Canetti 1962: 17).

'The voices,' Mr N went on, ignoring me, 'pay no attention to one another; each starts off in its own way and proceeds undeviatingly like clockwork, but when you take them all together, the strangest thing happens. It is as though you have a special key, which opens an overall effect unknown to the voices themselves' (Canetti 1986: 262).

'As if all the tracks are played at once. And the poet of this is the one who can hiphop from line to line, who can leap from furrow to furrow, yes.'

'The writer of that line,' Mr N says, 'also wrote "I am not the master – so to speak – of the people's usage, but it is of mine. As a helmsman ought to obey reason, and each one in the ship ought to obey the helmsman, so the people ought to obey reason, and we individuals ought to obey the people" (Varro 1938: 445). I am not to misjudge the old man: the parts he plays contain a wily wisdom. If there is nothing behind the person, that is something, the end of a stage illusion.'

I look out to sea. Yesterday's storm has left in its wake a stage effect of light-lanced clouds and sparkling water. It is a scene without focus, fading. I try to bring my gaze back to the Master, but I am losing my grip on him. The reality of his presence is fast draining away. The dome of his head is like a melon from a foreign country. It is fusing with the headland ... *Cosi divenni furia non mortale* (Ungaretti 1974: 251).

«»

It's a cruelly bright morning when I stagger out of the bar into Judenplatz. Climbing up the steps, I am like Orpheus returning home - *and* I've lost my Eurydice.

I find a café and call her: 'I feel like Fridolin in *Traumnovelle*. And my head! What *did* we take? Where are you?' I order a coffee. She says: 'I am in a room. There is a table with a book on it. I pick up the book to see what it is called. But the book has no spine, and when I open it, it falls apart, the pages scattering in every direction. I kneel on the floor, trying to gather up the stray leaves. But each page I touch turns into another book – another volume without a spine which, when I try to open it, also falls apart. I try to read the pages, hoping they will show me what to do. On one page I read: "What way in life shall I follow?" On another: "Yes and No." A man appears and begins calmly gathering up the papers. He organizes them into books, which he shelves with their backs to us. When he has completed the task, I find I am outside, in a small square. In the middle of the square is a house made of books. The books have their backs to me. The house is a mausoleum without a door.'[13]

The mobile drops out. I glance at the newspaper: the famous scourge of public reputations, the playwright ... has died. 'The helmsman dies because he lacks flexibility, falling victim to a desire for an absurd, rock-like immortality', the master once wrote, alluding to his reputation as the scourge of his nation's public life. Can he now, the obituary wonders, escape becoming 'an immortal Fury'? In the theatre of everyday life, who can tell what will happen?

I glance up and in the shop window see a ghost. It is Eurydice returning from the grave.

NOTES

1 For an evocation of the context of Apollinaire's 'Les Fenêstres', see Butor 1968:202-3.

2 In the period leading up to his first Olympian dream, Descartes 'found himself caught in a continual contention in which he could find diversion neither in walking nor in human society' (Cole 1992:32).

3 Adrien Baillet's version of Descartes' first Olympian dream transposed into the present tense (see Cole 1992:33).

4 With reference to Lefebvre (1993:166), who confines his discussion of theatrical space to the particular conception of space associated with the classical drama, which, because it offers us reflections and mirages, holds out a prospect of fulfilment that is ultimately unattainable. This produces 'great nostalgia'.

5 George Dennis lived 1814-1898.

6 The allusion is to Descartes' second Olympian dream (see Cole 1992:34-5).

7 According to www.quantavolution.org/vol_12/ka_18.htm

8 Michael Balint says these types inhabit a world 'of friendly expanses dotted more or less densely with dangerous and unpredictable objects' (1955:225-41, esp. 227).

9 Quoting Rosalind Deutsche and Esther da Costa Meyer.

10 From a description by Robert Hamilton (1749-1830) of 'a case of a soldier suffering from nostalgia, who received sensitive and successful treatment'. See en.wikipedia.org/wiki/Nostalgia

11 See V. Benedikt, 'On "Platzschwindel"', originally published in German in 1870. I am grateful to Mary Dwarka for directing my attention to this paper - and for supplying me with an English translation.

12 Of course these genealogies are part of my fiction. For further information, see F. Lennox Campello, '"Delerium", A Performance by Stanya Kahn' at www.geocities.com/SoHo/Gallery/7246/delerium. html

13 Besides the obvious reference to Rachel Whiteread's Jewish Holocaust Monument in Vienna, Eurydice's dream incorporates elements of Descartes' third and final Olympian dream (see Cole 1992:35-6).

REFERENCES

Balint, Michael (1955) 'Friendly Expanses - Horrid Empty Spaces' in *International Journal of Psycho-Analysis* XXXVI/4.

Butor, Michel (1968) *Inventory*, (ed. R. Howard), New York: Simon and Schuster.

Canetti, Elias (1962) *Crowds and Power*, London: Gollancz.

Canetti, Elias (1986) *The Play of the Eyes*, (trans. R. Manheim), New York: Farrar Straus Giroux.

Carter, Paul (2002) *Repressed Spaces*, London.

Cole, John R. (1992) *The Olympian Dreams and Youthful Rebellion of Rene Descartes*, Urbana: University of Illinois Press.

Dennis, George (1907) *The Cities and Cemeteries of Etruria*, vol. 2, London: J. M. Dent.

Goodman, Paul (1947) *Kafka's Prayer,* New York: The Vanguard Press, Inc.

Honegger, Gitta (2001) *Thomas Bernhard, The Making of an Austrian*, New Haven: Yale University Press.

Lefebvre, Henri (1993) *The Production of Space*, (trans. D. Nicholson-Smith), Oxford: Blackwell.

Mason, Bim (1992) *Street Theatre and Other Outdoor Performance*, New York and London: Routledge.

Schnitzler, Arthur (1977) *Doppio Sogno* [Traumnovelle], Milano: Adelphi Edizioni.

Specht, Karin (1994) 'The Little Red-Hot Man' in Katrin Sieg, *Exiles, Eccentrics, Activists: Women in Contemporary German Theater*, Ann Arbor: University of Michigan Press.

Ungaretti, Giuseppe (1974) 'Recitativo di Palinuro' in *Vita D'Un Uomo*, Milan: Mondadori.

Varro, Marcus Terentius (1938) *Varro on the Latin Language*, (trans. R. G. Kent), vol. 2, Cambridge (Massachusetts): Harvard University Press.

PAUL RAE

Why there is Wind: Power, Trees, Performance

1 If the future is now, when is tomorrow?

On 7 November 2004, Singapore's elder statesman Lee Kuan Yew planted a tree in his Tanjong Pagar constituency as part of the city-state's annual Clean and Green Week. To the extent that the event could be staged, it was thoughtfully done: decked out in matching green and blue batik shirts with floral motifs, Lee and his fellow Members of Parliament were veritable avatars of Cleanliness and Greenliness. Like baby-kissing, though, there's only so much pizzazz the performance of popular politics can or should support. A spade is a spade, whoever's digging, and the act itself was nothing new. In 1963, Lee, then Prime Minister,[1] initiated a planting campaign that has since seen the addition of over half a million trees to the otherwise densely populated, highly urbanized Southeast Asian island.[2] While the vast majority have been planted by the armies of workers from Thailand, Burma and the Indian subcontinent whose low-cost labour has been integral to the rapid infrastructural development of Singapore since full independence in 1965, a search at the National Archives reveals several hundred images of Lee, spade in hand and surrounded by onlookers, ministrating to a series of likely-looking saplings. This is how political performance secures the certainties of the present against the caprices of the future – again, and again, and again.

It is, after all, an iconic image, condensing some of the most distinctive characteristics of modern Singapore. On the one hand, a verdant Garden City in the tropics, easy on the eye in line with a general trend towards user-friendliness, which has in turn drawn foreign investment and multinational corporations, and kept an increasingly affluent population overwhelmingly in a state of uncomplaining contentment.[3] On the other hand, an authoritarian government practically synonymous with the state and continuously overseen by the paternalistic Lee for almost half a century, that exercises high levels of control over both its people and its environment. '[I]n 1967, I launched the Garden City program to green up the whole island and try to make it into a garden', recalled Lee in 1995 (1). Subsequently, the greening of Singapore by means of fast-growing imported exotics proceeded in tandem with an extensive social engineering program which, most explicitly in this connection, included a eugenicist and civilizational dimension aimed at improving the quality of Singapore's stock.[4]

It is important, however, to understand that the image of Lee Kuan Yew planting a tree does not merely *symbolize* the Singaporean condition, for, in a strict sense, interpretation is unnecessary. In the *Analects*, Confucius states: 'The virtue of the gentleman (*junzi*) is like the wind; the virtue of the small man is like grass. Let the wind blow over the grass and it is sure to bend' (1979: 12.19). In so far as Singaporean ministers style themselves as *junzi*,[5] the effect of Lee's iconic performance is direct

and unmediated. Appearing sporadically in the pages of Singapore's politically constrained media over the course of forty years, the image reiterates and legitimates the social order and interpellates the viewer accordingly. It is by means of such repetitions that Lee's People's Action Party has combined radical socio-economic transformations with a deepening acceptance of the political status quo. Yet even under a semiotic regime as carefully policed as Singapore's, the tree-planting image falls foul of a fatally anthropocentric hubris. Gathered in sequence, the persuasive power of the single act recedes before the cumulative effect of the whole series: against the unvarying repetition of the props – spade, sapling, eager onlookers – Lee grows older. From a stripling bedding down his plant-kingdom familiars, he becomes the octogenarian custodian of spry whippersnappers, and where the formers' futures entwine, the latters' bifurcate: now the sapling stands in mute testament to a Leeless future. Worse: although the accompanying plaque may memorialize him when he is gone, the tree as such is indifferent, a splinter of otherness, materializing a concept otherwise almost as inconceivable as death itself.

Official steps have been taken to stabilize the meanings of trees in Singapore. In 2001, the Heritage Trees Scheme began to identify specific trees that would 'help to create a sense of permanence and identity to the place we live' (NParks 2004a). [6] Meanwhile, Singaporeans have been collectively framed as aging alongside the trees, then-Deputy Prime Minister Lee Hsien Loong stating in 2003 that 'as Singapore matures as a society and our people develop a natural affinity for greenery, the Government's role [in realizing the vision of a Garden City] should increasingly be complemented by civic participation' (2003). [7] Re-visiting the 7 November 2004 planting, one notes its dovetailing into more pragmatic reflections on the future. In the following day's front-page story 'Future bright with polls results', Lee reportedly observed that the US, Australian and Japanese election results augured well for Singapore, despite an ongoing loss of jobs to outsourcing giants like India and China. Urging jobseekers to retrain for the service industries, he stated: 'I feel that the future for the next 10 years...will be as bright as it has been for the past 30 or 40 years' (in Chia 2004). As if to shade the future from the three- or fourfold-glare of the past, the caption accompanying the image salved the sunstroked logic of Lee's non-sequitur by informing readers that the sapling 'is the scion of the last Hopea Sangal (chengal) tree found in Singapore' (Chia 2004). Relief. A reminder that just as Lee's singular achievements in growing and greening Singapore make him one of a kind in the eyes of admirers and detractors alike, so a scion has recently taken root to retard the prospect of a Leeless future for one more generation. In August 2004 Lee Kuan Yew's son, Lee Hsien Loong, was sworn in as Singapore's third Prime Minister.

Even here, though, the smooth extension of the present into the future is thwarted, for if there is one thing that resonates even more profoundly in the Singaporean imaginary than the fortunes of the Lee family, it is an enduring, if sporadically expressed, attachment to stray fauna and threatened flora. Indeed, despite the caption's evasiveness on the subject, who amongst the *Straits Times*' readers could encounter a reference to 'the last Hopea Sangal (chengal) tree found in Singapore' and not recall the saga of a mere two years earlier? In September 2002, jubilant nature enthusiasts announced the positive identification of a 150-year-old Hopea Sangal tree, previously thought extinct on the island. Two months later, a developer illegally felled it, claiming it was a threat to nearby buildings, and that they were unaware of its uniqueness. The news unleashed a flurry of angry letters to the press and galvanized debate about the costs of development on Singapore's 'natural' habitat. The developer received a stiff fine, the trunk was turned into a sculpture park at the zoo, and seeds from the tree were hot-housed for Lee's planting two years hence. In their own way, all these events sought to repair the damage done by the felling, yet they inevitably fall short. The tree's age and indigeneity demand reparations that cannot be met in a single generation, if at all. In contemplating its fate, one confronts an association with place and a span of time that vaults beyond any one person's lived experience. Lee's planting ritual, and its

implicit association with his son's recent inauguration, is an attempt to domesticate the uncanny disinterest of trees by means of performance. But even at the tender age of two years, the sapling signifies otherwise. Looking carefully at the picture on the front page of the *Straits Times*, one realizes that where its leaves overlap with Lee's batik shirt, they blend into the pattern. Ironic intimation: that it should be one of the earth's youngest, reaching out to reclaim him.

2 The Silly Little Girl and the Funny Old Tree

On first acquaintance, *The Silly Little Girl and the Funny Old Tree*, by the late doyen of Singapore theatre, Kuo Pao Kun, is a simple, even simplistic, play. A misfit girl whose parents work long hours strikes up a relationship with a tree in the carpark of her school. They dance, sing songs and talk about time and human behaviour. An attempt is made to exorcize the Tree, but when bulldozers come to clear it for a housing development, the Girl stages a protest. She is removed to a sanitorium, and although the Tree is allowed to remain standing, its unruly branches are hacked back so that, as the developer says, 'it will blend in perfectly with the new landscape design' (Kuo: 2000: 115). The Tree dies, and the Girl dances in homage.

First staged in 1987 against a backdrop of rapid industrialization and urbanization, the play can be described as a cautionary tale about the intangible costs of materialism to the human spirit. As such, all the tropes are present and correct: the child as preternaturally sensitive to her surroundings; the Tree as a source of timeless wisdom; rapacious developers and philistine

authority figures who interpret the girl's behaviour as evidence of insanity. This strand arcs through the play from beginning to end, tracing an anthropocentric trajectory, whereby, as the Girl says, 'trees are like people' (99), and her relationship with the Tree symbolizes those aspects of *human-to-human* interactions that are threatened by over-zealous development.

There is, however, a second strand to the play that complicates and compromises the first. It can be discerned in three different operations.

Thematically, the Tree disavows the too-eager attribution of wisdom by the Girl by consistently turning questions back on her or refusing outright to answer them. This side-stepping of the reciprocal and the dialogic clears the ground for a more tangential procedure. When the Girl states that trees can only sing and dance when there is wind, the Tree replies: 'That's what the wind says. Actually, it's only when we sing and dance is there wind; only when our leaves and branches swing is there wind. Wind mustn't be so proud' (107). In this de-linking of cause and effect there is an implicit political challenge to the Confucian dictum that would see the people bending obediently to the will of the *junzi*, and there is also a demand that the Girl re-think her own position in less anthropocentric terms. Later, when she goes to the Tree at night, she is at first startled that it sees her in the dark, but goes on: 'Why can't humans see in the dark? Because human eyes are made to see only light. (*Reflecting for a moment*)' (110). In this reflection lies not only a moment of personal realization, but a space for the audience, too, to think through the ecologized epiphany that derives not so much from the precise answer as from the shift in logic that it entails.

Structurally, this ecological aspect constantly derails the linear trajectory of its human story, and suggests alternative temporalities along the way. The Tree tells long, digressive stories without a clear denouement, suggesting that in their entirety they last longer than the span of a human life. Both Girl and Tree return periodically to a refrain from the Chinese song 'Longing for the Spring Breeze'. Even more disjunctive is the physicality of the performance, and the physical relationship between Girl and Tree. The stage directions are simple but gnomic, demanding real inventiveness in the staging: 'The little one teaches the old one to sing the song from the distant past'; 'The Old Tree ... goes through a series of mimed actions tracing its own past before coming back to reality and tells her the story in words' (103); 'The Tree goes into a series of movements, turning and going around, shaking and wagging. Girl totally absorbed, but can't understand' (109).

This latter direction describes the Girl's encounter with

what the Tree calls the Bee Dance, and it is in this that the Girl – and the performer – feel out a less human-focused relationship with the Tree, and therefore a more inventive interaction with the audience. Another dance, the Tree Dance, is described, but the Tree is pruned before the Girl can learn it. As the Tree describes it, this dance has a revolutionary flavour, where trees interlink not only to withstand but to thrive from a storm, 'caressing the wind as they arch' (113). The storm over, 'the trees have become deeper rooted, the branches have become tougher, the leaves have become greener and lusher' (114). The Bee Dance, by contrast, is a solo: 'With this dance, the bee is telling its comrades: There, there is honey that way. In the direction such an angle to the sun, there is honey' (109). At the close of the play, '[p]ainstakingly, she executes the Bee Dance in solemn seriousness.... In stark concentration, she searches her memory and the environment' (116). The image is a complex one. Far removed from whimsy or New Age mysticism, it combines the becoming-bee of both Girl (by way of the Tree) and performer, with a gesturing towards political possibilities whose contours remain unclear. It is perhaps no surprise that the first actress to play the

Girl was Ang Gey Pin, a remarkable physical performer, who went on to practice extensively at the Workcenter of Jerzy Grotowski and Thomas Richards in Italy. Even today, and having not seen the original production, my personal response to Ang's combination of exploratory and intensive physicality is a sense of being bound in to an affective relation with a practice that carries the trace of those initial actions in Kuo's play.[8]

A final challenge to a strictly humanist reading of *The Silly Little Girl* concerns the figure of Kuo himself, who died in 2002. In a strange pre-figuring of the Hopea Sangal incident, the Old Tree in the play is identified as the last of its kind, and when reflecting on Kuo's unique character and influence, it is tempting to identify him with one or both of these trees.[9] Once again, though, this assumes that 'trees are like people', a claim subtly refuted by one of the most thoughtful responses to Kuo's death, the installation *A Tree in a Room* by the artist and performer Zai Kuning. Installed in a former Methodist chapel in early 2004, *A Tree in a Room* consisted of a thick, 6-metre-long horizontal tree trunk which had been sawn in two and 'stitched' back together again with hundreds of crisscrossed nails and wire. The accompanying text referenced an earlier project, made when Kuo was still alive, which took the form of a tree sculpture for the premises of Kuo's Theatre Training School. The tree is therefore associated with Kuo, and recalls not only *The Silly Little Girl*, but other well-known plays of his such as *The Coffin is too Big for the Hole* (1985) and *Descendents of the Eunuch Admiral* (1995).[10] And yet, however one tries, something about the actuality of the trunk – its dense mass and monumental presence – deflects any attempt to identify it directly with Kuo, or Kuo in it. The very treeness of the tree affirms itself, as mere correspondences recede. One is left, instead, with a sense of the labour of sawing and nailing required to meet this materiality. Between imagining this physical act and confronting the raw heft of a once-living-and-still-organic object, one encounters a depersonalized, dispersed remembrance of Kuo. The Chinese critic Yu Yun described him as 'a rude intruder in a beach resort' (2000: 55), and *A Tree in a Room* reinforces the sense that Kuo's perpetual untimeliness is more closely associated with the *longue durée* of tree-time than it is the more self-serving notion that 'his spirit is still with us'.

3 Why there is Wind

On 8 February 2004, Zai Kuning staged a performance in the gallery where the tree lay. In a series of choreographed actions he moved towards the trunk, then walked casually back to his starting position. He repeated this sequence for approximately twenty minutes. It was his version of the Bee Dance, and as time passed, and actions accumulated, my attention fastened on the way in which trees – or, more properly, our perplexity in their presence – draw performances out of us. Some, like politicians' tree-planting ceremonies, establish a comprehensive and instrumentalist framework to infuse the present with the promise of future growth. Others, such as the exorcism carried out at the foot of the Old Tree in Kuo's play, draw on established cosmologies and belief systems for the purposes of accommodation or appeasement.[11] A few, like Kuo's own act of writing, and Zai Kuning's response, endeavour to encounter the indifference of trees, and to open human experience to a temporality where assumptions of futurity are as flawed as describing what's past in terms of 'heritage'. This is why there is wind[12]. This is why there are trees. People mustn't be so proud.

NOTES

1. Lee Kuan Yew was Prime Minister of Singapore from 1959–90, whereupon he took on the title of Senior Minister. When Lee Hsien Loong became Prime Minister in August 2004, his predecessor, Goh Chok Tong, became Senior Minister, and Lee Kuan Yew adopted the title Minister Mentor.

2. Singapore is 647 sq km (250 sq mi) in size. It has a population of 4.2 million, of which 77 percent are of ethnic Chinese origin, 14 percent Malay, 8 percent Indian, and 1 percent other ethnicities.

3. The conjunction of these factors was vividly illustrated in the 2004 National Day Parade during a section in which Garden City themes were realized in a mass display by the government-linked People's Association. As over a thousand participants thronged the field of the National Stadium in brightly colored costumes, the two announcers providing the television voice-over interpreted their actions:
'This beautiful sea of green now … shows a giant leaf, aptly representing growth and diversity.'
'You know, this choice is very significant – leaves are where every part of the plant gets its life from and similarly Singapore can be thankful for its pioneers, who upon Independence, took the task of building Singapore upon them.'
'That's right. Bending and swaying in the wind the participants portray Singapore's flexibility and strength.'
'And now watch as the garden begins to blossom. 240 orchids streaming into the field now, and they will help to complete the formation representing Singapore as a Garden City.'
'The orchids are about 1.5-metres-tall each, and they are accompanied by forty butterflies fluttering in the wind. A graceful progression there as the garden blooms.'
'This really ties in with Singapore's transformation over the years into a cosmopolitan modern city one that attracts butterflies – or multinationals – to come and work here and set up office.'
'This Garden City concept goes beyond representing Singapore as a Clean and Green city. The Garden concept reflects Singapore as a Garden City where flowers of all types – people of all races – grow in harmony. Where our cultural diversity – like the many flowers in a garden – complement one another, and bring out the beauty of each ethnic group' (NDP 2004).

4. In the past, Lee Kuan Yew has made statements with a strongly eugenicist flavour, noting, with reference to the controversial book by Charles Murray and Richard Bernstein that 'the Bell Curve is a fact of life' (cited in Mauzy and Milne 2002: 55). The Graduate Mother Scheme of 1984 offered financial benefits for graduate mothers having more than two children, and sterilization services to women with little education who already had one child and whose household income fell below a certain level. The scheme was unpopular, and was replaced by another in 1987, which made no reference to educational levels, but continued to discriminate in favour of those on higher incomes.

5. This was most clearly articulated by then-Prime Minister Goh Chok Tong on the witness stand when he, then S. M. Lee, and a number of other members of the Singapore cabinet sued opposition candidate J.

B. Jeyaretnam for defamation for comments made during an election rally: 'In Singapore, we believed that leaders got (sic) to be honorable men, what we called jun zi (gentlemen)….We are different from the western societies. The way elections are fought over there, maybe there you can just knock your opponents backward with accusations about their integrity, nothing is done. But here, if ministers and politicians do not defend their integrity, they are finished, This is, by and large, in the Asian society with a very large component of Chinese, very Confucianist in their values…' (Jeyaretnam 2003: 84–5). The damages awarded to the claimants bankrupted Jeyaratnam, and he was obliged to relinquish his seat in Parliament. In the last election (in November 2001), the People's Action Party won 82 out of 84 seats.

6. Substantial contributions to the Garden City Fund, which was established in 2003 and provides for tree conservation, infrastructure development and botanical research, are rewarded with the dedication of a Heritage Tree. Intriguingly, a press release from the National Parks Board states that the 'Tembusu Tree featured on Singapore's $5 notes was dedicated to HSBC (Hong Kong and Shanghai Banking Corporation)' (NParks 2004b). Further investigation clarified that it was the original tree that was dedicated to HSBC, rather than the image on the note.

7. In a 1991 speech, then-Acting Minister for Information and the Arts, Brigadier General George Yeo, used an arboreal analogy to explain how he envisioned the relationship between the state and civic institutions, which included the arts community: 'The problem now is that under a banyan tree very little else can grow. When state institutions are too pervasive, civic institutions cannot thrive. Therefore it is necessary to prune the banyan tree so that other plants can also grow'. However, he went on to caution that 'we cannot do without the banyan tree. Singapore will always need a strong centre to react quickly to a changing competitive environment…. In other words, we prune judiciously' (1991: 9, 11).

8. This rather compressed point might usefully be expanded with reference to Gilles Deleuze and Félix Guattari's attempts to understand the relations between animals, plants, people and things in non-signifying terms. In the present context, it is an intriguing coincidence that one of their key examples concerns bees and orchids: '[T]here is constituted a conjunction of the flux of deterritorialization that overflows imitation which is always territorial. It is in this way also that the orchid seems to reproduce an image of the bee but in a deeper way deterritorializes into it, at the same time that the bee in turn deterritorializes by joining with the orchid: the capture of a fragment of the code, and not the reproduction of an image' (1986 [1975]: 14). In the case of *The Silly Little Girl*, I am suggesting that the Bee Dance, as demonstrated by the Tree and recalled with reference both to memory and environment by the Girl, is better understood as an attempt by the Girl to deterritorialize into both bee and Tree, than simply to represent a bee. Additionally, I propose that Ang's subsequent performances can be understood as tracing what Deleuze and Guattari call a 'line of flight', which was initiated by a deterritorialization out of the play.

9. The basis for identifying Kuo with these trees can be found in a

book of extracts and tributes published shortly after his death, where a central motif is the drawing of a stalk of maize, accompanied by a poem, which Kuo made during his political detention in 1977. Kuo is implicitly and explicitly aligned with the stalk, and one of the lines from the poem, 'and love the wind and rain', is taken as the title of the book (Kwok and Teo 2002). It might also be noted in passing that the discovery of the Hopea Sangal tree was announced just two days after Kuo's death on 10 September 2002. These are the kinds of coincident events whose significance becomes entwined as they pass into memory. In the furore that followed the felling of the tree two months later, the Chinese language newspaper, *Lianhe Zaobao* consistently referred to the Hopea Sangal as the '*lao shu*', or 'old tree'. Finally, I should like to insert a caveat regarding the implicitly dichotomous relationship in the structure and argument of this article between Lee Kuan Yew and Kuo Pao Kun, for there are important similarities, too. Despite the relatively rapid emancipation of women in Singapore following pragmatically (rather what in Euro-American terms would be called 'progressively') motivated legislation in the decade following independence to encourage them into the workforce, in the Singaporean imaginary, the figure of the patriarch continues to loom large. While Lee, as 'founding father' of the nation, is by far the most pervasive and visible embodiment of this figure, it is evident from the tenor of many of the tributes and eulogies that poured in following Kuo's death that within the theatre community at least, he played a similar role. No doubt, Kuo realized this role in a more benevolent fashion than Lee's 'tough love' act, but the very fact of his elevation to such a status, and the hierarchical, conservative structures of patronage and social organization that it represents, are something that Singaporean theatre practitioners have yet to address. Kuo famously described Singaporeans as 'cultural orphans', but the orphaning of its artists by his passing is an interpretation that needs to be resisted.

10. *The Coffin is too Big for the Hole* is a monologue recounting a stand-off between a mourner and a bureaucrat over his grandfather's coffin, which is too ostentatiously large for the standard-sized graves the government-run cemetery allows. *Descendents of the Eunuch Admiral* draws a parallel between emasculated office workers and Zheng He, a Chinese eunuch of the fifteenth century, and includes a description of how, at death, eunuchs would have their severed penises sutured back in place to ensure reincarnation as a man. (I am grateful to Lee Weng Choy for drawing this latter connection to my attention).

11. The images accompanying this article were taken by Yuen Chee Wai on several strolls with the author around the Little India area of Singapore, December 2004 - March 2005.

12. My title owes a debt to Matthew Goulish, himself referencing Yoko Ono: 'I considered a book that might result from following some simple instructions: 1) fill your book with seeds, 2) cut holes in it, 3) hang it where there is wind.' Matthew Goulish (2000) 39 Microlectures: in *Proximity of Performance*. London and New York: Routledge, p. 8.

REFERENCES

Chia, Sue-Ann (2004) 'Future bright with polls results', *Straits Times*, 8 November.

Confucius (1979) *The Analects*, trans. D. C. Lau, London: Penguin.

Deleuze, Gilles and Guattari, Félix (1986 [1975]) *Kafka: Toward a Minor Literature*, trans. Dana Polan, Minneapolis and London: University of Minnesota Press.

Jeyaretnam, J. B. (2003) 'Cross-examination by Mr George Carman, QC' in *The Hatchet Man of Singapore*, Singapore: Jeya Publishers.

Kuo Pao Kun (2000) 'The Silly Little Girl and the Funny Old Tree' in *Images at the Margins: A Collection of Kuo Pao Kun's Plays*, Singapore and Kuala Lumpur: Times Books International, pp. 98–116.

Kwok Kian Woon and Teo Han Wue (eds.) (2002) *Kuo Pao Kun: And Love the Wind and Rain*, Singapore: Cruxible.

Lee Hsien Loong (2003) *Speech by DPM Lee Hsien Loong at the Official Launch of the Garden City Fund, 2 December 2003, 7pm, the Istana Lawn.*,<http://www.nparks.gov.sg/news/speech031018c.shtml> accessed on 9 December 2004.

Lee Kuan Yew (1995) *Speech by Mr Lee Kuan Yew, Senior Minister, at the Launch of the National Orchid Garden on Friday, 20 October 1995 at 6.00pm at the Singapore Botanic Gardens.* <http://www.sprinter.gov.sg> accessed on 9 December 2004.

Mauzy, Diane K. and Milne, R. S. (2002) *Singapore Politics under the People's Action Party*, London and New York: Routledge.

NDP (2004) *National Day Parade* 2004, live telecast provided by MediaCorp, screened on Channel 5, Singapore, 9 August.

NParks (2004a) *Heritage Trees Scheme*, <http://www.nparks.gov.sg/nat_conv/nat_con-her_tre.shtml> accessed on 9 December 2004.

NParks (2004b) *Media Statement – Heritage Trees Dedicated to Donors of Garden City Fund, 1 July*, <http://www.nparks.gov.sg/news/newsroom.shtml> accessed on 9 December 2004.

Yeo, George (1991) 'Civic Society – Between the Family and the State', *Speech by BG (Res) George Yong-Boon Yeo, Acting Minister for Information and the Arts and Senior Minister of State for Foreign Affairs, at the NUSS Society Inaugural Lecture 1991, 20 June 1991*, <http://www.sprinter.gov.sg> accessed on 9 December 2004.

Yu Yun (2000) 'The Soil of Life and the Tree of Art: A Study of Kuo Pao Kun's Cultural Individuality through His Playwrighting', trans. Kuo Jian Hong, in Kuo Pao Kun, *Images at the Margins: A Collection of Kuo Pao Kun's Plays*, Singapore and Kuala Lumpur: Times Books International, pp. 18-59.

Towards Tomorrow: Forward

Only towards? Yes, for tomorrow, of course, never comes, it is always subjunctive, contingent and hungrily subjective, an object of desire and fear, already inevitable, fixed by the prescience of today and proven in the ovens of yesterday ... or is it?

Having not previously marked anniversaries or birthdays, we decided to mark CPR's 'coming-of-age', the possible watershed of our thirtieth anniversary, by producing both this book, *A Performance Cosmology,* and an international conference in April 2005 entitled 'Towards Tomorrow?'.

But Towards Tomorrow? was not exactly a birthday party; unlike sections of this book, it was not planned as an assertion of CPR as subject. Rather - and like other sections of this book - the event observed the milestone as pretext, subtext, and context for consideration of broader issues of 'tomorrow' in relation to theatre, performance, and performance research; a gathering, a moment in the present to look back to the future and forward to the coming of the past.

From the early days of Cardiff Laboratory Theatre, 'thinking' through practice and 'practising' through thinking have remained a prime concern and motivation for us, and the Towards Tomorrow? gathering brought together a range of contributions across disciplines, and from a range of artists, both emerging and experienced, as well as the emerging and leading scholars in the field.

Functioning here neither as 'selected highlights' of that event - nor indeed as a trailer to the forthcoming *Towards Tomorrow?* publication arising from it[*] - we are including two *Towards Tomorrow?* contributions here (and *not* in the conference publication) as each of them, in their very different ways, traverse several pathways through the field station matrix, on the journey towards tomorrow.

Unlike the urgent final call by Gómez-Peña that opens the Field Station section, for example, neither of these represents a first or last stop on the journey through the matrix, but rather a dialogic journey on the way (*towards*) with reflections through and across the interstices of time by two authors, both theorists and practitioners, whose voices come from different points in the performance cosmology: 'speaking again' in textual format a text by Rustom Bharucha that was originally prepared as an 'ungrammatical script made to be spoken' and developed here for the page, and an interview with Richard Schechner that has been transcribed and edited to retain the immediacy of conversation.

* Towards Tomorrow is planned for publication in 2007.

COURTESY OF CEREDIGION MUSEUM, ABERYSTWYTH

MIXED BATHING AT ABERYSTWYTH

RUSTOM BHARUCHA

Towards Tomorrow? Processing the Limits of Performance into the Real of Time

Ever so slight, if not tentatively provocative, this sliver of a question – 'towards tomorrow? – circumvents larger categories of 'the future' and 'the millennium': tomorrow, after all, is just another day. As one enters the trajectories of 'tomorrow', however, one begins to realize the minefield of possible explosions that lie ahead in the disjunctive ground of this essay. At first glance, it would seem that there is no time for tomorrow as we face the events of the day, which are increasingly marked by ruptures, interruptions, disruptions and breakdowns: symptoms of the quickening pace of globalization. Indeed, the terror of tomorrow lies not in the fact that it is unknown but, rather, that it is only too predictable. Global warming, SARS, bird flu, chicken flu, the pandemic of AIDS, terrorism, wars on terrorism, and new forms of poverty are not likely to disappear in a hurry. In this essay, I will be engaging with some glimpses of this familiar global predicament, as I move from fables, metaphors and improvisations, through disruptions of performance into the indeterminacies of the real: this will be my trajectory of thought in the essay.

In a somewhat utopian register, I would like to question how one can break the ceaseless repetition of 'tomorrow *and* tomorrow *and* tomorrow', in what remains the most powerful rendering of suspended time in the English language. Macbeth's soliloquy is also the death-knell of theatre practice. Perhaps one way of avoiding repetition is to explore the phenomenological immediacy of theatre and performance, but one could also attempt to push the very limits of theatre and performance into the processes of everyday life, where 'immediacy' is absorbed in a multitude of mutating instants. The concluding sections of this essay will be concerned with precisely those instantaneous events that do not normally get represented in theatre or performance studies because they cross the limits of critical scrutiny. They lie beyond what one is expected to think about in theatre and performance, and inevitably, they call into question the protocols of writing in relation to the 'real'.

How does the 'real' relate to the 'now'? Is it possible to envision tomorrow not through repetition but as a white-hot glaring beacon that burns but, in the process, lights the immediacies of the now? This 'now' is our provisional shelter, but, sooner or later, it is bound to break down, leaving us in a no-man's land, an interstice, a gap, between a now that is no more and a tomorrow that has yet to come. Let us hold on to this gap, because the uncertainty it provides could be our strongest ally as we push the limits of performance into the real of time through the processes of life itself.

Parable

To begin with a parable by Kafka, which Hannah Arendt has interpreted as a 'thought-event' in her magisterial preface to *Between Past and Future* (1993). In this 'event', Kafka positions his protagonist – nameless, but gendered 'he' – on a fighting-line, in which he is caught between two forces of time-past and time-future converging on him from either side. Indeed, they are pushing him into each others' tracks, and, if he hadn't been around, they would probably have neutralized each other like galactic missiles in a Star Wars narrative. Kafka depicts this man dreaming that he can jump out of the fighting-line and assume the role of a celestial umpire in what Arendt describes as a 'timeless, spaceless, suprasensuous realm' (1993: 11), which does not satisfy her at all. Instead of these transcendental possibilities, she proceeds to re-visualize the fighting-line in very graphic terms by suggesting that the very insertion of the man causes the two forces of time past and time future to *deflect*, as they meet not head-on but at an angle. From this gap, which Arendt compares to the 'parallelogram of forces' drawn from the language of physics, there is a 'third force' which emerges on a diagonal (1993: 9-10). Unlike the first two forces, which have unknown origins but a very definite end, this third force has a very definite beginning but its end is 'infinite.' And that, for Arendt, is the perfect metaphor for the activity of thought itself.

Arendt is clear that she is dealing with a metaphor, and metaphors are useful in indicating not so much *what* to think but *how* to think. She is also critical of the 'rectilinear temporal movement' (1993: 11) of Kafka's representation of time: a linearity that is often linked with Western concepts of time as opposed to the cyclic, elliptical and loop-like configurations available in non-Western understandings of time. We need to be wary of such dichotomies. As the Indian historian Romila Thapar has pointed out in *Time as a Metaphor of History*

(1996), cyclic and linear times can co-exist; cosmological time can incorporate other forms of 'time-reckoning', with shorter, more fragmented time-spans; and there are 'grey areas' in which cyclic and linear times can overlap. Though Arendt does not acknowledge this overlap, she does describe the gap of time between past and future as a 'small non-time-space in the very heart of time' (1993: 13). I will return to this 'non-time-space' later in the essay and embody it in a way that Arendt might not have approved. Furthermore, she emphasizes that this gap can only be 'indicated' but it cannot be 'inherited and handed down from the past'; it has to be 'discovered' (and, one could add, constructed, invented and reinvented). The experience of 'moving in the gap' can only be achieved 'through practice, through exercises' (1993: 13–14).

These words are familiar to us in the theatre, which is the outcome of many 'practices' and 'exercises', relating to how to breathe, how to stand, how to move, how to dance, how to scream, how to listen, how to think. Indeed, the theatre could be one of the most concrete sites for visualizing movement and thought through time, structured around specific thought-events (or processes). Let me briefly insert two such structures of time that counter the rectilinear temporal movement of Kafka's parable.[1] Both of them are improvisations, and the first can be regarded as a warm-up for the experiments that follow.

Improvisation 1

There are four distinct beats in this exercise that you are free to punctuate within the contours of a minimal script, which is left open for your mental meanderings:

Someone is calling your name.
You respond to the call.
You travel in your mind to the source of the call.
You react to something in that space.

Stripped of embellishment, this four-part narrative follows an apparent sequence, causality and passage of time. But if someone is calling your name – and you are compelled to voice your own name while listening to it – then who are you at that point in time? You are not that someone. You are in another place. The voice is from somewhere else. There could be a time-lag in the transference and picking up of the voice depending on the distance: a time-lag which could be amplified and distended through echoes. Do echoes exist in the past or in the future? Do they resonate in relation to what has already been named, or do they anticipate the name that has yet to be uttered with a different cadence and resonance?

You suspend the voicing of your name. Now you have all the freedom to respond to the call by recognizing its otherness. You voice the other's name, not your own. A duality is comfortably established. However, this freedom is likely to produce a different kind of restlessness. Now you want to get to the source of the call. This is the point when it would seem that you are going back to a point in time, to something that has already passed but is not yet a memory. It is still there hanging in the air, waiting to be encountered in the future-continuous. In responding to the call, therefore, you do not go back to the past; if anything, you are going back to the future, towards a tomorrow that has yet to be fully realized.

You enter a drift of time as you travel in your mind to the source of the call. You arrive. Are you there yet? Only an unconscious act of will, an inner heightening of breath, can break the aporia of that moment. You break your waking dream, your sleep-walking. You disrupt the silence of the future-continuous by grounding it abruptly within the ordinariness of the present moment. This jolt has all the jarring familiarity of the alarm clock in the morning, which remains one of the most insistently timely reminders of the relentlessness of everyday life. 'We are not free, and it begins with coffee in the morning,' as Bertolt Brecht had reminded us with his mordant wit.

From this somewhat impressionistic *rite de passage*, we are alerted to shifting locations of time, as we search for the future in the past, and the past in the future, within the contingencies of the present moment. Clearly, the past, the present and the future are interchangeable and fluid. Within their imagined entities, there is more than one past, one present and one future: a truism that is often lost in the dogmas surrounding monolithic conceptions of time, where a pure Past is invariably fundamentalist, a pure Future the emptiest of utopias.

In the plurality of times, there are some that lose their bearings and enter different energy-fields, while others return compulsively to their own orbits. It is not just the flights of time that matter, therefore, but their points of return. No point of return is ever the same: even though one may be returning to the same point, one can never fully anticipate the imminence of irregularities, bumps, forced landings and near accidents along the way. Like a note in a raga that careens and sweeps through a vista of sounds, picking up all the deviations and varied textures of a particular melodic structure, the return of the note is invariably marked by an element of surprise. The note is there, and yet, it is not quite the same. It is somewhere else in time.

Perhaps the greatest enigma of time lies in the blurring, if not indivisibility, of those intersections in the points of departure and return, so that it is no longer clear whether one is coming or going, or indeed, whether one has left at all if one has just arrived. Such enigmas cannot be easily explained in the language of the social sciences. Historians, the chroniclers of time, are generally out of their depth in dealing with these temporal ambiguities. Physicists probably come closest to mapping the whirligigs of time. However, in order to see time moving back and forth and to challenge easy notions of chronology, sequence and duration, let us explore another improvisatory framework from a different performance tradition.

Improvisation 2

Instead of Arendt's nameless protagonist standing on a fighting-line between time-past and time-future, let us imagine an actor who is playing the role of Arjuna in the *Mahabharata*. He is not on a fighting-line but in the battlefield of life itself, where he stands in resplendent solitude at the centre of the stage. *In medias res* we catch him at some point in his life, when the five Pandava brothers are living in exile, wandering in the forest, and the Great War has not yet commenced. Unlike Kafka's protagonist who is not free to do anything but dream of jumping out of the fighting-line, this actor is free to imagine his journey and actually to shape time in the battleground of his narrative.

Significantly, instead of taking a step forwards towards tomorrow, he chooses to go backwards towards yesterday. And from this yesterday, he proceeds to retrace his biography through all his yesterdays, pushing into the past of his life, his ancestry, perhaps his former lives, into the 'first syllable of recorded time', which he invents for himself. From this vanishing point, he surveys his point of departure lying ahead of him, and, in between these points, there is not so much a gap as a gaping void. Now he chooses to return. But in returning does he move forwards into the past, or does he return to the future? Does he return in a split-second of time, a mere blink of an eye? Or does he choose to take a longer, more circuitous route: a different route from the one on which he traveled to the vanishing point of a provisional present?

I am extrapolating freely here from an improvised structure of performance called the *nirvahana*, which literally means 'to accomplish, to carry out', from the Indian performance tradition of Kutiyattam, in Kerala, which goes back at least 1200 years. From its structured fluidity, we learn how differentiated times in the nirvahana can coexist, meld, disappear, re-

appear, separate, elongate and then collapse into each other's trajectories. In an earlier lecture I had used the *nirvahana* metaphorically to structure my own back-and-forth journey in theatre, but I did not address my own directorial reinvention of the *nirvahana* in an experimental production called *Prakriya* (Process).[2] Here I intersected the journeys of two actors playing two characters: Abhimanyu, who begins his life by listening to the future in the womb of his mother, which culminates in his slaughter in the labyrinthine battle formation of the *chakravuha* in the *Mahabharata*, and Nina from Chekhov's *The Seagull*, who begins her life as an actress with a play dealing with the end of the world, culminating in that famous scene where she is caught in the interstice of being both a seagull and an actress, who eventually flies away to an endless round of tomorrows as a touring actress in a provincial company.

One limitation with the structure of the *nirvahana* as I worked on it in *Prakriya* is that it seemed to bind the notion of 'process' within a purely aesthetic modality. My experiment was frustrating to me because it seemed overly hermetic. I urgently missed the interruptive power of the historical present: the one time that traditions like Kutiyattam will not allow because they are only too aware of its immediacy, volatility, violence and potential to disrupt the sanctified protocols of performance. The present, as Arendt understood only too well, can be smothered by the mediating principles of 'tradition'.[3]

Interruption

For the interruptive power of the historical present, one turns inevitably to Brecht, whose *verfremdungseffekt* introduced, at least in the perspective of Walter Benjamin (1992), a 'consciousness of the present' that had the potentiality to 'explode' the 'continuum of history' itself (1982: 227). But, one is tempted to say, 'this is only theoretically so.' The actual execution of the *verfremdungseffekt* in its numerous derivations in different theatre cultures has been predominantly emotive, climactic, histrionic and, indeed, a testament to the habitual repetition of theatre. What was intended to be a thought-event in structural terms has become a stylistic convention through its very reiteration. Mother Courage's silent scream numbs thought today in its matter-of-fact virtuosity. Perhaps the actor needs to be spared the formalized inscription of her character's contradictory grief and need to survive.

If we seek the interruptive power of the historical present in theatre, not as a metaphor or a normative idea or political ideal, then we will have to agree with

Alain Badiou that 'theatre's interruption cannot be intentionally manufactured by stylistic devices or manipulated by politically motivated dramatic agendas'.[4] Badiou introduces the provocative notion of 'event', which is 'something that happens' through a 'breach in time', producing a temporary 'rupture within the narrative' that normally sustains itself through repetition (1999: 38, 127). The event, which is not an invasive force, 'occurs within a situation but does not belong to it'; rather, it 'supplements' the situation and brings into focus 'the void' (Kear 2004: 100), which can be described as that 'aspect of the situation that has absolutely no interest in preserving the status quo as such' (Hallward 2003: 114-15). The event is unconditioned, unpredictable, unprecedented and unexpected, and, in this crucial sense, it cannot be programmed. In a sense, it cannot even be imagined. At best one could say that one has no other option but to anticipate the suddenness of its blow, the eruption of its volcanic force, but this can only be acknowledged in retrospect of 'something' that has already 'happened' (Kear 2004: 100).

Event

Let me at this point share something that happened in my theatre experience, which approximates, and yet questions, Badiou's understanding of the event. On a perfectly innocuous day, 10 September 2001, to be precise, I found myself in Manila ready to start a rehearsal process culminating in a long-desired production of Genet's *The Maids*.[5] The tomorrow of the production was six weeks away, and everything seemed to be in place. My love for the play, bordering on obsession, was – and continues to be – seemingly unconditional, because this play challenges the notion of 'truth' in the theatre. Indeed, it makes a mockery out of philosophical statements like Arendt's when she claims that the gap between past and future is 'the only region perhaps where truth eventually will appear' (1993: 14). There is no such singularized truth in Genet's play not least because there are no clear divisions between past and future. Instead of one gap, the play embraces and slips between a multitude, a labyrinth, a kaleidoscope of gaps, with several conflicting times animated by a gamut of performance styles: acting, playacting, imitation, mimicry, dissemblance, lying, melodrama, burlesque, cross-dressing, bad acting, no-acting. In such a virtuosity of styles, blatantly fake and emphatically framed within the deadly artifice of repetition, what hope can there be for truth, or, as Badiou puts it more earnestly, 'truth procedures'?

Along with the desire for the text, there is always intentionality in one's concept as a director, as much as one may deny it. What I wanted *The Maids* to say through my *mise-en-scène* was irrevocably linked to the political and economic fact that 'the maid' is one of the biggest export items of the Philippines, earning more foreign exchange than almost any other commodity, and contributing to the global economy at large. Thousands of Filipina maids live and work in varied conditions of neo-slavery, away from their homes and families, in countries as far-flung as Saudi Arabia, Singapore and Japan. Social outcasts, neither residents in their own homes nor citizens in their places of work, they are occasionally humiliated, beaten, abused, raped and even, in one chilling event masterminded by the state of Singapore, executed. I wanted to use the live footage of Flor Contemplacion's body brought back to the Philippines after her execution in Singapore, where she had been

Flor Contemplacion

charged and subsequently executed for the alleged murder of a child. In a neo-Brechtian directorial mode, I wanted to interrupt Solange's orgasmic funeral dirge at the end of Genet's play with Flor Contemplacion returning home to the Philippines as a saint. In short, I was excited by the possibilities of introjecting this 'real' event, extravagantly mediatized and mythologized in Filipino public culture, into my *mise-en-scène* of Genet's text.

Before 10 September 2001, when this concept was already in the process of crystallizing, political demonstrations had erupted on the streets of Manila, mocking the civic and democratic people's protests of Edsas 1 and 2 that had raged against the corrupt administrations of former Presidents Marcos and Estrada, respectively. Now, rather like a badly timed sequel to Hollywood blockbusters like *Rocky* and *Jaws*, Edsa 3 was rearing its head in the form of disorderly and frenetic demonstrations of the outcasts of society, not dignified enough to be called 'the wretched of the earth' but more likely the down-and-out scum, scavenging in garbage and living off refuse in the jungle-city of Manila. These outcasts had taken to the streets ostensibly in support of Estrada: ex-action hero in B-grade Filipino movies, womanizer, gambler, master crook, now facing charges for plundering the nation. This criminal was the people's saint.

In language clearly inspired by Genet, my translator Rody Vera describes the moment of Edsa 3 seductively:

I saw the darkened, sweating faces of the very same despised outcasts [as Genet's thieves] in the streets of Mendiola, armed only with rocks and sticks, their brute faces pocked by smut and dried spit, their urine-scented legs standing firm ground, fuelled by an uncontrollable rage, padded by money bills they got from their instigators... Could anyone like Genet depict them as angels blaring their trumpets and floating above these phalanxes of police truncheons and shields?[6]

The street fighters of Edsa 3 broke all norms of civic protest. One such uncivil gesture reported by an outraged bourgeois media was their deposits of urine and shit in front of a hallowed shrine of the Virgin Mary, prototype of Genet's Our Lady of Flowers. This gesture is reminiscent of Genet's mythologizing of a discarded public urinal, marked and cordoned off by the police force, which becomes a shrine for gay outcasts in one of his fictions. Within his mythopoeic world affirming the rituals of the oppressed, the biological has the potential to be transformed into an etherealized fantasy through a libidinal investment in bodily fluids and waste: blood, semen, urine, shit and tears. Edsa 3 embodied this complex of elements in 'real' time and space.

Needless to say, I was thrilled, because this evidence of struggle on the streets was not so much an interruption as an infusion of energies reinforcing my interpretation of the play. The 'now' of the play and the 'real' of Filipino politics seemed to meld into each other's situations. Then, like all such tumultuous immediacies, there was a rupture: September 11. Perhaps no one could have predicted this Event of global magnitude with the exception of its audacious, deadly, suicidal perpetrators, and possibly George Bush and his cronies, who chose not to pay

11 September 2001, New York City, USA

heed to its calamitous potentiality. In Manila, watching September 11 on CNN, an experience triggered by a split-second of jubilation, synchronized with disbelief, followed instantly by horror, grief, remorse and then, at a later stage, solidarity with the victims and anger at the demonization of all possible suspects, I cannot deny that I was hit. More specifically, my somewhat overconfident conceptualization of the *The Maids* was attacked.

Now I could no longer take refuge in the reassurances of the real drawn voyeuristically from Edsa 3. I had to test my political affinities to Genet within the global terror of our times. Given his passionate commitment to the Palestinian struggle, his love for the *fedayeen*, his deeply controversial discrimination between 'violence' (of so-called terrorists) and 'brutality' (of the state), supplemented by his notorious defence of the Baader-Meinhof terrorists and deeply provocative charge that 'America is afraid', can there be any doubt of Genet's allegiance in the post-September 11 scenario? Would his loyalties be with the 'civilized' world headed by the likes of Bush and Blair? Or would they not lie unstintingly, passionately, with the so-called 'terrorists'?

Chaos

With these questions, one is compelled to rethink the phenomenological immediacy of theatre outside the familiar Artaudian premise that 'the same gesture can never be repeated the same way twice in the theatre'. How does one rethink 'once' in theatre in terms of an irretrievable moment, as opposed to 'now', which connotes a mixing of times in an unspecifiable duration? With due seriousness, which might appear to be irresponsibly perverse, I would suggest that the phenomenological complement of 'once' in the theatre can be most accurately detected within the act of terrorism, which strikes with deadly precision in a split second of irretrievable destruction. The detonation of a 'human bomb', following its disguise and masquerade in the cultures of everyday life, could be one of the most formidable metaphors on the existing notions of how thought *strikes* in the theatre.

With September 11, I also recognized the destabilizing power of chaos in the theatre: the chaos that lurks in our public space but to which we remain oblivious till it explodes in our face. Not unlike a terrorist attack, which erupts both with deadly precision and a totally unexpected concatenation of social, historical, political and economic forces, the chaos of the real is at once immediate and beyond one's control. It is this eruption of chaos that I find more thought-provoking than what I self-consciously inscribe in the *mise-en-scène*, simulating chaos, though it could be argued that the 'real' and the 'simulated' are linked at the level of the political unconscious in no particular order or causality.

All these philosophical remarks were written in retrospect of 'something' that 'happened' in the performance site of *The Maids*, which was staged in a marvelously atmospheric, beer-smelling bar and disco called the Republic of Malate. What happened did not take place during the production but in its immediate after-life, just days after the closing night of the production, when the Republic burned down. Nothing remained of its gay erotica and kitsch commemorating baroque nostalgia and the Wild West. Within minutes the theatre was reduced to ashes.

The reasons around this fire-event are not yet clear. If it was the result of an electrical short-circuit, then this threat of fire had been imminent during our occupation of the space. Given the absence of fire exits in the Republic, this could have proved fatal. If, on the other hand, the fire was an act of 'arson', then its motives could range from a homophobic attack to deliberate sabotage for the lucrative benefits of real estate. The motives underlying the event become more sinister as we cross-examine the maids themselves, who at one point fantasize themselves as 'arsonists', which was the Tagalog equivalent for the more eloquent 'incendiary' of the original text: a word that is almost caressed by one of the maids as a 'splendid title'. Adding to the hermeneutic dilemma of the Republic of Malate's destruction was the soap-opera histrionics of the owner of the Republic of Malate, a fervent Born-Again Christian, who appears to have railed on television against the Devil, the very accomplice of the maids in their sexual fantasies.

I am not arguing here for the destruction of the means of production in the actual site of performance for theatre to be considered significant. I am not an anarchist. But I do believe that when the theatre burns down there is something to be learned from this unprecedented event, and that to return to the practice of theatre with the metaphoric reassurance drawn from its habitual, phoenix-like, death-in-life process is to risk lapsing into a kind of regression, if not time-warp. From the ashes of the Republic of Malate, which continue to smoulder in my mind, I get two kinds of provocation: 1. 'You're lucky, you got away with it', and 2. 'Your theatre is so safe.' I regard that second remark as a taunt, a self-accusation, which compels me to draw some critical ballast from Badiou when he says that the event produces subjects out of individuals, whose 'fidelity to the event' compels them 'to *invent* a new way of being and acting in the situation' (2001: 42). Perhaps not just in the situation but in the processes that sustain it and go beyond its duration

in the act of living. 'Keep going! Never forget what you have encountered.' These are useful reminders, not least because 'not-forgetting is not a memory', but also because it is by 'following through on the consequences and implications of the event' that one is reconstituted as a subject (Badiou 2001: 52, quoted in Reinelt 2004: 90).

Process

Post-September 11, I've been trying to follow through on what happened in Manila at the Republic of Malate, and I've come to a point where I am revaluating the role of 'process' in theatre and cultural practice. I am no longer concerned specifically with the disciplinary procedures and protocols of the aesthetic process, which I had explored in *Prakriya*, or even the ethical dilemmas of so-called inter-Asian performative processes mobilized in workshops and then commodified through simulacra of such processes in spectacles designed for the international festival circuit.[7] The process that concerns me today is immersed in the structures of everyday life, and it is held less by a narrative, performance or even a specific time-and-space-bound event than by the intersection of several processes: the social, the political, the economic and the cultural that animate (and disturb) the public sphere at practically every moment but in states of seeming normalcy. 'Theatre' and 'performance' are dynamic – perhaps even catalytic – elements in these processes, but they are not the determining factors of their configuration.

I would stress here the *intersection* of processes and not merely their coexistence, which has the possibility of assuming a specious civic solidarity. Indeed, one has to guard against the populist notion that site-specific events are *ipso facto* more 'political' than the conventional staging of proscenium theatre, bound within norms of policed propriety, safety and entertainment. Site-specific public culture has every possibility of reinforcing civic norms even as it seems to flaunt them. Such was my experience while working on a site-specific reenactment of a massacre staged in the village of Lonoy on the island of Bohol in the Philippines: a massacre that the American forces had inflicted on 400 Boholano peasants in the early years of the occupation in Lonoy itself.[8] The genre of the 're-enactment' sounds radical, but one should keep in mind that it merely follows an established, time-tested performance tradition within the national-popular imaginary of the Philippines. Tantalizingly, it seems to assume that the 'real' event of the actual massacre was an enactment in its own right. Hence, the performance itself is described as a re-enactment. But, what is the purpose of re-enacting a terrible event from the past if it occludes the more terrifying present?

In the staging of this event in Lonoy, there were four parallel processes that were mobilized simultaneously:

1. A pedagogical process initiated by high school teachers of Lonoy who were concerned that the massacre in their town was not recorded in their history books.

2. A theatrical and performative process, which involved an epic orchestration of patriotic tableaux, lamentation and slow-motion fight sequences and death throes of around eighty residents of Bohol, ranging from grandparents to children.

3. A civic process in which the re-enactment of the massacre was placed in a larger Cultural Caravan for Peace spearheaded by NGOs and the Church more concerned with camouflaging the history of insurgency in Bohol under the spectre of 'peace' than dealing with the politics of war.

4. A political process in which the Governor of Bohol, who funded the reenactment, tried to ride piggy-back on the event as he kicked off his election campaign during the performance with a blatantly opportunistic speech supporting the Estrada government.

All these processes came together in a fiesta-like event, at once heartwarming, tearful and full of good intentions, which simply played into the hegemonic norms of the narrative of community. As I have written elsewhere, this re-enactment asserted itself through a problematic exclusion of minorities, notably Muslims, and a totally non-reflexive surrender to a generally feel-good attitude towards Uncle Sam.[9] Devoid of any critique of the war in Iraq and other less technocratic massacres and genocides, as inflicted in Lonoy a hundred years ago, the hoary history of US imperialism was simply let off the hook. It was not even recognized as a problem.

Needless to say, this kind of fiesta-like event – or, more precisely, non-event – is solidified by the event-management of a grassroots bureaucracy, fed with the developmental sincerity of NGOs surfeiting on the rhetoric of national culture and good citizenship. There can be no exposition of the 'real' in such a celebration of amnesia, if not bogus lies. The 'real' demands a different kind of risk-taking precisely because it can be accessed only against the propaganda mechanisms of the State or the Church or the agencies of civil society. Resisting the formulation of a ready-made discourse, it is that potential immediacy in the body politic that has the power to test the limits of existing theories of development. Once tapped and incorporated into action, it already ceases to be real.[10]

To expose the 'real' of the historical present, I will have to take you elsewhere to the borderlines of a more volatile public space in Durban, South Africa, where I have been involved in a site-specific public art project called Tangencya. Scattered in at least nine satellite points of intervention in different parts of the city, the projects of Tangencya were situated and staged in a downtown shopping center, taxi ranks, a municipal children's playground, local history museums, the periphery of a partially abandoned Hindu temple in the resettlement area of Cato Manor and the inner recesses of the township of Umlazi on the outskirts of Durban.[11] What I can offer here is not a thick description of the project, but a distillation of its principles in relation to different manifestations and disruptions of 'process'.

Touch

Tangencya, which is a Portuguese word for 'touch', also connotes the more geometrical category of the 'tangent': a point of contact between two surfaces, which brings them into collision without allowing them to intersect or penetrate. The politics of touch assumes an explosive significance in the post-apartheid space, which is still in the process of reconstructing the formidably rigid institutionalization of public space and the racially determined organization of movement that was legislated by the apartheid system. If you were black or coloured – and implicitly, if you were white – you could go here, but you could not go there; you could live in these quarters, but not in those; you could attend that school, not the other one; that library, that swimming pool, that restroom. If you went to the supermarket, you could enter through that door, not this one; you could not sit on this bench in the park, you had to sit elsewhere, or just walk. Now, in the New South Africa, space is ostensibly free and one can go anywhere, anytime, like any other citizen with equal rights, but as one crosses from one space to another, the gaps suddenly re-appear, the invisible booby-traps become visible, and one is caught in a no-man's land or *cul de sac*. It is in these gaps in the public space that something is most likely to happen and potentially strike. Nothing momentous like September 11, or a terrorist attack, or even a bomb explosion: merely the banality of everyday violence in the form of a random knifing, mugging, stealing, or shooting.

Moving in the interstices, the in-between spaces, of the different satellites in the Tangencya project, was probably the most challenging aspect of the project. It was in this act of transportation – and, more specifically, of transporting our own bodies – that the process was most decisively challenged. In Umlazi, some of the artists were held up with a gun as they attempted to enter the

The 'mega-taxi', part of the Tangencya Project, Durban, South Africa

community centre where they imagined they were 'at home'. Highly tuned strategic skills were necessary to circumvent this attack by talking the assailants out of it. In the taxi rank where a mega-taxi was being built out of junk and found objects, all the equipment for the project was stolen overnight and the guard was mugged and robbed of his meagre savings. A documentary filmmaker from Brazil working on another project was knifed while he was entering what he perceived to be a no-man's land with a video camera. In a more macabre incident, one of the participants had rocks hurled at her car: just a bit of random violence, no personal animosity intended.

Confronting the actual physical risks of doing art in such a cityscape where the 'Holy Trinity' of the artist, the artwork and the public is subject to random attack, how does one sustain a cultural process? More critically, why intervene in the public space in the first place? Stephen Wright puts it sharply when he urges us to think about what happens when 'artists do not do art. Or, at any rate, when they do not claim that whatever it is they are doing is, in fact, art – when they inject their artistic aptitudes and perceptual *habitus* into the general symbolic economy of the real' (2004: 535). Infiltrating the public space not through performances, but rather through a specific set of 'competencies', these artists capitalize on their 'skills', ranging from the 'technical' to the 'procedural' to

the 'perceptual', which are contextualized within 'the pragmatics of a situation' (2004: 536). Wright argues that instead of 'recycling the art-related skills and perceptions back into the symbolic economy of art, a growing number of artists are now filtering them into other economies and, in a gesture of extra-territorial reciprocity, opening up a space within the symbolic economy of art to other practices' (2004: 535–6). I would emphasize that it is not just the symbolic economy of art that is infused with 'other practices'; new processes of art-making are entering those very spaces that are denied the fundamental right to create or to think about art in the first place.

Zamukuziphilisa, a women's collective and community centre, is one such space, which has sustained itself over ten years of intense creative struggle in the poverty-stricken and violent district of Umlazi, notorious for its gangs, drug-trafficking and escalation of deaths through AIDS. For their livelihood, the women have been involved in beadwork, jewelry, stitching and embroidery. With extraordinary grace, they have embroidered their own stories relating to domestic violence and prenatal childcare: stories, which have been exhibited in galleries in Europe and the United States, constituting new evidence of the violence of patriarchy in South Africa. In counterpoint to this visible economy of their art, the Tangencya intervention by the artist-architect Maria van

223

Zamukuphilisa, women's collective and community centre

PHOTOS: THE TANGENCYA PROJECT ARCHIVE

Supporting rubber-tyre wall designed by artist architect Maria van Gass

Gass has risked being entirely invisible, in so far as her project has involved nothing less than the strengthening of the very ground of the community centre in an imperceptible, yet tangible way. The ground here is no metaphor but the very earth on which the center stands.

In response to the fragile ecology of Zamukuziphilisa, where the three bamboo-and-mud and tin structures personally built by the women are beginning to collapse,

and the soil on the ground is fast eroding through an excess of surface water, Maria's expertise as an artist-architect has been stretched into a new awareness of her competencies. Based on a professional survey of the tenuous boundaries of this patch of land, supplemented by aerial photographs, state documents, rudimentary mappings and verbal evidence based on informally negotiated uses of land, a boundary wall made out recycled of tyres has now been created on the outer site of Zamukuziphilisa. What strikes me about this wall is not just its pragmatic solution to the real problem of soil erosion, but its close tuning to the cultural ecology of the women's centre, which has been sustained through a ten-year process of creative struggle, always working against odds, but still resilient and driven by the determination to make Zamukuziphilisa stand and last for tomorrow.

One of the challenges of such invisible tangibility is to document its process of creation. How, indeed, does one record the process of a real cultural economy of art? In the rough chaos of Tangencya's practice, scattered in nine distinct sites, where there was little possibility of sustaining what anthropologists would describe as *communitas*, there was one daily event that enabled the tangents to interconnect regularly, yet briefly. At the end of each day's work, the participants would meet like intimate strangers in different locations in the city and introspect on the events of the day. 'What happened today?' was the question with which I invariably began these conversations. What unfolded was almost uncanny, because the events of the day had not yet passed. We were catching 'process' in process.

How ironic that in the most sophisticated civic centres in the world, in art galleries and theatres, where artists are hurtling from one meeting to another, one rehearsal to another, one interview to another, there is no time for conversation. But in a public art project stretched to the extremities of its meagre resources, barely surviving the assaults and blows of the public sphere, with no frills, not even money for a convivial meal together, there is time for conversation. How does one explain this curious anomaly? Conversations, I have come to learn, are not necessarily the social prerogative of the bored and the rich, who have the leisure to converse about things that don't really matter. Sometimes one can have a conversation about 'real' things, allowing the slippages and flow of the different comments from conflicting contexts to create their own fabric.

In holding these conversations, which so uncannily evoke Arendt's 'small non-time-space in the very heart of time', which I had mentioned at the start of the essay, were we 'constructing' time, which Badiou associates – and indeed validates – as the 'primacy of the will'?

Clearly, we were not submitting to what he has derided as 'an inaccessible mixture of agitation and sterility, the paradox of a stagnant febrility', which Janelle Reinelt has described as 'frantic alternations between speed and stasis, a contemporary imperative to "hurry up" and a belief that there is nothing to be done' (Reinelt 2004: 90). This, indeed, would seem to sum up the predicament of the art establishment today. In his 'Seven Variations on the Century', Badiou goes on to say that '[i]f we wish to attain the real of time, it must be constructed, and this construction finally only depends on the care taken in becoming the agent of the procedures of truth' (quoted in Reinelt 2004: 90). This 'care', I would emphasize, is linked not so much to 'construction', but to allowing a moment to *be* and to *pass* without expecting anything from it till something happens that annihilates the possibility of care altogether.

Death

What happened in Tangencya was more unexpected, more painful, more irretrievable, than the burning of the Republic of Malate, because it directly concerned the life of one of our participants: the sculptor Richard Shange. It is hard to put this evidence in words. As Tangencya was beginning to present its work to the public, Richard went home over the weekend, where he allegedly stole some money from his sister. There was a violent confrontation in which the police got involved. Richard, it seems, showed resistance and was locked up in a police station where he tried to commit suicide three days later by hanging himself with a wire noose. This 'suicide', however, could have been a pretext on the part of the police to camouflage their own violence inflicted on Richard, who was shifted to a hospital where he died a few days later, alone. No one in the family came to visit him, either in the prison or hospital. When the Tangencya team got to know about his death, it was just in time for his funeral. A shoddy affair. The coffin was placed on two chairs, not even a table. There were no songs, no flowers, no felicitations. Instead, with the family's prior approval, the neighbours ran him down as a bad boy, a bad son, a bad member of the community. When it came for Tangencya to speak, all that our spokesperson could do was to express disbelief and shock, and to affirm that Richard was our friend and, above all, an artist.

What does it mean to be an 'artist' in a post-apartheid context, where the much-valorized spirit of *ubuntu* (forgiveness) hailed in the discourse of Truth and Reconciliation is not evident in real life, when there are no tangents but gaping divides between the personal and the political? I bring up the event of Richard's death because none of us could have anticipated it, perhaps he could not have anticipated it. But if we have to take the process further, and establish some tangential points of contact between his/Tangencya's divided worlds of family and art community, poverty and cultural/intellectual capital, creative skills and communicative/human breakdown, then we will have to process his death and transform it into cultural practice. Perhaps, we can draw our inspiration from other performances inspired by real deaths, such as the public funeral-spectacles commemorating the death of AIDS activists in South Africa. One thing is clear: we cannot sit back and retreat into our respective practices and allow Tangencya to continue as if Richard's death was accidental or a mere aberration. 'Let the artists die', as Kantor's title continues to mock us? No way.

The death of the artist opens up the real of time in brutal ways beyond the domain of 'high art' in which Badiou, for all his seemingly radical theory, seeks protection. In Rajasthan, so seemingly remote from South Africa, another artist, different and yet not so different from Richard, a subaltern folk singer called Methi was beaten to death by her co-singer and this co-singer's husband and son, in a drunken brawl in her village. A tragic case of a phenomenal folk artist, composer of hundreds of songs, whose life was cut short by the accumulation of tensions relating to poverty, alcoholism, illiteracy and absence of adequate recognition. One is compelled to say that something should have been done, something should have happened, to circumvent this avoidable death. But there was no meaningful intervention in Methi's life, neither by activists nor artists, and her tomorrow has been cut short. The world is poorer for it.

The scholar-activist faces a quandary: how does one ameliorate the conditions of life and work of the subaltern artist without sacrificing or eradicating his or her cultural knowledge and practice? One cannot relegate this precious task to developmental activists, who are unaware for the most part of the complex linkages between subaltern creativity and its embeddedness in material reality. When I listen to Kalbelia nomadic women sing, for instance, I am alerted to strange enigmas of time that challenge the dominant repertoires in established singing and performance cultures. I notice, for instance, that at a certain point in a singing session, most of the Kalbelia women may not recognize a particular song sung by the lead singer in the group. As she sings that song, the rest of the women gradually pick up a few notes, hum a line or two, and then, before you know it, they are all singing the song as if they have sung it all their lives. So, how do they remember something that they might never have heard before? Or are they creating the song for the first time, improvising its verses, from the tropes and remnants of other such songs in their oral tradition? [12]

This collective memory of the body, cutting across cognition, reason and analysis, cannot be separated from the 'real': the actual living conditions of the women in a state of poverty and illiteracy. One cannot condone these realities, but the fact is that they enable the women to remember hundreds of songs in a repertoire that far exceeds that of a trained professional singer.

Aluta Continua (*The Struggle Continues*): a site-specific performance piece in Tangencya 2, linking the struggles against apartheid and AIDS, staged in the crowded market area of Warwick Triangle, Durban. Drawing on the archetypal anti-apartheid image of Hector Peterson, the student shot dead in Soweto in 1976 and carried through the streets by his friend, the poster pictured here, designed by Ernest Pignon-Ernest, depicts a young black man dying of AIDS , carried in the arms of an African woman. The poster is embodied in the performance.

PHOTOS: THE TANGENCYA PROJECT ARCHIVE

Facing this paradoxical situation, one is compelled to confront the imperatives of 'tomorrow' weighing on the realities of the non-modern 'present' and challenging the creative indeterminacies of the 'now', at once disappearing and reappearing in states of seeming unselfconsciousness. How does one respect a subaltern phenomenology of being while seeking ways of ensuring its cultural memory through the globalizing processes of museumization and archiving? While these are necessary procedures of cultural preservation, how can the capital that accumulates from their structures be shared with those whose knowledge has facilitated their existence in the first place? Here we are compelled to insert a dimension of ethics in our preservation of the 'now', which needs to take into account the real economies of subaltern communities and their desire for a more viable future, not just for themselves but for the generations to come.

At times, the intimations of such an ethics can be traced in subaltern practices themselves, so long as one is prepared to work against the camouflage of folklore. Among some desert communities of Rajasthan, it is said that the Sufi romantic epic of Heer Ranjha is sung during epidemics of foot-and-mouth disease.[13] Initially, this juxtaposition of disease and song seems incongruous, not least because there is no cogent thematic link between their realities beyond the fact that Ranjha is a buffalo-keeper by profession. What matters, however, is not the specific content or interpretation of the song as such, or its potentiality to exorcize disease at a ritualistic level, but the fact that it is sung for nights on end for as long as the disease lasts. This singing is accompanied by other concrete quarantine practices such as preventing the cattle from leaving their pens, restricting the movement of other animals and people from neighbouring villages, avoiding the lighting of fires or the cooking of fried food to prevent smoke fumes from filtering into the air, and disinfecting water with alum. Ordinary, everyday, 'real' practices of survival, which can so easily be dismissed as quaint and regressive.

And yet, what is the situation today when we in the global metropolis face foot-and-mouth disease, among other mysterious animal-related diseases like SARS and bird flu? 'Global panic' would seem to be the answer: a panic that legitimizes new forms of brutality. I am thinking of thousands of chickens on a poultry farm that were buried alive during the SARS scare in India, because it was too dangerous to kill them outright. After all, their blood could have infected us. So, the chickens were effectively 'culled' through a slow and torturous death in a pit of earth in which they were systematically smothered with mud: a more terrifying euphemism for

'killed' would be hard to find. Similar acts of 'culling' have been practised with impunity across the civilized world, amounting to the liquidation of millions of birds and animals. With all our expertise in epidemiology, we don't know how to cope with these diseases, or to deal with the ubiquity of contamination. Unable to draw lessons from the evidence of the past or to imagine a testimony from the future, we appear to be living in an increasingly irreconcilable gap between the past and the future. The strategy would seem to be: Kill the present. In critical hindsight, this is not so much a strategy as a means of heightening the deadly repetition of 'tomorrow and tomorrow and tomorrow', with no respite from the tyranny of time and its systematic accumulations of violence.

Instead of killing time, a more creative task could be to be more attentive to the shifting contours and intersections of multiple times, which this essay has attempted to inventory through a spectrum of experiments. The singing of Heer Ranjha does not offer a solution to the epidemics of our times. But perhaps, if we could find a way of translating its ethic of coping with the disasters of today, we could find a way of dealing with tomorrow with more civility, more circumspect awareness of our shared vulnerabilities, and far less submission to what Badiou so accurately describes as 'stagnant febrility'. 'Learning to learn' from the subaltern, from those marginalized sectors of society whose 'residues' of knowledge may yet resist 'the telematic postmodern terrain of information command' (Spivak 1998: 343), could be one way of renewing the politics of hope. In the process, one need not suffer the repetition or the deadly predictability of tomorrow; one can reinvent it today.

NOTES

1. These two structures of improvised time were first presented in the Kappen Memorial Lecture, which I delivered in Bangalore on 19 February 2000 and which has been reprinted in monograph (2000).

2. The LIFT Lecture 2001, delivered as part of the London International Festival of Theatre, at Riverside Studios, was entitled 'Between Past and Future: Re imagining our times in theatre today'. The production of Prakriya had been briefly described as a 'detour in my theatrical journey' in the 'Afterword' to my Theatre and the World: Performance and the Politics of Culture (1993: 248–9). Today I see this experimental production as a catalyst that set me thinking about 'process' outside the limits of performance.

3. In her Preface to Between Past and Future, Arendt emphasizes that the gap between past was future was 'bridged over by what, since the Romans, we have called tradition ... When the thread of tradition finally broke, the gap between past and future ceased to be a condition peculiar only to the activity of thought ... It became a tangible reality

and perplexity for all; that is, it became a fact of political relevance'
(1993: 13-14). The point that Arendt totally misses out on is that
the so-called attenuation of 'tradition' is irrevocably placed within a
Eurocentric grasp of history and knowledge.

4. I am drawing here on Adrian Kear's lucid exposition on 'Thinking
Out of Time: Theatre and the Ethic of Interruption' (2004: 99). For my
discussion of Badiou, I am indebted to this essay along with Janelle
Reinelt's 'Theatre and Politics: Encountering Badiou' (2004). Both of
these essays draw on *Rhapsodie pour le théâtre* (1990), among other
manifestos and publications by Badiou, which still await full English
translation. The finest introduction in English on the larger political
and philosophical canvas of Badiou's thought is Peter Hallward's
Badiou: A Subject to Truth (2003).

5. A fuller exposition of my production of Genet's *The Maids*, produced
by PETA in Manila, appears in my essay 'Genet in Manila: Reclaiming
the Chaos of Our Times' (2003c).

6. Quoted in the programme of *The Maids*, produced by PETA, Republic
of Malate, Manila, October 2001.

7. See the section on Ong Keng Sen's *Desdemona*, both in the context
of the Flying Circus Project workshop process and its deconstructive
mise-en-scène for international consumption, as examined in my
essay 'Foreign Asia / Foreign Shakespeare: Dissenting notes on Asian
interculturality, postcoloniality and recolonization' (2004).

8. My essay 'Muslims and Others: Anecdotes, Fragments and
Uncertainties of Evidence' (2003b), contains a fuller description of the
process leading to the 're-enactment' of the massacre. For historical
details on the massacre, see Jes Tirol's *Bohol: From Spanish Yoke to
American Harness* (1998).

9. See the special issue of *Inter-Asia Cultural Studies* (2004 5[3],
December), 'Facets of Islam', in which my essay 'Muslims and Others'
was reprinted.

10. In my voicing of the 'unrepresentability' of the real, there are some
similarities with Baudrillard's position in positing 'a real that is the
limit to all systems, a real that no system could ever entirely capture', as
explicated by Rex Butler in his excellent monograph *Jean Baudrillard:
The Defence of the Real* (1999: 137). At some level, I would even share
Baudrillard's fascination for the paradox that 'the closer representation
comes to the thing it resembles the less it resembles it', but I would
not, therefore, assume that 'it is at this point at which absolute
resemblance and absolute difference touch' that 'the real' manifests
itself (1999: 137). From my analysis of the differing levels of 'the real'
in the political build-up to my production of *The Maids*, leading to the
burning of the theatre, I would stress that the real, however mediatized,
fictionalized, performed and ultimately represented in the act of writing,
remains unassimilated. In the concluding section of the essay, which
emphasizes the materiality of the real, my points of departure from
Baudrillard's 'real' become more obvious.

11. For a fuller documentation of the project, see the Tangencya website
<www.tangencya.co.za>, now incorporated into the larger website of
Create Africa South <www.cas.org.za>.

12. A comprehensive overview on 'women's songs' in Rajasthan can be
read in Chapter 7 of my book *Rajasthan: An Oral History* (2003a) drawn

out of conversations with Komal Kothari. See in particular pp.. 156-80.

13. See the section on '*Hir Ranjha* and Foot-and-Mouth Disease' in my
Rajasthan: An Oral History (2003a: 60-3).

REFERENCES

Arendt, Hannah (1993) *Between Past and Future: Eight Exercises in
Political Thought*, Harmondsworth: Penguin Books.

Badiou, Alain (1990) *Rhapsodie pour le théâtre*, Paris: Le Spectateur
français.

Badiou, Alain (1999) *Manifesto for Philosophy*, Albany. States University
of New York Press.

Badiou, Alain (2001) *Ethics: An Essay on the Understanding of Evil*,
London: Verso.

Benjamin, Walter (1982) 'Eduard Fuchs: Collector and Historian', in
Andrew Arato and Eike Gebhardt (eds.) *The Essential Frankfurt School
Reader*, New York: Continuum Books.

Benjamin, Walter (1992) *Understanding Brecht*, London and New York:
Verso.

Bharucha, Rustom (1993) *Theatre and the World: Performance and the
Politics of Culture*, London and New York: Routledge.

Bharucha, Rustom (2000) *Enigmas of Time: Reflection on Culture,
History and Politics*, Bangalore: Visthar.

Bharucha, Rustom (2003a) *Rajasthan: An Oral History: Conversations
with Komal Kothari*, New Delhi: Penguin India.

Bharucha, Rustom (2003b) 'Muslims and Others: Anecdotes,
Fragments, and Uncertainties of Evidence', *Economic and Political
Weekly* XXXIII(40). Reprinted 2004 in an edited version in *Inter-Asia
Cultural Studies* 5(3) (December, special edition on 'Facets of Islam'):
472-85.

Bharucha, Rustom (2003c) 'Genet in Manila: Reclaiming the Chaos of
Our Times', *Third Text* 17(1).

Bharucha, Rustom (2004) 'Foreign Asia / Foreign Shakespeare:
Dissenting notes on Asian interculturality, postcoloniality and
recolonization', *Theatre Journal* 56(1).

Butler, Rex (1999) *Jean Baudrillard: The Defence of the Real*, London:
Sage Publications.

Hallward, Peter (2003) *Badiou: A Subject to Truth*, Minneapolis and
London: University of Minnesota Press.

Kear, Adrian (2004) 'Thinking Out of Time: Theatre and the Ethic of
Interruption', *Performance Research* 9(4).

Reinelt, Janelle (2004) 'Theatre and Politics: Encountering Badiou',
Performance Research 9(4).

Spivak, Gayatri Chakravorty (1998) 'Cultural Talks in the Hot
Peace: Revisiting the "Global Village"', in Pheng Cheah and Bruce
Robbins (eds.) *Cosmopolitics: Thinking and Feeling Beyond the Nation*,
Minneapolis and London: University of Minnesota Press.

Thapar, Romila (1996) *Time as a Metaphor of History: Early India*, New
Delhi: Oxford University Press.

Tirol, Jes B. (1998) *Bohol: From Spanish Yoke to American Harness*,
Tagbilaran City: University of Bohol Research Center.

Wright, Stephen (2004) 'The Delicate Essence of Artistic Collaboration',
Third Text 18(6).

RICHARD SCHECHNER

Towards Tomorrow? Restoring Disciplinary Limits and Rehearsals in Time?

Richard Schechner interviewed by Richard Gough, October, 2004, in New York City, USA

RG I would like to talk about three things:
- the formation of Performance Studies as a discipline, and particularly within that, issues to do with performance's relationship to theatre;
- most of all, I want to talk about where we are now, today, and what your hopes are for the future of the discipline;
- and thirdly, as we go, explore paradigm, paradigm shifts, parasites and paradoxes.

As early as 1988, in an editorial in *TDR* about Performance Studies, and a new paradigm for the theatre and the academy, you were making the case for a radical reconfiguration of theatre and drama departments in the US; proposing indeed a revolutionary shift to Performance Studies as the better discipline to embrace a multicultural and intercultural North America, and a more appropriate vehicle for academic training, a broad foundation for humanities as opposed to a semi-vocational training in anachronistic and extremely partial and oversubscribed theatre practices.

And subsequently in a *TDR* commentary in 1993, you asked how many theatre departments would be around in ten years time?

RS They're still here, but a lot of them have changed. One of the indications of change is that Performance Studies graduates used to have a hard time getting work and now they do not. Theatre departments are still here: formal institutional changes are very hard to accomplish, people don't want to give up departmental status, and departments are loathe to change their name, but they're less loathe to change some of their functions. So I don't think that what I predicted has come about, but neither has it not come about. Take an example like the University of California, Berkeley, which is now called The Department of Theatre, Dance and Performance Studies, this is the add-on approach.

I don't know how many others are also calling themselves 'Performance Studies', but they have Performance Studies people. What does that mean? It means that – in addition to studying drama and the enactment of drama and how people are prepared to enact drama or to study it in a scholarly way, all of that I would put as theatre studies – they also look at, for example, performance in everyday life, the performance of rituals, the relationship between aesthetic and non-aesthetic performance. So, I do see that, at least in the United States, there has been a continuing, if not radical, change, then shift, if not shift, then drift! But, certainly, a tendency towards an expanded vision of the field.

This goes back in my thinking and experiences that I had that pre-dated the codification of environmental theatre and my interest in non-aesthetic performances, which led me to ethnographies and anthropological literature. But, as I note in my introduction to *Performance Studies*, this is one of the genealogies of Performance Studies (2002). Another branch is quite different, the one that's represented by Northwestern University and many former speech and rhetoric departments that also have the term Performance Studies independent of the way I use it, and that comes out of an aural interpretation, an aural literature. It actually comes out of the anti-theatrical prejudice.

In middle America, especially the Midwest, there was a strongly entrenched Protestant value system where the idea of performing on stage in the theatre was looked on suspiciously not only for the conventional reasons – the relationship with theatre to sexuality, theatre districts to red light districts and so on – but in a deeper, more platonic level and – from Plato into Saint Augustine and Saint Aquinas and into the church – that theatre was a lie.

And so to take Austin, who is a Platonist in a sense, who [says] that theatre is 'etiolated', or further removed from the truth, because it's pretend (1962: 22). So that the Austinian performative does not occur on stage because actors are just pretending to say, 'I promise you I'll marry you', and so although I find Austin very useful from the point of view of Performance Studies, he's an anti-theatre person; he's *performative*, but not performance.

Because of this very deep anti-theatrical prejudice that is embedded in Protestantism, especially in the United States, people were not encouraged to develop stage plays. But there was a kind of histrionic appetite, and this appetite was satisfied by the development of preaching, rhetoric and debate. These were the three things that were allowed in universities, and certainly preaching, which was not thought to be theatrical at all but the opposite of theatre. It took a theorist like me to say why it was performance, not *performative*, but performance. It was not looked at as theatrical, but that God's word was the truth.

But still, the preacher needed to be trained. Also needing to be trained was the politician, the public speaker, and debate was a way of doing that, so that if you have in conventional theatre antagonists and protagonists, in debate teams you have position and anti-position, you still have that antagonistic situation, and in the Midwest of the United States where theatre was not allowed to be taught, debate *was* allowed to be taught, and there were many debate teams. There were at university level departments of speech and rhetoric rooted in Aristotle, and, later, rhetorics, training people to debate, for various professions from salesmanship to lawyering, and all of these were non-theatrical performance. They weren't theorized yet.

Out of this came Performance Studies of the aural interpretation and speech 'way', because even though they weren't allowed to do plays, they were allowed to read great literature. Again in the nineteenth century, in the United States, as indeed in the UK, people would read the novels allowed, and they would read them well, one would suppose, people were actually trained how to aurally interpret, how to read effectively, so this substituted for the theatre. So, that led to the Northwestern University brand of performance; so performance in that sense, from the speech perspective, was a positive value, while theatre was a negative value. So, there are two genealogies going on. I have direct experience only with one, but I do know the history of the other.

RG I came across you first as a theatre-maker, but also a theorist of theatre. Your book, *Environmental Theatre*, made a huge impact on me and my work (1973). How has your own practice as a theatre director influenced the development of Performance Studies? Unlike some of your colleagues – people like Barbara Kirshenblatt-Gimblett, Diana Taylor and Peggy Phelan who have also made significant contributions to the field – you are one of the few who has come directly from theatre practice.

RS I'm a theorist-practitioner, yes. I was practising theatre before I was involved in Performance Studies. I've been practising theatre all my life, more or less. When I was in High School (secondary school) I took part in radio dramas on the educational radio station. When I was at college (university) I wrote play reviews, and I started to write plays. When I was in the army I directed plays, this is in the 1950's. When I got out of the

army, I started a summer theatre, Provincetown, in the 1950s. So I've been directing plays since I was 21 or 22 years old, long before I had any inkling of Performance Studies. I consider myself a theatre director, a theatre artist. Theatre is the art that I love the most. I don't think of theatre and Performance Studies inside myself as in any kind of conflict; they are like sleeping and eating: I like to sleep but I also like to eat. I don't think they're the same thing, but they're not in conflict with each other, each in its own place. I would say that my theatre practice is much more directly personally, expressive, as art usually is. I don't attempt, when I direct a play, or write a play, to represent the theoretical position to understand anything, particularly in an objective way, historically. I am rather trying to express myself within the dynamics of a group, to tell a good story, to put something effectively on stage, but when I turn and put on my theorist's cap, I'm doing something else again. And I don't try to rectify or align the one with the other. That would make me crazy. That would mean that I would either have to enslave my practice, my artistry, to some abstract theory through deduction, or I would have to channel my theory through induction to a practice, and I don't want to do that.

RG Nevertheless I'm curious to know how practice of theatre might inform your theories differently, say, from some of your non-practitioner colleagues.

RS I can answer that to this degree: it makes me a profound and committed and unalterable pragmatist; handsome is as handsome does. In that sense, I'm very sympathetic to the theories of William James. I like behaviourism. I'm sympathetic to science in the hard sense: show me the data, show me the experiment, does it add up, does it compute? Because I think that's what theatre's about, it's about physical practice. So, I also think of theory as epiphenomenal. In other words, it is secondary.

Theories come from practice and are then confirmed by practice. So, theories are like the bridge between two more solid islands. So you have some practice, you need to explain it, so you construct a theory, but then further practice has to confirm it. Now this doesn't necessarily have to be artistic practice. Any kind of data that's from the world can confirm it. Now, I understand that, in certain ways, theory can lead practice, can inform it or can call it into existence, but in my work rarely. In my work, for example, you might get environmental theatre: that came out of the work I was doing in the theatre. Then, from the work I did in the theatre, from the work I saw around me and in the streets, I constructed the six axioms for environmental theatre. Then in the book *Environmental Theatre*, there's a chapter on space, a chapter on performance training, a chapter on directing, a chapter on participation, a chapter on nakedness, and so on. All of these are full of concrete examples from which I made a theory, and a theory is an organized explanation of phenomena.

A theory is not free-standing. So I sometimes have quarrels with the field that I have called into existence, because I feel, particularly for example in the post-structuralist version, theories sometimes are free-standing; they're thought to be primary. Constructiveness is primary, and if you want to call that a theory, that's fine. In others, there's no such thing as an original – that's in *Restoration of Behaviour* (1985). That theory of mine is also based on a rehearsal model of life. No event exists for the first time, it is always to some degree a re-enactment or a re-constitution, or a re-alignment, or a re-organization, what I call a restoration, and that the nature of the future – what I'm going to say to you, what you're going to ask – constructs what of the past I need to make the present inevitable. So that it's a bundle of relations. I know that I do theorize a lot, but I theorize on the basis of concrete experiences, and I test my theories against those experiences.

RG Why is it then that so many people have mis-understood the project of Performance Studies in relation to theatre? Why do so many people think that Performance Studies is in some ways an errant child?

RS One should be very careful not to conflate a field with an individual, and not to forget the historical process, that once you start something in process it develops in its own way and if it's successful it attracts other minds. I'm not Performance Studies: I'm not like the King of France, 'Les temps c'est pas moi!' My ideas are very clearly spelled out in fifteen or twenty books, and I think they're quite consistent. But I think of Performance Studies as a project, I'm in disagreement with some of it, but I was one of its founders. I am the father of my children. That doesn't mean they're me. So, Peggy Phelan's mind, Barbara Kirshenblatt-Gimblett's mind, Diana Taylor's mind and hundreds of other minds are now working on the Performance Studies project. I may have been one of the first to work on it as a project, I may still be a strong voice within it, but I am not the only voice within it.

RG Would you like to see the study of theatre, even mainstream theatre, more prevalent, as an object of study within Performance Studies?

RS *More* prevalent? The study of theatre ought to be part of what Performance Studies is, it's a broad spectrum. My claim is not that theatre should be thrown out of it but that other things should be brought into it. As a spectrum, the aesthetic genre is not just theatre but theatre, dance, music and all the related arts form one part of that spectrum, of which performance in everyday life - sports, rituals, public ceremony - all these together form the total spectrum. In Performance Studies you must study this whole spectrum in relationship to each of its component parts and in relationship to its over-riding theory, so a Performance Studies that only deals with theatre, only deals with dance or only deals with music would be truncated and incorrect. But a Performance Studies that excluded theatre and dance and music would also be truncated, incorrect.

The real question you want to ask is, 'is the model of Performance Studies a theatrical model, and is it the guiding metaphor'? That is a question I don't have an answer to exactly. So, if one wants to take the Goffmanian approach then you say that drama or theatre is the guiding metaphor underlying performance. So in the chapter on performance in *The Presentation of Self in Everyday Life* Goffman uses terms like 'backstage' and 'frontstage': he uses '*theatrum mundi*' but he means a social '*theatrum mundi*' (1959). Where Shakespeare saw the whole world as a theatre, Goffman sees social interaction as a drama that is staged in a rather conventional theatre.

Now, I do not see that. My basic model, as you well know, is this loop model, in which the theatrical informs the social and the social informs the theatrical. It is not really 'natural', it is also constructed, but it's not as consciously constructed an intention as that which is consciously constructed. So, for example, in everyday conversation, we speak English, which we know is constructive, without quite thinking about it, but if we were to make a sonnet we would then think about the construction of our language in terms of the number of lines, the kind of metre and so on. So I go along with Derrida and the post-structuralists, in believing that all experience is constructive, but within that construction there are, if you will, super constructions or additional constructions, and therefore, in relation to those additional constructions, certain things are *as if* natural. We don't think about them, and certain other things are also constructive, and that is also not a switch on and off, it's a gradation, so that right now, when I'm speaking to you, I am thinking about what I'm saying, while an hour ago in the restaurant, I thought very little about what I was saying. So that it's not a question of now I'm constructing my language, and now I'm not, now I'm theatrically performing and now I'm just socially performing. It's a gradation, so that there are micro bursts of theatrical performance, right inside long stretches of social performance, which are not highly thought-about, and ditto inside a great art work; there are micro bursts of social performance, unthought-out things; instant reactions that people cannot possibly think about but which they still enact, even though they're constructing their score to the very last. It's what Cieslak said, 'the flame within the glass'. In other words the breath of social life makes that flame flicker and that ignites a certain interest, but that's spontaneous, and when we say spontaneous, we're saying natural within that larger construction.

I think that my colleagues in Performance Studies who do not know practice, who have not experienced it, are in a certain sense restricted because they haven't had the experience of really dealing with things in a one-to-one correspondence, as they happen. Part of the problem of theorists, of theory untethered from practice, is you can make too big a leap. In cosmology you can make a big leap, but then you finally have to do an experiment: does light bend or doesn't it?

So you make the leap, but then you have to, through observation and mathematics, say that it does or doesn't, or are there quarks, are there stranger structures? So you build a cyclotron, you confirm it. Sometimes when we do theory in humanities, the theory, just the blather of it, just the talk of it is all that we ask for. I insist 'no'; we have to also find means of testing our theories.

RG Going back to whether theatre is the guiding metaphor, or could be the guiding metaphor for performance ways of working ...

RS Well, of course theatre could be one of the guiding metaphors, but for performance, *organicity* would be another guiding metaphor. Let's go back to Aristotle: his beginning, middle and end, as he describes tragedy. That is not a description of theatre, that's a description of organicity that he applied to theatre. Whereby, as lives have beginnings, middles and ends, natural processes that are organic have beginnings, middles and ends, he's asking 'does tragedy have a similar rhythm?' He's not saying that if tragedies are this, then life should have it!

So organicity is a metaphor, and what I call *doing* and *showing doing*. In my book *Performance Studies*, I think one of my best theoretical distinctions was the development from ontology to performativity. In other words, everything that is *is* - so that's *being*. All beings do something, in other words they're in motion, they're in action, they follow the trajectory of organicity,

beginnings, middles and ends. Whether it's inherent in the universe, or whether it's *put* on the universe, we still say it begins with a big bang and it will end in entropy and so on, and all the myths of the world deal with beginnings, middles and ends. So that, I would say, even if it's not the way nature really is, it's the way humans have constructed nature - to me it doesn't make any difference at this level.

And then there is *doing*: performing comes in when you *show* doing, and as I said earlier, that's not a question of a switch on and off, sometimes we *show doing* more than others. It's a kind of saturation. I like to think, when I use Rasa theory from Asia, of flavour or taste or saturation, saturation in terms of colour, saturation in terms of smell, so that performing - *showing doing* - is not a quality of 'yes it is' or 'no it isn't', but rather how much of it is there, how saturated, how conscious of it? So for example, in Noh drama, we're very conscious of the *showing of the doing*, and in a properly executed Stanislavskian version of Chekhov, we're not so conscious of it.

Even more in films: in certain films we're not conscious of it and certainly we're not so conscious of it in documentary films where the claim is that there's no *showing of doing* at all, the camera just happens to be there, but the *showing of the doing* is there in the editing. There's a gradation of saturation between a film that is a documentary, and a Bunuel film, which is obviously a film about film and still therefore the *showing of doing*.

Performance Studies is *understanding* the *showing of doing*. Performance Studies can also be applied to *doing* itself and to *being*, but its primary object of study is *showing the doing*. Its secondary objects of study are phenomenology and ontology: *being* is ontological, *doing* is phenomenological, and then *showing doing* is performative. And *studying* showing doing is Performance Studies.

I'll stick by that model, and then the second model is the binocular model of the relationship between social life and aesthetic life, which was first published in my 'Selective Inattention' essay and it's the model that Turner picked up on and used. So, these are operative models, they're not really dramatic models. Like Turner's social drama model of breach, crisis, redressive action, re-integration, which is a dramaturgical, or theatrical, model of the world. It's fine, but it's very limited because it's based on Western dramaturgy. My model is not based on Western dramaturgy, and it's not a theatrical model, it's a performance model.

RG One of the issues that Phil Auslander raised in his book *Liveness: Performance in a Mediatized Culture* was whether it was Performance Studies or performance, in that sense, that was truly a paradigm shift (1999). Or rather he pointed out that within science – as we've just been talking about it as hard science – a paradigm shift not only replaces the previous paradigm but invalidates it.

RS Not necessarily! The shift from the Newtonian to the Einsteinian universe did not function like that. Einstein did not invalidate Newton. All Einstein said was that Newton was a special case. Einstein didn't say that apples fall up or don't fall, but that gravity, and the laws of gravity, the mathematical laws of gravity and the three laws of thermodynamics all apply, but within a limited case. So new paradigms can sometimes absorb older ones. We know this culturally. For example, let's take Christianity and Northern European religious practice: certainly Christianity was a paradigm shift to the peoples of Northern Europe when they adopted Christianity, but it didn't obliterate the old religion. So we still have our Christmas trees, we still have our saturnalias. It absorbs, transforms, modulates, but still does not obliterate. In fact I would say that cultural memory is very strong.

Most of the time a new paradigm absorbs and changes the meaning of another paradigm and uses it. In art there is often a manifesto aspiration of obliteration, but in science, including social science, there's a perception of gradual transformation, evolutionism. So, art tries to function revolutionarily, but did Marx, when he tried to do a scientific theory of revolution, absorb capitalism and to some degree obliterate it? No, I would say Marx *did* revolutionize: capitalism obliterated medievalism, and communism obliterated capitalism.

In most of the sciences sometimes things are obliterated, but sometimes they're transformed and remembered in different ways. Let's take the move from the heliocentre, from the geocentric to the heliocentric universe, from Ptolemy to Copernicus. Now, obviously, when Copernicus gets accepted, the idea that the earth is the centre of the universe gets obliterated, but what does not get obliterated is the notion of circulating heavenly bodies. That's the underlying paradigm: that the heavenly bodies circulate. The argument is what circulates round what? And one could argue that that's a secondary argument. Ptolemy and Copernicus agree that the world is in motion, worlds are in motion, in a roughly circular way. They're just arguing about what's at the centre of it. And once you get away from Ptolemy to Copernicus, you're obliterating one part of the paradigm, but you're accepting the other part. In fact you're using the other part to prove the first part, because Ptolemy's universe made the earth go in very weird loops to make it

that way, and Copernicus's was much more elegant. And so, it accepted the notion of circulation but had – like Ockham's razor – a simpler explanation. So, I would be very careful about the manifesto set of mind.

RG What you're proposing here is like a palimpsest in that you can see previous texts ...?

RS Well, a palimpsest has still the previous, but built over, that's architecturally true. But I'm talking about transforming, and evolution, transformational acceptance.

Evolution is not a palimpsest. A palimpsest is what happens when the church comes in and rips down the Aztec temple, and builds their own with the same bricks and you can still see a little bit of the Aztec underneath the church. But evolution is where ontogeny recapitulates phylogeny, and that's different. So we still go through a stage, for example, in our own development, our own embryonic development, where we have gill slits. So we haven't rejected, as it were, the fish stage, it's been absorbed and used in a certain way as we move on through an ongoing process. It's a really different mode of thought.

Palimpsest is building in layers, evolution is development through code. So in a certain sense, the post-modern notion of code is very strictly adherent: we couldn't have the computer without Darwin, and we couldn't have Darwin without Mendel. Mendel said there's a code and a way of inheritance, Darwin applied it across species and used the notion of code to construct an artificial evolutionary situation.

RG So, to tie that back to our theme, in that sense are you saying that Performance Studies is an evolution of theatre studies?

RS Well, I don't know much about theatre studies – don't jump! Performance Studies is in evolution, theatre studies is one of its forebears. Culture is not quite the same; even with parents, you have two and then you have four, you have grand parents. So, yes, theatre studies is earlier, but I'm not going to be a Social Darwinist and say that Performance Studies replaces it in that sense; it develops from but then it remains operative, and parallel to, but paradoxically, culturally, theatre studies assumes a subservient position – a subaltern position, as it were – because it's one genre of performance among many.

RG A narrow band within the broad spectrum. As a cultural Darwinist, may we talk about survival? Much has been discussed recently concerning survival, many companies that are celebrating significant anniversaries, and even this interview is being conducted within the context of CPR's thirtieth anniversary; Odin Teatret have just had their fortieth, Forced Entertainment, just this last weekend had their twentieth, and *TDR* will have it's fiftieth in 2006. In a Derridian context, survival takes on the notion of living on: *sur vivre*. At what level might performance be a parasite upon the real? I'm thinking here of parasite, both in the biological sense of symbiosis, but also as it's originally defined in the OED, as 'one who eats at the table of another, and repays by flattery'. Let me simplify: in what sense can performance and theatre be seen to sit beside - *para* - the world, in order to gain their sustenance?

RS No, they're part of the world, so can't be aside from it. In Derrida's world, there's nothing outside the text. But Derrida was wrong when he said that there is nothing outside the text. There's a lot that's outside the text, but there's nothing outside of the world, the world defined as ... as *being*. What is is and there's nothing outside of *being*. Ontology can be extremely seductive, and because words are constructed, meanings are constructed and they're not hemmed in by their genealogies. This is true of the whole concept of the real, whether it's Lacanian, or in a more common-sense way. In *it is* I find I have great problems with *it*. The *is* I don't have much of a problem with, and performance is part of the *is*, so I don't see performance as a parasite. I mean that would be more like Austin's etiolation: that it's a parasite implies that it doesn't have its own strength to live by itself, because it feeds off something else. That comes much too close to the idea of art as representation, which I also reject.

Some art can be representational, but it's not a sine qua non of art or theatre to be representational, and, in fact, I think one of the things about liveness that I like is that there's a certain amount of it that is irreducibly non-representational. In other words, the actor may be representing something, but the actor is also something, and that can't be represented and that is what the actor *is*. So, the actor's *isness*, is used to represent the drama, or the gestures, or the code, or what have you. Once you get to a film or a painting, all you have *is* the representation, because the being that created it is no longer there. So performing does not necessarily map entirely onto representation.

RG Returning to Performance Studies, and referring to your essay 'What is Performance Studies Anyway?' in Peggy Phelan's and Jill Lane's book, *The Ends of Performance*, in which you stress the unpredictability of the direction of the discipline (1998). You likened it to a sidewinder snake, and talked of its inherent instability

due to its intergeneric, interdisciplinary, intercultural formation. To what extent might this be an impediment to the grander project of Performance Studies becoming a foundation course for humanities? Can such an inherently, perhaps even purposefully unstable discipline provide a formation, a foundation?

RS Probably not. That's a really big problem - Performance Studies is never going to be stable, but if I had to give up one or the other, I would give up the foundation.

So, the nature of performance, the nature of *showing doing* is that you can show a lie, you can move in indirect ways. Where it becomes foundational is that in *understanding* showing doing, it educates the student in the ways of the world, which are so often just acting. It certainly has a long leash on the actuality or the truth of the situation. So what training or Performance Studies allows one to do, or prepares one to do, is to be sceptical of those kinds of social interactions and political interactions. So that whilst performance is untrustworthy, Performance Studies may not be untrustworthy.

The performance is the showing of the doing, but then we can develop more or less trustworthy methodologies to study the showing of the doing. At the same time, I'm aware that I write a lot and [that] not all of what I write fits into one grand scheme. So sometimes it's more in my inclination to emphasize the slipperiness of performance and Performance Studies. Another time it's more in my interest to emphasize its perceptual or revolutionary status.

RG Yes, I enjoy that very much in your writing and your talking, and always have done. But I do remember, and I remember this being like a gunshot when you first said it to me in around 1985, when you talked about your hope for Performance Studies as a discipline becoming a sort of foundation discipline, or potentially so ...

RS I haven't given up on that, but it is a foundation that won't be entirely canonical. So therefore it's a foundation in the training of healthy scepticism rather than a foundation in the training of orthodoxies. Usually we think of foundations as being orthodox, but maybe in a world that is going to move from postmodernism to whatever, in an unstable world, maybe the best foundational training is one that is processual and shifting, rather than founded on canons that are going to be blasted away.

RG And if that's the nature of the discipline - instability and processuality - to what extent is there an institutionalization of Performance Studies - PSi, an international association, a proliferation of courses and new departments, publishing of a Performance Studies text book - and thus the creation of a canon a church and a dogma, and therefore a need of reining it in?

RS But it is what happens, and it's a danger. Knowledge, its processes, the way it works is from a certain kind of breakthrough to a molten stage into a kind of frozen stage, and then somebody has to break through again. So that that's a kind of ongoing dialectic, or ongoing process.

So now, the breakthrough stage may have been some of the things I and others said in the late fifties and sixties, and then the molten stage continues until around 2000 or so, and now we're in the kind of freezing it, or institutionalizing phase, and then somebody's going to come along around 2010 and break it apart again. If it weren't then we'd enter into a kind of long medieval period. We don't know whether it will be or not, but that will determine what kind of historical period we're in.

In other words, if Einstein didn't come along and blast Newton and Heisenberg didn't come along and blast Einstein - not destroy them but kind of shake them up - we would be in a continuing Newtonian orthodoxy, which would be a very different world. For my new book, *After the Avant Garde*, one of the essays I'm working on is called 'Post-Modernism and Medievalism, and there I expand further on the fact that one of the options facing us is a long period of conservative thinking. And it may be. In which case, if my ideas are the last words out there, they'll become institutionalized and canonical for a long time to come. Otherwise, the shelf life of such ideas is ten to twenty years, and then they get revised.

RG It's fascinating to consider - thinking back to 1985, only twenty years ago, when you were first saying that - how far Performance Studies as a discipline has come.

RS But that's what I predicted. It was inevitable, because theatre studies was limited and weak, and Performance Studies was young and robust and not so limited.

RG And, prompted by seeing on your couch the latest copy of *American Theatre*, I recall only four years ago your *TDR* Comment analysing the prevailing conservatism as revealed through its adverts.

RS Yes, and I didn't say theatre studies was going to be reformed, I said Performance Studies is going to take over! And that's not even theatre studies, that's actual theatre. The practice of theatre in Middle America, that's what *American Theatre* and the Theatre Communications

Group, the most conservative, is addressing. Because it's owned by bourgeois people and bourgeois values, basically white, middle class values, so that if a person of colour was to work in that theatre, they and their skin may be of colour, but their performance is not of colour. If their performance is of colour, it's exonified and celebrated as 'Wow! We have a real black person, speaking real black language!' instead of it being a natural part of the diversity of expression.

RG I do wonder in some ways if we have achieved better in the UK? I'm looking at the list, in the 1993 *TDR* Comment when you're talking about new paradigms, particularly in the academy, when you describe the performance pie and how US theatre departments might reconstruct, reconfigure themselves. I do wonder if in the UK a more experimental and innovative mix has come about through Performance Studies meeting Theatre Studies, *British* Theatre Studies? Partly, because in the UK there is a greater clarity between vocational practical training and study, and also because British Theatre Studies is perhaps much broader and progressive in its scope. But, it is interesting, how, certainly in the UK, at the moment, there seems to be much more integration between Performance Studies, in terms of it's broad spectrum approach, and the Theatre Studies approach. Would you wish that to happen? Do you think that could still happen here in the US, or do you think it's so entrenched?

RS No, it's irrelevant what I wish! I write manifestos of sorts, or calls to action, but at the same time, I basically write descriptively of things. So, of course, it would be nice to have what you say happen, but I also am very aware that the mechanics and the buildings and the institutions and the habits of theatre departments, theatre in the academy, are very strongly inscribed here, or entrenched. Now, in certain places like at Brown University in Providence, they're making a Performance Studies/ Theatre Studies amalgam, with a particular emphasis in Asian performance and also in performance theory. So, that's a very hopeful sign. There are different new configurations all over the place, and as these younger scholars and scholar-practitioners take their place, there will be a change. The last thing that will change is *American Theatre*, because those advertising in the journal represent the regional theatre, not the universities.

Universities advertise themselves there, and there's a kind of symbiotic relationship that the universities want to attract students, who want to attract the jobs in the regional theatres as actors. We need to convince more students that they can come out of Performance Studies and then go to law school, or go to medical school, or go into business, or go into radio, or go into making experimental performance, not making their living at it, but learning something by it. We don't think that the only outcome of so-called theatre studies is a lousy job, you know, occasionally being employed as an actor.

For example, at NYU we have a programme called 'Lawyering', about the performance of law, and also the basic theory of law and performance, in other words, the relationship between antagonistic and collaborative, between private and show, and so we're not just talking about how to make lawyers better lawyers, but understanding the law, as a performance genre. What Performance Studies opened up was the possibility of imagining performance in its broader sense, in relationship to a number of existing disciplines, and at the same time developing the intellectual muscular core of its own discipline, and not relying on theatre as its basic metaphor, or only ally. It won't be a sea-change that theatre departments will see the light; it will be that they slowly get eroded around them, and they change, they get new people in that will add a kind of side programme that then grows.

RG So as you are saying, that unpredictability through inter-disciplinarity, is, in a way, still there and is the driving motor for the development of Performance Studies.

RS Yes, but at the same time, Performance Studies itself becomes an increasingly strong discipline. So now there is the inter-disciplinarity between Performance Studies and x, rather than Performance Studies being an inter-discipline. So, at one and the same time, it is its own paradox: it is still an inter-discipline (but it was more of an inter-discipline fifteen years ago); now it is its own discipline, which is seeking allies in other disciplines.

RG Earlier you were talking about building bridges between Performance Studies and Theatre Studies. I'm currently co-editing an issue of *Performance Research* entitled; 'On Theatre', and this is one of the question we have put in the call for papers: 'is there anything to be gained from taking literally those philosophers who seem to use theatre as a metaphor for more general questions of representation? What if when they say theatre, they really mean theatre?' As editors we wonder whether the contemporary study of performance has avoided applying its insights precisely where they might gain the greatest traction: in the theatre? One of the bridges you were positing is with mainstream theatre and drama, are there other bridges that you've been thinking about within the area of theatre and Theatre Studies?

RS *TDR* will still be mostly not about drama, but we are doing a new section called European Masters, and also going to do a series of articles in *TDR* about drama, a series called the 'Drama Review', because I find certain things happening in drama – Sarah Kane, Richard Maxwell etc. – quite interesting. So I'm not averse to any of that, as long as theatre knows its generic place. So I feel secure enough that I can now entertain articles about drama and so on, and, although I still want *TDR* to be very aware of Africa, Latin America, Asia, Oceania and so on, Europe is also re-entering because we can afford now to look in that direction as we've made progress in the other directions. Also, in terms of theatre studies, the most recent 'TDR Comment' by Steve Tillis outlines a whole new way of teaching theatre history.

What happens if you take world theatre seriously? Even within theatre studies, why in Western theatre is it said that theatre begins with the Greeks? That's a stupid assertion! And shows how far behind theatre studies are. It's like saying civilization began in Rome. There's one kind of civilization [that] began in Africa, one kind in Australia etc. Even the notion of civilization is challenged, and yet at the same time one says "origins of theatre' and all of a sudden you have thousands of phallic dances and Aristotle's version. Which is fine, but that's only twenty-five-hundred years ago. There was no theatre before then? In my new book series, that I'm publishing with Seagull Books (Calcutta), there is Yann Montelle's dissertation on performances in the Palaeolithic caves – that's twenty-thousand years ago! That's a good model for the beginning of theatre, and not as ritual either but as entertainment! So theatre studies itself needs a lot of revising.

RG As we are discussing *TDR*, can we discuss the role of a journal in relation to a field of study? As we have mentioned *TDR* celebrates its half-centenary in 2006, and your leadership of *TDR* has been quite remarkable during that period, and for much of that fifty years.

RS Yes, I've been the editor for a long time. I have certain quarrels with journals that rotate to their editors too quickly. Maybe my thirty years of editorship is too long, but it keeps me young, it keeps me on my toes, and therefore I think that I can still do intellectual battle with the youngest of my colleagues. But I don't like the idea of what happens, as in *Theatre Journal*, which is the journal of American Theater Higher Education, where they rotate every two years. There are two kinds of journals: one that totally tries to pretend to be representative of the discipline, where editorship is rotated and where there's a board of editors that decide on what's being published, etc. in an attempt to be objective; or one based on literary journals, which *TDR* is, where there is an editor, or a group of editors, who have a sustained and overt programme.

So the role of a journal? It has several roles: one is, of course, to present new and challenging scholarship, and to present this in line with its role. I'm not saying that there be only one role, but *TDR*'s not going to publish something totally outside of our area of interest, or totally counter to our programme.

For example, the whole programme of the avant-garde of the sixties was really energized by *TDR* at that time, and this is prior to Performance Studies. And in the sixties also the notion of street theatre, politically engaged theatre. At the same time, underneath, in an essay called 'Approaches' I outline the schema for Performance Studies, but, except for that one essay, it did not rise to the surface of *TDR* until the seventies. And when *TDR* became less politically active, I was no longer the editor. I only edited one guest issue, called 'Theatre and the Social Sciences', which really outlined the schema for Performance Studies. Michael Kirby withdrew *TDR* from all political activism and did this series of special issues, some of them very excellent. He tried to be 'objective'.

Now when I became editor again in '85, Performance Studies was already in existence; the Department of Performance Studies at NYU was already five years old, by name, and fifteen years old by practice. So I re-titled *TDR* to *TDR: The Journal of Performance Studies* – not *A Journal of Performance Studies* but *The Journal of Performance Studies*. A little bit arrogant, but at that point I took it upon myself to make *TDR* an active participant in, and advocate of, Performance Studies.

RG To return to performance theory, we've already discussed *showing doing*, which I think is one of those very wonderful key clarifying concepts of Performance Studies, in that it is so simple. The other thing that I always liked very much was the *as/is* concept. And I remember you once wrote: 'The world appeared no longer as a book to read but as a performance to participate in', and this had a profound influence on me and the development of my own company, CPR, in our origins as Cardiff Laboratory Theatre, resonating with our early stated manifesto to be 'illiterate on purpose'. Whilst the concept of the world *as* performance is very helpful in understanding the world, I nevertheless begin to have some anxieties about seeing *everything* as performance. So I'd like to ask at this point whether there are any qualifications you would put on the *as/is* performance model?

RS No, I would not, because *as/is* is a voluntary operation,

as I've argued in other places, and I'll argue again here. The *as* construction is not just about performance: you can see the whole world *as* a book, you see the whole world *as* physics, and you can see the whole world *as* sculpting. In other words, *as* is an operation that allows you to apply the methodology of one discipline to whatever you want to apply it to. Therefore if you want to see the world *as* performance, this is fine. If you want to see this room as performance, this is fine. Where people make a mistake is they extend the *as* in two directions: one, that it's necessary instead of voluntary and, two, that the world is the only thing that the *as* applies to, when it can be applied to the smallest phenomenon, or the largest one. So therefore I would certainly not withdraw it, because it's a general assertion of methodology: it doesn't particularly belong to performance.

RG That's clear. What does participating in the world *as* performance mean for you?

RS Well, again that hasn't changed that much. It means looking at one's overall experience and the particulars of that experience – one's social life, one's aesthetic life, one's professional life, one's intimate life – as occurring under the aegis of rehearsal. This means under the aegis of twice behaviour, restoration of behaviour. Let's take this conversation: thinking slightly ahead, I am asking myself about the kind of effect I wish to have, what performance do I wish or what behaviour or effect do I wish to bring into existence? And that allows me to think behind what things have happened in my life that help construct my thinking, which then determines my present day behaviours, which is our conversation.

That's what rehearsals do, rehearsals look forward to a production, or some kind of public showing. They draw on former rehearsals to determine what's going on in today's rehearsal, so in a strange and paradoxical way, the rehearsal view of the world is that the future determines the past, because it is according to what one plans to do that one selects from the repertory of the past, what to repeat, or what to improve on, in the present.

Now this is one model of the world. The only other model that I accept is the Buddhist model, which is a total present. If you're a person who is 'illuminated', as it were, and you're free from the cycle of desire, that means if you live totally in the present, there's nothing in the future you wish, therefore there's nothing in the past that you need to recall. And therefore you're totally in the present moment. That is very rare, it belongs only to Buddha and Bodhisattvas because most people cannot, or do not wish to, put themselves in that immediacy, because that immediacy is the eradication of memory and the eradication of any desire, any future, which means desire. Most people don't really understand Buddhism. They're very glib about 'living in the present moment'. But they don't really want to live in the present moment, it's a very bleak place, or it's very full, but it's full without effect because in desiring nothing, one feels nothing. I have to confess I'm not an enlightened person, and therefore I can only imagine on the basis of reports what enlightenment and bliss are like, although I have had flashes, if not of illumination, of understanding this sense of the present. But I do accept that as another approach to experience. So I accept restoration of behaviour, which is this processual business, and I accept a present-centredness. I don't accept any other.

RG Whilst we're on restoration of behaviour, at one point yesterday you also mentioned Shakespeare's worldview *theatrum mundi* and all the world being a stage. Neil Hornick, this wonderful performance artist in London called Phantom Captain, once said, 'If all the world's a stage, where's the rehearsal room?' So, within the notion of restoration of behaviour, and in that view of the world, it's glib I know, in terms of where the rehearsal room is, but if yours is all a rehearsal room, is there a stage?

RS I'm not too concerned about the stage, I don't know where it is, it's not in my world view, because I think we're always in process. Let's say the stage is a convention of allowing people to watch a certain amount of your rehearsals, and when I actually do art work, that's the way I work: every day I meet with the actors, at a certain point we let the audience in, but it isn't finished, it's not like a painting.

When do you say, 'I'm not working on it anymore'? I'm always working on productions, so in that sense I'm always in rehearsals, and very early on in actual rehearsals, I have opened rehearsals to observers. And therefore I look at the performance as a continuation of the rehearsals under a different aegis. And that makes performance very different from art works that are trying to stop time.

Joseph Conrad, in the preface to *The Nigger of the 'Narcissus'* - very interesting preface, forget about the title of the book - talks about art as rescuing from the remorseless rush of time something that has status, and I can believe that film and painting and poetry all do that, all have as an objective a certain way of stopping time, of making 'times' when you stop, or making it a very short span of time from the beginning of the sonnet to the end of the sonnet, from the time I look at that little block print here, to the time I stop looking at it (1990).

But theatre is not that way. If I look at that block print now, tomorrow it will be different only because I've changed, or the circumstances changed, and a slight deterioration, but not one that the artist wishes to have. But in performance it's different: tomorrow will be different, not only for those reasons but *it* in itself will be different, *it* itself is never quite the same.

So, we could try to score a performance exactly as Grotowski or Robert Wilson might, but it's human actors living in real time. The paradox, or the contradiction is, in terms of restoration of behaviour, it's always a repetition - but it's always a repetition in Derridean terms of being an iteration, not a repetition - and it can never be an act of absolute simulation. So it's an iteration, which means it's a circle; it's exactly the same, but it's not quite the same. We're not capable of doing it that way, and that excites me.

Therefore, I see the world as an ongoing rehearsal. And I see the performance of theatre as an ongoing rehearsal. I see the static arts as attempting to stop the 'on going'. Sculpting does it quite well, but then of course the statues deteriorate over time. But they try to freeze in time. Photography is a great freezer in time, and it really works against the notion of performance.

RG This ties us back to the conversation we were having yesterday about the instability of the discipline.

RS Yes, well, I'm all for instabilities, subversion, process, change - I kind of like that. You're a cook, so you must like it also. Cooking is a process: to under-cook, to over-cook are both mistakes, but you have to catch it, you can't stop it, you catch it in that window of opportunity, when it's right. So it begins to get right at a certain point, it stays right for a certain duration, then it goes wrong again, but it's always changing, it's never just stopped. So you have that window of tasteful opportunity, that's what performance is also.

RG Talking about times and the times we live in, I want to talk about where we are now, and the future. Last weekend I was at the University of Lancaster with Forced Entertainment who, remarkably for a permanent ensemble, have just reached their twentieth anniversary.

The subtitle of the conference to celebrate this anniversary was '*We are searching for a theatre that can really talk about what it's like to live through these times*'. There was quite a bit of questioning during the conference proceedings about *which* times, because some people thought even Forced Entertainment work, for all it's decentred and disjointedness, was not really of these times, but was of a slightly earlier time. I'm interested in what ways you think performance – or, for that matter, theatre, given the conference subtitle – can address the temper of the times, in terms of times that we now live in?

RS I don't know, these are getting into these areas that make me uncomfortable, because I think it could get us into the area of wanting to claim [a] Matthew Arnold view of art, which is that art should be important, should duly address the times. Of course it does those things, but usually in an oblique way. I'm not so sure that when Picasso painted *Guernica* he was painting an intervention into the Spanish Civil War as much as he was painting his particular feeling in outrage about a particular event. And it's similar for Goya.

But they stand as great works of anti-war, and even if they intended it as that and they were addressing the times – the Napoleonic Wars, the Spanish Civil War – one can also say that they were taking advantage of those events in order to render their art more effectively, that they were exploiting those events. I think that artists, like shamans, are always involved in a kind of double or triple operation. Brecht is a person I admire because he was conscious of that operation. He was talking about the politics of his day, *and* he was building a good nest for himself. He wasn't a hypocrite about it. He'd be a good Marxist, but he drove a hard bargain. So, I admire that, I think most of us live what Sartre would call bad faith, and the rest of us are even worse, hypocrites. So, this kind of addressing the future, or taking a kind of principled stand always makes me uncomfortable.

Now, having said that, of course I write and I direct in relationship to my current circumstances, but, as I said, like Picasso and Goya, I take advantage of those circumstances and react to them. But at age seventy, I don't think I can guide them.

RG We ended yesterday talking about interculturalism, and you were saying how there are a number of terms you feel particularly proud of having introduced into the performance world. Where do you think we've got to in terms of interculturalism?

RS I didn't invent the concepts, but inventing a label or a name is very important, naming a baby is very important. As to interculturalism, I feel that the world is inalterably a social world, a political world. It's inalterably in motion. Colonialism is not to be undone, it is just that we're going to the next phases, which does not mean that evil has disappeared and good has triumphed. But nor does it mean that it's colonialism in the same way.

Let's take a specific example: China. China is an extraordinarily powerful entity. I use the word entity

because its government has one kind of power, its culture has another kind of power, its economics another again. These are not all identical. In fact, the Chinese government will find it harder to control the culture and the economy because it's a horse that they're riding, but they're not entirely guiding it. And yet China's presence on the world stage, if you will, if you want to use that phrase, is something that was inconceivable during the period of colonialism.

And during the pre-colonial period, China was also extremely powerful, but there wasn't any world or global stage. There were regional stages, there were local stages – there weren't even nation states (we're talking about the period of adoption of the Western calendar, from the fall of the Roman Empire to the Renaissance) – and their distinct Empires, that traded with each other, but they didn't have a global view in that sense. China was very powerful in this period. It had a much larger fleet than anything the West had, even at the time that the Portuguese and Spanish began their explorations. There's the famous eunuch admiral who sailed all the way to Africa with a Chinese fleet – thirty thousand people, several hundred boats, the largest of them ten or twelve times the size of Columbus' boats – but turned around because he said there was nothing out there that the Chinese needed. He brought back trophies, but otherwise there was no advantage for China to reach out into the world. And, in fact, the Emperor felt that at that point the relationship to the outside world might contaminate China, so he ordered the destruction of the fleet.

Otherwise there was no doubt they would have got to Europe. They could have gone across the Pacific. This makes everything that the Europeans did in their little boats look like peanuts. It's well documented in the histories of China and even the Western histories of China, but we don't know about it. So a global view first comes into existence with modern astronomy, with space travel, with photography from the moon, with going to the moon. I remember in 1972 I was in Papua New Guinea, just a year after the first moon walk, and up in Highland New Guinea, very far away, on finding out I was American, a boy pointed to the rising moon and said in pidgin English, 'You, how put man there?' So he knew in the highlands in New Guinea that somebody had been there, how did he?

So, modern astronomy changed everything. It's not 9/11 that changed everything in that sense. From Ptolemy to Copernicus to viewing the Earth from outside the Earth. Going back to your paradigm shifts of imagination, the round globe became a fact rather than an abstract. So now we're living in a global situation, and that global situation is tainted politically and economically of course.

So we have now a world military and economic situation, in which former colonial powers still have an edge, but former colonized powers also are rising, and they're all interacting, as well as many, many lesser powers economically and politically speaking, *and* culturally, *and* in the art scene, *and* in the performance scene. People do travel around, and the fact of the matter is that artists are promiscuous, and they get influenced by whom they get influenced by. So that if Suzuki Tadashi does a great piece of work, he's going to influence a lot of people. Interculturalism as a phenomenon of the collision of different cultural practices, of mutual influencing, of the development at the same time of what I would call global styles as well as local styles. That's going to continue. We see it – globalization – most vibrantly, not in theatre but in music.

In music we have world beat. We see styles move very swiftly because the CD and the Internet are much quicker transporters of music than they are any other art. So, for example, in Trinidad you have Chutney Soca, a combination of Indian, South Asian, North American, West African and Trinidadian influences. The *Soca* combines the *So* of Soul and the *Ca* of Calypso. Soul being North American music, Calypso is itself a hybrid from West Africa and Trinidad, with some influence perhaps from the native Caribs who were there. And Chutney uses Indian drumming and Indian rhythms. So Chutney Soca is a particular musical form in and of itself, and it influences other things.

Listening to Gambuh music on my ipod today on the bus, I was thinking of using it in my next production, traditional Balinese music.

I think that's the other thing: I think we're much too hypocritical about honouring. I don't ask somebody in Japan or in India or in Africa to honour what I do. If they like what I do, let them steal it, and I'll steal what they do! And that's the way of artists, actually.

I think it's as bad to exploit somebody by dominating them, as to exploit them by over-honouring them, and I think to some degree, our theatrical leaders over-honour: they try to pay the debt of colonialism

RG It surprises me that there's never been a theatre/ performance equivalent of ethnomusicology, the study of world music/s as proposed originally by UNESCO, to look at the different musics of the world in their own terms.

RS Well, for example, let's take Faye C. Fei's book, *Chinese Theories of Theater and Performance* (1999). So far, Western theories have penetrated the rest of the world and now what we need to work on is having other

theories penetrate the West. So Fei's book, my essay 'Rasaesthetics', the translations of the *Natyashastra*, the increasing awareness of the works of Zeami Motokiyo, as well as the popularity of the *Dictionary Of Theatre Anthropology* – these begin to open the road in the other direction to some degree. So, yes, we need more of that.

RG They are surprisingly, all still very specific, small developments in that sense. I am aware that many theatre departments in the UK, have only one module or one course on world theatre, or on interculturalism.

RS World music, as it were, is basically popular music, to some degree a little traditional music as well. But basically popular music is market-driven. It is very frothy, it tends to become homogenized. Now, if you do serious ethnomusicology then you'll want to see what is local, and *only* local, about a particular music. So it's unlikely that the Gambuh I was listening to will ever become popular in London or New York – except among people who might like Balinese stuff, which is not that many. So, theatre and live performance maintains that kind of particularity, so that Noh drama for example will never become popular in Indiana, or in Manchester, although some people may like it. On the other hand, some individual artists may take something from Noh and use it, as indeed Butoh artists took something from German expressionist dance and from Noh, and from Shinto, and made something that was, to some degree, at least artistically, popular. Similarly, probably Eugene O'Neill will never be really popular in rural China. It just doesn't speak to their cultural experience.

RG But the issue of popularity is a sort of second and third development, isn't it? When that remarkable UNESCO series of world musics was appearing in the sixties, wonderful studies, say of the polyphonic singing of the Gabon, or the Burundi calling, the ethnomusicologists really wanted to understand what was going on. The popularity came later.

RS So why don't we have a similar thing with dance and theatre?

RG Ethnotheatrology …

RS We're not talking about the ethnomusicology in the sense of the study of it. We're talking now about the harvesting, the collecting of it. I don't read ethnomusicology, in the sense that I haven't read studies of those musics. I just listen to the music. So, what we need to have is something similar, just phenomenologically, of those forms. And now we have digital means, so it is more possible.

RG The availability of the resources is happening. For example one can buy a set of forty DVDs of Keralan theatre forms, but it's still fascinating how, within the teaching of theatre studies and performance studies it's remarkably ...

RS *[interrupts]* Well, even in terms of ethnomusicology, very few places teach the singing of Gambuh, believe me. So what we do need is the resources there, because there just isn't time enough in life for each individual, personally to know everything about everything, and so educationally there's a number of possible approaches:
1. Whatever culture I'm in should take 80 percent of my attention and the remaining 20 percent should kind of familiarize myself that I'm in the rest of the world.
2. Allocate attention and resource according to demographic analysis of the world allocate: 40 percent of the curriculum on China, 25 percent on India, 10 percent on the West etc. That would probably not be acceptable to many people.
3. A third would be some kind of subjective judgement of 'what's important to quote'.

And that's what scholars always argue about. That's probably what we've come to, so that at present scholars still privilege the West, even if they are not in the West. For example, in India in English language education it is still more usual to read Shakespeare than the *Natyashastra*, partly because the Western classics can be read in their original and very few people read Sanskrit. But I would like to see a situation where in the West we at least spend 50 percent of our curriculum on non-Western materials, and then in the non-West a world curriculum is developed.

RG Following on from the 2005 Singapore Performance Studies Conference's focus on g/localization, what do you see as the opportunities and the threats for performance in today's globalized world?

RS I don't know, you want me to talk about what I don't want to talk about, because this is all futurology, and I really distrust futurology. I think people blather about the long-term future but have very little control about it. Once Marx's dictatorship of the proletariat went belly-up, I have very little faith in long-term futurology.

As to the global threats and opportunities, I think we have to act as decent human beings to each other and have to be careful about both the unjust exercise of power and, equally, about hypocritical masking of power.

RG In a similar political line: if one was to construct an archive, a resource centre, something of real practical educational use to scholars and practitioners of performance, what should such a resource contain?

RS Well, a horizontal and vertical database of performance genres. So let's say a vertical database would be to take the Stanislavski system and branch through film and writing and pictures ranging from Stanislavski's own performances through to the performances of his studio, Meyerhold as one branch etc., branching right on through to film realism and contemporary realism. And then certain further branches onto Stanislavskianism as practised in Asia, Stanislavskianism as practised in Europe, in Africa. And then also a vertical branch for Brecht and epic theatre and so on. And so through branches of world genres one would, for example, branch through Sarugaku to Noh, to Mishima's versions of Noh. It would have to be a vast, vast library of all the performances that one can imagine, from all the cultures one can imagine, cross-referenced and represented both through primary data – that is, film and video-recording of the actual events and documentary – as well as analysis. Then I would like to see a specialized library of associated disciplines: ethnology for example, or psychodrama – aspects of the various social sciences and hard sciences that have something to say to, or about, performance. This would also be vast, and need extensive cross-referencing so that for example Eckman and Friesan's *Unmasking the Face: A Guide to Recognizing Emotions from Facial Expressions* is cross-referenced with *Kathakali* and other forms that control the face, and then also with masks that 'do' the face. It would be a vast, vast undertaking because it would have at its core aesthetic and ritual performances and then radiate out to include, for example, a whole archive on performances in everyday life and so forth. An enormous undertaking – years and years of work.

RG So finally, in the spirit of a long-running BBC radio programme, *Desert Island Discs*, I am going to send you alone to a deserted island. In the radio programme, the soon-to-be castaway is given the Bible and the complete works of Shakespeare to take with them and are allowed to choose one other book, one of their eight pieces of music and one luxury item that they can also take with them.

RS I'm not too eager to have Shakespeare or the Bible. Can I substitute?

RG On *Desert Island Discs* you can't. No one ever questions about having the Bible! But yes, you may – just this once.

RS Well, probably I would take the collected works of Plato and the *Mahabharata*. Well, for the luxury I would like to have a masseuse. I love a massage, and if she'd also be a chess player, that would be fabulous, so a high-level chess-playing masseuse.

RG That might be fine in your desire and in your rehearsal, but in actuality you are going to be alone without any Person Thursday. So next I will allow you five theatre experiences to take with you.

RS I would take groups rather than performances. I would take Forced Entertainment, I would take Saint Martins of the Field Baroque Orchestra, so that they could play me Baroque music, endlessly – I would love that. I would take the Grand Kabuki Theatre. I would take the complete repertory of Meyerhold. And I'd probably take the Berliner Ensemble.

RG What if you had to say which were the five performances that you've seen, that have marked you and changed you, really illuminated your thinking?

RS Well, illuminated and marked and changed are different matters. Certainly *Acropolis*.

I can't decide between an afternoon – an evening of Noh or an evening of Kabuki, one of the two. [pause] This is a tough question. [pause] Also, Helene Weigel in *Coriolanus* with the Berliner Ensemble. Also – I can't be specific about it – but certainly one of the great anti-war or Civil Rights Movement marches of the sixties, for example, the march on the Pentagon in 1970. Another one would be *Einstein on the Beach* by Robert Wilson, though maybe it could have also have been *Deaf Man Glance*, which was his earlier piece: the extension in time, slow-motion pieces. There was a new, a new kind of aesthetic that I hadn't seen before. Well, in terms of affecting me – this is a kind of a bizarre one – also there was a performance of *Carousel* by The Neptune Music Circus when I was sixteen or seventeen years old, because I fell in love with theatre having seen that. It probably was a very bad performance, but it was summer theatre, and I started to work backstage there as a volunteer. So it was my first real experience and involvement in the theatre. It was somewhere between a circus and a performance and had a big effect on me because it drew me into the theatre, as a concrete, physical thing.

REFERENCES

Auslander, Philip (1999) *Liveness: Performance in a Mediatized Culture*, New York: Taylor & Francis.

Austin, J. L. (1962) *How to Do Things with Words*, Cambridge: Harvard University Press.

Conrad, Joseph (1990) *The Nigger of the Narcissus*, London: Penguin.

Fei, Faye Chunfang (ed. and trans.) (1999) *Chinese Theories of Theatre and Performance from Confucius to the Present*, Ann Arbor: University of Michigan Press.

Goffman, Erving (1959) *The Presentation of Self in Everyday Life*, Garden City, New York: Doubleday.

Schechner, Richard (1973) *Environmental Theatre*, New York: Hawthorne Books.

Schechner, Richard (1985) 'Restoration of Behavior' in *Between Theater and Anthropology*, Philadelphia: University of Pennsylvania Press.

Schechner, Richard (1998) 'What is Performance Studies Anyway?' in Peggy Phelan and Jill Lane (eds.) *The Ends of Performance*, New York: New York University Press.

Schechner, Richard (2002) *Performance Studies: An Introduction*, London and New York: Routledge.

3. Evidence of the Past

For the record, and with the benefit of hindsight

From the Laboratory to the Centre:
History, Training, the Academy and the Book

Daniel Watt: If we can cover the establishment of Cardiff Laboratory Theatre, your early involvement and continued work through the 1980s first, before moving on to the formation of Centre for Performance Research in the 1990s up to the present. You joined Cardiff Laboratory Theatre early on, fresh from school. What was it that attracted you to the group and the type of performance work that they offered?

Richard Gough: The question assumes that something existed and the fascinating thing, thinking back about that very early phase, is not so much that there was a group to join, rather that there was something in the mix, and something happening and people making work that I wanted to be a part of. And that was very much focused around the vision and charisma of Mike Pearson. I suppose I have to go back into school to trace my own interests, because in terms of my upbringing and my family there wasn't really much introduction to the arts or theatre at all, but somehow, at school, I got very fascinated in the process of the school play. So even in the fourth or fifth form I was helping backstage and felt the buzz, the excitement of making work, yet for some reason when I reached the sixth form the school play wasn't going to happen. I can't remember the details. But I and a few schoolmates staged, independently, a

production of Harold Pinter's *The Birthday Party*, and it was fascinating in the response it caused and in the way that we did it, without any schoolteacher involved. It was an act of rebellion in many ways. It was all part of a much larger organization that I'd set up called The Spyder Arts Movement, which organized, amongst other things, trips to Cardiff to see Moving Being. And we organized thematic evenings that looked at the Beat Generation, and we brought in the films and the records of Burroughs speaking.

The year before I was to leave school, Cardiff hosted the Student Drama Festival at The Sherman Theatre. It inaugurated the theatre. At that point I was thinking of myself as someone who wanted to be a theatre director. I had absolutely no interest in, and was actually very nervous about being a performer and wanted to be a director. I was fascinated with Beckett and Pinter. These were the authors that as a kid I was just reading endlessly. I knew that I wanted to go on, probably to Manchester University to study drama, but I saw three productions at that student drama festival that probably changed my life. One was a production by a Polish student company from Jagiellonian University: Teatr Pleonazmus. The title of the piece was *One Fire Engine would not be Enough*, and it was an entirely physical production, and I later learned that this was a very seminal production within the student

Heart of the Mirror, *1983*

work in Poland, and some of the people of Akademia Ruchu and Theatre 77 were part of that company. I then saw a show by a group called Ritual Theatre, which was a group of musicians and performers. And the third production I saw was called *Time of the Season*, which was directed by Mike Pearson from Llanover Hall Experimental Youth Theatre Club.

I was offered a place to study drama at Manchester University but decided to take a year out partly because I wanted to find out more about theatre. That summer I took part in *Summer Thing* at Llanover Hall, which was a two-week summer school. Llanover Hall was a fascinating place in Cardiff, very close to Chapter Arts Centre, then funded by the County Council, running courses in the arts for anyone between 16 and 21. This summer school was an extraordinary opportunity to work with John White on an experimental music programme. Then a one-week project with Mike Pearson. So that's when I finally got to meet Mike. I kept seeing him, and his gang, sort of hovering around the Sherman Theatre, but I finally got to meet them and work with them in the summer of 1974. So I knew then I would be spending more time in Cardiff, and I basically joined the gang.

The one piece that's missing in my remembering of the history, as I didn't see it, is *Abelard and Heloise*, which Mike made in early '74 with Siân Thomas, Maria Daly and Dave Baird. By that summer Mike gave me the manifesto of Cardiff Laboratory Theatre, which is what's published in *Glimpses of the Map*.[2] I remember reading it and thinking: 'That's amazing, I'd like to be a part of that'. I imagined a place that seemed to be described in this manifesto. I imagined this centre where there was a rehearsal studio and a wonderful library and all these extraordinary facilities. I imagined a darkroom and a small cinema for screening films. Of course none of it existed. I think later that summer I was finally taken to 127 Claude Road, which is where Mike lived in a top floor flat sharing with Steve Allison, and that was it. That was Cardiff Laboratory for Theatrical Research. There was no library, no studio, nothing. I've often wondered about how much of what I've done over that last 30 years has tried to bring to reality what I'd imagined; this thing that never was but had been proposed by Mike.

So there were a number of us - Dave, Siân, Maria, Brynley Goulding, John Anzani. These are all the original members of the Llanover Hall group, and then Mike effectively creamed off some of those people to be the founder members of Cardiff Laboratory for Theatrical Research as it was originally called. The first project I participated in was in autumn 1974. I followed the rehearsal of a piece based on the *Rime of the Ancient Mariner*, which at that point was their third production:

PHOTO: PAUL TURNER

Mike Pearson and Richard Gough – Death of a Naturalist, 1977

Abelard and Heloise, Lesson of Anatomy and then *Mariner*. So I sat in the corner and was just a young kid, runner, gopher and helped build the set. I just hung around and watched the rehearsals in Chapter and got really attached to the company and struck up a really good friendship with Mike. This was at the time when Mike was really working with Dave Baird and Dek Leverton. Siân was still at school in her final year. So it was the three men mainly. It was a fascinating piece, which introduced me to all sorts of concepts that I'd never really thought about. They were using Meyerhold's concept of the *Cabotin*.[3] So that was my initial introduction to Meyerhold. They were struggling a little with some of Meyerhold's concepts and trying to get their bodies around biomechanics; all things that very much fired me in those early years and that I was going to pursue later on. As a company Cardiff Lab really only came together for six weeks at a time and then dispersed.

It is perhaps significant that around that time I followed an extramural class organized by David Hurn, the famous Magnum photographer, who was then setting

The Origin of Table Manners (*First Version*), 1985

up the documentary photography course at Newport College of Art. He did a fifteen-week course in twentieth-century photographers, and to witness such work had a big influence on me during that period. Gradually Mike and I just used to hang around, spending a lot of time together. I learned a great deal from Mike just reminiscing about RAT Theatre (Ritual And Tribal theatre).

I got involved as a performer in a project Mike and I made called *Gorboduc*. We moved from project to project. I suppose based on your question: what was the attraction, the attraction was both an alternative vision of what theatre is, but also how it could be made and how it might function. It was a sense of wanting to be part of a gang, a group. I say that very much in the sense of growing up in the sixties and seventies with The Rolling Stones and The Beatles and a desire to be part of a group, who were rather odd, rebellious, not fitting in, doing things in a slightly different way and determining their own work and having a sense of ownership over their own work. The 'gang' were not in any way interested in conventional theatre, which in many ways was a bit of a tension for me because I kept thinking: 'No, I really ought to be moving on now, to take up that place at Manchester'. I delayed it another year. I think I delayed Manchester two years, or even three years running, until I never actually went.

In 1976 Mike and Siân went over to Denmark and met up with Eugenio Barba and Odin Teatret, which was to have a big influence on me but was first brokered by Mike. I didn't know anything about this man, or this company, in Denmark. Mike and Siân were subsequently invited to Belgrade for the first gathering of Third Theatre companies. Then we all went to the second gathering in Bergamo. But by that time I had actually begun some of my own work separate from Mike. What Mike was really

good and encouraging about was creating structure. We used to call Cardiff Laboratory Theatre an umbrella organization, and it really was, because the structure allowed me to make some projects of my own. In 1976 I formed a little group, which was actually friends of mine from school: John Hardy, a musician, and Gerry Pyves, who were both at Oxford by that summer, to make another production, *Kaos*, with a group, Wraecca's Vision, that was a subset within Cardiff Lab.

Where my own work really took off is in the *Guizer Project*, and particularly the production *Shadowlands*, which is quite well documented in the Guizer book, a photographic record of that project. [4] I staged a series of special events – one-off, usually site-specific performances. I think Mike would give me credit for actually coming up with this idea of what became quite common currency within Cardiff Lab, but in those days it was quite new. Mike had worked on the well-rehearsed experimental piece that was rehearsed over five or six weeks. What I began to introduce was a notion of 'fast' theatre, site-specific work using particular buildings in Cardiff and then putting the audience on busses and taking them to other sites. I don't know quite where the idea came from. I think it may have been from reading TDR, from Meredith Monk certainly and from the early productions of Robert Wilson. I just got very excited by the idea of taking the audience on a journey, literally. Mike gave me permission to do that and then also participated in some of the productions.

DW: There were some fairly critical moments in CLT's evolution: the split with Mike Pearson following the Odin visit and the difficulties concerning *The Heart of the Mirror*. In terms of the development of the company, these seem to have been quite fruitful reorientations enabling the development of new interests and new members whilst still retaining contact with those who'd left. Can you outline the most important moments in CLT's development and those crisis points that seemed most critical to you?

RG: I think the notion of a split was much stronger in other people's minds than it was in ours. Exactly what I've just described, we were more like a grouping – and there's a negative side to this. If you trace through that whole 1973 to 1980, those seven years, there were probably very few pieces that were co-authored. I will talk about *Heart of the Mirror* in a moment as a significant failure – and I use that word in a qualified sense – but the piece that was a milestone, which Mike and I did collaborate on, was *Moths in Amber*, which was the piece we made in 1978. I think in retrospect that it was probably quite a remarkable production. It probably could have toured a lot more extensively than we were interested or able to do. I remember Mike and I met Yoshi Oida, the famous Japanese performer who had worked with Peter Brook, who had seen the piece in Rennes (Brittany) and was interested in why we weren't performing it. He thought it was one of the most remarkable pieces he'd seen. We did perform it quite extensively, and it brought Mike and Siân and myself together. I'm struggling to think of what else did that.

I suppose I was more ambitious in the sense of wanting to get funding and wanting to employ people and have an administrator. So I pushed for that, appointing the first administrator and having that first prospectus with all the photographs and different project outlines. Those were all quantum leaps for the company. I remember feeling that I was pushing to achieve that. So in that sense there were some tensions. I must say I was really fascinated with what I encountered at Bergamo when we went and met the other groups: to realize there were like-minded groups working all over Europe and beyond with whom we could have connections and exchanges. This suddenly completely fired me. So I was very committed to seeing if we could host them, to see if we could present their work. I was also very committed to getting a space, feeling that we were three years old and still hadn't got any base. We hadn't got a studio, so I persuaded Chapter, Cardiff's independent Art Centre occupying an old Edwardian school, to acquire the Gym, which was never originally let to Chapter. We got it off the County Council.

We were very fortunate with having Gilly Adams as the Director of the Drama Department of the Welsh Arts Council. Gilly had followed my, and Mike's, work a great deal and had been a huge supporter and was very affected by and touched by the Odin in Wales project. For her, that was another major watershed in the history of our work in terms of hosting that project, what it revealed about performance in Wales and the possibilities and vision of

The Orchestra, *Madrid, 1983*

Postcards in a Glass Court, *1980*

another sort of theatre. What was very fortunate was that Mike and I were able to negotiate a way of continuing the projects without having to scramble over the same funding.

Many thanks are due to Gilly for her support of our work, and at the same time she also encouraged Mike to start Brith Gof. What made things a little easier is that Mike chose to move here, to Aberystwyth. It was tough in 1980. A whole number of possibilities were landing our way in terms of what we could achieve. We had been based for two years at Chapter Arts Centre. We'd just delivered a major project. The Odin in Wales project was a big project to manage both financially and legally, administratively and organizationally and the way it functioned in different parts of Wales and the hundreds of people involved in one way or another. So it was a big project and Mike by that point was wondering where the place for our own work was? There was a danger of Cardiff Laboratory Theatre becoming this huge organization and servicing the world. In some ways he was right to have those concerns.

He wanted to focus on his own creative work. So he struck out for that, and we agreed to part. There was a sort of moment at the end of the Odin in Wales project where it was grim, in the sense that it was a massive project to achieve, and I was the organizer of it, but Mike was wanting to work on his own work and not be that involved. There was a moment of friction, distance and dislocation, but it was probably only a few months. Within months we were talking again. For me it's funny how people perceive it as some major split. I don't know how Mike feels, but it didn't feel like that from the inside. It didn't feel that significant.

I was 'under the influence' of Barba and the Odin theatre in many ways, yet even right from the beginning I was not wanting to follow their aesthetic. I wanted to

see if we could achieve the sense of a group, but a group of individuals. I didn't want a sort of wholly harmonized ensemble. I really wanted to push that individuality within the group further. Of course as soon as you do that it becomes a minefield. In that way it is easier to have a common language, a common technique, a common training, a common ethos, but that didn't seem appropriate to me by the early 80s. Already there were other political issues that had to be addressed. In 1979 Thatcher was voted in, 1980-81 was when Thatcher decimated the Arts through her policies. So things were changing, it was a very odd time to be establishing an ensemble, against all odds in many ways but in six months Siân and I did put together a group.

Having within the company two people that were accomplished musicians was really significant. Both John Hardy and Simon Thorne were trained as composers, both went to Oxford, both were very concerned with the performance of music and the theatrical side of instrumental music. They were also engaged with contemporary music. They were very open and gifted musicians who were able to teach some of us who weren't gifted musicians at all. Also the voice, working on singing, all these practices and techniques came into the mix. That's when we brought in a tremendous number of teachers. We really began to organize through that process an autodidactic programme and on the back of that began to organize a public programme of work. I've often said when people ask, 'Well, why did you start organizing these workshop training programmes?', well, it was very selfish, because I wanted training. I hadn't had any training. Most of the people who were working with us weren't trained, or hadn't gone through any conventional training. We effectively constructed our own programme around that time and then began to do special events.

We were gaining quite a name for ourselves by creating special events, doing extraordinary installation and site-specific work: Lake Bracciano near Rome, Blaenau Ffestiniog in Wales. We really were working very intensively creating a tremendous amount of work. When we write up the chronology and the history it is this that will figure more than the formal pieces that we made. Across those four years we actually only made four formal productions: *The Orchestra*, which was a wonderful outdoor event, *The Wedding*, *Heart of the Mirror* and the *Dragon Procession*.

The Wedding was actually thrown together. I remember a Timeout critic described it as a 'wonderful greasy salad'. I recall we paused in the making *Heart of the Mirror*, and in that pause we made this piece. It was like everything was the opposite of *Heart of the Mirror*. It was free, creative and joyful. Whilst at that point I felt I had got really good at being able to deliver quite complex special events, working with a team, taking everyone's ideas, scripting a piece and delivering projects in Leicester, Rome, Madrid, Santarcangelo, the thing I was really struggling with was the production *Heart of the Mirror*. It was almost as if the desire to create the masterpiece was haunting me. I knew I had to make something that was serious and would put us on the map. It was fine to do all these special events and to be fêted and regarded as a great thing in terms of all these extraordinary and unusual site-specific pieces we were making. For me it had to be the equivalent of Odin theatre's *Ashes of Brecht* or *Min Fars Haus*, which were their 'serious' pieces alongside their other more comedic pieces like *The Million*. In my own thinking *The Wedding* was a bit like how *The Million* was to Odin Teatret in 1980. I wanted *Heart of the Mirror* to be a bit like *Ashes of Brecht*. But it was beyond me in an interesting way.

As a vehicle it was overloaded, overburdened by our enthusiasms and our concerns to create a piece that spoke volumes. It really was a case that less would have been more. But we really wanted to do more. I couldn't complete it, and then Joan Mills came in during the second phase. It did actually tour - it was one of the first pieces to appear at the London International Festival of Theatre (LIFT) - and it toured abroad. It was a monster of a thing, physically, as well. Just in terms of the size of the set. It was a big construction. It never quite coalesced. It never quite found a synthesis. It remained fragmented. It was a struggle, and people struggled with it. Joan tried her best to try and bring it together. But that had problems too. By that time we were a group, and Joan felt that she was brought in from the outside and felt like 'an outsider.' We were experimental theatre artists, and that created another set of problems because in some ways Joan was coming in with a much stronger sense of dramatic and narrative construction. We're very indebted to what Joan did on that part of the process, even though it did create a whole other set of tensions.

We were touring extensively – Spain one week, Norway the next, back into France, to Sweden, across to Denmark. As a company it was tough. So those tensions were beginning to come in, linked to the burden of literally carrying this show around and yet having these pieces that were actually quite joyful. There was a mixture of shifts within social and everyday life and company aspiration that then saw another split. Again I don't see that as entirely negative. Schechner uses the phrase schismogenesis (originally used by Gregory Bateson to describe how life evolves through splitting apart) to describe the New York scene when his Performance Garage split and became The Wooster Group, and out

The Orchestra, *Madrid, 1983*

of The Wooster Group different companies emerged. So Schechner has used the term, schismogenesis as a way to describe evolution in the development of the New York companies. I think that was very true for us. The funny thing is that because our role model was the Odin theatre, it felt like to split was awful. It felt like to split was to fail. I had already moved on and no longer thought that the Odin model was apposite or appropriate to the mid-80s. So for me as long as there were still meaningful relationships – that I could still work with Siân, I could still work with Philip, and I did – it didn't matter that the notion of the ensemble split.

DW: What were the circumstances of CLT's final demise? And was the resurrection of CLT as CPR a pragmatic necessity or was it really the realization of a more educative aspect of CLT's work that had been integral from its inception? Can you identify particular differences in CPR's goals from those of CLT, because you still continued, as a smaller group, to present performance work regularly until the mid-1990s?

RG: Technically, what finally happened was that our activities as an organizer, as an impresario really, were getting ever more ambitious. We did various projects, one of which was that Jill and Judie produced the inaugural *Magdalena Project* and festival in 1986. The other big project we did, in the autumn of that year was *Peking Opera Explorations* and brought over an entire troupe from Peking. In 1987 we were even more ambitious, and we organized a four-month-long European tour of a seventy-strong troupe from Shanghai – the Kunju style of Chinese Opera – with the production of *Macbeth* along with *Peony Pavilion* and other shorter pieces.

Effectively we went insolvent after this project that, in many ways, was hugely successful. *Peony Pavilion* and

Macbeth opened in August at the Edinburgh Festival and then continued to tour around the UK, Sweden and Denmark, and we were still hosting and producing up until the end of November, concluding at the Belfast Festival. In the middle two weeks of November we co-produced with Sadlers Wells, renting the London Palladium on a commercial basis as a conventional impressario. There was a point at the end of the first week when we realized we were in serious financial difficulty. There was actually no hope, unless it improved that night (drastically, by about a thousand people). There was no way it could recover.

What does one do at this point? Technically, I knew enough as an administrator to know that at the moment you are aware you are trading insolvently, you have to declare yourself insolvent and take measures so that you're not worsening the loss, because if you don't then you become personally liable. Cardiff Laboratory was a limited company, limited by guarantee. If you trade knowingly improperly, then all those protections lift. So we went to see a major, multi-national, firm of insolvency practitioners. They were fascinated by our case, because they had never done anything like this - insolvency impinging on a cultural exchange project. We actually convinced them, which was contrary to all usual notions of insolvency practice, that we should complete the show - at the moment you reach crisis usually you should suspend activity. But we actually pointed out that it was in our creditors' interests to complete the two weeks at the London Palladium and to actually go on and do the week in Belfast. In other words to continue trading for two more weeks, because we would then be able to get the seventy-strong company out of the country and earn more money from Belfast.

It was a very complicated deal that Judie and I did, and it took some convincing. The Chinese troupe and tour managers never knew the extent of the difficulty we were in. They knew that there was a smaller audience in London than there should have been, but they got paid fully. They got all their honorariums, and we got both them out, which was the big worry, and their five tonnes of equipment out of the country. My major concern was that the whole thing would suddenly unravel and fall apart. It was a fascinating period, and our insolvency practitioner had a very good bedside manner encouraging us to work again to build up another company.

So by January 1988 we were starting again with the Centre for Performance Research. We did take it as an opportunity. What marks a difference here is that those activities that had, up to that point, perhaps been regarded as marginal became more central. So all the work that led to that insolvency - which was being a

Caroline Lynch-Blosse and Siân Thomas, Epiphanies, *Leckwith Church, Penarth, 1978*

producer, an impresario, an organizer - but was regarded as being on the outside of the work, then shifted to being the centre of our work. The other thing that marks this is that it was then truly a partnership between Judie and myself, from that point on. You'd think it would be the other way, that after being stung so badly, we would then never want to produce work again. But on the contrary we thought we'd get back into the car and drive again. So one of the first things we did in 1988, the launch project, was the conference on Theatre, Anthropology and Theatre Anthropology. That's when we began to organize that series of Points of Contact, which has influenced the development of Performance Studies. So there was a marked shift there. I should say that even in that final phase of Cardiff Laboratory Theatre we were making work. It was like a third generation. If you regard the first generation as being Mike and Dave, Dek, Siân, Maria and latterly me, the second generation was Jill, Melanie, Helen and Simon, John and Philip and of course Siân and me . The third generation was another group of people: Jim Ennis, Chris Marshall, Tracy Gilman, Sally

Jim Ennis, Andrzej Borkowski and Richard Gough – From Honey to Ashes
(First Version), *1986*

Melissa Thompson: You have said that the devising work with Cardiff Lab was experimental in the truest sense of the word, meaning that when you have experiments, some of them are going to fail. What is experimenting and failing? I was wondering if you could talk a little bit about that in terms of its importance in devised performance and performer training?

RG: When I was talking then about trial and error and learning through trying and learning through failing, sometimes some of the exercises we did and some of the projects we did, we learned the most from the things that went wrong. Luckily, nothing went so disastrously wrong that someone broke a leg or anything, but sometimes things did go wrong.

It was very much an attempt at play, really, and in some ways it had the quality of play in the sense of children playing in the laboratory, in the playground, and some things worked. From those very open experiments, some exercises, some compositional approaches simply gelled and functioned. Often one of us was standing out watching what the other three or the other two were doing, so even though there wasn't a director as such amongst us, there was often one of us witnessing the work that took place.

But there are a couple of things there. I remember Grotowski wrote, in *Towards a Poor Theatre*, about the Niels Bohr Institute in Denmark and the foundation of a method of investigation and the 'collective memory' of the Institute. We often use to say as an experimental theatre we must have the right to fail – not an easy thing to say to one's funders or supporters. But I think one of the problems of so-called experimental theatre is that it's almost expected that every experiment should succeed. I think it was Beckett that said, 'Fail again, fail better', and through those failures learn more. We clearly held that close to heart, but we also practised the true sense of experiment in those early days. We had a studio. We had a space. We were paid very little, sometimes not paid at all. But we had the curiosity and the willingness to try and see what could be made with very little resources.

I think there is also something experimental about misunderstanding, too, in a way that misunderstanding can be very creative. I think we often misunderstood some of the exercises that we read about in TDR, or some in of the early books that appeared in the early 1970s, in Joe Chaikin's exercises or Barba's exercises. We would read these and try and do them. Now, obviously if you try and do an exercise from a book, it's very different from being taught it by a living practitioner or a master. The lineage is broken in some ways, and the opportunities for mistakes are great, numerous and rather wonderful. And I think

Thompson and we made *The Origin of Table Manners* it's fascinating because it has the exact same parallel with *The Wedding* - *The Origin of Table Manners* was a hugely successful piece and a joy to make; as a director I felt really in control and creative. Then came the piece that was hugely problematic: *The Burning of the Dancers* the flawed masterpiece, a companion and compatriot of *The Heart of the Mirror.*

That moves us on a little bit. In terms of your question about the educational aspect, well, Judie and I have often talked about the significance in the simple shift in name. Once we became the Centre for Performance Research, it sort of fore-grounded the educational and academic, perhaps in ways that we didn't always intend it to. When we arrived at the formulation of a centre for performance research, it was nothing to do with the academy in the sense of a university research centre. Performance research seemed to sum us up, but it wasn't actually until many years later that I came into contact with what research meant from a university perspective.

«»

that there's also something quite experimental and playful in that approach to trying. To elaborate methods and systems from a real blend of starting points.

I remember one year when I read the entire *TDR [The Drama Review]*, from the early *Tulane Drama Review* days when Richard Schechner was first editing it through the whole Michael Kirby editorship. The Cardiff University Library had a complete set. There was very little material I could find at that point, say in 1975, apart from *TDR*. There were a few books on non-Western theatre, whether it's Indian Dance or Kabuki theatre or the Chinese Opera, and there were a few books on the American theatre of the 1960s and 1970s that were emerging. But that avid reading of all this material was an extraordinary course, a foundation course that I put myself through. In a funny way, the construction of the CPR library and Resource Centre is an attempt to continue that project that probably began in 1975 - that yearning, that desire to have access to material that wasn't just the plays of Shakespeare or the plays of Beckett or the plays of Pinter, to actually try and get access to information on theatre, on the making of theatre, the process of theatre, the theory and the cultural theories attached to and surrounding theatre. That's really what I was yearning for and needing at that point - and found to some extent.

And it is very interesting how that in-depth reading of all the issues of *TDR* had a big influence on me. It was the practices of some of the experimentalists in New York, Mabou Mines, Squat, Robert Wilson or Meredith Monk, that were being written about at that time. It was those new discoveries that influenced me greatly. I think it's very fascinating to try and unravel how the readings of those works that we never saw, or never had the opportunity to see, fired our own imagination. So I

never saw that early work of Meredith Monk, and yet I think that had a very big influence on me in the sense of beginning to think about staging journeys, literal journeys, taking the audience literally on a journey, out of the theatre into the streets of Cardiff to unusual or unused or disused buildings. That was very much inspired by not only reading about Meredith Monk but other projects happening in the States at that time. So, experiment also comes from influence via other sources. The desire to experiment in that way was propelled by the reading.

MT: So even reading things like *TDR*, which is much more academic rather than practical - it is not a collection of exercises that people write in to *TDR* every issue - even that can translate into or be translated into what you did practically in the studio?

RG: Yes, absolutely. Also I do remember there was Mel Gordon's article on Meyerhold's biomechanics[5] and the description of the Living Theater's work,[6] and they really did describe the exercises. And I do remember working for weeks on that set of exercises as described in the *TDR*, to try and manifest, to make real, to embody them, working from the page into action. So I think I'm suggesting that there were two things. There were very real descriptions of exercises that we attempted to do from the text, and yet in doing probably made some creative misunderstandings - in other words created other exercises. And then there were descriptions of events, projects, happenings, that were truly inspirational but inspirational in a very active sense, as I've said, in compelling us, propelling us to try and stage something that followed that line of experiment.

Chris Rowbury and Joe James - From Honey to Ashes *(Second Version), Warsaw, 1992*

The Widow's Dream, *Llechwedd Slate Caverns, Blaenau Ffestiniog, 1981*

PHOTO: PAUL ROYLANCE

MT: I think it's a really intriguing juxtaposition between what happens when you try to earnestly reproduce something – you know, here is this exercise and I want to do it correctly in the spirit of the way in which it is written – leading to misunderstanding and then also having the liberty to take the exercises and manipulate them or embellish them or add upon them. It seems to be an interesting mix because it seems like you don't get that too often. Either you're a theatre company in the spirit of someone else's tradition and it is passed on and you learn the correct technique, or you are saying, 'This is all our own work, and we're going to do something new'. The way that's mixed together in your work seems unusual.

RG: That is true, and in that sense we were very fickle and unfaithful and magpie-like almost. We took that from there, and this glistening jewel-like article from there, we acquired and appropriated. In one sense, we stole. In another sense, we were doing research. We were doing background reading. We were finding things. But we did concoct a peculiar mix, which on one level was a sort of goulash of different influences, but I think that did mark us out slightly differently from some of the other companies that were emerging at that time in Europe.

It was fascinating to us how some of those companies followed the training with such exactitude that it almost looked like replicas even down to the same sort of training gear that they wore, the same bright oranges and striking reds and peculiar shoes and things. But we often felt completely different, isolated as if we were out on some island, as we were in the UK. We weren't part of that mainland European approach.

MT: One of the things you've mentioned that's also been a big influence on and inspiration for your work is music. What kinds of music? And how do you think they influence your work?

RG: Well, I'm not sure how I got fascinated in this, but from the early days, and I'm thinking even before I started working with Mike, I was very interested in what since has become termed 'world music'. In those days, it wasn't categorized as such. I remember there was one particular shop in London [Collett's Record Store] that stocked a mixture of jazz, blues, and then a little section that had music from around the world, a few labels. And I became very interested in just listening to the music, and particularly the singing traditions of other cultures. So I distinctly remember on trips to London I would buy – it was a vast expenditure at that time for me – I'd buy five or six LPs, which would be an entire week's wage, and come back and just listen to this extraordinary brass band in Mexico, or yodeling not just from Switzerland but from central Africa and elsewhere, or the polyphonies of Georgia and of the Polynesian Islands. So that was a real fascination, which has continued to this day. So on the one hand, the great traditions and the varied traditions of world music, and on the other hand – and I think it probably happened because they were in Colette's Records, too – I came across a set of records called 'obscure records', which was contemporary – at that point British, but then it began to include other composers and musicians – experimental music. And again at Chapter one of the formative experiences for me was being in an audience – I think it was probably with only three other people – that I heard Gavin Bryars play 'Jesus' Blood'.

When he put on a film of a tramp walking forward, he put it in some sort of loop and then he played and augmented around this tape of a tramp singing 'Jesus' Blood', which of course has since become quite famous as he re-recorded it with Tom Waits about twelve years ago. That piece was a major influence for me, and when I finally found it on record, I probably used it so much to the point when other colleagues got sick of hearing it.

So there are these two things running, which again I think is very interesting in relation to my interest in theatre, and to some extent my interest in cuisine and cooking because there's a parallel here: on the one hand, the ancient traditions of world culture in terms of music, and on the other hand the most contemporary, experimental, minimalist music of contemporary composers. And that reflects my interest in theatre in terms of being passionately curious about world theatre and the great traditions of Indian Dance, Chinese Opera and Japanese Theatre and yet at the same time the most avant-garde, the most experimental, the most uncompromising innovative contemporary theatre. And equally in relation to food, a fascination with world cuisine, with cuisines of other cultures, with the food and techniques of other cultures, and with the most contemporary fusions, hybrids and cross-over influences of these cuisines. So there's sort of a parallel there. But the music was always a great influence.

We would start from very different sources, and a lot of my work in the early 1970s, mid-1970s, would start from an image or a piece of music, so that for example singing of the hunters in Burundi – one track of Aka Pygmies – would be how we would start a short piece or maybe a track of the Mexican brass band all completely playing out of tune with each other. Or a gypsy song from Romania would be the track that I would start, not as background music, not as muzak to improvise to, but as the starting point of an experiment that we would work on for two or three hours to make a short piece. We might never have even played the track of music in performance, so the audience may not even be aware of what was the starting point for us because we may have simply taken it in in some way, and it would have had an influence on us. Also, often images, pictures, postcards and more frequently photographs were used, as were very particular fragments of music which may be of a singing technique of world music or a contemporary piece by Gavin Bryars or Brian Eno. In those early days it was always British experimental musicians; latterly, it's become broader, and now I use North American, Estonian and Japanese composers.

«»

Daniel Lambert Special Event, *Leicester, 1981*

DW: I wanted to address some of the issues of CPR's identity and the context of academic partnership. What prompted the move to Aberystwyth? And could you talk a little about the difficulties and opportunities you had envisaged in a partnership with an academic institution and how those difficulties and opportunities have manifested themselves either as foreseen or unexpectedly?

RG: Let's begin by saying a difficulty can also be an opportunity, and an opportunity can also be a difficulty. What prompted the move was a difficulty in the first instance.

DW: A difficulty being in Cardiff?

RG: Yes, being in Cardiff, being independent and not having any form of partnership funding. At this point, and I'm talking now of 1993, 1994. One of the concerns of the Welsh Arts Council – who'd been funding us, on and off for the best part of twenty years – was partnership funding. The Arts Council were determined to see that its clients found partnership funding either through local authorities, or through other sources. Now of course for many other theatre companies, whether they were community theatre companies or theatre in education companies, the possibility of finding a partnership with county councils or educational authorities was more possible than for an experimental theatre organization.

For many years we had been realizing projects with different Higher Education institutes throughout the UK. In a way those projects reach back even into the late seventies. Certainly when CPR emerged from the ashes of CLT, one of the very first projects we staged was the first 'Points of Contact' international conference on theatre and anthropology. We staged that in conjunction with De Montfort University – Leicester Polytechnic at that point. That led to a whole series of 'Points of Contact' being staged with other institutions; 'Theatre, Nature, Culture' with Dartington College of Arts, and one of the biggest ones, 'Performance, Politics and Ideology' with Lancaster University. We enjoyed those relationships immensely and found them both challenging and stimulating in all sorts of ways, particularly the kind of intellectual dialogue we began to have with quite different partners. The kinds of conversation we had at Dartington were very different from those we had at Lancaster because of the very different research interests of the faculty. We enjoyed that aspect of collaboration, and gradually our work, and conferences, began to be attended by many more academics, representing many different theatre departments from around the UK. When we had hosted people like Grotowski and Barba, and then developed and expanded to stage projects like ISTA [International School of Theatre Anthropology], we used to get very good attendance by academics.

So over ten years, from a position of seemingly on the fringe and supposed isolation and exploring work and contacts with artists who weren't in any way the focus of most of the mainstream British theatre departments, a shift happened, and what was more peripheral and marginal became more central and thus the activities that we had pioneered to some extent, and explored, gradually became of concern and an object of study to many more theatre departments. We began to organize projects with them. For example, when we staged the ambitious project on Process and Documentation, we formed a steering committee that had representatives from the Universities of Bristol and Kent, Dartington, Leicester and several others.

We had always matched the Arts Council grant with other sources of income. That's why the Arts Council were in an interesting position with us, because we always proved that we were very efficient with their funds, and that even as an experimental theatre company we were more than doubling their grant through other earned income and the ability to attract other grants. So this was first a gentle pressure that gradually became more assertive. But the question arose whether the natural partner for us would actually be a university, an institution, rather than a city or county council. Interestingly for us, the main partners we had were not in Wales. We had very little contact with the University of Wales in Aberystwyth [UWA]. Some of the faculty there attended our conferences, but not many. Roger Owen, who we were first introduced to by Chris Cairns, who was a lecturer here, was one of the primary contacts that we had. There were a lot of complex reasons why that might have been. Partly because when Mike and I split the company back in 1980, Mike moved to Aberystwyth, and so we respected that Aberystwyth was the territory, for want of a better word, of Brith Gof and Mike's work. We tended not to try and encroach upon that area. Actually, at that point, very few of the staff and faculty from Aberystwyth seemed to be interested in the areas that many of the departments in the UK had become interested in. So for a little while we had some extensive discussions with Lancaster University to see if we might make some form of move from Cardiff to Lancaster, then, more interesting to us because of its location and proximity, with Bristol University. The 'problem' is that they are all in England, and we'd had long-standing connections with Dartington and Leicester, but all of them are across the border. That presented an interesting dilemma, because in moving we would have lost our entire Welsh Arts Council grant. There could have been some similar funding from the English Arts Council, but it wouldn't have been automatic or guaranteed.

Then in 1993 and 1994 we organized some very significant tours. First Roberto Bacci's company from Pontedera, in Cardiff, Aberystwyth and Bangor. Again, through Chris Cairns, in Aberystwyth we organized a seminar, and in Bangor a whole series of workshops, training and director's talks. In 1994 we organized the tour of Enrique Vargas's *Ariadne's Thread - The Labyrinth* (Taller Imagen, Bogota), which had a huge success in Aberystwyth, and this brought us more into contact with the department and with the head of department, Ioan Williams. Around that time I was invited to give the keynote to the Standing Conference of University Drama Departments [SCUDD]. That's when I first met Ioan and had a long discussion with him. At that time I was teaching at Royal Holloway – a course in Indian Dance Theatre and aesthetics – and Ioan asked why I was going all the way to London, why wasn't I having more contact with Aberystwyth. The answer was very simple: we hadn't been invited. Ioan moved very fast on that. A discussion opened as to whether CPR would move.

Tracie Gillman and Phillip Mackenzie - The Funeral, 1984

Initially it was collaboration with University of Wales College Aberystwyth, and our first thought was that there might be a way of remaining in Cardiff in association with UWA through the Federal University of Wales (which was also based in Cardiff). At that point we hadn't envisaged a move, lock stock and barrel, from Cardiff to Aberystwyth. As negotiations progressed, it became obvious that to do the things that Ioan wanted, which was to participate in and nurture the research culture in the department, we needed to be here. They made certain offers and proposals, which we then had to discuss with the Welsh Arts Council because they were quite nervous about a client becoming a part of a university and then their funding being absorbed by the university.

So we had to think very carefully about the formation of a legal structure that would allow the Centre for Performance Research Ltd, the educational charity that Judie and I had formed, to continue to exist and for a new venture to be formed. A joint venture between CPR Ltd and the University of Wales, which would allow for many of the projects to take place in Aberystwyth, was proposed. From the outset we made it clear to UWA that we wanted the work to be located in other parts of Wales and for us to be free to collaborate with other

universities, which has happened. We've done projects with the Universities of Birmingham, Roehampton and have continued a relationship with the Royal College of Music and Drama in Cardiff.

So those were the circumstances, partly driven by funding but also by a development in our work, which had brought us closer to the concerns of the academy and the production of new knowledge and practice. So the very nature of our work, within a frame of twenty years from say 1974-75 through to 1994-95 had shifted from being right at the peripheral or marginal to not necessarily becoming central but certainly closer to the centre. So it was the confluence of these different demands and interests that gave rise to the move.

Perhaps I should add that there were things we had done right from the beginning, in terms of publishing a journal and teaching, and if we take Maskarade as our first journal, for example, you'll see that we had articles by Brook, Barba, Grotowski, Kantor.[7] When I look back on that, I think it is quite remarkable that at that point those figures were not part of theatre studies in the UK. We were endeavouring to publish a journal that contained those practitioners and theorists, and those interests and the accumulation of our library, the resource centre, were

Ma Mingquin teaches the initial steps of Peking Opera, Cardiff, 1996

all part of that strategy. Those activities, which we had started in the mid-1970s showed an interest in forming a sort of alternative academy that was very much driven by a sense of auto-didacticism and an alternative curriculum and self-determined programmes of education. So that was all part of our work which was, in the 1970s, at odds with the spirit of the times, the temper of the times. But which, over twenty years, had become much more central to it. By the early 1990s we had published, and I had edited, *The Dictionary of Theatre Anthropology* by Eugenio Barba and Nicola Savarese. So we had already entered into a field of academic publishing that had made us quite interesting to a number of institutions. We clearly had other ambitions. For us it wasn't being driven at all by a research imperative in the sense of the British University Research Assessment Exercise, which is something we had no idea about. We were innocently naïve of it in the early 1990s. We weren't doing the work because of that. But others felt the work of interest because of it.

DW: But what exactly was it that attracted you to a partnership with a university, beyond consolidating those things you've already discussed – the library and those facets that were already in existence. What were your original thoughts of the excitement of the project?

RG: Whilst we felt very connected with a network of theatre companies, artist, directors and thinkers, around the world and particularly in Europe, we did feel very isolated from the academy with regard to the UK. I do remember, in the late 1970s and early 1980s in many of our travels to Denmark and Italy, often feeling very envious of what I saw. This may be through rose-tinted glasses or a certain naivety, but I felt there was a group of scholars, in Italy for example, who were following the work. I can think of Franco Ruffini and Ferdinando Taviaini, Nicola Savarese, Fabrizio Cruciani, a whole group of them, who were writing about Eugenio's work or the work of ISTA. I saw it in Denmark, and to some extent in France. And I thought, 'We don't have that'. There were a few, key, isolated figures. Nick Sales for example, at Exeter. Even at the point we hosted Grotowski, in 1981, I remember there were very few people in Universities that we felt were allies. There was Emily Davies, from UWA. She was very significant and a great supporter of ours in the early 1970s. Sadly, she died in the mid-1980s. But it really was only a handful of people.

I know when the invitation came, and we were considering the move to Aberystwyth, one of the things I was excited about, was meeting other scholars from other departments, from Art, International Politics, from Geography and again naively thinking, 'Great, we'll be

in a situation where there are a number of thinkers, and makers, and doers who we can weave into the debate and be enriched by their presence'. That was true of what we *had* experienced. Sadly, I'm a little disappointed that we haven't tapped into that here in Aberystwyth yet. For example, when we did the project on Process and Documentation in Lancaster what was very exciting was the way in which our colleagues in Lancaster managed to involve a number of scholars from quite different areas, from Renaissance Studies, from Geography, Sociology, through to Psychiatry. They were involved in the conference. That had been the sort of stimulus, and I remember in the latter days in Cardiff we began to make contacts with Christopher Norris and people in Cardiff University pursuing Critical Theory, and we invited them. That was very enriching to have those kinds of people present putting their ideas forward, talking with us. And the sort of interdisciplinary approach that we'd encountered abroad, whether it was people like Schechner or people closer to home such as Susan Melrose. That was the hope, that it would be part of the daily mix of being in a University. It has happened in part. If I was to say what I'd like to do in the next ten years, I think I'd like to create projects here where we make greater effort to involve colleagues from other disciplines and other departments and really push that interdisciplinary enquiry a bit further.

DW: Am I right in thinking that there was no specifically performance element to the department before the arrival of CPR, because neither Mike Pearson (Brith Gof) nor Jill Greenhalgh (Magdalena Project) was here. So did that emerge from CPR's involvement?

RG: Partly. But that was also part of Ioan's vision. He was aware that developments were happening within the discipline. At that point, in 1994, I don't think there was a department in the UK that had a Performance Studies programme. He was aware that performance research, and performance studies, as a discipline was beginning to emerge. So one of the things we were partly invited to do was to nurture performance research and Performance Studies within the department. That coincided with me becoming very actively involved with PSi (Performance Studies international), the association for performance studies and then becoming the president in 1997, then hosting the secretariat of the association at Aberystwyth for three years. Heike Roms, who was at that point concluding her PhD here, became the administrator of the association (PSi) and the assistant director of *Here Be Dragons* the fifth Performance Studies international conference that we hosted and I chaired and directed.

So again there were a number of coincidences. Heike was also very keen on forming a Performance Studies reading group. She and I, and Adam Hayward – who came with us from Cardiff, as resource centre officer and archivist – began to organize that on a fairly regular basis and invited a number of people, Phil Auslander, Jatinder Verma and Peggy Phelan, for example, to come and speak. Yet, as you say, there was no Performance Studies programme at that point. Then Mike was visiting, and he was interested in seeing if he could return here and develop a distinctive 'Aberystwyth School' of performance, through collaboration and consultation with us.

Again a confluence of events: our coming here, the launch of the journal *Performance Research* in 1995, my presidency of PSi. So there were some major shifts happening that created a platform together with a constant flow of visitors from around the world, through our programmes and projects. That created both the culture and the context for the Performance Studies programme to emerge. But CPR wasn't specifically charged to do that, our remit was much broader. Mike Pearson was charged to do that. And then the programme has developed, and other appointments, Jill Greenhalgh and now Heike Roms, have been appointed to develop that and then to launch an MA in performance practice.

DW: Do you think that solidifying of performance into a facet of the department stopped the kind of interdisciplinary dialogue that you might have been hoping for from happening? In a sense, CPR could be filtered through the performance angle of the department, and so it made those interdisciplinary discourses less likely to occur. Performance seems to be a good way of generating interdisciplinary study – how performance can speak in so many ways to all these different disciplines. I do find it surprising that it hasn't happened.

RG: I suppose there is a danger in the formulation of those interests into a category and into a curriculum. Such formation can also mark the end of a movement, the demise of shifting ground – the setting of foundation stones. It is necessary, and required from the point of view of delivery of an undergraduate course, but when we return to 'was the ambition to create undergraduate course?' Well, obviously not. To some extent once we've entered into the academy there is a curious juggling act going on: on the one hand we want to create a distinctive school of performance here in Aberystwyth, but we don't want it to become fixed or dogmatic in that way. I think some of the things that interest Mike, Heike

and me create a permanent state of revolution. That it is continuously regenerating, reconsidering and rethinking itself is to some extent where I'd like to continue with it. The formulation of an undergraduate course, or even an MA, is the by-product of the main enquiry. It's not the end result.

One of the hopes, or promises, of coming into a working relationship with the university was that we would have more time to study, to enquire, to conduct experiments, to return to the notion of a foundry or laboratory. One of the hopes of coming to be part of the academy was, not that it would be safer or more protected, but that somehow there would be more infrastructure to allow the experiment to continue. That has been one of the disappointments. To deliver these programmes, even with a small MA, the work that's required to deliver them properly is quite considerable, and that doesn't leave enough time to continue what one might consider the main project – to be engaged with an emerging discipline and constant enquiry. The difficulty is trying to maintain a balance between locking down into programmes and curricula and yet also remaining a participant in the art form and the practice, and the aesthetic, and the thinking behind those practices. Again, that is both a difficulty and an opportunity.

DW: With current CPR publications exploring the future of performance both in practical terms but also as an instance of the academy, how do you see the interface with CPR's academic work developing? Is there a conscious strategy to elaborate ideas as a 'foreign body' within an institutional context? Is there an attempt to recover that initial urge or is there going to be a new direction?

RG: I think the spectrum between 'foreign body' and that term from Derrida you mentioned, 'dangerous supplement', is clearly quite extreme. Something much more subtle in the 'dangerous supplement' is more interesting. I think I would be deluding myself to think we were a foreign body, because in many ways we've become captured. I recall Julian Beck, in one of his writings on The Living Theatre, remarking that the biggest threat to revolutionary artists is containment, that his or her work would be contained or commodified. In that sense I think we are firmly part of the university and contributing to the academy, so we're not a foreign body, even though we would like to remember and have nostalgia for our 'alien' and 'other' origins. So there is that sense of having come in from the outside, but we have come in. We can though be some form of dangerous supplement, and it's interesting how we might function in that way. The interface between

The Widow's Dream – *Llechwedd Slate Caverns, Blaenau Ffestiniog, 1981*

the profession and the academy, between practice and research, I think is deeply problematic. That really is interesting in terms of the future.

DW: Do you mean how practice is made manifest within the confines of the academy, or are you looking out to what's happening in the wider environment?

RG: I think I'm at a point of confusion, but I don't see that as negative. I'm beginning to have some doubts about what is preoccupying some of us with theatre and performance, practice as research, and the current thinking that a piece of practical work can be theorized and written about after the event as part of a research output. I'm beginning to become somewhat conservative: feeling that I would prefer there to be real, hard research and real, hard practice. I think the research we've always been interested in has been a slightly different animal than that in any case. It's a different way of integrating the two, so that through practice we can be theorizing in the moment of doing. I was pleased in my recent workshop group when one person mentioned that it was like 'philosophy in action'. That through the practical work and the exercises they were being set they were invited to be creative but also to think about what was being done and the broader implications of that. That's

the sort of area of integrated practice and research that interests me. Yet I fear the academy is going in a different direction, somehow validating practice as research, in an entirely different way by 'writing it up', or even writing over, like a palimpsest, where you have the practice and the practical work and then this immense apparatus of writing that is attached to it, that is sometimes woefully inadequate in what it attempts to do.

On the other hand I'm very keen on attempting to apprehend aesthetic practice, which again I think is quite a different thing. So how do we develop the language, the methods and the thinking to describe and analyse performance practice as aesthetic practice, not the application of performance to everyday life? That for me is where the future lies, to reconfigure this relationship, in the formal sense of practice and research, not necessarily of practice as research.

I find it interesting to go back and read Grotowski's ideals for a laboratory theatre and then Mike's manifesto from 1973 of what Cardiff Laboratory for Theatrical Research actually does. There are so many aspects of that manifesto that we've come close to realizing, and yet there is still that aspect of open-ended or 'blue sky' research. That still very much interests me. A theorist doesn't have to be there just to write-up about what took place but perhaps to interject and collaborate in other

Philip Mackenzie and Melanie Thompson – The Secret of Alice: Faustus, *Trevignano, 1983*

ways. I think we're in danger of becoming very formulaic about this notion of how to validate practice as research. I'm more interested in other ways, and I do think that is something that CPR could make a greater contribution to from within the academy and especially as we are about to move into a space where we will have a studio again, a laboratory once more. We moved from Cardiff; with a wonderful studio and a terrible set of offices, so that any noise going on in the studio would always interfere with the administration. But now we have a situation where we have a suite of offices and live in wonderful isolation but have no studio, and that I think has been a major difficulty. To try to bring back those components – the administration, the research, the library and the studio/ laboratory as interconnected – would be a significant development that might allow us to develop those programmes and experiments that really push forward the enquiry into what the theorized practical experiment might be.

DW: Finally, I just wanted to discuss the nature of CPR's publishing imprint: Black Mountain Press. It was never begun as an academic publishing enterprise. Publishing seems to have been an important part of the history of the company, as both CLT and CPR.

RG: Absolutely. It indicates an interest in publishing but also the value of the book, the printed word, the text

and the image, as a correspondent to the action. I think that has remained with me right from the beginning. I don't know where this impulse to publish came from, but it was always a desire. Mike shared it too, and has continued to share a passion for writing. When it comes to having our own press, it really was a case of saying there's some wonderful material out there that simply isn't available in English, or it was published in a small run. Then there's the huge enterprise of the journal, and we're now into our thirtieth issue. It's a big enterprise and maybe some would say that's enough, but if we weren't doing the other then that couldn't happen. For me, they are two halves of the same project. They're just different expressions of it: publishing as a way of disseminating and amplifying what took place and sharing the thinking, methods and practices. For me it's a necessary part. It's not just an appendage.

DW: I think already written into the publishing projects – as we've been talking about the supplementary aspect – is that the supplement to the knowledge contained in those books is the aesthetics of the books themselves. So it's the covers of the Black Mountain Press titles, the kind of imagery and the way the journal is laid out. All those things will always elude, will always slip away from, the academy because it's about the experience of reading that can never be recovered. A lot of the books in CPR's collection are about the aesthetics of the book.

RG: Yes, the book as an object, the artefact, the book itself, its materiality. These were things that Ric, Claire and I, when we were setting up the journal, paid a lot of attention to, and thankfully Routledge provided a great original designer, Simon Josebery, who we could have that dialogue with.

Secondly, there's the notion of the book or journal as a site: a place, or foundry, or font for knowledge; that how the knowledge is constructed between the covers, and how it's arranged and organized – that curatorial process – is bringing an element of our theatre work to publishing too. So the look and feel of the cover, the quality of the paper, the design and layout of the photographs has always been crucial to us. If someone were to give us an extra £100,000 in future years, I suppose the area I would like to develop would be publishing material and texts that other publishers wouldn't necessarily touch. If we could find the distribution mechanism, I would really love to have a very small imprint that did very specialist works. That we would accept that only 500 people would be interested in that artist, but as long as it was out there that would be a very satisfying facet of our work that I hope we could continue.

ACKNOWLEDGEMENT

With thanks to Melissa Thompson for her collaboration and contribution.

NOTES

1 This is a selection of material from interviews Richard Gough gave with Daniel Watt on 14 July 2004 and 13 July 2005 and with Melissa Thompson on 24 August 2004.

2 Pearson, Mike (1979) *Cardiff Laboratory Theatre: Glimpses of the Map*, Cardiff: CLT.

3 A travelling minstrel player or storyteller.

4 Gough, Richard (1977) *Dream Train: A Photographic Record of the Guizer Project*, Cardiff: CLT.

5 Gordon, Mel (1974) 'Biomechanics', TDR 18:3 (T63): 73–88.

6 Ryan, Paul Ryder (1974) 'The Living Theatre's "Money Tower"', TDR 18:2 (T62): 9-19.

7 Gough, Richard (1977) *Maskarade, The Journal of Cardiff Laboratory Theatre.* Cardiff: CLT.

Rehearsal in progress, Blaenau Ffestiniog, 1981

PHOTO: PAUL ROYLANCE

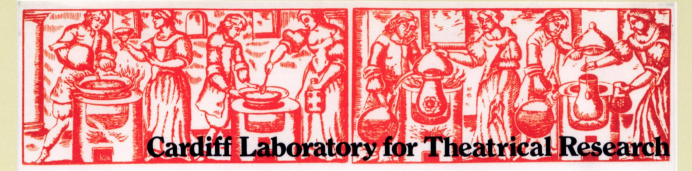

Cardiff Laboratory for Theatrical Research

THEATRE LABORATORY FIRST STATEMENT

What follows is an initial document setting out proposals for the founding of a
theatre laboratory in Cardiff. It is designed to draw essential comment, suggestions
and criticism.

The theatre laboratory will come into being early in 1974. It will function as a
body for intensive long-term research into theatrical methodology, with performance
and documentation as the application for a newly created language.

It will work essentially in the field of physical expression, developing a style
of performance which synthesises a variety of techniques into a language of bio-
energetics.

The laboratory will have a two-fold function.

Firstly, it will concentrate on research, even for the sake of research, without the
restrictions of performance dates and rehearsal schedules. A permanent performance
group will apply the fruits of research to experimental theatre pieces. Performances
may be extended over a period of time, perhaps one per week for several weeks so that
organic development may occur.

Secondly, it will have a major teaching role to make completed research more widely
available. Workshops will be arranged whenever required, preferably in a permanent
home, if the laboratory succeeds in finding one. Week-end and week-long courses will
be available in conjunction with other organisations. Thus, the research will have a
practical application in servicing the sadly neglected field of experimental theatre.

Documentation will be of the utmost importance in supplying an ideological base
for this type of work. There will be a quarterly publication of work from inside
and outside the laboratory, recording workshops, seminars, and performances and
presenting articles on methodology.

By necessity, the laboratory will be initially ephemeral, with workshops and
performances in a variety of locations. Obviously, such a venture will eventually
require a permanent home, a small plain space to fulfil the following functions:

1) Training, rehearsal and research work in a stable atmosphere.
2) Performance by members of the laboratory to small numbers of initially
   sympathetic public. These will be experimental in setting, subject matter and
   delivery.
3) Public demonstrations of technique. Regular workshops open to the public.
4) Seminars concerning the development of experimental theatre.
5) Guest performances and workshops by other groups and individuals working in
   the field of physical theatre.
6) A meeting place and forum for those concerned about the future of theatre.

Mike Pearson
October 1973

Centre For Performance Research
6 Science Park, Aberystwyth, SY23 3AH, Wales, UK
6 Parc Gwyddoniaeth, Aberystwyth, SY23 3AH, Cymru, y DU

TEL/FFÔN: +44 (0) 1970 622 133
FAX/FFACS: +44 (0) 1970 622 132

EMAIL/EBOST: cprwww@aber.ac.uk
www.thecpr.org.uk

A POSITION STATEMENT – 2005

The role of the Centre for Performance Research (CPR) in Wales is as a conduit and catalyst for change and exchange, for the development of the art form, and its wider appreciation and understanding. Through its participation and presentation programmes – working across a range of disciplines that include dance and theatre, installation and performance, music and multimedia projects, site specific and landscape-based events – the CPR promotes emerging artists and ideas, explores the relationship of innovation to tradition, and pursues (sometimes against prevailing trends and fashions) the questions underneath, in on-going long-term research and development.

To work towards an integration of theory and practice, and to make crucial and strategic interventions within education, research, and arts development, the CPR is located at the University of Wales Aberystwyth, working in close partnership with the Department of Theatre, Film and Television Studies and pioneering knowledge transfer principles and practice within the cultural industries. Whilst UWA is the home for the research activities, the public programmes of participation and presentation are staged on a pan-Wales basis. In autumn 2006, a purpose-built building to house CPR, containing studio and rehearsal facilities, library, resource centre and administrative offices will open and be known as Y Ffowndri. This will be a site to explore the interface between the profession and the academy, actively expanding knowledge transfer capability and the enhancement of skill and opportunity within the profession.

Inscribed within every project, every activity, mounted by CPR is the desire to affect change, with the key objectives being investigation, discovery and sharing. These objectives are to enable audiences and practitioners in Wales to engage with ideas, methods and practices from around the world and through this dynamic exchange foster a vibrant and distinctive theatre ecology in Wales, distinguished by its vitality, creativity, imagination, vision, openness, enthusiasm, curiosity and passion. They are also to enable the development of the art generally, its methods and techniques, and to extend the boundaries in these disciplines in new and ever-expanding contexts of communication.

This motivation connects and contributes to a wider cultural, social, and political agenda and Wales' place in Europe and the world. Theatre and performance must not merely enshrine cultural values and pronounce upon them with certainty, but rather contest them and offer a space/site for dynamic negotiation. The performing arts are a wide avenue for intercultural, intergenerational and social exchange, producing greater contact and understanding between people and between nations, and promoting open interaction, generative and transformative experiment and reflection, and the extension of boundaries and perceptions.

CPR wishes to promote the vigour of Wales as a project in process, constantly 'becoming' and continually redefining its past, present and future. Therefore, philosophically and in practice, the CPR does not desire to celebrate national culture falsely, and so gravitates towards the reflective, preferring to raise curiosity, to question and to challenge. As well as supporting initiatives that make strong links with countries and nations with a make-up similar to that of Wales, the CPR also believes that people and nations develop by engaging with difference, recognizing otherness and determining one's own unique characteristics through dynamic interaction.

The CPR's position in Wales may sometimes appear paradoxical, but to work through paradox and be paradoxically positioned within a culture is to be actively engaged. The position of Wales, on the periphery of Europe, is celebrated by CPR and transformed into a curatorial vision that takes a broad look at contemporary theatre and performance work, which includes:
• performance that makes the marginal central, celebrating diversity and all that which exists on the periphery, on the edge, on the border between different art forms and between social and aesthetic action – that which disturbs, illuminates, challenges the norm, takes a paradoxical position, is made off-centre, off-side, on purpose
• works that might previously have been thought of as disenfranchised, marginal or peripheral
• not only work that is 'the stuff' of the international festival circuit, but work that is made in and from a particular and specific set of circumstances
• work that is distinguished by its own sense of displacement and dislocation, that is angry and passionate, flagrant and partisan, speaking directly, visually and viscerally to a wide audience.

JUDIE CHRISTIE AND RICHARD GOUGH
APRIL 2005

Ar gyfer y chwilfrydig…agor bydoedd o berfformio
for the curious…opening up worlds of performance

Perfect Time : Imperfect Tense

An Object Exercise in Conditional Remembrance

PHOTO: LILITH GOUGH

This is a combined, and edited, version of material presented in two performance lectures:

'Fifth Column, Fourth Wall, Third Theatre (or Thirty-one Objects to Aid a Forgetting):
Cardiff Lab and CPR 1974-2004' (at 'C/O The Gym', 4-5 December 2004, Chapter Studio, Cardiff)

and

'Perfect Time: Imperfect Tense. An Object Exercise in Conditional Remembrance.'
(at 'Towards Tomorrow?', 6-10 April 2005, University of Wales, Aberystwyth.)

It is intended to be read as documentation of the performed event, an exploration of memories, meanings, identity and obligation, mediated through the enduring ability of objects to embody and evoke the transitory and ephemeral nature of performance and history.

Stage Directions

The Speaker is positioned centre-stage behind a lectern placed on a large low table. The table is covered in a pale, raw silk cloth, creating an open canvas, brightly-lit and defined, and flanked, to complete the tryptich, by two large upstage screens. The Speaker wears white archivist gloves and a black suit. To his left are two large wicker baskets, traditional theatre skips, in which all the objects are carefully contained, some wrapped in cotton, others sealed in plastic evidence bags.

As each new object is produced from a hamper, it is displayed and manipulated, dispassionately shown as if evidence in court, or lovingly caressed as treasured memento, or held forth as if for sale at auction, proffered for scrutiny, recognition and remark.

It is then positioned on the display table, and a still life of the objects evolves through accumulation and juxtaposition. Throughout, the Woman (base position stage-right), who should move with graceful stealth, slowly sweeps a video camera over the tableau and on the Speaker, focusing at times on the detail or a chance encounter, settling at other moments on the whole display, casting through live-feed onto screen upstage-right the moving imagery contrasting a random selection of thirty years of Cardiff Lab / CPR still images projected continuously on upstage left screen. Both projections at times complement and at others counter-point the words of the Speaker.

In the other version, there is a third character on stage: the Man (base station upstage-left), who should plod and shuffle with resentful deference; he slouches in a large leather armchair, and, in the dim light of a reading lamp, leafs through an enormous ledger. When each object has been introduced, the Man reluctantly leaves his post, collects each object from the Speaker and positions it in the display. These tasks are to be done in recalcitrant mode with specific attitude to each object, as butler, carer, porter, guardian or gaoler.

A soundtrack of music by Estonian composer Arvo Pärt and British composer Gavin Bryars accompanies the entire event.

1 The Egg

I want to begin with eggs. In this company, we know which came first; the chickens, both alive and dead, weren't to appear until *Mad Mex*, Guillermo Gómez-Peña, much later, and that is after hares, dead and alive, birds, bees, fish, goats and horses. The first object I can see used in a Cardiff Lab performance is an egg, and the egg runs through all our work, blown and painted, refilled, smashed, crushed and cherished. The one that Siân Thomas held, the one that Mike Pearson stuck in his mouth, the one that Simon Thorne and Helen Chadwick painted, celebrating Easter Polish-style with Akademia Ruchu, and the one that Megan Lotts and I recently boiled purple along with 500 others for *The Last Supper* in Madison. This is the way this talk begins, this is the way this talk proceeds, trying to put Humpty Dumpty together again, trying to re-member, before The Fall, the fall into time, the fall into pieces, to put it all back together again, and this is the way our future goes, bouncing, unpredictable, resilient.

He throws one of the eggs at the audience. It bounces and bounces and bounces and bounces … and rolls.

2 The Metal Bucket

I am not sure how early a metal bucket appears in a Cardiff Lab show but it seems to be the quintessential object for that very early phase. I missed the first year but I got to know it intimately through Mike Pearson and the photographs he showed me and the stories he told me over beers at Chapter, The Sherman, the Romilly, the Lexington and most of all in 127 Claude Road, Roath. Initially the distinctions between RAT Theatre, Transitions Trust, Llanover Hall Group and Cardiff Lab seemed blurred, but I soon got familiar and unravelled the threads. And tethered myself to Llanover and *SummerThing '74* and the gang that emerged from there – Siân Thomas, Maria Daly, David Baird, John Anzanni and Brynley Goulding. Reading *Abelard and Heloise* in an attempt to understand the amazing pictures of physical simplicity I saw of Mike, Dave, Siân and Maria; reading Artaud in the hope that the *Lesson of Anatomy* would reveal itself to me; and thoroughly acquainting myself with *The Rhyme of The Ancient Mariner* and Meyerhold's ideas of the *Cabotin* so that I, sat in the corner, could follow what Mike, Dave and Dek Leverton were dealing with in their latest show and for which I went out and bought the bucket!

3 The Coffee-Grinder

Of my own work and my early attempts to determine an aesthetic distinct within, yet drawing upon, the Cardiff Lab style - graciously supported and encouraged by Mike - the coffee grinder is symbolic.

I was drawn to objects that seemed to emerge into daylight from dusty attics, mouldy sheds, damp garages and, most of all, the junk shops along Cowbridge Road. I liked the patina, the sense of use and purpose, the scars and markings of an object well used, of functionality and distress; objects abandoned, discarded, rejected and forlorn. Struggling to assimilate Grotowski, Artaud and Brook, the writings and work of Duchamp, Bretton and Magritte perhaps held greater force. I liked to find objects, I liked found objects, I liked to find the action that went with the object and defined the found; I was inspired to liberate them from their moribund existence.

The Coffee Grinder was part of a group, a gaggle, an ensemble that included the old tricycle, the washboard, the bird cage, the antique child's pram, the box cameras, the magic lantern projectors, the broken umbrella, the cobbler's shoe stretchers - they were legion, they were loyal, they were ever so compliant, always ready to work, uncomplaining, delighted with this second life, this second order; this second being within a third theatre without a fourth wall, a sort of fifth column of radical objects with a sixth sense, in a seventh heaven, reborn on the eighth day.

In *Shadowlands*, the final part of *The Guizer Project*, all I did was grind coffee spinning carefully as Brynley and later Siân cycled a tricycle slowly in a spiral toward me leaving a trail of salt and John Hardy on the old 'found' harmonium sang nursery rhymes wistfully.

I did take delight the evening in Holstebro when Judy Barba told me that her ageing mother had said, 'Why don't you make shows like that Eugenio?' I don't think he has ever forgiven me.

He cranks and turns the handle around and around and spins slowly in the opposite direction.

4 Bird Whistles

Bird whistles
For creating a dawn chorus in the central piazza, Santarcangelo
For calling the birds in Bergamo who are not to be seen, blasted out of existence by gun-toting city hunters
For an evensong on the beach at Leckwith, Penarth
For a refrain in the slate caverns of Llechwedd, Blaenau Ffestiniog
For a flight of fantasy in the garden of Llanover Hall
For the re-appropriation of a decoy of death
For the dismantling and recasting of a gamekeeper's technique
For the hunted, for the trapped, for the caged, for the birds, for the sound, for the simplicity, for dawn and for dusk, in streets and in squares.

These are the earliest pieces of technical equipment I can recall us buying and in some ways, they are the most resilient, outlasting the dimmer racks, profile lamps, par cans and revox tape machines.

The moment in Bergamo was memorable. Mike, Siân and I were about to be introduced to Jerzy Grotowski by Eugenio Barba, but our attention was drawn more to the two guys at the far end of the garden, who appeared with guns, and shot out of the sky the tiniest of birds – all fair game to these hunters, delicacies for the table, flesh and bone consumed in crunchy delight. When Eugenio asked us to make a special event for Donizetti, a former citizen of Bergamo, to create a parade leading through the old town, we knew what to do. An event to evoke birds, to call the birds, to feed them, and mourn their loss and disappearance, a eulogy of calls.

He blows, pumps and turns the whistles, a brief chorus of trills, quacks and calls.

5 The Receipt

A receipt for three pairs of black underpants, bought by Mike Pearson on 25 May 1974. And this is by way of acknowledging all those administrators, book-keepers and accountants who have diligently filed receipts and certified expenditure on the bizarre and the ridiculous – sustaining the complex financing of projects through the ever-accommodating stationery budget – and have done so much more than process the receipts for the several million pounds worth of expenditure over the years, I know, not least significantly raising and earning the funds to pay for it.

A short list of not untypical items: a live mandarin duck; three tons of Colombian coffee beans; an S&M chastity belt; asphalt for road repairs; a deep sea-diver's helmet; 600 test-tubes. But there comes a time when even three pairs of black underpants need to be accounted for as company property. But now we can only find two ... ?

He calls out to the audience, offering an amnesty.

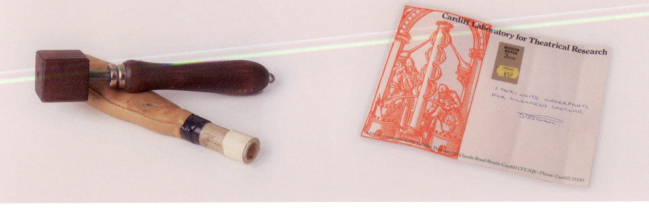

6 The Cigar-Box Violin

As if found along with the coffee grinder, this original cigar box violin (circa 1920) appeared early and made several aborted attempts to get into Cardiff Lab shows; excluded for being too enthusiastic, it sulked for years upstairs in the Gym. Siân and Ljiljana Ortolya rediscovered it when working with Jill Greenhalgh and Melanie Thompson on *Postcards in a Glass Court*, but it was not until 1982 (seven years of whining) that it found a home, gently coaxed, trained and stroked by Siân in *Heart of the Mirror*.

But I still don't particularly like it, and I include it here, in spite of itself and its sound, to represent music and to acknowledge all those company members who have brought a musical sensitivity and sense of musical composition to our work. I hear the sounds of the Redwing Empire Band, the street singing whilst hunting the wren, the shows entitled *The Orchestra* and *Orpheus*, the mountain *hollas* used in street processions, the *Anthem for Leicester*, the songs in the caverns at Llechwedd, the children's choirs in Belfast, the settings for *Paradise of the Soul* and *Labyrinth of the Heart* in Copenhagen. *The Georgian Feast* at St Stephens, the massed choirs of *Local Voices: Worlds of Song*.

The work that John Hardy and Simon Thorne conducted throughout the 1980s, on compositions, on show sound tracks and in nurturing a musical culture within the company – all whist fully participating as actor/performers – was significant for the contribution it made to integrate a musical and visual approach to the composition and structure of performance. John, Joan Mills and Paul Roylance collaborated on the first Voice Festival, Project Voice, in 1980, and Joan has continued since 1989 to develop Giving Voice and now Voice International as a distinct and distinctive division of CPR.

7 TDR

This is a first edition of the 1965 publication of TDR – the *Tulane Drama Review* as it was then – the Polish Lab issue. A remarkable convergence of four major figures of twentieth-century theatre: Eugenio Barba and Ludwig Flaszen writing the first articles on the work of Jerzy Grotowski and published by the then editor of TDR, Richard Schechner. Subsequently all of these men were to visit Cardiff and to work in our studio. Barba and Schechner several times, Ludwig Flaszen twice, Grotowski sadly only once.

But I don't include this journal in my collection of objects as a memory of the authors, editors and practitioners, rather more for it as a journal and the beginning of a collection. I bought this copy of TDR along with 52 others in Hay on Wye in 1975 and have been building up a library ever since. Frustrated by not being able to find information on the sort of theatre that Mike was talking about and we as a group were increasingly encountering, I became determined to construct an alternative library that placed a greater emphasis on the physical and visual aspects of theatre.

The library has been itinerant ever since it began: first in a shoe cupboard in the Gym, then in 5 Llandaff Road, in boxes for years, then above the Gym, then Unit 8, Science Park, Aberystwyth and now Unit 6, Science Park, Aberystwyth, and possibly in 2006 in a purpose-built building in Aberystwyth. The collection now comprises in excess of 3,800 books, 3,000 journals and 1,400 videos. Ric Allsopp was the first person to attempt to catalogue the collection in 1986, and Ric worked at various points in the years following. Since then a number of people have worked tremendously hard to try to maintain, promote and develop the collection. In addition to Ric, these are Jim Ennis, Adam Hayward, Rachel Rogers, Dan Rebbeck and now Jodie Bray.

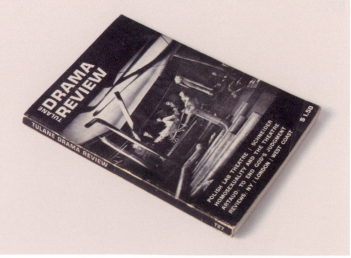

8 Catacomb Postcards

Postcards of the Capuchin Catacombs, in Palermo, Sicily. These images of the dead have lived with me for the past twenty-eight years. I have used them in shows, in talks, in lectures and presentations, in workshops, and in numerous devising processes. They disturb and attract me, in morbid fascination. I have wanted to return to Sicily, ever since we visited it in 1977, with Mike and Siân, presenting *Dancing on the Volcano*, in the Palermo *incontroazzione*, as part of a tour that would include Turin and the highly prestigious Nancy Festival.

Palermo shocked, challenged and changed me fundamentally. Despite travels with family to Canada and Norway, and school trips to France and Austria, this was my first real adventure. Following on from the success of *The Guizer Project*, I was pleased to accompany Mike and Siân and help in any way I could. I did well with the flight tickets, I recall, managing to get several re-routes, schedule changes, and even new destinations all included on the original ticket, a skill I still try to practise today with a trickster's slight of hand, being drawn to the 'non', in non-refundable, non-transferable, non-negotiable, non-exchangeable.

Palermo assaulted me, and became a measure by which other journeys and destinations were marked. It was exhilarating and exasperating. I recall the smells, the heat, the sweet pastries, and the freshly-squeezed orange juice. I recall two wizened old men, paying three million dollars to the teller in the bank. The wet fish market and the fruit and veg markets sprawling through a labyrinth of back streets, the Old Town, the docks, the danger, the guns, the puppets and the dead. The avenue of priests in agonized confrontation with their maker, suspended, frozen, captured and desiccated in the catacombs.

9 A Skull

A sheep's skull, it could have been a horse's, or any number of birds, dogs, cats, rats or foxes. Bones and the remains of animals have rattled through thirty year's work: *Moths in Amber, Burning of the Dancers, Postcards in a Glass Court*, in the street work of the late seventies and most notably in Mike's solo show, *Deaf Birds, Late Snow*. Lis Hughes Jones recently recalled that one of her haunting memories is of dragging entire horse skeletons out of Landimore marsh for the show *Trail of Tears*.

The animal remains remain, the shows disappear, and it has always been performances' fragility, their instability and their ephemerality that has attracted us, drawn us and seduced us. What remains? An archive of decay and detritus, forever struggling to evoke the event and its eventfulness, the momentary occurrence in time and place, fleeting, like lives, disappearing in its very moment of appearance.

But there was one skull that never performed, never appeared, at least not in one of our shows. I discovered it the night I first got the keys to enter The Gym, up in the top office, the storeroom of the old school gymnasium: a human head. Used, I was told later by South Glamorgan Education Authority, for life-drawing classes, no longer required, too real, not legal, discarded; 'use it in Hamlet, you're an actor', the man said. Alas … I never have. But now he finds a place in a still life, a *memento mori*.

He turns the skull to face him, as if to kiss.

10 The Bottle of Vodka

After all that death – fire and water: a bottle of Żubrówka Vodka, Bison Brand with the slither of aromatic grass, allegedly 'peed on by Bison to turn the Vodka a pale yellow'; offered in memory of all our colleagues, travels, collaborations, trials and tribulations, encountered, forged and found in Poland.

With Akademia Ruchu from Warsaw with Theatr Ósmego Dnia (Theatre of the Eighth Day) in Poznań, Grotowski's Laboratory in Wrocław, Tadeusz Bradecki and the Stary Theatre in Cracow, Theatr 77 in Łódź, Gardzienice Theatre Association in Lublin and Song of the Goat in Wrocław, together with many other individuals, scholars and practitioners.

Poland feels like a spiritual home to this company, and it influenced our origins significantly. Mike had already been, and Siân, James Castle and I made the journey to Warsaw and then to the lake district of Iława, guests of Akademia Ruchu in 1979, where we were to meet both Włodzimierz Staniesewski of the Gardzienice Theatre and Simon Thorne. The nights spent in the old town of Warsaw getting drunk on vodka and eating well due to black market money exchange, formed friendships and professional allegiances that continue to this day. And for eighteen years after this first visit, I went back to Poland at least twice every year.

He holds the bottle reverently, and then greedily gulps down a few slugs.
A little later, he quaffs again ... this time merrily.

11 IBM Golf Balls

The golf balls of an IBM typewriter. This needs some explanation. Difficult to understand no doubt that this was a major improvement on the Smith Corona, a real high-tech revolution enabling italics and alternative typeface; the more balls, the more fonts.

These were given to us by the designer, Steve Allison, who upgraded sometime in the early eighties to the unlikely contraption called an Apple Macintosh, and I include them to mark, underline, put in bold, increase point size, indent, centre align (all those things we can now do with a single control shift) the debt of gratitude we owe to all the administrators who have worked with and for Cardiff Lab and CPR over the last thirty years. The first person we thought of as an organizer, as an administrator was Norman Frisch, on a continuum that stretches to Helen Gethin. And it is a long list, but to name the key administrators whose personalities and commitment enabled the development of this company: Caroline Lynch-Blosse, Gill Sealby, Steve Fletcher, Celia Webb, Claire Swatheridge and Marcie Hopkins and two people are obviously missing, and missed in this world, who deserve special mention: Ceri Llewellyn and Paul Chandler.

Ceri who cared for us in the early eighties, Ceri who fumed and fought and laughed and railed against injustice, Ceri who created a drama, when there was just a crisis, who disappeared time and time again with Polish men, first Ludwig Flaszen, then Jerzy Grotowski, going for afternoon tea in posh hotels across Cardiff, knitting Grotowski a jersey emblazoned with a big letter 'G' – shame we have no photo.

And Paul, the administrator at Chapter Arts Centre, who with Mik Flood, helped us immensely in those early years and in getting this space as a permanent home. But Paul also, whom we met again as we moved to Aber, and with whom we began to work. Paul, so scrupulous and incisive of budgets and figures, so enraged by mis-spending, the mis-spoken, the mis-behaved, Paul, whom we took to Copenhagen like a secret weapon to unleash at the Kopenhagen International Theatre Festival (KIT).

Each administrator has created a distinctive regime, the history of the company could be written through the perspective of these organizational differences, but at the heart resides fortitude, resilience, creativity and sheer hard work.

12 Set of Early Publications

This is a set of the earliest publications of Cardiff Lab: *Masquerade, Dream Train*, the *Cardiff Lab Prospectus, Selected Documents* and *Glimpses of the Map.*

Two journals, two documentary booklets (one of a specific project, and one of the first six years), one prospectus and a promotional package. It is astonishing to me, looking back, that we had the wisdom and wherewithal to produce these at such an early phase in our work, and, setting aside the promotional, and autobiographical nature of some, the early attempts at a journal, with articles contributed by Peter Brook, Eugenio Barba, Tadeusz Kantor, Jerzy Grotowski and a certain Michael J. Pearson, were incredible, and in some ways this enterprise was preposterous, and precocious.

Having just completed Issue 1 of Volume 10 of the journal, *Performance Research*, entitled *On Theatre*, and continuing to work on issue 10.4 *On Technē*, I realize we are about to complete thirty-five issues of the journal. Founding *Performance Research*, with Ric Allsopp and Claire MacDonald back in 1995, was the realization of a long-term ambition, the seeds of which, for me, lie in this clutch of publications, and Ric and Claire likewise, I know, produced artists' books and specialist publications early in their careers. Clancy Pegg, Linden Elmhirst, and a host of production managers, editors and publishers at Routledge, Taylor and Francis, have enabled us to sustain this effort and output.

As for the early publications, whom were they for? I remember being terribly disappointed, when I returned a month later to Lears Bookshop in Cardiff, who I had persuaded to take ten copies of *Dream Train*, only to discover that three had been sold, but actually, on reflection, that seems rather good! Of course, these were the best visiting cards any upcoming theatre organization

13 Martin

Martin the polecat, Martin the fox, has remained in this box for the last twenty years, brought out occasionally to scare living cats and dogs, but most especially to frighten young children. Martin toured Europe in *Moths in Amber*, animated by hand and two walking sticks; me, the master-puppeteer of a great aunt's fur-wrap.

It is very strange for someone who has never been that excited by puppets and puppetry, and as someone who has disparaged mime and regards it as a debilitating disease, rather like amoebic dysentery, something you never quite get out of the system, I who have often been overcome with sympathy whilst watching a show, shaking my head, sadly muttering, 'he has had mime'. Now I look back on these pictures and see that half the time, I was a rather chubby mime and the rest of the time a rather naff puppeteer.

But this wasn't puppetry, this was animation of the inanimate, a transformation through human agency. We have all the language now, we can write up what we did.

He delves into a wooden box, and animates the fur – Martin; the dead animal surveys the audience, first with curiosity, then leerily, then mischievously and threateningly.

14 The Garden Spray

Used first in a show for which no document exists but in which I buried Mike alive, with me as some strange gardener tending to a desolate landscape, the writings of T, S, Eliot and Samuel Beckett scripting an entirely non-verbal enactment. I was later to use this Garden tool to spray the audience of *Moths in Amber* and usher them out of the all-white tent, the scent of orange blossom and rose water introducing once again, as with the coffee grinder, an olfactory sensation at the close of a densely visual and aural performance.

Sensory exploration continues as a fascination and concern for us, whereby synaesthesia, as artistic metaphor as well as mode, allows us to break the habitualized pathways of perception, 'the tyranny of the eye' (to quote Enrique Vargas), tapping deep into memory through smell and olfaction, using the eyes in your feet, listening through your shoulder or simply tasting the unfamiliar or the familiar in unusual ways.

He sprays the audience; the smell of rose water and orange blossom diffuses through the auditorium.

15 The Hot Dog

A hot dog sausage, a Danish hot dog sausage, a relative of the one that Mike and Jimmy Castle ate one night in Herning, or was it Aarhus, or was it Esbjerg, or maybe the outskirts of Copenhagen; somewhere in Denmark, having done *Moths in Amber*, having struck the set and packed the truck, we wandered the streets, looking for something to eat. Finding nothing but a caravan selling hot dogs, sold seemingly to accompany the streams of mustard, ketchup and mayonnaise to be poured along their backs (we can just visit Ikea nowadays), Mike and James staunchly, vehemently, admirably vegetarian, convinced themselves and us, that there was little meat content in this serially-concocted pink pig's penis of a Danish delicacy. I offer this in memory of all those meals had on tour.

And let us not forget the necessary ritual of splitting the group bill; a conclusion to any restorative restaurant forage that is bound to induce indigestion and at times instant nausea – 'well let's just split it equally'; 'no, that's not fair, I didn't eat the popadoms!' I am sure somewhere there is a theatre group still stuck in a restaurant trying to figure out a fair solution to this.

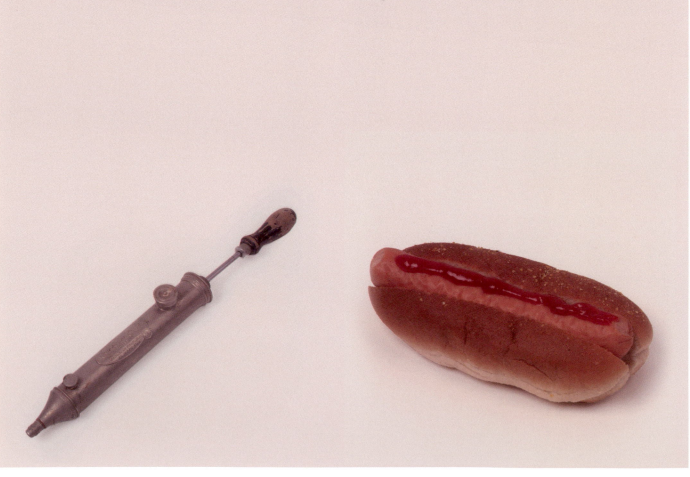

16 The Cookery Book

This is the companion to the copy of TDR. This is the inaugural book in another collection – a library of cookery books, specializing in the cuisines of other cultures. This is the anthropologists' cookbook, and I bought it, strangely enough, in Galloways, Aberystwyth, during our residency in 1979, one of the most productive and enjoyable residencies we ever did, giving workshops, presenting *Moths in Amber* and creating special events in the Old College and along the prom. I cherish this book for the memory of that time, for the start of a library and most of all, for the recipes, on how to cook a dog, how to prepare puffin pie and how to skin a cat.

Taking inspiration from this book and subsequent purchases on Japanese cookery, a few months later we even staged our first banquet. Twenty-five years have passed, and I am still trying to realize some of the hopes Mike, Siân, James and I had for that event. The most recent editions of the Last Supper in Florence, Italy, and Madison, Wisconsin, USA, have got closer to a seamless staging of banquet, edible installation and performance that evolves through a complex shift of calibrated structures.

In including this book, I should also like to record the happier moments of times on tour, in the company of others, sharing plans for the future, plotting and scheming and, most of all, shopping.

17 The Pink Teddy Bear

Given to us by Eugenio Barba and the members of Odin Teatret at the end of their residency in Cardiff in 1990. Found in a rubbish-skip in Canton, given with love and fondness and wrapped in a performance ceremony of great excess and sincerity. It's true, when it comes to presents it's in the giving not the receiving; it's the thought that counts. The dozen large panatone heaped onto me in Rome, the warrior knives from Tblisi, the chain mail armour from Tehran, a half-human-size china vase from Beijing, given at the point of departure and destined to encumber, or the kangaroo steaks brought to us from Sydney by someone who we knew had been delayed on a two-night stopover in Egypt. We're always grateful but sometimes cautious.

And so it was that as we were about to board the plane departing from Khartoum, Mr Gor gave Rachel Rogers and me a huge wooden camel as a gift for Judie. Sitting quietly, exhausted, in Cairo, the bulk of the camel between us, we noticed a poster depicting the pyramids. Where else should a camel reside and pose? We took a picture and then, silently, guiltily, feigning nonchalance, walked away from it, not turning back, hoping no-one would notice our careful abandonment. We gave Judie the picture. These gifts mark our encounters, links in a group culture and a network of charged symbols.

He looks ruefully at the bear and proceeds to manipulate it like a ventriloquist's dummy, momentarily with enthusiasm, and then casts it away.

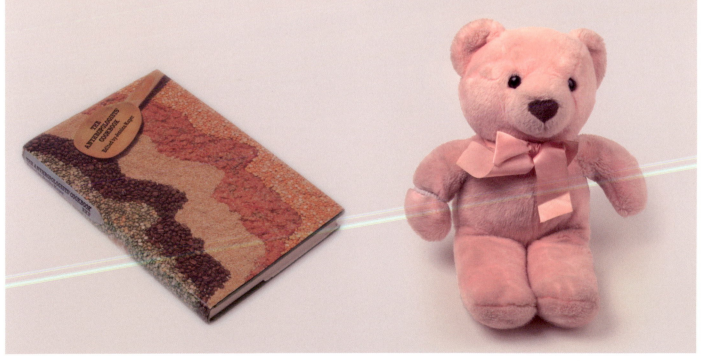

18 Georgian Herbs

A collection of herbs brought from Tblisi, Georgia, by Edisher Garakanidze and Joseph Jordania for the Georgian Feast to be staged as part of the Points of Contact conference *Performance Food and Cookery* in January 1994. A visit that opened up an exchange between Wales and Georgia, which is still developing today. The food was not to be as authentic as the singing and the toasting (and particularly the drinking), but it did include a great many walnuts and pomegranates.

It seemed to me that it was within the challenge to stage a Georgian Feast, and to reproduce the unfamiliar – the polyphonies, their harmonies and dissonance and the taste, textures and aromas of the food – that the lessons of understanding were to be learnt. How do we begin to understand the complexities of another culture and the ancient knowledge embedded deep in their structure? To adapt and mutate, worst still to approximate, seems like an act of arrogance, a strategy of assimilation; but to respect otherness and difference and then struggle to attain without compromise, in this case, of musical structure and cuisine, seems more like a constructive encounter.

In an opening address to one of Joan's *Giving Voice* conferences, *An Archaeology of the Voice*, I once asked if we could imagine the vocal folds of a nation, the vocal folds that form and help define a culture. I had in mind Georgian polyphony where the sounds not only enthral and excite but function as a sort of aural epiphany, an illumination through sound – a sonic/acoustic immersion of harmonies and dissonance – to an ancient world of unbroken tradition, where the vocal folds unfold and wrap around you – a polyphonic embrace!

And with these herbs, and in mentioning our two great Conference series *Points of Contact* and *Giving Voice*, I should like to thank all our conference curators and collaborators, Scott deLahunta, Heike Roms and many others who have staged these complex gatherings, the *Past Masters* series and many more: as packaged tours, as itinerant wandering, as academic enquiry, as multi-layered event, as peer-group gathering, as international association convention.

19 The Box of Tissues

A box of tissues – man-size – a required prop for every participant in Kristin Linklater's voice workshop, not only for clearing the throat, snot and mucus, sweat, but also for soaking up the copious floods of tears frequently released in the process of freeing the natural voice, tapping into the subterranean reservoirs of identity and self. But also included as a symbol for all the workshops and pedagogical programmes, organized and sustained over thirty years, thousands upon thousands of hours, many diverse techniques, methods, traditions, ways of working, ideas shared, transmitted. Explored.

A wave
A sign,
A blank page
A white square,
A blank canvas,
A lacrimal sign in Japanese Noh theatre,
The square grid of Goat Island,
The flowing water sleeves of Chinese National Treasure Madame Wu's
The white sheet in the game of the infinite possibilities in my own teaching
The Tissue, to remove Kathakali make-up

Pedagogy. Auto-didactic programmes begun in the early days because we had no training, then over the years grown, developed and sustained to share with others, offering opportunity to many, many thousands of participants in programmes led by countless artists from all over the world, programmes for the transmission of performance knowledge, theory literally incorporated, embodied, transmitted through action and experience, body to body. The tissue, for the blood, sweat and tears.

For each evocation he makes a corresponding tissue action; discarded, each tissue floats to the floor.

20 The Captain's Goblet

An old goblet. The captain's goblet from *The Origin of Table Manners*. A show that went through two incarnations, involving two different casts of two different generations of Cardiff Lab / CPR ensembles, but with Andzrej Borkowski, the captain, remaining a constant, an elegant and precise presence, transfixed upstage centre, omnipresent.

The Origin of Table Manners was a fun show to make; the process of making, comprehensive, exploratory and experimental, generating material that could never be contained in a single show: the blindfolded banquets, the dinner parties with bandaged bits, the silent supper and the singing supper, the endless boring conversationalists, the sad happy children's parties, the smashing Greek dinners, the Polish toasts, the Chinese visions of hell, the lettuce-eaters, the cream-cake lovers, the on-board entertainment, the after-dinner disco, the bread-and-water banquet, the abstinence and the excess.

Sometimes, the production of a production exceeds demand, the process of creating and creation more exhilarating than the fixed repetition of the show itself. Sometimes it is a struggle to capture, structure and compose, to do justice to what the devising process uncovered, created and unleashed. Sometimes the material resists and refuses to be laid down, sequenced, montaged, juxtaposed, provocative, productive, efficacious in unplanned ways, giving life to other projects and other shows. This was true for *Heart of the Mirror*, but in *Table Manners* we captured most of what we exposed, and the next object also represents a body of work that struggled to succeed: incoherent, inarticulate, awkward and edgy.

21 The Station Master's Lamp

The station master's lamp from *The Burning of the Dancers*, a show that Philip MacKenzie and I and all the team wrestled with for years. The best set we ever had, designed by Simon Banham, an extraordinary lighting plot simply composed by Paul Clay, and a great sound score by Simon Thorne. A show that never toured, a show that played only in Cardiff in different versions, a failure that I still regard as one of our best pieces from that middle phase.

It was formidable, relentless and unforgiving, but, once again, the memories of those all-night vigils of waiting in The Gym, our studio, in the waiting-room, generating a choreography of waiting, sitting, standing, of seemingly doing nothing, of encountering emptiness and abandon, are vivid and truly disturbing. So too, the films Philip made of the journeys we took, actual sojourns across snow and sand, in mist and sleet, an endless pilgrimage to find the show, which was the subject of the show, and let's not forget the subtitle: *The Solitary of the Lonely*. *Burning of the Dancers* was in many ways, the companion piece to *The Origin of Table Manners*, in much the same way that *Heart of the Mirror* was to *The Wedding*. Both were troubled siblings, and yet both contained the more profound indications for the future.

22 The Broken Globe

The much travelled globe, made in the 1920s, its expanses of imperial pink receding into faded patchy pointillism, which finally fell apart in my hands, in rehearsal in Londrina, Brazil, latitude 20.23 south of the equator, the glue of the hemispheric seam, melting, yielding, cracking open and fracturing at its point of weakness. The broken globe.

People-to-people, community-to-community, artist-to-artist. A new internationalism, or an old one? The politics of exchange, the multi-edged ambiguities of 'collaboration'.

Translation, mutation, betrayal, appropriation, exoticization, alterity, globalization, immunization, fundamentalism. East/west, north/south. The broken globe, breaking into more pieces.

Meeting ... daring ... trying ... needing ... to touch ... there, right there ... the handshake, a moment ... there ... in the middle of the shifting fundament, the matrixed minefield ... there, in the no-man's land ... there, on the border, transit papers in hand ... there, in the sucking, smothering sludge of bureaucracy ... there ... for some ... on the other side of barbed wire and trenches ...

We must.

He reveals the globe, at first intact, seemingly whole, and then allows it to fall apart in his hands.

23 An Espresso Cup

An espresso cup. A fancy espresso cup ... with a lid. A cup for serving a cappuccino of soup.

Savoured in a posh restaurant in Florence as guests of Roberto Bacci and Luca Dini, of Pontedero Teatro, Tuscany, Italy. In memory of Italy and all those encounters with directors, performers and musicians - romantic, professional, passionate, co-productive, infatuated, administrative, chaotic, sun-drenched, sexed, salty and seductive. And of course, it can all be said of Spain too ... but not Denmark.

Italy, Bergamo and Santarcangelo of the early days.

Italy, Volterra, Pontedera and Faenza of the middle phase.

Italy, Vicopisano and Firenze of recent times.

I love Italy. Italy, Spain, Brazil, Poland – and Denmark – have been great hosts and collaborators for our work over thirty years. Roberto, Luca, and Carla Pollastrelli, whom Mike and Siân first met in Belgrade in 1975, have remained close, faithful and loyal companions along this long path.

Italy is for me my adopted country; Schechner talked about how we have our country of birth and our country of work and domicile, but also we often have another country, where we feel most at home, that we adopt in our heart deep within. Many people through visiting us and working with us feel that about Wales, and when they tell me about how positively they felt about their time in Wales and being in Wales, I take pride. Wales is the country in which I was born and have lived and worked all my life. Yet also, there is a pang of guilt, a slight sense of betrayal, something within that says, 'yes, but I feel that about Italy. That's where I want to be'.

24 The Company Seal of Cardiff Laboratory Theatre

A symbol of legality, officialdom, conformity.

In memory and deep gratitude of all those trustees, Board members, and chairpersons of Cardiff Lab and CPR, who over the years, with no financial reward, have given hundreds of hours in support and defence of our work, with care, diligence, and responsibility.

Judie and I know too well the risks and dangers involved in the achievement of seemingly impossible projects. This seal should have been destroyed in November 1987 as Cardiff Laboratory Theatre went into insolvency. In the last few weeks of an otherwise immensely successful tour of the seventy-strong Shanghai Kunju Opera, which had begun as the highlight of the Edinburgh Festival in August. In November we hired the London Palladium, with Sadlers Wells, for two weeks, at the bargain price (then) of £5,000 per day. Whereas our previous year's Peking Opera season at Sadlers Wells had sold out and had had to extend its run, at the Palladium even a thousand people in the house was disturbingly reminiscent of a bad night in Chapter. The box-office takings failed to meet targets. It was clear we were in trouble, and it was beyond our accountant.

The insolvency practitioners of Arthur Young were fascinated by our case because, contrary to usual insolvency practice, it was better for the creditors for us to continue the tour for a further two weeks, to get to the end of the Palladium run, and go to the sold-out season at the Belfast Festival, and then to get the company safely back to China.

After we had sold all the company equipment and had the formal liquidation meeting with creditors, the insolvency managers took Judie and me aside and said, 'Well, it's an end, but not *the* end'.

For twelve months on a jobseekers allowance, we had no company and no board, but some great advisers, tremendous goodwill, determination and good fortune.

I mention here only a few names to evoke the many: Roger Tomlinson, Kaite O'Reilly, Ted Braun, Noel Witts, Michael Freeman, Roger Owen and Michael Anderson.

25 A Pair of Lederhosen

A pair of lederhosen, one of seven, worn by one of the von Trapp family, in our production, *The Sound of Muzak*, for which no documentation exists, only memories, and here are a few of my favourite things:

An all male chorus of bearded nuns.

The two Marias fighting over who should sing 'The Hills are Alive'.

The director of Chapter Arts Centre making a cameo appearance as a lonely goat-herd with twenty cardboard cut-out goats.

The audience having to make a choice of being nun or Nazi.

A sing-along with Sound of Music preceding by several years the phenomenal success of the sing-along film screenings.

The lederhosen von Trapp children, a mixture of Chapter and Cardiff Lab staff.

And these lederhosen are offered in memory of all of those people, many of whom are not actors or performers, who have taken a part in special events or one-off productions, installations, street processions and pageants, from Leicester to Londrina, from Madrid to Madison, from Belfast to Blaenau in Florence, Copenhagen, Amsterdam – the list is long.

26 Hotel Shampoo

A collection of complimentary shampoo, garnered from around the world, reflecting the more mature comfort of the last fifteen years, rather than the cheapskate, back-packing sojourns of the first. As a theatre company we were more accustomed to being put up in doss-houses, dives and dormitories that always seemed to be on the shady red-light edge of a railway station. And then in schools, monasteries, farms and churches in Italy, Spain, Portugal and Poland. But I include these toiletries in memory of the thousand hotel rooms booked in Cardiff and Aberystwyth, and elsewhere in Wales and the UK, that we have arranged for guests and in doing so have supported the economy of our country, to remember that side of our organization which is part travel agency, accommodation office, catering, social and welfare Inc. We affirm that we realize all these exchanges of scholars and practitioners, and all the international theatre festivals, tours, gatherings, symposia, workshops and conferences to enable the worldwide migration, dissemination and liberation of hotel complimentary toiletries.

27 The Monkey King Boots

The Monkey King boots worn by Mr Law, Peking Opera Master from Hong Kong, guest artist and director for the Cardiff Lab production *Journey to the West*, a production created as part of the Peking Opera Exploration project, and one of a large consignment of Chinese Opera goods, seventy trunks, inveigled through customs as the personal luggage of diva, and Chinese National Treasure, Madame Wu.

Monkey King boots are introduced to this canvas to represent the many thousands of artists from around the world whom we have hosted from the early project on Kathakali and Balinese dance with I Madé Bandem and family and Krishnan Namboodiri to the many others including Grotowski Laboratorium, Gardzienice, Akademia Ruchu, Song of the Goat, all from Poland; taller Imagen, Columbia; Els Comediants, Spain; Pontedera Teatro, Italy; Les Kurbas, Ukraine; Theatre Bazi, Iran; P'ansori Opera, Korea; Sameveda chanters from India; A Filleta, Corsica; Maya Rao and Dashka Seth, India; Bill Shannon, USA; William Yang, Australia; Jant-bi, Senegal, to name just a few. All these artists have touched us deeply and offered insight to other ways of 'being, of doing and of showing doing' (Richard Schechner). We continue to pioneer and promote the best of traditional and contemporary world theatre.

28 The Toothbrush

This is the toothbrush that Trisha Rhodes bought for the conference delegate who asked her for one, who asked her to nip out and buy one for him, and this is in memory of all such demands, no matter how great or small, that were done in the name of customer care and genuinely done to please. But this toothbrush is actually an impostor, for Judie intervened, telling Trisha not to go – a step too far, a demand beyond the call …

So this toothbrush appears here as a warning, a marker in the sand but also as a memory for all those more reasonable requests that we have genuinely and graciously fulfilled with care and humility. And I mean to thank here all those project assistants, bursary barters and internees who in more recent years have been at the front line and cut their teeth.

He holds the object with distaste, an offending article – suspect evidence – and brandishes it in warning.

29 The Mexican Hat

The Mexican hat given to me by *Mad Mex*, border-artist Guillermo Gomez-Peña, crowning me chief honcho at the end of our collaborative production, *Club Raw*; one of many occasions working with Guillermo, sometimes as guest artist/director, and sometimes as producer of the work of his company La Pocha Nostra.

And this by way of celebrating all those occasions when we have worked with other artists, individuals from companies, directors, performers and visual artists in a collaborative process, when one's own techniques methods and assumptions confront, challenge and accommodate (transform, mutate) those of our guests and our own are similarly apprehended by our guest. This is a tough process requiring mutual respect and understanding, and we have been blessed over the years with some extraordinary opportunities with Odin Teatret in 1980 and then especially with the small team of Odins in Blaenau, with Akademia Ruchu in Cardiff, with Theatre 77, Divadlo na Provisku and Den Blau Hest on the *Together Project* in Copenhagen – Lorette Van Heteren, Meredith Monk, Guillermo Gomez-Peña, Roberto Sifuentes, Peader Kirk, Frankie Armstrong, Philip Zarilli, Rachel Rosenthal, William Yang, Tess de Quincey, the list could go on.

He parades the hat and wears it proudly, seeking the most flattering tilt.

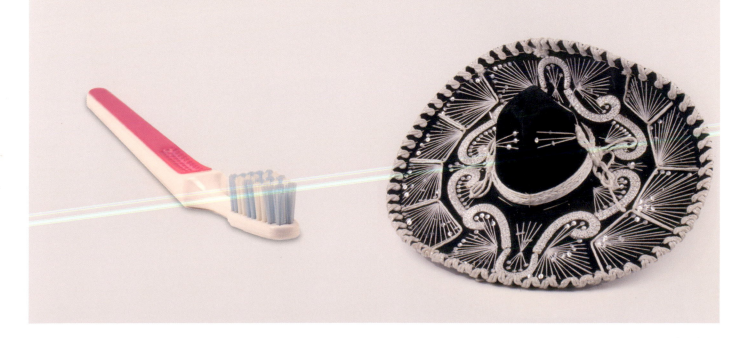

30 The Hay Cutter

Hearing how members of Odin had each been funded to travel to somewhere in the world and learn the techniques of another theatre culture, back in the late seventies we decided that we could each have five pounds to spend on an object for use in devising. The streets of Canton were to be our world – go forth and discover – and this is what Mike came back with. I am sure he did a strange sort of dance with it, I am sure I felt this could lead to a bloody end. It was never used.

And I include this for all the objects that never appeared in a show but that desperately wanted to and by extension, all the shows that were discussed but never made: the one about the Ranters and the English Civil war; the one on Welsh convict women; the one for the tin mines at Parys mountain and Cwmystwyth; the one for the gaol at Beaumaris (which connected with the one on Welsh convict women); the one entitled *Morris and his Men*, about neo-fascist vigilantes disguised as Morris dancers; the one about optometry, opticians, sight and vision; the one on time, the one on memory and the one on love.

He grasps the cutter in unwieldy fashion, and clumsily reinvokes a mimetic action.

31 Index Cards

And finally, the thirty-first object: a pack of unused index cards, for the future. For the unwritten scenarios, for the plans, productions and programmes of the next thirty years. For the categorization and the ordering of things. For the writing of lists of hopes and dreams. For the labelling of the uninvented. For a taxonomy of the as-yet unseen. For the yearning. For the longing. For the blankness. For the unmarked card.

The index card, the tool and the method I learnt from Mike to structure shows, to record the building blocks, to re-order scenarios by re-shuffling the pack, to re-configure the stepping stones, used today to order these objects, used tomorrow to …

The luxury item I would ask for on a desert island – an endless supply of index cards with a never-ending pencil: cheap, sad, lo-tech and disposable, bio-degradable, tangible.

But I could never survive without Judie or Joan in any case, and throughout the last twenty and more years of this narrative runs their presence. To the future and with thanks to each of you for the past. Towards Tomorrow!

He carefully places the small packet on the display table and completes the arrangement of evidence, standing back to reflect on this still … the still life.

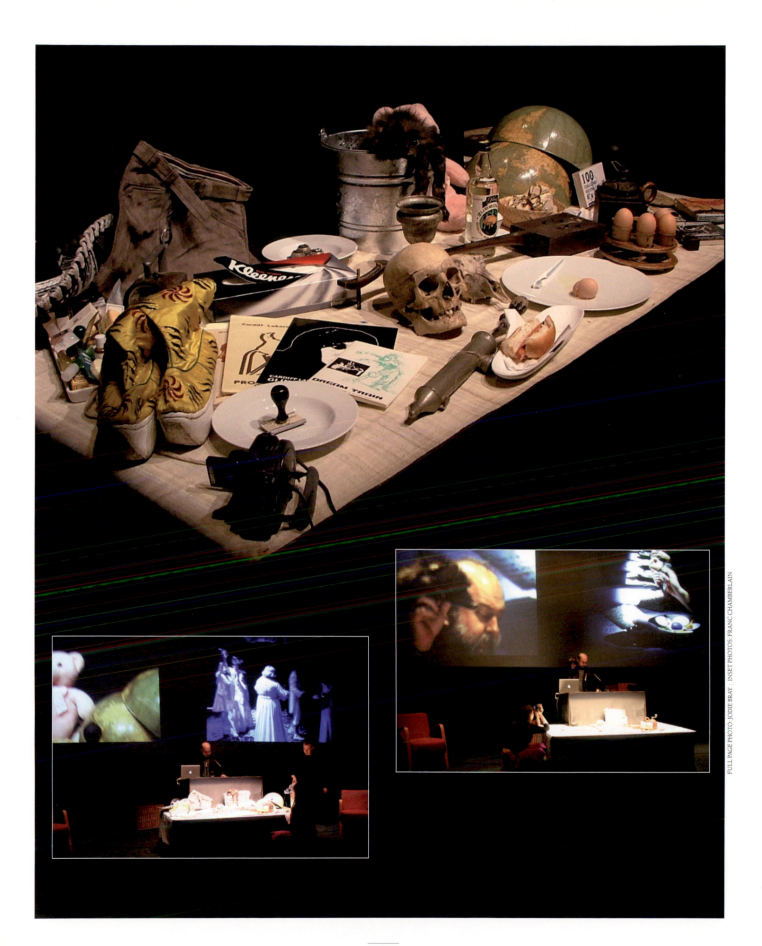

FULL PAGE PHOTO: JODIE BRAY : INSET PHOTOS: FRANC CHAMBERLAIN

Bibliophobia : An Oneiric Fable

It was late in the evening when the call came that would seal my fate and lead down this inescapable path of madness and despair, a path that I have followed, with gladness and devotion, because of a love of books. I was invited by a man whose name seemed vaguely and disturbingly familiar: a Professor R. A. Evermore. My trade, until then, had been as a sort

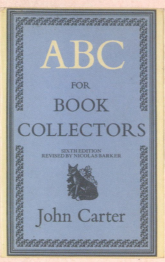

of book detective. I would track down treasured stolen volumes, priceless antique books lost in transit (most of them insurance scams no doubt). My job – if that's what you could call it – was to trace books: out-of-print, rare, stolen and occasionally entirely imaginary.

Professor Evermore wanted me to do some work in an archive held by an organisation called the Centre for Performance Research in the small Welsh town of

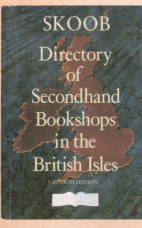

Aberystwyth. I had never been before and it sounded interesting enough. The pace of London had worn me down, and a few months, maybe even a year, in a seaside town would probably do me some good. Although the initial outline of the work was unclear it seemed that I would be working closely with the Director of the Centre and would have access to the

sizeable and somewhat idiosyncratic collection that the Centre had amassed. I was to explore and hopefully to publish some of its more obscure holdings. Some quick explorations on the web served to intrigue me further:

As well as containing extensive collections of familiar texts ranging from Stanislavski to Craig, from Artaud to Copeau, there are also collections of material that can not be found

elsewhere. Extensive collections of material on Kathakali, Kunju Theatre, Pansori Opera, Balinese Dance are placed alongside the more traditional material to provide a broad-ranging and comprehensive living resource. (Centre for Performance Research 2006)

I had a couple of weeks to finish other work there in the city, and make a few final arrangements. Yet I found myself continually returning to that name, R. A. Evermore, as though some suspicion sought to bring itself to consciousness: some memory I had buried. Indeed the friends that gathered on my final night, in what they called 'civilization', all said how familiar Evermore's

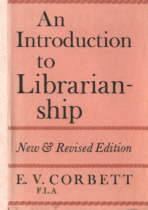

name was, yet none was able to quite articulate where, or why, they might have encountered him.

The train journey there was itself a nightmare, yet one softened by the beauty of the scenery, as I passed vast mountains and valleys and wild expanses dotted with grazing sheep. Aberystwyth was attractive, with its huddled backstreets revealing themselves enticingly yet awkwardly, beside the theme bars and game stores of

modernity, as though they might lead one quite literally into the past.

The Centre was not really what I had expected, located on an industrial estate just above the university buildings (that seemed to perch above the town with a possessive air). It was a low building, a suite of offices that apparently had provided 'temporary' accommodation for over nine years. As I made my way to the doors, a piece of lined notepaper swirled across the car park and danced a couple of times about me before ceasing its windy jig at my feet. Brushing off the dirt I was able to read, in a spidery pencil:

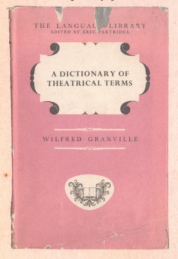

On the one hand, the archive is made possible by the death, aggression and destruction drive, that is to say by originary finitude and expropriation. But beyond finitude as limit, there is … this properly in-finite movement of radical destruction without which no archive desire or fever would happen. (Derrida 1988: 94)

My initial thought was that this formed part of some student's notebook, some jottings taken in a lecture. However the lack of context, with no further explanation on the page and no reference made me sceptical. So too did the script, which seemed to belong to another time. The anachronistic fervour of the calligrapher was there; someone older must have written it – and then cast it to the wind. I was intrigued enough to pocket it anyway and proceeded nervously to my first meeting with CPR.

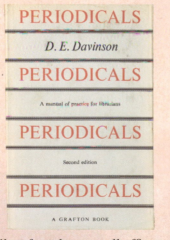

Evermore, whose connection to the place I was still unclear about, had informed the Centre of my arrival. The staff, of which I was now a part, were welcoming and friendly. I found my small office very appealing, both secluded and sociable. It afforded a view of the hill overlooking the town, finished off with some monumental column (which I would later learn to have been in commemoration of the Battle of Waterloo). The window had horizontal bars across it, and I joked with my colleagues concerning whether these were to keep me in or something else out. A brief murmur of guilty laughter informed me that indeed there were secrets to be found in this Centre.

After settling in I spent the afternoon familiarizing myself with the archive which contained videos, DVDs, music recordings on various media, academic journals and – of most interest to me – books. On first being shown into the library, I was immediately in my element, the rich array of spines, colourful and alluring, beckoned me forward. Over those few hours I began my first explorations of the hazy world that I now know exists between knowledge and practice, between the word and its flesh. For within minutes I had begun to notice the idiosyncrasies of this collection's existence: I do not think I would be claiming too much by saying that it seemed, even from a brief examination, to have a personality.

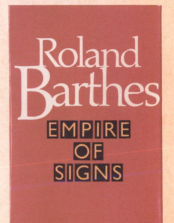

Who had devised such a collection? There on the shelves such titles as Aries's *The Hour of Our Death* and Fergusson's *Dancing Gods* were to be found alongside the standard texts on theatre and performance such as Schechner's *Performance Studies*, Auslander's *Theorizing Practice, Practising Theory* and Turner's *The Ritual Process*. *The Old Gods* of Patrick Logan and Porteous's *Beauty and Mystery of Well-Dressing* stood cover to cover alongside books on Kabuki, Clowns and Puppets, Masks, Mime and Ballet. Texts on primitive song and Indian dance could be found beside the *Unaussprechlichen Theater* of Von Lunzt and a text on Soviet Russian Theatre. Even George Witley's *The Meltdown Shards* was propped – as though by chance – against a copy of Hugard's and

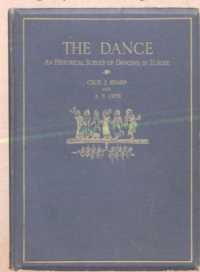

Braue's *The Royal Road to Card Magic*. This curious juxtaposition of texts intrigued me all the more, and I began browsing through the more obscure works: lovely editions, beautiful texts, superb illustrations. Hours drifted by as I familiarized myself with the collection. I have often thought that a library is more like a friend, a strange friend with many idiosyncrasies, a friend that it will take years to know, to understand, to get *acquainted* with. Finally, with night drawing on, I opened the exquisitely bound *Chinese Opera and Painted Face* of Pe-Chin Chang. Just beneath the contents I found a passage, written in faded pencil, by the same

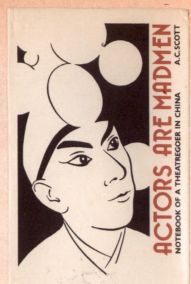

spidery hand that had penned the sheet that had come to rest before me earlier, it read:

> Have you ever thought about faking an historical item? Maybe during research on a particular historical occurrence in arts or politics, when you began to think that something special should have been said or done? Or because you suspected that there had actually been another voice that the archive for some reason had failed to record? Have you ever been tempted – have you ever smiled and realized that you would probably have the expertise to succeed with it? That you would know what the item should look like, and where exactly it would have to be found (accidentally!), and how it would have to be introduced into the debate? (Peters 2002: 122)

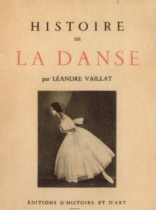

I dismissed the coincidence – always a mistake – and closed the book. It had certainly been a curious first day, and yet as the weeks and months slid by with progress made in unearthing boxes of material, programmes, funding reports, posters, flyers and letters, I gradually forgot the strange beginnings of the archive work. Even Evermore had slowly faded from my memory, so absorbed was I in the task at hand, a task I now know to be intimately bound up with destruction, life, death, memory and ghosts. As with this type of work, there is the continual battle against the gradually expanding archive: adding more seems to conspire against any attempt to investigate its depths thoroughly. Boxes of new materials would arrive: books,

records, papers, CDs and records, all gathered from disparate countries and cultures, variously packaged and posted to join the growing walls of material. The Director of the Centre did not help in this regard, or rather to say that he would continually arrive with further items and obscure texts gathered on his travels. Often I would glance over from my office to see another package or box brought in and a number of my colleagues would gather eagerly around these new arrivals, carefully unwrapping them, cataloguing and ordering them for future reference. Yet when I would venture into the library later to discover these new items for myself, I found them impossible to trace. Everything seemed to be absorbed into the enormous wall labelled 'New Acquisitions', but despite its obvious, gradual and unrelenting expansion I was never able clearly to discern the new from the old in terms of

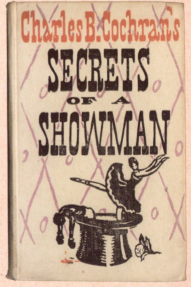

these 'acquisitions.' In fact I began to develop a strange suspicion that these new materials never really found their way into the library by the conventional manner but rather that they, and I know the word will seem odd, assimilated themselves into its walls by some innate and almost sentient means.

It was with this preposterous notion in my mind that I resolved one day to follow the Director to one of these book 'haunts' that I knew he frequented: Hay-on Wye. I had been there before and thoroughly enjoyed losing myself for hours amidst the dusty mouldering shelves of obscure books and magazines propped against pulp editions and rare etchings. Each shop seemed to generate its own little corridors of interest and seclusion. I wanted to follow him to discover the source of these marvellous editions, to track the archive to one of its origins.

Following his car through the winding roads of mid-Wales was difficult enough, as each treacherous bend loomed unexpectedly through the gloom of a dreary grey day. Added to this was the driving rain that seemed to conspire against any attempt to keep his vehicle in sight. Eventually we came into the 'town of books', and I kept a good distance behind him hoping to glimpse the first shop that he would visit. But it was not to a shop that he went, rather to a plain house on the main street. He talked for a few moments to a stooped and suspicious looking gentleman before passing him a card. The man went inside, leaving the Director on the doorstep for a few minutes, before returning with a small box, which was exchanged amidst furtive glances up and down the road. I had ducked into the doorway of a coffee shop but kept an eye on him as he returned to the car with the package.

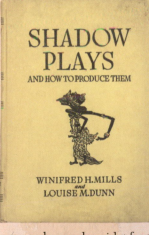

That afternoon I followed him from house to house as these acquaintances he visited yielded up packages, boxes and volumes of books and papers that had obviously been specifically acquired for him. The library grew through these personal associates, each watching and waiting for the necessary texts to make the thing whole and complete. I trudged back to the car soaked and perplexed. Something in the way that the Director had gathered his collection seemed so strange, yet also so simple: he had obviously cultivated a loyal group of enthusiasts who passed these works on to him and yet I had seen no money change hands or any other item given in return. Perhaps the cards he handed over at each visit held some secret, a ticket to a performance, a phone number, a website. It would have to remain just that: a secret.

That night on my return I slept long but dreamed of many visitors heading towards the Centre, each with a gift, and that these steadily filled the library until there was no room left to even open the door and from within there came a low groaning and straining as the shelves sagged with the attempt to hold together the incredible collection.

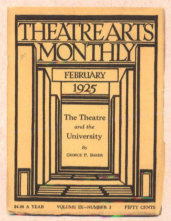

Many months passed, during which I was able to put behind me the strange furtive compulsion I had had to unlock the secrets of the library and its sources. But the peculiarity of the place was to return to me as a true and powerful revenant.

In the late summer I found myself working late. To take a break from the glare of the computer screen I resolved to look through some of the music in the archive. I scanned down the list: Swiss Yodelling, Indonesian Funerals and Fertility Feasts, Bengalese Songs of the 'Madmen' and the Ceremony of the Kadiri Dervishes. I listened to quite a number of the records and CDs that evening and as the clock paced towards midnight my head was filled with many voices and sounds that seemed so unreal, as though from another world. As I searched through a box to find the final

CD I had chosen: Diamanda Galás's Masque of the Red Death, I happened upon a sheet of printed paper. It was a statement, in a short, typed letter that reminded me of the nature of the archive:

> The documentation of our previous projects – embracing theatrical theory, training methodology, scenario construction and critical considerations of performance works – and the information collected through encounters with other groups and audiences together form, in a sense our group's memory. We thought that the synthesis of these two collections of documentary material could be the beginning of a resource preserving and reflecting some of the creation that a performance project spawns beyond merely 'the show'. (Gough 1979)

What struck me particularly was the notion of

'spawning', and I instantly recalled the first words I had read, from the website, concerning the Centre's archive: that it was a 'living resource'. The notion of spawning, of a multitude of possible births, from the closeted confines of the archive was incomprehensibly vast. A network of connections and possibilities opened up. I stared out towards the black night sea and thought of all the fish, all the fish-like things, which now writhed and spawned, creating their own living resource, of replication and difference.

The next afternoon, after everyone had left, I returned to the copy of *Chinese Opera and Painted Face*, half-knowing, half-dreading what I would find there. The pencilled text still remained but had also changed; it now read:

> There is idealism inherent in the perception of an archive as unchanging and unchangeable. The curatorial responsibility towards preservation, conservation and restoration belies the myth of the stability of the artefact. Nowhere is this more the case than in performance studies, which grapples to find appropriate styles in which to catalogue and shelve its ghosts. (Iball 2002: 59)

Had I time then to reflect on the true horror of the metamorphosed text, and what it now said about the mutability and transitory nature of the archive, I would have collapsed. Yet before I was able to think further

on this, the book seemed to shift slightly in my hand in a manner that I can describe only as fidgeting.

Had the book truly moved in my hands? I cannot be certain. Perhaps it was my own hand that shook? Certainly the months here in this seaside town had taken their toll on me. As winter gave

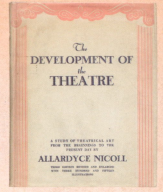

way to the bluebells of spring I had spent more time thinking about the library, gradually transforming my own shelves at home to begin to resemble those in that collection; sourcing obscure texts from shady dealers in far off countries and spending my time, more and more often, in the calming confines of those walls of books. Yet surely my nerves were not that shot. I held my hand out to gauge its steadiness: not a tremor. And then it happened again, only this time more noticeable and for considerably longer. The book did not move as such but rather breathed. Yes! Its pages and cover seemed to expand, as in the first stretch of a balloon inflating, and then contracted. I placed the text back on the shelf and was sure I heard a faint exhalation of air as it resumed its rightful place.

Shaken and concerned I left the library heading back

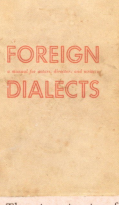

towards my small office and was sure I saw a figure slip by outside, through the frosted glass, along the corridor. Was I being followed, and watched? Would they object to my presence here so late? Then my phone gave a couple of shrill beeps, indicating a message had come through. I saw it was from Evermore, the first communication in months (and a cryptic one). It read:

> The time is ripe fr the scholarly stalker 2 recognize hw academia defers the desire fr affection, displacing it frm the subject of thr obsession (Iball 2002: 62)

Perplexed I slumped in my chair, allowing the little breeze that there was drift past me through the window. It had been a very hot day, and the view from my barred window showed the stark white-washed houses creeping up Pen Dinas Hill, with the sea spread out beside them. This idyllic scene shimmered in the evening haze, blending homes and sea, hill and sky. Then I heard a dull rumble from the library, a deep grumbling sound that reminded me of a hungry stomach aching for food, or of something lonely and forlorn. An email came through:

> The possibility of the archiving trace, this simple possibility, can only divide the uniqueness. Separating the impression from the imprint. Because this uniqueness is not even a past present. It would have been possible, one can dream of it after the fact, only in so far as its iterability, that is to say its immanent divisibility, the possibility of its fission, haunted it from the origin. The faithful memory of such a singularity can only be given over to the spectre. (Derrida 1988: 100)

And just below, by way of signing off: 'Have you dreamed it all, then, after the fact? Best Wishes, A Friend.'

Again the rumbling noise from the library, and my head pounded with all the messages and information. I remembered ghosts and memories, and a strange thought occurred that it might just be possible for a library to be truly alive. To have a sort of sentience comprised of the thematic material that it had collated (my rational faculties were quite evidently crumbling rapidly). And what then, my addled brain conjectured, would a hungry, lonely archive consume? Itself.

I raced through to the library, hearing now a cacophony of groans and rumbles from all around me as though standing inside the stomach of a great beast. I picked up the first book that came to hand: *The Dead Memory Machine*, by Pleśniarowicz, flicking through I found the first few pages blank, rifling through the book I finally came to some text about halfway through. Yet it was disappearing before my eyes, each black letter unravelling into nothing like a picked thread undoes

a garment. Staring at that page, as its ink was untraced in a bizarre mirroring of the process of writing, I think I understood that there was indeed something missing, misplaced, in the library. It was memory itself: a memory that all libraries attempt to preserve, to enclose against the creeping ruination of time. I picked another book from further along the shelf and flicked through it. Blank. Moving quickly across the stacks there were so many already gone. I managed to catch the last few pages of a book on Noh theatre, as the words faded away. Continually surging in my ears was the breathing or groaning noise, which now seemed desperate and urgent, like a drowning body that has made it to the surface struggling for air. The archive was feeding on itself, or rather it was assimilating those words into some kind of physical being (one that I was unable to see but nevertheless was certain existed). There, amidst the shelves of empty works (their words devoured by a ravenous *living* archive with a subterranean intelligence now embodied in the building itself and in those who had used it), I realized that I would never open another book as long as I should live but would instead dwell forever beneath the weight and shadow of their spectrality.

NOTE

1. With apologies to H. P. Lovecraft and to the staff of CPR who are far less sinister than herein portrayed (I hope).

REFERENCES

Centre for Performance Research website 2006: http://www.thecpr.org.uk/archive/index.html

Derrida, Jacques (1998) *Archive Fever: A freudian Impression*, trans. Eric Prenowitz, Chicago and London. University of Chicago Press

Gough, Richard (1979) 'Resources' in *Cardiff Laboratory Theatre, Selected Documents* Summer/Autumn 1979, Cardiff: CLT

Iball, Helen (2002) 'Dusting Ourselves Down' *Performance Research 7 (4):pp.59-63

Peters, Sibylle (2002) 'The Academic Laboratory of Fake and as – a Proposal', *Performance Research* 7(4): pp.121-125

Circumstantial Evidence

Despite an early emphasis in our work upon the potential for creative interplay between archive and studio, the actual chronicle of CLT and CPR work has been partial and the documentation of process fragmentary.

For this family album we have undergone a process of remembering, putting-back together month-by-month, and committing years from memory into writing. In this process of re-assembly, we have tried to recall and record an extended family, listing names of people, productions, places and participants. Individuals remaining luminous but with calendars fleeting and facts obscured, we have attempted to reconstruct an accurate roll-call; in this reconditioned almanac, however, we are aware there are some missing slivers, lost souvenirs and misplaced relatives.

1974

FEBRUARY
Abelard and Heloise
Performance
PERFORMERS: Dave Baird, Maria Daly, Mike Pearson, Siân Thomas
CHAPTER ARTS CENTRE, CARDIFF, WALES

MARCH
Labyrinth
Workshop/Performance
PERFORMERS: CLT members
LLANOVER HALL THEATRE, CARDIFF, WALES

JUNE
The Philosopher's Stone
Performance
CLT in collaboration with Keith Wood Group
SHERMAN ARENA THEATRE, CARDIFF, WALES

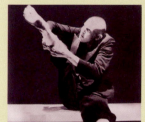

JULY
The Lesson of Anatomy:
The Life, Obsessions and
Fantasies of Antonin Artaud
Performance
Joint project with Théâtre du Double (Paris)
DIRECTORS: Jean Gremion, Patrick Guinand
PERFORMERS: Dave Baird, Ritva Lehtinen, Dek Leverton, Mike Pearson
THE OVAL HOUSE, LONDON, ENGLAND
SHERMAN ARENA, CARDIFF, WALES

Time of the Season
Workshop/Performance
LED BY: Mike Pearson
PERFORMERS: John Anzani, Dave Baird, Wendy Balfour, Gaynor Bernard, Karen Chandler, Maria Daly, Bryn Goulding, Mandy Seagroatt, Siân Thomas, Clive Walters
LLANOVER HALL, CARDIFF, WALES

Image
Workshop/Performance
LED BY: Mike Pearson
PERFORMERS: Dave Baird, Maria Daly, Mike Pearson, Siân Thomas
LLANOVER HALL, CARDIFF, WALES

AUGUST
Summerthing
School/Retreat
LED BY: Mike Pearson
LLANOVER HALL, CARDIFF, WALES

Mariner
Performance
PERFORMERS: Dave Baird, Dek Leverton, Mike Pearson, Siân Thomas
CHAPTER ARTS CENTRE, CARDIFF, WALES

Nighthawk
Performance
CLT in collaboration with Keith Wood Group
CHAPTER ARTS CENTRE, CARDIFF, WALES

1975

MARCH
Gorboduc
Performance
PERFORMERS: Dave Baird, Richard Gough, Dek Leverton, Mike Pearson
CHAPTER ARTS CENTRE, CARDIFF, WALES

JULY
Triad
Performance
PERFORMERS: Maria Daly, Mike Pearson, Siân Thomas
LLANOVER HALL, CARDIFF, WALES

NOVEMBER
Bricolage
Special Event
PERFORMERS: Richard Gough, Mike Pearson
LLANOVER HALL, CARDIFF, WALES

1976

FEBRUARY
Gilgamesh
Performance
PERFORMERS: Richard Gough, Diana Heppenstall, Mike Pearson
CHAPTER ARTS CENTRE, CARDIFF, WALES

JUNE
Nest of Ninnies
Performance
PERFORMERS: Richard Gough, Mike Pearson, Gerry Pyves
LLANOVER HALL, CARDIFF, WALES

AUGUST
Owls or Flowers?
Performance
PERFORMERS: Mike Pearson, Siân Thomas
CARDIFF, WALES

CLT at the Odin Teatret Seminar

Including:
Demonstrations, Presentations, Discussions and Workshop/ Training Sessions
HOLSTEBRØ, DENMARK

Owls or Flowers?
Performance
PERFORMERS: see above
ÅLBORG, DENMARK

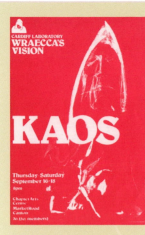

CLT at the International Encounter of Group Theatre (Third Theatre)

Including:
Demonstrations, Presentations, Workshops, Discussions
Owls or Flowers?
Performance
PERFORMERS: see above
BELGRADE, YUGOSLAVIA

SEPTEMBER

Wraecca's Vision – Kaos
Performance
DIRECTOR: Richard Gough
PERFORMERS: Christine Favre, Richard Gough, John Hardy, Gerry Pyves
ST DONATS ARTS CENTRE AND CHAPTER ARTS CENTRE, CARDIFF, WALES

1977

JANUARY-FEBRUARY

Roundabout and Circular
Performance
DIRECTOR: Richard Gough
PERFORMERS: Richard Gough, Bryn Goulding, John Hardy
FROM CHAPTER ARTS CENTRE - TO - EAST MOORS YOUTH CENTRE, CARDIFF, WALES

FEBRUARY

Death of a Naturalist
Performance
DIRECTOR: Richard Gough
PERFORMERS: Richard Gough, Mike Pearson
FROM CHAPTER ARTS CENTRE - TO - KING'S ROAD CHURCH HALL, CARDIFF, WALES

Dancing on the Volcano
Performance
PERFORMERS: Mike Pearson, Siân Thomas
CHAPTER ARTS CENTRE, CARDIFF, WALES

Owls or Flowers?
Performance
PERFORMERS: see above
CHAPTER ARTS CENTRE, CARDIFF, WALES

MARCH

For a Lost Hour
Performance
DIRECTOR: Richard Gough
PERFORMERS: George Auchterlonie, Mike Baker, Mick Brennan, Richard Gough, John Hardy, Mike Pearson, Barry and Eve Pilcher, Gerry Pyves, Pol ar Ruz, Peter Thomas
FROM CHAPTER ARTS CENTRE, CARDIFF - TO - ST MARY'S WELL BAY, SULLY, WALES

MARCH-APRIL

Shadowlands
Performance
DIRECTOR: Richard Gough
PERFORMERS: Richard Gough, Bryn Goulding, John Hardy, Gerry Pyves
CHAPTER ARTS CENTRE, CARDIFF, WALES

APRIL-MAY

CLT tours Italy and France

Dancing on the Volcano
Performance
Owls or Flowers?
Performance
PERFORMERS: see above
FESTIVAL MONDIAL DU THÉÂTRE, NANCY, FRANCE; INCONTROAZIONE FESTIVAL, PALERMO (AND THROUGHOUT SICILY) AND TURIN, ITALY

JULY

Maskarade
The Journal of Cardiff Laboratory Theatre (eds. Richard Gough and Mike Pearson)
A CPR PUBLICATION

AUGUST

Clean of Body, Clean of Clothes
Performance
PERFORMERS: Mike Pearson, Siân Thomas, Inga Bjarnason, Nigel Watson
CHAPTER ARTS CENTRE, CARDIFF, WALES

SEPTEMBER

CLT at the International Encounter of Group Theatre (Third Theatre)

CLT activities included:
Special Events, Streetwork, Workshops and Demonstrations of Technique
PERFORMERS: George Auchterlonie, Richard Gough, John Hardy, Mike Pearson, Gerry Pyves, Siân Thomas
BERGAMO, ITALY

NOVEMBER

CLT participates in Chapter Arts Centre Residency

COMPANY IN RESIDENCE: Pip Simmons Group - The Woyzeck Project
CHAPTER ARTS CENTRE, CARDIFF, WALES

Dream Train
A Photographic Record of the 'Guizer Project' with a commentary including Maps and Music
A CPR PUBLICATION

1978

JANUARY

Epiphanies - Observance of Twelfth Tide
Performance
DIRECTOR: Richard Gough
PERFORMERS: Tim Baker, Richard Gough, John Hardy, Caroline Lynche-Blosse, Peter Thomas, Siân Thomas
FROM CHAPTER ARTS CENTRE – TO – LLECHWEDD CHURCH, PENARTH, WALES

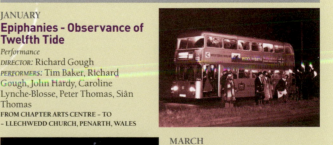

MARCH

Deaf Birds, Late Snow
Performance
PERFORMER: Mike Pearson
CHAPTER ARTS CENTRE, CARDIFF, WALES

MAY
Handshake
two 36 hour Workshops
WORKSHOP LEADERS: Richard Gough, Mike Pearson
CHAPTER ARTS CENTRE, CARDIFF, WALES

JUNE
CLT participates in Chapter Arts Centre Residency
COMPANY IN RESIDENCE: Waste of Time
(Amsterdam, the Netherlands)
CHAPTER ARTS CENTRE, CARDIFF, WALES

JULY
'The Gym' CLT moves to first permanent home 'The Gym' - Chapter Arts Centre, Cardiff, Wales

SEPTEMBER
CLT in Residence at Chapter Arts Centre

Including
Moths in Amber: Glimpses of a Nomad Opera
Performance
PERFORMERS: Cathy Frost, Richard Gough, Gerry Pyves, Mike Pearson, Siân Thomas
Whose Idea Was the Wind? *Performance*
PERFORMER: Mike Pearson
Shadowlands *(Second Version)*
Performance
DIRECTOR: Richard Gough
PERFORMERS: Richard Gough, John Hardy, Siân Thomas
Deaf Birds, Late Snow
Performance
PERFORMER: Mike Pearson
The Special Feast
Workshops
CHAPTER ARTS CENTRE, CARDIFF, WALES

Early Streetwork
PERFORMERS: Dave Baird, James Castle, Mike Pearson, Gerry Pyves, Siân Thomas
VARIOUS, WALES

SEPTEMBER – OCTOBER
CLT Tours Denmark
Including:
Performances and Residencies
Shadowlands
Performance
Moths in Amber: Glimpses of a Nomad Opera
Performance
DIRECTOR AND PERFORMERS: see above
ÅRHUS, BRABRAND, HOLSTEBRØ AND NAERUM SLAGELSE, DENMARK

OCTOBER
CLT at the Steirischer Herbst Festival
Including:
Moths in Amber: Glimpses of a Nomad Opera
Performance
PERFORMERS: James Castle, Cathy Frost, Richard Gough, Mike Pearson, Siân Thomas
GRAZ, AUSTRIA

NOVEMBER
CLT tours Brittany
Moths in Amber: Glimpses of a Nomad Opera
PERFORMERS: James Castle, Richard Gough, Mike Pearson, Siân Thomas
INCLUDING: THE RENNES FESTIVAL AND ST BRIEUC, BRITTANY, FRANCE

DECEMBER
The Wren Hunt
Performance Tour
PERFORMERS: Dave Baird, James Castle, Mike Pearson, Siân Thomas
VARIOUS, SOUTH WALES

Cardiff Laboratory Theatre

HANDSHAKE
a week-end meeting

JANUARY - MARCH
CLT tours Wales
Moths in Amber
Performance
PERFORMERS: see above

Aberystwyth Residency
Activities included:
Moths in Amber
Performance
PERFORMERS: see above
Aberystwyth Event
Special Event/Performance
DIRECTOR: Richard Gough
PERFORMERS: Peter Brooks, James Castle, Richard Gough, Mike Pearson, Siân Thomas
Workshop Series
UNIVERSITY OF OF WALES, COLLEGE ABERYSTWYTH, ABERYSTWYTH, WALES

FEBRUARY-MARCH
Mold Residency
Including:
Moths in Amber
Performance
PERFORMERS: see above
Mold Event
Special Event/Performance
DIRECTOR: Richard Gough
PERFORMERS: Peter Brooks, James Castle, Richard Gough, Gill Lloyd, Mike Pearson, Philip Thomas, Siân Thomas
Plas Teg
Special Event/Performance
DIRECTOR: Richard Gough
performers: James Castle, Richard Gough, Mike Pearson, Philip Thomas, Siân Thomas
MOLD, WALES

Bangor Residency
Including:
Moths in Amber
Performance
PERFORMERS: see above
Special Event
PERFORMERS: James Castle, Richard Gough, Mike Pearson, Philip Thomas, Siân Thomas
Workshop Series
UNIVERSITY OF WALES, COLLEGE BANGOR, BANGOR, WALES

MARCH
A Celebration of Homecoming and a Coming of Age
Performance to mark 5th anniversary
DIRECTOR AND PERFORMERS: members of CLT
THE GYM, CARDIFF, WALES

Moths in Amber
Performance
PERFORMERS: see above
THE GYM, CARDIFF, WALES

MAY – OCTOBER

The Summer Project
Including:

The Redwing Empire Band
Performance
PERFORMERS: Dave Baird, Lis Hughes Jones, Mike Pearson, Philip Thomas, Siân Thomas

The Bear Hunt
Performance
PERFORMERS: Dave Baird, Lis Hughes Jones, Mike Pearson, Philip Thomas

Blodeuwedd
Performance
PERFORMERS: Dave Baird, Lis Hughes Jones, Mike Pearson, Philip Thomas, Siân Thomas, Jeremy Turner, Christine Watkins, Sera Williams

The Distant Travellers *Performance*
PERFORMERS: Dave Baird, James Castle, Lis Hughes Jones, Mike Pearson, Philip Thomas, Siân Thomas
62 PERFORMANCES IN 39 WELSH TOWNS INCLUDING: BUILTH WELLS, BLAENAU FFESTINIOG, CAERPHILLY, CARDIFF, HAY-ON-WYE, LLANDRINDOD WELLS, MACHYNLLETH, MONMOUTH, NEWPORT, NEWTON, RHAYADER, WORCESTER AND WELSHPOOL.

JUNE

CLT at the Alternative Inspirations for the Actor's Work and New Theatre Houses Festival
COLLABORATING COMPANIES: Centro Ricerca e Sperimentazzione Teatrale di Pontedera (Italy), Gardzienice Theatre Association (Poland), Kathakali Kerala Kara Kendram (India) and Teatru Ósmego Dnia (Poland)
ILAWA, POLAND

Intensive Working Session
COLLABORATING COMPANIES: Akademia Ruchu (Poland) and Den Blå Hest (Denmark)
WARSAW, POLAND

Collaboration/Performance
Solo performance pieces for village of Veruchio
PARTNER COMPANY: Akademia Ruchu (Poland)
SANTARCHANGELO THEATRE FESTIVAL, ITALY

JULY

Summer School
WORKSHOP LEADERS: Tom Fjordefalk of Odin Teatret, Richard Gough, Mike Pearson, Siân Thomas of CLT
THE GYM, CARDIFF, WALES

JULY – OCTOBER

The Outdoors Indoors
Performance/Event
Activities included:

Redwing Empire Band
Performance
PERFORMERS: see above

The Distant Travellers
Performance
PERFORMERS: see above
CHAPTER ARTS CENTRE, CARDIFF, WALES

OCTOBER

CLT Organized Performance
Company: Patrick Beckers (Belgium)
Depaysage
Performance
CHAPTER ARTS CENTRE, CARDIFF, WALES

CLT at the Steirischer Herbst Festival
Including:

'Open House'
Special Event commissioned by the festival

Redwing Empire Band
PERFORMERS: see above

The Distant Travellers
PERFORMERS: see above

The Bear Hunt
PERFORMERS: see above

The Sleepwalkers
Special Event
A celebration of the life and work of Johannes Kepler
PERFORMERS: Dave Baird, James Castle, Richard Gough, John Hardy, Lis Hughes Jones, Mike Pearson, Philip Thomas, Siân Thomas
GRAZ, AUSTRIA

Selected Documents
Journal
(ed. Richard Gough)
A CLT PUBLICATION

NOVEMBER-DECEMBER

CLT Organised Residency/ Performance Tour
Company: Akademia Ruchu (Poland)
Performances/Demonstrations/Workshops
LONDON AND DARTINGTON, ENGLAND

Residency
CARDIFF, WALES

1980

JANUARY-MAY

CLT Tours Europe
Postcards in a Glass Court
An Academy of Fantasy
Performance
DIRECTOR: Richard Gough
PERFORMERS: Richard Gough, Jill Greenhalgh, Ljiljana Ortolja-Baird, Siân Thomas, Melanie Thompson
CHAPTER ARTS CENTRE, CARDIFF, WALES ÅRHUS, COPENHAGEN, HERNING AND HOLSTEBRO, DENMARK; ROTTERDAM, NETHERLANDS; GOTHENBERG, SWEDEN

APRIL

The Village Project
- to examine ways of presenting theatre in small communities
Residencies
PERFORMERS: Dave Baird, Lis Hughes Jones, Ljiljana Ortolja-Baird, Mike Pearson
VARIOUS, WALES

CLT Tours Wales

Postcards in a Glass Court - An Academy of Fantasy
Performance
DIRECTOR AND PERFORMERS: see above
ABERYSTWYTH, BANGOR, BUILTH WELLS AND MOLD, WALES

JUNE/JULY
Kathakali/Balinese Project
CLT Curated Residency
Activities included workshops, lectures, performances, films, barters, community meetings and presentations at Welsh festivals
COMPANIES: I Made Bandem and Family (Bali), Barbara Laishley (England: UK), Krishnan Nambudiri and Associate (India), Tara Rajkumar and VM Karunakaran Nair (India)
CHAPTER ARTS CENTRE, CARDIFF, WALES

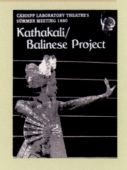

CLT Residency at Santarchangelo Festival

Including:

Workshops and Demonstrations

Special Event
IN COLLABORATION WITH Centro Ricerca e Sperimentazzione Teatrale di Pontedera (Italy)

Special Event
IN COLLOBORATION WITH The Mike Westbrook Band and Phil Minton (England:UK)

Women of The Dreaming *Performance*
DIRECTOR: Richard Gough
PERFORMERS: Lilijana Ortolja-Baird and Siân Thomas

Joking Apart *Performance*
DIRECTOR: Richard Gough
PERFORMERS: Jill Greenhalgh, Melanie Thompson
SANTARCHANGELO, ITALY

Women of The Dreaming
Performance
DIRECTOR AND PERFORMERS: see above
CHAPTER ARTS CENTRE, CARDIFF, WALES

Joking Apart
Performance
DIRECTOR AND PERFORMERS: see above
CHAPTER ARTS CENTRE, CARDIFF, WALES

AUGUST

Odin in Wales Residency of Odin Teatret (Denmark)
CURATION: Richard Gough
Activities included: Streetwork, Outdoor Performances, Formal Indoor Productions, Workshops, Films, Exhibitions and a Conference
CHAPTER ARTS CENTRE, CARDIFF, WALES

Street Performances, Presentations & Barters
BALA, BLAENAU FFESTINIOG, CARMARTHEN, LLANUWCHLLYN, NARBETH, NEWCASTLE EMLYN, MERTHYR TYDFIL, WALES

Collaborative Projects and Special Events
DENBIGH, LAMPETER AND MACHYNLLETH, WALES

Glimpses of the Map
Cardiff Laboratory Theatre, 1974-1980
A chronicle written by Mike Pearson
A CLT PUBLICATION

CARDIFF LABORATORY THEATRE
GLIMPSES OF THE MAP

OCTOBER

Joking Apart
Performance
DIRECTOR AND PERFORMERS: see above
CHAPTER ARTS CENTRE, CARDIFF, WALES

1981

FEBRUARY

The bi-lateral separation of CLT and formation of two autonomous companies

Mike Pearson and Lis Hughes Jones form Brith Gof and establish a base in Aberystwyth and Siân Thomas and Richard Gough continue under the name Cardiff Laboratory Theatre and establish a new permanent ensemble

MARCH - MAY

Spring School
CURATION: Richard Gough
A series of weekend workshops
LEADERS INCLUDED:
Frankie Armstrong, Patricia Bardi(USA), Roberta Carreri (Italy), Toni Cots (England: UK), Roma Choudhury (India), Peter Cusak (England:UK), Max Eastley (England:UK), Peter Ellis (England:UK), Will Gaines (England:UK), John Hardy (England:UK), Gordon Jones (England:UK), Maggie Nichols (England:UK), Michael Nyman (England:UK), Melvyn Poore (England:UK), Mike Pearson (Wales:UK), Emil Wolk(England:UK), and Simon Thorne (Wales:UK)
THE GYM AND CHAPTER ARTS CENTRE, CARDIFF, WALES

JUNE

Project Voice Inauguration
Presentation of Programme at the ITI General Assembly
MADRID, SPAIN

Leicester Residency
Including:

Daniel Lambert Event
Street Parade and Opening Ceremony

A Flush of Civic Toilets
Opening Event

The Life and Times of Thomas Cook
Travelling Special Event from Leicester to Loughborough and back
DIRECTOR: Richard Gough
PERFORMERS: Andrzej Borkowski, Yvonne Cheal, Jill Greenhalgh, John Hardy, Philip Mackenzie, Joan Mills, Geraldine Pilgrim, Siân Thomas, Melanie Thompson, Simon Thorne

An Evocation of the Jarrow Crusade
Outdoor Installation and Street Processions
LEICESTER, UK

JULY

CLT hosts Jerzy Grotowski
Including:

Encounters with Grotowski
Weekend public symposium

Month-long residency
CHAPTER ARTS CENTRE, CARDIFF, WALES

SEPTEMBER-OCTOBER

Blaenau Ffestiniog Residency

Including:

The Dragon Procession

An interchangeable sequence of outdoor performances
DIRECTOR: Richard Gough
PERFORMERS: Yvonne Cheal, Jill Greenhalgh, John Hardy, Philip Mackenzie, David Southern, Siân Thomas, Melanie Thompson, Simon Thorne

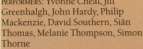

The Widow's Dream

Performance in the Slate Quarries
DIRECTOR: Richard Gough
PERFORMERS: Yvonne Cheal, Jill Greenhalgh, John Hardy, Philip Mackenzie, Joan Mills, David Southern, Siân Thomas, Melanie Thompson, Simon Thorne

Wedding Breakfast and Cabaret for Dragons

Streetwork/Performance
DIRECTOR: Richard Gough
PERFORMERS: Yvonne Cheal, Jill Greenhalgh, John Hardy, Philip Mackenzie, David Southern, Siân Thomas, Melanie Thompson, Simon Thorne

Street Parades, Processions and Outdoor Work

CLT members in collaboration with actors of Odin Teatret
BLAENAU FFESTINIOG, WALES

Outdoor work

In collaboration with Odin Teatret (Denmark)
VARIOUS, WALES

NOVEMBER-DECEMBER

Autumn School

Series of week-long and weekend workshops
WORKSHOP LEADERS INCLUDED: David Hykes (USA), Zygmunt Molik (Poland), Enrique Pardo (Peru/France)
THE GYM AND CHAPTERR ARTS CENTRE, CARDIFF, WALES

1982

FEBRUARY

The Wedding

Performance
DIRECTOR: Richard Gough
PERFORMERS: Helen Chadwick, Jill Greenhalgh, John Hardy, Philip Mackenzie, Melanie Thompson, Siân Thomas, Simon Thorne
CHAPTER ARTS CENTRE, CARDIFF, WALES

APRIL

CLT tours Wales

Dragon Procession

An interchangeable sequence of outdoor performances
DIRECTOR AND PERFORMERS: see above
INCLUDING ABERAERON, CARDIGAN, CARMARTHEN, DOLGELLAU, HARLECH, LAMPETER, MACHYNLLETH, NEWCASTLE EMLYN AND NEW QUAY

MAY

CLT tours Denmark

Including:

The Wedding

Performance
DIRECTOR AND PERFORMERS: see above
COPENHAGEN, HERNING AND HOLSTEBRØ

Århus Residency

The Wedding

Performance
DIRECTOR AND PERFORMERS: see above

Workshops at Århus Theatre Academy

ÅRHUS, DENMARK

CLT Tours Spain

The Wedding

Performance
DIRECTOR AND PERFORMERS: see above

Dragon Procession

An interchangeable sequence of outdoor performances
DIRECTOR AND PERFORMERS: see above

Streetwork

VARIOUS, SPAIN

JUNE-JULY

CLT tours Wales

Dragon Procession

An interchangeable sequence of outdoor performances
DIRECTOR AND PERFORMERS: see above

The Wedding

Performance
DIRECTOR AND PERFORMERS: see above

The Wedding Breakfast and Barter

A community arts interaction
INCLUDING: BALA, BLAENGWYNFI, BARMOUTH, CARDIGAN, CROESERW, DOLGELLAU, GLYNCORRWG, LLANDYSSUL, NEWTOWN, MERTHYR AND RHONDDA

SEPTEMBER

CLT Tours Italy

The Wedding

Performance
DIRECTOR AND PERFORMERS: see above
SANTARCHANGELO THEATRE FESTIVAL, VOLTERRA THEATRE FESTIVAL AND PONTEDERA, ITALY

Volterra Residency

Including:
Creation and performance of

The Orchestra

An outdoor concert
DIRECTOR: Richard Gough
PERFORMERS: Helen Chadwick, Jill Greenhalgh, John Hardy, Philip Mackenzie, Melanie Thompson, Siân Thomas, Simon Thorne

Workshops, Presentations and Meetings

CLT at the Festival of the Twin Towns
The Orchestra
An outdoor concert
DIRECTOR AND PERFORMERS: *see above*

Streetwork and Special Events
NANTES, FRANCE

NOVEMBER

CLT Curated Residency

Company: Grotowski's Teatr Laboratorium (Poland)
Including:
Workshops and Lectures
COMPANY WORKSHOP LEADERS: Irena Rycyk,
Rena Mirecka-Kadziolka, Zygmunt Molik,
Stanislaw Scierski, Ludwik Flaszen
THE GYM, CARDIFF, WALES

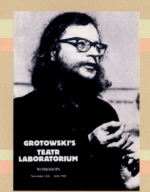

Project Voice Festival
Festival Launch Event
DIRECTOR: *John Hardy*
Including:
Workshop and Symposium
WORKSHOP LEADERS AND PRESENTERS INCLUDED: Lars Af Malmborg (Sweden), Patricia Bardi
(USA/Netherlands), Wilfrid Mellers (England:UK), Zygmunt Molik (Poland), Enrique
Pardo (Peru/France), John Potter (England:UK)
CARDIFF, WALES

1983

FEBRUARY
The Heart of the Mirror
Performance
DIRECTORS: *Richard Gough, Joan Mills*
PERFORMERS: *Helen Chadwick, Richard
Gough, Jill Greenhalgh, John Hardy,
Phillip Mackenzie, Melanie Thompson,
Siân Thomas, Simon Thorne*
THE GYM, CHAPTER ARTS CENTRE, CARDIFF,
WALES

CLT tours France
The Heart of the Mirror
Performance
DIRECTOR AND PERFORMERS: *see above*
MULHOUSE, FRANCE

MARCH – APRIL
Chapter Arts Centre Residency
EXPOSITION
*The complete performance work of Cardiff Laboratory Theatre, workshops and guest performances
from Akademia Ruchu (Poland) and Piccolo Theatre (Italy)*

CLT Performances
For a Lost Hour (Version 2)
Performance
DIRECTOR: *Richard Gough*
PERFORMERS: *CLT members*

Special Celebration
Performance/Installation/Celebration
DIRECTOR AND PERFORMERS:
CLT members

The Wedding
Performance
DIRECTOR AND PERFORMERS: *see above*

The Heart of the Mirror
Performance
DIRECTOR AND PERFORMERS: *see above*

The Sound House
Performance/Musical Collaboration

Easter Fools
Collaborative Performance
PARTNER COMPANY: *Akademia Ruchu
(Poland)*
PERFORMERS: *members of CLT and
Akademia Ruchu*

Akademia Ruchu Performances
English Lesson
Other Dances

Piccolo Teatro Performances
Il Giardino
Puccini
CHAPTER ARTS CENTRE, CARDIFF, WALES

CLT Organised Tour

COMPANY: **Centro Ricerca e Sperimentazzione Teatrale di Pontedera** (Italy)
INCLUDING: CARDIFF, WALES; LONDON AND DARTINGTON, ENGLAND

CLT Organized Residency

Part of the "Adopt a Host" programme
Company: **Akademia Ruchu** (Poland)
Performances:
Other Dances
English Lesson
Autobus
Daily Life After the French Revolution
Europa
Center – Polish Tatra

Workshops and Seminar Workshops
Film Screenings
INCLUDING LONDON, BRISTOL, LEICESTER,
TORRINGTON, DARLINGTON AND YORK, ENGLAND;
CARDIFF, WALES

MAY
San Isidro Residency
Centered around fiestas of San Isidro,
Spain
Including:
The Orchestra *Performance*
DIRECTORS AND PERFORMERS: *see above*

The Heart of the Mirror *Performance*
DIRECTOR AND PERFORMERS: *see above*

Special Event in Retiro Park
Workshops and Seminars
MADRID AND OUTLYING AREA, SPAIN

JUNE

CLT at the Gjøglernekommer Theatre Festival
Including:

The Wedding
Performance
DIRECTOR AND PERFORMERS: see above

The Heart of the Mirror
Performance
DIRECTOR AND PERFORMERS: see above

The Orchestra
Performance
DIRECTOR AND PERFORMERS: see above

Streetwork
OSLO, NORWAY

JUNE/JULY

CLT at The Fools Festival
Including:

The Together Project
The Labyrinth of the World
The Paradise of the Heart
a commissioned collaborative performance:
DIRECTORS: Richard Gough (Wales:UK), Zdzislaw Hejduk
(Poland), Alexander Jochveldt (Denmark), Joan Mills (Wales:UK),
Petr Oslzly (Czechoslovakia), Peter Schernhaufer (Czechoslovakia)
PERFORMERS: members of CLT, Theatr 77 (Poland), Divadlo Na
Provazku (Czechoslovakia) and Den Blå Hest (Denmark)

Heart of the Mirror
Performance
DIRECTOR AND PERFORMERS: see above

The Orchestra
Performance
DIRECTOR AND PERFORMERS: see above
COPENHAGEN, DENMARK

AUGUST

CLT at the London International Theatre Festival (LIFT)

Including:

The Wedding
Performance
DIRECTOR AND PERFORMERS: see above

The Orchestra
Performance
DIRECTOR AND PERFORMERS: see above

The Heart of the Mirror
Performance
DIRECTOR AND PERFORMERS: see above

Theatre and Voice Workshops
LONDON, ENGLAND

SEPTEMBER

CLT at: 1st Trevignano International Theatre Festival
Including:

The Orchestra
Performance
DIRECTOR AND PERFORMERS: see above

The Wedding
Performance
DIRECTOR AND PERFORMERS: see above

The Heart of the Mirror
Performance
DIRECTOR AND PERFORMERS: see above

Journey to the Castle
Collaborative Performance
Part of **The Alice Project**
DIRECTOR AND PERFORMERS: members of
CLT, Grenland Friteater (Norway) and
Odin Teatret (Denmark)

The Secret of Alice
Collaborative Performance
DIRECTOR AND PERFORMERS: members of
CLT, Grenland Friteater and
Odin Teatret
LAKE TREVIAGNO, ROME, ITALY

CLT at the 2nd Valladolid International Theatre Festival
Activities included:

The Wedding
Performance
DIRECTOR AND PERFORMERS: see 1982

The Orchestra
Performance
DIRECTOR AND PERFORMERS: see above
Workshops and Discussions
VALLADOLLID, SPAIN

DECEMBER

Blaenau Ffestiniog Residency

Including formation of:
local adult drama/theatre group,
Community Arts Committee, the
advancement of stilt club previously
established

Feast of the Firebird
celebration with local artists
DIRECTOR: Richard Gough with
Michael McCarthy (Apprenticeship
Scheme Theatre Director)
PERFORMERS: community members
and CLT
BLAENAU FFESTINIOG, WALES

1984

JANUARY
Llandysul Residency
Activities included:

Feast of the Firebird
Outdoor Event
DIRECTOR: Michael McCarthy
PERFORMERS: community members and CLT

Streetwork
Workshops
Collaborations with local artists
LLANDYSUL, WALES

FEBRUARY
CLT Organised Tour
COMPANY: **Théâtre de l'autre Rive** (France)
CARDIFF, WALES

CLT Organised Tour
PERFORMER: **Richard Fowler**
CARDIFF, WALES

Curated Residency
K.N.Pannikar & Colleagues (India)
Programme included performances and workshops
CARDIFF, WALES

CARDIFF LABORATORY THEATRE
Flight Into Winter

MARCH
CLT Tours Wales

Orpheus Opera Project *Performance*

DIRECTOR: Michael
McCarthy
PERFORMERS: Jill
Greenhalgh, John
Hardy, Philip
Mackenzie, Mike
Rafferty, Dorota
Kwiatowska, Simon
Thorne, Siân Thomas
MUSICIANS: Glynn Perrin,
Mike Rafferty, Ali
Robinson
INCLUDING ABERGAVENNY,
ABERYSTWYTH, BANGOR,
BLAENAU FFESTINIOG,
BRECON, CARDIFF,
CARMARTHEN, DOLGELLAU,
LLANDRINDOD WELLS,
LLANDYSUL, NEWTOWN
WALES

APRIL
CLT tours Wales
Manact
Performance
PERFORMERS: Philip Mackenzie, Simon Thorne

NOVEMBER-DECEMBER
The Funeral
Performance
PERFORMERS: Jim Ennis, Tracie Gillman, Chris Marshall, Philip Mackenzie
CHAPTER ARTS CENTRE, CARDIFF, WALES

CLT tours Poland
The Funeral
Performance
DIRECTOR AND PERFORMERS: see above

Manact
Performance
DIRECTOR AND PERFORMERS: see above
INCLUDING: LODZ AND WARSAW, POLAND

1985

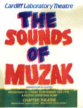

FEBRUARY
CLT Tours Wales

MARCH
The Funeral
Performance
DIRECTOR AND PERFORMERS: see 1984
VARIOUS, WALES

MAY
The Centre for Performance Research
Established as the resource centre of Cardiff Laboratory Theatre, 5 Llandaff Road, Cardiff, Wales

JUNE
CLT at the Midsummer Music Carnival
Workshops, Streetwork and Special Events
DIRECTOR: Richard Gough
PERFORMERS: Frankie Armstrong, Andrzej Borkowski, Jim Ennis, Tracie Gillman, Philip Mackenzie, Chris Marshall
BELFAST, NORTHERN IRELAND

AUGUST
Captive Waves
Performance
Magdalena '86: Pilot Project
DIRECTOR: Jill Greenhalgh
PERFORMERS: Charlotte Buchanan, Kari Furre, Jill Greenhalgh, Claire Hughes, Ali Robinson, Sandra Salmaso
CHAPTER ARTS CENTRE, CARDIFF, WALES

CLT Presented Performance
Company: Els Comediants (Spain)
Alè
Performance
ST DAVID'S HALL, CARDIFF, WALES

SEPTEMBER
Commedia Dell'Arte
CLT Organized Residency
WORKSHOP LEADERS: Carlo Boso and Stefano Perocco (Italy)
CHAPTER ARTS CENTRE, CARDIFF, WALES

Streetwork and Special Events
CARDIFF CITY CENTRE, CARDIFF, WALES

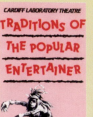

OCTOBER
CLT Presented Performance
Company: Divadlo na Provazku (Czechoslovakia)
Commedia Dell'Arte
Performance
ST DAVID'S HALL, CARDIFF, WALES

OCTOBER - DECEMBER
Traditions of the Popular Entertainer Festival
CURATION: Richard Gough
WORKSHOP LEADERS INCLUDED: Gerry Cottle (England:UK), Edwin E. Dawes (England:UK), Alan Felton (England: UK), Penny Mindelsohn (England:UK), Bolek Polivka and Divadlo na Provazku (Czechoslovakia), Mike Simkin (England:UK), George Speight (England:UK), Rogan Taylor (England:UK), John Warren (England:UK)
CHAPTER ARTS CENTRE, CARDIFF, WALES

The Origin of Table Manners
Performance
DIRECTOR: Richard Gough
PERFORMERS: Andrzej Borkowski, Jim Ennis, Tracie Gillman, Jill Greenhalgh, Philip Mackenzie, Chris Marshall, Sally Thompson
CHAPTER ARTS CENTRE, CARDIFF

NOVEMBER
CLT Organized Workshop
Le Jeu
WORKSHOP LEADER: Philippe Gaulier (France)
CHAPTER ARTS CENTRE, CARDIFF, WALES

Cardiff Laboratory Theatre, Theatre Papers The Fifth Series No 3
(ed. Peter Hulton)
DARTINGTON: THEATRE PAPERS
A CLT PUBLICATION

DECEMBER
The Sounds of Muzak
Performance
DIRECTOR: Richard Gough
MUSIC DIRECTOR: John Hardy
PERFORMERS: Jim Ennis, Tracie Gillman, Jill Greenhalgh, John Hardy, Chris Marshall, Joan Mills, Sally Thompson and staff members of Chapter
CHAPTER ARTS CENTRE, CARDIFF, WALES

1986

JANUARY-FEBRUARY
From Honey to Ashes
Performance/Installation
DIRECTOR: Richard Gough
PERFORMERS: Andrzej Borkowski, Jim Ennis, Richard Gough
CHAPTER ARTS CENTRE, CARDIFF, WALES

FEBRUARY-MARCH

Faustus

Performance
PERFORMER: Philip Mackenzie
with a special appearance by Tracie Gillman
CHAPTER ARTS CENTRE, CARDIFF, WALES

MARCH-APRIL

Expo 86 Chapter Arts Centre Residency

Including **Workshops, Presentations, Exhibitions**

The Origin of Table Manners

Performance
DIRECTOR AND PERFORMERS: see above

From Honey to Ashes

Performance/Installation
DIRECTOR AND PERFORMERS: see above

Faustus

Performance
PERFORMERS: see above

Lost Voices

Performance
DIRECTOR: Richard Gough
PERFORMERS: Frankie Armstrong, Joan Mills
CHAPTER ARTS CENTRE, CARDIFF WALES

Research Trip to China

INVITED ARTISTS: Richard Gough and Chris Marshall
HONG KONG, BEIJING AND SHANGHAI, CHINA

AUGUST

Magdalena '86: International Festival of Women in Theatre, Phase 1

Including **Workshops, Discussions, Performances, Presentations**

PROJECT DIRECTOR: Jill Greenhalgh
PRODUCER: Judie Christie
WORKSHOP LEADERS INCLUDED: Geddy Aniksdal, Anne Erichsen and Elin Lindberg (Norway), Brigitte Cirla (France), Helen Chadwick (England:UK), Maria Consagra (USA/Italy), Lis Hughes Jones (Wales:UK), Zofia Kalinska (Poland), Ida Kelarova and Iva Bittova (The Czech Republic), Stacey Klein and Andrea Dishy (USA), Kozana Lucca (France), Netta Plotzky (Russia/Israel), Graciela Serra (Argentina), Isabel Soto (France)
PERFORMANCES: Geddy Aniksdal, Anne Erichsen and Elin Lindberg (Norway), Helen Chadwick (England:UK), Cora Herrendorf (Italy), Jolanta Biela Jelzmyk and Jolanta Gadeczek (Poland), Brigitte Kacquet (Belgium), Zofia Kalinska, Ida Kelarova and Iva Bittova (Czechoslovakia), Jolanta Krukowska and Marta Sutkowska (Poland), Anna Lica (Denmark), Netta Plotzky (Russia/Israel), Sandra Salmaso and Cinzia Mascherin (Italy), Graciela Serra (Argentina)
CHAPTER ARTS CENTRE, CARDIFF, WALES

Phase 2

Collaborative Performance
PERFORMERS: festival artists
EDWARD ENGLAND POTATO WAREHOUSE, CARDIFF, WALES

SEPTEMBER

Peking Opera Explorations Festival 86-87

Peking Opera School Residency

Lectures, Concerts, Exhibitions, Demonstrations and Film Screenings

CURATION: Richard Gough and Chris Marshall
WORKSHOP LEADERS: Ma Mingqun (P.R.C.), Wang Peilin (P.R.C.), Wu Suqui (P.R.C.), Luo Cho Yi (Hong Kong), Guo Yi (P.R.C./UK), Guo Yue (P.R.C./UK)
PRESENTATIONS: Members of the Company
CARDIFF, WALES

Peking Opera Explorations Festival 86-87

China Day: A Festival of Chinese Culture

CURATION: Richard Gough and Chris Marshall
PRESENTATIONS: Jessica Cohen and Richard Farmer (England:UK), Dai Bai Fung (P.R.C./UK), the Guo Brothers (P.R.C./UK), Lorette van Heteren (Netherlands), Ma Ming Qun (P.R.C.), Ng (P.R.C.), Jo Riley (England:UK), Wu Suqui (P.R.C.), Luo Choi Yi (Hong Kong)
WELSH COLLEGE OF MUSIC AND DRAMA, AND CHAPTER ARTS CENTRE, CARDIFF, WALES

Peking Opera Explorations Festival 86-87

Peking Opera & 20th Century European Theatre

International Symposium
Presentations, Demonstrations and Film Screenings

CURATION: Richard Gough and Chris Marshall
CHAIR: Richard Gough
PERFORMANCES: Wu Suqui (P.R.C.), Ma Mingqun (P.R.C.) and Luo Choi Yi (Hong Kong)
PRESENTATIONS: William Dolby (England:UK), Richard Gough (Wales:UK), Tao Ching Hsu (Taiwan/UK), Colin Mackerras (Australia), Jacques Pimpaneau (France), Jo Riley (England:UK), Nicola Savarese (Italy), Elizabeth Wichmann (USA)
WELSH COLLEGE OF MUSIC AND DRAMA CARDIFF, WALES

OCTOBER-NOVEMBER

Peking Opera Explorations Festival 86-87

Peking Opera Tour

CPR Organized Tour

PRODUCER: Judie Christie

Havoc in Heaven
The Monkey King
500 Years On
The Red Maid
The Complexion of Peach Blossom
Stealing the Magic Herbs
The Jade Bracelet
Two Shots at the Wild Goose

Performances
DUBLIN AND GALWAY, EIRE; BARNSTAPLE, BIRMINGHAM, BRIGHTON, CANTERBURY, DARTFORD, HULL, LONDON, NORWICH AND SOUTHEND, ENGLAND; BELFAST, N. IRELAND; EDINBURGH, SCOTLAND AND CARDIFF, WALES

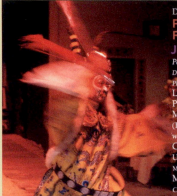

DECEMBER
Peking Opera Explorations Festival 86-87
Journey to the West
Performance
DIRECTOR: Richard Gough (Wales:UK)
PERFORMERS: Jim Ennis (Wales:UK),
Lorette van Heteren (Netherlands),
Philip Mackenzie (Wales:UK), Chris
Marshall (Wales:UK), Sally Thompson
(England:UK), Luo Choi Yi (Hong Kong)
with special appearances by: Jessica
Cohen (Wales:UK), Jill Orram (Wales:
UK), Paula Vickers (Wales:UK)
MUSICIANS: John Hardy (Wales:UK),
Michael Rafferty (Wales:UK)
CHAPTER ARTS CENTRE, CARDIFF, WALES

Honey to Ashes *Performance*
DIRECTOR AND PERFORMERS: see above
CHAPTER ARTS CENTRE, CARDIFF, WALES

Faustus *Performance*
DIRECTOR AND PERFORMERS: see above
VARIOUS, WALES

1987

JANUARY–FEBRUARY
Research Trip to China
INVITED ARTISTS: Judie Christie, Richard Gough,
Chris Marshall, Sally Thompson
SHANGHAI, CHINA AND TAIWAN

MARCH
Reconnaissances to Ireland *CPR AND*
GARDZIENICE ARTISTS: Judie Christie, Jim Ennis,
Wlodzimierz Staniewski
VARIOUS, EIRE AND N.IRELAND

APRIL
Centre for Performance Research: Catalogue One 1987–88
COMPILED AND EDITED BY Ric Allsopp
A CLT PUBLICATION

AUGUST-NOVEMBER
Peking Opera Explorations Festival 86-87
CPR Organized Tour of The Shanghai Kunju Theatre
The Kunju Macbeth
The Woman Warrior
The Peony Pavilion
Performances
PRODUCERS: Judie Christie, Richard Gough, Chris Marshall
COPENHAGEN AND HERNING, DENMARK; BARNSTAPLE, BRIGHTON, BRISTOL, CAMBRIDGE,
GUILFORD, IPSWICH, LEICESTER, LONDON, MANCHESTER, PRESTON, PLYMOUTH, SOUTHAMPTON
AND STRATFORD, ENGLAND; BELFAST, N. IRELAND; EDINBURGH, INVERNESS AND GLASGOW,
SCOTLAND; LINKÖPING, SWEDEN; CARDIFF, WALES

Peking Opera Explorations Festival 86-87
Shanghai Kunju Theatre – Souvenir Programme
A CLT PUBLICATION

OCTOBER-NOVEMBER
Peking Opera Explorations Festival 86-87
Secrets of the Pear Garden
Peking Opera School II
A series of workshops, masterclasses and presentations by company members and
invited experts
CURATION: Judie Christie, Richard Gough, Chris Marshall
WORKSHOP LEADERS: Zhang Chun Hua (P.R.C.), Ma Mingqun
(P.R.C.), Chen Xilan (P.R.C.)
PRESENTATIONS INCLUDED: Michael Gissenweher (Germany),
Jaques Pimpaneau (France), Jo Riley (England:UK), Charles
Scott (England:UK), Zhang Chun Hua (P.R.C.)
CHAPTER ARTS CENTRE, CARDIFF, WALES

NOVEMBER
Peking Opera Explorations Festival 86-87
Translation, Mutation and Betrayal
*An international symposium on tradition and experiment in the
exchange of theatres east and west*
CURATION: Judie Christie and Richard Gough
CHAIR: Richard Gough
CONTRIBUTORS INCLUDED: James Brandon (USA), Tsai Chin
(Hong Kong/UK), Michael Gissenweher (Germany),
Richard Gough (Wales:UK), Tao Ching Hsu (Taiwan/UK),
Dana Kalvodová (Czechoslovakia), John Martin (England:
UK), Jacques Pimpaneau (France), Jo Riley (England:UK),
Nicola Savarese (Italy), Members of the Shanghai Kunju
Theatre Company and the Peking Opera (P.R.C.)
RIVERSIDE STUDIOS, LONDON, ENGLAND

DECEMBER – MARCH '88
***The dissolution of the formal entity
Cardiff Laboratory Theatre Ltd.***
due to insolvency arising from losses on the
London season of Shanghai Kunju Theatre tour

APRIL - JULY

CPR successor to CLT Formation of the formal entity and educational charity, Centre for Performance Research Ltd.

Points of Contact: Theatre, Anthropology and Theatre Anthropology
Conference
CURATION: Judie Christie and Richard Gough
CHAIR: Richard Gough
PERFORMANCE: Roberta Carreri (Italy/Denmark)
PRESENTATIONS: Nicholas Arnold (England:UK), Eugenio Barba (Italy/Denmark), John Blacking (N. Ireland:UK), Mette Bovin (Denmark), Roberta Carreri (Italy/Denmark), Richard Gough (Wales:UK), Franco Ruffini (Italy), Nicola Savarese (Italy), Richard Schechner (USA), Ferdinando Taviani (Italy)
LEICESTER POLYTECHNIC, LEICESTER, ENGLAND

OCTOBER - DECEMBER
Act 88
Workshop Series
WORKSHOP LEADERS: Cicely Berry (England:UK), Paul Clements (Wales:UK), Richard Gough (Wales:UK), Frank Rozelaar Green (Wales:UK), Mary Hammond (England: UK), Andrew Neil (Wales:UK), Joan Mills (Wales:UK), Echo Studios (Wales:UK), David Tinker (Wales:UK)
THE GYM AND CHAPTER ARTS CENTRE, CARDIFF, WALES

DECEMBER – MARCH '89
'The Practice'
Formation and training of the new performance ensemble of the CPR

JANUARY–FEBRUARY
The Fool School
Workshops, Talks, Performances and Presentations
CURATION: Judie Christie and Richard Gough
WORKSHOP LEADERS INCLUDED: Carlo Boso (Italy), Pierre Byland (Switzerland), Ken Campbell (England:UK), I Nyomen Catra (Bali), Richard Gough (Wales:UK), Joan and Barry Grantham (England: UK), Zhang Chun Hua (P.R.C.), Jonathan Kay (England:UK), John Lee (England:UK), Karunakaran Nair (India)
CHAPTER ARTS CENTRE, CARDIFF, WALES

JANUARY–MARCH
The Burning of the Dancers
Performance
DIRECTORS: Richard Gough, Philip Mackenzie
PERFORMERS: Chris Durnall, Jo Law, Phillip Mackenzie, David Murray, Nicki Rainsford, Chris Rowbury, Susan Vidler
PRODUCTION AND DESIGN: Simon Banham, Paul Clay, Juliet Marsh
CHAPTER ARTS CENTRE, CARDIFF, WALES

MARCH
Frankie Armstrong Voice Workshop
CARDIFF, WALES

APRIL
Gardzienice Theatre Association, Centre for Theatrical Practices, Poland
A Photographic Essay with articles and interviews to accompany the Gardzienice Project UK
(*EDS.* Judie Christie and Richard Gough)
A CPR PUBLICATION

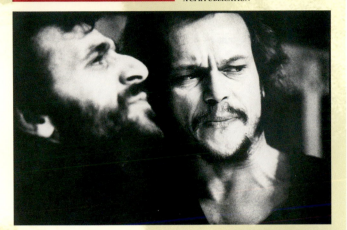

Points of Contact :Performance, Nature, Culture
Conference and Exposition of Gardzienice Theatre Association
CURATION: Ric Allsopp, Judie Christie, Richard Gough
PRESENTATIONS: Brith Gof (Wales:UK), Richard Demarco (Scotland:UK), Malgorzata Dziewulska (Poland), Gardzienice Theatre Association (Poland), Richard Gough (Wales:UK), Horse and Bamboo (England:UK), I.O.U. (England:UK), Lumiere & Son (England:UK), Janusz Majcherek (Poland), Wlodzimierz Staniewski (Poland)
DARTINGTON COLLEGE OF ARTS, ENGLAND

Gardzienice Project '89, Phase 1
CPR Organized Tour
Performances, Post-show Discussions and Presentations
PRODUCER: Judie Christie
Avvakum, with Gathering
Performances
BRIGHTON AND DARTINGTON, ENGLAND; GLASGOW, SCOTLAND; CARDIFF, WALES

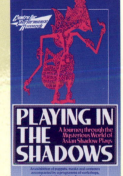

The Burning of the Dancers *Performance*
DIRECTOR AND PERFORMERS: see above
CHAPTER ARTS CENTRE, CARDIFF, WALES

The Resurrection of the Body
CPR Organized Residency
Company: Gardzienice Theatre Association (Poland)
DRUIDSTONE HAVEN, WALES

MAY - JUNE
Playing in the Shadows: A Journey through the Mysterious World of Asian Shadow Plays
Exhibitions
Exhibition of puppets from the Musée Kwok On Collection Paris, France, accompanied by a programme of workshops, demonstrations and performances
CURATION: Judie Christie and Richard Gough
THE OLD LIBRARY, THE HAYES, CARDIFF, WALES

The Origin of Table Manners
Performance
DIRECTOR: Richard Gough
PERFORMERS: Andrzej Borkowski, Chris Durnall, Jo Law, David Murray, Nicki Rainsford, Chris Rowbury, Susan Vidler
CHAPTER ARTS CENTRE, CARDIFF, WALES

OCTOBER-NOVEMBER

The Practice tours the UK
The Origin of Table Manners
Performance
DIRECTOR AND PERFORMERS: see above
VARIOUS, ENGLAND, SCOTLAND AND WALES

Act '89 Workshop Series
A season of weekend workshops
WORKSHOP LEADERS INCLUDED: Richard Gough, Joan Mills, Lloyd Newson, Julia Wilson-Dickson
CHAPTER THEATRE, CARDIFF, WALES

1990

APRIL

Points of Contact:
Performance, Politics and Ideology *Conference*

CURATION: Judie Christie and Richard Gough in collaboration with Baz Kershaw
CHAIR: Richard Gough
WORKSHOP LEADERS: Margaretta D'Arcy (Eire), Hugo Medina (Chile), Kolé Omotoso (Nigeria), Petr Oslzly (Czechoslovakia), Richard Schechner (USA), Joel Schechter (USA)
PRESENTATIONS: John Arden (Eire), Clive Barker (England:UK), Augusto Boal (Brazil), Chris Cairns (Wales:UK), Mick Dillon (England:UK), Utpal Dutt (Bangladesh), David Edgar (England:UK), Dario Fo and Franca Rame (Italy), Gillian Hanna (USA), Albert Hunt (England:UK), Mine Kaylan (Turkey/UK), Deborah Levy (England:UK), Hugo Medina (Chile), Richard Schechner (USA)
DEPARTMENT OF THEATRE STUDIES, UNIVERSITY OF LANCASTER, ENGLAND

Giving Voice Inaugural Festival and Symposium
DIRECTOR: Joan Mills
PERFORMANCES/DEMONSTRATIONS: Roberta Carreri (Italy/Denmark)
P'ansori Opera performers: Eun Hee-Jin, An Sook-Hun and Chong Hwa-Young (Korea)
WORKSHOP LEADERS: Frankie Armstrong (Wales: UK), Brigitte Cirla (Belgium), Richard Farmer (Wales:UK) and Joan Mills (Wales:UK), John Francis (England:UK), Derek Gale (England: UK), Mary Hammond and Geoffrey Osborn (England:UK), Eun Hee-Jin (Korea), Chong Hwa-Young (Korea), Kristin Linklater (USA), Kozanna Lucca (Argentina), Zygmunt Molik (Poland), Ronald Murdoch (England:UK), Gilles Petit (France), Ellen Mueller Preis (Germany) and Louise Bourbeau (Germany), An Sook-Hun (Korea), Barnaby Stone (England:UK)
SYMPOSIUM PRESENTATIONS: Frankie Armstrong (Wales:UK), Cicely Berry (England:UK), Brigitte Cirla (Belgium),
Sara Collins (Wales:UK), Derek Gale (England:UK), Mary Hammond (England:UK), Tom Harris (England:UK), Keith Howard (England:UK), Jacob Lieberman (England: UK),
Kristin Linklater (USA), Kozanna Lucca (Argentina), Zygmunt Molik (Poland), Ronald Murdoch (England:UK), Inok Paek (Korea), Gilles Petit (France), Ellen Mueller Preis (Germany)
CARDIFF, WALES

Augusto Boal Workshop
CPR Organized Workshop
UNIVERSITY OF LANCASTER, ENGLAND

The Practice tours Colombia
The Origin of Table Manners
Performance
DIRECTOR: Richard Gough
PERFORMERS: Andrzej Borkowski, Joe James, Jo Law, David Murray, Nicki Rainsford, Chris Rowbury, Susan Vidler
BOGOTA, CALI, MEDELLIN, COLOMBIA

JUNE

Directors' Training Module 1
Intensive Workshop for Directors
INVITED DIRECTOR: **Augusto Boal** (Brazil)
THE GYM, CARDIFF, WALES

SEPTEMBER

Odin in Wales: Ten Years On
CPR Organized Residency
Workshops, Performances, Film Screenings, Demonstrations
CURATION: Judie Christie and Richard Gough

Odin Performances
Talabot
Judith
Traces in the Snow
The Castle of Holstebro

The Practice Performances
The Origin of Table Manners
The Burning of the Dancers
ODIN WORKSHOP LEADERS: Eugenio Barba, Richard Fowler, Iben Nagel Rasmussen, Torgier Wethal
PRESENTATION: Project Groenseland

Symposium: Theatre: Autobiography and Anthropology
CONVENOR: Eugenio Barba

Nordisk Teater Laboratorium Administrators' Forum
PRESENTATION: Eugenio Barba, Søren G. Kjems, Sigrid Post, Julia Varley
THE GYM AND CHAPTER ARTS CENTRE, CARDIFF, WALES

The Burning of the Dancers *Performance*
DIRECTOR: Richard Gough and Philip Mackenzie
PERFORMERS: Jo Law, Philip Mackenzie, Roger McKern, David Murray, Nicki Rainsford, Chris Rowbury, Susan Vidler
CHAPTER ARTS CENTRE, CARDIFF, WALES

Great Reckonings in Small Rooms?
Visions for a New Theatre *Conference*
CURATION AND CHAIR: Richard Gough
PRESENTATIONS: Roberto Bacci (Italy), Eugenio Barba (Italy/Denmark), Jean-Norman Benedetti (England:UK), Edward Braun (England:UK), Fabrizio Cruciani (Italy), Mike Elster (Wales:UK), Richard Gough (Wales:UK), Shomit Mitter (India/UK), Zbigniew Osiński (Poland), Carla Pollastrelli (Italy), Franco Ruffini (Italy), Nicola Savarese (Italy), Nicholas Worrall (England:UK)
CARDIFF, WALES

Directors' Training Module 2
Intensive Workshop for Directors
INVITED DIRECTOR: **Eugenio Barba** (Italy/Denmark)
THE GYM, CARDIFF, WALES

JUNE
The Burning of the Dancers *Performance*
DIRECTOR: Richard Gough
PERFORMERS: Brendan Charleson, Joe James, Roger McKern, Nicki Rainsford, Chris Rowbury, Tracy Spottiswoode, Susan Vidler
THE GYM, CARDIFF, WALES

From Honey to Ashes: The Spirit of the Hive
Performance
DIRECTOR: Richard Gough
PERFORMERS: Joe James, Susan Vidler, Chris Rowbury
THE GYM, CARDIFF, WALES

JULY
The Practice Tours Italy

Performances and Special Events
From Honey to Ashes
Performance
DIRECTOR AND PERFORMERS:
see above

From Honey to Ashes: The Foundation of the City
Performance
DIRECTOR: Richard Gough
PERFORMERS: Brendan Charleson, Athena Constantine, Joe James, Roger McKern, Chris Rowbury, Tracy Spottiswoode, Susan Vidler

Special Events
DIRECTOR AND PERFORMERS: The Practice members
VOLTERRA AND FAENZA, ITALY

OCTOBER
A Dictionary of Theatre Anthropology: The Secret Art of the Performer
by Eugenio Barba and Nicola Savarese
CPR Book edited by Richard Gough and published by Routledge, London and New York
A CPR PUBLICATION

JANUARY-MARCH
Meeting Ground Workshop Series
Evening Meetings, Discussions and Workshops for Local Practitioners
CHAPTER ARTS CENTRE, CARDIFF

JANUARY
Voice and Body Workshops *Workshop Series*
WORKSHOP LEADER: Zygmunt Molik (Poland)
CHAPTER ARTS CENTRE, CARDIFF, WALES

FEBRUARY
Directors' Training Module 3: Woyzeck Project
INVITED DIRECTOR: Tadeusz Bradecki (Poland)
THE GYM, CARDIFF, WALES

The Practice tours Poland
From Honey to Ashes
DIRECTOR AND PERFORMERS: see 1991
INCLUDED: KRAKOW, GDANSK, POZNAN, WARSAW, POLAND

From Honey to Ashes
Performance
DIRECTOR AND PERFORMERS: see 1991
CHAPTER ARTS CENTRE, CARDIFF, WALES

APRIL
International School of Theatre Anthropology ISTA - 10th Session, Working on Performance, East and West/Subscore

CPR Organized Festival
Performances, Presentations, Workshops, Discussions and Working Sessions
PRODUCERS: Judie Christie and Richard Gough
CONVENOR/DIRECTOR: Eugenio Barba (Italy/Denmark)
ISTA ARTISTS INCLUDED: Fabrizio Cruciani (Italy), Dharma Shanti Company (Bali), Kanichi Hanayagi (Japan), Patrice Pavis (France), members of Odin Teatret (Denmark), Mark Oshima (Japan), Sanjukta Panigrahi and ensemble (India), Franco Ruffini (Italy), Ferdinando Taviani (Italy), Nicola Savarese (Italy)
PERFORMANCES INCLUDED: Desak Made Suarti Laksmi and ensemble (Bali), Kanichi Hanayagi (Japan), Odin Teatret (Denmark), Sanjukta Panigrahi and ensemble (India)

Theatrum Mundi
Performances with ensembles and local artists
Intensive work session with Odin Teatret and ISTA artists
BRECON, WALES

Fictive Bodies, Dilated Minds, Hidden Dances
Conference
Eugenio Barba (Italy/Denmark), Fabrizio Cruciani (Italy), Carol Martin (USA), Patrice Pavis (France), Ferdinando Taviani (Italy), Members of Odin Teatret (Denmark) and Sanjukta Panigrahi (India), Franco Ruffini (Italy), Nicola Savarese (Italy), David Williams (England:UK)
CHAPTER ARTS CENTRE, CARDIFF, WALES

East & West
CPR Organized Programme of Residencies and Performances
PERFORMANCES: A Multi-Cultural Variety Show (various), Dharma Shanti Company (Bali), Kanichi Hanayagi Company (Japan), Odin Teatret (Denmark), Sanjukta Panigrahi (India)
BRECON AND CARDIFF, WALES

Refusing to Act: Acts of Refusal
CPR Organized Workshop
WORKSHOP LEADER: Nigel Watson
CHAPTER ARTS CENTRE, CARDIFF, WALES

MAY
The Practice tours England
From Honey to Ashes
Performance
PERFORMERS: Josie Ayers, Joe James, Chris Rowbury
BRIGHTON FESTIVAL SHOWCASE AND VARIOUS, ENGLAND

JUNE
The Practice tours Brazil
From Honey to Ashes
Performance
DIRECTOR AND PERFORMERS: see above
LONDRINA AND SAO PAULO, BRAZIL

The Tempest Special Event
Large-scale site specific series of events made for Londrina
with local artists and The Practice team: Josie Ayers, Simon Banham, Judie Christie, Geoff Haynes, Joe James, Roger McKern, Beatrice Pemberton, Chris Rowbury
DIRECTOR: Richard Gough
LONDRINA, BRAZIL

SEPTEMBER–OCTOBER

New Polish Realities

Converging residencies of three Polish companies across the UK with a programme of performances, lectures, workshops, demonstrations and post-show discussions/presentations
PRODUCER: Judie Christie

COMPANY: **Akademia Ruchu**
Everyday Life after the Revolution II
Performance
LONDON AND MANCHESTER, ENGLAND; CARDIFF, WALES

COMPANY: **Teatr Ósmego Dnia**
(Theatre of the Eighth Day)
No Man's Land
Performance
CREWE, LONDON AND NOTTINGHAM, ENGLAND; GLASGOW, SCOTLAND; CARDIFF, WALES

COMPANY: **Gardzienice Theatre Association**
Avvakum with Gathering Carmina Burana
Performances
LONDON, NOTTINGHAM AND STRATFORD-UPON-AVON, ENGLAND; CARDIFF, WALES

The Practice tours England and Scotland
From Honey to Ashes
Performance
PERFORMERS: see 1991
LANCASTER, LONDON, ST. AUSTEL, TORRINGTON, TOTNES AND YORK, ENGLAND AND ABERDEEN, SCOTLAND

1993

JANUARY

Points of Contact: Performance, Ritual and Shamanism
Conference
CURATION: Richard Gough and Scott de Lahunta
chair: Scott de Lahunta
PERFORMANCES: Alastair MacLennan (N. Ireland:UK), Nick Stewart (England:UK)
WORKSHOP LEADERS: Alessandro Fersen (Italy), Nicolás Núñez (Mexico)
PRESENTATIONS: Brian Bates (England:UK), Etzel Cardena (USA), Enzo Cozzi (England:UK), Alessandro Fersen (Italy), Sam Gill (USA), John Green (USA), Frances Harding (England:UK), Christopher Innes (Canada), Dan Noel (USA), Nicolás Núñez (Mexico), Osita Okagbue (Nigeria), Julius Sonny Spencer (Sierra Leone), Michael Tucker (England:UK), Edith Turner (USA)
CHAPTER ARTS CENTRE, CARDIFF, WALES

FEBRUARY

Performance: Process and Documentation, Devising and Documentation, Phase I
Conference and gathering
CURATION: Richard Gough and Chris Rowbury
PERFORMANCES: Desperate Optimists, Clock, Man Act
PRESENTATIONS INCLUDED: Mary Brennan (Scotland:UK), Martin Coles (England:UK), Steven Copley (England:UK), Chris Crickmay (England:UK), Michael Cummins (England:UK), Barry Edwards (England:UK), Tim Etchells (England:UK), Terence Hawkes (Wales:UK), Anthony Howell (Wales:UK), David Hughes (England:UK), Mine Kaylan (England:UK), Joe Lawlor (Eire), Mark Long (England:UK), Chris Lucas (Wales:UK), Claire MacDonald (England:UK), Philip Mackenzie (Wales:UK), Julian Maynard-Smith (England:UK), Luke Mckeown (England:UK), Joyce McMillan (Scotland:UK), Fred McVittie (England:UK), Susan Melrose (England:UK), Christine Molloy (Eire), Cristopher Norris (Wales:UK), Alison Oddey (England:UK), Louise Oliver (England:UK), Mike Pearson (Wales:UK), Andrew Quick (England:UK), Kenneth Rea (England:UK), Penny Saunders (England:UK), Tessa Speak (England:UK), Nigel Stewart (England:UK), Julian Thomas (Wales:UK), Simone Thorne (Wales:UK), Jason Walsh (England:UK), Carran Waterfield (England:UK), David Wheeler (England:UK)
CHAPTER ARTS CENTRE, CARDIFF, WALES

AUGUST

Performance: Process and Documentation, Phase II
Summer retreat of practical investigations
CURATION: Richard Gough and Chris Rowbury
WORKSHOP LEADERS INCLUDED: Black Mime Theatre (England:UK), Brith Gof (Wales:UK), Forced Entertainment (England:UK), Hijinx Theatre (Wales:UK), Industrial & Domestic (England:UK), Natural Theatre (England:UK), Second Stride (England/Wales:UK), Station House Opera (England:UK)
PRESENTATIONS: Dangerous Men (England:UK), Das Wunden (Wales:UK), Susan Melrose (England:UK), Roland Miller (England:UK), Arnold Wesker (England:UK)
BRECON, WALES

1994

JANUARY

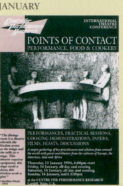

Points of Contact: Performance, Food and Cookery
Conference and Festival
CURATION: Richard Gough and Scott de Lahunta
PRODUCER: Judie Christie
CHAIR: Richard Gough
PERFORMANCES: Bobby Baker (England:UK), Gunter Berghaus (Germany) and Bristol University Drama Department students (England:UK), Shirley Cameron (England:UK), East Coast Artists (USA), Roland Miller (England:UK), Alicia Rios (Spain), Evelyn Silver (England:UK), Jane Sutcliffe (England:UK), Silvia Ziranek (England:UK)
WORKSHOP LEADERS: Edisher Garakanidze with Joseph Jordania (Republic of Georgia), Gillian Hadley (England:UK), Alicia Rios (Spain)
WORKSHOPS AND THEMATIC DISCUSSIONS: Gunter Berghaus (Germany/UK), Peter Brears (England:UK) and Lynette Hunter (England:UK), Shirley Cameron (England:UK), Doreen Fernandez (Philippines) and Jeremy MacClancy (England:UK), Gillian Hadley (England:UK), Tom Jaine (England:UK), Peter Lichtenfels (England:UK), Roland Miller (England:UK), Amy Trubeck and Barbara Wheaton (USA), Sri and Roger Owen (UK/Indonesia), Richard Schechner (USA), Silvia Ziranek (England:UK)
FOOD DEMONSTRATIONS: Chikako Cameron (Japan), Gilli Davies (Wales:UK), Lawrence Green (Switzerland), Satish Kumar (India/UK), Adrian Innocent (Wales:UK), Elisabeth Luard (Wales:UK), Giovanni Malacrino (Italy), Sri and Roger Owen (UK/Indonesia), Mary Roberts (Wales:UK), Jane Sutcliffe (England:UK), Franco Taruschio (Italy/Wales)

PRESENTATIONS: Bobby Baker (England:UK), Jane and Rod Bell (Wales:UK), Gunter Berghaus (Germany/UK), Peter Brears (England:UK), Chikako Cameron (Japan), Shirley Cameron (England:UK), Terry Chinn (Wales:UK), Alan Davidson (England:UK), Gilli Davies (England:UK), Doreen Fernandez (Philippines), Darra Goldstein (USA), Lawrence Green (Switzerland), Gillian Hadley (England:UK), Lynnette Hunter (England:UK), Adrian Innocent (Wales:UK), Tom Jaine (England:UK), Eve Jochnowitz (USA), Barbara Kirshenblatt-Gimlett (USA), Satish Kumar (India), Peter Lichtenfels (England:UK), Elisabeth Luard (Wales:UK), Jeremy MacClancy (England:UK), Giovanni Malacrino (Italy), Susan Melrose (England:UK), Roland Miller (England:UK), Sri and Roger Owen (UK/Indonesia), Mary Roberts (Wales:UK), Richard Schechner (USA), Franco and Ann Taruschio (Italy/Wales), Amy Trubek (USA), Barbara Wheaton (USA)
THE GYM AND CHAPTER ARTS CENTRE, CARDIFF, WALES

Georgian Polyphonic Singing
CPR Organized Workshop/Performance Banquet for Points of Contact Festival
WORKSHOP LEADER: Edisher Garakanidze with Joseph Jordania (Republic of Georgia)
ABERYSTWYTH, WALES

THE CENTRE FOR PERFORMANCE RESEARCH, CARDIFF, PRESENTS
EAST COAST ARTISTS FROM NEW YORK
FAUSTgastronome

Organized Performance and Lecture Tour
Company: East Coast Artists (USA)
Faust Gastronome
Performance
DIRECTOR AND LECTURER: Richard Schechner
INCLUDING: BRISTOL, DARTINGTON, LANCASTER, LONDON AND NORWICH, ENGLAND; GLASGOW, SCOTLAND

FEBRUARY

CPR Organized Performance and Workshop/Meeting Tour
Company: Compagnia Laboratorio di Pontedera (Italy)
Fratelli Dei Cani (The Brothers of Dogs) and
Il Cielo Per Terra (The Sky Underground)
Performances
CARDIFF, ABERYSTWYTH AND BANGOR, WALES

THE CENTRE FOR PERFORMANCE RESEARCH, CARDIFF PRESENTS
COMPAGNIA LABORATORIO DI PONTEDERA FROM ITALY IN FRATELLI DEI CANI THE BROTHERS OF DOGS AND IL CIELO PER TERRA THE SKY UNDERGROUND

Directors' Training Module 4: Five Senses of Theatre Workshop/ Meeting
Roberto Bacci and the work of the Foundation/Institute Pontedera Teatro
including talks and film screenings
BANGOR, WALES

APRIL

Giving Voice # 2:
The Voice in Performance – A Geography of the Voice
Festival and Symposium
DIRECTOR: Joan Mills
PERFORMANCES: Purna Das Baul and Subhendu Das Baul (India), Elfed Lewys (Wales: UK) and Enrique Pardo (Peru/France)
WORKSHOP LEADERS: Helen Chadwick (England: UK), Kristin Linklater (USA), Enrique Pardo (Peru/France), Anna Petrova (Russia), Anna Zubrzycka (Poland)
SYMPOSIUM PRESENTATIONS: Cicely Berry (England: UK), Caroline Bithell (Wales:UK), Joanna Campion (England:UK), Roma Choudhury (India/Wales), Martin Duckworth (England:UK), Richard Gough (Wales:UK), Mary Hammond (England:UK), Alison Hindell (Wales:UK), Tim Ward Jones (England:UK), Stephen Langridge (England:UK), Venice Manley (England:UK), Joan Mills (Wales:UK), Michael McCarthy (Wales: UK), Janet Ritterman (England:UK), Jenny Roditi (England:UK)
WELSH COLLEGE OF MUSIC AND DRAMA, CARDIFF, WALES

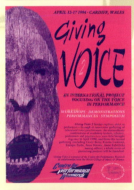

Giving VOICE
AN INTERNATIONAL PROJECT FOCUSING ON THE VOICE IN PERFORMANCE
WORKSHOPS · DEMONSTRATIONS
PERFORMANCES · SYMPOSIUM
APRIL 13-17 1994 · CARDIFF, WALES

MAY

Directors' Talkshop:
Peter Brook (France)
CPR Organised Workshop/ Meeting
CHAPTER ARTS CENTRE, CARDIFF, WALES

JULY - AUGUST

Performance: Process and Documentation
International Conference and Summer School in collaboration with the Department of Theatre Studies, Lancaster University (England:UK)
PROJECT DIRECTOR: Chris Rowbury

Chasing Shadows
International Summer School
WORKSHOP LEADERS: Brith Gof (Wales:UK), Pete Brooks (England:UK), Gay Sweatshop (England: UK), Graeae Theatre Company (England:UK), Geese Theatre Company (England:UK), Wendy Houston (England:UK), IOU (England:UK), Alastair MacLennan (N. Ireland:UK), Natural Theatre Company (England:UK), Paines Plough (England:UK), Tara Arts Group (England:UK), Welfare State International (England:UK)

LANCASTER UNIVERSITY CENTRE FOR PERFORMANCE RESEARCH
SUMMER SCHOOL OF THEATRE
JULY 18 - AUGUST 12 1994 · LANCASTER UNIVERSITY, UK
CHASING SHADOWS

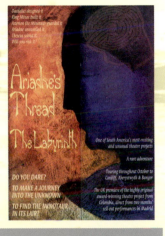

JULY

CPR Summer Retreat
CURATED AND LED BY CPR artists
DRUIDSTONE HAVEN, WALES

OCTOBER

CPR Organized Performance and Workshop Tour
Company: Taller de Investigacion del Imagen Teatral (Colombia)
Ariadne's Thread – The Labyrinth
Performance
CARDIFF, ABERYSTWYTH AND BANGOR, WALES

Sensory Image Workshops
WORKSHOP LEADER: Enrique Vargas (Colombia)
BANGOR AND CARDIFF, WALES

DECEMBER

Launch of PR.Axis
PR.Axis later to become the journal Performance Research

WOULD YOU LIKE THE CHANCE TO WIN AN ARMCHAIR FULL OF THE LATEST THEATRE BOOKS FROM ROUTLEDGE?
OF COURSE YOU WOULD!

Ariadne's Thread The Labyrinth
One of South America's most exciting and unusual theatre projects
A rare adventure
DO YOU DARE? TO MAKE A JOURNEY INTO THE UNKNOWN TO FIND THE MINOTAUR IN ITS LAIR?
Touring throughout October to Cardiff, Aberystwyth & Bangor
The UK premiere of the highly original award-winning theatre project from Colombia, direct from two months sell-out performances in Madrid

1995

APRIL

Giving Voice # 3:
A Geography of the Voice
Festival and Symposium
DIRECTOR: Joan Mills
PERFORMANCES: E.L.A.N. (Wales:UK), Sianed Jones (Wales:UK), Kindred Spirits (England:UK), Phil Minton (England:UK), Aaron Williamson (England:UK), Benjamin Zephaniah (England:UK)
WORKSHOP LEADERS: Frankie Armstrong (Wales:UK), Patricia Bardi (Netherlands/USA), Helen Chadwick (England:UK), E.L.A.N. (Wales:UK), Common Lore (England: UK), Steve Chicurel (USA), Edisher Garakanidze and Joseph Jordania (Republic of Georgia), Ulrike Jungmair (Austria), Venice Manley (England:UK), Phil Minton (England:UK), Sheetal Mukherjee (India), Wlodzimierz Staniewski (Poland), Andrew Wade (England:UK), Julia Wilson-Dickson (England:UK), Keith Yon (St. Helena), Benjamin Zephaniah (England:UK)
SYMPOSIUM PRESENTATIONS: Frankie Armstrong (Wales:UK), Patricia Bardi (Netherlands/USA), Steve Chicurel (USA), Lyn Darnley (England:UK), Veronica Doubleday (England:UK), Paul Farringdon and Heather Williams (England:UK), Edmond Fivet (England:UK), Vic Gammon (England:UK), Edisher Garakanidze (Republic of Georgia), Gardzienice Theatre Association (Poland), Siwsann George (Wales:UK), Richard Gough (Wales:UK), Richard Gwyn (Wales:UK), Trân Quang Hai (Vietnam/France), Ken Hunt (England:UK), Adam Jaworski (Poland), Gruffudd Jones (Wales:UK), Ulrike Jungmair (Austria), Joseph Jordania (Republic of Georgia), Venice Manley (England:UK), Joan Mills (Wales:UK), Patrick de le Roque (France), Srikant Sarangi and Virpi Ylanne-McEwen (India/UK), Julia Wilson-Dickson (England:UK), Keith Yon (St. Helena/UK)
WELSH COLLEGE OF MUSIC AND DRAMA, CARDIFF, WALES

JUNE–JULY
Summer Retreat: Eros and Psyche
CPR WORKSHOPS: Richard Gough and Joan Mills
GUEST ARTIST AND PROJECT LEADER: Enrique Pardo (Peru/France)
DRUIDSTONE HAVEN, WALES

SEPTEMBER – OCTOBER
CPR @ Aberystwyth
Richard Gough appointed Senior Research Fellow in the Department of Theatre Film and Television Studies at the University of Wales, Aberystwyth and CPR forms joint venture (CPR @ Aberystwyth), with the University of Wales, Aberystwyth

The Sound House
Collaborative Performance/Commissioned Concert Tour
DIRECTOR AND COMPOSER: Meredith Monk (USA) in conjunction with Katie Geissinger (USA) and Tom Bogdan (USA)
PERFORMERS: Caroline Bithell (Wales:UK), Stacey Blythe (Wales:UK), Helen Chadwick (England:UK), Guy Dartnell (England: UK), Pauline Down (Wales:UK), Jonathan Goldsmith (England:UK), Venice Manley (England:UK), Joan Mills (Wales:UK), Ian Morgan (Wales:UK), Philipa Reeves (Wales: UK), David Shepherd (Wales:UK), Simon Thorne (Wales:UK)
ABERYSTWYTH, BANGOR, CARDIFF, HARLECH, MOLD, RHAYADER, SWANSEA , WALES AND ULEY, ENGLAND

OCTOBER
Pastmasters: Vsevolod Meyerhold

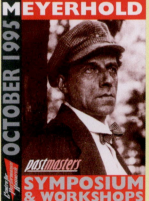

Symposium and Workshops
CURATION: Richard Gough and Nick Sales
CHAIR: Richard Gough
WORKSHOP LEADERS: Gennadi Bogdanov (Russia), Alexei Levinski (Russia)
CARDIFF, WALES
SYMPOSIUM PRESENTATIONS: Eugenio Barba (Italy/Denmark), Jörg Bochow (Germany), Gennadi Bogdanov (Russia), Edward Braun (England:UK), Stella Duff (England: UK), Mel Gordon (USA), Richard Gough (Wales:UK), Lars Kleberg (Sweden), Robert Leach (England:UK), Alexei Levinski (Russia), Nikolai Pesochinski (Russia), Beatrice Picon-Vallin (France), Ralf Räuker (Germany), Vadim Sherbakov (Russia), Maya Sitkovetskaya (Russia), Richard Taylor (Wales:UK), Maria Valentey (Russia), Thilo Zantke (Germany), Phillip Zarrilli (USA)
UNIVERSITY OF WALES, ABERYSTWYTH, WALES

1996

MARCH
Launch Event of the journal Performance Research
PRESENTATIONS: Ric Allsopp, Richard Gough, Claire MacDonald, Mike Pearson, Talia Rodgers
OLD OPERATING THEATRE, LONDON, ENGLAND

Performance Research
The journal published trianually initially and then quarterly, is published by Routledge for ARC, a division of the Centre for Performance Research

Performance Research
Volume 1/1 : The Temper of the Times
(*EDS.* Ric Allsopp, Richard Gough and Claire MacDonald)
LONDON: ROUTLEDGE
A CPR PUBLICATION

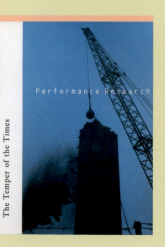

APRIL
Giving Voice #4: An Archaeology of the Voice
Festival and Symposium
DIRECTOR: Joan Mills
WORKSHOP LEADERS: Edisher Garakanidze (Republic of Georgia), Michele George (Canada), Brigitte Kloareg (France), Kristin Linklater (USA), Jacqueline Martin (Australia), Trân Quang Hai (Vietnam/France)
PRESENTATIONS: Caroline Bithell (Wales:UK), Helen Chadwick (England:UK), Sioned Davies (Wales:UK), Robert Evans (Wales:UK), Larry Gordon (USA), Jovan Howe (USA), Mike Pearson (Wales:UK), Irina Raspopova (Russia), Christina Shewell (England:UK), William Taylor (USA/UK)
CARDIFF, WALES

MAY
CPR moves to Aberystwyth, Wales

JUNE/JULY
CPR Summer Retreat: King Lear Project
CPR WORKSHOPS: Richard Gough and Joan Mills
GUEST ARTIST AND WORKSHOP LEADER: Kristin Linklater (USA)
DRUIDSTONE HAVEN, WALES

AUGUST
Kalarippayattu Workshop
WORKSHOP LEADER: Phillip Zarrilli (USA/UK)
ABERYSTWYTH, WALES

Performance Research
Volume 1/2 : On Risk
(*ED.* Claire MacDonald)
LONDON: ROUTLEDGE
A CPR PUBLICATION

SEPTEMBER
Points of Contact: Performance, Tourism and Identity

Conference and Festival of Itinerant Presentations
CURATION: Richard Gough and Judie Christie with Adam Hayward
PERFORMANCES: Guillermo Gómez-Peña (Mexico/USA) and Roberto Sifuentes (USA), Mary Lemley (UK/USA)
PRESENTATIONS: Simone Abram (England: UK), Robin Arthur (England:UK), Rustom Bharucha (India), Edward M Bruner (USA), Coco Fusco (USA), Guillermo Gómez-Peña (Mexico/USA) and Roberto Sifuentes (USA), Richard Gough (Wales: UK), Ron Jenkins (USA), Eve Jochnowitz (USA), Barbara Kirshenblatt-Gimlett (USA), Dean MacConnell (USA), Dorothy Noyes (USA), Patricia Peach (England:UK), Mike Pearson and Michael Shanks (Wales:UK), Ned Thomas (Wales:UK), Jatinder Verma (Tanzania/UK)
BEGINNING IN ABERYSTWYTH AND JOURNEYING THROUGHOUT WALES

OCTOBER
MA Theatre and the World launched
A taught Masters Programme delivered by the Department of Theatre Film and Television Studies, University of Wales, Aberystwyth in close collaboration with CPR. The MA Theatre and the World runs annually from this point.

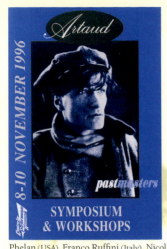

8-10 NOVEMBER 1996

Artaud

pastmasters

SYMPOSIUM & WORKSHOPS

NOVEMBER
Pastmasters: Antonin Artaud
Symposium and workshops
CURATION AND CHAIR: Richard Gough
PERFORMANCES: Georges Baal (France), Gerard Nauret (France), Aaron Williamson (England:UK)
WORKSHOP LEADERS: Michael Caven (Eire), Dave Levitt (Wales:UK), Mike Pearson (Wales:UK), Brian Singleton (Eire)
PRESENTATIONS: Georges Baal (France), Mark Batty (England:UK), Gunter Berghaus (Germany), Ross Birrell (Scotland:UK), Neil Borland (England:UK), David Brady (England:UK), Michael Caven (Eire), Steve Dixon (England:UK), Helga Finter (Germany), Tony Gardner (England:UK), Jane Goodall (Australia), Dave Levitt (Wales:UK), David MacLagan (England: UK), Charles Marowitz (USA), Gerard Nauret (France), Florence de Meredieu (France), Mike Pearson (Wales:UK), Peggy Phelan (USA), Franco Ruffini (Italy), Nicola Savarese (Italy), Claude Schumacher (Scotland:UK), Brian Singleton (Eire), Tor Arne Ursin (Norway), Nigel Ward (England: UK), Aaron Williamson (England:UK), Sarah Wilson (England:UK)
UNIVERSITY OF WALES, ABERYSTWYTH, WALES

DECEMBER
Performance Research
Volume 1/3: On Illusion
(*ED.* Ric Allsopp)
LONDON: ROUTLEDGE
A CPR PUBLICATION

1997

APRIL
Giving Voice #5:
An Archaeology of the Voice
Festival and Symposium
DIRECTOR: Joan Mills
PERFORMANCES: A Filetta (Corsica), Frankie Armstrong (Wales:UK), Celtic Ceilidh (Various/UK), Michele George (Canada), The Grandmothers of Bistritsa (Bulgaria), Nóirin Ní Riain (Eire), Trân Quang Hai and Bach Yen (Vietnam/France)
WORKSHOP LEADERS: A Filetta (Corsica), Frankie Armstrong (Wales:UK), Roberta Carreri (Italy/Denmark), Louis Colaianni (USA), Cusan Tan (Wales:UK), Nelli and Bair Dougar-Zhabon (Siberia), Michele George (Canada), Siwsann George (Wales:UK), The Grandmothers of Bistritsa (Bulgaria), Trân Quang Hai (Vietnam/France), Kristin Linklater (USA) and Enrique Pardo (Peru/France), Venice Manley (England:UK), Joan Mills (Wales:UK), Nóirín Ní Riain (Eire), Irina Raspopova (Russia),
PRESENTATIONS: A Filetta (Corsica), Dina Ancheva (Bulgaria), Douglass Bailey (Wales: UK), Caroline Bithell (Wales:UK), David Burbidge (England:UK), Lyn Darnley (England: UK), Nelli Dougar-Zhabon (Siberia), Jovan Howe (Russia), Benny Kalanzi (Uganda), Brigitte Kloareg (France), Enrique Pardo (Peru/France), Mike Pearson (Wales:UK), Trân Quang Hai (Vietnam/France), Iegor Reznikoff (Russia), Patsy Rodenburg (England:UK), Christina Shewell (England:UK), Bach Yen (Vietnam)
ABERYSTWYTH, WALES

AN INTERNATIONAL FESTIVAL OF THE VOICE
3 to 13 APRIL 1997 ABERYSTWYTH

giving voice

A 'working holiday' in beautiful surroundings by the sea for everybody with an interest in their voice

Performance Research
Volume 2/1: Letters from Europe
(*EDS.* Ric Allsopp, Richard Gough and Claire MacDonald)
LONDON: ROUTLEDGE
A CPR PUBLICATION

MAY
Making the Body 'All Eyes'
CPR Organized Workshop
WORKSHOP LEADER: Phillip Zarrilli (USA/UK)
ABERYSTWYTH, WALES

Performance Studies international
Richard Gough voted inaugural president of the new association for Performance Studies, (later PSi). First secretariat created at the University of Wales Aberystwyth. Heike Roms subsequently appointed first administrator.

JUNE-JULY
CPR Summer Retreat: Landscapes, Bodyscapes, Escapes
CPR WORKSHOPS: Richard Gough and Joan Mills
GUEST ARTIST: Phillip Zarrilli (USA/UK)
DRUIDSTONE HAVEN, WALES

JULY
The Beckett Project *Collaborative Performance*
DIRECTOR: Phillip Zarrilli (USA/UK)
ABERYSTWYTH, WALES

CPR Summer School
Cancelled due to the death of the leading guest artist

AUGUST
Making the Body 'All Eyes'
CPR Organized Workshop
WORKSHOP LEADER: Philip Zarrilli (USA/UK)
THE SPACE, CARDIFF, WALES

Performance Research
Volume 2/2: On Tourism
(*EDS.* Richard Gough and Heike Roms)
LONDON: ROUTLEDGE
A CPR PUBLICATION

SEPTEMBER
The Black Dinner
Performance/Edible Installation
DIRECTORS: Judie Christie and Richard Gough
Collaboration with DasArts Block 7 students
AMSTERDAM, NETHERLANDS

Modern Miracles
Schools Outreach Programme
CPR Organized Workshop Series
WORKSHOP LEADER: Richard Gregory
ABERYSTWYTH, WALES

OCTOBER
CPR Presented Performance
Company: Victoria Theatre Company (Belgium)
Bernadetje
Performance
ABERYSTWYTH ARTS CENTRE, WALES AND CO-ORGANISED TOUR TO NEWCASTLE AND LONDON, ENGLAND, GLASGOW, SCOTLAND

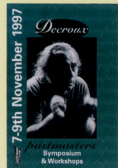

NOVEMBER
Pastmasters: Etienne Decroux
Symposium and Workshops
CURATION: Judie Christie and Richard Gough with Adam Hayward
CHAIR: Richard Gough
PERFORMANCES: Thomas Leabhart (USA), Steve Wasson and Corinne Soum (England:UK)
WORKSHOP LEADERS: Thomas Leabhart (USA), Georges Molnar (Canada), Leonard Pitt (USA)
SYMPOSIUM PRESENTATIONS: Jean Asselin (Canada), Ineke Austen (Netherlands), Denise Boulanger (Canada), Anne Dennis (Spain), Thomas Leabhart (USA), Yves Lebreton (France), Martina Leeker (Germany), Annie Loui (USA), Yves Marc and Claire Heggen (France), Marco de Marinis (Italy), Kathryn Wylie Marques (USA), Georges Molnar (Canada), Patrice Pavis (France), Leonard Pitt (USA), John Schranz (Malta), Steve Wasson and Corinne Soum (England:UK)
UNIVERSITY OF ABERYSTWYTH, ABERYSTWYTH, WALES

Georgian Singing
CPR Organized Workshop
WORKSHOP LEADER: Edisher Garakanidze (Republic of Georgia)
ABERYSTWYTH, WALES

DECEMBER
Performance Research
Volume 2/3: On Refuge
(EDS. Ric Allsopp and Claire MacDonald)
LONDON: ROUTLEDGE
A CPR PUBLICATION

1998

APRIL
Performance Research
Volume 3/1: On America
(ED. Nick Kaye)
LONDON: ROUTLEDGE
A CPR PUBLICATION

MARCH - JUNE
The Blazing Heart
A Community Choir Project of workshops and rehearsals leading to a public performance as part of the Giving Voice programme
PROJECT DIRECTOR: Joan Mills
COMPOSER: Helen Chadwick
PERFORMERS: David Shephard, Matthew Bailey, Frankie Armstrong, Sue Jones-Davies, Helen Chadwick, Joan Mills, Siân Croose and the Heartsong Community Choir
ABERYSTWYTH ARTS CENTRE, ABERYSTWYTH, WALES

JUNE - JULY
CPR Summer Retreat: Landscapes, Bodyscapes, Escapes
WORKSHOP LEADER: Richard Gough
DRUIDSTONE HAVEN, WALES

Making the Body 'All Eyes'
Workshop
WORKSHOP LEADER: Phillip Zarrilli (USA/UK)
CARDIFF, WALES

JULY
CPR Summer School
Performances, Workshops, Residencies
Performative Writing
WORKSHOP LEADER: Peggy Phelan (USA)
Training with the SITI Company
WORKSHOP LEADERS: Saratoga International Theatre Institute (USA)
Alice Underground
Collaborative Performance
DIRECTOR: The SITI Company
The Water Station
Collaborative Performance
DIRECTOR: Phillip Zarrilli (USA/UK)
UNIVERSITY OF WALES, ABERYSTWYTH, WALES

AUGUST
Performance Research
Volume 3/2: On Place
(EDS. David Williams and Mark Minchinton)
LONDON: ROUTLEDGE
A CPR PUBLICATION

SEPTEMBER
Points of Contact: Performance, Places and Pasts
Conference and Festival of Itinerant Presentations
GUEST CURATORS: Mike Pearson and Michael Shanks
CHAIR: Adam Hayward
PERFORMANCES: Margaret Ames (Wales:UK), Sean Tuan John and John Rowley (Wales:UK), Branislava Kuburovic (Serbia) and Boedi S. Otong (Indonesia), Mike Pearson and Mike Brookes (Wales:UK), Marc Rees (Wales:UK), Mala Sikka (Wales:UK), Simon Whitehead (Wales:UK)
PRESENTATIONS: David Austin (Wales:UK), John Barrett (England:UK), Ken Brassil (England:UK), Paul Carter (Australia), Mary Anne Constantine (Wales:UK), Jez Danks (Wales:UK), Eddie Ladd (Wales:UK), Lisa Lewis (Wales:UK), Clifford McLucas (Wales:UK), Keith Morris (Wales: UK), Roger Owen (Wales:UK), Mike Pearson (Wales:UK), Allan Pred (USA), Fran Rhydderch (Wales:UK), Heike Roms (Germany/Wales), Mike Shanks (Wales:UK), Ulf Strohmayer (Germany), Ned Thomas (Wales:UK)
BEGINNING IN ABERYSTWYTH AND JOURNEYING THROUGHOUT WEST WALES

NOVEMBER
Pastmasters: Bertolt Brecht and Sergei Eisenstein
Symposium and Workshops
CURATION: Richard Gough and Adam Hayward
CHAIR: Richard Gough
Baal
Performance
DIRECTED BY Ralf Räuker with UWA Theatre Studies students
WORKSHOP LEADERS: Clive Barker (England:UK), Robert Leach (England:UK), Jorg Mihan (Germany)
PRESENTATIONS: Sally Banes (USA), Clive Barker (England:UK), Rosamund Bartlett (England:UK), Birgit Beumers (England:UK), Martin Brady (England:UK), Dietmar Hochmuth (USA), Lars Kleberg (Sweden), Robert Leach (England:UK), Jorg Mihan (Germany), Meg Mumford (Scotland: UK), Amy Sargeant (England:UK), Ralf Räuker (Germany), Janne Risum (Denmark), Richard Taylor (Wales:UK), Peter Thomson (England: UK), Elizabeth Wright (England:UK)
UNIVERSITY OF WALES, ABERYSTWYTH, WALES

DECEMBER
Performance Research
Volume 3/3: On Ritual
(ED. Gunter Berghaus)
LONDON: ROUTLEDGE
A CPR PUBLICATION

1999

FEBRUARY
David Zinder on the Michael Chekhov Technique
CPR Organized Workshop
WORKSHOP LEADER: David Zinder (Israel)
ABERYSTWYTH, WALES

Tribute to Jerzy Grotowski

Public Symposium

CURATION AND CHAIR: Richard Gough
PERFORMANCES: Sculptured in Smoke: Hilary Becket (Wales:UK), Belinda Neave (Wales:UK), Geoff Moore (Wales:UK), Nigel Watson (Wales:UK)
PRESENTATIONS: Marianne Ahrne (Denmark), Eugenio Barba (Italy/Denmark), Ned Chaillet (England:UK), Mike Elster (Wales:UK), Jerzy Gurawski (Poland), Jenna Kumiega (Poland/UK), Michael Kustow (England:UK), Zbigniew Osiński (Poland), Carla Pollastrelli (Italy), Richard Schechner (USA)
CARDIFF, WALES

Launch of Black Mountain Press
Publishing House of CPR

Land of Ashes and Diamonds:
My Apprenticeship in Poland followed by 26 letters from Jerzy Grotowski to Eugenio Barba
by Eugenio Barba
ABERYSTWYTH: BLACK MOUNTAIN PRESS
A CPR PUBLICATION

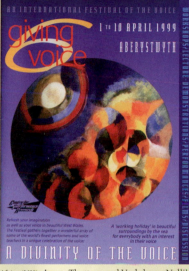

APRIL
Giving Voice #6:
A Divinity of the Voice
Festival of performances, workshops, demonstrations and presentations
PROJECT DIRECTOR: Joan Mills
PERFORMANCES: Barbara Acker and David Vining (USA), A Filetta (Corsica), Frankie Armstrong (Wales:UK), Patricia Bardi (Netherlands/USA), Helen Chadwick (England:UK), Sue Jones Davies (Wales:UK), ELAN (Wales:UK), Flamenco/Fado (Spain), Gardzienice Theatre Association (Poland), Siwsann George (Wales:UK), Heartsong Community Choir (Wales:UK), Aram and Virginia Kerovpyan (Armenia), M'tiebi (Republic of Georgia), Hossein Omoumi (Iran), Iegor Reznikoff (Russia), Sinfonye (England:UK), The Shout (England:UK), The South African Gospel Singers (South Africa/UK), Aryan Thottam and Vashdevan Nellikat (India), Zarjanka (Russia)
WORKSHOP LEADERS: A Filetta (Corsica), Patricia Bardi (Netherlands/USA), Helen Chadwick (England:UK), Vivien Ellis (England:UK), Argentina Santos with Jorge Fernando (Spain), Vic Gammon (England:UK), Michele George (Canada), Chloë Goodchild (England:UK), Trân Quang Hai (Vietnam/France), M'tiebi with Joseph Jordania (Republic of Georgia), Aram and Virginia Keroupyan (Armenia), Luzili Mulindi King (Kenya/UK), Hossein Omoumi (Iran), Noah Pikes (England:UK), Jill Purce (England:UK), Iegor Reznikoff (Russia), Aryan Thottam and Vashdevan Nellikat (India), Irina Raspopova with Zarjanka (Russia), Pinise Saul (South Africa/UK), Tomas de Utrera with Eloy Abad (Spain), Kalinka Vulcheva (Bulgaria), Mirka Yemendzakis (Greece)
PRESENTATIONS: included workshop leaders and the following: Orlando Gough (England:UK), Kimberly Holton (England:UK), Alexander Knapp (Germany), Deborah Procter (England:UK), Bernice Johnson Reagon (USA), Uri Sharvit (Israel), Geraint Vaughan-Jones (Wales:UK)
ABERYSTWYTH, BRECON, WALES AND LONDON, ENGLAND

International Performance Festival
CURATION: Judie Christie and Richard Gough
PERFORMANCES: Barbara Acker and David Vining: The Chants of Florence Farr (England:UK), A Filetta (Corsica), Patricia Bardi (Netherlands/USA), Brith Gof (Wales: UK), Helen Chadwick (England:UK), ELAN, Forced Entertainment (England:UK), Gardzienice Theatre Association (Poland), Goat Island (USA), Iberian Voices: Flamenco – Deep Song (Spain) and Fado – Voices From the Sea (Portugal), Virginia Kerovpyan (Armenia), M'tiebi (Republic of Georgia), Hossein Omoumi (Iran), La Pocha Nostra (Mexico/USA), Maya Rao (India), Bernice Johnson Reagon (USA), Iegor Reznikoff (Russia), Sacred Voices of Wales (including Heartsong Community Choir, Frankie Armstrong, Helen Chadwick, Siwsann George, Joan Mills, Cusan Tan, Plethyn), The Shout (England:UK), Sinfonye: Symphonia – Hildegard of Bingen (England:UK), The Song of Ancient India: Chants from the Samaveda, The South African Gospel Singers, Theatreworks (Singapore), Zarjanka: Sacred Songs of Russia (Russia)
ABERYSTWYTH, WALES

5th Performance Studies international Conference

Here be Dragons: boundaries, hinterlands and beyond
International Conference of workshops, performances, presentations, installations, papers, talks and panel discussions promoting the exchange between scholars and practitioners in the field of Performance Studies
CURATION: Richard Gough and Heike Roms
CHAIR: Richard Gough
WORKSHOP LEADERS: Barry Edwards (England:UK), Leslie Bentley (USA), Larry Bogad (USA)
PERFORMANCES: all performances of the International Performance Festival as well as: Rhonda Blair (USA), Henry Daniels (England:UK), Galinsky (USA), Hui-Wen Chen/U-Man-Zoo Theatre (Wales:UK), Luba Agonistas Performance Group (Mexico), Sophia Lycouris (England:UK), Fred McVittie (England:UK), Helen Paris (England:UK), Alice Stefania (Brazil), John Troyer (USA), Jason Winslade (USA), Woestijn (Belgium)
INSTALLATIONS/PRESENTATIONS: Gill Goddard (England:UK), Debbi Sutton (USA)

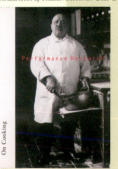

PRESENTATIONS: over 170 international conference delegate panel presentations
KEYNOTE PRESENTATIONS: Richard Gough (Wales: UK), Amy Guggenheim (USA), Bernice Johnson Reagon (USA),
Heike Roms (Germany/Wales), Richard Schechner (USA), Wlodzimierz Staniewski (Poland), Hanne Seitz (Germany), Phillip Zarrilli (USA/UK)
UNIVERSITY OF WALES, ABERYSTWYTH, WALES

APRIL
Performance Research
Volume 4/1: On Cooking
(*ED.* Richard Gough)
LONDON: ROUTLEDGE
A CPR PUBLICATION

JUNE
CPR Summer School: Hotel Wales
GUEST ARTISTS AND PROJECT LEADERS: Guillermo Gómez-Peña (Mexico/USA) and Roberto Sifuentes (USA) of La Pocha Nostra

Museum of Fetishised Identities
Performance/Installation
DIRECTORS: Guillermo Gómez-Peña (Mexico/USA) and Roberto Sifuentes (USA) of La Pocha Nostra together with Judie Christie and Richard Gough
PERFORMERS: participants of Hotel Wales and local artists
CEREDIGION MUSEUM, ABERYSTWYTH, WALES

AUGUST
Performance Research
Volume 4/2: On Line
(*EDS.* Ric Allsopp & Scott deLahunta) **LONDON: ROUTLEDGE**
A CPR PUBLICATION

SEPTEMBER

CPR Artist in Residence at DasArts
Residency included leading the 'thematic block' of the study programme and directing performances and installations
ARTIST: Richard Gough

The Last Supper
The White Dinner
Performances
AMSTERDAM, NETHERLANDS

Directors' Talkshop: Anatoli Vasiliev (Russia)
CPR Organized Workshop/Meeting
CHAPTER ARTS CENTRE, CARDIFF, WALES

OCTOBER
CPR On Tour
Singing Workshop
with Michele George (Canada) and Joan Mills (Wales:UK)
UNIVERSITY OF WALES, BANGOR, WALES

Theatre - Solitude, Craft, Revolt
by Eugenio Barba
ABERYSTWYTH: BLACK MOUNTAIN PRESS
A CPR PUBLICATION

NOVEMBER

Pastmasters: Michael Chekhov
Symposium and Workshops staged in collaboration with the Department of Drama and Theatre Arts, University of Birmingham and the Birmingham School of Speech and Drama
CURATION: Richard Gough and Adam Hayward
CHAIR: Adam Hayward
WORKSHOP LEADERS: Jörg Andrees (Germany)
WORKSHOP DEMOS: Sarah Kane (England: UK), Joanne Merlin (USA)
PRESENTATIONS: Jörg Andrees (Germany), Lendley Black (USA), Lisa Byckling (Finland), Franc Chamberlain (England:UK), Jack Colvin (USA), Lisa Dalton (England:UK), Graham Dixon (Australia), José Luis Gómez (Germany), Douglas Hankin (England: UK), Marina Ivanova (Russia), Sarah Kane (England:UK), Katya Kamotskaia (Russia), Andrei Kirillov (Russia), Jobst Langhans (England: UK), Joanne Merlin (USA), Bernardas-Gitis Padegimas (Lithuania), Mala Powers (USA), Deirdre Hurst du Prey (Canada), David Zinder (Israel)
UNIVERSITY OF BIRMINGHAM, ENGLAND

DECEMBER
Performance Research
Volume 4/3: On Silence
(ED. Claire MacDonald)
LONDON: ROUTLEDGE
A CPR PUBLICATION

2000

YEAR-ROUND
Community Voice Projects
Worlds of Song
Workshops, voice development classes and performances in collaboration with Aberystwyth Arts Centre and Heartsong Community Choir
ABERYSTWYTH, WALES

FEBRUARY-APRIL

CPR on Tour
Workshop
with Lorna Marshall (Australia/UK)
BRECON, WALES
Workshop
with Luzilli Mulindi King (Kenya/UK)
CRICCIETH, WALES
Workshop
with David Zinder (Israel)
ABERYSTWYTH, WALES
Workshop
with Enrique Pardo (Peru/France)
ST DONAT'S, WALES
Workshop
with Stuart Lynch (Australia)
ABERYSTWYTH, WALES

APRIL
Performance Research
Volume 5/1: Openings
(EDS. Ric Allsopp and David Williams)
LONDON: ROUTLEDGE
A CPR PUBLICATION

JULY
CPR Summer School : Landscape and the Body

WORKSHOP LEADERS: Richard Gough (Wales: UK), Navtej Jahor (India), Joan Mills (Wales: UK), Mike Pearson (Wales:UK), Phillip Zarrilli (USA/UK)
ABERYSTWYTH, WALES

Archaeological Dances *Performance*
DEVISED BY: Mike Pearson and John Rowley (Wales:UK) with members of the Summer School
PRESELI MOUNTAINS, WALES

AUGUST
Performance Research
Volume 5/2: On Animals
(ED. Alan Read)
LONDON: ROUTLEDGE
A CPR PUBLICATION

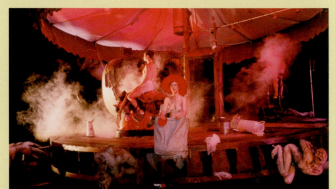

SEPTEMBER-OCTOBER
Restless Gravity
Month long festival of workshops, residencies, parades, events, performances, expeditions, organized by CPR in collaboration with Aberystwyth Arts Centre, Theatr Gwynedd and Theatr Taliesin
CURATION AND DIRECTION: Judie Christie and Richard Gough with the Restless Gravity Consortium Board, Sybil Crouch, Alan Hewson and Dafydd Thomas
PERFORMANCES: Arad Goch (Wales:UK), Armagh Rhymers (Eire), Barabbas (Eire), Bebia (Bulgaria), The Corn Exchange (Eire), Desperate Optimists (Eire), Earthfall Dance (Wales:UK), Lucy Gough (Wales:UK), Richard Gough (Wales:UK), Sioned Huws (Wales:UK), Jant-Bi (Senegal), Sean Tuan John (Wales:UK), Eddie Ladd and Tystion (Wales:UK), William Lang (Australia), Pearson/Brookes (Wales:UK), Maya Rao (India), Bill Shannon 'CrutchMaster' (USA), Jo Shapland (Wales:UK), Steel Wasp (Wales:UK), Teatr Piesn Kozla (Poland), Theatr Bara Caws (Wales:UK), Theatr Wladol Iddewig (Wales:UK), Theatr Y Byd (Wales:UK), Théâtre de la Mezzanine (France), U-Man-Zoo (Wales:UK), Victoria (Belgium), Simon Whitehead (Wales:UK), Young @ Heart Chorus (USA)
WORKSHOP LEADERS: Armagh Rhymers (Eire), Barabbas (Eire), Bebia (Bulgaria), Desperate Optimists (Eire), Jant-Bi (Senegal), Maya Rao (India), Rachel Rosenthal (USA), Rhiannon (USA), Alan Schacher (Australia), Bill Shannon 'CrutchMaster' (USA), Teatr Piesn Kozla (Poland)

Mapping Wales
Performance
EXPEDITIONS: John Baylis (Australia), Guillermo Gómez-Peña (Mexico/USA), Sean Tuan John (Wales:UK), Eddie Ladd (Wales:UK), Mike Pearson (Wales:UK), Rachel Rosenthal (USA), Bill Shannon CrutchMaster (USA), Simon Whitehead (Wales:UK), William Yang (Australia)
ACROSS MANY CITIES, TOWNS AND THE COUNTRYSIDE OF WALES INCLUDING: ABERYSTWYTH, BANGOR, CARDIFF, NEWTOWN AND SWANSEA

OCTOBER
The Last Supper
Performance
DIRECTOR: Richard Gough
THE CHAPEL, UNIVERSITY OF WALES, ABERYSTWYTH, WALES

NOVEMBER
Pastmasters: Tadeusz Kantor & Cricot 2
Symposium and workshops
CURATION: Richard Gough and Rachel Rogers
CHAIR: Richard Gough
WORKSHOP: Ludmila Ryba (Poland)
PRESENTATIONS: Jacquie Bablet (France), Andrzej Bialko (Poland), Wieslaw Borowski (Poland), Richard Demarco (Scotland:UK), Brunella Eruli (Italy), Elizabeth Hare (England:UK), David Hughes (England:UK), Jaromir Jedlenski (Poland), Zofia Kalinska (Poland), Michal Kobialka (USA), Martin Leech (England:UK), Grzegorz Musial (Poland), Cordelia Oliver (Scotland:UK), Krzysztof Pleśniarowicz (Poland), Ludmila Ryba (Poland), Guy Scarpetta (France), Mischa Twitchin (England:UK), Duncan Ward (England:UK), Noel Witts (England:UK)
UNIVERSITY OF WALES, ABERYSTWYTH, WALES

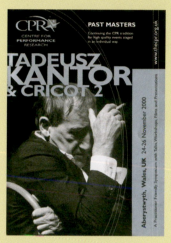

DECEMBER
Performance Research
Volume 5/3: On Memory
(EDS. Adrian Heathfield and Andrew Quick)
LONDON: ROUTLEDGE
A CPR PUBLICATION

2001

YEAR-ROUND
Local Voices, Worlds of Song
Community Voice Projects including:
Workshops, voice development classes and performances in collaboration with Aberystwyth Arts Centre and Heartsong Community Choir. Choral Song series commissioned for Heartsong Community Choir. Workshops and song teaching sessions throughout Wales.
CURATION: Joan Mills and Roxane Smith
ABERYSTWYTH, WALES, UK

APRIL
Performance Research
Volume 6/1: Departures
(ED. Claire MacDonald)
LONDON: ROUTLEDGE
A CPR PUBLICATION

JULY
CPR Summer School: Landscapes of the Senses
WORKSHOP LEADERS: Richard Gough (Wales: UK), Stuart Lynch (Australia), Joan Mills (Wales:UK), Enrique Vargas (Colombia)
ABERYSTWYTH, DRUIDSTONE HAVEN, PRESELI MOUNTAINS, WALES

Points of Contact: Performance, Homes and Gardens
Cancelled because of the outbreak of Foot and Mouth disease

AUGUST
Performance Research
Volume 6/2: On Maps and Mapping
(ED. Richard Gough)
LONDON: ROUTLEDGE
A CPR PUBLICATION

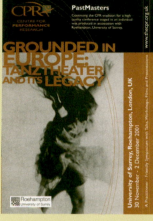

OCTOBER-NOVEMBER
Pastmasters: Grounded in Europe - Tanztheater and its Legacy
Symposium and workshops produced in association with the Drama Department, Roehampton, University of Surrey
CURATION: Richard Gough and Rachel Rogers
CHAIRS: Rachel Rogers and Alan Read
PERFORMANCES: Liz Aggiss (USA), Michele Cuomo (USA), Silke Mansholt (Germany), Nola Rocco (USA)
PERFORMANCE LECTURE: Carol Brown (New Zealand)
WORKSHOP LEADERS: Isa Partsch Bergsohn (Germany), Monika Koch (Germany), Valerie Preston-Dunlop (England:UK), Ana Sanchez-Colberg (Puerto Rico), Geraldine Stephenson (USA)
PRESENTATIONS: Liz Aggiss (USA), Isa Partsch Bergsohn (Germany), Carol Brown (New Zealand), Guy Cools (Belgium), Michele Cuomo (USA), Matthew Goulish (USA), Sondra Fraleigh (USA), Marion Kant (England:UK), Monika Koch (Germany), Rebecca Loukes (England:UK), Silke Mansholt (Germany), Nancy Mauro-Flude (Australia), Meg Mumford (Scotland:UK), Larraine Nichols (England:UK), Valerie Preston-Dunlop (England:UK), Nola Rocco (USA), Ana Sanchez-Colberg (Puerto Rico), Geraldine Stephenson (USA)
UNIVERSITY OF SURREY, ROEHAMPTON, LONDON, ENGLAND

DECEMBER
Performance Research
Volume 6/3: On Navigation
(EDS. Ric Allsopp & David Williams)
LONDON: ROUTLEDGE
A CPR PUBLICATION

2002

YEAR-ROUND
Local Voices, Worlds of Song
Voice in Common workshops, voice development classes and rehearsals
ABERYSTWYTH, WALES

MARCH
Performance Research
Volume 7/1: On Editing
(EDS. Claire MacDonald and William H. Sherman)
LONDON: ROUTLEDGE
A CPR PUBLICATION

APRIL
Local Voices, Worlds of Song
WORKSHOP LEADERS: Frankie Armstrong (Wales:UK), Esyllt Harker (Wales:UK), Kate Howard (England:UK), Natalia Zumbadze (Georgia), Michael Harper (UK), Una May (Jamaica/UK), Mouthful (England:UK)

Voice in Common
PERFORMERS: Community choirs
ABERYSTWYTH ARTS CENTRE, ABERYSTWYTH, WALES

Giving Voice #7:
The Voice Politic: Politics, Society and the Voice

Festival of performances, workshops, demonstrations and presentations
PROJECT DIRECTOR: Joan Mills
PERFORMANCES: Frankie Armstrong (Wales:UK) and Leon Rosselson (England:UK), Imbizo (Zimbabwe), Neil Kinnock in Conversation with Patrick Hannan (Wales:UK), Local Voices, Worlds of Song – Community Choir Concert (Wales:UK), Political Poetry in Performance (UK), Politicians Live on Stage (UK), Jeremy Turner and Bethan Bryn (Wales:UK), Voices to Light Our Way (various), Patience Agbabi (England:UK), Nigel Jenkins (Wales:UK), Gwyneth Lewis (Wales:UK), Mouthful (England:UK)
WORKSHOP LEADERS: Frankie Armstrong (Wales:UK) and Leon Rosselson (England: UK), Guy Dartnell (England:UK), Susan Hale (USA), Michael Harper (USA), Kristin Linklater and Carol Gilligan (USA), Marya Lowry (USA), Phil Minton (England:UK), Nat'o Zumbadze (Republic of Georgia), Peter Morgan Barnes (Wales/New Zealand), Simon Rainbow Banda (Zimbabwe:Africa), Juliet Russell (England:UK)
PRESENTATIONS: included workshop leaders and the following: Max Atkinson (England:UK), Cicely Berry (England:UK), Caroline Bithell (Wales:UK), Roz Comins (England:UK), Mark Langley (England:UK), John Powles (England:UK), Nigel Osborne (Scotland:UK), Denise Armstrong (England:UK), Bill Hopkinson (England:UK), Richard McKane (England:UK)
ABERYSTWYTH AND CARDIFF, WALES

CPR Organized Tour
PRODUCER: Judie Christie
Company: Theatre Bazi (Iran)
The Mute who was Dreamed That's Enough! Shut Up!
Performances
INCLUDING LONDON, ENGLAND; GLASGOW, SCOTLAND; ABERYSTWYTH AND CARDIFF, WALES

MAY
The Last Supper
Collaborative Performance
COLLABORATIVE PARTNER: Pontedera Teatro
CO-DIRECTORS: Richard Gough, Peader Kirk
PERFORMERS: Gigi Agyropolou (Greece), Electa Behrens (USA), Giovanni Berti (Italy), Jodie Bray (Wales:UK), Silvia Bruni (Italy), E-tong Chen (Taiwan), Tiziana Ciasullo (France), Antonia Doggett (England:UK), Martina Favilla (Italy), Antonio Ferrazzoli (Italy), Richard Gough (Wales:UK), Berith Hjelmgard (Denmark), Vikram Iyengar (India), Luciana Mari (Italy), Joan Mills (Wales:UK), Caterina Nacci (Italy), Paola Pallini (Italy), Daria Palotti (Italy), Stefano Parigi (Italy), Ailsa Richardson (Wales:UK), Stephanie Sachsenmeier (Germany/UK), Raffaella Santucci (Italy), Giorgia Scalmani (Italy), Dries Van Dorp (Belgium), Natassa Xydi (Greece)
PRODUCTION AND DESIGN: Simon Banham (Wales:UK), Peter Lochery (Wales:UK), Cathy Piquemal (France/Wales)
VOICE DIRECTOR: Joan Mills
FABBRICAEUROPA FESTIVAL, FLORENCE, ITALY

JUNE
Performance Research
Volume 7/2: Translations
(*EDS.* Ric Allsopp and Caroline Bergvall)
LONDON: ROUTLEDGE
A CPR PUBLICATION

Bodyweather Workshop
CPR Organized Workshop
WORKSHOP LEADER: Tess de Quincey
ABERYSTWYTH, WALES

JULY
CPR Summer School: The Summer Shift
WORKSHOP LEADERS: Richard Gough (Wales:UK), Joan Mills (Wales:UK), New World Performance Lab (USA), Mike Pearson (Wales:UK), Tess de Quincey (Australia), Daksha Sheth (India)
ABERYSTWYTH, WALES

SEPTEMBER
Performance Research
Volume 7/3: On Fluxus
(*EDS.* Ric Allsopp, Ken Friedman and Owen Smith)
LONDON: ROUTLEDGE
A CPR PUBLICATION

Situated Appetites
Performance/Installation
DIRECTOR: Richard Gough
PERFORMERS/MAKERS: Jodie Bray, Judie Christie, Jack Gough, Richard Gough, Antony Pickthall, Ailsa Richardson, Rachel Rogers
ABERYSTWYTH ARTS SCHOOL, ABERYSTWYTH, WALES

NOVEMBER
CPR Organized Workshop
Voiceworks: Stemwerk
WORKSHOP LEADERS: Jean-René Toussaint and Anne-Marie Blink of Stemwerk (Netherlands)

DECEMBER
Performance Research
Volume 7/4: On Archives and Archiving
(*EDS.* Richard Gough and Heike Roms)
LONDON: ROUTLEDGE
A CPR PUBLICATION

2003

YEAR-LONG
Community Voice Projects
Evening Voice Development Classes, Heartsong Community Choir Classes, Weekend Voice Workshops and Voice in Common
PROJECT DIRECTOR: Joan Mills
ABERYSTWYTH, WALES

JANUARY
Cross Currents: Dance workshop
with **Allajotas** (Nigeria)
CARDIFF, WALES

FEBRUARY
Cross Currents: Skinner Release
Movement Technique
WORKSHOP LEADER: Gabi Agis (England:UK)
BANGOR, WALES

Cross Currents: Bodyweather Workshop
WORKSHOP LEADER: Stuart Lynch (Australia)
ABERYSTWYTH, WALES

MARCH
Performance Research
Volume 8/1: Voices
(*ED.* Claire MacDonald)
LONDON: ROUTLEDGE
A CPR PUBLICATION

Cross Currents: Guerrilla Retreat
WORKSHOP LEADERS: Helen Paris and Leslie Hill (UK/USA)
ST. DONAT'S, WALES

Voiceworks: Song, Dance, Rhythm, Movement, Gesture and the Spoken Word
WORKSHOP LEADER: Grzegorz Bral (Poland)
BANGOR, WALES

Cross Currents: Finding the Funny
WORKSHOP LEADERS: Ridiculusmus (England:UK)
BRECON, WALES

Cross Currents: Constructing Maps and Memory: Documentation and Representation
WORKSHOP LEADERS: Reckless Sleepers (England:UK)
CHAPTER ARTS CENTRE, CARDIFF, WALES

Cross Currents: Developing the Soliloquy
WORKSHOP LEADER: SuAndi (England:UK)
CARDIFF, WALES

Cross Currents: Introduction to Koodiyattom
WORKSHOP LEADER: Sreenath Nair and Arya Madhavan (India)
ABERYSTWYTH, WALES

Voiceworks: Voic(e)motion
WORKSHOP LEADER: Guy Dartnell (England:UK)
MOLD, WALES

APRIL
Cross Currents: Presence – Physical and Vocal Work
WORKSHOP LEADER: Gary Carter (Netherlands/South Africa)
WREXHAM, WALES

Voiceworks: Voice in Action
WORKSHOP LEADER: Natalka Polovynka (Ukraine)
ST. DAVID'S, WALES

Voiceworks: Yodelling
WORKSHOP LEADER: Hans Köhl (Austria)
MACHYNLLETH, WALES

MAY
Surrealist Banquet
Special Event/Performance Banquet/ Installation as part of:

Surrealism Laid Bare, Even
Third International Symposium on Surrealism
DIRECTOR: Richard Gough (Wales:UK)
PERFORMERS: Tessie Beavers (Netherlands), Jodie Bray (Wales:UK), Alice Briggs (Wales: UK), E-tong Chen (Taiwan), Antonia Doggett (England:UK), Richard Gough (Wales:UK), Marcie Hopkins (Germany/ UK), Vikram Iyengar (India), Jack James (England:UK), Antony Pickthall (Wales: UK), Rachel Rogers (Wales:UK), Stephanie Sachsenmeier (Germany/UK)
WEST DEAN COLLEGE, WEST SUSSEX, ENGLAND

Voiceworks: Voices
WORKSHOP LEADER: Viviane de Muynck (Belgium)
ABERYSTWYTH, WALES

Voiceworks: Welsh Folk Song
WORKSHOP LEADER: Julie Murphy (Wales:UK)
NARBERTH, WALES

Voiceworks: Speaking Shakespeare
WORKSHOP LEADER: Peter Morgan Barnes (N. Ireland:UK)
AMMANFORD, WALES

Voiceworks: Zulu Singing
WORKSHOP LEADER: Doreen Thobekile (South Africa/UK)
BANGOR, WALES

Voiceworks: Mongolian Throat Singing
WORKSHOP LEADER: Michael Ormiston (England:UK)
ST DONAT'S, WALES

JUNE-JULY
Performance Research
Volume 8/2: Bodiescapes
(*EDS.* Peter M. Boenisch and Ric Allsopp)
LONDON: ROUTLEDGE
A CPR PUBLICATION

CPR Summer School
The Summer Shift
WORKSHOP LEADERS: Guillermo Gómez-Peña (Mexico/USA), Richard Gough (Wales:UK), Les Kurbas Theatre Company (Ukraine), Joan Mills (Wales: UK), Mike Pearson (Wales:UK), Goat Island Performance Group (USA), Phillip Zarrilli (USA/UK)
ABERYSTWYTH, WALES

Club Raw
Performance
DIRECTORS: Guillermo Gómez-Peña (Mexico/USA) with Richard Gough and Judie Christie
PERFORMERS: participants of the Summer Shift and local artists
CASTLE THEATRE, ABERYSTWYTH, WALES

Directors' Talkshop
Goat Island (USA)
ABERYSTWYTH, WALES

CPR Organized Performance and Workshop Tour
Company: **Les Kurbas Theatre Company** (Ukraine)
ABERYSTWYTH AND AMMANFORD, WALES

SEPTEMBER
Performance Research
Volume 8/3: On Smell
(*EDS:* Richard Gough and Judie Christie)
LONDON: ROUTLEDGE
A CPR PUBLICATION

OCTOBER
The Wildebeest Lounge
CPR Presented Performance
CREATED AND PERFORMED BY: Gary Carter and Neil McCarthy
MARINE HOTEL, ABERYSTWYTH, WALES

Cross Currents: Butoh Workshop
WORKSHOP LEADER: Marie-Gabrielle Rotie (England:UK)
SWANSEA, WALES

NOVEMBER
Übung CPR Organized Tour (Voiceworks)
Company: **Victoria Theatre Company** (Belgium)
CHAPTER ARTS CENTRE, CARDIFF, WALES

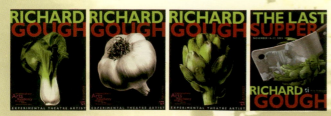

CPR Artist in Residence at University of Wisconsin, Madison

Residency included leading a study programme on performance, food and cookery, a practical course on devising theatre and directing a performance/installation
ARTIST: Richard Gough

The Last Supper
Performance
MADISON, USA

Cross Currents:
Stand-up Comedy
WORKSHOP LEADER: Oliver Double (England:UK)
ABERYSTWYTH, WALES

Cross Currents:
Mongolian Throat Singing
WORKSHOP LEADER: Michael Ormiston (England:UK)
BANGOR, WALES

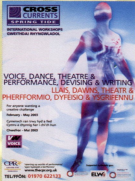

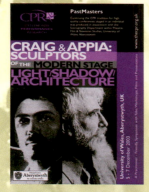

DECEMBER
Performance Research
Volume 8/4: Moving Bodies
(*EDS.* David Williams and Ric Allsopp)
LONDON: ROUTLEDGE
A CPR PUBLICATION

Pastmasters: Craig & Appia:
Sculptors of the Modern Stage
Conference
CURATION: Richard Gough and Rachel Rogers
CHAIR: Richard Gough
PERFORMANCES: U-Man Zoo (Wales:UK)
PRESENTATIONS: Simon Banham (Wales:UK), Christopher Baugh (England:UK), Richard Beacham (USA), Kirsten Dehlholm (Denmark), Hugh Denard (England:UK), Richard Downing (Wales:UK), Cat Fergusson (England: UK), Harvey Grossmann (USA), Dorita Hannah (New Zealand), Christopher Innes (Canada), Vikram Iyengar (India), Henryk Jurkowski (Poland), Ruth Mandel (Belgium), Selma Odom (Canada), Simon Rees (Wales:UK), Mischa Twitchin (England:UK), J. Michael Walton (England:UK)
UNIVERSITY OF WALES, ABERYSTWYTH, WALES

Directors' Talkshop:
Kirsten Dehlholm (Denmark)
ABERYSTWYTH, WALES

Cross Currents:
Contact Improv
WORKSHOP LEADER: Matilda Leyser (England:UK)
LLANDRINDOD WELLS, WALES

2004

YEAR-ROUND
Community Voice Projects
Voice Development Classes, Weekend Voice Workshops
VARIOUS, WALES

FEBRUARY-APRIL
Cross Currents:
Speaking Shakespeare
WORKSHOP LEADER: Peter Morgan Barnes (N. Ireland:UK)
ABERYSTWYTH, WALES

Cross Currents:
Vocal Dance
WORKSHOP LEADER: Patricia Bardi (Netherlands/USA)
ST. DONAT'S, WALES

Cross Currents:
Movement
WORKSHOP LEADER: Ultima Vez (Belgium)
SWANSEA, WALES

MARCH
Cross Currents:
Dance Improvisation
WORKSHOP LEADER: Rosemary Lee (England:UK)
LLANDRINDOD WELLS, WALES

Local Voices Worlds
of Song
CPR organized Wales community choir events including:
Gatherings, workshops and performances and the Traveller Project with CPR commission 'Travels with My Uncle' by Karl Jenkins.
ABERYSTWYTH, WALES

APRIL
Giving Voice #8:
Thinking Voice, Feeling Voice
– Towards a Philosophy and
Psychology of the Voice
Festival of workshops, performances, demonstrations and presentations
DIRECTOR: Joan Mills
PERFORMANCES: Jonathan Hart Makwaia (USA/UK), Mariana Sadowska (Ukraine), Stepanida (Siberia), Volcano Theatre Company (Wales:UK)
WORKSHOP LEADERS: Anne Marie Blink (Netherlands), Jonathan Hart Makwaia (USA/UK), Sreenath Nair and Arya Madhavan (India), Enrique Pardo (Peru/France), Tomasz Rodowicz (Poland), Mariana Sadowska (Ukraine), Judith Shahn (USA), Åsa Simma (Sweden), Stepanida (Siberia), Jean Rene Toussaint (France/Netherlands)
PRESENTATIONS: included workshop leaders and the following: Frankie Armstrong (Wales:UK), Yvon Bonefant (Canada), Andrew Kimbrough (USA), Alice Lagaay (UK/Germany), Tara MacAllister (USA), Ralf Peters (Germany), Joanna Weir-Ouston (England:UK), Linda Wise (Kenya/France)
UNIVERSITY OF WALES, ABERYSTWYTH AND ROYAL WELSH COLLEGE OF MUSIC AND DRAMA, CARDIFF, WALES

99 Georgian Songs:
A Collection of
Traditional Folk, Church
and Urban Songs from
Georgia
PLANNED AND INTRODUCED BY Edisher Garakanidze
EDITED BY Joan Mills
NOTES AND TRANSLATIONS BY Joseph Jordania
ABERYSTWYTH: BLACK MOUNTAIN PRESS
A CPR PUBLICATION

Performance Research
Volume 9/1: Correspondence
(*EDS.* Claire MacDonald and Ric Allsopp)
LONDON: ROUTLEDGE
A CPR PUBLICATION

Eating Words

Performance Banquet on the occasion of the Standing Conference of Drama Departments (SCUDD) being held at UWA
DIRECTOR: Richard Gough
ABERYSTWYTH, WALES

APRIL - DECEMBER

Traveller

8 month long Community Choir Project involving gatherings of choirs from throughout Wales in classes, workshops and rehearsals PROJECT DIRECTOR: Joan Mills
REGIONAL TUTORS: Pauline Down, Roxanne Smith and Sarah Harman
INCLUDING: MACHYNLLETH, SOUTH WALES, MID/WEST WALES, NORTH WALES, AND A NATIONAL GATHERING AT ABERYSTWYTH, WALES

JUNE-JULY

CPR Summer School
The Summer Shift

WORKSHOP LEADERS: Carol Brown and Dorita Hannah (New Zealand), Elevator Repair Service (USA), Richard Gough (Wales:UK), Joan Mills (Wales:UK), Motiroti (England:UK), Mike Pearson (Wales:UK), Aida Redza (Malaysia), Taal Fusion (UK/India)
ABERYSTWYTH, WALES

Performance Research
Volume 9/2: On the Page
EDS. Ric Allsopp and Kevin Mount
LONDON: ROUTLEDGE
A CPR PUBLICATION

SEPTEMBER

Performance Research
Volume 9/3 – Generation
(*ED.* Claire MacDonald with Laura McGough)
LONDON: ROUTLEDGE
A CPR PUBLICATION

NOVEMBER

Cross Currents: Ensemble Physical Improvisation
WORKSHOP LEADER: Quiddity Theatre (Australia)
LLANDRINDOD WELLS, WALES

Cross Currents: Devising/Site-Specific
WORKSHOP LEADER: Geraldine Pilgrim (England:UK)
ABERYSTWYTH, WALES

Cross Currents: Physical and Vocal Training
WORKSHOP LEADER: Kelman Group
UNIVERSITY OF GLAMORGAN, WALES

DECEMBER

c/o The Gym

A 30-year anniversary celebration bringing together past and current members of CPR and CLT including an exhibition, site visits, talks and discussions

Fifth Column, Fourth Wall, Third Theatre (or Thirty-one Objects to Aid a Forgetting)
Performance/Presentation
by Richard Gough

Other Chapters in the Cardiff Book of Performance (Index, Postscript, Erratum)
Presentations/Papers
WITH Janek Alexander, Mik Flood, Philip Mackenzie, Geoff Moore, Richard Huw Morgan, Mike Pearson, Heike Roms, Ceri Sherlock, Simon Thorne, Roger Tomlinson
CHAPTER ARTS CENTRE, CARDIFF, WALES

Performance Research
Volume 9/4: On Civility
(*ED.* Alan Read)
LONDON: ROUTLEDGE
A CPR PUBLICATION

Traveller Performance

*A promenade concert presented in collaboration
with St Donat's Arts Centre including:*

Travels with My Uncle

COMPOSER: Karl Jenkins
PERFORMERS: 100 singers from
community choirs throughout Wales
ST DONAT'S, WALES

2005

FEBRUARY
The Dead Memory Machine: Tadeusz Kantor's Theatre of Death

BY Krzysztof Pleśniarowicz, *TRANSLATED BY* William Brand
ABERYSTWYTH: BLACK MOUNTAIN PRESS
A CPR PUBLICATION

Cross Currents: A Live Art Experiment

WORKSHOP LEADER: Silke Mansholt (Germany)
POWYS DANCE, LLANDRINDOD WELLS, WALES

MARCH
Cross Currents: Loss and Bereavement

WORKSHOP LEADER: Luke Dixon, Nomad Theatre (England:UK)
ABERYSTWYTH, WALES

Unmentionable Cuisine at the Federal Reserve

*Performance Banquet for the 11th PSi
conference – Becoming Uncomfortable,
Brown University, Providence, Rhode
Island*
DIRECTOR: Richard Gough
(Wales:UK)
PERFORMERS: Jodie Bray (Wales:
UK), Carrie Coon (USA), Julia
Hinderlie (USA), Alicia Rios
(Spain), Melissa Thompson
(USA), Ryan Winkles (USA),
Mark Young (USA) and
students of Brown University
PROVIDENCE, USA

APRIL
Towards Tomorrow?

An International Gathering

Conference and Festival
CURATION: Judie Christie
and Richard Gough
CHAIR: Richard Gough
with Daniel Watt
PERFORMANCES: Alice
Briggs (Wales:UK),
Irish Modern Dance
Theatre (Eire), Rabab
Ghazoul (Iraq/UK), Zoe
Laughlin (England:UK),
Silke Mansholt (Germany),
Shazia Mirza (England:UK),
Ailsa Richardson (Wales:UK),
Louise Ritchie (Wales:UK),
Stelarc (Australia), Victoria Theatre
(Belgium), Volcano Theatre Company
(Wales:UK)
WORKSHOP LEADERS: Julia Lee Barclay (USA/
UK), Simon Bayly (England:UK), Shimon
Levy (Israel), Faith Wilding (USA)
KEYNOTE PRESENTATIONS: Philip Auslander (USA),
Rustom Bharucha (India), Steven Conner
(England:UK), Jane Goodall (Australia), Guillermo
Gómez-Peña (Mexico/USA), Richard Gough
(Wales:UK), Dragan Klaic (Serbia/Netherlands),
Hans Thies Lehman (Germany), Alphonso
Lingis (USA), Bonnie Marranca (USA), Jon
McKenzie (USA), Shazia Mirza (England:UK),
Susan Melrose (England:UK), Victoria Nelson
(USA), Marian Pastor Roces (Philippines),
Patrice Pavis (France), Mike Pearson (Wales:
UK), Alan Read (England:UK), Freddie Rokem
(Israel), Stelarc (Australia)

PRESENTATIONS: Joshua Abrams (USA/UK),
Electa Behrens (USA), Iwan Brioc (Wales:
UK), Piet Defraeye (Canada), John Elsom
(England:UK), Peter Falkenberg and Sharon
Mazer (New Zealand), Josette Féral (Canada), Alison Forsyth (Wales:UK), Karoline
Gritzner (Germany/Wales), Dror Harari (England:UK), Alison Hodge (England:
UK), Helen Iball (England:UK), Jude James (England:UK), Isabel Jones (England:
UK), Adrian Kear (England:UK), Joe Kelleher (England:UK), Karen Juers-Munby
(England:UK), Michal Kobialka (USA), Ray Langenbach (Malaysia), Martina Leeker
(Germany), Rita Marcalo (England:UK), Julian Maynard-Smith (England:UK),
Avanthi Meduri (India/UK), Daniel Meyer-Dinkgräfe (Germany/Wales), Sreenath
Nair and Arya Madhavan
(India), Kristine Nutting
(Canada), Jan Overfield
(England:UK), Jennifer
Parker-Starbuck (USA/UK),
Pam Patterson (Canada),
Shannon Payne (USA),
Krzystof Pleśniarowicz
(Poland), Paul Rae
(Singapore/UK), Nicholas
Ridout (England:UK), Petra
Sabisch (UK), Marko
Stamenkovic (Serbia)
SYZGY: Jennifer Verson,
Rebecca Woodford-Smith
and MikYoung Pearce
(England:UK), TRAWS: Jill
Greenhalgh, Richard Huw
Morgan, Paul Jeff, Lisa
Lewis, Roger Owen, Mike
Pearson, Steve Robins,
Heike Roms, Nic Ros and
Daniel Watt (Wales:UK),
Mischa Twitchin (England:
UK), Mick Wallis (England:
UK), Martin Welton
(England:UK)
ABERYSTWYTH, WALES

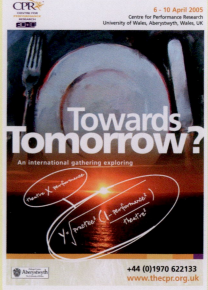

A Roll Call of Other Key People

(in addition to the founding members, directors, performers and curators credited in the preceding pages)

Administrators
Caroline Lynch-Blosse (1978-79)
Gill Sealby (1979-81)
Ceri Llewellyn (1981-83)
Meurig Parry (1983-84)
Steve Fletcher (1984-85)
Celia Webb (1993-95)
Claire Swatheridge (1996-2004)
Marcie Hopkins (2002-04)

Assistant Administrators
Yvonne Cheal (1982-83)
Kevin Thomas (1983-84)
Cathy Saunders (1983-84)
Katie Dymoke (1985-86)
Paula Vickers (1986-87)
Sheila Stockton (1988-90)
Alison Jones (1991-92)
Trisha Rhodes (1996-97)
Fiona Smith (1997-99)
Gwen Davies (2000)
David Gillam (2000)
Amanda Jones (2001)
Sam Morton (2001)
Elen Chick (2001-03)

Performance Research Journal Administrators
Clancy Pegg (1995-2001)
Linden Elmhirst (2002-)

The Practice Administrator
Howard Cooper (1991-92)

PSi Administrator
Heike Roms (1998-2001)
Jelena Majerhofer (2001)

Marketing and Development
Celia Webb (1990-93)
Deborah Procter (1999-2000)

Archivists
Ric Allsopp (1985-87)
Jim Ennis (1988-89)
Adam Hayward (1996-99)
Aysegul Kürkçüoglu (1999-2000)
Dan Rebbeck (2001-02)

Research Assistants and Book Club Managers
Adam Hayward (1996-99)
Rachel Rogers (1998-2004)
Jenny Norris (2004)
Ailsa Richardson (2005)

Publications Assistant
Daniel Watt (2004-06)

Project Co-ordinators
Norman Frisch (1978-79)
Paul Roylance (1981)
Joan Mills (1981 & 1983)
Paul Chandler (1983 & 1995)
Jill Greenhalgh (1985 & 1986)
Chris Marshall (1986 & 1987)
Jo Riley (1986 & 1987)
Jim Ennis (1987-88)
Ken Cockburn (1989-90)
Scott deLahunta (1993-94)
Chris Rowbury (1993-94)
Ric Allsopp (1993 & 1994)
Nick Sales (1995-96)
Adam Hayward (1998-99)
Roxane Smith (2001)
Peader Kirk (2002)
Rachel Rogers (2000-04)

Design & Production
Thony Christie (1974-75)
Pete Brooks (1978-79)
Paul Downton (1978 & 1980)
Peter Furness (1979-80)
Tony Welch (1982-83)
Trisha Webb (1984-86)
Trevor Turton (1984-85 & 1991)
Wiard Sterk (1986)
Brian Williams (1986-87)
Russell Harvey (1987)
Gilly Thomas (1989)
Juliet Marsh (1989-90)
George Davis-Stewart (1989-94)
Sid Marchant (1992)
Giles Parberry (1993 & 1994 & 2000)
Gerald Tyler (1992 & 2000 & 2002)
Peter Lochery (2002)
Simon Banham (1989-90 & 1992 & 2002)
Ian Buchanan (1999-2000 & 2002 & 2004)

Interns
Scott de LaHunta (1992)
Rebecca Gabittas (1993-94)
Rabab Ghazoul (1993-94)
Bridget Keehan (1993-94)
Clare Wallace (1993-94)
Kendra Fanconi (1994-95)
Sara Brady (1995-96)
Misha Myers (1997-98)
Michael Stubblefield (1997-98)
Louisa Colzani (2000)
Liz Holmes (2002)
Electa Behrens (2002)
Annouchka Bayley (2002-03)
Alice Briggs (2002-03)
Jessica Jeske (2003)
Abi Lake (2003)
Jenny Norris (2003-04)
Siu-lin Rawlinson (2003-04)
Gemma Harris (2003-04)
Dominique Fester (2004)
Grace Looi (2004)
Julia Hinderlie (2004)
Melissa Thompson (2004)
Vanessa Williams (2004-05)
Sarah Hak (2004-05)
Nick Minns (2004-05)
Ruth Peer (2005)
Sam Ek (2005)
Melissa Dunne (2005)
Leah Bradford Smart (2005)
Stephanie Ward (2005-06)
Marc Oliver Krampe (2006)
Lisa Mildenhall (2006)
Shamsher Virk (2006)
Danny Furness (2006)

Members of CLT and CPR Boards of Management
George Auchterlonie (1978-80)
Mike Pearson (1978-80)
Mike Baker (1978-80)
Gill Sealby (1981-87)
Sue Harris (1981-84)
David Greer (1981-96)
Kath Ukleja (1983-87)
Griff Taylor (1983-87)
Martin Banham (1988-91)
John Beatlestone (1988-91)
Edward Braun (1993-2003)
Wendy Crockett (1999-2003)
Chris Ricketts (2000-03)
Caitlin O'Reilly (1996-2004)

Current CPR Ltd. Board of Management Members: 2006
Noel Witts (1988–)
Roger Owen (1992–)
Roger Tomlinson (1993–)
Michael Freeman (1999–)
Michael Anderson (2002–)

Current CPR Team: 2006
Artistic Director:	**Richard Gough** (1975–)
Executive Producer:	**Judie Christie** (1986–)
Marketing & Development Director:	**Antony Pickthall** (2000–)
Administrative Director:	**Helen Gethin** (2004–)
Voice Director:	**Joan Mills** (1990–)
Projects Co-ordinator:	**Cathy Piquemal** (2001–)
Archivist:	**Jodie Bray** (2002–)
Research Assistant & Publications Manager:	**Siu-lin Rawlinson** (2005–)
Publications Assistant:	**Electa Behrens** (2006)

ABERYSTWYTH
Where the Holiday pound buys more fun

COURTESY OF ABERYSTWYTH MUSEUM

Notes On Contributors

PAUL ALLAIN is Professor of Theatre and Performance at the University of Kent, Canterbury. He collaborated with the Gardzienice Theatre Association from 1989 to 1993 and published the book *Gardzienice: Polish Theatre in Transition* (1997). He co-edited the *Cambridge Companion to Chekhov* (2000), and his book *The Art of Stillness: The Theatre Practice of Tadashi Suzuki* was published by Methuen (2002) and Palgrave Macmillan, USA (2003). Routledge published his *Companion to Theatre and Performance*, co-written with Jen Harvie, in early 2006. Paul is currently researching the legacy of Grotowski's work.

RIC ALLSOPP is a co-founder and joint editor of *Performance Research*, a quarterly international journal of contemporary performance (London and New York: Routledge) *http://performance-research.net* and is Reader in Performance Research at Dartington College of Arts, Devon, UK. Publications include *The Connected Body?* (1996) with Scott deLahunta, and numerous articles on performance, writing and contemporary practice for various journals and books.

FRANKIE ARMSTRONG is an internationally acclaimed singer who has been singing and recording professionally since 1964. In 1975 she began leading voice workshops and pioneered new methods of teaching and singing based on traditional methods of singing and song. Her workshops focus on releasing the natural song, song interpretation, performance skills and the 'Voices of the Archetypes of Myth'. She currently works throughout the UK, Europe and Australia, as well as Eire and North America. She has published her autobiography, *As Far as the Eye Can Sing*, and *Well-tuned Women: Growing Strong through Voice Work*, with Jenny Pearson.

PHILIP AUSLANDER is Professor in the School of Literature, Communication and Culture of the Georgia Institute of Technology in Atlanta, where he teaches in the areas of Performance Studies, Media Studies and Popular Music. His books include *Liveness: Performance in a Mediatized Culture* (Routledge 1999), for which he won the prestigious Callaway Prize, and *Performing Glam Rock: Gender and Theatricality in Popular Music* (Michigan 2006). In addition to his scholarly work on performance and music, Professor Auslander writes art criticism for *ArtForum* and other publications.

CHRISTOPHER BALME currently holds the Chair in Theatre Studies at the University of Munich. He was born and educated in New Zealand where he graduated from the University of Otago. He has lived and worked in Germany since 1985 with positions at the universities of Würzburg, Munich and Mainz. In 2004 he was appointed to the Chair in Theatre Studies at the University of Amsterdam. He has published widely on German theatre, intercultural theatre and theatre and other media. He is past-president of the German Society for Theatre Research, is on the executive committee of the IFTR and is Senior Editor of *Theatre Research International*. Recent publications include *Decolonizing the Stage: Theatrical Syncretism and Postcolonial Drama*, (Oxford 1999); *Einführung in die Theaterwissenschaft* (Berlin 2003); *Crossing Media: Theater – Film – Photographie – Neue Medien*, edited with Markus Moninger (ePODIUM, 2004). Forthcoming is a study of performative encounters around the Pacific, *Pacific Performances* (Palgrave 2006).

RUSTOM BHARUCHA is an independent writer, director, cultural critic and dramaturg, based in Calcutta. He is the author of several books including *Theatre and the World, The Question of Faith, In the Name of the Secular, The Politics of Cultural Practice, Rajasthan: An Oral History* and a forthcoming monograph on the inter-Asian affinities and differences of Rabindranath Tagore and Okakura Tenshin, entitled *Another Asia*. A member of the International Advisory Council of the Prince Claus Fund for Culture and Development, Rustom is also actively involved in cultural networks such as TADIA (The African Diasporas in Asia), among other initiatives concerning subaltern communities, religious minorities and cultural activism around AIDS.

JOHANNES BIRRINGER is a choreographer and artistic director of AlienNation Co., a multimedia ensemble based in Houston (*www.aliennationcompany.com*). He has created numerous dance-theatre works, digital media installations and site-specific performances in collaboration with artists in Europe, North America, Latin America and China. He is the author of several books, including *Media and Performance: Along the Border* (1998), *Performance on the Edge: Transformations of Culture* (2000) and *Dance Technologies: Digital Performance in the 21st Century* (forthcoming). After creating the Dance and Technology programme at Ohio State University, he now directs the Interaktionslabor Göttelborn in Germany (*http://interaktionslabor.de*) and is Professor of Performance Technologies at Brunel University, London.

PAUL CARTER is a writer and artist. His recent books include *Repressed Spaces* (Reaktion Books, 2002), *Material Thinking* (Melbourne University Press, 2004) and *Mythform: The Making of Nearamnew* (Melbourne University Press, 2005) – an account of the public artwork he created at Federation Square (Melbourne). He is Professorial Research Fellow in the Faculty of Architecture, Building and Planning, University of Melbourne.

FRANC CHAMBERLAIN is editor of both the Routledge Performance Practitioners series and Routledge Companions to Theatre Practitioners. Author of *Michael Chekhov* (Routledge, 2004) and devisor/performer of Interruptions (2003–ongoing), he is currently based at University College Cork, Ireland. Together with Tom Leabhart he is working on the Routledge Companion to Decroux as well as continuing research on the Vidya project in Ahmedabad in collaboration with Ralph Yarrow and Frances Babbage.

JUDIE CHRISTIE is Executive Producer for CPR. After gaining her MA in Theatre Studies and Fine Art, Glasgow, she worked variously as community theatre worker, designer, administrator and production manager, prior to joining Cardiff Laboratory Theatre in 1986 as project co-ordinator for Peking Opera Explorations and the first Magdalena International Festival. Since founding the CPR with Richard Gough in 1988, she has produced and curated its many programmes of cultural exchange and collaboration, performance-making and touring, education, training and research. A member of the *Performance Research* editorial board, Judie co-edited the issue 'On Smell' (September, 2003).

LAURIE BETH CLARK is a professor in the Art Department of the University of Wisconsin at Madison where she teaches studio courses in Performance, Video and Installations and seminars on topics in Visual Culture. She produces large-scale site-specific installations and performances as well as more modestly scaled single-channel video tapes and virtual environments. She also writes essays for conferences and publications. Recent projects and works in progress explore veracity and mendacity, virtuality and materiality, trauma and memory.

ENZO COZZI is a lecturer at Royal Holloway University of London. His subjects are the ecology of mind and performance and the relationships between healing, learning, ritual and cosmology. He is also an applied performance practitioner, specializing in adapting devotional and festive ritual forms to learning and healing contexts. He has published in *La Escena Latinoamericana* (Mexico), *Investigación y Crítica* and *Ecovisiones* (Chile) and *Journal of Latin American Cultural Studies, New Theatre Quarterly* and *Performance Research* (all in the UK). He has been a consultant/teacher in ritual theatre and education with the Ministry of Education and various local education authorities in Chile. He also teaches part-time in the Universidad Mayor and Universidad Finis Terrae in Chile. He co-directs the 'Analema' (Analogical Learning Matrixes) research centre based in Chile.

TIM ETCHELLS is an artist and writer best known for his work as director of the UK performance ensemble Forced Entertainment. He has also collaborated with a wide range of other artists to create works in diverse media and contexts. Since the mid-1980s he has developed a unique voice in writing for and about performance. Published work includes *Certain Fragments* (Routledge, 1999) and *The Dream Dictionary (for the Modern Dreamer)* (Duck Editions, 2001). Recent Forced Entertainment performances include Etchells's solo *Instructions for Forgetting*, which blurs the borders between confessional performance, video and documentary essay, the absurd vaudeville of failure *First Night* and the deconstructed ironic rock spectacle *Bloody Mess*. Etchells is currently Creative Fellow in the Department of Theatre Studies at Lancaster University, UK.

ANNA FENEMORE is currently Research Fellow at the University in Cheshire at Crewe and Alsager. She is also the Artistic Director of Pigeon Theatre, a Manchester-based physical-performance company, and performer with The Chameleons Group multimedia performance company. Her current research interests are: spectating embodiment, performer bodywork training, multi-sensory performance, performance and phenomenology and theories of performance space.

GUILLERMO GÓMEZ-PEÑA is a performance artist and writer based in San Francisco. He is the Artistic Director of La Pocha Nostra performance troupe and a contributing editor of *TDR* magazine (MIT Press). He has written seven books, the most recent being *Ethno-Techno: Writings on Performance, Pedagogy and Activism* (Routledge, 2005). Descriptions of his current projects can be found on his website: *www. pochanostra.com*.

JANE R. GOODALL is the author of *Artaud and the Gnostic Dream* (1994 Oxford), and most recently, *Performance and Evolution in the Age of Darwin* (2002 Routledge), which won the Rob Jordan biennial prize for the best book in theatre and performance studies from the Australasian Drama Studies Association. She has held positions at several Australian universities, teaching drama and performance, cultural history and history of science. Currently, she teaches Contemporary Arts at the University of Western Sydney. She is also a successful crime novelist, including most recently The Walker (Hodder, 2004) and *The Visitor* (Hodder, 2005).

RICHARD GOUGH is Professor of Theatre and Performance in the Department of Theatre, Film and Television Studies at the University of Wales, Aberystwyth, as well as Artistic Director of the CPR. He has dedicated the past thirty years to developing and exploring interdisciplinary, experimental performance work. He has curated and organized numerous international theatre projects, including conferences, summer schools and workshop festivals, and has produced nationwide tours of experimental theatre and traditional dance/theatre ensembles from around the world. He has directed over seventy productions, many of which have toured Europe, and he has lectured and led workshops throughout Europe and in China, Japan, Colombia, the United States and Brazil. He edited *The Dictionary of Theatre Anthropology* (Routledge, 1990), is the general editor of the Routledge (Taylor and Francis) quarterly publication *Performance Research* (Journal of Performing Arts) and publisher and series editor of Black Mountain Press.

MATTHEW GOULISH co-founded the performance group Goat Island in 1987 with director Lin Hixson. He has collaborated on nine performance works and several writing and film projects with the company. He has published and lectured widely, and his *39 Microlectures – in proximity of performance* was published in 2000. In 2004 he received a Lannan Foundation writing residency in Marfa, Texas. He teaches writing at The School of the Art Institute of Chicago.

JILL GREENHALGH works extensively in Europe, Australasia and the Americas as producer, director, performer and teacher. In 1986, after seven years with Cardiff Laboratory Theatre, she founded the Magdalena Project – International Network of Women in Contemporary Theatre. This network spans forty-seven countries, with autonomous national groups regularly organizing Magdalena Festivals. Currently, Jill is Lecturer in Performance Studies at the University of Wales, Aberystwyth, and involved in a long-term collaboration with a Mexican performance artist examining the unsolved killings of hundreds of young women in the border regions of the USA and Mexico.

ADRIAN HEATHFIELD writes on and curates contemporary performance. He is the editor of a number of books including *Live: Art and Performance* (Tate Publishing, 2004) and *Shattered Anatomies: Traces of the Body in Performance* (Arnolfini Live, 1997). He co-curated the *Live Culture* event at Tate Modern, London, in 2003 with Lois Keidan and Daniel Brine.

HELEN IBALL is a lecturer in Drama at the University of Hull. Her articles have appeared in *Performance Research* and *Contemporary Theatre Review*, and these reflect her interests in theatrical aesthetics, particularly in the staging of bodily appetite/invasion. She has recently published on the international touring of Bobby Baker in *Casting Gender: Women and Performance in Intercultural Contexts* (New York: Peter Lang). She is writing a study of Sarah Kane's *Blasted* (London: Continuum), which is due for publication in 2007, and monographs on recent British theatre and theatricality.

AMELIA JONES is Professor and Pilkington Chair in Art History and Visual Studies at the University of Manchester. Jones edited the volume *Feminism and Visual Culture Reader* (Routledge, 2003) and has published the books *Postmodernism and the En-Gendering of Marcel Duchamp* (1994), *Body Art / Performing the Subject* (1998) and *Irrational Modernism: A Neurasthenic History of New York Dada* (2004). Her edited anthology *A Companion to Contemporary Art Since 1945*, a handbook and intellectual survey, includes twenty-seven original essays and is forthcoming from

Blackwell. Her book, *Self Image: Technology, Representation and the Contemporary Subject*, on artists' use of technologies of representation to interrogate the boundaries of the self, is being published in 2006-7 by Routledge. Jones has received ACLS, NEH, and Guggenheim fellowships.

ADRIAN KEAR is Head of Drama, Theatre and Performance Studies at Roehampton University, London. He is the co-editor of *Psychoanalysis and Performance* (Routledge, 2001) and *Mourning Diana: Nation, Culture and the Performance of Grief* (Routledge, 1999). He contributes to the academic journals *Contemporary Theatre Review*, *Parallax* and *JPCS*, as well as frequently writing for *Performance Research*. He is currently completing a book entitled, *Theatre and Event* (forthcoming, 2007).

JOE KELLEHER teaches in the School of Arts at Roehampton University, London. He writes on contemporary theatre and performance. He is co-editor with Nicholas Ridout of the forthcoming book *Contemporary Theatres in Europe* (Routledge, 2006). His work has appeared in journals such as *Contemporary Theatre Review*, *Frakcija*, *PAJ* and *Performance Research*, and books such as *Blairism and the War of Persuasion*, edited by Steinberg and Johnson (Lawrence and Wishart, 2004) and *Live: Art and Performance*, edited by Adrian Heathfield (Tate Publishing, 2004). He is the author of a series of essays on Societas Raffaello Sanzio's *Tragedia Endogonidia*, published in *Idioma, Clima, Crono* (Cesena, 2002-4), and is currently collaborating on books with the Societas and with Italian performance collective Kinkaleri. Joe is a member of London-based theatre group PUR.

DRAGAN KLAIC is a theatre scholar and cultural analyst with strong research interests in contemporary performing arts, European cultural policies, strategies of cultural development and international cultural cooperation, interculturalism, festivals and cultural memory. He serves as a permanent fellow of Felix Meritis Foundation in Amsterdam, teaches Arts and Cultural Policy at the University of Leiden and is the author and editor of several books, most recently *Europe as a Cultural Project* (Amsterdam: ECF, 2005). He is completing a handbook on international cultural cooperation.

MICHAL KOBIALKA is Chair and Professor of Theatre at the Department of Theatre Arts and Dance, University of Minnesota. His book on Tadeusz Kantor's theatre, *A Journey Through Other Spaces: Essays and Manifestos, 1944-1990* (University of California Press) was published in 1993. He is the editor of *Of Borders and Thresholds: Theatre History, Practice and Theory* (University of Minnesota Press, 1999) and a co-editor (with Barbara Hanawalt) of *Medieval Practices of Space* (University of Minnesota Press, 2000). His book on the early-medieval drama and theatre, *This Is My Body: Representational Practices in the Early Middle Ages* (University of Michigan Press, 1999) received the 2000 ATHE Annual Research Award for Outstanding Book in Theatre Practice and Pedagogy. He has just finished a critical book-length study of Tadeusz Kantor's theatre.

ALPHONSO LINGIS is Professor of Philosophy at Pennsylvania State University and author of numerous books including *Abuses* (1994), *The Community of Those Who Have Nothing in Common* (1994), *Foreign Bodies* (1994) and most recently *Dangerous Emotions* (2000). His translations of philosopher Emmanuel Levinas and his philosophical grounding within the work of Kant, Heidegger, Merleau-Ponty and Nietzsche inform his unique speculations on passion, emotion and beauty. His areas of specialization include phenomenology/existentialism, modern philosophy and ethics. His reviewers and critics have called Alphonso Lingis everything from a 'poet in disguise' to a 'brilliant philosopher.'

CLAIRE MacDONALD is a writer and editor whose interests lie at the intersection of fiction, performance and the visual arts. A co-founder of both Impact and Insomniac theatre companies, she was a theatre-maker and performer before turning to plays and fiction. As a critic she publishes widely on the visual arts, writing and performance. She has taught writing and performance in universities in the UK and the USA. She is a founding editor of the journal *Performance Research*, and a contributing editor to *Performing Arts Journal*. She is currently a research fellow in Performance and Publication at Central St. Martins College of Art in London.

JON McKENZIE is Coordinator of Modern Studies and Assistant Professor of English at the University of Wisconsin–Milwaukee, where he teaches courses in performance theory, post-modern theatre and performance, and civil disobedience. He is author of *Perform or Else: From Discipline to Performance* (Routledge) and co-editor of *Contesting Performance: Global Genealogies of Research* (forthcoming). His essays include 'Laurie Anderson for Dummies', 'Genre Trouble: (The) Butler Did It' and 'Democracy's Performance', and his work has been translated into Croatian, French, German, Japanese, Polish, and Portuguese. Jon's current research project focuses on global performativity, digital activism and experience design. He has also worked in the new media industry as a writer and information architect.

SUSAN MELROSE is Professor of Performance Arts and Research Convenor for Performing Arts, in the School of Arts, Middlesex University, UK. After completing her doctoral research in performance analysis at the Sorbonne Nouvelle in the early 1980s, she established and ran postgraduate profession/vocation-linked theatre and performance studies courses at the Central School of Speech and Drama and Rose Bruford College, London, before taking up her professorship at Middlesex. She is widely published in the fields of performance analysis, performance writing and critical semiotics. Her *Semiotics of the Dramatic Text*, for Macmillan, appeared in 1994. In 2005 she co-edited *Rosemary Butcher: Choreography, Collisions and Collaborations* for Middlesex University Press. A number of presentations and keynote papers are web-published at *http://www.sfmelrose.u-net.com*.

JOAN MILLS is a theatre director, voice practitioner, the CPR's Voice Director and Fellow in Voice and Performance at the Department of Theatre, Film and Television Studies, University of Wales, Aberystwyth. She has directed a wide range of theatre over the past thirty-five years, from new writing to TIE, classical text to visual performance, and has created a number of original theatre pieces. Her work is influenced by her understanding of voice practice from various cultures, particularly since 1990, through her curation of 'Giving Voice' for the CPR. For eight years she was Head of Voice and Movement at the Royal Welsh College of Music and Drama, and has taught workshops in voice, acting and writing throughout the UK, Europe and the USA. She founded the community choir Heartsong and has recorded three CDs in collaboration with Frankie Armstrong, as well as her own teaching CD.

PATRICE PAVIS is Professor of Theatre Studies at the University of Paris 8, France. He is the author of *Dictionnaire du Théâtre* (Paris: Dunod, 1996), which is now available in English as *Dictionary of the Theatre: Concepts and Analysis* (Toronto University Press, 1998). Other books include *The Intercultural Performance Reader* (Routledge) and *Performance Analysis* (University of Michigan Press). In 2005 he gave the Leverhulme lectures at the University of Kent.

MIKE PEARSON is Professor of Performance Studies, Department of Theatre, Film and Television Studies, University of Wales, Aberystwyth. Between 1971 and 1997 he helped pioneer and develop innovative approaches in the practice, theory and pedagogy and documentation of performance, particularly in Wales, in a series of companies including RAT Theatre (1972-3), Cardiff Laboratory Theatre (1973-81) and Cwmni Theatr Brith Gof (1981-97). His interests include physical theatre, devised performance and site-specific work. He continues to make performances as a solo artist and in collaboration with Mike Brookes in Pearson/Brookes. He is the co-author with Michael Shanks of *Theatre/Archaeology* (Routledge 2001), and his monograph *'In Comes I': Performance, Location and Landscape* (University of Exeter Press) is forthcoming.

SIBYLLE PETERS studied literature, theatre and philosophy in Hamburg, Germany, where her research focus was on the production of meaning in postdramatic theatre and tactical media and time. Since 1997 she has been a researcher and lecturer at the universities of Hamburg, Munich, Basle and Berlin. Her current research is on the academic lecture as performance. Her work, as both director and performer, include performances and real fictions on the boundaries of art and science / art and politics. She has published on theatricality and knowledge, rhetorics and audiences, economies of the public, time and media, performative evidence and the improbability drive.

MICHAEL PETERSON teaches Theatre and Performance Studies at the University of Wisconsin-Madison. He is the author of *Straight White Male* (University of Mississippi Press, 1997), a critical study of form and identity-privilege in monologue performance art and comedy, and is completing a book-length performance study of a tourist city, *Las Vegas Culture*. Other works-in-progress include essays on televisual place and on audience interpretations of show business, and – in the very long-term – performance projects including a multi-part work on the physical culture of urban bodies of water and a portable performance, *DarkRoom*, concerned with some of the themes of his essay for this volume.

PAUL RAE is a writer and the director of the Singapore-based performance company spell#7 (*www.spell7.net*). He makes performances, lectures and participatory public art events, and has published articles on interculturalism, cosmopolitanism and contemporary Southeast Asian theatre in *Performance Research, Contemporary Theatre Review* and *The Drama Review*. In 2004 he co-ordinated the tenth Performance Studies international (PSi) conference, held in Singapore. In 2007 he will collaborate with Martin Welton to co-edit an issue of *Performance Research* entitled 'On the Road'.

ALAN READ is Professor of Theatre in the Department of English at King's College, and director of the Centre for Theatre Research in Europe. He is the author of *Theatre and Everyday Life: An Ethics of Performance* and editor of *The Fact of Blackness: Frantz Fanon and Visual Representation* and *Architecturally Speaking: Practices of Art, Architecture and the Everyday*. He is a founding member of the journal *Performance Research* and was the guest editor of 'On Animals'. He is currently responsible for the five-year Arts and Humanities Research Board project 'Performance Architecture Location'. As part of this work, the international symposium 'Civic Centre: Reclaiming the Right to Performance' took place across London in April 2003.

AILSA RICHARDSON is a performer and director of site-specific and collaboratively-devised performance that has a strong relationship to audience. She is particularly interested in devising structures and training that expand perception, awareness and the process of re-membering. Other current interests are states of ecstasy, performance and transformation and creative communities. She trained in Fine Art in Bristol and in Theatre (MA) in Aberystwyth. Since 1997 she has worked with By Word of Mouth, Kneehigh Theatre, Richard Gough and CPR, the de Quincey company (Australia), U-man Zoo and her own company, Fan Yma. Ailsa is in ongoing training in Bodyweather, a performance training devised in Japan by Min Tanaka. She is currently Associate Artist with CPR.

FREDDIE ROKEM is Professor of Theatre Studies at Tel Aviv University, where he served as Dean of the Faculty of Arts from 2002 to 2006. His *Performing History: Theatrical Representations of the Past in Contemporary Theatre* received the ATHE Prize for best book in theatre studies for 2001. His most recent book, *Strindberg's Secret Codes*, was published in 2004. He has also published numerous articles in scholarly journals and books. Rokem is editor of *Theatre Research International* (2006-9) and associate editor *Theatre Journal and Assaph: Studies in the Theatre*. He is a translator and a dramaturg and serves as vice president of Performance Studies international (PSi) and as a member of the executive committee of The International Federation for Theatre Research (IFTR).

HEIKE ROMS is a lecturer in Performance Studies at the University of Wales, Aberystwyth. She has published on contemporary performance practice and theory, in particular on work originating in Wales. Forthcoming publications include a co-edited volume (with Jon McKenzie and C. J. Wan-Ling Wee) entitled *Contesting Performance: Global Genealogies of Research* (for Palgrave Macmillan). A consultant editor for *Performance Research* since its inception, Heike co-edited with Richard Gough the issues 'On Tourism' and 'On Archives and Archiving'. Between 1998 and 2001 she served as the administrator of PSi Performance Studies international under Gough's presidency and co-organized the Fifth Performance Studies Conference in Aberystwyth in 1999 in collaboration with CPR. Originally from Germany, Heike has lived in Wales since 1995.

RICHARD SCHECHNER is one of the pioneers of Performance Studies. A scholar and director, he is University Professor of Performance Studies at the Tisch School of the Arts at New York University and Editor of *TDR: The Journal of Performance Studies*. He is the author of *Performance Studies: An Introduction, Public Domain, Environmental Theater, The End of Humanism, Performance Theory, Between Theater and Anthropology* and *The Future of Ritual*. His books have been translated into Spanish, Korean, Chinese, Japanese, Serbo-Croat, German, Italian, Hungarian and Bulgarian. He is the general editor of the Worlds of Performance series published by Routledge.

EDWARD SCHEER is a senior lecturer in the School of Media, Film and Theatre at the University of New South Wales in Sydney, Australia. He is a founding editor of *Performance Paradigm*, an online journal of contemporary culture and performance. He has completed a book-length study of Mike Parr's Performance Art (to be published by Schwartz Press in late 2006) and is editor of *100 Years of Cruelty: Essays on Artaud* (Power

Publications, 2000) and *Antonin Artaud: A Critical Reader* for Routledge (2004).

REBECCA SCHNEIDER directs the MA and Ph.D. in Theatre and Performance Studies at Brown University. She is the author of *The Explicit Body in Performance* (Routledge, 1997) and co-editor of a book on twentieth-century directing practice and theory titled *Re:Direction* (also with Routledge). She has written numerous essays, among them 'Hello Dolly Well Hello Dolly: The Double and Its Theatre' in *Psychoanalysis and Performance*, 'Solo Solo Solo' in *After Criticism: New Responses to Art and Performance* and 'Performance Remains' in the journal *Performance Research*. Schneider is a contributing editor to *The Drama Review* and on the board of *Theatre Survey*. She is co-editor (with David Krasner) of the book series Theatre: Theory/Text/Performance for the University of Michigan Press.

DANIEL WATT is a lecturer in English and Drama at Loughborough University. He holds an MA in Philosophy and Literature from the University of Warwick and his D.Phil. thesis (University of Sussex) examined 'The Future of the Fragment: Transformations of Writing in the Work of Blanchot, Beckett, Coetzee, Derrida and Jabès'. His research interests include fragmentary writing, ethics and literature, and philosophical and literary influences on theatre and performance in the twentieth century. He has published articles in *The Oxford Literary Review*, *Performance Research* and *Wormwood: writings about fantasy, supernatural and decadent literature*.

MICK WALLIS is Professor of Performance and Culture and Director of Research in the School of Performance and Cultural Industries, University of Leeds, UK. His principal research focus at present is in cultural histories of performance with a particular focus on non-canonical performance in Britain 1919–51. He is conducting an AHRC-funded survey of village theatre in England. Recent work includes *Drama/Theatre/Performance* (Routledge 2004) with Simon Shepherd, an essay in Volume 3 of the Cambridge History of British Theatre (2004) and an essay on presence on the neoclassical stage in Performance Research 10(1) (2005). He is co-editor (with Richard Gough) of *Performance Research* 10(4) (2005), 'On techne'. Mick is co-founder of the Inter-War Rural History Group and the Performance Robotics Research Group. He is co-ordinator of the Arts Work With People Project (AWP), a collaboration with arts charity Salamanda Tandem.

DAVID WILLIAMS has worked as a teacher, writer, translator, director, dramaturg and performer in Australia and England. At present, he is Professor of Theatre and Senior Research Fellow at Dartington College of Arts, Devon, England. He has edited books about the work of Peter Brook's CIRT and Ariane Mnouchkine's Théâtre du Soleil. Recent research relates to animals and/in performance (particularly horses, birds and dogs), fire, water and a history of skies. Current collaborative projects include work with Gregg Whelan and Gary Winters (Lone Twin) and Emilyn Claid.

Photography Credits

Birringer, Johannes pp.90-92 (videostills)
Bray, Jodie p.283 (full page image)
Butcher, Rosemary p.135
Carter, Paul and Ed pp.201-205 (all)
Casid, Jill p.57
Ceredigion Museum pp.215, 317
Chamberlain, Franc pp.41-46 (all), 283 (insets)
CPR Archive pp.18, 48, 49, 52, 55, 60, 164-167 (all in right hand column), 248, 250, 253, 254, 256, 257, 262
Giles, Mary p.33
Glendinning, Hugo pp.7, 22, 24
Gómez-Peña, Guillermo pp.75 77 (videostills)
Gough, Lilith p.266
Gough, Richard pp.xi, 3, 53
Hudson, Keith p.35
Jones, Lewis p.162
Hunt, Kristin p.62
Keller, Aline Vasquez p.32
Kinkaleri (Performance Group) pp.127-131
Koolwijk, Reyn van pp.50, 51, 54, 56, 63-65
Laurie Beth Clark Archive pp.164-167 (all in left hand column)
London Tate Gallery p.196
Lowe, Linton p.258
Martinez, Daniel Joseph p.80 (all)

McCormick, John p.89
Morris, Keith pp.30, 11 (lower), 59, 61, 267-282 (all)
Oliver, Barnaby p.13 (all maps)
Pearson, Mike pp.121, 122
Pavis, Patrice p.176 (all)
Wai, Yuen Chee pp.207-212
Rastl, Lisa p.88
Roms, Heike pp.10 (all), 11 (upper), 12 (all), 14
Roylance, Paul pp.37, 39, 40, 246, 249, 251, 255, 261, 263
Rusz, Jan p.21
Sakauchi, Futoshi p.36
Tangencya Project Archive pp.223-226 (all)
Tarr, Brian p.47
Turner, Paul pp.247, 252
Williams, Cody cover, p.58
Unknown title page, p.111
www.civil.usyd.edu.au/latest/wtc.php p.220
www.geocities.com/Richard.clark32@btinternet.com/flor.html p.219

Bibliophobia

Covers from the following books (in order of appearance):
Carter, John. *ABC for Book Collectors*. Revised by Nicolas Barker Hertfordshire: Granada, 1980.
Hamilton, D.A, and Mei P.Ong, eds. *SKOOB: Directory of Secondhand Bookshops in the British Isles*. London: SKOOB Books Publishing Ltd., 1991.
McKerrow, Ronald B. *An Introduction to Bibliography for Literary Students*. Oxford: Clarendon Press, 1928.
Corbett, E.V. *An Introduction to Librarianship*. London: James Clarke & Co Ltd., 1966.
Cranville, Wilfred. *A Dictionary of Theatrical Terms*. London: André Deutsch, 1952.
Davinson, D.E. *Periodicals: A Manual of Practise for Librarians*. London: André Deutsch, 1964.
Sharp, Cecil J. and A.P. Oppé. *The Dance: A Historical Survey of Dancing in Europe*. London: Halton & Truscott Smith, Ltd., 1924. New York: Minton, Batch & Company, 1924.
Barthes, Roland. *Empire of Signs*. Translated by Richard Howard London: Jonathan Cape Ltd., 1983. Jacket Design by Mon Mohan
Scott, A.C. *Actors are Madmen: A Notebook of a Theatregoer in China*. Wisconsin & London: The University of Wisconsin Press, 1982. Jacket Design by Ed Frank.
Vaillat, Léandre. *Histoire de la Danse*. Paris: Editions d'histoire et d'art, Librairie Plon, 1942.
Hoffman, Prof. Louis. *Later Magic*. London: George Routledge & Sons, 1904.
Cochran, Charles B. *Secrets of a Showman*. London: William Heineman Ltd., 1925.
De Zoete, Beryl. *The Other Mind: A Study of Dance & Life in South India*. London: Victor Gollancz Ltd., 1953.
Caffin, Caroline & Charles H. *Dancing & Dances of Today: The Modern Revival of Dancing as an Art*. New York: Dodd, Mead & Co, 1912.
Baker, George P. *The Theatre and the University* Isaacs, Edith J.R. Theatre Arts Monthly Volume IX, Number 2, February 1925.
Mills, Winifred H and Louise M. Dunn. *Shadow Plays and How to Produce them*. New York: Doubleday, Doran & Co., 1938. Cover Illustration by Corydon Bell
Shalett Herman, Lewis & Márguerite. *Foreign Dialects: A Manual for Actors, Directors & Writers*. New York: Theatre Arts Books, 1973. Jacket Design by Owen Scott.
Hiatt, Charles. *Henry Irving: A Record and Review*. London: George Bell & Sons, 1899.
Nicoll, Allardyce. *The Development of the Theatre: A Study of the Theatrical Art from the Beginnings to the Present Day*. London: George G. Harrap and Company Ltd., 1949.
Calmour, Alfred C. *Fact and Fiction About Shakespeare*. Stratford-on-Avon: George Boyden, 1894.
Morley, Henry. *Memoirs of Bartholomew Fair*. London: Chapman & Hall, 1859. Cover Illustrations by the Brothers Dalziel.
Brient, Michel, ed. *Revue d' Histoire du Théâtre* Number IV Paris: Publications de la Société d'Histoire du Théâtre, 1956

Chronology Photography Credits

Every effort has been made to credit photographers for their work; the Editors apologise for any unintentional omissions and welcome corrections and enquiries. The photographs in this section are from the CPR Archive except for the following:
Allison, Steve p.290 (Years 1974 + 1975)
Barrance, Tom p.298 (The Funeral)
Chamberlain, Franc p.316 (Towards Tomorrow – Kristine Nutting)
di Gregorio, Alessandra p.315 (c/o The Gym)
Glendinning, Hugo p.301 (Gardzienice Theatre Association)
Keller, Aline Vasquez p.315 (Eating Words)
Morris, Keith p.308 (Summer School: SITI and Points of Contact), p.309 (Summer School: Hotel Wales)
Richardson, Simon p.308 (Edisher Garakanidze)
Roylance, Paul pp. 294 – 297 (Years 1981 – 1984)
Tarr, Brian p.303 (From Honey to Ashes)
Turner, Paul pp. 290 -292 (Years 1976 – 1979)
van Koolwijk, Reyn p.307 (Black Dinner), p.309 (CPR Artist in Residence at DasArts)

CPR

CENTRE FOR PERFORMANCE RESEARCH

LOCATED IN WALES

working nationally and internationally

FOR THE CURIOUS

opening worlds of performance

The Centre for Performance Research is a pioneering and multi-faceted theatre organization located and rooted in Wales, working nationally and internationally. CPR produces innovative performance work, arranges workshops, conferences, lectures and masterclasses (for the professional, the amateur and the curious), curates and produces festivals, expositions and exchanges with theatre companies from around the world, publishes and distributes theatre books, as well as the journal Performance Research, and houses a resource centre and library that specializes in world theatre and performance and maintains an archive on contemporary Welsh performance.

CPR aims to develop and improve the knowledge, understanding and practice of theatre in its broadest sense, to effect change through investigation, sharing and discovery and to make this process as widely available as possible. Its programmes of work combine cultural co-operation, collaboration and exchange, practical training, education and research, performance, production and promotion, documentation and publishing, information and resource.

CENTRE FOR PERFORMANCE RESEARCH
6 Science Park
Aberystwyth SY23 3AH
Wales UK
Tel +44 (0)1970 622 133
Fax +44 (0)1970 622 132
Email cprwww@aber.ac.uk
web: www.thecpr.org.uk

CPR gratefully acknowledges the support and continued investment of:

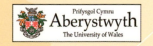

a specialist journal that promotes a dynamic interchange between scholarship and practice in an expanding field of performance. Interdisciplinary in vision and international in scope, its emphasis is on research in contemporary performance arts within changing cultures.

Performance Research

Routledge
Taylor & Francis Group

www.tandf.co.uk/journals

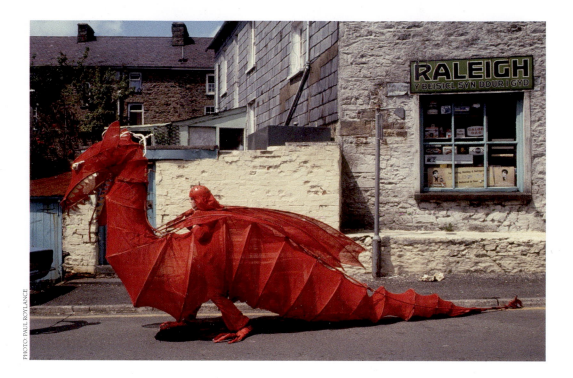